W9-ALT-546

Globalization and the sustainability of cities in the Asia Pacific region

Note to the reader from the UNU

The objective of the United Nations University Programme on Mega-cities and Urban Development, initiated in 1990, is to examine the social, economic, and environmental consequences of the development of large metropolitan agglomerations, particularly in developing countries.

Following the release of *Mega-city Growth and the Future* (Tokyo: UNU Press, 1994), *Emerging World Cities in Pacific Asia* (Tokyo: UNU Press, 1996), *The Mega-city in Latin America* (Tokyo: UNU Press, 1996), and *The Urban Challenge in Africa* (Tokyo: UNU Press, 1997), this book provides new insights into the mega-city phenomenon in the Asia Pacific region.

The United Nations
University

UNU/IAS
Institute of Advanced Studies

Globalization and the sustainability of cities in the Asia Pacific region

Edited by Fu-chen Lo and Peter J. Marcotullio

United Nations
University Press

TOKYO · NEW YORK · PARIS

United Nations University Press
The United Nations University, 53-70, Jingumae 5-chome,
Shibuya-ku, Tokyo, 150-8925, Japan
Tel: +81-3-3499-2811   Fax: +81-3-3406-7345
E-mail: sales@hq.unu.edu
http://www.unu.edu

United Nations University Office in North America
2 United Nations Plaza, Room DC2-1462-70, New York, NY 10017, USA
Tel: +1-212-963-6387   Fax: +1-212-371-9454
E-mail: unuona@igc.apc.org

United Nations University Press is the publishing division of the United Nations
University.

Cover design by Andrew Corbett

Printed in the United States of America

Library of Congress Cataloging-in-Publication Data

Globalization and the sustainability of cities in the Asia Pacific region /
edited by Fu-chen Lo and Peter J. Marcotullio.
    p.   cm.
Includes bibliographical references and index.
ISBN 92-808-1060-X
1. Urbanization—East Asia. 2. Urbanization—Pacific Area. 3. Cities and
towns—East Asia—Growth. 4. Cities and town—Pacific Area—Growth.
5. Sustainable development—East Asia. 6. Sustainable development—
Pacific Area. 7. Globalization. I. Lo, Fu-chen. II. Marcotullio, Peter, 1957–
HT384.E18 G56 2001
307.76′095—dc21   2001004006

Contents

Case studies: The post-industrial capital exporters

The entrepôt borderless cities

The industrial cities

The amenity cities

Conclusion

List of tables and figures

Preface

The beginning of the millennium has been an auspicious time for the United Nations University Institute of Advanced Studies (UNU/IAS). The UNU/IAS is emerging from its status as a "new" institute. First, the UNU/IAS is entering its sixth year of fruitful operation and, thanks to those that have worked to secure its future, it has a well-founded basis of research work upon which to build. Second, the direction of research and the various programme management responsibilities have recently been transferred from the "founding fathers" to the next generation of IAS staffers. It is both with sadness that long-time friends have left the institute and with great expectation that the new era will provide continued successful efforts that this Preface celebrates the accomplishments of and provides a glimpse of what might be in store for the urban programme at the institute. This text is an especially appropriate venue for this retrospective and prospective, as the research herein provides a bridge between the efforts of the past and what is planned for the future.

The past 10-year urban research agenda was formulated at the United Nations University Centre and was later transferred to the UNU/IAS in 1996. The Mega-cities and Urban Development Programme within the UNU/IAS began the implementation of a series of projects that addressed the pressing problems of mega-cities around the world.[1] Some may not be aware of the UNU and the UNU/IAS, so after a brief introduction to these organizations, the Preface presents the Mega-cities and Urban Development Programme's history, achievements, and current research projects. This short introduction to the programme will also provide the reader with the larger context under which the work herein was undertaken.

The United Nations University[2]

The United Nations University is an international academic organization designed to contribute, through research and capacity-building, to efforts to resolve the pressing global problems that are of concern to the United Nations, its peoples, and its members states.[3] It provides and manages an institutional framework for bringing together the world's leading scholars to address pressing global issues. In the process the University's activities alleviate the isolation of researchers in developing countries.

U Thant, the former UN Secretary-General, made the original proposal for the University in 1969 to promote international scholarly cooperation, undertake problem-oriented, multidisciplinary research on urgent global concerns, and strengthen research and training in developing countries. The UN General Assembly adopted the University Charter in 1973 and Japan made a pledge of US$100 million to the UNU's Endowment Fund. By May 1996, pledges and payments to the Endowment Fund totalled US$308 million. In June 1992, reflecting the willingness of the Japanese people to invest in the University, the Japanese government made available a permanent UNU headquarters building in the Shibuya ward of Tokyo.

The UNU is an autonomous body of the United Nations with academic freedom guaranteed by its charter. It receives no funds from the regular budget of the United Nations. Financial support is entirely by way of voluntary contributions from governments, agencies, foundations, and individual donors. The UNU's 2000–2001 biennium budget was roughly US$76 million. Major donor countries include Japan, Finland, Macau/People's Republic of China, the Netherlands, the UK, Canada, Iceland, and Venezuela.

In its activities the UNU works closely with the UN Secretariat, UNESCO, and other UN organizations, often acting as the link with the world's academic community. The UNU engages in multidisciplinary studies based on principles and priorities set by the University Council, a body that determines the principles and policies of the UNU. The Secretary-General of the United Nations and the Director-General of UNESCO appoint 24 of its 28 members, who come from all parts of the world.

The UNU is organized on a networking principle. The University provides specialized training through the world. It has no student body in the traditional sense: its "faculty" consists of its international network of scholars, while it "students" are mainly young researchers and other professionals from developing countries who receive postgraduate training as UNU fellows. The UNU headquarters centre is the hub and coordination point of the worldwide system. The chief academic and administrative officer of the University is the Rector.[4]

Much of the research carried out by the University occurs through work performed in various research and training centres/programmes (RTC/Ps). These institutes are individually mandated to work on specific global problems that require sustained efforts. Currently, the University has 13 RTC/Ps around the world (in alphabetical order):

- BIOLAC – UNU Programme for Biotechnology in Latin American and the Caribbean (Caracas, Venezuela)
- Food and Nutrition Capacity-Building – Cornell University (Ithaca, NY, USA)
- FTP – UNU Fisheries Training Programme (Reykjavik, Iceland)
- Governance Programme (Barcelona, Spain)
- GTP – UNU Geothermal Training Programme (Reykjavik, Iceland)
- IAS – UNU Institute for Advanced Studies (Tokyo, Japan)
- IIST – UNU International Institute for Software Technology (Macau)
- ILA – UNU International Leadership Academy (Amman, Jordan)
- INCORE – UNU Initiative on Conflict Resolution and Ethnicity (Ulster, Northern Ireland)
- INRA – UNU Institute for Natural Resources in Africa (Accra, Ghana; with a mineral resources unit in Lusaka, Zambia)
- INTECH – UNU Institute for New Technologies (Maastricht, Netherlands)
- INWEH – UNU International Network on Water, Environment, and Health (Hamilton, Canada)
- WIDER – UNU World Institute for Development Economics Research (Helsinki, Finland)

The Institute of Advanced Studies[5]

The RTC UNU/IAS was officially inaugurated in April 1996.[6] The founding director of the UNU/IAS was Tarcisio Della Senta.[7] He and a distinguished group of scholars have been instrumental in constructing the Institute's statutes and initiating in the UNU/IAS the original research programmes and projects.[8]

The IAS, located on the grounds of the UNU headquarters building in Tokyo, Japan, conducts research and postgraduate education both in-house and in cooperation with a worldwide network of academic institutions and international organizations. Guided by its statutes, the institute has attempted to "create a vigorous, in-residence community of scholars dedicated to research and learning at the frontiers of knowledge".[9] The in-house faculty includes senior researchers, research associates, visiting research fellows, fellows, and visiting professors, who are working on a full-time or part-time basis. In addition, adjunct professors from Japanese universities participate in academic activities. The network faculty is composed of a number of scholars from institutions in Asia and other regions of the world. They are involved in both the research and postgraduate education activities conducted by the UNU/IAS. Their association with the institute is for specific tasks, or for the duration of a given research project.

The vision that guides the research at the UNU/IAS is that through "eco-restructuring" of human activities and lifestyles a sustainable future can be achieved. In order to do this a multifaceted knowledge system must be created to support research activities. This knowledge system is based upon multidisciplinary approaches and creative solutions to major problems of humankind.

The areas of research are flexible and multithematic. While they are all concerned with the interactions of societal and natural systems, they can be grouped under four themes: sustainability and development; environmental multilateralism and diplomacy; mega-cities and urban development; and science, technology, and society. These themes should not be seen as independent activities; rather, they all represent different aspects of the process of eco-restructuring. Of these programmes, the one which focuses on mega-cities and urban development has the longest history.

The Mega-cities and Urban Development Programme

This overview of the Mega-cities and Urban Development Programme includes a short history followed by a list of the programme's achievements to date. Thereafter is a brief introduction into the perspectives used to study global urban development, followed by a description of how the research on globalization and the sustainability of cities in the Asia Pacific region is placed in the context of the programme's evolving research agenda.

History

The mega-cities and urban development area follows a tradition of several years of UNU-sponsored research on globalization and urban challenges. Fu-chen Lo, former deputy director of the UNU/IAS, inherited the agenda for this programme in the early 1990s when he was asked by the then vice-Rector, Roland Fuchs, to study urban phenomena worldwide. The programme moved to the UNU/IAS when the RTC was opened in 1996. Working with Fu-chen Lo over the past decade in succession have been Juha Uitto, Jacob Park, and Peter J. Marcotullio. In April 2000, Peter Marcotullio accepted the position of programme manager and is moving the research agenda in new directions. This book is a cross-over between the previous focus on globalization and urban development and urban "sustainability".

Originally, the focus of the programme's research was on "mega-cities" – those cities with more than 8 million inhabitants, as defined by the United Nations. Later studies turned to focus on "world" or "global" cities. Thus, emphasis shifted from a descriptive-based account of cities to one that explores the underlying causes of urban growth. The term "global city" is predicated on a set of theories that attempts to define the contours of contemporary urban development on a global scale through cross-border transactions.

During the course of various research projects a series of workshops and conferences were sponsored. The UNU/IAS Mega-cities Programme, through various research efforts, has sponsored at least 16 urban workshops and two international conferences (in cooperation with UNESCO and the UNCHS). Further, during the 10 years of the programme, links were forged with other UN agencies, such as the UNCRD, the UNCHS, and UNESCO.

Achievements

The programme's achievements can be listed by category: a network of scholars, edited books, and UNU/IAS working papers.

Network of scholars

One of the main achievements of the programme has been the creation of a worldwide network of scholars. Over 100 academics and practitioners from 36 countries have participated in past research efforts. Approximately half of these participants have been from developing countries.[10]

Volumes published

Thus far the work has resulted in five major edited publications:[11]

- Roland J. Fuchs, Ellen Brennan, Joseph Chamie, Fu-chen Lo, and Juha I. Uitto (eds). 1994. *Mega-city Growth and the Future*. Tokyo: UNU Press.
- Fu-chen Lo and Yue-man Yeung (eds). 1996. *Emerging World Cities in Pacific Asia*. Tokyo: UNU Press.

Table P.1 Distribution of scholars by research effort

Name of effort	Number of scholars involved
Mega-cities around the World	19
Asia Pacific Cities	11
Latin America Cities	17
Africa Cities	14
Global Cities around the World	23
Central and Eastern European Cities	15
Globalization and Urban Sustainability in the Asia Pacific	15
Global Cities, Telematics, and Transnationalism	16
Total	130[12]

- Alan Gilbert (ed.). 1996. *The Mega-city in Latin America*. Tokyo: UNU Press.
- Carole Rakodi (ed.). 1997. *The Urban Challenge in Africa*. Tokyo: UNU Press.
- Fu-chen Lo and Yue-man Yeung (eds). 1998. *Globalization and the Urban Future*. Tokyo: UNU Press.

The distribution of scholars by completed research effort is shown in Table P.1.

Working papers

To date over 15 UNU/IAS working papers have been produced in the programme area.[13]

Research perspectives

A brief introduction to the perspectives of so many scholars cannot do justice to their work. While many different viewpoints have been put forward in the various texts, however, at least five points can be highlighted as common to much of the research conducted: emphases on the concepts of globalization, urbanization, regionalism, world systems theory, and world city formation.

Globalization

During the past few decades, the world economy has experienced structural adjustments affecting production, distribution, and resource utilization. Cross-border functional integration of economic activities and growing interdependency among regional economic blocs are part of a set of processes defined as "globalization" which have been a major theme to the work of the programme. As functional integration is progressing through the speeding up and increased stretching (geographical widening) and intensity (deepening) of international linkages, evidence used in the studies centres on such indicators as trade and financial flows, foreign direct investment (FDI), communications (information flows), and personal and business travel between cities that have become nodes within the flows.

Increasing cross-border economic integration has been underpinned by technological developments. Together these forces have been called the techno-economic paradigm for development. Scholars who have submitted chapters to the various texts have participated in the discussion of the role of technology in urban development. One concluding project, coordinated by Saskia Sassen, is focused on this important topic.

Urbanization

Within a decade or so, more than 50 per cent of the world's population will live in cities. This trend is particularly important in the developing world, since almost 90 per cent of all urban citizens will live in Asia, Africa, and Latin America. Furthermore, national urbanization rates in many parts of these regions are predicted to continue increasing beyond 2025.

One striking aspect of this global urbanization process is the rise of "mega-cities" (those with more than 8 million inhabitants). While in 1950 there were two mega-cities, both located in industrialized countries, the new geography of the megalopolis is dominated by developing nations. Of the 28 cities predicted to have populations of over 8 million by the year 2000, 22 will be in developing regions.

In combination with the techno-economic determinist viewpoint, studies of global urbanization have taken on greater significance and provided breakthroughs in current understandings of the development process. The UNU/IAS has attempted to be at the forefront of understanding these trends.

Regional emphasis

There have been three general ways in which regions and nations have experienced uneven economic adjustments associated with globalization. First, the structure of production within advanced economies of the North has changed from one based on industrial manufacturing growth and employment to service-dominated economies. Second, a manufacturing belt has emerged in East and South-East Asia. Third, those regions, nations, and localities unable to take part in the global integration of production have been marginalized.

In order to explore fully the variation among regions in urban transformations, the studies at the UNU/IAS have largely been regionally based, concentrating on developing areas. To date, studies have been completed of Asia Pacific, Latin America, and Africa. A current project focuses on urban transformations in Central and Eastern Europe.

World systems theory

Working off the deficiencies of dependency theory, another approach to urban and regional development evolved that stressed the increasing importance of the global economy to cities. This approach concentrates on the international economic transactions among different cities. This was a significant departure from previous urban and regional planning approaches. Most post-war regional and urban analyses were limited to a national planning framework, although dependency theory provided the first break from that line of exploration. With growing cross-border linkages in terms of trade, investment, finance, people, and information, attention turned to outward-looking policies that enhanced connections to non-domestic sources of growth.

This perspective, in large part, originated with interdependency theory (or world systems analysis) that proposed a single interpretation for global urbanization. Like dependency theory, world systems analysis treated activities throughout the globe as a single entity, the capitalist world economy. Like dependency theory, the argument via this route rejected a country-by-country analysis of social change. Country analyses were piecemeal, so the argument went, and needed to be replaced by a single society assumption. Within this theory, urban development is therefore a product of the emergence of a capitalist mode of production and subsequent transformations in space relations. In its most determinist format, the world system culminated in the emergence of a single integrated capitalist world economy which incorporates most nation-states. The capitalist mode of production and the development of nation-states were interdependent structurally. Spatial changes set in motion circular and cumulative processes of population concentration that affected the world at different times and in different places over the past three centuries. It differed from dependency theory in that relationships between developed and developing countries were conceived as interdependent. Further, this relationship was not defined solely by trade, but included the role of transnational organizations among other cross-border relationships. Also, interdependency recognized that some "semi-peripheral" nations could emerge from the constraints imposed on them by the system.

World city formation

Globalization studies also include the emergence and growing importance of "world" or "global" cities. Scholars have performed examinations of the role of cities within the global system. They argue that cities act as the linchpins to the world economy. One crucial outcome is the emergence of a world city system with "global cities" as key points controlling much of the world's economic activities. Within this paradigm, the development of the world system of cities is a spatial outcome of global capitalist development. Cities were important because they were the locations of concentrated and centralized economic power. On the one hand, manufacturing was decentralizing from traditional blue-collar cities in Europe and North America to other locations, including developing countries. At the same time some cities were increasingly the centres for the centralization of command and control functions (transnational corporation – TNC – headquarters)and specialized business service functions), also known as control and management functions (CMF).

As cities increase their number and intensity of linkages to the world system, they undergo social, economic, and physical changes. Key to these changes are infrastructure advancements that enhance transnational flows, such as cargo ports, teleports, and airports among other developments. UNU/IAS urban studies have moved from a focus on large cities to those that play a key role in the global economy. Common to all studies sponsored at the institute is the notion of the importance of cities to the world economic system. Also common to these studies is the identification of key changes within cities as they increase their functional linkages to the world economy.

The context for this study

This Mega-cities Programme research agenda is currently concluding. Among those projects that will be published within the next year or so are "Global Cities and the Impact of Telematics and Cross-Border Relationships" and "Globalization and Urban Transformations in Central and Eastern Europe". The bases for the studies on globalization and urban development were the variations in the impact of transnational flows on different parts of the world. Although single volumes cannot do justice to the complexity of interactions between cities and international flows, they provide a basis for an understanding of the differences among regions. When published these volumes will provide a complete set of studies covering the major developing regions of the world. There is no other collection like it.

Among the eight texts, however, there are two that stand out as providing a different point of departure. These are the study on the role of telematics in urban development and this volume on urban sustainability. They have concentrated on specific pressing aspects of urban development. Both of these studies have been key in helping to push the research into new fields.

This particular text is providing a link to a new set of studies that will examine issues of urban "sustainability" in more detail. This change was prompted by the completion of the regional studies, promotion of the inclusion of environmental issues in urban studies by the UNU/IAS Board, and through the advice of over 35 prominent urban scholars interviewed to help in picking a relevant and timely focus.[14] The programme name has tentatively been changed to the Regional and Urban Development Programme in anticipation of future studies that will take us into the next millennium.

The editors would like to thank all the participants in the programme, past and present. Their hard work and dedication helped to make each UNU/IAS urban project a success. While all the contributors deserve thanks, the editors would like highlight the efforts of the project coordinators, Ellen Brennan, Kaliopa Dimitrovska-Andrews, Roland Fuchs, Allen Gilbert, F. E. Ian Hamilton, Yue-man Yeung, Carole Rakodi, and Saskia Sassen, who provided the energy and enthusiasm necessary to complete projects and whose intellectual leadership was nothing less than inspirational. The copyeditor, Cherry Eleins, contributed significantly to the preparation of this large volume. Any mistakes in the volume are the responsibilities of the editors and chapter contributors. Lastly, the UNU/IAS Urban Programme would like to acknowledge generous financial support provided by the Sasakawa Foundation. This aid facilitated much of this research and therefore we owe the Foundation special thanks.

Notes

1. The programme name has recently been changed to Urban and Regional Development Programme, but throughout this volume it is referred to as the Mega-cities Programme.
2. This section was taken largely from two documents: "The United Nations University" pamphlet produced by the UNU headquarters public affairs section; and "The United Nations University Institute of Advanced Studies: Research and Postgraduate Education" pamphlet produced by the UNU/IAS.
3. For more information on the University see their homepage at http://www.unu.edu.
4. J. A. van Ginkel, formerly Rector Magnificus at the University of Utrecht, the Netherlands, assumed the post of the fourth UNU Rector on 1 September 1997.
5. For more detail on the work of the entire Institute see *UNU/IAS Report, April 1997–April 1999*. Tokyo: UNU/IAS.
6. For more information on the Institute of Advanced Studies see the UNU/IAS homepage at http://www.ias.unu.edu.
7. The current director is A. H. Zakri from Malaysia.
8. The UNU/IAS appointed founding board members included Sir John Kendrew (UK), Lawrence Klein (USA), and Hiroyuko Yoshikawa (Japan). Current board members include Abdul-Latif Yousef Al-Hamad (Kuwait), Jean-Pierre Contzen (Belgium/chair), M. G. K. Menon (India/former chair), Gertrude Mongella (Tanzania), and Jose Israel Vargas (Brazil).

9. UNU/IAS Statute, Article 2, section 1.

10. A scholar receives this designation only if the institute or university that he or she is from is based in a developing country *and* he or she is currently working in an institute that is located in a developing country.

11. For information on how to obtain these publications contact the United Nations University Press, United Nations University, 53-70, Jingumae 5-chome, Shibuya-ku, Tokyo 150, Japan. Tel: (81-3) 3499-2811. Fax: (81-3) 3499-2828.

12. The total number is greater than the approximate number of scholars previously mentioned because some scholars participated in more than one project.

13. The UNU/IAS, as of January 2001, has published 87 papers in the working paper series. Paper topics range widely and several urban and non-urban UNU/IAS scholars have written on topics related to urban development. In the future, in order to record progress in this area, as was recently implemented by the Environmental and Multilateral Diplomacy Programme, a separate set of working papers should be organized for the programme.

14. Tarcisio Della Senta prompted the members of the Mega-cities Programme to undertake a small project entitled "Reflections into the Future", which entailed interviewing urban scholars to obtain their views on the most important urban issues for the new millennium. The results of this work helped to formulate a new research agenda.

1

Introduction

Peter J. Marcotullio and Fu-chen Lo

The project planning meeting for the development of this volume was held in Jakarta, Indonesia, in July 1997. Most of the participants, at the time, were bullish on globalization and its growth impact on the region's cities. None understood what exactly was happening at that moment. Within a short time, however, the importance of the growing crisis became clear. Many of the "miracle" Asia Pacific countries underwent an economic crisis of unprecedented proportions. By August of the next year, at the project review meeting, the cracks in the system were clear. As 1998 ended, five of the former "high-performance economies" were on a downward trend. The Republic of Korea, a proud new member of the Organization for Economic Cooperation and Development, required an IMF bail-out. After a decade of annual growth rates of 10 per cent, some economies contracted by as much as 15 per cent. Stock market values were more than halved, Asia's total of bad loans was estimated to be US$1 trillion, and some currencies lost between 30 and 70 per cent of their value (*FEER* 1999). The crisis provided the unexpected backdrop against which the studies of cities in the region were performed.

The next 18 months were difficult. As a whole, developing Asia's growth slowed down from 5.8 per cent in 1997 to 1.6 per cent, and for the first time in the 1990s it was lower than in Latin America or Africa (Table 1.1). Only China and a few countries in South Asia managed to sustain the growth rates of recent years (UNCTAD 1999).

Aggregate GDP of the four newly industrializing economies (NIEs)

1

Table 1.1 World output, 1990–1998

Region/country	% change over previous year			
	1990–1995[a]	1996	1997	1998[b]
World	1.9	3.3	3.3	2.0
Industrialized countries	1.7	2.9	2.9	2.2
USA	2.3	3.4	3.9	3.9
Japan	1.4	5.0	1.4	−2.8
European Union	1.3	1.6	2.5	2.7
Transition economies	−8.2	−1.5	1.4	−1.4
Developing countries	4.9	5.8	5.4	1.8
Latin America	3.3	3.6	5.4	2.1
Africa	1.1	3.9	2.7	2.9
Asia	6.4	7.1	5.8	1.6
China	12.4	9.6	8.8	7.8

Source: UNCTAD 1999, Table 1.1, p. 4
a. Annual average.
b. Estimate.

Table 1.2 World economic output projections

Country/region/area	Annual % change			
	1997	1998	1999	2000
World	4.2	2.5	2.3	3.4
G7	3.0	2.2	1.9	2.0
Japan	1.4	−2.8	−1.4	0.3
Asian NIEs	6.0	−1.5	2.1	4.5
Developing countries	5.7	3.3	3.1	4.9
Africa	3.1	3.4	3.2	5.1
Asia	6.6	3.8	4.7	5.7
ASEAN-4	3.8	−9.4	−1.1	3.0
China	8.8	7.8	6.6	7.0
Countries in transition	2.2	−0.2	−0.9	2.5

Source: IMF 1999, Table 1.1, p. 2

contracted by 1.5 per cent in 1998, in contrast to an expansion of 6 per cent in the preceding year (Table 1.2). Two of the four NIEs suffered recessions in that year. Taiwan survived the financial turmoil relatively unscathed (Table 1.3), and was able to fight off crisis because of its pre-emptive devaluation and large foreign exchange reserves built up from current account surpluses (UNCTAD 1999). The decline in growth for the economy was contained at 4.8 per cent, against 6.8 per cent growth in

Table 1.3 Growth in selected developing countries, 1990–1998

Country	1990–1995[a]	1996	1997	1998[b]
Hong Kong	5.5	4.5	5.3	−5.1
Korea	7.4	7.1	5.5	−5.5
Singapore	8.5	6.9	7.8	1.5
Taiwan	6.4	5.7	6.8	4.8
Indonesia	7.1	7.8	4.9	−13.9
Malaysia	8.7	8.6	7.7	−6.2
Philippines	2.2	5.8	5.2	−0.5
Thailand	8.3	5.5	−0.4	−8.0
China	12.4	9.6	8.8	7.8
Argentina	6.0	4.4	8.0	4.2
Brazil	2.7	2.9	3.8	0.2
Mexico	1.5	5.5	7.1	4.8

Source: UNCTAD 1999, Table 1.2, p. 10
a. Annual average.
b. Estimate.

1997. Hong Kong, on the other hand, experienced its first recession in 13 years. Output declined by 5 per cent that year in contrast to a growth rate of over 5 per cent in 1997. In Singapore, growth fell to 1.5 per cent in 1998 from nearly 8 per cent in 1997, but the city-state was able to fight off a contraction. In both Singapore and Hong Kong, wages and employment were allowed – and in the case of Singapore, forced – to fall in order to maintain an external balance of trade and competitiveness (UNCTAD 1999). The recession in the Republic of Korea was due to the severe contraction of both domestic and external demand, resulting in output falling by approximately 5.5 per cent. Because other countries in Asia were the destinations for about half of Korea's exports prior to the crisis, the fall in external demand was followed by the deepening of the financial crisis in the country.

In ASEAN, income for the group as a whole fell by 9.4 per cent in 1998, in contrast to an increase of 3.8 per cent in 1997. The first to be struck by speculative attack in 1997, Thailand implemented a series of financial and other structural reforms to stem capital outflows. Despite these attempts, the country's economy still suffered an 8 per cent con-traction. Indonesia's economy bore the brunt of the crisis as exports and investment collapsed, resulting in a contraction of nearly 14 per cent in output. The country's troubles were exacerbated by the effects of El Niño on agricultural production and continued civil unrest. The economic contraction in the four ASEAN countries reflected the impact of currency depreciation and generalized debt deflation, and produced widespread insolvencies as a massive reversal of private capital flows ensued. In the Philippines, the relatively low level of financial leverage (about 60 per cent of GDP) and continued strong export demand helped save the country from some of the worst effects of the crisis (ADB 1999): the decline in the Philippine economy was around 0.5 per cent. Malaysia chose a different path, introducing capital controls and expanding the government's economic role in an attempt to shield the domestic economy from the volatility of international capital flows. At first the country appeared to avoid the worst effects of the crisis, but capital outflows brought growth down to −6.2 per cent.

Since that time, however, things have again dramatically changed. Many nations and many cities within these nations have weathered the storm. The authors believe this was due, in large part, to the underlying structures developed within the region by the major metropolitan centres. These structures include, foremost, the development of physical infrastructure and institutions that support the growing interconnectedness of the region's cities. It seems that the worst of the 1997 crisis for many cities is over, and new developments are under way.

The region's urban centres did not survive without problems. The financial stampede followed by nationwide political uprisings deeply and continuously impacted on Indonesia, turning Jakarta from a "global city" to a "city in crisis" (Firman 1999; see also Chapter 11 of this volume).

Notwithstanding this almost miraculous comeback, many challenges remain. Of importance are those threats to the continued "sustainability" of these cities. These issues emerged before the crisis, and no doubt will grow if ignored in the future. They were brought home to the members the Mega-cities project group unexpectedly, at the same time that the group broached the question of sustainability.

While the timing of the study was dramatically appropriate, it was also challenging for the authors as they attempted to understand the transformations that had taken place over the recent past. The main focus of the chapters in this book is the impact of transnational flows. Globalization has been particularly strong in the region, and its impacts have been seen throughout the region's cities. There are three major lessons that can be gleaned from the work presented here. First, globalization processes have created a strong and solid set of linkages among the cities in the region. These connections have weathered a crisis and proven to be structurally sound. It is the authors' belief that the most affected nations were able to bounce back from their economic turmoil because of the regional economic production system. Second, while the contemporary forces of growth have been strong, they do not necessarily promise "sustainability". A sustainable future, in terms of the development of "liveable" cities in all aspects of urban life, must be created, produced, struggled for. It isn't inevitable. Indeed, globalization has brought with it patterns of social tension and environmental degradation evident in various cities throughout the Asia Pacific region. Lastly, while regulating and controlling the negative aspects associated with rapid development have often been discussed in the context of urban management, there is a limit to the effectiveness of local policies. Cities are not autonomous entities, and therefore their sustainable development must also be approached through global, regional, national, and local policies.

Themes of the book   ─ to what

The focus on the transnational character of urban sustainability provoked the discussion of a variety of themes by authors. The foremost include globalization, world city formation, the functional city system, and urban sustainability. While each author has his or her own perspective on each of these dynamics, there was still, at a general level, a degree of convergence in thought.

The first note of importance is the definition of the Asia Pacific region. In previous UNU/IAS studies, the Asia Pacific region was defined as the area bordering the Pacific ocean, but exclusively including the Asia continent (Lo and Yeung 1996). As Terry McGee and Chung-Tong Wu (Chapter 4) have pointed out, however, a narrow definition is increasingly harder to defend. This follows the processes of globalization which are making it increasingly difficult to define strictly the limits of this region's (or any other's, for that matter) activities and impacts.[1]

The volume includes the nations typically included in a study of the Asia Pacific, as well as Australia and Canada. At first glance it might seem odd to add these nations but not those in South Asia. This can be explained by the increasing cross-regional block movements of people and goods that are examined in several chapters in the volume (see for example Chapters 2, 4, 13, and 14). It is the authors' contention that, while South Asian cities are also increasingly integrated into the Asia Pacific, cities such as Sydney and Vancouver are already intensely linked to the regional urban system.

Globalization

The debate over "globalization" is contentious, with a variety of emerging conceptualizations concerning its history, internal dynamics, and structural outcomes. Potentially, the broadest definition and one that all contributors agreed upon is the "the widening, deepening and speeding up of worldwide interconnectedness in all aspects of contemporary social life, from the cultural to the criminal" (Held *et al.* 1999: 2). Furthermore, while there are an increasing number and variety of flows that are stretching and widening and increasing their speed around the globe, authors in this volume have concentrated on a select few. Predominately, these include economic (investment, trade, and information) and migration flows. Together the movements of goods, services, people, and information connect the various Asia Pacific nations to the regional and world economy. While this has its drawbacks, as many authors note the importance of other issues – the globalization of media, culture, etc. – the concentration on economic and migration issues is understandable given their importance in shaping the region and the discourse on the subject. Indeed, if not for the growth experienced in the four "tigers" and ASEAN, the concept of globalization would have an entirely different character.

Further, although globalization has a much longer history, the most dramatic impacts of these processes, particularly in the Asia Pacific region, have been experienced during the post-war period. Again, considering the importance of growing interdependency in trade and investment flows within the world and the movement of people during this period in the region, this is not surprising. This is not to say, however, that authors do not appreciate the "long *durée*", but rather, for the sake of focus and coherence, have concentrated on contemporary transformations.

Underlying the trends in current flows are technological developments in the areas of telecommunications and transportation, among others, often associated with the fourth (or possibly fifth) Kondratieff wave. Increasing cross-border economic integration has been supported by technological developments. Together, the technological advances and increasing importance of cross-border flows are defining the techno-economic paradigm for development.

In their analyses of these trends, many of the authors in this volume subscribed to a variant of the "one-world" analysis. This perspective emanates, but is significantly different, from "dependency" theory. The approached stressed herein concentrates on the international economic transactions among different cities, with the outcome of interdependency. This perspective rejects a country-by-country analysis of social and economic change. Country analyses are piecemeal, so the argument goes, and need to be replaced by a single world society assumption. Within this theory, urban development is therefore a product of the emergence of particular forms of the capitalist mode of production and subsequent transformations in space relations. The new international division of labour (NIDL) is the outcome of the process, and is often mentioned in terms of "complementarity" as opposed to "exploitation". One important way that this perspective differs from dependency theory is the view that relationships between developed and developing countries were conceived as interdependent and lack the "core/periphery" distinction (for a different view see Chapter 8 on Hong Kong).

World city formation and the Asia Pacific functional city system

Evidence for the geographical scope of global processes includes the specific locations or nodes within the flows. These "cotter pins" to the global economy (Feagin and Smith 1985: 4) include cities among other places, and in the Asia Pacific such cities are largely major metropolitan centres along coasts. It is here, in these locations, where the work of globalization gets done (Sassen 1994).

In their studies of the relationship between globalization and urban centres many scholars have concentrated on what have come to be called "world" or "global" cities (see for example, Sassen 1991). Within this perspective, the development of the world system of cities is the spatial outcome of global capitalist development. Cities are important as the locations of concentrated and centralized economic power and as centres for the production and innovation of specialized services. That is, while manufacturing has decentralized to other locations (including suburban areas), cities have become centres for the centralization of command and control functions (headquarters and specialized business service functions), also known as control and management functions (CMF). At the same time they are the sites of innovations in and production of a vast array of services that, in part, provide for the infrastructure of global capability.

Too often, however, cities which are important sites of manufacturing production are left out of this analysis. In the context of this volume, however, the authors consider the entire regional system of cities and the important role of all types of economic functions, including, for example, industrial and amenity functions. Stressing whether a city is "global" is not as important as understanding the processes by which it enhances its international connections. This work follows previous UNU/IAS studies which have argued that economic growth, integration, and the resultant interdependency within the region have led to the emergence of a functional city system, defined as "a network of cities that are linked, often in a hierarchical manner based on a given economic or socio-political function at the global or regional level" (Lo and Yeung 1996: 2).

The functional city typology has been a useful tool in making economic, social, and environmental distinctions among cities within the re-

Table 1.4 Characteristics and roles of cities in the Asia Pacific functional city system

City	Economic characteristics	Functional role
Tokyo	Post-industrial	Central management
Seoul	Industrial/services	Central management
Taipei	Industrial/high tech	Central management
Hong Kong	Entrepôt/finance/regional HQ	Borderless
Singapore	Entrepôt/finance/regional HQ	Borderless
Bangkok	Industrial	Industrial production
Jakarta	Industrial	Industrial production
Shanghai	Industrial	Industrial production
Vancouver	Post-industrial/port/immigration	Amenity
Sydney	Post-industrial/finance/immigration	Amenity

gion, and provides a coherent framework within which the material is presented. Each chapter, or set of chapters, adds elements, based upon the typology, to an understanding of the puzzle of Asian urban development. On the other hand, however, the typology is also limited in that it captures only a few dimensions of each of the enormously complex cities discussed in the text. The authors understand that this formalization remains problematic in its inability to deal with the growing density of international linkages and complexity of domestic conditions both within and among cities.

Notwithstanding these restrictions, the functional city system concept has helped the authors connect globalization processes to local transformations. That is, as cities articulate to this system, they undergo a process of development commensurate with their dominant transnational economic roles. These changes have been referred to as the world city formation process (Friedmann and Wolff 1982). The resultant general patterns of development have been discerned based upon the intensity of the prevailing international currents (Table 1.4). Key to these changes in the Asia Pacific have been infrastructure advancements that enhance transnational flows, such as cargo ports, teleports, and airports, among other developments. Common to the studies in this volume is the identification of key changes within cities as they increase their functional linkages to the world economy.

Urban sustainability

Limiting "globalization" to the study of economic and immigration flows immediately restricts the scope of "sustainability". The chapters in this volume have concentrated on economic, environmental, and social issues as, in the authors' perspective, these tend to be the most important challenges urban centres are currently facing.

What came out of the studies was that globalization is a doubled-edge sword bringing both promises and perils in almost everything associated with it (Yeung 1998). In the past it had been argued that globalization, Asian style, was bringing with it social equity (World Bank 1993). The Asian financial crisis, however, a globalization-driven event, displayed that the equitable growth achieved in the region was fragile. For example, Indonesia, which was making strides in lowering the numbers of its poor, saw sharp increases in the number of those in poverty after the crisis (McGee 1998). Even before the crisis, studies have noted that social tensions and conditions within cities needed attention (Schmidt 1998; ADB 1997).

Rapid economic growth in the region has also been achieved at the cost of severe environmental problems (ADB 1997). A series of studies have demonstrated the environmental problems associated with rapid and intensive urban growth, bringing into question the "grow now, clean later" attitude (see Chapter 15). The case study chapters in this volume provide detailed accounts of the growing environmental awareness in cities throughout the region. Yet the issues are not the same in all locales. There are differences in both the quality and degree of environmental degradation. These differences, it is argued, are related in part to the functional role of the city within the regional city system.

Notwithstanding the rebound of many of the economies in 2000, a new era in development thinking is emerging (McGee 1998; Douglass 1998). These changing conditions require a new urban and regional theory paradigm. One way forward is to incorporate "sustainable development" into globalization discourse. The two concepts of globalization and sustainability are not incompatible, and can be used together to prescribe a development strategy that attempts to tackle some of the problems associated with globalization-driven growth alone. Their combination implies, for cities, reaching way beyond administrative borders. While there is much that cities can do to control their internal environments (see for example Chapters 8 and 9 on Hong Kong and Singapore), solutions must also be sought at the international level.

There is a growing body of literature that approaches urban sustainability from the international scale (see, for example, Harris 1992; Stren, White, and Whitney 1992; Burgess, Carmona, and Kolstee 1997; Low *et al.* 2000). Within this corpus of literature on "sustainable cities", however, there are limited international comparative studies available. Indeed, in a recent compendium of seminal writings on urban sustainability,

David Satterthwaite (1999) noted this lacunae in current research. The authors hope that the attempts in this volume begin to fill this need, and in doing so generate new thinking concerning the management of cities.

Construction of the book

The first set of chapters in the text outline the general processes that the authors believe are important to understanding the growth and sustainability of the entire regional city system. These chapters are followed by a series of case studies divided by the type of city suggested by the functional city system concept (Table 1.4). Each of these case studies identifies how the city region has been articulating to the regional system and how, in turn, the linkages have impacted on development. Most of the case study authors have also focused on the most relevant social and environmental constraints to urban growth in their specific contexts. The final chapter in this section attempts to summarize the results of the studies by placing urban sustainability into an international context.

The overview chapters start out with a map of the trajectory that globalization forces have taken in the region and the development of the functional city system. Fu-chen Lo and Peter J. Marcotullio's Chapter 2 argues that urban development in the region has been underpinned by economic globalization, started by Japanese investment in the region during the 1980s (first in the NICs and later in ASEAN). Following the Japanese were the NICs, Korea, Taiwan, Singapore, and Hong Kong, and thereafter were the ASEAN four, Indonesia, Malaysia, the Philippines, and Thailand. This "wild flying geese" model of development was accompanied by growing interconnectedness of cities as they carved out a variety of functions. Thus the growth of coastal cities precipitated the emergence of a massive urban corridor, or functional city system, that stretches from Tokyo to Jabotabek and then out to Sydney and Vancouver.

An examination of the role of foreign direct investment (FDI) in the region follows this analysis. In Chapter 3, Sung Woong Hong describes the importance of these flows, their impact on receiving countries, and how the financial landscape has changed with the advent of the financial crisis of 1997. While encouraging the continuation of FDI flows, he warns of the dangers of "hot money" and short-term loans. These aspects of financial globalization, according to Hong, have had negative impacts on nations and cities throughout the region. As FDI remains an important vehicle for development, he discusses how countries now must emphasize a variety of factors to attract investment, including "created assets", such as human capital, and urban infrastructure and promotion policies.

This leaves open the question of how the creation of these assets will be financed.

In Chapter 4, the last of the overviews, Terry G. McGee and Chung-Tong Wu describe the importance of international migration flows to urban development in the region. They focus on the main features of the region's immigration flows, and analyse these movements by using a topology based upon sources and destinations. Importantly, they point out a series of four challenges that have accompanied these trends: the changing role of governments, the integration of migrants into city regional economies, building liveable residential communities, and creating social harmony with increasing diversity. In their conclusions they identify policy areas that, arguably, could provide a means to tackle these issues and make cities in the region more liveable. A high priority is "social sustainability", related directly to the continuing rising trends in international migration. This, they argue, can only be accomplished by implementing policies at both international and local levels.

The chapters following these overviews are case studies of individual cities, divided along the lines of the major economic functions of various cities. The first set of case studies is from the main capital exporters of the region, including such cities as Tokyo, Seoul, and Taipei. In Chapter 5 on Tokyo, Tetsuo Kidokoro, Takashi Onishi, and Peter J. Marcotullio discuss some of the transformations and the planning responses to those trends within Tokyo, as it became a "global" city. Given this background, they criticize the newest national capital regional development plan. In terms of international competitiveness, environmental protection, and development policy, they find that the plan falls short of providing an appropriate guidance tool. This mis-specified set of policies was created, according to the authors, by an imbalance in the decision-making processes, which lacked citizen participation during the formulation of the plan. The preparation of the region's plans in the future should therefore include more than just the national government, as there are an increasing number of other stakeholders (private-sector TNCs, non-profit organizations, and local and prefectural governments) emerging within Japanese society.

In Chapter 6 Won-yong Kwon discusses how globalization processes within Seoul have sharpened the conflicts between the urban "haves" and "have-nots" and negatively impacted on the environment. He describes and analyses what Seoul is and how it has come to be, focusing on globalization and the growth of the metropolitan area. The impact of the recent crisis has encouraged decision-makers within the city to reconsider growth in the light of sustainable development. Particularly important and previously unmet challenges for the local citizenry include transportation congestion, the green belt, and solid waste management. In his conclusion Kwon gives five lessons from Korea's experience in policy responses to globalization.

In Chapter 7, Ching-lung Tsay discusses the growth of Taipei in relation to the economic development of Taiwan. Through an examination of the urbanization process in Taiwan the author describes how a national system of cities that approximates to the ideal rank-size distribution developed. Within the Taipei metropolitan area, deconcentration helped the city avoid some of the problems that would have occurred otherwise. Tsay notes that the continuation of the growth of the city has been relatively smooth, and the population has continued to distribute itself throughout the country despite the increasing externalized linkages of its economy.

Next the section provides two chapters on entrepôt or borderless cities: Singapore and Hong Kong, once both "city-states". Their special status has enabled a unique type of growth. In Chapter 8, Victor F. S. Sit discusses the growth of the Hong Kong extended metropolitan region (EMR), and how this development was intimately related to the city's articulation with the global economy and the penetration of economic and social pressures into the city region. He uses Castells's (1977) phrase of "dependency urbanization" to describe the various aspects of urban development in the Hong Kong, Macau, and Pearl river delta area. In so doing, he attempts to reveal the spatial pattern of urbanization and functional division of labour in different parts of the Hong Kong EMR. At the macro level he points out the various aspects of global flows, while at the local level he insists upon the importance of the dual forces of polarization and dispersal. As a result of this type of development, the author argues that the city of Hong Kong has been able to move smoothly to a "sustainable future", but the peri-urban and peripheral areas have developed severe pollution, environmental, and infrastructure problems. Sit provides some policy recommendations to help ease the problems and move towards more regionally coordinated sustainable development.

Chia Siow Yue's Chapter 9 on Singapore argues that the city-state has become a regional hub and global city, and highlights how the physical and economic constraints of being a small island nation were overcome by careful physical planning and the strategy of integration with the region and global economy. The city-state's efforts have been successful, as Singapore has undergone rapid growth and development and now has a per capita GDP higher than that of the USA (World Bank 1999). As a regional and international city it hosts 5,000 foreign multinationals and international companies, giving it one of the highest FDI penetrations in the world. Importantly, Chia points out that while the nation has borders, its economy has become borderless.

At the same time, the author stresses that Singapore has become a "garden city" with high environmental standards. She argues that several factors have facilitated the city's ability to grow and yet remain clean and green. For example, Singapore does not face the rural-urban migration problem that confronts other city planners; migration is essentially cross-border and subject to border controls, making it easier to project population size. Its Land Acquisition Act gave the government legal power to acquire land speedily and at low cost early on, and has enabled Singapore to implement its public housing, urban renewal, urban infrastructure, and industrialization projects. Further, Chia suggests that the limited land area has made Singapore policy-makers and planners highly conscious of the need to balance economic development with environmental protection and conservation. Lastly, the author points out some of the key elements of Singapore's environment management strategy: long-term planning and preventive control; strict environmental legislation and effective enforcement; comprehensive monitoring of environmental quality; provision of environmental infrastructure; and use of appropriate environmental technology. A close look at Singapore's experience with environmental management demonstrates that despite rapid population growth, urbanization, and industrialization, negative impacts on the environment can be effectively controlled and managed in the core area of a growth triangle through appropriate policy planning and implementation. The author does not, however, mention the conditions in the neighbouring areas of Johore, Malaysia, and the Riau islands of Indonesia.

Thereafter are descriptions of some of the region's industrial centres. This category includes Shanghai, Jakarta, and Bangkok. While these cities have undergone tremendous globalization-driven growth over the last few decades, they have also become highly polluted urban centres. Ning Yuemin's Chapter 10 on Shanghai covers the most contemporary aspects of the globalization process. As China was isolated from the world economic system from the 1950s to 1978, it has only recently been opened to outside investment and Shanghai has taken up its former position as one of the country's premier industrial cities.

Ning describes in detail the processes by which the city has grown, paying particular attention to the latest phases of development and social and environmental issues affecting Shanghai. He points out that since the 1980s the government has loosened the household registration system and a large floating population has appeared, moving in search of employment. Within the city, this non-native floating population has contributed to the economic development of the city, but has also brought many social problems. He suggests that the management of this floating population has become one of the most important issues for Shanghai's social sustainability.

Other important issues, according to the author, include strengthening population control and mediating environmental pollution. Ning goes to great lengths to emphasize that one of Shanghai's greatest challenges is to maintain sound environment quality. He states that for a long period of time the environmental quality in Shanghai was satisfactory, but over the last few decades the city has developed a multitude of environmental problems, including air and water pollution and growing solid waste production. The good news is that, as Ning reports, Chinese leaders are responding to these challenges with strategies of sustainable development. While these are major positive steps, Ning provides some further suggestions as to what the city needs in the future.

Budhy T. S. Soegijoko and B. S. Kusbiantoro's Chapter 11 describes the positive and negative aspects of globalization in an Indonesia city and identifies the economic, social, and environmental consequences to the city region of Jabotabek. The chapter illustrates the various impacts of the globalization process on Jabotabek by demonstrating the relationship between global flows of goods, services, FDI, people, and information and the spatial and functional transformation of the region. After identifying how the processes of globalization developed within the mega-urban region, the authors provide a detailed description of how the Asian financial crisis has impacted on the city and the necessity to turn towards sustainable development. Their description of the impacts of the Asian financial crisis is a chilling portrayal of the dark underside of the process.

Among environmental and social issues they highlight growing water supply and air pollution issues, accompanied by high levels of poverty and increasing social unrest (due to the increasing disparity of quality of life for the urban region's citizens). Finally, the authors give general strategies that will arguably minimize negative impacts of the globalization process through emphasizing the competitive (product/output) over comparative advantages of the city region.

In Chapter 12, Sauwalak Kittiprapas discusses the overall trends in urban and regional development in Thailand and the recent changes to the extended Bangkok region (EBR). Urbanization pressures, globalization forces, and the financial crisis have provided strong impetus for change, and Kittiprapas recommends specific policies in that regard. The author presents an overview of the internal and external factors impacting on spatial development and urban transformation in Thailand, while also addressing problems resulting from the current economic crisis. Thereafter, Kittiprapas examines the migration and industrial location trends over the recent past, noting that while firms have moved out of Bangkok proper, they are still largely concentrated in the extended Bangkok region. After discussing both recent and future urbanization trends in Thailand and the EBR, she focuses on the impacts of linkages to the global and regional economy. In her concluding sections, she presents some policy responses for sustainable development and a discussion of policy options.

The last set of chapters cover what have been termed the "amenity cities". From these studies it can be concluded that some cities linked to the regional city system are growing in ways that include environmental awareness. Peter A. Murphy and Chung-Tong Wu, in Chapter 13, describe the relationship between globalization and ecological sustainability in Sydney. The city represents the challenges present for Australia's urban system as it strives to achieve sustainability. Sydney is unique because of its size and physical setting, which highlight the importance of environmental issues. The natural amenity of the city is tied to its position within the regional city system, and the authors describe how the citizenry are increasingly aware of the environment. The authors present, in their conclusions, a framework for how globalization has impacted on the capacity and willingness of governments to implement ecologically sustainable development objectives in metropolitan Sydney. They suggest, however, that Sydney's increasing articulation to the global web of flows has blocked managerial objectives of urban governance, concluding that globalization has been an obstruction to the maintenance and improvement of Sydney's environmental quality.

In Chapter 14, Terry G. McGee emphasizes the liveability of cities as a prime goal of urban development in Vancouver, a "sub-global" urban region. His study demonstrates that city regions can develop strategic planning processes which provide liveability and reinforce the competitive strength of an urban region. As the city's growth increasingly relies on tourism as opposed to exports, the tension between growth and the environment has heightened, with the resultant plans promoting growth management and liveability. Yet here, as in the previous chapter, McGee is concerned that the push for "global" status and efficient land usage will severely degrade the current beautiful environment. From the conclusions of these two chapters, it is far from clear that increased globalization will bring environmental quality, even in cities that theoretically use their high and abundant amenity as part of their comparative advantage.

In Chapter 15, Peter Marcotullio attempts not only to draw together some of the ideas and conceptual lessons provided in the preceding chapters, but also to provide a framework within which globalization forces in the region can be connected to urban, social, and environmental sustainability. This chapter is not so much a conclusion as a conceptual piece that points to a specific research agenda. Globalization and environmental and social urban conditions in the Asia Pacific region are distinguished through the usage of the functional city typology. While Chapter 2 describes a framework within which globalization-driven economic development in the region can be understood, this chapter attempts to use this framework to understand the environmental and social challenges within the cities. Rather than being a definitive statement, however, this chapter only sketches out some interesting relationships that need further exploration. The conclusion is that globalization is not only driving the growth of cities in the region, but also impacting on their social and environmental conditions. To deal with challenges in these areas, the author suggests, will take more than good management and local policies. It will increasingly require national, regional, and global policies and institutions.

Notes

1. The major trade and economic organization in the region, the Asia Pacific Economic Cooperation (APEC), created in response to the growing interdependence among Asia Pacific economies, includes the Asian countries mentioned in the text along with Canada, Australia, New Zealand, the USA, Mexico, Chile, and Peru.

REFERENCES

Asian Development Bank (ADB). 1997. *Emerging Asia: Changes and Challenges*. Manila: ADB.

Asian Development Bank (ADB). 1999. *Asian Development Outlook*. Hong Kong: ADB and Oxford University Press.

Burgess, Rod, Marisa Carmona, and Theo Kolstee. 1997. *The Challenge of Sustainable Cities*. London: Zed Books.

Castells, M. 1977. *The Urban Question*. Cambridge, MA: MIT Press.

Douglass, Michael, 1998. "Urban and Regional Policy after the Era of Naïve Globalism", paper presented at the UNCRD Global Forum on Regional Development Policy, 1–4 December, Nagoya.

Far Eastern Economic Review (FEER). 1999. "Environment", in *Asia 1999 Yearbook: A Review of Events of 1998*. Hong Kong: FEER, pp. 58–61.

Friedmann, John and Goetz Wolff. 1982. "World city formation: An agenda for research and action", *International Journal of Urban and Regional Research*, Vol. 6, No. 3, pp. 309–343.

Feagin, Joe R. and Michael Peter Smith. 1985. "Cities and the new international division of labor: An overview", in Michael Peter Smith and Joe R. Feagin (eds) *The Capitalist City*. Oxford: Basil Blackwell, pp. 3–34.

Firman, Tommy. 1999. "From 'global city' to 'city of crisis': Jakarta metropolitan region under economic turmoil", *Habitat International*, Vol. 23, No. 4, pp. 447–466.

Harris, Nigel. 1992. "Wastes, the environment and the international economy", *Cities*, August, pp. 177–185.

Held, David, Anthony McGrew, David Goldblatt, and Jonathan Perraton. 1999. *Global Transformations: Politics, Economics and Culture*. Stanford: Stanford University Press.

IMF. 1999. *World Economic Outlook May 1999*. Washington, DC: IMF.

Lo, Fu-chen and Yue-man Yeung. 1996. *Emerging World Cities in Pacific Asia*. Tokyo: United Nations University Press.

Low, Nicholas, Brendan Gleeson, Ingemar Elander, and Rolf Lidskog (eds). 2000. *Consuming Cities: The Urban Environment in the Global Economy After the Rio Declaration*. London: Routledge.

McGee, Terry G. 1998. "Rethinking regional policy in an era of rapid urbanization and volatile globalization", paper presented at the UNCRD Global Forum on Regional Development Policy, 1–4 December, Nagoya.

Sassen, Saskia. 1991. *The Global City: New York, London, Tokyo*. Princeton: Princeton University Press.

Sassen, Saskia. 1994. *Cities in a World Economy*. Thousand Oaks, CA: Pine Forge Press.

Satterthwaite, David (ed.). 1999. *Sustainable Cities*. London: Earthscan Publications.

Schmidt, Johannes Dragsbaek. 1998. "Globalization and inequality in urban South-East Asia", *Third World Planning Review*, Vol. 20, No. 2, pp. 127–145.

Stren, Richard, Rodney White, and Joseph Whitney (eds). 1992. *Sustainable Cities: Urbanization and the Environment in International Perspective*. Boulder, CO: Westview Press.

United Nations Conference on Trade and Development (UNCTAD). 1999. *Trade and Development Report 1999*. New York: United Nations.

World Bank. 1993. *The East Asian Miracle*. Oxford: Oxford University Press.

World Bank. 1999. *World Bank Development Report 1999/2000*. Oxford: Oxford University Press.

Yeung, Yue-man. 1998. "The promise and peril of globalization", *Progress in Human Geography*, Vol. 22, No. 4, pp. 475–477.

Overview chapters

2

Globalization and urban transformations in the Asia Pacific region

Fu-chen Lo and Peter J. Marcotullio

Introduction

During the past few decades the world economy has experienced increasingly rapid structural adjustments, affecting production, resource utilization, and wealth creation. Cross-border functional integration of economic activities and growing interdependency of nations and regional economic blocs define "globalization", the catchword for the trends. Networks of flows in goods and services, capital, finance, people, and information are linking nations through the activities performed in major metropolitan centres.

The logic of globalization-driven growth has privileged some regions and cities over others. In general, the developed world and some developing and newly industrialized economies (NIEs) have benefited, while many developing countries have been marginalized. Within developed countries the centres of finance and advanced business services as well as those with high-tech industries have benefited, while cities dominated by traditional blue-collar employment have stagnated. Among developing nations, the resulting sets of economic arrangements have been, up until recently, particularly beneficial to East and South-East Asian countries.

Important elements in the evolution of the global system are the expansion of trade, capital flows (particularly direct investments), and a wave of new technologies. Cities have become the nodes in the global web of economic flows and linkages. The result, particularly evident in the Asia Pacific region,[1] is the emergence of a functional city system (Yeung and Lo 1996a).

This chapter attempts to place the economic growth and increasing interdependence of countries in the Asia Pacific region in the context of the developing global economy, and in the process highlight the importance of cities. Further, the emerging character of the urban system and the pattern of urban development within cities in the region will also be presented. The first part of the chapter outlines the processes of globalization by underscoring in different sections how uneven development is part of the globalization process, how interdependency has grown over the last few decades, and how economic growth and interdependency evolved within the Asia Pacific region.[2] The second part of the chapter focuses on the role and changing characteristics of cities in the region by describing the structural linkages among cities and the emergence of an Asia Pacific urban corridor through the development of a functional city system. Among cities integrated in this system, these changes have contributed to a new process of urban development that has been referred to as "world city formation" (Friedmann and Wolff 1982).

Globalization and the Asia Pacific region

Uneven global development

There have been three general ways in which regions and nations have experienced the uneven economic adjustments associated with globalization. First, the structure of production within advanced economies of the North has changed from one based on industrial manufacturing growth and employment to service-dominated economies. Second, a manufacturing belt has emerged in East and South-East Asia. Third, those regions, nations, and localities unable to take part in the global integration of production have been marginalized.

For the past few decades there has been considerable growth in the service sectors of the economies of the OECD countries (Table 2.1). The increases in service activities have occurred rapidly and correspond to national economic structural changes. While industrial production has not disappeared from these economies, the service sector now plays a more dominant role in the growth of national outputs. A result of this change has been higher levels of unemployment, as jobs lost in the manufacturing sector have not been replaced adequately with growth in service employment.[3]

While most of the world's manufacturing production is still located in OECD countries like the USA, Japan, and nations in Western Europe,

Table 2.1 Share of service sector in GDP of G7 countries, 1960 and 1993

Country	1960	1993	% change
USA	58	75[a]	29.31
UK	53	65	22.64
France	52	69	32.69
Germany	41	61	48.78
Japan	42	57	35.71
Canada	60	71	18.33
Italy	46	65	41.30

Source: World Bank, *World Development Report* (various years)
a. 1991 figure.

Table 2.2 Share of manufacturing sector in GDP of selected countries, 1960 and 1993

Country	1960	1993	% change
USA	29	18[a]	−37.93
UK	32	25	−21.88
France	29	22	−24.14
Germany	40	27	−32.50
Japan	34	24	−29.41
Korea	14	29	107.14
Taiwan	35[b]	39[b]	11.40
Singapore	12	37	208.33
Malaysia	9	19[c]	111.11
Indonesia	8	22	175.00
Thailand	13	28	115.38
Philippines	20	24	20.00
China		38	
Argentina	32	20	−37.50
Brazil	26	20	−23.08
Mexico	23	20	−13.04

Source: World Bank, *World Development Report* (various years)
a. 1991 figure.
b. ADB, *Asian Development Outlook* (various years).
c. 1985 figure.

there have been significant changes in the geography of manufacturing output (Table 2.2). The flip side of rapid growth in services in the economies of the developed countries was a substantial loss in manufacturing activities. In all of the G7 countries the share of manufacturing in GDP dropped significantly from 1960 to 1993. In the USA, from 1979 to 1995, 24.8 million blue-collar jobs were extinguished and the new employment created was not in the manufacturing sector (*New York Times*

1996). This decrease in manufacturing employment translated directly into lower production levels: in terms of world share, the manufacturing output from the USA declined from 34.4 per cent in 1965 to 25.7 per cent in 1992.

At the same time an industrial belt has been emerging in the Asia Pacific region, marking the second uneven development consequence of globalization processes. The Asian NIEs, followed by the ASEAN countries, were able to take advantage of the shifting location of industrial manufacturing jobs, while other developing nations have not. The Asian NIEs experienced spectacular manufacturing-sector-driven growth during the past few decades. The percentage of the Republic of Korea's GDP output accounted for by manufacturing increased from approximately 14 per cent to 29 per cent between 1960 and 1993. Singapore's manufacturing component jumped from 12 per cent to 37 per cent of the city-state's GDP during the same period.

The expansion of manufacturing output in these countries has been responsible for their impressive economic achievements. Taiwan, Indonesia, Hong Kong, Singapore, and the Republic of Korea were among the top 10 countries with the highest positive change in GDP per capita in the world between 1965 and 1990 (World Bank 1993). One of the most dramatic cases was Korea, which attained average annual growth rates of almost 8.6 per cent in the 1960s, 10.3 per cent in the 1970s, and 9.7 per cent in the 1980s (Table 2.3). Taiwan's per capita income jumped from US$1,518 in 1962 to US$3,313 in 1972 and US$11,590 in 1992.[4] The island's economy experienced 9.7 per cent annual growth in the 1970s and 7.8 per cent growth in the 1980s. However, only a small set of nations, mostly located in this region, capitalized on the shift in manufacturing production and economic growth.

A third uneven effect of globalization has been the marginalization of a large portion of the developing world. Both Latin America and Africa have felt the negative effects of globalization and were not able to benefit from the positive aspects. Historically, these regions depended on primary product exports for up to 90 per cent of their total export trade. As late as 1990, for all non-Asian developing nations, primary products accounted for over 70 per cent of exports and in sub-Saharan Africa primary products accounted for over 88 per cent of total export earnings (Todaro 1997). In the early 1980s these economies were badly hurt by the fall in both world primary commodity prices and fuel-oil prices. During the period from 1980 to 1992, economic growth per capita in Latin America and the Caribbean averaged −0.2 per cent and in Africa it was −0.8 per cent (ibid.).

The low economic growth in these regions was complicated by the emergence of debt crises for many nations. As countries lost income from

Table 2.3 GDP annual average growth rates of selected economies, by decade

Country	1960–1970	1970–1980	1980–1990
USA	4.3	2.8	3.4[b]
UK	2.9	2.0	3.1
France	5.7	3.2	2.2
Germany	4.4	2.6	2.1[b]
Australia	5.5	3.0	3.4
Japan	10.5	4.3	4.1[b]
Korea	8.6	9.6	9.7
Hong Kong	10.0	9.2	7.1[b]
Taiwan[a]		9.7	7.8
Singapore	8.8	8.3	6.4
Malaysia	6.5	7.9	5.2
Indonesia	3.5	7.2	5.5
Thailand	8.2	7.1	7.6
Philippines	5.1	6.0	0.9
China	9.2	–	9.5
Argentina	4.2	2.5	−0.4
Brazil	5.4	8.1	2.7
Mexico	7.2	6.3	1.0

Source: World Bank, *World Development Report* (various years)
a. ADB, *Asian Development Outlook* (various years); the figures for Taiwan
   cover 1971–1980 and 1981–1990.
b. Estimates.

the drop in world primary commodity prices, interest rates in the USA
were raised to fight inflation. The result was that primary exporting high-
debt countries were unable to pay back debt on loans from both international financial institutions and private banks. By 1990, national debts in
African and Latin American countries had become the heaviest among
the developing world. In 1989, of the 17 countries with a net external debt
of 100 per cent or more of the national GDP, 15 were in Africa, Latin
America, and the Caribbean. For both Latin America and Africa the
1980s were a "lost decade" for development.

The pattern of global economic activity described above is arguably
simplified. For example, the recent growth in the economies of Mexico,
Argentina, Botswana, and Brazil demonstrates that the patterns are not
uniform. However, the industrial belt developing in coastal cities of the
East and South-East Asia Pacific region continues to grow and strengthen
as it attracts investments from Japan, the USA, and Europe. Further,
there is a widening gap in the adoption of new technologies that underpin
economic growth between countries. While the nations that are currently
networked into "globalization" processes are developing and enhancing

the infrastructure necessary for the smooth functioning of global networks, both Africa and Latin America are conspicuously missing from
the plans/projections for advanced telematic hookups (Dicken 1992: 10)
and transportation super-hubs (Rimmer 1997: 459). These and other uneven growth conditions suggest that the pattern of development identified
will not change over the short or medium term (Lo 1994).

Spatial integration and interdependency

One of the most significant features of globalization is the extensive coverage of world commerce by trade, investment, and new technologies that
underpin development. The importance of these constituent elements is
revealed in their size and growth rates. Together these flows, along with
related trends, are enhancing the integration of nations and cities and
promoting the spatial differentiation of economic activities.

World trade has been growing rapidly since 1950 (Table 2.4). From
that time to 1992 the annual average growth rate topped 11.2 per cent,
bringing the net value of global trade from US$61 billion to over US$3.7
trillion (UNCTAD 1994). However, these growth rates are not only
unprecedented, they are also higher than those of global production.
While in 1950 merchandise exports were 7.0 per cent of world GDP, by
1992 global exports accounted for 13.5 per cent of total world output
(Maddison 1995). The expansion of trade is a defining characteristic of
the post-Second World War world economy.

Trade has expanded quickly in East and South-East Asian nations after
the 1950s (Table 2.5). The rapid increases follow a pattern that begins in

Table 2.4 Annual average growth rates of trade, by region

Region	1950–1960 %	1960–1970 %	1970–1980 %	1980–1990 %
World	6.5	9.2	20.3	6.1
Developed market economies	7.1	10.0	18.8	7.8
North America	5.1	8.7	17.0	5.9
EC^a	8.4	10.2	19.3	8.3
Developing countries	3.1	7.2	25.9	2.2
South America^b	2.3	5.1	20.6	2.3
Sub-Saharan Africa	4.8	7.8	20.0	−2.0
South and South-East Asia	0.2	6.7	25.8	10.8

Source: UNCTAD 1994, Tables 1.5 and 1.6, pp. 16–25
a. Includes Belgium Luxembourg, Denmark, France, Germany, Greece, Ireland,
   Italy, the Netherlands, Portugal, Spain, and the UK.
b. Includes Argentina, Brazil, Chile, Mexico, Paraguay, and Uruguay.

Table 2.5 Annual average growth rates of trade, by country

Country	1950–1960 %	1960–1970 %	1970–1980 %	1980–1990 %
USA	5.1	7.8	18.2	5.9
UK	4.8	6.3	18.4	5.8
France	6.4	9.8	19.8	7.7
Germany	16.6	11.4	19.1	9.6
Australia	0.9	7.7	15.9	6.3
Japan	15.9	17.5	20.8	8.9
Korea	1.4	39.6	37.2	15.1
Hong Kong	−0.4	14.5	22.4	16.8
Taiwan	6.5	23.2	28.6	14.8
Singapore	−0.1	3.3	28.2	9.9
Malaysia	0.6	4.3	24.2	8.6
Indonesia	−1.1	1.7	35.9	−1.3
Thailand	1.5	5.9	24.7	14.0
Philippines	4.5	7.5	17.5	3.8
China	19.1	1.3	20.0	12.7
Argentina	−0.2	4.8	18.0	2.1
Brazil	−2.0	7.2	21.7	5.1
Mexico	3.4	6.0	25.7	2.4

Source: UNCTAD 1994, Tables 1.5 and 1.6, pp. 16–25

Japan and is then experienced by the Asian NIEs in the 1960s, then sub-sequently explosive growth rates of trade in ASEAN countries. Further, while the 1970s had brought growth in trade to most countries around the world (average annual world growth rate in trade was 20.3 per cent), the Asian NIEs and the ASEAN countries experienced a particularly rapid expansion in their exports and imports. In the 1980s world trade slowed due to the fall in primary commodity prices and a global recession in the first part of the decade, among other factors, but trade for those countries in Asia continued to grow. The exceptions were Indonesia and the Philippines. Indonesian trade was depressed by the fall in demand for its agricultural and fuel-oil products (particularly in the first half of the decade), and the political instability during that period hurt Philippine economic growth.

Notwithstanding its magnitude and rapid expansion, an important aspect of global trade during the past few decades is the growing complexity of international goods and services commerce. The cross-country arrangement of production processes and the global relocation of their different components have not only helped to expand the importance of this flow, but have also led to increased intrafirm trade. The movement of goods and services within the same company that has plants and offices in different nations has helped to create and sustain international economic linkages.

A significant trade-related phenomenon has been the development of the global finance system. While the world finance system developed to keep the global trade system working smoothly, the flows of global finance alone have subsequently taken on unique importance. Peter Drucker (1986) has suggested that this development represents a separation of the "real economy" of the production and trade of goods and services from the "symbol economy" of credit and financial transactions. This separation is significant in that each "economy" has since then operated independently.

The importance of the international finance system can be seen in the absolute size of and increases in foreign currency trade. For example, in mid-1980s, foreign currency trade exceeded US$150 billion a day, which annually amounted to 12 times the value of world trade in goods and services for that year. By the late 1980s the total was up to US$600 billion a day, no less than 32 times the volume of international commercial transactions worldwide (Drucker 1986; Strange 1994). Transactions in the Eurocurrency markets have risen from US$3 billion in the 1960s to US$75 billion in 1970 and US$1 trillion in 1984 (Strange 1994). These transactions have been encouraged by a global network of 24-hour capital market transactions concentrated in cities such as New York, London, and Tokyo (Sassen 1991).

The institutional structure of the emerging global financial system contributes to its importance. Since the global financial system is a hybrid of states and markets, it is therefore not solely within the command of governments. As the "symbol" and "real" economies have separated, the influence of global markets for money has grown and the power of governments to influence or control these markets has diminished. This system is vulnerable and considered to be the "Achilles' heel" of the global economy (Strange 1994). If confidence in the system fails, decades of achievement can be wiped out in a relatively short period of time. Further, since the financial system is embedded in international transactions, "shocks" in one place are quickly felt in another. While the Mexican financial crisis raised questions for investors and policy-makers, it was the 1997 currency and capital market crises that provided evidence of the interconnected nature of the global finance system. Within a period of days, the stock markets of Bangkok, Kuala Lumpur, Hong Kong, New York, London, Tokyo, Frankfurt, Paris, New Zealand, Brazil, Argentina, and Mexico fell. The current climate within the global financial system demonstrates that given impetus, the reaction on the part of investors to reduce their exposure, even in well-managed economies, can be translated quickly around the world.

While the growth of trade and financial flows is linking the nations of the world, one of the dominating forces of global integration is the rapid increase in flows of foreign direct investment (FDI).[5] The major channel of FDI is the transnational corporation (TNC). This institution may be the most important force creating "global shifts" in economic activity (Dicken 1992). The growth of FDI has been an integral part of the general economic growth in the world economy (UNCTAD 1997).

TNC activity was relatively unimportant until the late 1950s. The total accumulated stock of foreign direct investment rose from US\$14.3 billion in 1914 to US\$26.4 billion in 1938, before soaring to reach US\$66 billion at the end of the 1950s (Dunning and Archer 1987). However, during the 1960s FDI inflows began to explode, and grew at twice the rate of growth of world gross national product and 40 per cent faster than world exports. In the late 1980s FDI inflows to countries around the world grew at the rapid annual average growth rate of over 24 per cent (Table 2.6). In subsequent years the rate of growth of FDI more than doubled that of world trade. By 1996, FDI inflows had reached US\$3 trillion, FDI stocks had reached approximately US\$3.2 trillion, rising from US\$1 trillion in 1987, and the sales and assets of TNC foreign affiliates (US\$6.4 trillion) was higher than total world trades of goods and services (US\$6.1 trillion). The growth of the international production system reflects rapid changes

Table 2.6 Selected indicators of FDI and international production, 1986–1996

Item	Value at current prices (US\$ bn)		Annual growth rate (%)			
	1995	1996	1986–1990	1991–1996	1995	1996
FDI inflow	317	349	24.4	17.1	32.6	10.3
FDI inward stock	2,866	3,233	18.7	11.7	18.7	12.8
Sales of foreign affiliates	5,933[a]	6,412[b]	17.3	4.0[c]	12.5[a]	8.1[b]
Total assets of foreign affiliates	7,091[a]	8,343[b]	19.9	11.2[c]	13.1[a]	17.7[b]
Gross fixed capital formation	6,088	N/A	10.7	4.5[d]	12.4	N/A
Exports of goods and non-factor services	5,848	6,111	14.3	7.4	16.2	4.5

Source: UNCTAD 1997, Table 1.1, p. 4
a. 1993.
b. 1994.
c. 1991–1994.
d. 1991–1995.

in corporate structures and is being pursued through foreign investment channels (UNCTAD 1997).

FDI has been overwhelmingly dominated by TNCs from developed countries. The resultant investment transactions have been described as mainly limited to a "triad" including the EU, North America, and East and South-East Asia (focused on Japan) as the dominant regional blocs (Ohmae 1985). While transnational investment is primarily concentrated in the developed market economies, developing countries are increasingly playing an important role (Table 2.7). Cross-investment between the major developed market economies has increased substantially. The percentage of total global FDI captured by developing countries has increased from 18 per cent in the mid to late 1980s to over 36 per cent in 1996. Asia has captured more than 60 per cent of FDI flows to the developed world. Further, a considerable number of TNCs from a small number of developing countries, most obviously some of the Asian NIEs, have emerged. Among a list of 1995's top 50 TNCs based in developing economies, 34 are home institutions of the four Asian NIEs and China. These 50 firms have total assets ranging from US$1.3 million to US$40 million, total sales ranging from US$366,000 to US$36 million and total number of employees ranging from 7,434 to 200,000. Two of them are included in the 1996 list of the top 100 global TNCs (UNCTAD 1997).

A third key factor that has facilitated and enhanced global restructuring has been the new wave of technological innovations. Advances in micro-electronics, telecommunications, robotics, biotechnology, and new materials have come in rapid succession in developed countries and selected NIEs. As one observer has noted: "[t]echnology is, without doubt, one of the most important contributory factors underlying the internationalization and globalization of economic activity" (Dicken 1992: 97). The world economy is facilitated by new information technologies, in which ideas, capital, and people move rapidly and in large numbers (Lo 1994).

The new wave of technologies has created new growth markets in both developed and developing countries as outdated products and production processes decline in demand. Information technologies play a key role in increasing global integration and speeding economic transactions. The Internet and related telecommunications technologies will make markets more transparent and continue to drive globalization processes as they drive prices for long-distance transactions down. For example, a three-minute telephone call between New York and London has fallen in price from US$300 (in 1996 dollars) in 1930 to US$1 in 1997 (*The Economist* 1997). According to a UN forecast, the potential from information technology will increase 10 times between 1990 and the year 2000 (United Nations 1990). By the year 2000, more than half of the capital goods

Table 2.7 FDI inflows, by host region and economy, 1985–1996

Host region/economy	US$ bn			Cumulative growth 1991–1996 (US$ bn)	Average FDI inflow 1991–1996 (US$ bn)	% change 1991–1996
	1985–1990 (annual average)	1991	1996			
World	141.9	158.9	349.2	1,455.3	242.5	17.1
Developed countries	116.7	114.8	208.2	929.7	155.0	12.6
European Union	52.7	78.8	99.4	526.3	87.7	4.8
North America	53.9	25.5	91.3	317.6	52.9	29.0
Other	10.2	10.5	17.5	85.8	14.3	10.8
Developing countries	24.7	41.7	128.7	479.9	80.0	25.3
Latin America	8.1	15.4	38.6	140.6	23.4	20.2
South, East, and South-East Asia	12.4	21.2	81.2	298.3	49.7	30.8
Other	4.2	5.1	8.9			11.8
Central and Eastern Europe	0.5	2.4	12.3			38.0
Republic of Korea	0.7	1.2	2.3	7.4	1.2	14.4
Singapore	3.0	4.9	9.4	33.6	5.6	14.1
Thailand	1.0	2.0	2.4	11.6	1.9	3.8
Indonesia	0.6	1.5	8.0	19.7	3.3	40.0
Malaysia	1.1	4.0	5.3	28.0	4.7	5.8
Philippines	0.4	0.5	1.4	6.5	1.1	20.9
China	2.7	4.4	42.3	155.0	25.8	57.5
Viet Nam	0.0	0.2	2.2	6.0	1.0	56.6

Source: UNCTAD 1997, Table B.1, pp. 303–307

31

industries of the industrialized countries will be dominated by newly developed high technologies (Lo and Nakamura 1992).

While the major breakthroughs in the transport of goods and services occurred in the nineteenth century, modern enhancements such as large cargo freighters and jumbo jets have improved the movement of goods and services. More importantly, the expansion and development of commercial high-speed passenger transportation have allowed for a tandem rise of annual distance travelled and personal income. That is, while people from different classes and societies are spending the same average amount of time travelling per day,[6] those with higher incomes are travelling further. Thus, as world GDP per person has increased, so has total person kilometre miles (PKM). For example, total PKM travelled has increased by over four times from 5.5 trillion PKM in 1960 to 23.4 trillion PKM in 1990, and is expected to more than double by 2020 to 53 trillion PKM (Schafer and Victor 1997). This has helped to create a community of global travellers that has increasingly significant social consequences. Innovations and advances in information and transportation are but a few of the new wave of technologies that are enabling truly large-scale revolutionary change. Together they have helped to bring about a new "techno-economic paradigm" based on knowledge-intensive production (Lo 1994).

The internationalization of production, finance, banking, and services, coupled with advances in telecommunications, information, and transportation, have helped to minimize the importance of national boundaries in decisions to locate production plants (Friedmann 1986; Nakakita 1988). Increases in trade, finance, and investments have the effect of creating a "borderless" global economy (Ohmae 1990). This "borderless" economy has become a distinctive feature of the new global economic system and it symbolizes the interpenetration of transnational economic activity among national economies. The growing interdependence that accompanies these linkages is based on complementary relationships among different entities. Although examples of regional complementary and cooperative relationships are rare, they are developing.[7] The end of the 1980s saw growing interest in economic cooperation as a result of major global political changes, acceleration in the pace of liberalization, and the perceived need, particularly in Asia Pacific economies, to maintain competitiveness in the global economy.

Economic growth and structural interdependence in the Asia Pacific region

As mentioned previously, the economies in the Asia Pacific region have been undergoing rapid and intensive economic growth (Table 2.3). Since the 1960s, nations in East Asia and the Pacific have had higher growth rates than any other region of the world. Indeed, the progress of some countries in the region has been described as nothing short of a "miracle" (World Bank 1993).

The rapid rise of Asian economies and the region's developing structural interdependence began with Japan's recovery from the Second World War. Starting with the Korean War in the early 1950s, Japan's economy revived and expanded dramatically. Japan's GDP growth soared in relation to that of the USA. In 1960 Japan's production output was 8.5 per cent of that of the USA. By 1970 it was 20 per cent of that of the world's largest economy, and by 1990 Japan's GDP was 55 per cent of that of the USA. (World Bank, *World Development Report*, various years). By 1992, Japan's GNP per capita was second in the world to that of Switzerland, and amounted to US$28,190. Japanese economic power was housed in large institutions, including 10 of the world's largest banks and 315 of the world's top 1,000 corporations. They also controlled a leading position in 25 of 34 technologies considered essential for a post-industrial world (Nester 1990). Between 1986 and 1990 Japanese firms received 44 per cent of all the patents issued around the world for robot technology and 33 per cent of patents on optical fibre technology (National Science Board 1994). Japan's current account balance for 1992 was the largest in the world, totalling, after official transfers, US$118 billion. However, Japan's role was not limited solely to providing new prominence to the region as an emerging economic giant. More significantly, it led the way in reshaping the economic activity in East and South-East Asia through trade and intraregional investment. Indeed, the region has developed in Japan's embrace (Shinohara and Lo 1989; Hatch and Yamamura 1996).

Japanese trade and investments in the Asia Pacific region have been the key to both the initial success of the region and the restructuring of many of the area's economies. Japanese exports have been increasingly directed to nations in the region. For example, between 1975 and 1985 the value of Japanese products exported to the Republic of Korea, Singapore, Malaysia, and Thailand increased by 202 per cent, 226 per cent, 378 per cent, and 121 per cent respectively (Akita, Lo, and Nakamura 1997). By 1987, Japan's trade with the Asian NIEs had increased so sharply that it was of roughly the same magnitude as its trade with the 12 countries of the then European Community (Yeung and Lo 1996b). By 1996, Japan's exports to the world amounted to US$400.5 billion and over 45 per cent of that went to Asia (JETRO 1997).

Japanese trade in Asia grew with the importance of intrafirm trade among Japanese companies. Many Japanese TNCs have subsidiaries located in the region with which they trade parts and services. In this way

Japanese trade has strengthened its economic linkages to developing countries in the region. Therefore the basis for increased Japanese trade with the Asian NIEs and ASEAN originated and developed with FDI. At its height, the region's catch of Japanese FDI reached 11.7 per cent in 1988 at US$5.2 billion (Yeung and Lo 1996b).[8] It is the accumulation of Japanese FDI and the technologies that have accompanied these investments that have provided the original impulse for the region's growth and strengthened its interdependency.

The historical pattern of regional economic development within East and South-East Asia is related to three waves of spatially concentrated investments. The first wave began with the relocation of Japan's manufacturing industries to offshore sites in the Republic of Korea, Taiwan, Singapore, and Hong Kong. During the 1960s and 1970s Japanese firms, experiencing escalating labour and material costs of production at home, were looking for sites elsewhere (Kojima 1978). At that time, Japanese investments in Asia were in labour-intensive manufacturing, and the Asian NIEs not only provided cheaper labour but also new markets for goods. The host countries welcomed the employment, capital infusion, and technological uplift that accompanied the investments.

The second wave occurred in the 1970s and 1980s, when the comparative advantage of countries in ASEAN attracted Japanese investment. At first, industrial investment decisions to relocate factories were related to the factor endowments and the comparative advantages of specific localities. This industrialization pattern became the catalyst for the "flying geese" pattern of development (Yamazawa 1990).[9] In this industrialization process, latecomers successfully entered sectors in which they had an increasing comparative advantage in terms of cost. They also imported technology from already mature economies whose competitive advantage in that industry was declining. They later invested in new industrial products using new technologies and know-how for which they had the innovative edge.

Japan led the region in relocating light manufactured goods industries to NIEs in the 1970s. The Asian NIEs responded and shifted their exports to light manufacturing, and subsequently to durable consumer goods and machinery products. Almost simultaneously the ASEAN group shifted from raw material exports to manufacturing exports and then light manufacturing. The movement of industrial production followed the shift of investment, from Japan to the NIEs and then to ASEAN.

Since then Japanese interindustrial linkages with the NIEs and ASEAN have diversified into chemical products, metal products, machinery and transport equipment, construction, and even high-tech industries. These industries were dominated by interindustry structures that were not easily replicable. They therefore did not conform to the flying geese model as experienced previously. Many of these types of industries were relocated based on so-called "borrowed technology", and depended on Japan and other industrialized economies for capital goods, technology, and direct investment (Lo, Salih, and Nakamura 1989). The inflows of FDI and technology took on a "billiard ball" pattern where parts of the production process for one product were located in a variety of different localities (Ohta, Tokuno and Takeuchi 1995). While the pattern of development no longer strictly resembles the flying geese model, the resultant East Asian industrial belt has been further strengthened by the intraregional structural linkages among Japan, the NIEs, and ASEAN nations (Lo and Nakamura 1992).

The flow of Japanese capital was enhanced by a seemingly unrelated set of events in foreign relations. Exchange rate alignments among the major developing countries not only helped to sustain a long economic boom over the latter half of the 1980s for developed nations, but also impacted on the economic flows of goods, services, and investment to developing nations in the Asia Pacific region. The appreciation of the yen (*endaka*) as a result of the Plaza Accord of September 1985 helped to provide further incentive for Japanese investment into Asian NIEs and later into ASEAN and China (Lo 1994).

Although after the Plaza Accord the leading recipients of total Japanese investment were still the USA and European countries, the gravity of Japanese manufacturing investment shifted to the NIEs and ASEAN nations. Japanese companies were anxious to relocate their production processes abroad in order to maintain a competitive edge. During the short period from 1985 to 1988, Japanese investment cases in ASEAN rose from 292 different investments amounting to US$9.3 billion to 825 investments amounting to US$27.1 billion (Yamashita 1991). Japanese investment stock accumulated in Asia from 1985 to 1987 totalled US$422 million, compared to an accumulated stock of US$593 million from the previous three decades (Nakakita 1988).

The appreciation of the yen was followed by a similar appreciation of the currencies of the Republic of Korea and Taiwan in 1986 and 1987. These "little tigers", in turn, also enhanced their export manufacturing competitiveness by relocating domestic industries to cheaper locations. FDI from Taiwan, Hong Kong, and Singapore exhibited a gravitational tendency and remained in neighbouring nations in Asian. Taiwan first, followed by Korea, Singapore, and Hong Kong, were extremely important as sources of FDI for ASEAN during the late 1980s (Yamazawa and Lo 1993). For example, by 1986 Taiwan ranked second in value to Japan in its investments in Thailand (Lo, Salih, and Nakamura 1989). Korea invested over US$250 million in cumulative stock in 1988 in ASEAN. However, Korea's overseas investment continued to rise. By 1990, it hit a record of US$959 million, an increase of 68 per cent over the previous year (Clifford 1991).

Hong Kong and Singapore followed the lead of Korea and Taiwan. Hong Kong provided FDI to China, and especially to its immediate hinterland, the Pearl river delta. Vast quantities of manufacturing investment poured out of Hong Kong into neighbouring Guangdong province. It was estimated that Hong Kong businesses employed some 2 million workers in that region in thousands of small factories. Hong Kong has also been a substantial provider of investment in Indonesia and Thailand (Yeung 1994). Singapore's direct investments also flow to its neighbourhood. Two-thirds of the total investments from Singapore are located in Malaysia, and another 24 per cent went to Indonesia. Singapore's two closest neighbours were the recipients of almost 90 per cent of its total investment in Asia (Dicken 1992).

The inflows of FDI facilitated structural changes in trade orientation and economic development in ASEAN countries. As a result of the FDI, ASEAN countries underwent major economic restructuring, particularly from being commodity exporters in the 1960s to being manufacturing exporters in the 1980s. Starting in the mid-1980s, the share of manufacturing exports began to rise dramatically in these countries. Just as primary commodity prices dropped in the early 1980s, the inflow of investment provided the ASEAN countries with timely and critical support for the development of new export industries. Export-oriented FDI stimulated the manufacturing sector in these countries. During the period from 1980 to 1990 manufacturing industry exports almost tripled from 21.8 per cent to 59.8 per cent for all ASEAN countries. Indonesia's manufacturing share of exports increased 15.6 times, while Singapore and Thailand also made impressive gains (Yeung and Lo 1996b). In general the exports from the Asia Pacific region increased dramatically after 1985. The four Asian NIEs and the ASEAN countries accounted for only 12 per cent of world exports in that year, but by 1993 their share had climbed to 19 per cent. It has been estimated that Asia Pacific exports will reach 23 per cent of total world trade in 1998, and this figure does not include Japan's contribution, nor China's increasingly significant one (*US News and World Report* 1993). Outward-oriented export expansion-based growth has been the most important factor in explaining Asia Pacific nations escaping the fate of African and Latin American countries during that period. For example, Indonesia was hard hit by the drop in oil prices, but still overcame the "Dutch disease"[10] in the mid-1980s as it switched from oil revenue to other types of goods and services for its export-led growth (Saldi 1989). The structural changes associated with FDI inflows allowed Asian NIEs and ASEAN nations to switch first to export manufacturing before subsequently increasing their production capacities.

The third wave of foreign investment and development occurred after the mid-1980s and centred on China. In the early 1980s four special economic zones in Guangdong and Fujian in southern China saw rapid development because of their special privileges in setting policies to make foreign investment attractive and propitious. With positive results from this experiment, Premier Zhao Ziyang was able to introduce an ambitious plan to extend the practice of encouraging FDI to 14 other cities along the coast in 1984. Then, in 1990, a successful new development area was designated in the Pudong area near Shanghai. The governmental efforts in the Pudong New Area of Shanghai helped to turn the city from a domestic economic centre to an international metropolis between 1990 and 1995, with the inflow of US$8.52 billion (Ning and Wang 1996). As China's general open policy gathered momentum, FDI converged on its coastal cities, making them the generators of over 53 per cent of the total Chinese GDP.

China has now become the magnet for FDI in the region. In 1992 China approved 48,764 foreign investment projects, with the contracted amount reaching US$58.1 billion, of which US$11 billion was utilized. These are increases of 276 per cent, 385 per cent, and 152 per cent respectively over the previous year (Xiaoji 1995). Although as early as 1986 more than half of China's import and export trade went into the Asia Pacific region (Yu 1989), the massive inflow of FDI into Chinese coastal cities, particularly from Japan,[11] has tightened regional economic integration and secured China's role in the region's growth.

In the early 1990s the region experienced increased investments from the Asian NIEs, ASEAN, and non-regional economies. By 1994, FDI from the individual Asian NIEs into the region was approaching the levels of flow from Japan, and in the case of Hong Kong tripled Japanese investments (Table 2.8). During that year, the investments from these countries were primarily directed at ASEAN and China. However, Japan has maintained a considerable investment interest despite its sagging post-bubble economy. In the early 1990s, Japanese manufacturers, particularly machine-makers, continued to invest heavily in the region. The share of Japanese manufacturing FDI in Asia has grown from 19.8 per cent in 1990 to 32.9 per cent in 1993, while falling from 43.9 per cent to 37.2 per cent in North America and from 29.7 per cent to 18.3 per cent in Europe over the same period (Fukushima and Kwan 1995). Japanese FDI increased sharply in Thailand during 1993 and 1994 as Casio, Sony, Toyota, and Honda expanded their production capacities. Japanese firms have also recently increased investments in the Philippines, Indonesia, Malaysia, and China (Hatch and Yamamura 1996). Heightening the draw of investment is the growing market for final consumption of goods and services among many developing countries in the region.

While in general the percentage ratio of FDI to domestic capital for-

Table 2.8 Intraregional flows of FDI in East and South-East Asia, 1994

US$ million

In Out	Japan	NIEs	Korea	Taiwan	Hong Kong	Singa-pore	ASEAN	Thai-land	Malay-sia	Philip-pines	Indo-nesia	China	Total FDI outflows
Japan	–	1,667	428	391	249	598	4,894	2,556	673	103	1,563	2,075	8,636
NIEs	226	543	128	402	13	0	15,945	1,282	1,989	631	12,043	24,959	41,673
Korea	66	5	–	5	N/A	N/A	2,049	29	156	15	1,849	723	2,843
Taiwan	25	68	65	–	3	N/A	4,325	475	1,059	268	2,488	3,391	7,809
Hong Kong	77	267	43	224	–	N/A	6,874	211	333	288	6,042	19,665	26,883
Singapore	58	203	20	174	10	–	2,697	567	405	60	1,664	1,180	4,138
ASEAN	1	29	6	8	15	0	–	766	75	5	216	469	499
Thailand	0	2	1	1	0	N/A	72	–	4	56	12	235	309
Malaysia	0	23	5	3	15	N/A	650	68	–	160	422	201	874
Philippines	1	3	0	3	N/A	N/A	43	6	1	–	36	140	187
Indonesia	0	1	0	0	1	N/A	0	0	0	0	–	116	117
China	7	25	6	N/A	19	N/A	25	89	7	17	91	–	57

Source: Japan Development Bank 1996

mation in NIEs and ASEAN is not large, it is still vitally important to these countries. By 1996, the ratio of FDI inflows to gross domestic fixed capital did not exceed 8.2 per cent in developing countries, but was much higher for Asian countries like Singapore (24.6 per cent), Malaysia (17.9 per cent), and China (25.7 per cent) (UNCTAD 1997). Further FDI flows into the NIEs and ASEAN represent continuous technological uplift. For example, Japanese joint ventures promoted technology transfer through on-the-job training (OJT), quality control (QC), and production management (Yamashita 1991). In 1992, of 231 affiliates surveyed, 54 per cent of all TNCs operating in South, East and South-East Asia had transferred their management technologies and quality control (UNCTAD 1995). Technological diffusion is having a cumulative impact on economic growth. Domestic firms in Malaysia, for example, have acquired substantial operation and process adaptation knowledge and experience in the production processes in the electronics industry through foreign investments (Salleh 1995).

The flows of FDI and transfers of technologies have had a synergistic effect on both inter- and intraregional trade, and have made the region economically complementary. Since the economies of Japan, Asian NIEs, ASEAN, and China are at different stages of economic development and have different population sizes, resource endowments, and structures of production, the combination of shifting comparative advantage for certain industries and interregional FDI investment flows has strengthened structural interdependency. This has stimulated plans for the manufacturing of entirely regional products. Nissan, for example, has announced plans to assemble the "first truly regional, strategic vehicle", called the NV (new vehicle), with parts coming from Thailand, Taiwan, Malaysia, the Philippines, and Japan (Hatch and Yamamura 1996: 26). Over the recent past the spread of industrialization from Japan to the NIEs and then to ASEAN has facilitated the international division of labour and allowed countries at different stages to climb up the comparative advantage ladder (Yamazawa and Lo 1993). The East Asian industrial belt that has developed will only get stronger with continued political stability, the growing openness of China, and the trend away from trade and investment protectionism.

Urban transformations in the Asia Pacific region

At the centre of global integration are the interlinkages of cities and major metropolises into a world city system. The rise and then stagnation of OPEC cities, the debt burden of Latin American metropolises, the stagnation of import-substitution industries in African urban centres, and the rising role of Tokyo and other Asian cities as new trade and financial centres in the world economy clearly demonstrate how the major metropolitan centres in the world have been affected by global structural adjustments.

Previously urban scholars believed that cities, metropolises, or megalopolises took their shape and character from the economic and social processes largely operating within the limits of national territories. However, the movements of capital, people, and information have expanded urban hinterlands across national boundaries. The new "borderless" economy has resulted in the development of an international hierarchical system of cities, and international transactions now impinge on city form. The system of cities that has developed in East and South-East Asia is based on integrated sets of economic functions. This section reviews the structural linkages between cities in the region and the development of the Asia Pacific city system. The differentiated process of world city formation has further compelled cities to enhance their international roles. The resulting patterns of urban development demonstrate that both domestic and international forces order city forms.

The structural linkages of cities in the Asia Pacific region

Among a variety of developing urban networks within the Asia Pacific region, the emergence of a large urban corridor has been identified (Yeung and Lo 1996a). This corridor stretches between the Tokyo area and north-east China via the two Koreas to Malaysia, Indonesia, and the Philippines. A bird's-eye view of the area suggests that the urban corridor is composed of a set of smaller-scale urban corridors including the Pan-Japan Sea Zone, the Pan-Bohai Zone, and the South China Zone, among others. Choe (1996) has provided the best illustration of a mature transnational subregional urban corridor, in which an inverted S-shaped 1,500 km urban belt from Beijing to Tokyo via Pyongyang and Seoul connects 77 cities with over 200,000 inhabitants each into an urban conglomeration of over 97 million people (Figure 2.1)!

In the past urban scholars thought that echelons of connected cities organized by city size, the operations they performed for the immediate surrounding area, and the nature of local trading relationships constituted urban systems. Central-place theory attempted to address urban system structures (in terms of size, spacing of cities, and the configuration of their market areas) by concentrating on the interdependence of urbanization and local (national) trade. However, given recent changes in the global economy and the changing nature of trade, it is useful to consider urban system development in the light of the central role of cities in the "borderless" economy. City size alone is no longer a good indicator of

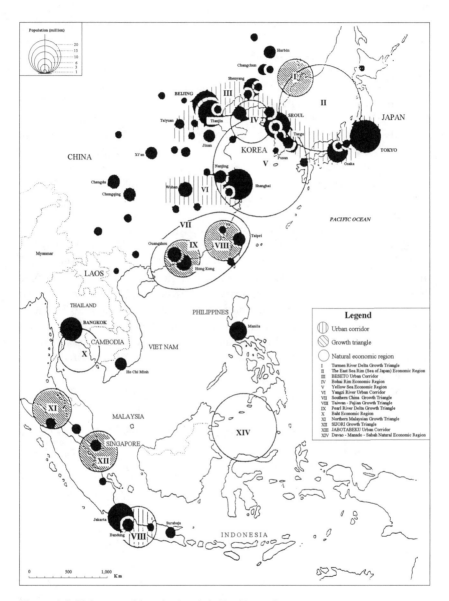

Figure 2.1 Urban corridors in the Asia Pacific region
Source: Choe 1998, Figure 7.3

41

importance (Chase-Dunn 1985; King 1990), rather the basis of a city's centrality in the global system is its articulation into a functional network of cities (Heenan 1977; Friedmann and Wolff 1982; Timberlake 1985; Henderson and Castells 1987).

The urban corridor in the Asia Pacific region is not simply a set of mega-cities exclusively providing goods and services, markets, and governmental services for individual nations. It is a transnational system of functionally integrated cities. This network of cities links, in a hierarchical manner, the nations in the region through the imperatives (trade, finance, investments, transportation, commerce, banking, services, government administration, manufacturing production, and so on) of globalization. It has therefore been referred to as a functional city system (Yeung and Lo 1996a). The implication of this system is that the accumulation of networks provides the basis for development and the measure of a city's international importance.

However, the functional city system in the Asia Pacific region is enhanced through the dual importance of networked cities as both international and domestic centres of growth. Table 2.9 demonstrates how important some individual cities in the region are to their domestic economies. These figures are conservative estimates, and show that both the population and percentage share of GDP are concentrated in single urban centres. If the boundaries of these cities were extended to encompass the extended metropolitan area for each locality, the shares of these indicators would increase substantially. In 1992 DKI Jakarta and its

Table 2.9 Comparative scale of metropolitan economies in major East Asian cities, 1993

City	Population		Gross domestic product		Share of FDI	
	Number (10,000)	National share %	Amount (US$100,000)	National share %	Inner city %	Extended metroplitan area %
Singapore	293	100.0	551	100.0		
Kuala Lumpur	115	6.5	71	11.2	0.4	20.5
Bangkok	555	9.9	531	42.6		46.8
Manila	793	13.6	175	32.2	14.7	56.1
Jakarta	826	4.6	201	12.7	15.2	45.7
Shanghai	953	0.8	262	4.4	8.9	20.6[a]
Hong Kong	606	100.0	1,164	100.0		
Taipei	265	12.7	305	13.5		
Seoul	1,061	24.4	819	24.6		

Source: Japan Development Bank 1996
a. Yangtze delta area.

surrounding administrative districts, collectively called Jabotabek,[12] accounted for over 23 per cent of the GDP of Indonesia (Soegijoko 1996b). Notwithstanding the importance of the metropolitan region, the figures in this table demonstrate the importance of these central city areas to the domestic production of their respective countries.

At the same time these cities are the sites of international transactions, such as FDI flows, international trade, and transportation and communication networks, as discussed previously. As Table 2.9 also indicates, a large proportion of the FDI into the nations in the region flows into the major urban centres. In many nations FDI inflows are predominately directed to these primate cities. In 1993, Bangkok, Manila, and Jakarta all received over 40 per cent of all foreign investments into their respective countries. These relationships represent developing trends. Between 1967 and 1991, investment in Jakarta accounted for one-fifth and one-third of total domestic and foreign investment projects, respectively. These shares would double if the Botabek region outside Jakarta were included. Bogor, Tangerang, and Bekasi accounted for more than half of domestic investment and almost 50 per cent of foreign investment cumulatively from 1967 to the end of 1990 (Soegijoko 1996a). In Bangkok, from 1979 to 1990, 67.8 per cent of all approved foreign direct investment for Thailand was located in the surrounding five provinces (inner ring) of the city (Krongkaew 1996).

International trade also flows through these cities. Singapore and Hong Kong, as city ports, represent extreme cases of trade-city nexus. Singapore's exports of goods and non-factor services were 170 per cent of its GDP in 1990, and during the same year Hong Kong's exports were 137 per cent of its GDP trade (World Bank 1992). While the large volume of trade does not represent the imports of goods consumed in the city and amounts of exports are not strictly related to internal production, the traffic adds significantly to urban economic growth via the necessity to service trade flow. In other cities, trade from domestically produced and consumed goods and services is important to economic growth. In Jakarta, Indonesia, the 1989 value of the city's exports accounted for one-third of Indonesia's exports (excluding oil and gas), and the city's share of trade has been increasing since 1986. During that same year, 50 per cent of all imports to the country moved through the city (Soegijoko 1996a).

Global and regional integration is highly dependent on transportation and communication networks. Transportation networks are developing rapidly in the region. Eleven of the top 25 container ports that dominate world container traffic are now located in East and South-East Asia, and the region also has six or seven of the busiest airports in the world, carrying both passengers and freight to global destinations (Rimmer 1996). Meanwhile, the diffusion of information technologies has progressed in few developing countries, but among those nations where it has begun to proliferate are the Asian NIEs, including Hong Kong, the Republic of Korea, Singapore, and Taiwan (Soubra 1995).

Regional integration is also based on political relations among nations and cities. Many nations in the region have attempted to enhance their integration into the global economy by liberalizing FDI, finance, and trade policies (World Bank 1993). Urban areas in North-East Asia and the Asia Pacific region have also been initiating regional cooperative efforts on a city-to-city basis. Some medium-sized cities (Kobe, Kitakyushu, and Niigata in Japan; Khabarovsk, Sakhalin, and Irkutsk in the Common-wealth of Independent States; and Jilin, Dalian, and Hunchun in China) are actively engaged in political efforts to establish cross-national link-ages (Hong 1996).

These conditions strongly suggest that within the Asia Pacific region an integrated system of urban-based networks is developing into a large urban corridor. Those cities integrated into the system have been under-going changes related to their roles. These changes have a profound im-pact on the physical form of the city.

World city formation Asia Pacific style[13]

While local economic, political, and social influence continues to play a major role in shaping cities, the changing world economy has brought attention to regional and global impacts on the physical character of urban centres, particularly those articulated to the world economy (Sassen 1994). A number of works have attempted to identify the urban centres that should be included in the category of "world cities" (Cohen 1981; Friedmann 1986; King 1990; Sassen 1991). These attempts usually char-acterize world cities as those that provide advanced financial services, business services, headquarters of TNCs, and international institutions and transportation linkages. Therefore a valuable approach to the study of the cities in the Asia Pacific region is to identify the physical changes that have accompanied their integration into the larger system. Identifying changing patterns in urban form and conceptualizing world city formation as a process are critical to the understanding of the functional city system.

In order to be effective in the global and regional economies, cities in the region have been preparing themselves in a variety of ways. Many cities have spared no efforts or costs in infrastructure investment, creating space within their administrative boundaries and improving themselves, physically and economically, so as to be able to enhance their roles as command posts, financial centres, headquarters venues, transport hubs, and industrial centres. The improvements to urban infrastructure to ac-commodate globalization needs include new transportation facilities, technological-oriented modern buildings, financial districts, and new town development. International economic flows have also been facilitated by a variety of government policies to attract investments and direct FDI to specific locations.

Asia Pacific governments have been investing heavily in transportation and telecommunications developments. One popular project has been the large futuristic airport, such as the recently opened Chek Lap Kok in Hong Kong, Kansai airport in Osaka, the Seoul metropolitan airport, and Nong Ngu Hao in Bangkok. Indeed, the concept of the "Pearl river delta" could be marketed only because of the plethora of new airport openings in the region. Locations besides Hong Kong include an airport capable of receiving large aircraft in Shenzhen, a modern new air facility in Macau, another in Zhuhai (a city adjoining Macau), and approval from Beijing for one in Guangzhou (Vittachi 1995). Before the Asian financial crisis of 1997, 11 new airports were planned for opening within the next 10 years in different cities throughout this area (Yeung 1996). Those cities in the region with large airport terminals are in the process of upgrading them. Cities such as Taipei and Singapore[14] already have large modern facilities, but are planning for future expansions (Japan Development Bank 1996).

Another set of transportation improvements include road and rail access to large cities. In the period 1965–1975 highway usage increased at a rate of 10.7 per cent per year, and truck tonnage increased by 7.19 per cent compared with the annual growth rate of 4.7 per cent. In road and rail transport, Hong Kong and Japan have been the high infrastructure investors. During the post-war years Japan successfully pioneered high-speed trains (*Shinkansen*) that revolutionized short-distance travel. Between 1990 and 1993, Hong Kong truck tonnage grew at 15.3 per cent annually and passenger numbers grew by 8.9 per cent (Yeung 1996). This represents the result of heavy investment in roads. Both cities have also invested heavily in bridges. In 1994 alone, Hong Kong awarded six "considerable size" bridge contracts to international construction conglomerates (Thornton 1995). Hong Kong's newly opened Tsing Ma bridge is the biggest railway suspension bridge in the world. Hong Kong recently finished a US$20 billion transportation project and is committed to spending another US$30 billion on future transportation infrastructure over the next five years (Leung 1998).

The Republic of Korea and Malaysia have also invested in transportation facilities. Korea started its transportation investment with the Seoul-Pusan, Seoul-Incheon and Daejon-Jeonju express highways in the late 1960s, and by 1990 had completed over 1,551 km of expressway (Hong 1997). Korea is also building a high-speed railway system (Thornton 1995). Kuala Lumpur recently finished the first line of an urban light-rail system. Malaysia's Renong group also completed an 800 km north-south highway for US$2.3 billion in 1994. Renong is currently vying for a US$725 million contract to build a high-speed "tilting train". Once completed this train will slash travelling times between Rawang, Kuala Lumpur, and Ipoh, 174 km to the north (Jayasankaran 1997).

The volume of trade generated by the region has facilitated the development of the world's largest cargo ports. Most of the import and export traffic flows through selected cities. For example, 80 per cent of Korea's imports and exports go through Pusan (Thornton 1995). It's no surprise then that 12 of the "top 25" container ports for 1992 are located in the region (Rimmer 1996).[15]

Another important response to global economic pressures has been the development of infrastructure for high-speed transmissions of information. As mentioned previously, although the region is lagging behind the rest of the world, business services, and hence rapid transmission of information, are of growing importance in selected cities (Edgington and Haga 1998). In general, large cities in the region are the best providers of telecommunications services. Two to three times the percentage of urban dwellers enjoy telecommunications links in the cities of Bangkok, Manila, Jakarta, and Shanghai than those in smaller cities or rural areas of their respective countries (Japan Development Bank 1996). But in some Asian cities, information technologies have taken on extra importance. Singapore has attempted to restructure its economy toward the creation of an information city. A 1991 government publication set out the key role of the information economy in meeting the city-state's needs. Singapore is aiming to make itself a hub of communications, finance, and travel. Information technology is at the core of plans for the city's future (Perry, Kong, and Yeoh 1997). The Teleport project in Tokyo, less than six kilometres from downtown, was planned as an information and futuristic city. The estimated construction cost of the area's infrastructure alone is approximately US$20 billion (Tokyo Metropolitan Government 1996). Malaysia's "multimedia super corridor", Cyberjaya, that would stretch from Kuala Lumpur 50 kilometres to the south, ending at a new international airport, has begun construction (Jayasankaran 1997). This project is envisioned as a setting for multimedia and information technology companies and is being promoted through government incentives (Sirat 1998).

Location decisions for TNCs not only include consideration of the amount of infrastructure but also its type and quality, as particular industries have specific requirements (Peck 1996). Asia Pacific governments, in efforts to provide incentives to firms, have developed "industrial parks" on the outskirts of cities. Much of this development has been concentrated in and around major metropolitan cities in the region. In Singapore, Taipei, and Seoul, industrial parks have operated with success, prompted and supported by government and private investments.

One important and controversial device to stimulate exports and foreign investment has been the development of export processing zones (EPZs). An EPZ is a relatively small, separated area that is designated as a zone for favourable investment and trade conditions (compared with the host country). In effect they are export enclaves within which special concessions apply, including extensive incentives and often exemption from certain kinds of limiting legislation. The government provides the physical infrastructure necessary for industries. What is important about EPZs is that they are set up for manufacturing. While some EPZs have been incorporated into airports, seaports, or commercial free zones located next to large cities, others have been set up in relatively undeveloped areas as part of a regional development strategy. Asia contains 60 per cent of all EPZ employment in developing countries. Hong Kong and Singapore are, in effect, entire free zones, but with export processing activities concentrated in a number of industrial estates. In 1986, total employment in such zones was 89,000 in Hong Kong and 217,000 in Singapore. The other major concentrations are in Taiwan (80,469 employed in four EPZs), Malaysia (81,688 in 11 EPZs), the Republic of Korea (140,000 in three EPZs) and the Philippines (39,000 in three EPZs)(Dicken 1992).

Apart from these publicly financed infrastructure projects, the private sector has also been intimately involved in the world city formation process in Asia Pacific cities. Large-scale urban redevelopment projects, funded in many cases by the private sector, are seen as a way to restructure land uses and stimulate the local economy (Amborski and Keare 1998). For example, well-located areas previously occupied by railroad facilities, related transportation, and industrial uses have been left abandoned in many cities as more goods are now shipped in containers from a small number of ports and terminals. These areas represent opportunities for redevelopment and have helped to advance the inner-city mega-project developments that came into vogue at the end of the twentieth century. Over three dozen have been identified around the world (Olds 1995). In Tokyo the four largest redevelopment projects are the Tokyo Metropolitan Government, Yebisu Garden Plaza, the Tokyo International Forum, and the Tokyo Teleport. These projects represent redevelopment efforts that have been compared in scale to the rebuilding undertaken after the great Kanto earthquake in 1923 and the city's reconstruction after the 1945 Second World War bombings (Cybriwsky undated). The city has been expanding (more quickly during the 1980s) in all directions possible:

up to new heights; out to the edges of the Kanto plain; off into Tokyo Bay; and down below the ground.

These mega-projects often include high-profile "prestige" buildings. As one architect suggested, "[m]any Asian countries see the tall building as a device to move them quickly into the 21st century, to catch up quickly".[16] According to the Tall Building Council, in 1986 the 10 tallest buildings in the world were all in the USA. In 1996, four of the top 10 were in Asia (Petronas Towers, Malaysia; Central Plaza, Hong Kong; Bank of China Tower, Hong Kong; Shun Hing Square, Shenzen). Typically these projects are conceived of as landmarks to "symbolize the prosperity of the city ... and embody the hopes and lofty ideals of the people".[17] The Mitsui New No. 2 Building in Tokyo, completed in 1985, is regarded as the first built in Asia. Others include the 32-storey Stock Exchange Centre in Manila, which is run by an electronic nerve centre, and Seoul's Sixty-four Building.

A similar aspect among many of these Asian infrastructure projects is that they are on "reclaimed" land. For example, much of the central city area of Singapore has been uplifted since the 1960s. The east coast area has been reclaimed over the last two decades, giving way to new commercial and business centres such as Marine Parade. The Kansai, Chek Lap Kok, and Seoul airports are all built on reclaimed land. Tokyo has been expanding through landfills along Tokyo Bay since the 1960s. Much of Tokyo's Teleport project is on reclaimed land, and so is Haneda airport, only 15 km from the city centre. The demand for space in Hong Kong since the mid-nineteenth century has necessitated land reclamation from its deep-water harbour.

Another type of important development changing the urban landscape in the region is large research and development (R&D) facilities. Asian cities have invested in R&D complexes that are typically located outside the city core. In Japan, the government has encouraged the construction of entire technologically advanced cities or "technopolises", such as Tsukuba science city located 60 km north-east of Tokyo. Tsukuba is a small city built for high-tech industries, research institutes, residential housing, and universities. Taiwan used this model to create a science park, a new R&D and high-technology manufacturing centre located in Hsinchu outside Taipei. Due to the success of this park, the government is currently planning on the construction of an even larger facility in the southern part of the island.

World city formation is a continuing and varied process. An understanding of this process neither provides a prediction as to whether a particular city in the region will be able to participate in globalization-driven growth in the future, nor will it make possible the determination of a defined development path for all cities. Urban growth is a highly complex phenomenon and is influenced by national and local circumstances. For example, not all cities promote similar infrastructure developments. However, within the large number of cities in the region that are articulated to the functional city system, the recent and rapid changes to cities are both a result of and a preparation for global and regional integration. A general pattern is emerging within those cities based on the hierarchical functions performed within their boundaries.

The last section presents a generalized pattern of development among cities in the Asia Pacific region. This categorization is not meant to be exhaustive, but rather demonstrates some of the various ways that international functional networks are impacting on city growth and development.

Emerging patterns of urban development

The previous section focused on how urban development has converged, the characteristics of the convergent forms, and the underpinning economic elements in this trend. However, Asia Pacific cities are also diverging in form and function. Although globalization connotes an increasingly homogenized world, and has led to the use of such labels as "global village", "global marketplace", or "global factory", claims of movements towards seamless urban space are oversimplifications. The "global city" concept connotes a uniform development that obscures the multifaceted dynamics of growth for cities in the world city system. Thus, rather than focus on the singular form of "global cities" this section presents world city formation as a multifaceted process. Economic interdependency and government interventions have allowed for divergence in urban growth and development among cities in the region. As cities outside the Asia Pacific region, as defined in the beginning of this chapter, are incorporated into the regional city system, they too take on unique and important functional characteristics. Further, as the functions of cities within the regional system vary, so do their development patterns.

Although directed in many ways, the government-backed pursuit of growth through the free market has privileged the process of capital accumulation. Many city public officials have formed an implicit coalition with either land-based entrepreneurs or business conglomerates. The weak tradition of local autonomy and lack of decentralization among nations in the region has inhibited the formation of intermediate institutions and organizations for tighter regulation. Hence, growth has followed the broad outlines delimited by the particular unique functional role of the city in the regional and global economy (Yeung and Lo 1996a).

Cities networked into the functional city system in the Asia Pacific region have not developed uniformly. The demands of the emerging city system in the region have been different for each city depending on a variety of factors, but predominately upon the economic functions performed. Those cities that are on the top of the hierarchy include the urban locations of major capital exporters. Within these cities business firms play important command and control roles within the world and the region (for example, Tokyo, Japan, and to a lesser extent Seoul, Korea, and Taipei, Taiwan). These cities are developing differently to those cities that are FDI recipients (such as Jakarta, Indonesia, Shanghai, China, and Bangkok, Thailand). Further, the two entrepôts (Hong Kong and Singapore) have demonstrated a level of cross-border development not experienced as intensely in other metropolitan centres. Lastly, some cities in the system have been developing as "amenity" cities. These, as mentioned above, are taking steps to enhance their ecological environments as a way to attract investment and economic activity.

Capital exporters (post-industrial cities)

The post-industrial city is dominated by the processing of information and knowledge (Savitch 1988). Tokyo, Seoul, and to a lesser extent Taipei exemplify the Asia Pacific style of post-industrial development. Sassen (1991) has identified the economic and social order of "global cities", of which New York, London, and Tokyo are examples. By now the argument is familiar to the reader. These cities are the sites of concentrations of TNC headquarters, multinational banks, and producer and business services. In Tokyo employment in manufacturing is decreasing and employment in the service sector is increasing (Honjo 1998). It houses a high concentration of central management function (CMF), R&D firms, and government agencies within Japan. At the same time the city is expanding, leaving inner-city workers with longer commutes as many of the jobs remain in the inner-city area.

Like Tokyo, Seoul has a disproportionate share of the national population (23 per cent in 1995). Service and high-tech activities are also highly concentrated within the Seoul metropolitan area. In 1992, 57 per cent of the total industrial establishments and 51 per cent of their workers were located in the Seoul metropolitan area (Hong 1997). All of the Republic of Korea's TNCs are based in the capital city and enjoy close contact with the central government, a necessary condition for Korean business deals. While new "downtowns" across the Han river have been created by moving the various back offices into locations close to the new towns of Pyongchon, Sanbon, and Bundang, Seoul city retains the most important control and management functions (Kwon 1996). Also, similar to Tokyo, the amount of inbound FDI is small compared to that of outbound flows. In the single year of 1996, outbound flows of FDI from

Seoul reached US$4.2 billion. Compare this with US$6.25 billion, the total accumulated stock of inbound FDI in the city as of 1996.

These relations take on specific forms in the urban landscape. Both cities have concentrations of large mega-projects, particularly those with large high-rent residential and commercial spaces, R&D centres, and recreational/entertainment facilities for the upper-income service-sector employees. Teleports for the smooth transmission of information and gleaming "intelligent" buildings housing banks and other important financial institutions are developed in central business districts. Nodal clusters of spatially differentiated economic activities have appeared. This multicentric structure is seen in Tokyo, as areas such as Shibuya, Ikebukoro, Maronuchi, Kasumigaiseki, and Shinjuku each capture different economic roles within the city's economy. While other cities in the region have similar types of developments, in Tokyo they have evolved extensively to meet the needs of a post-industrial urban centre. Tsukuba science city, one of Japan's first technolopis centres, is only 60 kilometres from central Tokyo and includes both living and working facilities in a satellite town (Figure 2.2). It has attracted 120 private research establishments, including international giants such as Du Pont, ICI, Intel, and Texas Instruments, and since 1985 private company researchers and their support staff have risen to 5,000, almost matching the 6,700 government researchers (Edgington 1994).

Seoul has also undergone significant industrial restructuring and spatial reorganization since the 1980s. Manufacturing industries have decentralized while advanced services are concentrated in the core regions of the city. Seoul's emerging multicentric structure is closely related to intraregional specialization of producer services, as each centre has distinctive characteristics in terms of local interfirm networks and firm structure (Park and Nahm 1998). Because of Seoul's continued growth, the government is considering abandoning the "green-belt" ring concept and therefore intensifying use of a once protected area.

Sites of FDI: Industrial cities

Industrial manufacturing processes are vitally important to the growth and development of the regional city system, and hence these centres play an important role in the functional city system. Industrial centres include urban areas such as Bangkok (Krongkaew 1996), Jakarta (Soegijoko 1996a), and Shanghai (Cui 1995). These urban centres have recently experienced a decline in agriculture and an increase in industrial concentration in the outer rings of the city. Employment data for Jabotabek demonstrate this trend (Tables 2.10 and 2.11). From 1971 to 1990, while employment in agriculture declined in Jakarta, manufacturing employ-

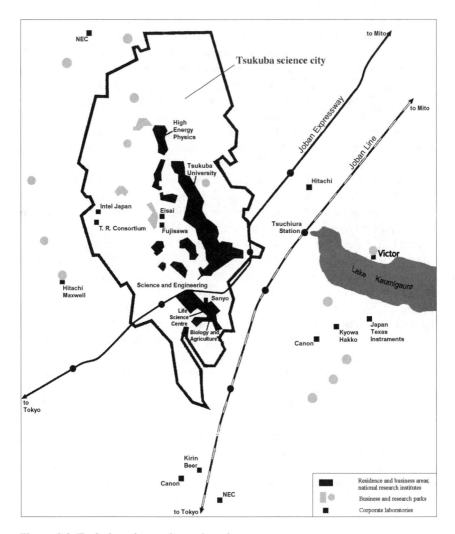

Figure 2.2 Tsukuba science city and environs
Source: Edgington 1994

ment increased in the outer administrative districts (*kabupatens*) of
Bogor, Tangerang, and Bekasi. Manufacturing development continues to
be stimulated by various government-sponsored activities, including the
creation of industrial parks within these districts.

   Areas outside the urban cores have relatively more available land and
somewhat less stringent regulatory controls on manufacturing-related
growth and investment by multinational corporations. Hence, industrial
activity start-ups resulted from the inflow of foreign direction investment.

Table 2.10 Trends in the spatial distribution of employment by sector in Jabotabek, 1971–1990

Region/district	1971 %	1980 %	1990 %
DKI Jakarta			
Primary	12.3	7.1	5.3
Secondary	66.4	64.9	51.0
Tertiary	74.2	71.8	59.6
Botabek			
Primary	87.7	92.9	94.7
Secondary	33.6	35.1	49.0
Tertiary	25.8	28.2	40.4

Source: Soegijoko 1996b

Table 2.11 Trends in the spatial distribution of employment by sector in Jabotabek, 1971–1990

Region/district	1971 (000)	1980 (000)	1990 (000)
DKI Jakarta			
Primary	46,122	51,510	49,910
Secondary	202,901	428,533	810,231
Tertiary	895,377	1,447,591	2,071,711
Botabek			
Primary	329,087	674,662	900,085
Secondary	102,848	232,067	777,681
Tertiary	311,089	568,222	1,404,191
Jabotabek			
Primary	375,209	726,172	949,995
Secondary	305,749	660,600	1,587,912
Tertiary	1,206,466	2,015,813	3,475,902

Source: Soegijoko 1996b

Global integration has affected the pattern of development by producing a ring of manufacturing plants concentrated in a doughnut fashion around the city cores. In Jabotabek during the early 1990s real estate, mining, and industrial-activity-oriented FDI dispersed to the outer area while construction, trading, and service-oriented FDI concentrated in the centre (Table 2.12).

The Bangkok metropolitan region (BMR) of Thailand is located centrally, adjacent to the Gulf of Thailand. The Greater Bangkok area includes the Bangkok metropolitan area and the administrative regions of Nontha Buri, Pathum Thani, and Samut Prakan. The Greater Bangkok area is considered the urban portion of the BMR. In the 1980s, manu-

Table 2.12 Spatial distribution of foreign direct investment in Jabotabek, 1990–1994

Sector	DKI Jakarta %	Botabek %
Construction	100.0	0.0
Trading	100.0	0.0
Hotels and restaurants	94.3	5.7
Agriculture	90.9	9.1
Transport, warehouses, and communications	86.0	14.1
Other services	83.5	16.5
Wood industries	24.2	75.8
Non-metal mineral industries	22.8	77.3
Food industries	19.4	80.6
Textile industries	14.2	85.8
Metal products/machinery	10.7	89.4
Chemicals	6.7	93.3
Other industries	4.4	95.6
Paper industries	3.1	96.9
Basic metal industries	2.0	98.0
Mining	0.0	100.0
Real estate	0.0	100.0

Source: Soegijoko 1996b

facturing value added in the BMR accounted for more than 75 per cent of the nation's total manufacturing production. In the early 1990s there was a significant shift of industrial production location to outside the BMR and to Rayong, Chon Buri, Chachoengsao, Samut Sakhon, and Nakhon Pathom, but particularly the eastern region. The Thailand Board of Investment suggests that the eastern seaboard's share of industrial investment increased from 34 per cent to 63 per cent between 1991 and 1996 (see Chapter 12 in this volume).

The flows of FDI into the industrial cities of Bangkok and Jakarta create a urban form that includes industrial firms' development in the suburban or ex-urban fringes and commercial development in the centre. While this chapter has only described these two cities, the same is happening in other places such as Shanghai. This development is distinctly different from that associated with the capital exporters described earlier.

The entrepôts: Borderless cities

Economic globalization has stimulated subregional economic cooperation in several locales. Successful growth triangles, a uniquely Asian development pattern, are localized economic zones involving several countries whose centre is a major metropolitan area. These can be viewed as "borderless" economies where the international division of labour has developed to the urban centre's advantage (Thant, Tang, and Kakazu 1994). Cities that have been impacted by borderless economies can no longer be considered distinct economies, but are really part of a larger extended metropolitan region (EMR) (Ginsburg, Koppel, and McGee 1991; Macleod and McGee 1996). EMRs may stretch up to 100 km from an urban core and are characterized by high levels of economic diversity and interaction, a high percentage of non-farm employment, and a "deep penetration of global market forces into the countryside" (Macleod and McGee 1996: 418). EMR growth implies the increasing need for development to be seen as regional rather than rural or urban.

An existing "borderless" economy has grown between Singapore, Malaysia (Johore), and Indonesia (Riau islands), and is called Sijori. It revolves around the city-state of Singapore, which has recently reached out to acquire the benefits that rural industrialization can provide (see Chapter 9 in this volume). The growth of the outer reaches of Singapore's core was directly related to Singapore's maturing economy. The flows of people and goods from the city to the outlying areas accompanied an increasing level of cross-border capital flows.

Another example of cross-border cooperative development involving capital, technological, and managerial inputs is the integration of Hong Kong, Taiwan, and China's southern provinces of Guangdong and Fujian. Hong Kong is the centre of the Zhujiang delta and has emerged as a financial and headquarters centre (Chapter 8 in this volume). A large proportion of the manufacturing production in Hong Kong has been relocated to southern Guangdong in China. Apart from Guangzhou, Shenzhen, Zhuhai, and Huizhou, most other cities within the delta are basically labour- and land-intensive production areas. They are dominated by manufacturing with a small tertiary sector. About 3–5 million workers in this part of China are reportedly employed in factories funded, designed, and managed by Hong Kong entrepreneurs. Further, by the early 1990s about 20.8 per cent of Hong Kong's imports were from the interior of China and 31 per cent of her exports went to China (Sung 1991). Between Hong Kong and Shenzhen alone 805,000 TEUs of goods pass through road checkpoints, in addition to the 281,000 TEUs (20-foot equivalent units) ferried between the two areas by river vessels (Chu 1996).

In July 1997, China reabsorbed Hong Kong. However, the "borderless" economy of the city still exists, perhaps even more so. Taiwanese capital has been attracted to the city, and much of it has been channelled through Hong Kong intermediaries to the mainland. This is particularly true for Taiwanese investments in rapidly growing cities such as Shanghai

(Ning and Wang 1996). Also trade relations between China, Hong Kong, and Taiwan are highly integrated and considered an important part of each country's continued growth (Hwang, 1995).

Amenity cities

Notwithstanding the lack of attention given to environmental issues in some, predominately industrial, cities within the regional city system, globalization provides the impetus for the development of ecologically "sustainable" policies. Evidence of this trend can be seen emerging in Sydney and Vancouver. These two cities have three important aspects in common: post-industrial economies integrated into the Asia Pacific regional economy; "inviting" natural environments or high concentrations of "amenities"; and economic development accompanied by a sufficiently high level of per capita welfare and political acceptance to maintain and enhance the environment.

Globalization forces impacting on Vancouver and Sydney include financial and capital flows consistent with their post-industrial economic structures, trade in goods (for Vancouver), and immigration flows. Sydney is the capital of New South Wales and Australia's most global city. Vancouver, as part of "Cascadia", has been considered an emerging "sub-global world city" (see Chapter 14 in this volume).

Among Australia's cities, Sydney has the largest share of regional headquarters of transnational corporations serving the Asia Pacific region. Sydney also hosts three-quarters of the international and domestic banks operating in Australia. It has the largest stock exchange and the country's only futures exchange. Sydney is increasingly the preferred location for multinational regional HQs in the Asia Pacific. Of the regional head offices of the top 20 firms in four sectors – accounting, advertising, management consulting, and international real estate – 39 per cent are in Sydney. These concentrations of functions relate to both the cities' post-industrial economy and their roles as command and control centres (see Chapter 13 in this volume).

Trade is to Vancouver as information and financial flows are to Sydney. Among the trading connections the Vancouver–Hong Kong connection has perhaps received the most attention. However, the city and its region have had significant linkages with Japan. Due to the need to secure large quantities of Canadian agricultural and industrial resources, 11 of Japan's major general trading companies, called *sogo shosha*, established subsidiaries in Canada. Of these 11, five chose Vancouver as their local headquarters. This is because 60 per cent of the *sogo shoshas'* trade is done through the port of Vancouver. While Japan accounted for only 6 per cent of Canadian export destinations in 1988, it made up 27 per cent of those of British Columbia. Further, Japanese trade with Canada expanded between 1960 and 1990, and the Canadian-based branches of the Japanese *sogo shoshas* generated most of the business (Chapter 14 in this volume).

Both Vancouver and Sydney have recently been the targets of Asian immigrants. In 1991, Sydney had 28.5 per cent of the total number of persons born overseas within Australia, and 42 per cent of all immigrants to the country were from Asia. For Sydney the growth of foreign-born residents is twice as fast as the growth of the total population. Sydney's greater integration with the global economy, including the local airport's (Kingsford Smith) dominance as a hub of air traffic, plays an important role in these flows. Vancouver is one of the most rapidly growing urbanized regions in North America. Between 1981 and 1996 the population of the region increased from 1.2 million to 1.9 million. Of these, 600,000 people, almost one-third, arrived in the years 1991–1994. Most significantly, net international migration increased from 33 per cent in the 1980s to 59 per cent between 1991 and 1994. Many of these migrants are from Asia.

The cities' environmental amenities (climate, harbour, beaches, mountains, low levels of pollution) and multicultural character are key to each city's competitive advantage. Vancouver is part of a wide region of "geographical affinity" which stretches from southern Oregon to the ski resort of Whistler, 120 km north of the city. However, one problem for Vancouver is managing growth, as city expansion is sandwiched between the ocean and the foothills of the Rocky Mountains. Sydney has many beaches, a beautiful harbour, and climate attractions that can be considered environmental amenities. The state of New South Wales and many local governments have come to appreciate that these amenities need protection. In a large part, this is because both Sydney and Vancouver are major tourist stops within the region. Because of their natural amenities they attract a large and economically important number of tourists to their respective areas.

The local factor in the creation of amenity cities is essential. In the state of New South Wales, planning includes two phases (strategic and developmental). Consideration of implications of development on the environment is mandated in both phases. As a result, large areas of land earmarked for urban development in Sydney's west and south-west were put on hold in the early 1990s due to air pollution concerns. At the project level environmental impact assessment applies to both public and private developers. Further, citizens and non-governmental organizations continue to press for more regulation and greater consideration of the environmental impacts of development. In Vancouver the urban region has attempted to develop strategic planning processes that provide for both liveability and reinforced competitiveness. The Greater Vancouver

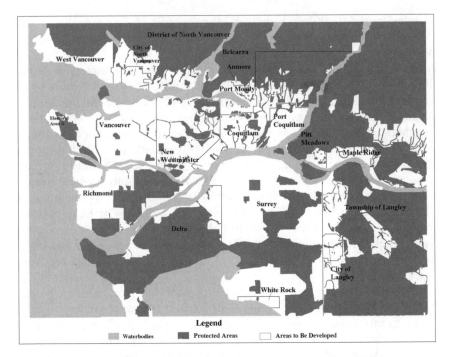

Figure 2.3 The Greater Vancouver Regional District Green Zone Plan
Source: Based on GVRD 1996.

Regional District Authority (GVRD), made up of 20 municipalities and
two electoral areas, has developed a "liveable region strategic plan for
2021". Important components of this plan include, *inter alia*, implementing a transportation system that involves a mix of private and public systems, implementation of environmentally acceptable policies of waste
removal and treatment, water provision and pollution control, and committing more than two-thirds of the GVRD's land base to a green zone to
protect watersheds, parks, ecologically important areas, working forests,
and farmland (Chapter 14 in this volume) (Figure 2.3). Together Vancouver and Sydney are carving out a niche within the regional city system
that includes the provision of a high-quality environment. This environment invites both business (TNCs) and immigrants, and can be viewed as
part of its comparative advantage.

Summary

The patterns described for individual cities are, at best, general development patterns. Therefore it is not expected that every city in the Asia

Pacific functional city system will fit into this typology. The patterns do, however, represent the impacts of international influences on the growth and development of cities. For example, Bangkok is both the primate city and capital of Thailand, and holds an important position among the network of cities in the region.

Conclusions

This chapter has attempted to explain the logic of globalization and how this logic has played out in the East and South-East Asia regions. Global transactions and relationships have been shaped by increased international trade, investments, financial flows, telecommunications, and new waves of technologies, among other factors. The result has been a more integrated yet functionally differentiated spatial pattern of economic activity.

At the centre of this global economic integration and structural adjustment is the interlinkage of mega-cities and other major metropolises to form a functional city system. Cities are the engines of economic growth in the new global economy. In the Asia Pacific region, because of intense economic integration and interdependence, an urban corridor has developed.

Those cities integrated into the functional city system are undergoing the process of world city formation. Whether they are labelled as "world cities" is irrelevant. Their inclusion in the system has had direct effects on their form and growth. The demands of the new economic and social order within the region have selectively included cities within the urban corridor running from Tokyo to Jakarta, favouring large coastal cities with good transportation and communications access. More trade and economic interactions are translated directly into a growing number of airports, container ports, and teleports. These major infrastructure provisions are but a few examples of the world city formation process in action.

The urban system in the region is composed of hierarchically integrated cities. Typical examples of cities that are considered the nerve centres of the system are Tokyo, Seoul, and Taipei. While they have retained the command and control roles of the regional and global economy, other aspects of production and distribution have decentralized to locations in other NIEs and ASEAN countries. At a lower intensity of decentralization, cities such as Hong Kong and Singapore have developed "borderless" economies, although their economies have retained a strong neighbourhood character. Finally, the industrial centres, such as Jakarta, Shanghai, and Bangkok, have developed an urban growth pattern resembling a doughnut, with commercial development occurring in the centre of the city and manufacturing firms locating around the periphery. Each of these types of cities is integrated into the developing urban corridor of East and South-East Asia, and they make up essential components of the Asia Pacific city system.

The integration within the world city system enhances polarization within a particular nation and locality. Those areas that have been included act as magnets which continually draw people from the countryside. The rapidity of these changes has created urban environmental stress that will challenge each city's growth potential in the future. It is necessary for city managers to understand both the domestic and the international roles of their cities in order to confront the challenges before them and position their cities for continued growth in the twenty-first century.

Notes

1. In this chapter the Asia Pacific region includes those nations bordering the South China Sea and the western Pacific Ocean. Also included in the study are cities in Oceania (Sydney) and Canada (Vancouver).
2. While not attempting to downplay the significance of a variety of social and political processes associated with globalization, this chapter concentrates largely on economic changes and impacts.
3. Notwithstanding fluctuations and the recent drop in unemployment in the USA, among 17 OECD members unemployment levels as a percentage of the labour force have risen during three periods from 1950–1973, 1974–1983, and then 1984–1993 (Maddison 1995). In the USA, despite the total gain of 27 million jobs from 1979 to 1995, the loss of 43 million jobs during the same period prompted the *New York Times* (1996) to run a seven-article series on "The downsizing of America". As one observer has noted, within the new global economy, employment and production have become "uncoupled" (Drucker 1986).
4. Measured as constant 1990 dollars. See Maddison 1995, Table D-1e, pp. 204–205.
5. "Foreign direct investment" is defined as an "investment involving a long-term relationship and reflecting a lasting interest and control of a resident entity in one economy (foreign direct investor or parent enterprise) in an enterprise resident in an economy other than that of the foreign direct investor". (UNCTAD 1997: 295). It is simply direct investment that occurs across national boundaries, but differs from "portfolio investment" in that it is structured to gain control of the firm.
6. The average "travel-time" budget for travelling is typically between 1.0 and 1.5 hours per person per day in a wide variety of economic, social, and geographic settings.
7. The most developed and sustained instance has been among the ASEAN countries.
8. Since that point the relative share of Japanese FDI in the region has decreased, yet Japan is still a major influence in the Asia Pacific.
9. As Walter Hatch and Kozo Yamamura (1996: 27) have explained:

   Japanese economist Akamatsu Kaname developed this theory of economic development. Like Vernon's [1966] product cycle theory, it spelled out a protracted process, driven by the gradual and international diffusion of technology, in which a developing country upgrades its export and industrial structures. In the 1970s and 1980s, the theory was modified to explain the synergistic pattern of economic development and integration in Asia. Japan was the "lead goose" followed by the Asian NIEs, then the ASEAN, then China, and so on. As it flies forward, becoming more and more technologically advanced, Japan pulls the entire V-formation along with it. It does so by successively shedding industries in which it no longer holds a comparative advantage. Through FDI, these industries ultimately find a new home among the less developed countries ("follower geese") of Asia. Over time, these developing countries master the new technology, upgrade their own industrial structures, and themselves begin shedding outdated industries.

10. The "Dutch disease" is a term used to describe a phenomenon first observed in the Netherlands in the 1970s. When oil was discovered and exported, it caused an appreciation in the real exchange rate of the Netherlands, making its exports less competitive and causing a relative decline in its manufacturing sector.

11. In 1994 there were 636 cases of FDI from Japan alone slated for the Chinese mainland (Hatch and Yamamura 1996).

12. In 1973 DKI Jakarta was incorporated into a larger metropolitan region through the promulgation of Jabotabek. This urban agglomeration combines the metropolitan area of Jakarta (Ja) with the surrounding *kabupatens* (administrative regions) of Bogor (Bo), Tangerang (Ta), and Bekasi (Bek). A joint development cooperative board was established, with the responsibility of coordinating development in this region.

13. See Yeung and Lo 1996b for an earlier version of this section. This working paper was later published under the same title in Lo and Yeung 1998.

14. Singapore has plans to enlarge Changi airport; the extension includes a third runway and terminal, to be finished by 2010. These additions will increase the airport's capacity by 50 per cent: in 1994 Changi's capacity was approximately 24 million passengers a year, and this capacity was 90 per cent utilized; the extension will bring the capacity to 36 million passengers a year.

15. These are, in rank order, Hong Kong (1), Singapore (2), Kaohsing (4), Pusan (5), Kobe (6), Keelung (10), Yokohama (11), Tokyo (14), Bangkok (19), Manila (21), Nagoya (24), and Tanjung Priok (25).

16. Eugene Kohn, architect with the firm of Kohn Pedersen Fox, architects, in New York, as quoted in Gebhart 1997.

17. Yoshito Kato, managing director of Mori Bini Architects and Engineers in Tokyo, as quoted in Gebhart 1997.

REFERENCES

Akita, Takahiro, Fu-chen Lo, and Yoichi Nakamura. 1997. "Interdependence and growth in the Asia Pacific region: An international input-output analysis." UNU/IAS Working Paper No. 29.

Amborski, David and Douglas Keare. 1998. "Large-scale development: A teleport proposal for Cordoba", *Land Lines*, newsletter of the Lincoln Institute of Land Policy, September, pp. 4–5.

Asian Development Bank (ADB). 1990. *Asian Development Outlook 1990*. Manila: ADB.

Asian Development Bank (ADB). 1995. *Asian Development Outlook 1995 and 1996*. Hong Kong: Oxford University Press.

Asian Development Bank (ADB). 1998. *Asian Development Outlook 1998.* Hong Kong: Oxford University Press.

Chase-Dunn, Christopher. 1985. "The system of world cities, AD 800–1975", in Michael Timberlake (ed.) *Urbanization in the World Economy.* Orlando, FL: Academic Press, pp. 63–85.

Choe, Sang-Chuel. 1996. "The evolving urban system in North-East Asia", in Fu-chen Lo and Yue-man Yeung (eds) *Emerging World Cities in Pacific Asia.* Tokyo: United Nations University Press, pp. 498–519.

Choe, Sang-Chuel. 1998. "Urban corridors in Pacific Asia", in Fu-chen Lo and Yue-man Yeung (eds) *Globalization and the World of Large Cities.* Tokyo: United Nations University Press, pp. 155–173.

Chu, David K. Y. 1996. "The Hong Kong-Zhujiang delta and the world city system", in Fu-chen Lo and Yue-man Yeung (eds) *Emerging World Cities in Pacific Asia.* Tokyo: United Nations University Press, pp. 465–498.

Clifford, Mark. 1991. "A trickle, not a flood", *Far Eastern Economic Review*, No. 28, December, p. 67.

Cohen, R. B. 1981. "The new international division of labour, multinational corporations and urban hierarchy", in Michael Dear and Allan J. Scott (eds) *Urbanization and Urban Planning in Capitalist Society.* London: Methuen, pp. 287–315.

Cui, Gonghao. 1995. "Development of Shanghai and the Yangtze delta", in Anthony Gar-On Yeh and Chai-Kwong Mak (eds) *Chinese Cities and China's Development, A Preview of the Future Role of Hong Kong.* Hong Kong: University of Hong Kong Press, pp. 241–254.

Cybriwsky, Roman. Undated. "Urban development and internationalization of Tokyo: Examples from four recent high-profile projects", unpublished paper.

Dicken, Peter. 1992. *Global Shift: The Internationalization of Economic Activity*, 2nd edn. New York: Gilford Press.

Drucker, Peter. 1986. "The changed world economy", *Foreign Affairs*, No. 64, pp. 768–791.

Dunning, John H. and Howard Archer. 1987. "The eclectic paradigm and the growth of UK multinational enterprise, 1870–1983", *Business and Economic History*, Vol. 16, pp. 19–49, reprinted in Geoffrey Jones (ed.). 1993. *Transnational Corporations: A Historical Perspective.* New York: Routledge, pp. 23–62.

The Economist. 1997. "One world", *The Economist*, Vol. 345, No. 8039, 18 October, pp. 99–100.

Edgington, David W. 1994. "Planning for technology development and information systems in Japanese cities and regions", in P. Shapira, I. Masser, and D. W. Edgington (eds) *Planning for Cities and Regions in Japan.* Liverpool: Liverpool University Press, pp. 126–154.

Edgington, David W. and Hiro Haga. 1998. "Japanese service sector multinationals and the hierarchy of Pacific Rim cities", *Asia Pacific Viewpoint*, Vol. 39, No. 2, August, pp. 161–178.

Friedmann, John. 1986. "The world city hypothesis". *Development and Change*, No. 17, pp. 69–83.

Friedmann, John and Goetz Wolff. 1982. "World city formation: An agenda for research and action", *International Journal of Urban and Regional Research*, Vol. 6, No. 3, pp. 309–343.

Fukushima, Kiyohiko and C. H. Kwan. 1995. "Foreign direct investment and regional industrial restructuring in Asia", in Normura Research Institute and Institute of Southeast Asian Studies, *The New Wave of Foreign Direct Investment in Asia*. Singapore: ISAS, pp. 3–39.

Gebhart, Fred. 1997. "View from the top, Asian cities reach for the sky", *CAAC Inflight Magazine*, pp. 46–50.

Ginsburg, N., B. Koppel, and T. G. McGee (eds). 1991. *The Extended Metropolis: Settlement Transition in Asia*. Honolulu: University of Hawaii Press.

Greater Vancouver Regional District (GVRD). 1996. *Creating Our Future, Steps to a More Livalde Region 1996*. Burnaby, BC: GVRD Communications and Education, p. 18.

Hatch, Walter and Kozo Yamamura. 1996. *Asia in Japan's Embrace, Building a Regional Production Alliance*. Hong Kong: Cambridge University Press.

Heenan, David A. 1977. "Global cities of tomorrow", *Harvard Business Review*, May–June, pp. 79–92.

Henderson, Jeffrey and Manuel Castells (eds). 1987. *Global Restructuring and Territorial Development*. New York: Sage.

Hong, Sung Woong. 1996. "Seoul: A global city in a nation of rapid growth", in Fu-chen Lo and Yue-man Yeung (eds) *Emerging World Cities in Pacific Asia*. Tokyo: United Nations University Press, pp. 144–178.

Hong, Sung Woong. 1997. *Building a Power House*. Seoul: Korea Research Institute for Human Settlements.

Honjo, Masahiko. 1998. "The growth of Tokyo as a world city", in Fu-chen Lo and Yue-man Yeung (eds) *Globalization and the World of Large Cities*. Tokyo: United Nations University Press, pp. 109–131.

Hwang, Jing-huei. 1995. "Taipei's role in the regional development of China", in Anthony Gar-On Yeh and Chai-Kwong Mak (eds) *Chinese Cities and China's Development: A Preview of the Future Role of Hong Kong*. Hong Kong: University of Hong Kong Press, pp. 277–294.

Japan Development Bank. 1996. "Office location environment in major East Asian cities", *Research*, Vol. 219, September.

Japan External Trade Organization (JETRO). 1997. *White Paper on International Trade Japan 1997*. Tokyo: JETRO.

Jayasankaran, S. 1997. "Diverging tracks, cracks appear in Malaysian railway consortium", *Far Eastern Economic Review*, 17 April, p. 67.

King, Anthony D. 1990. *Global Cities: Post Imperialism and the Internationalization of London*. New York: Routledge.

Kojima, Kiyoshi. 1978. *Direct Foreign Investment: A Japanese Model of Multinational Business Operations*. London: Croom Helm.

Krongkaew, Medhi. 1996. "The changing urban system in a fast-growing city and economy: The case of Bangkok and Thailand", in Fu-chen Lo and Yue-man Yeung (eds) *Emerging World Cities in Pacific Asia*. Tokyo: United Nations University Press, pp. 286–334.

Kwon, Won-Yong. 1996. "Globalization and mega-city development: A case of Seoul", paper presented at the UNU/UNESCO workshop in Hong Kong and Tokyo, October.

Lo, Fu-chen. 1994. "The impacts of current global adjustment and shifting techno-economic paradigm on the world city system", in Roland J. Fuchs, Ellen

Brennan, Joseph Chamie, Fu-chen Lo, and Juha I. Uitto (eds) *Mega-City Growth and the Future*. Tokyo: United Nations University Press, pp. 103–130.

Lo, Fu-chen, Kamal Salih, and Yoichi Nakamura, 1989. "Structural interdependency and the outlook for the Asian Pacific economy towards the year 2000", in Miyohei Shinohara and Fu-chen Lo (eds) *Global Adjustment and the Future of Asian-Pacific Economy*. Tokyo: APDC, IDE, pp. 80–107.

Lo, Fu-chen and Yoichi Nakamura. 1992. "Uneven growth, the mega-trends of global change and the future of the Asia Pacific economics", in S. P. Gupta and S. Tambunlertchai (eds) *The Asia Pacific Economies: A Challenge to South Asia*. Bangalore: Macmillan, pp. 25–64.

Leung, Kenneth K. S. 1998. "Infrastructure development under economic crisis in Hong Kong", paper presented at a conference on Infrastructure Development and International Cooperation during an Economic Crisis in the Asia Development Countries, Tokyo, Japan, November.

Maddison, Angus. 1995. *Monitoring the World Economy 1982–1992*. Paris: OECD Development Centre.

Macleod, Scott and Terry G. McGee. 1996. "The Singapore-Johore-Riau growth triangle: An emerging extended metropolitan region", in Fu-chen Lo and Yue-man Yeung (eds) *Emerging World Cities in Pacific Asia*. Tokyo: United Nations University Press, pp. 417–464.

National Science Board. 1994. *Science and Engineering Indicators: 1993*. Washington: US Government Printing Office, pp. 177–185.

Nakakita, Toru. 1988. "The globalization of Japanese firms and its influence on Japan's trade with developing countries", *The Developing Economies*, Vol. 26, No. 4, December, pp. 306–322.

Nester, William. 1990. "The development of Japan, Taiwan and South Korea: Ends and means, free trade, dependency or neomercantilism?", *Journal of Developing Societies*, No. 6, pp. 203–218.

New York Times. 1996. "The downsizing of America", *New York Times*, 3–9 March.

Ning, Yuemin and Dezhong Wang. 1996. "Foreign direct investment and economic development of Pudong New Area", paper given at the UNU/UNESCO conference on Mega-cities, January.

Ohmae, Kenichi. 1985. *Triad Power: The Coming Shape of Global Competition*. New York: Free Press.

Ohmae, Kenichi. 1990. *The Borderless World: Power and Strategy in the Inter-linked Economy*. New York: McKinsey & Co.

Ohta, Hideaki, Akihiro Tokuno, and Ritsuko Takeuchi. 1995. "Evolving foreign investment strategies of Japanese firms in Asia", in Normura Research Institute and Institute of Southeast Asian Studies, *The New Wave of Foreign Direct Investment in Asia*. Singapore: ISAS, pp. 43–63.

Olds, Kris. 1995. "Globalization and the production of new urban spaces: Pacific Rim megaprojects in the late 20th century", *Environment and Planning A*, No. 27, pp. 1713–1743.

Park, Sam Ock and Kee-Bee Nahm. 1998. "Spatial structure and inter-firm networks of technical and inforamtion producer services in Seoul, Korea", *Asia Pacific Viewpoint*, Vol. 39, No. 2, August, pp. 209–220.

Peck, F. W. 1996. "Regional development and the production of space: The role of infrastructure in the attraction of new inward investment", *Environment and Planning A*, No. 28, pp. 327–339.

Perry, Martin, Lily Kong, and Brenda Yeoh. 1997. *Singapore, A Developmental City State*. New York: John Wiley and Sons.

Rimmer, Peter. 1996. "Transport and telecommuncations among world cities", UNU/IAS Working Paper No. 14, July.

Rimmer, Peter. 1997. "China's infrastructure and economic development in the 21st century", *Futures*, Vol. 29, Nos 4/5, May/June, pp. 435–465 .

Saldi, Mohammad. 1989. "The oil problem – with special relevance to Indonesia", in Miyohei Shinohara and Fu-chen Lo (eds) *Global Adjustment and the Future of the Asian Pacific Economy: Papers and Proceedings of the Conference on Global Adjustment and the Future of Asian Pacific Economy*. Tokyo: Institute of Developing Economies and the Asian and Pacific Development Centre, pp. 249–257.

Salleh, Ismail Md. 1995. "Foreign direct investment and technology transfer in the Malaysian electronics industry", in Normura Research Institute and Institute of Southeast Asian Studies, *The New Wave of Foreign Direct Investment in Asia*. Singapore: ISAS, pp. 133–159.

Sassen, Saskia. 1991. *The Global City: New York, London, Tokyo*. Princeton: Princeton University Press.

Sassen, Saskia. 1994. *Cities in a World Economy*. Thousand Oaks: Pine Forge Press.

Savitch, Hank V. 1988. *Post-Industrial Cities: Politics and Planning in New York, Paris and London*. Princeton: Princeton University Press.

Schafer, Andreas and David Victor. 1997. "The past and future of global mobility", *Scientific American*, October, pp. 58–61.

Shinohara, Miyohei and Fu-chen Lo (eds). 1989. *Global Adjustment and the Future of the Asian Pacific Economy: Papers and Proceedings of the Conference on Global Adjustment and the Future of Asian Pacific Economy*. Tokyo: Institute of Developing Economies and the Asian and Pacific Development Centre.

Sirat, Morshidi. 1998. "Producer services and growth management of a metropolitan region: The case of Kuala Lumpur, Malaysia", *Asia Pacific Viewpoint*, Vol. 39, No. 2, August, pp. 221–235.

Soegijoko, Budhy. 1996a. "Jabotabek and globalization", in Fu-chen Lo and Yueman Yeung (eds) *Emerging World Cities in Pacific Asia*. Tokyo: United Nations University Press, pp. 377–416.

Soegijoko, Budhy. 1996b. *Impact of Strengthening in International Urban Linkage: The Case of Jabotabek, Jndonesia*. Indonesia: National Development Planning Agency (BAPPENAS), NLI Research Institute.

Soubra, Yehia. 1995. "Trends and current situation in the diffusion and utilization of information technology", in United Nations Conference on Trade and Development, *Advanced Technology Assessment System, Information Technology for Development*, Issue 10, Autumn. New York: United Nations, pp. 48–63.

Strange, Susan. 1994. "The structure of finance in the world system", in Yoshikazn Sakamoto (ed.) *Global Transformation: Challenges to the State System*. Tokyo: United Nations University Press, pp. 228–249.

Sung, Yun-wing. 1991. *The China-Hong Kong Connection*. Cambridge: Cambridge University Press.

Thant, Myo, Min Tang, and Hiroshi Kakazu (eds). 1994. *Growth Triangles in Asia: A New Approach to Regional Economic Cooperation*. Hong Kong: Oxford University Press.

Thornton, Emily. 1995. "Asian infrastructure: Big, bigger and biggest", *Far Eastern Economic Review,* 6 April, pp. 37–44.

Timberlake, Michael (ed.). 1985. *Urbanization in the World Economy*. Orlando, FL: Academic Press.

Todaro, Michael P. 1997. *Economic Development*, (6th edn.) New York: Longman.

Tokyo Metropolitan Government (TMG). 1996. *Creating Rainbow Town, a New Waterfront City*. Tokyo: Bureau of Port and Harbour, TMG.

United Nations. 1990. *Global Outlook 2000*. New York: United Nations.

United Nations Conference on Trade and Development (UNCTAD). 1994. *Handbook of International Trade and Development Statistics*. New York: United Nations.

United Nations Conference on Trade and Development (UNCTAD). 1995. *World Investment Report 1995: Transnational Corporations and Competitiveness*. New York: United Nations.

United Nations Conference on Trade and Development (UNCTAD). 1997. *World Investment Report 1997: Transnational Corporations, Market Structure and Competition Policy*. New York: United Nations.

US News and World Report. 1993. 17 May, p. 61.

Vernon, R. 1966. "International investment and international trade in the product cycle", *Quarterly Journal of Economics*, No. 80, pp. 190–207.

Vittachi, N. 1995. "The Orient's new pearl", *Far Eastern Economic Review*, 6 April, pp. 52–54.

World Bank. 1978. *World Development Report 1978*. New York: Oxford University Press.

World Bank. 1981. *World Development Report 1981*. New York: Oxford University Press.

World Bank. 1986. *World Development Report 1986*. New York: Oxford University Press.

World Bank. 1992. *World Development Report 1992*. New York: Oxford University Press.

World Bank. 1993. *The East Asian Miracle*. New York: Oxford University Press.

World Bank. 1994. *World Development Report 1994*. New York: Oxford University Press.

Xiaoji, Zhang. 1995. "Foreign direct investment in China's economic development", in Normura Research Institute and Institute of Southeast Asian Studies, *The New Wave of Foreign Direct Investment in Asia*. Singapore: ISAS, pp. 223–242.

Yamashita, Shoichi (ed.). 1991. *Transfer of Japanese Technology and Management to the ASEAN Countries*. Tokyo: University of Tokyo Press.

Yamazawa, Ippei. 1990. *Economic Development and International Trade: The Japanese Model*. Translated from Japanese. Honolulu: East-West Center, Resource Systems Institute.

Yamazawa, Ippei and Fu-chen Lo. 1993. "Introduction", in Ippei Yamazawa and

Fu-chen Lo (eds) *Evolution of Asia Pacific Economies: International Trade and Direct Investment*. Kuala Lumpur: Asian and Pacific Development Centre, pp. 1–17.

Yeung, W. C. Henry. 1994. "Hong Kong firms in the ASEAN region: Transnational corporations and foreign direct investment", *Environment and Planning A*, No. 26, pp. 1931–1956.

Yeung, Yue-man. 1996. "Urban infrastructure in Pacific Asia: Profile, priorities and prospects", Department of Geography, Chinese University, Occasional Paper No. 131.

Yeung, Yue-man and Fu-chen Lo. 1996a. "Global restructuring and emerging urban corridors in Pacific Asia", in Fu-chen Lo and Yue-man Yeung (eds) *Emerging World Cities in Pacific Asia*. Tokyo: United Nations University Press, pp. 17–47.

Yeung, Yue-man and Fu-chen Lo. 1996b. "Globalization and world city formation in Pacific Asia", UNU/IAS Working Paper No. 16. Tokyo: UNU/IAS.

Yeung, Yue-man and Fu-chen Lo. 1998. "Globalization and world city formation in Pacific Asia", in Fu-chen Lo and Yue-man Yeung (eds) *Globalization and the World of Large Cites*. Tokyo: United Nations University Press, pp. 132–154.

Yu, Yong-ding. 1989. "China's economic policy towards Asian-Pacific economies", in Miyohei Shinohara and Fu-chen Lo (eds) *Global Adjustment and the Future of the Asian Pacific Economy: Papers and Proceedings of the Conference on Global Adjustment and the Future of Asian Pacific Economy*. Tokyo: Institute of Developing Economies and the Asian and Pacific Development Centre, pp. 176–204.

3

FDI in Asia in boom and bust: Sustainability of cities and economies in Asia

Sung Woong Hong

Introduction: Sustainability, globalization, and financial crisis in the Asia Pacific region

Economic and environmental sustainability are two interacting attributes of urban systems. Economic sustainability, in a normative sense, supports a level of environmental sustainability chosen by society. The condition of the human-made environment, such as urban infrastructure, requires massive capital investment financed by either domestic or foreign sources and makes up an important aspect of a sustainable economy. On the other hand, economic sustainability, to a large degree, is also determined by environmental sustainability. Clean water and air are the prerequisites for efficient industrial development. In addition, the human-made environment is an important determinant in attracting foreign capital inflows. Environmental quality is a pull factor for foreign capital. Therefore, environmental sustainability is an important part of the foundation of economic sustainability, and vice versa.

Prior to the Asian financial crisis in 1997, developing countries had been actively participating in international capital markets. Their capital markets were increasingly opened to foreign investors. Bond issues had increased and new financing schemes were developed to attract overseas investors. The engagement of developing countries in international capital markets was encouraged in international dialogues, such as at the Uruguay Round of GATT and the WTO. Many developing countries were strongly encouraged to accept the new wave of liberalization and privatization as a necessity for growth and development. And growth, liberalization, and privatization all went hand in hand with increases in foreign investment.

In recent years, inflows of foreign capital in developing countries increased in various forms. Inflows of foreign direct investment (FDI) constituted the largest portion of overseas financing to the developing countries. FDI in developing countries quadrupled during the 1990s, reaching US$120 billion in 1997. The share of global FDI inflows to these countries increased from 21 per cent in 1991 to 36 per cent in 1997 (World Bank 1998).

This was due, in part, to the attractiveness of Asian developing countries to transnational corporations (TNCs), especially after the mid-1990s financial crisis in South America. The newly industrialized countries of ASEAN, notably Malaysia, Thailand, Indonesia, and the Philippines, along with other rapidly growing Asian countries, such as China, attracted more FDI than any other developing countries in the world.

Studies indicate there is a strong positive correlation between rapid growth and FDI inflows.[1] This was evident in Asia. The newly industrializing countries (NICs) in the region, along with the ASEAN-4 countries, recorded an extraordinarily high economic growth rate over the last few decades. Their economic performance paralleled massive inbound FDI flows. It was a good time for Asia. It was a time of prosperity.

The dramatic performance of the Asian countries was manifested in their major metropolitan centres. Visitors to those cities gasped at seeing the rapid rise of fashionably designed and elegantly built offices and hotels, some of which are owned or managed by the TNCs. The physical changes within cities, along with their economic performance, were dazzling. But there have been other changes in those cities too. The mode of urban life in Asian cities has changed. Inflows of capital have accompanied an influx of telecommunications and news media services from the industrialized countries. These have also been influencing Asian life in style and quality.

In 1997, however, a reversal of the upward trend of economic growth and capital inflows occurred as the Asian financial crisis deepened. Most of those fast-growing Asian economies, the four ASEAN countries, and the Republic of Korea experienced foreign exchange crises and have been in economic depressions of varying degrees since then. They have suffered a decline in the gross flows of capital since the third quarter of 1997 (World Bank 1998: 11). The credit ratings of those countries also dropped and, despite financial bail-outs from the International Monetary Fund (IMF), they were subsequently forced to handle difficulties in overseas financing. From the second quarter of 1999, however, most Asian

economies have been recovering from the economic crisis and are expected to achieve positive growth in the coming years.

With depreciated Asian currencies and general economic depressions,
asset deflation was a common phenomenon. The "fire sale" of assets
in some Asian countries was spectacular (Krugman 1998). Many Asian
economies recorded minus growth rates after the end of the first quarter
of 1998. Korea recorded −3.7 per cent, Indonesia −9 per cent, and Thailand −7 per cent (*Business Week* 1998). In Korea, in dollar terms, asset
values declined to roughly half of those prior to the crisis. Unemployment
and bankruptcies hit record highs in almost all the highly affected countries. Private industries and governments faced acute shortages of cash.
In addition to the foreign debt service, governments need money to
finance industrial restructuring and unemployment compensation. The
fiscal crunch in revenues thus put Asian public investment plans in
jeopardy, and many countries and cities faced difficulty in domestically
financing infrastructure development. As a result, these entities had to
turn to foreign sources to finance their debt services and infrastructure
developments.

The foreign exchange shortage was caused by the sudden withdrawal of
short-term loans by foreign financial institutions. Increases in inbound
FDI are therefore a hopeful solution. With the hard-learned lessons of
the dangers of short-term loans and hot money without proper risk management and supervision, Asian countries are now out to secure greater
levels of foreign investment.

Competition for foreign capital, however, has become keener. For
those Asian countries in financial crises, it has become increasingly important to create hospitable environments to attract TNCs. In the global
economy, the low cost of labour and other resources are no longer sufficient, in and of themselves, to attract overseas capital. Further, policies to
liberalize trade and capital markets have not provided a competitive edge
over other competing countries in the global capital market (UNCTAD
1998). Thus, there is growing emphasis on "created assets" as determinants of capital inflows. Characteristics such as urban development levels,
infrastructure, and technology are increasingly a determinant in attracting foreign capital within the competitive global capital market.

This chapter discusses FDI in Asia. The first section presents overall
global trends and those within the region. The second section discusses
the impacts of FDI on economies in the region by concentrating on the
spatial, infrastructural, industrial, and technological aspects of the flows.
The third and last section discusses the role of globalization and capital
markets in the quest for urban sustainability. Immediately, a distinction must be made between portfolio or equity investments and those
that are made for the long term. The first set of investments have played

a significant role in creating the Asian financial crisis, while FDI has become an increasingly important, stable, and therefore sought-after growth determinant.

FDI in Asian emerging economies

FDI in the global capital market

FDI can be defined as the governance of business by a foreign entity through the exercise of significant influence on the management of the firm (UNCTAD 1997). Although the criteria vary by country, generally foreign portfolio investments between 10 and 25 per cent of the total capital are classified as FDI.[2] These investments can take the form of sole investments, joint ventures, and mergers and acquisitions (M&As). FDI is usually carried out in forms of equity or debt. Actual inflows of capital, however, are not necessarily an intrinsic part of FDI. FDI, for example, includes the foreign investment accompanying a loan from a third country, where the TNC may bring in their patent rights, technology, and machinery, instead of capital, to the host country (Lee 1997).

The amount of FDI inflows is related to the competitive advantage of industries in the source and host countries. The push factors include high labour costs, strong trade union activities, and an unfavourable business environment in the source country. Growing concern about the environment and strict pollution control at home are other possible push factors. Poor technology in a country can also be a push factor in the developing countries, as it encourages industries to go abroad to obtain higher levels of technology.

Traditionally, pull factors in developing countries have been an abundant labour force and natural resources. The labour market of a developing country is generally flexible and trade unions are less active compared with those of the industrialized countries.[3] On the other hand, FDI can also be attracted to the technology level and large potential market of developed countries. Membership in a regional economic bloc with trade barriers could also be a pull factor. For instance, TNCs invest in the UK in order to sell their products in the European market where there are strong trade barriers to non-members. Tax concessions and other forms of incentives to foreign investors are pull factors. An adequate level of infrastructure and utilities are also pull factors.

The policy emphasis on enhancing FDI has shifted from trade and investment liberalization and privatization policies to macro-economic and organizational policies traditionally not considered as a part of FDI policies. The importance of natural resources as a determinant of FDI has also shifted to "created assets" such as human capital, urban agglomeration, accessibility to the international market, etc. As a result, in order to promote inflows of foreign capital, governments in developing countries cannot rely on a single attractive feature, but must advance a variety of different pulls. They must therefore enhance the effectiveness of investment policies and promote "created assets".

Inflows of foreign capital translate into increases in capital accounts in the balance of payments of the host country. This eases financial constraints and helps further increase investment, and consequently raises economic performance. In given instances, foreign capital can also promote export or import substitution. In both cases, FDI brings positive impacts on the balance of payments (Kim, Kim, and Wong 1998). FDI also has the potential to bring some detrimental impacts to the host country. In the case of FDI inflows through M&As, foreign investors may reduce the number of employees when they take over and restructure the local firm.[4] Foreign investors could import raw materials and semi-final goods from their source countries so that the host country would have to increase imports. In addition, FDI may involve loyalty payments, remittance of profits, and the repayment of foreign loans, which could increase capital outflows later. Also, in cases of M&As, loss of control over domestic firms may become a controversial political issue.

FDI trends in Asia

About 20 years ago, 90 per cent of all international capital flows were due to trade in real goods and only 10 per cent were investment related. Today, this situation is reversed. About 90 per cent of international capital flows are investment related, whereas 10 per cent emanate from international trade (Armstrong 1997; Goldberg and Klein 1997).

FDI continued to grow in 1997 for the seventh consecutive year, and reached a record high. Worldwide FDI inflows increased by 19 per cent, reaching US$400 billion, with outflows of US$424 billion (UNCTAD 1998). During that year, the ratio of FDI stock (inward and outward) to global GDP was 21 per cent, and foreign affiliate exports were one-third of the global exports.

Between 1990 and 1996, FDI outflows increased by over 43 per cent. FDI in developing countries jumped to US$119 billion in 1996 and US$120 billion in 1997, which was five times more than in 1990. FDI shares of world GDP increased from 0.8 per cent to 2.0 per cent from 1991 to 1997. The share of FDI going to the developing countries (Figure 3.1) also increased, from 21 per cent in 1991 to 36 per cent in 1997 (World Bank 1998).

FDI inflows in Asia accounted for only 2.9 per cent of Asian GDP in

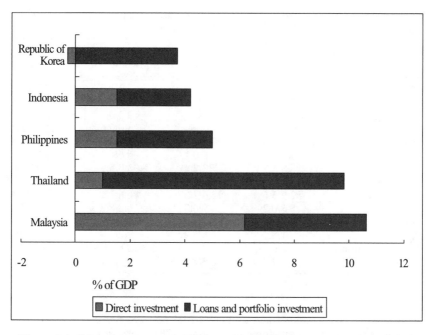

Figure 3.1   Annual average net private capital inflows between 1991 and 1997
Source: *The Economist* 1998

1980, but increased to 12.1 per cent in 1994. In 1996, Malaysia and Singapore had the highest ratios of FDI inflows to GDP, which reached 27 per cent and 22 per cent respectively (Table 3.1).

During the 1990s, the proportion of FDI inflows to gross fixed capital formation also increased in Asia countries. FDI inflows into Asia were approximately 3.1 per cent of the gross fixed capital formation in 1990, and increased to 7.2 per cent by 1996 (Table 3.2). In China, the share of foreign compared to gross domestic capital increased from 2.6 per cent in 1990 to 24.5 per cent in 1996. Singapore also has a relatively high FDI proportion in its capital formation, though its share decreased over the period from 47.1 per cent in 1990 to 23.5 per cent in 1996. The proportions of FDI inflows to the gross fixed capital formation in Japan and Korea were relatively low, recorded as 0.1 per cent and 0.6 per cent, respectively, in 1994.

Increases in FDI inflows to China have been remarkable, as the country alone received US$42 billion in FDI inflows in 1996, whereas Singapore had about US$10 billion in the same year (UNCTAD 1997: 78). In 1990, the total amount of FDI inflows to Asia was US$22.12 billion, which was less than 10 per cent of the world total at the time. By 1996, the inflows increased to US$84.28 billion, which represented approxi-

Table 3.1 Shares of inbound and outbound FDI stock as a percentage of GDP by region and economy, 1980–1995 (inbound/outbound)

Country/region	1980 %	1985 %	1990 %	1995 %
Asia	3.5/0.6	7.3/0.8	7.3/1.9	14.2/6.0
Korea	1.8/0.2	1.9/0.6	2.3/0.9	2.3/2.2
Thailand	3.0/–	5.1/–	9.3/0.5	10.3/1.4
China	–/–	1.2/–	3.6/0.6	18.2/2.3
Hong Kong	6.3/0.5	10.5/7.0	18.7/18.5	22.7/88.8
Indonesia	14.2/–	28.6/0.1	36.6/–	25.2/0.3
Malaysia	24.8/1.7	27.2/2.4	33.0/5.3	52.1/12.6
Philippines	3.8/0.5	4.2/0.6	4.7/0.3	9.2/1.6
Singapore	52.9/5.6	73.6/7.5	86.6/12.7	67.4/38.4
Taiwan	5.8/0.2	4.7/0.3	6.2/8.2	7.3/11.2
Japan	0.3/1.8	0.4/3.3	0.3/7.0	0.3/6.0
USA	3.1/8.1	4.6/6.2	7.2/7.9	7.7/9.8
European Union	5.5/6.3	8.2/10.4	10.8/11.8	13.2/14.6
World	4.6/4.9	6.3/5.9	8.3/8.1	10.1/9.9

Source: UNCTAD 1996, 1997

Table 3.2 Shares of inbound and outbound FDI flows as a percentage of gross fixed capital formation, by region and economy, 1984–1995 (inbound/outbound)

Country/region	1984–1989 annual average %	1990 %	1991 %	1992 %	1993 %	1995 %
Asia	2.3/1.2	3.1/1.6	3.4/1.2	4.1/2.6	6.5/3.9	7.5/4.9
Korea	1.4/0.3	0.8/1.1	1.0/1.3	0.6/1.1	0.5/1.1	1.1/2.1
Thailand	4.4/0.3	7.1/0.4	4.9/0.4	4.8/0.3	3.5/0.5	2.9/1.3
China	1.8/0.5	2.6/0.6	3.3/0.7	7.8/2.8	20.0/3.2	25.7/1.4
Hong Kong	12.2/15.6	8.5/11.7	2.3/11.6	7.7/28.7	7.1/74.5	8.4/100.6
Indonesia	1.6/0.1	2.8/–	3.6/–	3.9/0.1	3.8/–	6.5/0.9
Malaysia	8.8/2.6	23.8/3.8	23.8/2.3	26.0/2.6	22.5/5.9	17.9/11.2
Philippines	5.1/–	5.2/–	6.0/−0.3	2.1/0.1	7.9/–	9.0/2.4
Singapore	28.3/3.6	47.1/17.2	33.5/7.0	13.3/7.4	24.6/8.8	24.6/13.9
Taiwan	3.3/9.6	3.8/15.0	3.0/4.4	2.4/5.1	2.4/6.5	2.7/4.6
Japan	–/3.4	0.2/5.1	0.2/4.0	0.3/2.0	–/1.2	–/1.5
European Union	4.7/7.7	7.0/9.5	5.5/7.6	5.5/7.5	5.8/7.2	6.8/9.2
USA	5.8/2.2	6.0/3.4	3.0/4.5	2.2/4.9	4.7/7.8	5.9/9.0
World	3.1/3.3	4.0/4.7	3.1/4.2	3.2/3.9	3.8/4.2	5.2/5.6

Source: UNCTAD 1996, 1997

mately 25 per cent of the world total (Table 3.3). Nearly half of FDI inflows in Asia were designated for China (Figure 3.2).

The influx of FDI in developing countries in the 1990s was accelerated

Table 3.3 FDI inflows, by host region and economy, 1984–1996

US$ million

Country/region	1984–1989 annual average	1990	1991	1992	1993	1994	1995	1996
Asia	11,540	22,122	23,129	29,632	50,924	57,507	65,249	84,283
Korea	592	788	1,180	727	588	809	1,776	2,308
Thailand	676	2,444	2,014	2,114	1,730	1,322	2,003	2,426
China	2,282	3,487	4,366	11,156	27,515	33,787	37,500	40,180
Hong Kong	1,422	1,728	538	2,051	1,667	2,000	2,100	2,500
Indonesia	406	1,093	1,482	1,777	2,004	2,109	4,348	7,960
Malaysia	798	2,333	3,998	5,183	5,006	4,348	5,800	5,300
Philippines	326	530	544	228	1,238	1,591	1,478	1,408
Singapore	2,239	5,575	4,887	2,204	4,686	5,480	6,912	9,440
Taiwan	691	1,330	1,271	879	917	1,375	1,559	1,402
Japan	81	1,753	1,730	2,756	210	888	41	220
European Union	37,702	97,387	78,777	83,793	81,029	72,395	110,884	99,416
USA	43,938	47,918	22,799	18,885	43,534	49,903	60,848	84,629
Australia	4,306	7,077	4,903	4,912	2,687	4,423	13,094	6,043
New Zealand	176	1,686	1,698	1,090	2,200	2,796	2,483	2,928
World	115,370	203,812	158,936	173,761	218,094	238,738	316,524	349,227

Source: UNCTAD 1996, 1997

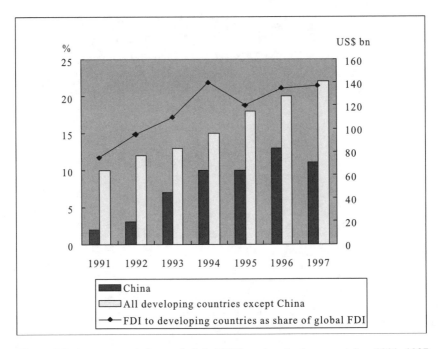

Figure 3.2 Amount and share of global FDI to developing countries, 1991–1997
Source: UNCTAD 1997

by the liberalization of the trade and capital markets, and also by privatization. The major sources of the capital flows were from the USA,
Japan, Germany, the UK, and France. A notable feature of the outbound
FDI during this period was the addition of some developing economies,
such as Korea, Singapore, and Hong Kong, as capital exporters. In Asia
alone, outflows of capital from developing countries have increased. FDI
from the developing countries increased to US$51.5 billion in 1997, up
from US$47 billion in 1996 and US$8.3 billion in 1990. The share of total
outbound FDI from the developing countries increased from 4 per cent in
1990 to 15 per cent in 1996. As it can be seen from Table 3.4, Asian FDI
outflows jumped from 5 per cent of the total in 1990 to 15 per cent of the
total in 1996. By 1996, Asian FDI from NICs, ASEAN, and other developing countries amounted to US$46.8 billion and was twice the size of
that of Japan (US$23.4 billion). Hong Kong's outward FDI amounted to
US$27 billion in that year. This gave it the distinction of being the largest
capital exporter among the group (58 per cent). Singapore (US$4.8 bil-
lion) and Korea (US$4.2 billion) are next, followed by Taiwan (US$3.1
billion), China (US$2.2 billion), Malaysia (US$1.9 billion), and Thailand
(US$1.7 billion) (Table 3.4).

Table 3.4 FDI outflows, by source region and economy, 1984–1996

US$ million

Country/region	1984–1989 annual average	1990	1991	1992	1993	1994	1995	1996
Asia	5,984	11,816	7,819	18,695	31,042	35,913	42,437	46,816
Korea	137	1,056	1,500	1,208	1,361	2,524	3,529	4,188
Thailand	41	140	167	147	233	493	886	1,740
China	581	830	913	4,000	4,400	2,000	3,467	2,200
Hong Kong	1,833	2,448	2,825	8,254	17,713	21,437	25,000	27,000
Indonesia	16	11	13	52	356	609	603	512
Malaysia	233	532	389	514	1,325	1,817	2,575	1,906
Philippines	4	–5	–26	5	374	302	399	182
Singapore	610	2,034	526	1,317	2,021	3,104	3,906	4,800
Taiwan	1,999	5,243	1,854	1,869	2,451	2,460	2,678	3,096
Japan	20,793	48,024	31,620	17,390	13,830	18,090	22,510	23,440
European Union	62,641	132,959	106,362	110,521	96,596	112,836	149,118	160,372
USA	16,847	27,175	33,456	38,978	74,837	51,007	92,929	84,902
Australia	3,338	186	3,022	854	1,768	5,243	4,092	1,343
New Zealand	276	2,365	690	792	1,300	1,571	924	–157
World	121,630	240,253	198,143	201,465	239,090	251,117	338,729	346,824

Source: UNCTAD 1996, 1997

Japan has sustained a balance of payments surplus for decades. This condition, along with an unfavourable business environment at home, stimulated firms to invest abroad. Korea, however, has had balance of payments deficits since the late 1980s. Nevertheless, inward FDI to Korea increased dramatically over the last few years. This is partly because of the degrading business environment within the home countries, and partly due to relaxed foreign investment policies in Korea.

Impacts of FDI

Spatial implications

In most Asian countries over the last three decades, rapid industrialization has been accompanied by rapid urbanization. Within all growing economies, large numbers of underemployed and unemployed people migrated into the urban centres looking for jobs. Industrial activities moved into the urban centres to take advantage of the urban infrastructure and the large labour pool, making real estate in these centres a scarce resource. Both industrial firms and individuals were attracted to urban centres to take advantage of agglomeration economies. Consequently, the demand for housing and urban land development increased rapidly. Urban concentration was also accelerated through government policies that directly and indirectly influenced their development. Industrialization and urban concentration fed each other in a cumulative and circular fashion. Thus, investment from both private enterprises and government in urban facilities, residential structures, production facilities, and infrastructure expanded as the economy grew.

The pattern of FDI location differs by industry and by the unique characteristics of the economic geography of the host country. Notwithstanding these differences, the investment choices of TNCs largely relate to efficiency, resource, and market characteristics. In Asia, these behaviours resulted in three main outcomes. First, there has been a concentrated location pattern of FDI in the region's capital cities and their peripheries. Second, encouraged by government-sponsored industrial estates with access to port facilities, some production sites of FDI have been located in the provincial areas with good access to material sources and/or air or sea port facilities. Third, natural resource development industries dispersed to locations of high concentration of the resource.

In essence, the location pattern of FDI in developing Asian countries followed the trend of domestic investment, but more intensively. Foreign investments have not only located in the urban centres, however, but they have also concentrated in the capital cities. In Japan, for example, about 80 per cent of the headquarters of foreign firms are located in the Tokyo metropolitan area (Japan Development Bank 1996: 21). The lion's share of inbound FDI, around 50 per cent, in the Philippines, Thailand, and Indonesia are located in Manila, Bangkok, and Jakarta, respectively (see Table 2.9).

In the case of Korea, most foreign affiliates in manufacturing tend to be located in the peripheries of urban centres in the provincial areas. On the other hand, the central offices of the affiliates are mostly located in the Seoul metropolitan region. FDI inbound within the city boundary of Seoul reached 52.5 per cent in a number of cases, and 19.5 per cent in terms of value. However, the larger portion of FDI in manufacturing is spread out to the peripheries of the provincial urban centres.

Service- and manufacturing-related FDI companies tend to locate their headquarters and branch offices in the urban centres to take advantage of the built-up environment. Urban centres often provide benefits in terms of access to global information networks that are essential to contacting the parent companies and overseas clients. Furthermore, in many Asian countries the central government plays the dominant role in development strategies. Key agencies are often concentrated in the major urban centres, the capital, and provincial capital cities. Consequently, foreign firms prefer such locations for their main offices so as to be close to these officials. Service-related FDI in particular has concentrated in the urban centres of the host countries, which provide amenities of international standards and the best accessibility to the global network essential to businesses.

FDI and infrastructure

Infrastructure investment in many countries is a vehicle for economic sustainability and growth. In the developing countries, the human-made environment is also an important determinant for foreign capital inflows as well as for social welfare. The public provision of infrastructure is considered as a cost-free input for private industry which serves to promote the economic sustainability of society. Despite large investments, with rapid industrialization Asian countries have been continuously in need of infrastructure investment. For example, during the period of fast growth in the East Asian countries, the financial requirements for infrastructure amounted to approximately US$1.4 trillion. For China alone it was estimated to be US$700 billion. A larger sum of funds, however, is still required to meet demand. The rapidly industrialized countries, without exception, have limited funds for these capital investments. The bottlenecks in infrastructure have hampered the efficiency of the economy, hindered inflows of FDI, and slowed growth in enhancing the quality of urban life.

Most of these fast-growing Asian economies face severe bottlenecks in financing infrastructure using only domestic savings. The involvement of TNCs in overseas infrastructure projects has been increasing, but slowly. Infrastructure financing takes various forms of FDI, such as greenfield investments or acquisitions through privatization, build-own-operate (BOO), build-operate-transfer (BOT), and build-transfer-operate (BTO).

Privatization has been an important channel for attracting FDI in infrastructure projects. In developing countries, the revenue from privatization amounted to US$40 billion in the period 1988–1995, representing 37 per cent of revenues from global infrastructure privatization activities, while FDI accounted for half of the revenues. Generally, infrastructure investments require a long-term commitment from a foreign source and influence their management decisions (UNCTAD 1996: 18–29).

Infrastructure investment by overseas sources has only recently started in Asia. The legal framework for BOT for infrastructure investment was established in Viet Nam in 1993 and in China in 1995. In Korea, the overseas investment law was revised in June 1998 to attract overseas capital for major infrastructure investments. In spite of these efforts, because of the long gestation period and high fixed cost of the infrastructure projects, as well as host country regulations on price and other operation details, overseas investors have avoided making extensive commitments. Instead, they have preferred to provide commercial loans and finance debt through issuing bonds.

There is potential for TNCs to participate in infrastructure development projects. Partly, this is due to technological advancements that enable dividing huge infrastructure projects into many separate projects that can be handled by private investors. Since the financial crisis, Asian governments have been competing to attract overseas financing. Deregulation and liberalization are progressing much faster than previously.

On the issue of infrastructure, it is worth emphasizing that these investments are not only necessary to enhance the productivity of domestic industry and the quality of life for residents, but are also an important determinant in attracting further FDI. In other words, infrastructure investment is not only the desirable destination of FDI, but the provision of an efficient infrastructure network is an element in determining the location of TNC investments. This is a "Catch 22" dilemma faced by many developing countries. It is especially significant for those Asian economies with foreign exchange shortages.

FDI and industry

One dominant feature of FDI in the 1990s was the increasing share of service-related investments. Recently, some Asia Pacific countries have

Table 3.5 Share of GDP and FDI inflows by sector in selected Asian countries

Country	Primary sector		Secondary sector		Tertiary sector	
	GDP	FDI	GDP	FDI	GDP	FDI
Korea (1997)	5.7	0.6	25.9	33.9	68.4	65.5
Taiwan (1996)	3.3	0.0	28.5	38.0	68.2	62.0
Singapore (1994)	0.2	0.8	23.8	34.8	76.0	64.4
Thailand (1996)	11.8	0.0	29.3	33.9	58.9	66.1
Indonesia (1995)	11.7	3.5	32.2	67.4	56.1	29.1
Philippines (1995)	21.70	0.0	24.0	71.5	54.3	28.4
Japan (1995)	1.9	0.0	24.9	38.2	61.8	61.8

Source: The Economist Intelligence Unit 1997

been attracting service-sector FDI. Korea, Indonesia, and Thailand are some of the countries demonstrating rapid growth in capital inflows in the service sector.

The sectoral shares of capital inflows are quite different from the share of domestic industries. FDI by TNCs is generally based on firm-specific elements related to the enhanced competitiveness gained from overseas operations. The elements of competitive advantage of overseas affiliates are in technology, organization, marketing knowledge, goodwill, brand name, etc. On the other hand, the market structure and competitiveness of the host countries also influence the TNCs' choice of industrial sector investment. As shown in Table 3.5, the service sector has the major share of inbound FDI in Taiwan, Korea, Singapore, and Thailand, while FDI shares in the manufacturing sector are largest in Indonesia and the Philippines.

An analysis of industries at the one-digit level of standard industrial codes (SICs) reveals that inflows of capital are more or less concentrated in a few manufacturing sectors. In Taiwan, 64 per cent of the capital inflows are in electricity and electronics. In Indonesia, 72 per cent of FDI is invested in one sector of chemicals, petroleum, and rubber. In Korea, 36 per cent of the FDI is in the food and beverage and tobacco industries. The industrial quotients in Table 3.6 indicate the degrees of relative concentration of FDI, and the ratio of shares of FDI to the relative shares of production by domestic industries.

Table 3.6 Industrial quotients (IQs)[a]

Industries	Korea (1995)	Taiwan (1995)	Indonesia (1995)	Japan (1995)
Metal	0.07	0.15	0.11	0.02
Chemicals, petroleum, coal, and rubber	0.55	0.86	4.51	5.04
Non-metallic products	0.00	0.27	0.45	0.00
Paper, paper products, printing and publishing, wood products	1.69	0.03	0.76	0.00
Fabricated metal products, machinery, and equipment	0.78	0.25	5.25	0.25
Electricity and electronics, medicine	0.82	3.34	0.00	0.45
Transport equipment	0.93	1.00	0.00	0.02
Food, beverage, and tobacco	3.23	0.21	0.24	0.27
Textiles, wearing apparel, and leather	0.90	0.20	0.10	0.46
Others	0.50	0.00	0.14	1.62

Sources: UNIDO 1998; JETRO 1997; Korean Ministry of Finance and Economy 1997; Bank of Korea various years

a. $IQ = \dfrac{FDI_i}{\sum FDI_i} \Big/ \dfrac{X_i}{\sum X_i}$ where FDI_i : FDI_i in sector i, X_i; output in sector i.

Japanese FDI is quite diversified. The sectoral share of Japan's FDI is similar to that of the Japanese economy in the 1980s, as suggested in the "flying geese" type of development pattern. On the other hand, the FDI from the USA to Asian countries falls largely in a few selected industries, resource development, petroleum, and electronics (Goldberg and Klein 1997).

The USA and Japan are the major FDI source countries for service-sector activity. The service sector accounted for 58 per cent of FDI from Japan and the share of the service sector doubled in the stock of FDI from the USA over the past decade. A similar pattern can be observed in FDI outflows from the other industrialized countries.

There are several factors that contribute to the fast growth of FDI in the service sector. First, service-sector activities in developing countries are the fastest-growing sectors within their economies, and are considered the most lucrative markets. Furthermore, the service sector requires a commercial presence in the market because of the nature of the business. Second, FDI in the service sector is increasingly attractive due to developments in telecommunications technology that allow close supervision and coordination of affiliates. Third, the privatization of public services in developing countries contributed to the growth of FDI in the service sector. About 40 per cent of the revenue generated by privatization programmes in the developing countries in the 1990s has been directed to service-sector activities.

FDI and technology transfer

A positive impact of FDI has been technology transfer. With the opera-tion of overseas affiliates, production technology from industrialized coun-tries has been transmitted to local labour forces in the developing world through on-the-job training or exchange programmes between parent companies and affiliates. Technology transfer, among other things, helps to increase the productivity and occupational mobility of local workers.

Accompanying technology transfer is the spillover of knowledge to local firms. FDI also boosts competition among local rivals for the acqui-sition of better technologies. The vertical integration of interfirm link-ages by the foreign company forces the domestic firm to meet standards practised in the source countries. In the process, FDI serves to develop human resources in the host countries. It provides on-the-job training opportunities for the workers in the affiliates, and promotes the mobility of labour.

In this vein, the choice of technology transferred has been a con-troversial issue. The technology of the affiliates is a reflection of source countries that are capital rich and technologically advanced. These tech-nologies may not, in all cases, be suitable for the development of the host economy. Studies report that over 70 per cent of technology adopted by the affiliates of TNCs are technologies originated from the source coun-tries. In some cases, there is difficulty adapting the new technology at the local level because of large factor price differences enhanced by technical rigidity (Marsh, Newfarmer, and Moreira 1983).

The transfer of technology to host countries favours two different routes. One is where technology imported through FDI substitutes for the local R&D. Another is where the imported and domestic technologies are complementary to each other. In the cases of Taiwan, Korea, and Singa-pore, studies found the export-oriented affiliates of TNCs applied tech-nology similar to their parent companies (Chung and Lee 1980; Jo 1980). Kumar (1996), on the other hand, concluded that technology adopted by the affiliates depends on market orientation.

In the cases of Korea and Japan, technology and capital imports have been decoupled. This provides the host country with the opportunity to undertake its own initiative in shaping R&D. In general, however, one can expect that the production technology of the parent company, which uses the environmental standards of the host country, could be trans-mitted to the affiliates. Consequently, affiliates are likely to assimilate the practice of the parent firms in the source country. The technology of the parent firm, transmitted to the affiliates under contractual modes, out-right licensing, or capital good imports, tends to be adjusted through re-verse engineering such that recipient countries export technologies to the source country. So, while the first generation of plants were built using the technologies of the host countries, following generations were built using locally created technologies based on newly adopted knowledge and reverse engineering (Westphal, Rhee, and Pursell 1979; Kim 1988; Amsden 1989).

The location of production is generally subject to centralized decision-making. Thus, the affiliates in developing countries undertake R&D only when it fits in their global strategy. Though TNCs tend to decentralize R&D functions to affiliates, they still largely remain in industrialized countries.

Globalization, capital markets, and sustainability

Globalization and the Asian crisis

Liberalization of capital markets has been advocated as a means to prosperity. In particular, developing countries were strongly advised to open up their capital markets. This, it was argued, would enable them to fuel growth using both domestic and external capital from the global market. In Korea, until recently, the government refrained from promoting foreign capital inflows. Korea then joined the OECD in 1997, following Mexico, and they were advised to open up their capital markets.

In 1997, the end of Asian miracle came about suddenly with the region's financial crisis that severely damaged five countries: Indonesia, Malaysia, Korea, Thailand, and the Philippines. Together, in 1994 these countries had net private inflows of US$41 billion, and the amount jumped to US$93 billion in 1996. The inflow exceeded the total current account deficit, allowing the governments to accumulate US$37 billion in additional reserves. At the start of the crises in 1997, net inflows turned into net outflows of US$12 billion. In a one-year period, the swing in the net supply of private capital was US$105 billion (Wolf 1998).

Foreign investors pulled out and banks and financial institutions refused to rollover short-term loans. The Asian financial markets, which had been providing higher interest rates than in the USA, Europe, and Japan, were no longer attractive for hedge fund investments. The miraculous Asian economic growth period came swiftly to a halt.

Economic growth in Asian countries is built upon a high-debt model of development. Export-oriented rapid growth in those countries was possible with the expansion of a few selected industries and enterprises. Governments actively supported these activities. Firms expanded their capital to attain an economic scale that enabled them to compete in the international market. This was possible because of the exceptionally high domestic savings and the governments' unspoken guarantee that domestic financial agencies would be solvent during all periods. The high-debt growth model is predicated upon the close coordination of activities among the government, banking, and business sectors.

After the financial crisis, the fabric of the Asian system has been disintegrating. The start of this process was the liberalization of the financial market. Hasty liberalization triggered banks and businesses, mainly the *"Chaebol"* in Korea, to expand their borrowing indiscriminately. With rampant overinvestment, the return on capital has dwindled. In the early 1990s when the Western industrial countries were in a depression and Mexico was gripped by its own financial crisis, opportunities in the Asian economies provided the best options available to the global investor. The high debt of Asian economies was fuelled by the massive influx of capital from the industrialized countries in the West and also from a few Asian countries, such as Japan, Korea, Hong Kong, and Taiwan. However, in 1997, economic conditions in the USA and the EU turned around, which made the terms provided on investment in Asian countries inferior. The exodus of foreign capital started.

In these Asian countries, low-interest foreign capital poured into the real estate sector. High-rise office buildings and downtown condominiums mushroomed in metropolitan areas in most of these countries. Following the appreciation of the Japanese yen against the dollar in 1996, the current account balances for many Asian countries fell deeper into deficit. In Thailand, deficits amounted to US$14.7 billion and in Korea the deficits reached US$23.7 billion (Table 3.7). The same general trend was also seen in Indonesia, Malaysia, and the Philippines. Despite deficits, the value of the domestic currencies was kept artificially high by manoeuvring the exchange rate in these countries. With a large gap between the real and the nominal exchange rates, financing institutions opened themselves up to the rapid and strong influence of short-term global capital flows, such as those controlled by hedge funds and the like.

Table 3.7 Current account balance of Asian countries

Country	US$100 million							
	1990	1991	1992	1993	1994	1995	1996	1997
Korea	−22	−87	−45	−48	−45	−90	−237	−86
Thailand	−73	−76	−64	−70	−84	−136	−147	−32
Indonesia	−30	−43	−28	−21	−28	−68	−78	−
Malaysia	−9	−42	−22	−28	−45	−74	−61	−
Philippines	−27	−10	−10	−30	−30	−20	−44	−

Source: World Bank 1998

In the current situation, businesses find themselves in overindebted situations with heavy debt service payments, while being short of cash. In order to stay alive they have liquidated their real estate assets, among others. There has been a drastic decline in the value of real estate in most of these countries. For example, in many cases the price of real estate decreased by half within a year of the start of the crisis.

As a result of the crisis there has been a general decline in the economic performance of the once rapidly growing Asian countries. With a few exceptions, the GDP growth in most of these countries during 1998 was negative: −5.2 per cent in Hong Kong, −16.5 per cent in Indonesia, −6.8 per cent in Malaysia, −1.2 per cent in the Philippines, and −6.6 per cent in Korea. Most of these countries were going through painful industrial restructuring. The rate of unemployment and bankruptcy created social unrest in Indonesia. Industrial production has decreased by more than 10 per cent in Malaysia, the Philippines, Thailand, and Korea as of late 1998. Manufacturing plants have been closing in provincial regions and the suburbs of metropolitan areas. Vacant stores and office space and unsold housing units are increasing in urban areas. There have been many incidents of reverse migration of laid-off workers from the cities to rural areas.

FDI and economic sustainability

Prior to the crisis, direct equity investments in Asia increased in a stable manner. Capital inflows from non-bank private creditors were also stable, with a net inflow of US$18 billion in 1996 and US$14 billion in 1997. Portfolio equity, however, changed drastically from US$12 billion inflows during 1996 to similar outflows in 1997. But the most radical changes accompanying the Asian crisis were in commercial bank flows, which went from US$24 billion in 1994 and US$56 billion in 1996 to reversing net payments of US$21 billion in 1997 (Wolf 1998).

In the middle of the financial crisis, FDI became an important source of capital inflows for Asian countries. In the five Asian countries most affected by the crisis, Indonesia, Malaysia, the Philippines, Thailand, and Korea, foreign portfolio equity flows and bank loans dropped sharply and turned negative in 1997 (UNCTAD 1998: 17). Unlike other foreign capital inflows, such as portfolio equity investment or official government assistance, FDI inflows to Asian countries have continued to be stable source of capital.

FDI is essentially more a transfer of control than movement of capital *per se* (Kindleberger 1969). If the financial crises in Asian countries were all panic without moral hazard, Krugman suggests that current investors in these countries are purchasing firms at "fire sale" prices. Foreign firms bought ownership of these domestic businesses for less than the "right" price (Krugman 1998: 7).

Some consequences of the financial crisis are conducive for FDI inflows in Asian countries. Because of the drastic decline in asset prices in these countries, real estate and other assets cost much less for foreign investors. The crisis became an opportunity for businesses seeking strategic positions in Asia, and there is evidence that firms from the USA and EU are taking advantage of the situation.

Recently, in the midst of the economic meltdown, the Korea Exchange Bank, the second largest in Korea, announced it was selling 29.7 per cent (US$250 million) of its stake to Germany's Commerz Bank AG. Mr H. Vogt, the chief representative of the German bank, explained to reporters that their decision to buy is based on Korea's long-term economic potential, despite current troubles in the stock market and financial sectors (*Korea Herald* 1998). After the drastic decline of inbound FDI following the IMF bail-out, inbound FDI has been increasing in Korea. In particular, after the revision of the Foreigner's Land Acquisition Act in June 1998, real estate investment by foreigners increased. During the four months after the revision, foreign investment in real estate reached US$660 million. In the turmoil of the financial crisis, FDI may be the type of investment that the Korean economy needs, although M&A entry may cause a social backlash as the national government loses control over domestic firms.

On the other hand, the crisis has had adverse effects on FDI inflows. The declines in domestic demand adversely impact on domestic-market-oriented FDI. Foreign affiliations in the service sector are more susceptible to a depression in the local economy. Furthermore, the general depression in the Asian economy reduces the intraregional FDI in Asia that has been an important part of its capital inflows.

After the Asian economic crisis, there have been innumerable discussions about how to prevent such a situation occuring in the future. Some of the causes of the crisis are related to domestic conditions. Stanley Fischer of the IMF summarized these causes as failures to dampen overheating, manifested in large external deficits and asset price bubbles; maintenance of pegged exchange rates, which stimulated excessive external borrowing; lax financial regulations, which allowed a sharp deterioration in the quality of bank portfolios; and lack of commitment to make needed adjustments when the crisis was under way (Wolf 1998). One of the remedies put forward has been the Tobin tax, which argues that a cross-border payment of tax on the inflows of foreign capital may impact on the horizon of financing and therefore discourage volatile capital movements. However, Dornbusch (1998) argues that the Tobin tax will not work for the Asian cases because "Asia was not brought down by shortsighted round tripping" of foreign capital. Rather, he suggests that under the extensive depreciation of Asian currencies, reaching over 50 per cent at times, the small financial penalty generated by the Tobin tax would not be an effective tool to discourage rapid capital movements.

Many economists now recommend a system of preventive capital controls that limit capital inflows. In order to structure their maturity, priority of the capital inflows is advised in a three-step fashion. The first priority is for equity investments. The second priority is for long-term bonds, and the third is for short-term borrowing.

Asian countries have been struggling to cope with the radically changing global economic environment. With bail-out financing, the IMF has prescribed tight money and high-interest policies for some Asian countries. However, the IMF prescription does not seem to be curing the sickness fast enough. Asset devaluation tied to high interest rates is further dampening investment and consumption, and creating another hurdle for industrial restructuring and fast recovery. The Asian nations are now ready to remake a recovery plan. They are searching for a better approach that fits the current economic situation and the inherent structures of their economies. In an effort to sustain the economy from further deterioration, the Korean government announced a 1999 budget plan that expands public spending to facilitate domestic consumption and investment. The government will invest US$8.5 billion, close to 15 per cent of the total budget, in infrastructure and housing construction until the end of 1999. Furthermore, in early 1998 the government allocated US$1.2 billion to support unemployed people.

Conclusions

The major lesson from the financial crises is that globalization has two sides. Previously, globalization was viewed uncritically as the engine of growth for nations able to participate. Since 1997, however, many countries in the Asia Pacific region have been forced to face the negative consequences of global capitalism.

In the period of rapid economic growth in Asia, FDI played an important role in providing capital for infrastructure development and the expansion of industries in these countries. The rapid growth of Asian economies has been, in part, sustained by the inflows of foreign capital. These inflows were viewed as a boon to rapidly urbanizing Asian nations with limited capital to invest in the urban infrastructure, such as roads, water, and the sewerage systems.

All foreign capital inflows, however, are not alike. Under the financial crises, some Asian countries also experienced the dangers of ebbs and flows of "hot money" in the form of portfolio investments, which rolled like "a can on the deck in the storms". FDI, on the other hand, has been a stable source of capital for some Asian countries which need hard currency for debt servicing while they undergo a foreign exchange crisis. Those countries are desperate to attract foreign capital for economic recovery. At the same time, they have to compete with other countries to attract foreign capital by expanding "created assets", which also require capital investments. This is a dilemma shared by those Asian countries in need of capital.

These Asian countries are in danger of making unsound capital investment decisions in the heat of the financial crisis. One danger is that they may be forced to take in more polluting industries through inbound FDI than would normally be the case. Also, they may jump at M&A-type investments and thus lose management control and business interests, thereby jeopardizing their national interest. More foreign capital inflow is necessary for economic recovery and sustainability in these countries. An important question here is how to attract foreign capital, FDI in particular, without sacrificing environmental and economic sustainability of an urban system or a system of cities. In this crisis, developing countries must make prudent decisions.

In addition to moral hazards or crony capitalism, the financial crisis may stem from inherent problems within the global capital market. To prevent a recurrence of a financial crisis in the future, prudence in management of global capital is necessary for the sustainability of cities throughout in the world.

Notes

1. Inbound FDI and per capita income and growth rate in the host countries are an important determinant of FDI, although their relation appear to have a simultaneity problem in econometric findings.
2. The OECD classifies investments as FDI if portfolio investment exceeds 10 per cent of the total capital (Kim, Kim, and Wong 1998).
3. Some countries have strong union activities, which divert inward FDI inflows to other countries.
4. Structural adjustment is normally accompanied by a reduction in the number of employees, especially if participating firms originate from developed countries.

REFERENCES

Amsden, Alice. 1989. *Asia's Next Giant: South Korea and Late Industrialization.* New York: Oxford University Press.
Armstrong, Martin. 1997. *Global Market Outlook to 2003.* Princeton: Princeton Economics Institute.

Bank of Korea. Various years. *National Account*. Seoul: Bank of Korea.

Business Week. 1998. "The global impact", *Business Week*, 1 June, pp. 18–35.

Chung, B. S. and Chung H. Lee. 1980. "The choice of production techniques by foreign and local firms in Korea", *Economic Development and Cultural Change*, No. 29, pp. 135–140.

Dornbusch, Rudi. 1998. *Capital Controls: An Idea Whose Time Is Gone*. Internet: http://web.mit.edu/rudi/www/acapcpn~1.html.

The Economist. 1998. "Keeping the hot money out", *The Economist*, 24 January. Internet: http://www.economist.com/archive.

The Economist Intelligence Unit. 1997. *Country Report*, various countries including Korea, Taiwan, Singapore, Thailand, Indonesia, the Philippines, and Japan. London: EIU.

Goldberg, Linda S. and Michael W. Klein. 1997. *Foreign Direct Investment, Trade and Real Exchange Rate Linkages in Southeast Asia and Latin America*. Cambridge, MA: National Bureau of Economic Research.

Japan Development Bank (JDB). 1996. *JDB Research Report*, September, No. 219 (in Japanese).

Japan External Trade Organization (JETRO). 1997. *World and Japan FDI*. Tokyo: JETRO (in Japanese).

Jo, Sung-Hwan. 1980. "Direct private investment", in Chong Kee Park (ed.) *Macroeconomic and Industrial Development in Korea*. Seoul: Korea Development Institute, pp. 129–182.

Kim, Kwan-ho, Jun-dong Kim, and Yoon-jong Wong. 1998. *The Status of FDI and its Proposal for Enhancement*. Seoul: KIEP (in Korean).

Kim, Linsu. 1988. "Technological transformation in Korea and its implications for other developing countries", *Development and South-South Cooperation*, Vol. 4, No. 7, pp. 19–29.

Kindleberger, C. P. 1969. *American Business Abroad: Six Lectures on Direct Investment*. New Haven: Yale University Press.

Korea Herald. 1998. "German Commerz Bank to buy 29.7 per cent stake of KEB", *Korea Herald*, 29 May. Internet: http://www.koreaherald.co.kr/kh0529/m0529b03.html.

Korean Ministry of Finance and Economy. 1997. *Trends in International Investment and Technology Inducement*. Seoul: Ministry of Finance and Economy (in Korean).

Krugman, Paul. 1998. *Fire Sale FDI*. Internet: http://web.mit.edu/krugman/www/FIRESALE.htm.

Kumar, Nagesh. 1996. *Foreign Direct Investments and Technology Transfers in Development: A Perspective on Recent Literature*. Internet: http://www.intech.unu.edu/publicat/discpape/dp-full/9606-f.htm.

Lee, Se-Gu. 1997. *The Inducement of FDI in Seoul*. Seoul: Seoul Development Institute (in Korean).

Marsh, L., R. Newfarmer, and Lino Moreira. 1983. *Employment and Technological Choice of Multinational Enterprises in Developing Countries*. Working Paper No. 23. Geneva: International Labour Office.

UNCTAD. 1996. *World Investment Report 1996: Investment, Trade and International Policy Arrangements*. New York and Geneva: UNCTAD.

UNCTAD. 1997. *World Investment Report 1997: Transitional Corporations, Market Structure and Competition Policy*. New York and Geneva: UNCTAD.

UNCTAD. 1998. *World Investment Report 1998: Trends and Determinants Overview*. New York and Geneva: UNCTAD.

UNIDO. 1998. *International Yearbook of Industrial Statistics 1998*. Vienna: UNIDO.

Westphal, Larry E., Y. W. Rhee, and Gary Pursell. 1979. "Foreign influences on Korean industrial development", *Oxford Bulletin of Economics and Statistics*, No. 41, pp. 359–388.

Wolf, Martin. 1998. *Flows and Blows*. Internet: http://www.stern.nyu.edu/~nroubin./Capital Flows-IIF-Wolf-FT398.html.

World Bank. 1998. *Global Development Finance 1998: Analysis and Summary Tables*. Washington, DC: World Bank.

4

International migration, urbanization, and globalization in the Asia Pacific region: A preliminary framework for policy analysis

Terry G. McGee and Chung-Tong Wu

Introduction

The current era of globalization has introduced fundamental changes in communication and information flows, a greater acceleration of capital transfers, and increased population movement between states. The manner in which these globalization processes have impacted upon the urbanization process in the Asia Pacific region has been the subject of many studies sponsored by the UN University (Fuchs *et al.* 1994; Lo and Yeung 1996; Lo and Yeung 1998). These studies all recognize the importance of natural population increases and rural-urban migration in contributing to the growth of cities, but little attention has been paid to the accelerating volume of international migration that is now experienced by cities in the region. This chapter focuses upon five aspects of this international migrant movement as it influences cities in the region.

First, the technical and definitional problems of assessing population mobility between nations are analysed. Second, the main features of Asia Pacific urbanization and city systems are presented as a foundation for the analysis of the role of international migration in the growth of cities which makes up the third part. Fourth, the major challenges of international migration to these cities are discussed. The final part deals with the policy issues arising from this process, particularly as they affect liveability and sustainability of cities.

A brief disclaimer

The topic that this chapter covers is large, and while there is a substantial literature on international migration and in particular on the role of international migration in individual cities, there have been few attempts to unravel the dimensions of international migration within a broad regional context. In tackling this task the authors have been greatly helped by reading Kritz and Zlotnik (1992), Hugo (1997) and Skeldon (1997a), who provide general overviews of the process. Thus, what is attempted in this chapter in effect is a preliminary framework for policy analysis.

Clearing the decks: Definitional problems

The four major identifying terms of this paper – international migration, urbanization, globalization, and the Asia Pacific region – are all problematic: balloons into which writers blow their own breath. In this respect the current authors are no different; the definitions that follow are, in essence, working definitions to permit the subsequent analysis.

Urbanization

There is general agreement that urbanization is a process involving the growth of population in urban places. The level of urbanization is defined as the increase in the population in urban places in relation to the total population of a given country. At the global scale, the level of urbanization is growing rapidly, and is currently expected to be more than 50 per cent by 2020 (McGee 1998). This overall figure masks sharp differences in the level of urbanization between developed and developing countries. In the countries currently identified as developed, the levels of urbanization began to increase almost 200 years ago, allowing most of these countries to achieve higher urbanization levels much earlier than countries identified as developing. Most developed countries had reached urbanization levels of more than 50 per cent by the early twentieth century. By comparison, most developing countries will reach this level by the middle of the twenty-first century. Further, because a major part of the global population (two-thirds) is located in developing countries, much of the urban increase between 1998 and 2025 will occur in this part of the world. Forecasted growth in developing countries during this period is over 1.8 billion people (United Nations 1999). Almost 80 per cent of this increase will occur in Asia!

Demographic components of the urbanization process

There is considerable debate about the continuation of the various demographic components of urban population growth. The population of
urban places can grow in four ways: by natural increase (excess of births
over deaths); by migration from non-urban places to urban places within
a given country, which is most frequently labelled rural-urban migration;
by international migration of people from one country to the urban places
of another country; and by the reclassification of urban places with the
inclusion of non-urban places.

This chapter focuses on the third component of the demographic contribution to urbanization, namely international migration.

International migration

Historically, international migration is primarily a result of the political
demarcation of global territory that accompanied the growth of nation-
states, beginning in the nineteenth century. Prior to this time, while there
was migration between various regions of the globe, it took the form of
population movements associated with trade colonization and frontier
development etc. across ill-defined boundaries. With the growth of the
nation-state it became necessary to define membership of the nation-state
by birth, residence, language, religion etc., and people who changed residence between states became international migrants. In the post-1960
period, however, as globalization increased the possibilities for population movements between states, the term has become somewhat more
problematic as nations have found it difficult to prevent large-scale illegal
migration and there is a growing fluidity in population mobility, often
allowing people to maintain residences in two or more countries (McGee
1997a; Skeldon 1997b). This chapter will adopt a very broad definition
of international migration that assumes a shift of residence from one
country to another and a specified period of residence in the in-migration
country.

Globalization

Globalization is a general term used to describe economic and technological processes that facilitate movement of capital, people, and commodities between states (see McGee 1997a for further discussion). The
authors accept the premise that these processes have changed radically
during the post-1945 period. They underpin major changes that effectively lead to space-time collapse and are crucial to an understanding of
international migration.

The Asia Pacific region

There are many understandings of the Asia Pacific region, but this chapter utilizes McGee's (1997b) definition that includes the countries focused
on the Pacific region. The authors recognize, however, that the processes
of international migration cannot be so narrowly defined. For example,
the numbers of international in-migrants from the South Asian region are
growing rapidly in the region, and out-migration from many countries of
the region (particularly the Philippines) to the Middle East is an important feature of international migration.

Urbanization in the Asia Pacific region

It is now well understood that the Asia Pacific region as defined in the
previous section is an emerging integrated subglobal region. This recognition is realized in the emergence of new regional organizations such as
APEC. At the same time there are considerable problems in measuring
the emergence of the Asia Pacific system. Apart from the problems of
defining spatial components of this system there are real difficulties in
measuring the degree of interaction in, for example, the case of international migration. Table 4.1 presents data for the region. Clearly the
region is characterized by a high degree of inequality in terms of wealth
that is reflected in the sharp variance between the developed and developing countries' overall levels of production.

Indeed, as Table 4.1 shows there are distinctive subcomponents of
the system – the two supereconomies of Japan and the USA; the white
settler economies of Canada, Australia, and New Zealand; the newly industrialized economies of Korea, Hong Kong, Taiwan, and Singapore;
the other Asian countries, including the population giant of China, which
contains about 50 per cent of the region's population; and the larger
Latin American countries of the Pacific Rim. Of interest as well is the fact
that the distribution of GDP was remarkably stable in the 25-year period
from 1965 to 1990. The recent fiscal turmoil in Asia is likely to have seen
the USA increase its proportion of the regional GDP. Despite the much-
heralded rise of the NIEs, the largest shift in GDP has been in Japan's
share of the Asia Pacific output, essentially at the expense of the USA. A
final characteristic of the Asia Pacific system is that the disparity between
the very large proportion of population in the less-developed parts of the
region and the small proportion in the richer supereconomies and white
settler colonies is an important reality. The fact that 80 per cent of the
population produces only 20 per cent of the GDP is reflected in their low
national levels of living.

Table 4.1 Percentage of gross domestic product and population of Asia Pacific rim: 1965–1990

	1965 GDP %	1965 Population %	1979 GDP %	1979 Population %	1983 GDP %	1983 Population %	1990 GDP %	1990 Population %
Supereconomies	77.8	21.5	74.4	18.6	75.2	18.4	79.2	17.4
USA	69.7	14.3	52.6	12.3	56.8	12.2	49.9	11.7
Japan	9.1	7.2	21.8	6.3	18.4	6.2	29.3	5.7
White settler	8.1	2.3	8.4	2.0	8.9	2.1	6.94	2.1
Canada	5.2	1.4	5.1	1.2	5.6	1.2	4.40	1.2
Australia	2.3	0.8	2.9	0.7	2.9	0.8	2.50	0.8
New Zealand	0.6	0.1	0.4	0.1	0.4	0.1	0.04	0.1
NICs[a]	0.9	3.3	2.6	3.4	2.8	3.4	3.6	3.4
Other Asian[b]	8.2	64.8	8.5	66.0	7.2	67.7	6.0	68.4
Latin America[c]	5.1	7.6	6.2	8.5	5.9	7.9	3.5	8.6
Total[d]	100.1	99.5	99.5	100.2	99.5	100.2	99.4	99.9

Source: World Bank 1991
a. NICs: Korea, Hong Kong, Taiwan, Singapore.
b. Other Asian countries: People's Republic of China, ASEAN (except Singapore).
c. Latin America: Mexico, Columbia, Peru, Chile, Argentina.
d. Percentages do not sum due to rounding.

Despite these subregional differences, researchers have begun to show that the transactional components of the Asia Pacific system are experiencing increasing interaction in communications and information flows (Rimmer 1992, 1994; Dick and Rimmer 1993; Rohlen 1995). Their general conclusion is that the technological revolution in communications, containerization, and wide-bodied jets has accelerated the movement of capital, goods, and people throughout the region. The dimensions of this transactional revolution are important to understand, for they underlie the considerable growth in international migration.

These developments can be illustrated through a brief analysis of the transportation patterns in the region. In the last 20 years there has been a significant shift in scheduled air-traffic routes in favour of the Asia Pacific over other regions of the globe. By 1996, prior to the Asian fiscal crisis, air traffic within the Asia Pacific region doubled the European and US markets. It was estimated in 1996 that by 2010 there will be a fourfold increase in the number of air passengers to 375 million and at that point the Asia Pacific will generate 51 per cent of the world's scheduled passenger traffic, although these estimates may have to be revised in view of the current Asian recession. Business travel will increasingly be added to by tourism and family visits. The movement of freight, via cargo, air, and landbridges in the region, has continued to grow, enhanced by the development of a few major points of intermodal transportation (Rimmer 1994). Information flows through various forms of telecommunications have grown rapidly, and in the period 1990–1995 Asia absorbed almost 50 per cent of global foreign direct investment in developing countries. These are the netscapes about which Appardurai (1990) and Castells (1996) have written so expressively.

This combination of economic growth, while slowing after the 1997–1998 fiscal crisis, and increased transactive capacity will still continue to fuel urbanization growth in the region. One feature of this will be the continuing emergence of major urban nodes that are the connectivity points of the region. Often these nodes form part of corridors of linked transactive networks that are the major focus of economic growth. Because these corridor regions are economically the most rapidly growing regions of the world, they act as a focus for both internal and international migration.

A framework for the analysis of international migration in the Asia Pacific

Any framework for the analysis of international migration in the Asia Pacific region must recognize that, as Skeldon reminds us, "the global

Table 4.2 Major demographic variables for selected countries arranged by development tier, Asia Pacific region

	Population mid-1994 (millions)	Annual growth labour force %	Proportion urban^a %	Migrant stock 1990 %^b	No. of migrants 1990 (000s)	Remittances as % of foreign exchange	Total fertility rate 1994^a	GNP per capita 1994 (US$)
Old core								
USA	260.6	1.1	76.0	7.9	19,603	0.1	2.0	25,880
Canada	29.2	1.1	77.0	15.5	4,266^c	0.7	1.9	19,510
Australia	17.8	1.6	85.0	23.4	3,916	2.2	1.9	18,000
New Zealand	3.5	1.5	86.0	15.5	519	7.0	2.1	13,350
New core								
Japan	125.0	0.6	78.0	0.7	868	0.1	1.5	34,630
Singapore	2.9	1.0	100.0	15.5	418	–	1.8	22,500
Hong Kong	6.1	0.8	95.0	–	–	–	1.2	21,650
Taiwan	20.9	1.0	75.0	–	–	–	2.0	10,852
Korea	44.5	1.9	80.0	2.1	900	0.5	1.8	8,260
Core extensions and potential core								
Malaysia	19.7	2.7	53.0	4.2	745	0.2	3.4	3,480
Thailand	58.0	1.5	40.0	0.6	314	2.5	2.0	2,410
China	1,190.9	3.7	29.0	–	346	1.0	1.9	320
Mexico	88.5	2.9	75.0	0.4	339	7.6	3.2	4,180
Chile	14.0	2.2	86.0	0.8	106	–	2.5	3,520

Labour frontier							
Philippines	67.0	2.6	53.0	0.1	38	13.4	3.8	950
Indonesia	190.4	2.5	34.0	0.1	96	0.8	2.7	880
Viet Nam	72.0	2.1	21.0	–	21	–	3.1	200
Laos	4.7	3.6	21.0	0.4	14	2.9	6.6	320
Cambodia	10.0	2.3	12.0	0.3	22	–	5.3	–
Myanmar	45.6	2.1	47.8	0.2	100	0.5	4.0	–
Resource rich							
Kuwait	1.6	2.3	97.8	71.7	1,503	–	3.0	19,420
Papua New Guinea	4.2	2.3	16.0	0.7	27	0.7	4.9	1,240

Source: Skeldon 1997a

a. Percentage of urban population in a given country.
b. Percentage of total population born outside the country.
c. Number of people who immigrated to country as of 1990. Note this is not the same as migrant stock since it excludes people born outside the country to Canadian citizens.
d. Calculated as the number of live births as a ratio of women in the child-bearing age group, 15–45 years old.

international migration system has changed dramatically over the last 150 years" (Skeldon 1997a: 52). In the late nineteenth and early twentieth centuries, the major migration movements were from Europe to North and South America, Australia, and New Zealand and from China and India to other parts of the world, particularly South-East Asia. Only the European pattern continued after the disruption of the Second World War. It was never to resume major importance, however, as the international migration system became more complex after the 1960s. This complexity involved a shift from a transatlantic to a transpacific system of migration.

Skeldon, in his most recent book, *Migration and Development: A Global Perspective* (1997a), puts forward a spatial framework for the analysis of this international migration. He divides the world into a series of "development tiers" that "tries to capture the idea of transition in types of economies" (Skeldon 1997a: 50) from agricultural to non-agricultural economies (Table 4.2). The first tier within the Asia Pacific region is the "old core" area of North America and Australia. The second tier covers the "new core" regions of East Asia and Latin America that include Japan, the Republic of Korea, Hong Kong, Taiwan, and Singapore. A third development tier is made up of an "actively expanding core" including the coastal zones of China, some countries in ASEAN (Malaysia, Thailand), and parts of Latin America such as Chile and border areas of Mexico. A fourth tier is a labour frontier that includes countries such as Myanmar, the Philippines, Indonesia, and much of Mexico. These countries make important contributions to population flows to the core regions. Finally, Sheldon defines a "resource rich" tier, which attracts specialized flows of migrants for resource extraction on frontier developments such as inland China, Kalimantan, and some of the Pacific countries like Papua New Guinea.

Within this spatial model there are several different explanatory typologies of international migration. The best established focuses upon motivational or functional dimensions of migration. Since these two dimensions are inextricably linked it is not always possible to separate the two. In addition, the classification of international migration is complicated by the blurring of categories of short-term and long-term migration that were often used to distinguish between immigrants and labour contract workers.

As a basis for analysing the patterns of migration to urban areas in the Asia Pacific region, the authors have developed the following typology that reflects the "development tier" put forward by Skeldon.

International migration within the "core" regions

The migration movements in largely urbanized countries of the region, including the USA, Canada, Australia, Japan, and the NIEs, tend to be interurban. It is often argued that international migration to these countries is primarily associated with the increasing internationalization of economic activity and is characterized by the movement of professionals engaged in business information industries and other service industries (Sassen 1991). An example of this type of movement is the growth in numbers of foreign residents (excluding illegals) in Japan, estimated to have risen from 100,000 to 300,000 in the last 10 years. The majority of these immigrants reside in the urban corridor that stretches from Tokyo to Osaka. Many writers have begun to focus on this group of mobile migrants as essentially transnationals who move throughout the Asia Pacific developing a lifestyle that is labelled "translocal". Good examples are the so-called "astronauts" who move back and forth between Hong Kong and Canada, maintaining residences in each society. This latter phenomenon is also prevalent in Australia (Pe-Pua *et al.* 1998).

International migration from the "labour frontier" to the "core" regions

International migration from the "labour frontier" constitutes by far the largest volume of transfers in the Asia Pacific region, and it most frequently involves movement from "labour surplus" regions to "urbanized" tiers. The majority of these migrants come to live in the city regions of the developed core.

Broadly, in functional terms there are four different streams of migrants. First are the legal immigrants who have applied to immigrate to core countries. In the last 20 years the major streams of this type of migration are from countries such as Hong Kong, Taiwan, China, and the Philippines (Table 4.3). Second, there are flows of refugee immigrants who have moved to the core from countries such as China, Viet Nam, and other Indochinese countries. They make up an important part of international migration.

Third, there is the international movement of short-term contract workers. While they are supposed to return to their home countries at the end of their contracts, they increasingly stay on as illegal migrants or apply for legal migrant status (Table 4.4). International students, while often not supposed to work, also fit into this category.[1] An example of one of the best-known groups of migrants in this short-term category is Filipino domestic workers. Table 4.4 shows the significance of the flow and stock of short-term contract workers within the East Asian host economies, an important feature of the recent rapid economic growth of the region.

Fourth, there are illegal migrants. By far the largest volume of illegal migrants has moved from Mexico to the USA, where they dominate US cities along the Mexican border and make up a majority of the

Table 4.3 Ten major source countries of Australian and Canadian immigrants, 1981–1996

	Australia % of total			Canada % of total		
	1981–1982	1990–1991	1995–1996	1981	1990	1996ᵃ
	UK 31.3	UK 17.0	New Zealand 12.4	UK 14.7	Hong Kong 10.8	Hong Kong 10.5
	New Zealand 9.9	Hong Kong 11.1	UK 11.4	China 7.6	Poland 7.7	China 8.5
	Viet Nam 9.4	Viet Nam 10.9	China 11.3	India 7.3	China 6.6	India 6.9
	Poland 4.9	New Zealand 6.1	Hong Kong 4.4	USA 6.8	Lebanon 6.0	Philippines 6.9
	South Africa 2.8	Philippines 5.2	India 3.7	Viet Nam 6.3	Philippines 5.9	Sri Lanka 4.3
	Philippines 2.8	Malaysia 4.7	Viet Nam 3.6	Philippines 4.6	India 5.9	Taiwan 3.6
	Germany 2.6	India 4.2	Philippines 3.3	Poland 3.2	Viet Nam 4.3	Poland 3.6
	Netherlands 2.0	Taiwan 2.9	South Africa 3.2	Hong Kong 3.1	Portugal 3.6	Taiwan 3.1
	Malaysia 2.0	Sri Lanka 2.7	Sri Lanka 2.0	Haiti 2.9	UK 3.2	Viet Nam 3.1
	Cambodia 1.8	China 2.7	Indonesia 1.8	Portugal 1.8	USA 2.6	USA 2.8
	Other 30.5	Other 32.4	Other 42.9	Other 40.8	Other 43.6	Other 50.3

Source: Adapted from Inglis, Birch, and Sherrington 1994, pp. 10–11; Statistics Canada 1996; Department of Immigration and Multicultural Affairs, Australia 1997
a. For the period between 1991 and the first four months of 1996.

Table 4.4 Stocks of migrant workers in East Asian and GCC host economies by country of origin, 1997

	Hosts										
	New core					Core extensions and potential core			East Asia total (000s)	Gulf CC[a] total (000s)	Country total (000s)
Origins	Japan (000s)	Hong Kong (000s)	Singapore (000s)	Korea (000s)	Taiwan (000s)	Brunei (000s)	Malaysia (000s)	Thailand (000s)			
Asia total	500	311	200	78	265	62	1,100	890	3,406	720	4,126
South Asia	5	20	30	10		6	100	50	216		216
Indonesia		20	0	2	6	2	650	0	685	200	885
Philippines	280	115	60	15	100	9	300	0	879	500	1,379
Myanmar	15							600	615		615
Malaysia	50	14	60	0	2	24	0	0	150		150
Singapore				1		1			1		1
Thailand	70	24	50	40	150	20	50		365		365
China	10	100			5			100	255		255
Korea	70								70	20	90
Japan	18	18							18		18
Other Asia				10	2	1		140	153		153

Source: Adapted from Stahl 1998. Classification of "core" and "core extensions and potential core" are based on Skeldon 1997

a. Gulf CC (Gulf Cooperation Council) members states are Bahrain, Kuwait, Oman, Qatar, Saudi Arabia, and the United Arab Emirates.

inhabitants of the Los Angeles metropolis. Amnesties have meant that many of these migrants eventually become legal citizens. The number of illegal migrants moving into Japan has increased greatly in the last 10 years, and the movement from Indonesia to Malaysia is said to be in excess of 1 million people (Hugo 1999: 22).

International migration from "labour surplus areas" to the "resource frontiers"

While this type of migration is of less relevance to the study of international migration and urbanization in the Asia Pacific region, it cannot be ignored, for some of the Asia Pacific countries, including the Philippines (flows to the Middle East), are major sources of out-migration and "remittances". Studies of international migration show that this form of international migration often leads to subsequent movement of migrants to the core countries in a form of step migration.

Major challenges of international migration to the cities of the Asia Pacific region

It is obvious from the preceding section that the volume of international migration is increasing, and is being directed to the city nodes and corridors of the Asia Pacific. The factors that produce this acceleration of migration are often analysed as pushes from sending areas and pulls from the receiving area in terms of relative inequities of job opportunities and levels of living. While these factors are important, it is necessary to stress that international migration is also facilitated by accelerated information flows between sending and receiving countries, the existence of migrant networks in which family reunion is pre-eminent, and a developing immigration industry in which recruiting agencies, travel agents, and lawyers play a major role. Together these factors have significant explanatory power within the "development tier" system outlined above. These forces, essentially motivational or functional dimensions of migration, fit within the development tier system and help to provide insights into why immigrants have chosen "cities" as translocal destinations.

Notwithstanding the reasons for immigration, the basic fact that international migration is increasing in the region provides challenges to cities. These challenges deal with directing the incoming migration traffic, facilitating and enhancing the integration of migrants into city region economies, providing adequate housing for migrants, and maintaining social harmony and order within cities.

Challenge one: Government's role in directing flows and conditions of immigration

International migration occurs within a governmental framework that attempts to regulate the flows and conditions of international migration; at the international level there are a number of international conventions that govern the movement and acceptance of refugees, and international labour conditions are monitored by the International Labour Office. It is, however, at the level of the nation-state that the major legal systems of regulation on international migration operate. The national state is concerned with legal matters relating to immigrant application, the issuing of immigrant/employment visas, and the policies that concern costs and benefits of inflows of people from abroad. Government regulations can also attempt to extract income from migrants, as is the case for Filipino migrants' remittances to the Philippines and entrepreneur migrants to the USA, Canada, and Australia. A major concern for national governments has been the commitment of immigrants to permanent residence in their new countries. This concern particularly focuses upon citizenship, which most states are unwilling to give unless immigrants make a major commitment to ongoing residence and employment (Ip, Inglis, and Wu 1997). The increasing "translocalization" of international migration has caused some states to permit dual passport holding (Canada and Australia), while others insist upon a single country of citizenship (Malaysia and Singapore).

The major challenge that immigration poses to city governments of the region is that, with few exceptions (for example Singapore), they have virtually no capacity to control immigration flows into their cities. While some forms of national government-sponsored migration attempt to settle migrants outside the major cities, this type of activity is not very successful. Thus, "city regions" are the main locations where immigrants reside. An extreme example of this is the case of Los Angeles County (which is roughly equivalent to the Los Angeles urban region). In 1990, LA County had 3.2 million of its 9.4 million residents born abroad, of whom about one-third were not proficient in English (Clark 1998: 61). The two streams of these migrants exhibited what has been called "segmented assimilation", which means that well-educated immigrants migrate to the suburbs where they blend with native residents, while lower-income immigrants are concentrated in *barrios* where language and cultural traits are reinforced. This lack of assimilation creates difficulties for group members when it comes to accessing education and jobs, and has ultimately led to a "segmentally rejected" population which places a considerable burden on city services. While the federal government has many programmes to assist with these situations, there is still a heavy burden placed on city administrations (Waldinger and Bozorgemehr 1996). This type of segmentation appears to be particularly prominent in some North American cities.

In Australia, where settler immigrants tend to gravitate to the few large cities such as Sydney, Melbourne, Brisbane, and Perth, successive governments have tried policies of enticing new immigrants to the secondary centres, but without much success. One metropolitan area, Sydney, continues to attract close to half of all settlers arriving in Australia.

Challenge two: Integrating international migrants into city region economies

While there is an ongoing debate concerning the economic contribution that international migrants make to national economies, the contribution that immigrants make to city region economies has not been carefully evaluated. Generally research evidence indicates that over a long period of time immigrants have a major positive impact on city economies. First, the majority of migrants move into sectors where job opportunities are most available and least sought after by the host society populations. Thus, migrants work in service and industrial occupations where long hours, low pay, and sometime dangerous activities are commonplace. While not advocating this type of treatment, there is no arguing that the work migrants undertake in these sectors is an important contribution to urban economies. Second, networks which span countries become important sources of additional employment through new businesses such as travel agencies, restaurants, specialized food shops, and video stores selling national films and TV programmes from the immigrants' countries of origin (Tseng 1997). Third, the "professional migrants" often bring investment capital that is used in "high-technology" industry as well as for the purchase of high-priced real estate. Finally, the "contract workers" provide labour in occupations that are short of workers, such as the construction industry in Japan, Malaysia, and Singapore or domestic labour in Hong Kong and Canada.

All these migrant categories undoubtedly contribute to the economic growth of host societies, but it is the last category of contract workers that is potentially most troublesome for host societies. The economic advantage of this type of migrant to employers is considerable: first because the period of the contract is generally short and thus lifetime benefits are not expected to be paid by the employer; and second because the temporary nature of the employment means that the legal and political status of the labour migrant is not recognized by the host society and their conditions of work can be very exploitative. This situation poses great difficulties for host societies, which have to try to protect foreign workers against abuses that often become major political issues as unions and civil rights groups within the host societies campaign against them. For example, the supportive activities of the ILO and the formation of lobby groups with respect to contract domestic servants in Canada have greatly improved their conditions of work. In some cases, "contract worker" conditions or activities can become an important source of tension between the migrants' countries and the host country (Gibson and Graham 1996; Goss and Lindquist 1995).

Challenge three: Building liveable residential proximity in the city regions of the Asia Pacific

This "segmented labour market" described in the previous challenge is also reflected in the pattern of residence of migrants. In the past the ecological patterns of residence of immigrant groups were dominated by inner-city residence, but this is now being replaced by the movement of immigrants into the middle and outer rings of cities. Thus, for instance, in Sydney and Vancouver there are sizeable communities of Hong Kong/ Taiwan migrants living in Chatswood (Sydney) and Richmond (Vancouver) in areas which have little resemblance to the "Chinatowns" that grew up in the nineteenth century. It is important to stress that this growth of "immigrant identity" reflected in such "ecological niches" is often encouraged by cities in countries such as Canada and Australia, to create a more cosmopolitan and "global" image of their city. Thus, for instance, "Chinatowns" have been developed as tourist attraction in many cities. The best known is San Francisco's Chinatown. It is interesting to reflect on the concept of immigrant districts, which are based on the idea of liveable immigrant districts in juxtaposition with non-immigrant districts, being viewed as a positive benefit by many city administrations rather than the negative consequence of racism and residential exclusion (see Burnley, Murphy, and Fagan 1997 and Ley 1997 for a discussion of this aspect in Sydney and Vancouver). To summarize, city governments face a challenging tussle in handling the creative tension in the need to create "cosmopolitan" and yet homogeneous national cities.

Challenge four: Building social harmony and order in the cities of the Asia Pacific region

Almost certainly the most difficult challenge for creating liveable cities in the Asia Pacific region is developing social policies that are designed to avoid conflict between migrant and host societies. At the national level, several policies have existed among the core countries. Historically they have tended to be exclusionist on the basis of cultural homogeneity. Thus,

Australia, Canada, the USA, and Japan adopted exclusionist policies for immigrants who lacked the host societies' dominant language skills. As the core societies' demand for specialized labour increased, however, these countries moved towards more inclusionist policies that involve recognizing the needs of the host society (family, reunion, special labour needs, etc.). Even Japan, which was previously exclusionist, has moved towards a more inclusionist policy. This, in part, is provoked by a rapidly ageing population and shortages of unskilled labour, despite a growing unemployment rate reflecting the slowdown in Japanese growth.

The principal effect of the shift in national immigration policies, particularly when it has been associated with a growing inability by the state to control and regulate migration, has been to increase the diversity of immigrants economically, socially, and ethnically. But the process has increased the social volatility of international migration. Even the most cursory review of the recent social conditions of the major city regions produces large numbers of examples of "tension" and "social problems" that are created by international immigration.

These examples range widely. Immigrants are often assumed to play a major role in drug activities, using their networks to facilitate the trade. Immigrants' cultural preferences present different cultural practices that do not necessarily fit into the dominant society. The immigrant professionals exhibit lifestyles that make the middle-class host society groups jealous. Immigrants are accused of putting too much pressure on social costs by demanding extra language training. This list is very long indeed.

The reaction of the national governments is of course quite diverse. In some of the core countries, such as Canada and Australia, an emphasis has been placed on multiculturalism, with a strong recognition that the societies are made up of a mixture of different cultures. In Australia, the state of New South Wales increasingly uses the notion of "multicultural advantage" as a selling point. In others, of which Japan is representative, immigrants can only be accepted after learning to speak the language and experiencing many years of residence. The growth of immigration has produced considerable "backlash" which has racial elements and is causing some governments (Australia, Canada, New Zealand, the USA) to develop policies which emphasize "national values". This has been labelled by some researchers as "a new Americanization".

Conclusion and policy issues: International migration, liveability, and sustainability in the Asia Pacific city regions

Current debates on the future of urbanization in the Asia Pacific region focus quite correctly on the problems of sustainability in city regions. They concentrate on the demands that future population growth will place upon creating a functioning urban infrastructure, an acceptable level of living, and an environment that does not deteriorate to the point when these two other needs cannot be met. These problems are most stark in the heavily populated regions of the Asia Pacific. However, there is virtually no discussion of the issue of social sustainability, a concept that is central to the structure and types of urban societies that will emerge in the Asia Pacific region. In fact the creation of urban societies in which there is a clear commitment on the part of city inhabitants to a type of society that accepts increasing international migration is perhaps the most difficult task for city and government administrations. It will involve creative policy building educational institutions that reach this attitude as a central part of "citizenship".

If the authors' assertion that international migration will continue to accelerate and play a major role in the growth of Asia Pacific urban regions is correct, then it is imperative to develop policies that recognize "social sustainability" as an important goal of creating liveable city regions. This means that policy discussions will have to involve at least three dimensions. The first is developing effective policies regarding international regulation of migration. For example the growth in the international surveillance of illegal migration is an example of such a policy. Second, national governments will need to develop policies for international migration in conjunction with the local governments (municipalities etc.) that have the problem of implementing policies which respond to population movements over which they have little control. Finally, there will have to be a realization that the social structure of the cities of the future is likely to be more ethnically and culturally diverse, more open to international influences, and more stratified than in the cities of the present. There are some who see this mixture as extremely volatile and threatening to social stability. It therefore becomes imperative that policies are developed which recognize the social mixture of cities as strengths that reinforce societies at large.

Notes

1. The number of international students in Canada is 62,235 (1996/1997), and there are 457,984 in the USA (1996/1997), and 62,974 in Australia (1997). Close to 55 per cent of the international students in Australia originate from South-East Asia. For the USA, 36 per cent came from East Asia and only 10 per cent from South-East Asia (IIE 1998).

REFERENCES

Appardurai, A. 1990. "Disjuncture and differences in the global cultural economy", *Public Culture*, Vol. 11, No. 2, pp. 1–24.

Burnley, I., P. Murphy, and R. Fagen. 1997. *Immigration and Australian Cities*. Sydney: Federation Press.

Castells, Manuel. 1996. *The Rise of Network Society, Vol. 1. The Information Age: Economy, Society and Culture*. Oxford: Blackwell.

Clark, William A. V. 1998. *The California Cauldron*. New York: Gilford Press.

Department of Immigration and Multicultural Affairs, Australia. 1997. *Australian Immigration: Consolidated Statistics 1995–96*, No. 19. Canberra: DIMA.

Dick, Howard and P. J. Rimmer. 1998. "The trans-Pacific economy. A network approach to spatial structure", *Asian Geographer*, Vol. XII, Nos 1–2, pp. 5–18.

Fuchs, Roland J., Ellen Brennan, Joseph Chaimie, Fu-chen Lo, and Juha Uitto (eds). 1994. *Mega-City Growth and the Future*. Tokyo: United Nations University Press.

Gibson, K. and J. Graham. 1996. "Situating migrants in theory: The case of Filipino migrant construction workers", *Capital and Class*, No. 3, pp. 131–149.

Goss, Jon and Bruce Lindquist. 1995. "Conceptualizing international labor migration: A structuration perspective", *International Migration Review*, Vol. 25, No. 2, pp. 317–351.

Hugo, Graeme. 1997. "Migration and mobilization in Asia: An overview", in E. Laquian, A. Laquian and T. G. McGee (eds) *The Silent Debate: Asian Immigration and Racism in Canada*. Vancouver: Institute of Asian Research, University of British Columbia, pp. 157–192.

Hugo, Graeme. 1999. "Undocumented migration in South-East Asia", in Tseng, Yeu-Feu, Allan Borowski, Meyer Burstein, and Lois Foster (eds) *Asian Migration: Pacific Rim Dynamics*. Taipei: Interdisciplinary Group for Australian Studies, National Taiwan University, pp. 15–48.

Inglis, Christine, Anthony Birch, and Geoffrey Sherrington. 1994. "An overview of Australian and Canadian migration pattern and policies", in Howard Adelman *et al.* (eds) *Immigration and Refugee Policy: Australia and Canada Compared*, Vol. 1. Melbourne: Melbourne University Press.

International Institute of Education. 1998. *Open Doors 1996/96*. New York: IIE.

Ip, David, Christine Inglis, and Chung-Tong Wu. 1997. "Concepts of citizenship and identity among recent Asian immigrants in Australia", *Asian and Pacific Migration Journal*, Vol. 6, Nos 3–4, pp. 363–384.

Kritz, M. and H. Zlotnik. 1992. "Global interactions, migration systems, processes and politics", in M. Kritz and H. Zlotnik (eds) *International Migration Systems: A Global Approach*. Oxford: Clarendon Press.

Ley, David. 1997. "The rhetoric of racism and the politics of explanation in the Vancouver housing market", in E. Laquian, A. Laquian, and T. G. McGee (eds) *The Silent Debate: Asian Immigration and Racism in Canada*. Vancouver: Institute of Asian Research, University of British Columbia, pp. 316–331.

Lo, Fu-chen and Yue-man Yeung (eds). 1996. *Emerging World Cities in Pacific Asia*. Tokyo: United Nations University Press.

Lo, Fu-chen and Yue-man Yeung. 1998. "Globalization and urbanization", UNU/IAS Working Paper No. 39.

McGee, Terry G. 1997a. "Globalization and international migration in the Asia Pacific region", in E. Laquian, A. Laquian, and T. G. McGee (eds). *The Silent Debate: Asian Immigration and Racism in Canada*. Vancouver: Institute of Asian Research, University of British Columbia, pp. 359–368.

McGee, Terry G. 1997b. "Building research networks in the Asia Pacific region: It's a basis for cooperation", *Asian Perspectives*, Vol. 21, No. 2, pp. 9–36.

McGee, Terry G. 1998. "Urbanization in an era of volatile globalization: Policy problematiques for the twenty-first century", paper presented at the UNCRD Global Forum, Nagoya.

Pe-Pua, Rogelia, Colleen Mitchell, Stephen Castle, and Robyn Iredale. 1998. "Astronaut families and parachute children: Hong Kong immigrants in Australia", in Elizabeth Sinn (ed.) *The Last Half Century of Chinese Overseas*. Hong Kong: Hong Kong University Press, pp. 279–297.

Rimmer, P. J. 1992. "Megacities, multi-layered economies and development corridors in the Pacific economic zone: The Japanese ascendancy", in *Conference Paper on Transportation and Urban Development*. Vancouver: Centre for Human Settlement, University of British Columbia, pp. 7–56.

Rimmer, P. J. 1994. "Transport and communications in the Pacific economic zone during the early 21st century", in Yue-man Yeung (ed.) *Pacific Asia in the 21st Century, Geographical and Developmental Perspectives*. Hong Kong: Chinese University Press, pp. 195–232.

Rohlen, Thomas P. 1995. *A Mediterranean Model for Asian Regionalism: Cosmopolitan Cities and Nation-States in Asia*. Stanford, CA: Asia Pacific Research Centre, Stanford University.

Sassen, S. 1991. *The Global City, New York, London, Tokyo*. Princeton, NJ: Princeton University Press.

Skeldon, Ronald. 1997a. *Migration and Development. A Global Perspective*. Harlow: Addison Wesley Longman.

Skeldon, Ronald. 1997b. "From multiculturalism to diaspora. Changing identities in the context of Asian migration", in E. Laquian, A. Laquian, and T. G. McGee (eds) *The Silent Debate: Asian Immigration and Racism in Canada*. Vancouver: Institute of Asian Research, University of British Columbia, pp. 193–212.

Stahl, C. 1998. "Some observations on trade and the export of labour services", Working Paper No. 2, Asia Pacific Centre for Human Resources and Development Studies, University of Newcastle.

Statistics Canada. 1996. *1996 Census*. Ottawa.

Tseng, Yen-Fen. 1997. "Ethnic resources as forms of social capital: A study on Chinese immigrant entrepreneurship in Los Angeles", *Taiwanese Sociological Review*, No. 1, pp. 169–205.

United Nations, Population Division. 1999. *World Population Prospects: The 1998 Revision*. New York: United Nations.

Waldinger, Roger and Mehdi Bozorgemehr (eds). 1996. *Ethnic Los Angeles*. New York: Russell Sage Foundation.

World Bank. 1991. *World Development Report 1991*. New York: Oxford University Press.

Case studies: The post-industrial capital exporters

5

The impacts of globalization and issues of metropolitan planning in Tokyo

Tetsuo Kidokoro, Takashi Onishi, and Peter J. Marcotullio

Introduction

Globalization trends have changed the conditions for urban planning in cities around the globe. Enhancing transnational cross-border activities has become a key factor in urban and regional development strategies as metropolitan planners attempt to increase the international competitiveness of their urban centres (Cox 1995). These strategies include more than mediating economic trends, however, as globalization-related flows have also influenced various aspects of social life through, among other ways, the spatial restructuring of the city. Further, as Machimura mentions (1998: 184), "No 'global city' story can be understood without reference to the local processes which give it its substantial form." Considering the growing importance of keeping cities competitive and the extent of globalization's impacts on the spatial and social formation of cities, an evaluation of responses in terms of metropolitan planning has become an urgent issue. An urban centre's ability to deal constructively with these trends will determine, to a large extent, the future quality of life for its citizens.

This chapter attempts to describe the impacts of economic globalization on the Tokyo metropolitan area (TMA),[1] the history of planning efforts to control these effects, and the current major planning issues within the urban field, or greater Tokyo area. With this insight, the chapter presents a framework of metropolitan planning in Tokyo, in terms of both strengthening competitiveness and enhancing sustainability, in response to the current trends of globalization.

The impacts of globalization on the spatial formation of Tokyo

The most important contemporary spatial trend within Tokyo has been the concentration of employment in the central city area. In 1995, within the national capital region (NCR), composed of the TMA and the seven surrounding prefectures, 11 per cent of all jobs were found in the central three wards. Approximately 36 per cent of all jobs are located within the 23 wards area.

The concentration of jobs is related to the high levels of commercial services demanded within the urban economy, and to rising land values in the inner-city wards. As Tokyo's economy switched from manufacturing to commercial services, inner-city areas were the sites for the construction of buildings to house these activities. Demand sky-rocketed during the late 1980s, and as a result, by 1990 the office floor area in four wards (the three wards in Tokyo's CBD and a new central business district) exceeded the office floor area available in Manhattan, New York (Itoh 1990). On the other hand, commercial high-rise buildings, particularly those for international-oriented firms, pull in the highest rents, forcing residents to seek housing further from the city core. For example, the rent for a single-family home within the 23 wards area, for an average middle-class manager in his 50s, would cost him 10 times his annual income (Itoh 1990). Japanese inner-city land prices increased rapidly, reflecting the rapid and large-scale concentration of capital and population as well as land speculation. Further, the government was not able to provide effective measures to control them (in other words, taxes on increases in land prices and development profits) (Alden, Hirohara, and Abe 1994).

The increasingly high concentration of business activity has had two related impacts on the inner city. First, over the last three decades the nighttime population density of the central three wards has fallen to approximately 6,000 persons per square kilometre, making the density less than half of the ward average (13,047 persons per square kilometre). Second, the high intensity of business activity during the daytime in the inner areas of the city has given rise to a daytime/nighttime population ratio of over 10:1, creating traffic and congestion problems (Togo 1995), housing problems (Itoh 1990; Togo 1995), and straining infrastructure (see, for example, Onishi 1993). This ratio is significantly higher than similar ratios for central areas of large cities like New York, Paris, and London (which range from 1.5:1 to 2.5:1).

The high concentration of jobs in Tokyo has accompanied a transformation in urban employment structure, and more recently masks some important employment location outcomes. First, there has been a significant shift from industrial employment to employment in the service sectors. This has largely been due to the growing importance of transnational and regional headquarters' activities in the Tokyo economy. As shown in Table 5.1, in 1996 35 per cent of all company headquarters listed on the Tokyo Stock Exchange were in the central three wards and 58 per cent were in the 23 wards area. Although these shares have slightly decreased over the last 10 years, the numbers of headquarters of these major companies located in both the central three wards and the 23 wards are increasing. Within the Tokyo metropolitan region (TMR), composed of the TMA and the three neighbouring prefectures, the rate of concentration of headquarters also continues to increase.

Second, while the rate of national job concentration within the TMR continues to increase (Table 5.2), the job share of the three central wards has actually decreased since 1965. This is largely because the shares of the three prefectures adjoining the TMA have increased over the last 30 years. While the total number of jobs in the NCR has nearly doubled from 1965 to 1995, numbers in the central areas did not. Notwithstanding the absolute growth in the surrounding prefectures, a significant number of jobs remain concentrated in the central area.

While the concentration of commercial employment in the central areas of Tokyo is a direct result of globalization processes, the movement of jobs out to the three surrounding prefectures has been due, in part, to government policies. In terms of the globalization of Tokyo city, two influences have been important: the location of foreign direct investment (FDI); and the globalization of Japanese manufacturing production.

During the late 1980s, under what is now considered the "bubble economy" era, the number of foreign-affiliated companies increased rapidly. This trend stabilized in the first half of the 1990s. Under the current regime of deregulation in the financial and retail sectors, among others, FDI into Japan has increased again. Most of this increase is accounted for in developments within Tokyo. Directly after the economic bubble burst, FDI inflows into Japan decreased. The peak "bubble" year for FDI was in 1992, when foreign investments in the country reached US$2.8 billion (UNCTAD 1998). Recently, however, FDI inflows have not only increased, but have exceeded previous high levels. In 1997, foreign investments in the country reached a record high of US$6.8 billion (Table 5.3).

Within Japan, foreign-affiliated companies have spatially concentrated

Table 5.1 Concentration of head offices of major companies in Japan

	TMA	Tokyo 23 wards	Tokyo three central wards	Tama area	Neighbouring three prefectures within 60 km range	Four prefectures within 100 km range	NCR total	Whole nation
1986	890	867	588	23	109	19	1,018	1,499
(%)	(59.4)	(57.8)	(39.2)	(1.5)	(7.3)	(1.3)	(67.9)	(100)
1996	1,031	998	614	33	162	29	1,222	1,772
(%)	(58.2)	(56.3)	(34.7)	(1.9)	(9.1)	(1.6)	(69.0)	(100)

Table 5.2 Number of jobs by workplace in the national capital region

	Area		1960		1995	
	(km²)	(%)	(000)	(%)	(000)	(%)
Tokyo three central wards	42	0.1	1,290	11.5	2,242	10.6
Tokyo 23 wards	618	1.7	4,551	40.6	7,249	35.8
TMA	2,183	5.9	5,006	44.6	8,769	41.4
Neighbouring three prefectures within 60 km range	11,365	30.8	3,385	30.2	8,435	39.8
Four prefectures within 100 km range	14,399	39.0	2,821	25.2	3,975	18.8
NCR total	36,879	100	11,213	100	21,179	100

Source: National Land Agency 1997, p. 5, Table 1.1.2

within the city of Tokyo (Figure 5.1), and the lion's share of these investments went into the non-manufacturing sector. This sector accounted for over 60 per cent of all FDI. Of these investments, nearly 80 per cent were concentrated in the TMA and over 50 per cent of these operations found locations within the central three wards. Despite this concentration, an interesting new trend is that the number of foreign-affiliated companies located in the three neighbouring prefectures is also steadily increasing, although the absolute stock accumulated is still small when compared with the amount invested in the central areas of Tokyo.

Thus, part of the impact of globalization is the spatial concentration of foreign-affiliated companies in the central areas of Tokyo. This reflects the importance of Tokyo's service functions within the global city system. Globalization processes continue to strengthen the international service function role of the city and the spatial outcome of this is a continuing concentration of commercial development in the central areas of the region.

The concentration of headquarters of major companies within Tokyo sets the foundation for its role in the global economy. Most of the headquarters deploy production and sales networks worldwide. Tokyo functions as the international service centre of Japanese TNCs. The many research institutions located in the areas adjoining the central area, particularly in the western corridor of the TMR, give the city the additional characteristics of a world service and R&D centre complex. Importantly, Tokyo is different from cities like New York, London, Singapore, and Hong Kong in the sense that Tokyo primarily services Japanese TNCs, while the other cities function as international service centres for foreign companies as well. This concentration of Japanese service and R&D functions within the city limits its international character, and is illustrated by a comparison of the number of international conferences held

Table 5.3 FDI inflows to Japan

	1995		1996			First half of 1997		
	No.	Amount US$ million	No.	Amount US$ million	(%)	No.	Amount US$ million	(%)
Total	1,272	3,837	1,304	6,841	100	648	2,108	100
Subtotal manufacturing industry	190	1,467	211	2,762	40.4	91	746	35.4
machinery	56	191	73	1,383	20.2	30	519	24.6
chemicals	69	1,132	59	617	9.0	19	154	7.3
metal	3	1	10	468	6.8	2	0	0.0
rubber/leather	2	22	7	95	1.4	0	0	0.0
petroleum	21	20	34	73	1.1	14	29	1.4
textiles	5	24	3	8	0.1	8	8	0.4
foods	7	43	3	3	0.0	7	19	0.9
glass/ceramic	1	0	1	0	0.0	1	2	0.1
other	26	31	21	115	1.7	10	16	0.8
Subtotal non-manufacturing industry	1,082	2,373	1,093	4,079	59.6	557	1,363	64.6
service	315	503	341	2,095	30.6	186	401	19.0
trade	591	706	610	1,477	21.6	298	391	18.5
finance/insurance	63	1,044	50	243	3.5	35	171	8.1
real estate	19	16	44	234	3.4	13	380	18.0
telecommunications	66	56	29	19	0.3	13	16	0.8
transport	14	13	10	9	0.1	10	3	0.1
construction	3	1	4	0	0.0	7	0	0.0
other	11	34	5	1	0.0	4	1	0.0

Source: JETRO 1998, p. 67, Table III.6

120

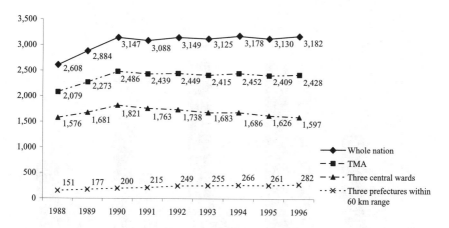

Figure 5.1 Location of foreign-affiliated companies in Japan
Source: National Land Agency 1997, p. 9, Figure 1.3.1

by country and city. For the last 10 years, among nations the USA has
hosted the most international conferences, followed by France and the
UK. Japan ranked number 11 for hosting international conventions in
1995. Among cities, in 1995 Paris was the leading convention city, followed by London and Singapore. Tokyo ranked 28th. It may be said that
Tokyo is not becoming more of an international centre in the sense of
openness to a diversity of peoples or deep cultural exchanges (Douglass
1993), and given present conditions, it will not be one in the near future.
This obvious contradiction to the 'global city' image of Tokyo represents a peculiar combination of both resistance and positive adjustment
to globalization forces. It is one of many contradictions evident in the city
that frame politics at the local level (Machimura 1998).

Recent changes in the industrial structure of the city reflect the concentration of both foreign and domestic economic activities. Since the
1980s, the number of jobs in manufacturing industries within the TMA
has decreased, while those in the service industries have increased.
Within service-sector employment, the largest share of growth has been
generated in computer-related service industries. This reflects the national
concentration of information-related industries within the region. Approximately 70 per cent of the 880,000 new jobs created between 1981
and 1991 were in service industries, defined narrowly as services not including commercial, financial, real estate, etc. Within this definition of
services, the major field has been computer-related services, which accounted for 30 per cent of the new service jobs during this period. Information technology has been a driving force prompting the increased
concentration of business activities to Tokyo.

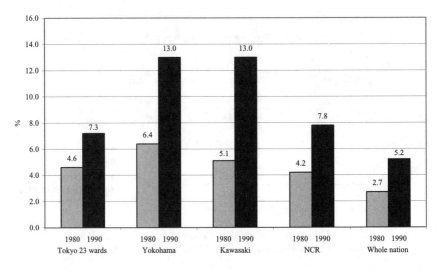

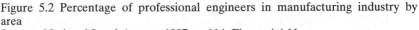

Figure 5.2 Percentage of professional engineers in manufacturing industry by area
Source: National Land Agency 1997, p. 114, Figure 4.4.11

These industries have been concentrated in the western corridor of the TMR, which includes the western parts of the 23 wards and Tama area and the east side of neighbouring Kanagawa prefecture. The coastal area west of Tokyo Bay, called the *Keihin* industrial belt, is the major petrochemical and steel industrial complex in Japan. The inland area of the *Keihin* industrial belt has grown as a production centre for automobile, electronics, and machinery industries. Against the background of the existing accumulation of various types and sizes of companies in the manufacturing industry, the western corridor of the TMR has now emerged as a major global R&D centre with the establishment of a large number of research institutions, particularly in manufacturing industries.

Evidence of this concentration is revealed in the numbers of professional engineers employed in manufacturing industries in the area. The engineering share as a proportion of the total workforce has increased from 5 to 13 per cent in Yokohama city and Kawasaki city, which are core cities in the western corridor of the TMR (Figure 5.2).

The continued concentration of commercial FDI and Japanese services within inner Tokyo and the emergence of the *Keihin* industrial belt have caused concern among planners. In reaction, several sets of policies were enacted to counter these trends. Recently, government planning officials have attempted to encourage investment in areas outside the centre of the city. This, it was hoped, would turn the outer areas into major business centres, as seen in the peripheries of cities in North America. Yet

decentralization is a global issue
Regionality

Equalizing factors of — *for*
— *the*

while some changes have occurred, in general the decentralization policies of the government have had mixed results. An understanding of the
role of government planning strategies in the spatial formation of Tokyo
requires an examination of the historical relationship between changes in
the Japanese economy, national development policies, and the changing
position of Tokyo within Japan and the world city system.

housing
infras
employ

Globalization and decentralization policy in Japan

Spatial decentralization to counter problems caused by overconcentration
in Tokyo has been one of the major focuses of national urban development policies in Japan. Since the 1960s, five national development plans
(NDPs) and four national capital region development plans (NCRDPs)
have been formulated by the national government.[2] Those plans attempted to decentralize economic activities from Tokyo as well as to alleviate problems caused by the overconcentration of these activities. The
effects of the policies have been mixed, and have depended on the economic context of national development, the type of industry regulated,
and the infrastructure required by the industry. A review of the history
of decentralization policies provides a fuller understanding of the limits
of Japanese regional and urban policy. This history can be divided into
three stages, covering industrial manufacturing growth pole strategies,
high-tech growth pole strategies, and bubble era strategies.

Manufacturing growth pole strategies

driving force

The basis for Japan's present-day economy was secured in the late 1940s
and early 1950s. With heavy manufacturing as the driving force of the
economy and a willing and able-bodied workforce, it took Japan only
a decade to recover from the Second World War. These preconditions
were helped by external factors. The Japanese economy began to grow
again in the 1950s, stimulated by the Korean War. The demand for strategic goods lifted the Japanese economy into a boom. The "special pro-
curements" (the special demand for goods and services generated by the
war) and rapid expansion of exports were particularly beneficial to the
country. By 1955, production output surpassed wartime peak levels, but
Japan's economy was still was 16 times smaller than that of the USA. At
the same time, it stood poised at the beginning of the "era of high-speed
growth".

Beginning in the early 1960s, Japan's national priorities centred on
doubling the national income. This was achieved by emphasizing the acquisition of low-cost energy resources and other raw materials and the

GNP

expansion of the manufacturing production system through a regional development scheme. These national priorities, with a variety of other practices, were supported by a stable political regime and a complex web of cooperation between national bureaucracies, large businesses, and the labour force, which together became known as Japan's "industrial policy".

As part of the industrial development strategy for the country, Japan promoted the development of new industrial cities (NICs) and special industrial districts (SIDs). These were included in the first NDP in the early 1960s, and involved the decentralization of smokestack industries from large cities. The first and second NCRDPs (1958 and 1965, respectively) were also aimed at decentralizing factories. This effort was promoted through the designation of new urban development areas on the fringes of the NCR. In these areas new factories were encouraged to locate, and at the same time restrictions on the establishment and expansion of factories within the built-up areas, such as Tokyo's 23 wards, were promulgated. These policies aimed at decentralizing the main industries of the period, including energy, steel, automobiles, ships, petrochemicals and chemicals, and transportation infrastructure. Before the decentralization programme many of these industries were located in the major urban centres, including Tokyo, but they found it increasingly difficult to do business in an urban setting because of rising land prices and a labour force in the cities inadequate for their needs. They quickly took advantage of the government incentives and infrastructure provided by relocating to the 20 coastal areas that the government promoted.

Central government policies were augmented by activities at the local level. Many communities combined forces with local politicians with a "pipeline to the centre" to create amenable conditions for economic growth. The pipeline allowed for the flow of a variety of forms of government assistance, including large infrastructure projects. Communities were allowed a tax holiday in the hopes of luring new plants and factories.

By 1970, Japan's economy was second in size only to the USA. The country had seen the change from an agricultural society to an urbanized society in around 20 years. In the late 1950s about 40 per cent of Japan's workforce were employed in agricultural activities, but by 1970 only 15 per cent were working on farms or in related activities. Most areas designated as NIC/SIDs grew successfully with the economy. Indeed, their growth far exceeded national averages. Thereafter, however, the economic growth rates of those areas dropped to levels much lower than the national average, and some continued to decline or stagnate. Much of the reason for the change in fortunes for these industrial growth poles, as well as the entire economy, can be found in the changing development trajectory of Japan and influences from external sources.

High-tech and R&D growth pole strategies

As industrial development proceeded, localities became aware of the negative externalities of industrial development. Especially serious was the problem of environmental disruption from the heavy chemical industries. Towards the late 1960s, these problems became a major national issue and public opinion began to regard industrial growth as negative. Among the most important environmental concerns were air pollution, water pollution, waste disposal, noise and vibrations, and ground subsidence. Activists included pollution victims who were forced into action by physical suffering and financial loss. Grass-roots outcry peaked with the "big four" court cases in the early 1970s.

A partial response to this and other societal problems was the election of progressive local governmental leaders, such as Minobe Ryokichi of Tokyo. Indeed, the 1970s marked the heyday of centrist and progressive party movements in Japan. Minobe concentrated his efforts on improving the quality of life in the city. Because Tokyo had prospered and continually attracted industry throughout the era of high growth, by the early 1970s it was choking on its success. The governor directed special attention to the environment and social services.

While the Japanese public became more aware of the despoliation of the environment, global economic forces and new technologies were at work in shaping the future of the country and of Tokyo. Specifically, a crucial turning point for Japanese economic and urban development came in 1973 with the worldwide energy crisis. As a result of the tripling in the price of oil, the rate of national economic growth dropped from 5.1 per cent in 1973 to −0.5 per cent in 1974. The oil shocks of 1973–1974 and 1978–1979 led to a decline in the Japanese manufacturing sector. Heavy industries, such as steel and shipbuilding, were hit hard. Steel production dropped from a peak of 119 million tonnes in 1973 to about 106 million tonnes in 1988, and this level was dependent on the government's public works projects. In the shipbuilding industry, after peak annual production of 17 million tonnes in the 1970s, production fell to 8.2 million tonnes in 1987. Automobile production continued to grow, but at a slower rate than before. Approximately 8 million cars were produced in 1988, compared with slightly over 7 million in 1980 and 4.6 million in 1975. The production of chemicals and petrochemicals also lagged behind the forecasts of the 1970s, due primarily to increased oil prices. Naphtha production declined steadily from the mid-1970s. Ethylene production, which stood at 5.3 million tonnes in 1977 and was forecast to be 15 million tonnes in 1985, was in fact only 4.3 million tonnes in 1986.

The oil and environmental crises enhanced the perception that the income-generating industries of the time could no longer support Japan's future economic growth. The crises accelerated the replacement of these industries by newly emerging high-tech industries such as microelectronics (semi-conductors, computers, and communication equipment) and other related manufacturing industries, such as automobiles and consumer durable goods. Through industrial restructuring, heavy industry was replaced by high-tech-based light and knowledge-intensive industries. While heavy industries moved out of the cities to more suitable locations in coastal industrial zones, high-tech industries moved inland to areas of clean air and water, high-speed transportation, and markets.

The economic restructuring of the country's economy was facilitated by the promulgation of R&D and high-tech production growth centres through government planning efforts. The Ministry of International Trade and Industry's "technopolis policy" (1980) and complementary policies for the regional development of knowledge-based and information-based services in the fourth comprehensive land development plan (1987) were launched in an attempt to complement the ongoing restructuring of the national economy from a heavy to high-tech industry base and balance growth (Edgington 1994). If the growth pole policy for industry manufacturing worked, why couldn't the same be applied to other industries?

Notwithstanding substantial government funding, however, among the designated technopolis growth poles areas only a few grew to become high-tech industrial production centres. Successful areas attracted significant private investment, as was seen in Nagaoka in Toyama prefecture, Hamamatsu, Oita, and Kyushu (*ibid.*). In general, though, the technopolis programme did not produce R&D centres in high-tech industry.

Further, many successful R&D firms and high-tech industries continued to concentrate within the TMR. At one point the Tokyo metropolitan area accumulated the largest manufacturing agglomeration in the nation. However, like its urban counterparts, Tokyo lost 349 factories (1,000 square metres or more in size) between 1975 and 1984, although high-tech industrial development and R&D investments continued to increase within the national capital area.

Bubble era strategies

The anomaly of Tokyo's continued attraction to industry despite handsome government incentives to locate elsewhere can be explained by the concomitant growth of new techno-economic-based industries, and then the rise of the service sector within the city. Early on the service sector had been an important part of Tokyo's economy, but during the late 1970s onward it took on a special significance. The service sector covers those activities associated with public, private, and not-for-profit services, including the activities of banks, securities firms, investment banking offices, real estate development offices, accounting firms, advertising, law firms, research and development organizations, trucking, warehousing, and the retail and wholesale trade among others. While the entire country was struggling through the restructuring of the manufacturing sector, Tokyo was becoming more dependent on services, and the urban economy in Japan was undergoing a sectoral restructuring.

Whereas the traditional secondary sector stagnated after its rapid postwar expansion, during this later period the tertiary sector started to expand. From 1970 to 1994, while the manufacturing sector continued to account for approximately 26 per cent of GDP, the service sector rose from 26 to almost 34 per cent of Japanese GDP. Further, Tokyo was becoming increasingly important to both Japan's and the world's economies through its command and control functions. Tokyo was becoming an "global" city.

Japan's emphasis on saving energy, pollution control, and automation devices provided dividends in improved productivity, and resulted in increased competitiveness abroad. As a result, export surpluses increased and the Japanese trade volume quadrupled from 1970 to 1990. These surpluses contributed to the growth of financial reserves, which further enhanced Japan's commitment to international finance and assistance.

Japan's change from heavy industries to high-tech industries such as robotics, automobiles, optics, electronics, and computers allowed their firms more production flexibility. These industries could "outsource" production to other localities. Hence Japanese high-tech industries could produce their products by having low-skilled, low-paid workers in other parts of Japan and in foreign countries do much of the work. This flexibility allowed for the movement of Japanese investments to developing nations in Asia. Their dominance in the robotics field also helped them to compete successfully in foreign markets. They controlled a major share of the world's robots and put them to work successfully. For example Toyota, using modern robotics, could produce an automobile using far fewer man-hours then their international competitors.

After 1985, Japanese FDI outflows, stimulated by the results of the Plaza Accord, increased dramatically. The Plaza Accord of 1985 between Japan and the USA weakened the dollar to the disadvantage of the yen. At this time the USA was suffering under a double deficit: the government deficit (the government was spending more than it was taking in), and a trade deficit (more American dollars were being spent on imports than other comparable money spent on American exports). President Reagan wanted to weaken the dollar to boost the sale of American products overseas. James Baker, US Secretary of the Treasury, nego-tiated with the Japanese and other nations to increase the value of their currencies. These talks resulted in a rise of the value in the yen (*endaka*) against the dollar from 221.68 per US$ in 1985 to 138.45 per US$ in 1987.

The direct result of this change was that it was cheaper for the Japanese to buy American goods and Japanese goods became more expensive in the USA. The indirect result was a challenge to Japanese industrial sys-tem to achieve even lower production costs. This was met by Japanese firms through the movement of their production sites into other countries within Asia, including locations in Indonesia and Malaysia. While in the past Tokyo had been the centre of the Japanese national economy, after the movement of Japanese FDI out of the country the Japanese economy developed into a transnational system with Tokyo at the centre. Hence a by-product of this new investment was the creation of a functional eco-nomic system within Asia with Tokyo as an important centre of its man-agement functions.

At the same time that Japanese industries were decentralizing from urban centres and globalizing, or relocating firms in areas outside Japan, they were leaving their headquarter functions in Japanese urban centres, especially in Tokyo. A central dynamic to the new global economy is that the more globalized the Japanese economy becomes the higher the ag-glomeration of central functions within Tokyo. Integral to these activities are the control and management functions (CMFs) for Japanese firms, including those activities related to finance, insurance, and wholesale and business services. CMFs are the top decision-making procedures in the planning and management of various sectors, public as well as private, and are also closely linked to research/development and information functions, supported by the work of myriad clerks, bureaucrats, and secretaries.

A growing number of national headquarters functions were locating in Tokyo as early as the 1960s, but Tokyo's position as a centre of the growing Asian urban functional city system and global economic sys-tem facilitated further CMF development (Honjo 1998). This activity was complemented by a complex of organizations dedicated to running the dispersed network of factories, offices, and service outlets as well as the production of financial innovations. The concentration of CMFs in Tokyo was enhanced by the development of the city's stock exchange, which joined New York's and London's as a major worldwide stock trading institution. The large national financial reserve and Tokyo's geographic location, which made it possible to operate a world stock market on a "round-the-clock" basis, increased the city's international importance. Tokyo's stock exchange opens shortly after New York's closes, and it closes shortly before the stock exchange in London starts the day.

The new stage of decentralizing strategies promoted by the government responded to the ever-increasing role of the services in economic development in Japan and the concentration of these functions in Tokyo. These policies were intended to promote business service centres, and included the Multi Core Promotion Act and the Regional Core City Promotion Act. In the third NCRDP (1976) an idea emerged that in order to decentralize Tokyo, the government needed to promote other core cities. In this way, they would attract offices as a counter-magnet to the central areas of Tokyo. The fourth NCRDP (1986) clearly identified this idea as a main objective and focused on the reorganization of Japan's urban system from a monocentric structure to a multicentred one with multiple subregions (Figure 5.3).

The concept of multiple centres as counter-magnets to the concentration of office construction in Tokyo was named the "business core city" (BCC) policy, and cities like Yokohama/Kawasaki, Urawa/Omiya, Hachioji/Tachikawa, and Tsuchiura/Tsukuba science city were designated as BCCs. These centres were situated between 30 and 50 km from the centre of Tokyo. They were cities of considerable size, and were located along railways extending radially from the capital. Prefecture governments in consultation with the concerned cities formulated the BCC development framework plan. The minister of the National Land Agency approved each administered plan and the projects were implemented under the initiative of the prefecture or local governments. The national government supported the projects listed in the development framework plans through additional grants for public works, tax exemptions, and the provision of credit for the development of core facilities. These core facilities were constructed and managed as public-private joint ventures.

Core facilities and the functions of each node vary depending on the characteristics of each BCC. In the case of Chiba city, a convention and exhibition centre, a smart office complex, a monorail line, and an extension of the urban rail system were constructed through this programme. The plan includes the provision of low-interest loans to private companies through the Japanese National Development Bank, under the condition that the private firms move all or part of their headquarters to the BCC. A total of 3,100 million yen was provided through this scheme in 1992 and 1993. Due to the recession that hit the country, however, no further funds under this programme have been authorized in this area since then.

Considerable employment has been generated within BCCs during the 1990s. *Makuhari*, the new centre in Chiba city, and MM21, the new centre in Yokohama city, started their development in the 1990s as the core projects of each BCC. Both projects are located on reclaimed land within Tokyo Bay. The *Makuhari* plan included a workforce of 150,000 and a residential community of 26,000, all on a 522 ha site. The MM21 plan

Present structure

Future structure

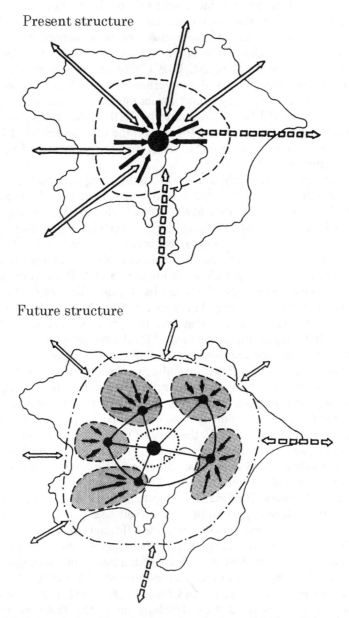

Figure 5.3 Concept of multi-nucleus structure in the national capital region, 1986
Source: Kawakami 1990, p. 17, Figure 7

130

included a 190,000-person employment level and 10,000 residents on a 186 ha site. As of March 1997, much of the commercial section of *Makuhari* had been completed. This includes a convention and exhibition centre, office complexes, hotels, condominiums, and other facilities. Approximately 350,000 people work in the area. The residential section has not been completed and only 5,000 people currently live there. MM21's convention centre, office complex, hotels, commercial complex, and other facilities have been completed and approximately 250,000 people have jobs in the area.

Many company headquarters have moved to these two areas. BMW Japan moved its headquarters to *Makuhari*, and a significant number of foreign-affiliated manufacturing company headquarters have recently located in MM21. This success may reflect the importance of the western corridor of the TMR, including Yokohama city as an R&D centre within Japan, rather than the success of the government policy. Though the number of jobs in the Tokyo 23 wards area increased by 1,040,000 (1.6 per cent), from 6,230,000 to 7,270,000, between 1980 and 1995, Yokohama city and Chiba city have grown even faster. The number of jobs in Yokohama city increased by 360,000 (35.1 per cent), from 1,030,000 to 1,390,000, and the number in Chiba city increased by 130,000 (45.7 per cent), from 280,000 to 410,000, over the same period. As a result, the share of employment controlled by the 23 wards area within the entire TMR has decreased from 49.0 per cent to 43.6 per cent. At the same time the employment share held by the BCCs, including Yokohama city and Chiba city, increased from 13.8 per cent to 15.2 per cent.

While planners have welcomed these changes, the issues related to concentrated employment in the centre of the city have not been relieved. For example, the daily flow of commuters and other visitors to the 23 wards area from outside the city increased from 2.64 million in 1980 to 3.69 million persons in 1995. The movement of jobs to these BCC sites did not counter the significant out-migration from the 23 wards area to the suburbs that occurred during this period. At the same time as Tokyo experienced suburbanization, the absolute number of jobs in the 23 wards area increased. As a result, the daily flow of commuters to the 23 wards from outside increased significantly. While a considerable number of jobs were generated in BCCs, the reorganization of the monocentric spatial structure of the TMR, which was the main objective of the fourth NCRDP, has not been successfully accomplished.

In summary, urban policy in Japan over the last 40 years was largely a regionally based programme that consistently attempted to achieve rapid economic growth. Urban policies were designed to support those goals. Upon a closer look, decentralization policies, part of the regional scheme, have changed their focus from heavy industry to electronics and machinery industries, and finally to R&D and services. These changes have been commensurate with the economic development structure of Japan. The growth pole strategy was successful in the case of heavy industries because, in part, these types of firms were heavily regulated and protected by the national government. They also relied on governmental infrastructure provision such as the development of industrial ports. Yet the same strategy did not work for electronics and machinery industries, nor for R&D and service industries. This is because these particular industries did not necessarily depend upon the government to provide special large-scale infrastructure projects. They could therefore choose their locations in a freer manner than heavy industries. Under market mechanisms, which provided for location incentives, these industries positioned themselves in major urban centres and along highway routes rather than in concentrated "science centres". Furthermore, even medium-sized Japanese manufacturing companies have increasingly deployed their production nets over the entire globe. As aforementioned, the R&D as well as service activities concentrate within the TMR because of the better access to international information, domestic services, and governmental bodies. Under the conditions of globalization the measures taken by the Japanese government to promote specific areas, such as tax exemptions and provisions of credit, have not become the decisive factors in location decision-making. Hence, national government policies implemented after the manufacturing growth poles have not been successful in attempting to distribute economic activities spatially.

Due to rising land values in Tokyo, the provision of housing and infrastructure became difficult, leading to the desolation of inner-city communities and the need to improve the quality of life for citizens. This is increasingly important to Tokyo's planners and decision-makers. Of the five major current strategies put forward by the city, four deal with social and environmental issues. High on the list is the creation of an appealing and liveable city (TMG 1999).

Current issues in planning the national capital region

The third interim report of the Subcommittee on NCR Development of the Advisory Committee on National Development (hereinafter referred to as "the report") was published in July 1998.[3] The report set forth the goal of the fifth NCRDP as the realization of a "decentralized network structure" throughout the capital region by reorganizing the present monocentric spatial structure of the NCR through the promotion of telework and increased residential activity in the central areas of Tokyo (Figure 5.4). The major programmes endorsed in the fifth NCRDP were

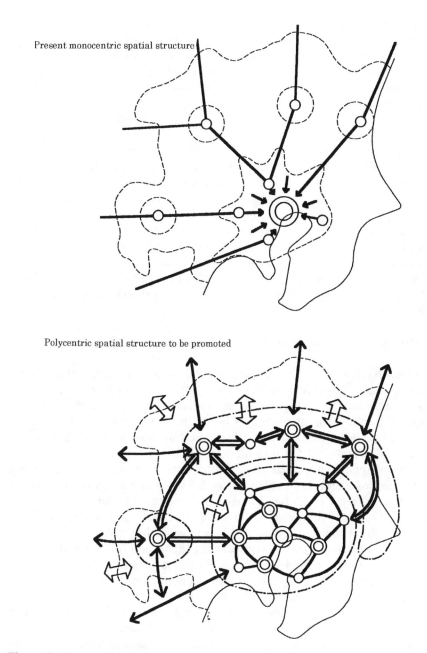

Present monocentric spatial structure

Polycentric spatial structure to be promoted

Figure 5.4 Present discussion of the reorganization of the spatial structure of the national capital region
Source: Subcommittee on NCR Development 1998

133

the promotion of habitation in the central area of Tokyo and the promotion of the growth of BCCs as well as the growth of regional core cities (RCCs), which are located around 100 km from the centre of Tokyo, the improvement of circumferential transport networks to strengthen the link between BCCs and RCCs, and the improvement of telecommunications networks.

The report's stated objectives were "the promotion of creative activities of individuals and the improvement of quality of life", "the formation of environmentally sustainable metropolitan areas", and "the promotion of economic activities with international competitiveness". The report further stressed that a decentralized network structure is key to the achievement of those objectives. In this section, the discussion will focus on whether the directions that the NCRDP expressed in the report are indeed moving Tokyo towards a "sustainable" future. This analysis is presented from the standpoint of the present trends of globalization and the impacts of these processes on the spatial formation of the NCR. Three aspects are of particular importance to the sustainability of Tokyo: international competitiveness, environmental protection, and development policy.

International competitiveness

Enhancing linkages with areas outside the NCR is not stressed in the report despite the critical importance of this aspect in strengthening the city's international competitiveness. Indeed, the report barely touches upon this matter, mentioning that the NCR should function as a node of both domestic and international horizontal network systems. Yet Tokyo has a horizontal relationship with only a few cities around the world, and probably none within Japan. Rather, the world city system has developed into a set of hierarchical relations, with Tokyo and a few other cities at the top in terms of global finance and services. In fact, as mentioned earlier, the TMR functions as the location of CMF and R&D complexes for the global Japanese economy. This relationship necessarily strengthens the hierarchy of cities involved with Japanese production processes. Therefore, to strengthen Tokyo's international competitiveness, the city must maintain and strengthen it global economic functions. This is critical to the city's international linkages.

In the age of globalization, it is not possible to discuss reorganization of the urban spatial structure without considering access to international linkages. Two important aspects that determine these linkages and are of importance to Tokyo are the location of the airport hub and the spatial organization of internationally related business activities within the city area.

The role of transportation systems, particularly access to international airports, is of critical importance. In Tokyo, questions arise over the current access to two existing airports in the NCR, Narita and Haneda.[4] Narita is Tokyo's link to other countries, while Haneda is used for domestic travel. Narita airport is located on the eastern fringe of the TMR. Compounding the inconvenient location of the airport is its relationship to the location of the management and R&D complexes that extend to the west. In order to alleviate this significant mismatch between the city's major international airport and the growth areas in business, a proposal to expand the functions of Haneda airport as the international airport has been floated. Haneda is located close to the centre of Tokyo and would be an ideal spot for meeting the demand for international arrivals and departures. For example, Haneda could be used for the international flights to East and South-East Asia, since the flight time to those countries is fairly short and thus access time to the airport becomes comparatively important.

In addition, the functional linkages forged through business activities (international, professional, and information services and management and R&D functions) from the "mother headquarters" to the globally dispersed set of factories should be effectively strengthened. For many businesses in Tokyo these activities are located in the form of a chain along the western corridor extending from the central area. The report misses these key relationships when it stresses the decentralized network structure. If one looks at the NCR as a unit, as in paradigms of past regional plans, this static structure put forth in decentralization plans may be justified, but it is not a reality of today. For example, while the planned circular expressway around the suburban fringe (20 to 30 km from the city's centre) will help to decrease traffic flows in the central area and support movements within the corridors, the circular highway planned at a distance of over 100 km from the centre is unnecessary.

Environmental protection

The report's findings can be questioned in terms of protecting the environment. The report's proposed idea of a "decentralized network structure" is antithetical to the creation of an energy-efficient society. The decentralized network structure illustrated in Figure 5.4 will strengthen the creation of an automobile-dependent society similar to those typically observed in cities in North America. This is a problematic structure from the standpoint of environmental sustainability. Few cities in the world have grown to be mega-city size and maintained a viable subway and railway system, as has Tokyo. In that sense, the city's mass-transit experience is highly valuable. The duty of metropolitan planning for Tokyo in the twenty-first century is to continue this tradition. The present problems caused by its extended radial structure, such as long commuting time, extremely crowded railways during rush hours, and little housing space, among others, can be partly solved through enhancing the public transportation system. In this sense, the reorganization of habitation and economic activities within railway corridors seems more appropriate than promoting a decentralized structure that will encourage more automobile traffic.

Economic activities should be located in such a way as to be woven together with business linkage needs. The commuting pattern of residence to workplace is simple if people live near to their workplaces. Thus it seems that there is no reason to scatter the workplaces and living places throughout the entire NCR to alleviate the problems of commuting in the TMR. The report ultimately contradicts itself. While the promotion of habitation in central areas of Tokyo and telework could lessen commuting demand, the promotion of a decentralized urban structure with a circular highway system in areas far from the existing metropolitan areas of Tokyo may lead to the creation of longer commutes.

Development strategy

Finally, the report proposes the promotion of BCCs and RCCs as nodal points of regional linkage through the financial assistance of the national government. Yet, as discussed previously, regional development in the age of globalization and information technology makes publicly guided location policy inefficient. Unlike the case of steel and petrochemical complex promotion, which necessarily relies on large-scale public investment, current economic activity is less dependent on governmental action. The economic location policy to drive economic development that the national government promotes should be abandoned. Location policies should be limited to land-use management from environmental and cultural viewpoints, or for social policy measures such as the creation of jobs in areas hard hit by drastic globally related economic structural change. In the case of Japan, the limits of land seriously hinder efficient urban development. Thus it is often difficult for the private sector to embark upon large-scale urban development projects, particularly in built-up areas. Yet the urban development projects themselves should be conducted with the aim of public-private partnerships. The government should limit its role in land assembly to only those cases that are justified. In sum, economic activities should be allowed to locate freely within the restraint of the land-use and social policies of the government (to ensure equity). The result will eventually be an efficient spatial formation.

Conclusions

The present spatial impact of globalization on the Tokyo metropolitan area is the concentration of commercial activities in the central city wards. The unique characteristics of Tokyo in terms of spatial formation are that the world headquarters of Japanese TNCs are concentrated in the central area and R&D functions are located along the railway corridors extending from the centre, particularly to the west. They have close linkages and form a corridor in this part of the region.

After considering these spatial characteristics, the present NCRDP's proposals to create a decentralized network structure within the city seem inappropriate at best. On the contrary, what is needed is a railway corridor structure to make the TMR both economically competitive and environmentally sustainable.

Finally, the authors would like to point out the problems in the process of formulation of the NCRDP. At present, the NCRDP is formulated by the national government as a part of the planning of national development. Yet, given the growing complexity of Japanese society, top-down decision-making seem out of date. Tokyo has matured into a "global" city and suffers from various problems. To solve these problems, city bureaucrats will need the help of the general citizenry. It is true that the metropolitan planning in the TMR covers the areas of many local governments and several prefecture governments, and thus the national government should take the coordination role in the process of formulating the plan. The national government, however, is only one of several players within the region that are affected by these decisions. Other stakeholders include local governments, prefecture governments, the private sector, and non-profit organizations (NPOs). It is becoming increasingly obvious that one player cannot decide all the rules of the game. It is strongly suggested that the national government should not only allow, but should also facilitate the involvement of local and prefecture governments as well as the representatives of the private sector and NGOs/NPOs in the future decisions concerning planning in the national capital region.[5]

Notes

1. The areas in and around the Tokyo metropolitan area are defined as:
   - Tokyo metropolitan area (TMA): the area governed by the Tokyo metropolitan government (TMG); total area 2,187 km^2, population 11.8 million in 1995, including the 23 special wards area that covers 621 km^2; the TMA also encompasses the Tama area

- Tokyo metropolitan region (TMR): the area covered by the TMA and neighbouring three prefectures which are commonly understood as actual metropolitan areas of Tokyo; area 13,553 km^2, population 32.6 million in 1995
- national capital region (NCR): the area covered by the TMA and surrounding seven prefectures; area 36,884 km^2, population 40.4 million in 1995
- wards area: the area covered by the 23 wards of Tokyo which are commonly understood as Tokyo proper; area 621 km^2, population 8.0 million in 1995
- Tama area: the rest of the TMA except for the wards area; area 1,566 km^2, population 3.8 million in 1995. The Tama area consists of 26 cities, five towns and one village, tablelands, hills, and mountains, extending to the west of the special wards area, and has a total area of 1,159 km^2, and finally there are a string of islands south of Tokyo Bay
- central three wards area: the area covered by the three central wards (Chiyoda, Minato, Chuo); area 42 km^2, population 0.24 million in 1995.

2. The agency responsible for the formulation of both the NDPs and the NCRDPs is the National Land Agency (NLA), headed by the minister of the NLA. NCRDPs are basically revised in line with the NDPs.

3. The subcommittee members are appointed by the prime minister to give technical advice upon consultation of the prime minister on the direction of NCR development. The committee members are composed largely of experts on physical planning and economics. The secretariat is made of the staff of the National Land Agency.

4. Before Narita airport was opened, Haneda served as both an international and a domestic airport.

5. The TMR, which is thought to be the actual metropolitan area of Tokyo, is appropriate as the planning unit rather than the NCR, which is the conceptual space as a region of the nation. Using the TMR will encourage relevant bodies to participate in the planning process.

REFERENCES

Alden, Jeremy, D., Moriaki Hirohara, and Hirofumi Abe. 1994. "The impact of recent urbanization on inner-city development in Japan", in Philip Shapira, Ian Masser, and David W. Edgington (eds) *Planning for Cities and Regions in Japan*. Liverpool: Liverpool University Press, pp. 33–58.

Cox, Kevin R. 1995. "Globalization, competition and the politics of local economic development", *Urban Studies*, Vol. 32, No. 2, pp. 213–224.

Douglass, Michael. 1993. "The 'new' Tokyo story: Restructuring space and the struggle for place in a world city", in K. Fujita and R. C. Hill (eds) *Japanese Cities in the World Economy*. Philadelphia: Temple University Press.

Edgington, David W. 1994. "Planning for technology development and information systems in Japanese cities and regions", in Philip Shapira, Ian Masser, and David W. Edgington (eds) *Planning for Cities and Regions in Japan*. Liverpool: Liverpool University Press, pp. 126–154.

Honjo, Masahiko. 1998. "The growth of Tokyo as a world city", in Fu-chen Lo and Yue-man Yeung (eds) *Globalization and the World of Large Cities*. Tokyo: United Nations University Press, pp. 109–131.

Itoh, Shigeru. 1990. "Dispersion possibility of its monocentric urban structure", paper presented at the Symposium on the Mega-city and the Future: Population Growth and Policy Responses sponsored by the Population Division, United Nations and the United Nations University, October.

Japanese External Trade Organization (JETRO). 1998. *Hakusho Toushihen* (JETRO White Paper on Investment). Tokyo: JETRO

Kawakami, H. 1990. *Kyodaitoshi Tokyo no keikakuron* (Planning in Mega-city Tokyo). Tokyo: Shokokusha

Machimura, Takashi. 1998. "Symbolic use of globalization in urban politics in Tokyo", *International Journal of Urban and Regional Research*, Vol. 22, No. 2, pp. 183–194.

National Land Agency (NLA). 1997. *Shutoken hakusho* (White Paper on National Capital Region). Tokyo: NLA.

Onishi, Takashi. 1993 "A capacity approach for sustainable urban development: An empirical study", *Regional Studies*, Vol. 21, No. 1, pp. 39–51.

Subcommittee on NCR Development. 1998. *Third Interim Report.* Tokyo: Advisory Committee on National Development.

Togo, Hisatake. 1995. "The metropolitan strategies of Tokyo: Towards the restoration of balanced growth", in L. J. Sharpe (ed.) *The Government of World Cities: The Future of the Metro Model.* Chichester: John Wiley & Sons, pp. 177–201.

Tokyo Metropolitan Government (TMG). 1999. *Tokyo, Current Issues.* Tokyo: TMG.

United Nations Conference on Trade and Development (UNCTAD). 1998. *World Investment Report 1998.* New York: United Nations.

6

Globalization and the sustainability of cities in the Asia Pacific region: The case of Seoul

Won-yong Kwon

Introduction

Globalization is characterized by increasing functional and spatial integration of economic activities among countries, and has intensified competition among cities articulated to the world's urban system. Sustainability concerns economic growth and environmental quality. While globalization was once thought of as the answer to continued growth and development, recent impacts, including the ongoing Asian financial crisis, have forced Asians seriously to reconsider the role of transnational flows and the integration of the cities of the region.

Globalization processes have sharpened the conflicts between the urban "haves" and "have-nots". They have also generated a rift between those who promote global infrastructure to increase urban competitiveness and those interested in delivering basic services and providing jobs for the poor. These tensions have materialized within the Republic of Korea's largest and most globalized city, Seoul. As an important member of the regional and world city system, Seoul is the location of Korean domestic and transnational corporation headquarter's functions. It has therefore grown and benefited from increased functional integration of economic activities within the regional and global marketplaces. It has also been severely hurt by the recent Korean economic crisis.

As the Asian financial crisis has been painful to citizens of the city, it has forced a re-evaluation of priorities. Amid the recent turbulence created by globalization, this chapter argues that Seoul's relentless growth

140

should be reconsidered in the light of "sustainability". The first section presents an overview of the urbanization trends in Korea from 1960 to 1995, explains the development of Korea's urban order, and highlights the predominance of Seoul within this system. The government counter-measures to relieve heavy urban concentration in Seoul are briefly out-lined. In the second section the changing spatial patterns are described in conjunction with the decentralization of population and manufactur-ing employment from Seoul. Emphasis is placed on the need for metro-politan planning and management. In the third section the dynamics of Seoul's urban economy are discussed from the globalization perspective, and in relation to the expansion of international transactions, producer services, and urban competitiveness. The final section examines the deli-cate balance between the maintenance of economic and environmental sustainability. This section focuses on quality of life (QOL) issues such as transportation congestion, the green belt, and solid waste disposal.

The overall objective of this chapter is to describe and analyse what Seoul is and how it has come to be, rather than to present its prospects for the future. The conclusion summarizes and reflects on some of the lessons learned from the Korean urbanization experience, and identifies policy constraints and opportunities. It is hoped that this work will provide the basis for Seoul's sustainable development into the twenty-first century.

Urbanization in Korea: An overview

Trends: 1960–1995

Over the past 30 years, the Republic of Korea has experienced an un-precedented increase in the rate of urbanization in both absolute and relative terms. The number of cities with a population of more than 50,000 increased from 27 in 1960 to 73 in 1995. During that period, the level of urbanization skyrocketed from 35.8 per cent in 1960 to 85.0 per cent in 1995, reaching the saturation point (Table 6.1).

Urban growth can be measured in terms of size, speed, and spatial balance. Since 1960, the size of the Korean urban population has in-creased by 15.8 million, more than the increase in the total national pop-ulation over the same period. As shown in Table 6.2, the speed of urbanization accelerated between 1966 and 1970 directly after the imple-mentation of the country's first five-year economic development plan (1962–1966). Government efforts to modernize Korea played a decisive role in its urban growth. For example, an industrial town, Ulsan, was constructed in 1963 by vigorous government initiatives, which thereafter ignited remarkable industrial growth throughout the 1960s and 1970s.

Rapid urbanization itself, however, does not imply a spatial problem.

Table 6.1 Urbanization in Korea and population concentration in Seoul

Year	Total population (000)	Urbanization level (%)	Population concentration in Seoul (%)	Davis primacy index[a]
1960	24,989	35.8	9.8	1.09
1970	31,434	49.8	17.6	1.53
1975	34,707	58.4	19.9	1.51
1980	37,436	66.7	22.3	1.43
1985	40,467	73.8	23.8	1.39
1990	43,520	79.6	24.4	1.35
1995	44,609	85.0	23.0	1.21

Source: Economic Planning Board, *Population and Housing Census*, various years
a. Refers to the ratio of the primate city population divided by the total population of next three largest cities.

Table 6.2 Speed of urbanization as measured by the population growth rate

Period	Urban area (A) %	Whole country (B) %	Speed (A−B) %
1960–1966	5.0	2.6	3.4
1966–1970	6.3	1.9	4.4
1970–1975	5.2	2.0	3.2
1975–1980	4.2	1.9	2.3
1980–1985	3.7	1.6	2.1
1985–1990	3.0	1.4	1.6
1990–1995	1.8	0.4	1.4

Source: Economic Planning Board, *Population and Housing Census*, various years

The major urban problems in Korea arise from heavy population concentration in the capital city, Seoul, leading to a skewed pattern of urban development. Korea suffers from an urban spatial imbalance. For example, Seoul's share of the national population increased from 7.3 per cent in 1955 to 23.0 per cent in 1995. The recent national census revealed that the population of Seoul has already reached more than 10 million, while the second largest city, Pusan, reached 3.8 million, and the third largest, Taegu, 2.4 million. Currently Seoul, covering approximately 0.63 per cent of the national territory, accommodates nearly a quarter of the national population.

Causes of Seoul's growth

Urbanization in Korea can only be discussed in conjunction with the rapid expansion of urban manufacturing that absorbed the inflow of cheap

Table 6.3 Urbanization and industrialization in Korea

Year	Urbanization level (A) %	Industrialization level (B)[a] %	Difference (A−B) %
1966	42.1	42.1	0.0
1970	49.8	49.6	0.2
1980	66.7	66.0	0.7
1985	73.8	75.1	−1.3
1990	79.6	81.7	−2.1
1995	85.0	87.4	−2.4

Source: Economic Planning Board, *Population and Housing Census*, various years
a. The industrialization level means the ratio of manufacturing and service-sector employment to national total employment.

labour from rural areas. In Korea, urbanization and industrialization have been strikingly correlated (Table 6.3). The particular pattern of urbanization and industrialization, however, privileged the growth of Seoul over other urban centres. Both economic and policy factors have contributed to population concentration in Seoul.

The dramatic growth of Seoul is largely attributed to the export-led industrialization programmes of the Korean government. The initial expansion of labour-intensive industries in Seoul caused a large number of rural residents to move into the city. The dominance of Seoul's economy over the rest of the country was reinforced by the continued influx of rural migrants that further fuelled growth. As the city expanded and manufacturing industry grew, Seoul functioned as the development engine for the entire national economy.

A survey of urban migrants to Seoul by the Korea Research Institute for Human Settlements (1980) demonstrated that economic motives underlay the movement of many Koreans to the nation's capital. More than 40 per cent of the respondents mentioned job-related, job-seeking or business convenience factors as the principal motivation for their migration to the city (Table 6.4). Initially, manufacturing firms accompanied the movement of population. They created Seoul's comparative advantage in labour, information, finance, and government administrative services benefits (Kim 1995). The country's strong centralist tradition enhanced the city's attractiveness to firms, as it meant access to government decision-making. As more business headquarters located in Seoul, it enhanced the opportunities for jobs.

More recently, the tertiary sector of the urban economy has become the economic base of Seoul. The number of white-collar jobs for professional, managerial, and clerical workers has been rising, while the number of blue-collar jobs has been falling. Despite the change in urban eco-

Table 6.4 Reasons for residing in Seoul

Reasons	Response %
Job-related	26.3
Born in Seoul	23.9
Education of household head or children	17.9
Joining family	11.7
Job-seeking	8.2
Convenience for business transactions	7.8
Influence of friends or relatives	2.1
Other	2.1

Source: Korea Research Institute for Human Settlements 1980

nomic structure, high incomes and job creation associated with the expansion of the new urban economy have continued to induce a steady and sizeable flow of migrants to the city.

Consequences of population concentration

There are at least three unfavourable consequences of having one very dominant city in a country (Kwon 1981). First, regional disparities arise from the uneven distribution of population and economic activities. The distorted spatial organization resulting from Seoul's dominance in the national urban system has undeniably contributed to interregional inequity. For example, the concentration of population has led to high housing rents and crowded schools within Seoul. At the same time within rural communities there is an abundance of vacant houses and under-utilized schools.

The second consequence is the diseconomies within Seoul itself and the strain they place on the city's management. Rapid population growth resulted in severe urban problems such as traffic congestion, land speculation, housing shortages, overcrowding, pollution, and backlogs in infrastructure development. Combined with municipal financial difficulties, the provision of urban services has continued to be a critical problem. The third and possibly the most important consequence concerns national defence. The location of this very large agglomeration within range of the Democratic People's Republic of Korea's artillery is disadvantageous in terms of military security.

The Korean government responded to the abovementioned consequences in the form of population decentralization policies. A host of strong policy measures have been adopted to fight concentration and centralization since the 1970s. These included development control by a rigid zoning system and establishment of green belts, industrial re-location, and dispersal of government offices and universities from Seoul. The goal of these government efforts was simply to reverse the tendency for people to concentrate in Seoul.

Despite controversy, population decentralization policies that endeav-oured to relieve the primate city phenomenon were not successful (Choe 1990; Hong 1997). There are several reasons for these failures. First, the influence of government programmes *vis-à-vis* market forces remains unclear. Even if the programmes were successful, their ability to decon-centrate population may well have been overcome by economic forces. Second, there was an inevitable mismatch between the rhetoric of plan-ning and spatial policy implementation. What was called a deconcentra-tion policy was not implemented as such. Third, neglecting local auton-omy was a mistake. The systematic devolution of government power might have relieved the heavy concentration in Seoul, but it was not tried. Lastly, Korea had already reached the stage of "mature urbanization" by the time the policies were implemented. Thus, the population decentral-ization problem became a metropolitan management problem, not a re-gional problem.

Metropolitan growth and change

The metropolitan region, as a planning unit, includes the surrounding area that has socio-economic linkages and interdependency with the cen-tral city. In this context, population distribution and employment location are two major determining variables whose changes bring about patterns of metropolitan settlement. Similarly, metropolitan commuting patterns reflect energy-related environmental sustainability trends. Therefore, new town development is regarded as a strategically important policy instru-ment, in so far as its aim is to accommodate the spillover of people and jobs from the central city to outlying areas.

Seoul is endowed with a beautiful landscape that changes dramatically with each season. The two main geographical features that dominate the city are the mountain axis extending from the north to the south and the Han river flowing from east to west. Figure 6.1 demonstrates how these factors affected the spread of Seoul's urban development and the expansion of the transportation network from 1958 to 1990. Due to rapid population growth since the early 1960s, building sites have encroached upon agricultural and forest lands. Over the last three decades, the Seoul metropolitan region (SMR), consisting of Seoul city and its adjoining Kyonggi province, grew to occupy the entire area within a 50–60 km radius from the city's centre (an area of 11,726 square kilometres). At

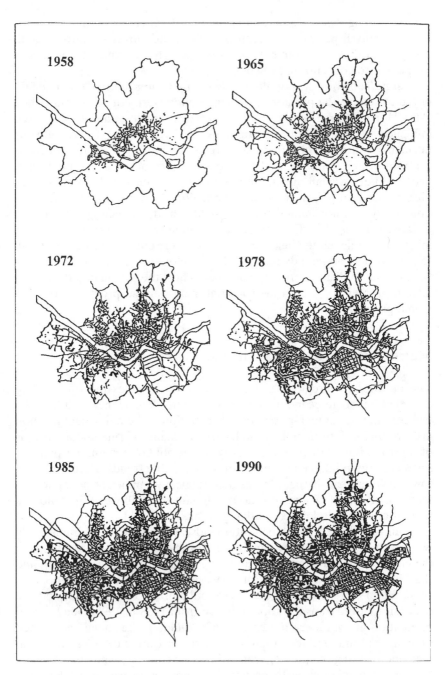

Figure 6.1 Physical expansion of built-up area in Seoul
Source: Seoul Metropolitan Government 1997

present, about 45 per cent of Korean people live and work in the SMR as a functional urban region.

Population distribution

Before the 1970s, Seoul was a monocentric city spreading out from a point located principally north of the Han river. This basic urban structure remained despite a doubling in land size since 1963. The central business district (CBD) covers 9.2 square kilometres (1.5 per cent of the total land area of Seoul), and is the central core from which all major arterial roads radiate. The CBD of Seoul was formerly a residential zone. Through "invasion and succession", commercial offices and various facilities have replaced older residential areas (Kwon 1987). The consequence of the outward movement of people resulted in the transformation of the built environment. For example, many elementary schools in the CBD had to close due to the decline in the school-age population. Currently, the core functions as a centre of commercial employment, white-collar jobs in government institutions, and headquarters of business firms, banks, and insurance companies.

Concomitant with the decrease of residential buildings in the centre, there has been an increase in the residential population south of the Han river and the gradual emergence of two subcentres: Yoido (once a riverside island) and the Youngdong area. The south's share of the city population rose from 21.8 per cent in 1970 to 49.3 per cent in 1995 with the construction of large high-rise apartment complexes south of the river. Recently, another movement of commercial office buildings has followed the residential shift. Table 6.5 presents the current status of the deconcentration of office space from the centre to these subcentres. Commercial and residential development in these areas are part of their emergence as secondary CBDs.

While Seoul has gradually transformed into a multicentric city, it also underwent a metropolitan growth process. This process began with the completion of the subway (line number one) in Seoul and two suburban

Table 6.5 Office floor space distribution in Seoul, 1993

Total[a]	CBD (downtown)	Youngdong (subcentre)	Yoido (subcentre)	Others
1,695	419	494	384	397
(%)	(24.7)	(29.2)	(22.7)	(23.4)

Source: Park 1996, p. 75
a. Includes public, commercial, and office buildings with more than 10 storeys or floor space of 100,000 square metres.

Table 6.6 Population growth in the Seoul metropolitan region

	1960	1970	1980	1990	1995
Seoul (A)	2,445	5,433	8,364	10,613	10,231
Kyonggi (B)	2,749	3,358	4,934	7,974	9,958
SMR (A + B)	5,194	8,791	13,298	18,587	20,189

	Annual percentage growth rate			
	1960–1970	1970–1980	1980–1990	1990–1995
Seoul (A)	7.9	4.3	2.4	−0.7
Kyonggi (B)	1.8	3.8	4.8	4.4
SMR (A + B)	5.4	4.1	3.3	1.7

Source: Economic Planning Board, *Population and Housing Census*, various years

rail transit systems (from Seoul to Inchon and from Seoul to Suwon) in 1974. Suburban access by rail facilitated commuting and led to rapid urban development along two main transportation corridors dispersing the SMR population.

As shown in Table 6.6, the population of the SMR increased from 5.2 million in 1960 to 20.2 million in 1995. During this same period the nation's total population increased from 25.0 million to 45.5 million. This indicates that the growth in Seoul accounted for approximately 73 per cent of the total national population growth. Since the 1980s, however, the speed of population growth within Seoul has slowed considerably. The residential population has dispersed to the outer fringes of the city. Table 6.6 also demonstrates that the population growth rate in Kyonggi province doubled that of Seoul in the 1980s. This distribution has been perceived as a state of "relative decentralization", in the sense that the population is increasing in the outlying areas of the city much faster than within Seoul itself (Klaassen, Molle, and Paelink 1981).

It is also noteworthy that the sources of population growth in Seoul are changing, and the metropolitan expansion is increasingly dependent upon natural increase rather than in-migration. With higher levels of urbanization, the impact of rural migration became increasingly less significant. Presently, there are extremely few young people among farm workers in Korea, which implies a virtual exhaustion of the "rural migration stock". Subsequently, the migration pattern within Korea has changed from a rural-to-urban to an urban-to-urban type. In 1988, the year of the twenty-fourth Olympiad, Seoul achieved the status of a mega-city in terms of its sheer size by recording a population of 10 million. Only two years later, in 1990, Seoul experienced a net out-migration (91,000 persons) for the first time. It is premature, however, to conclude that the SMR is now entering into a phase of "absolute decentralization".

In view of the prospect of urbanization in the 1990s and beyond, new forms of regionwide planning and management are necessary. Many urban services, for example, spill over political jurisdictions. Transportation, electric power, water supply, and air pollution pay no attention to local political borders. Thus, in Seoul, controversial issues that have focused policy attention include the coordination of metropolitan transportation networks; location of public facilities (such as garbage and solid waste disposal sites and cemeteries); allocation of new towns containing industrial and housing estates; and environmental conservation. Among these, protecting the water quality of the Han river is undeniably of vital importance to achieve sustainable development for the SMR.

Employment location and commuting

Since the 1970s, Seoul has experienced an absolute decline in manufacturing jobs and a decrease in the share of the total population within the SMR. At the same time, Kyonggi province has gained in both population and jobs. Table 6.7 indicates that such deconcentration of the Seoul population to its satellite cities and suburban areas occurred simultaneously with a shift in manufacturing employment.

Despite the continuing decentralization of manufacturing employment to the outer rings of the SMR, the shift in population is also due to high housing costs and housing shortages within Seoul. According to the 1995 census, there were 7.3 million commuters in the SMR as a whole, and approximately 0.8 million suburban residents commute daily to Seoul. Table 6.8 reveals that the average commuting distance has increased substantially between 1980 and 1995. Further, cross-commuting has been

Table 6.7 Distribution of manufacturing employment and population between Seoul and Kyonggi province

	1973 %	1978 %	1983 %	1988 %	1995 %
Manufacturing employment*a*					
Seoul	70.6	52.3	45.7	36.5	26.8
Kyonggi	29.4	47.7	54.3	63.5	73.2
Total	100.0	100.0	100.0	100.0	100.0
(000 persons)	(581)	(1,031)	(1,019)	(1,515)	(1,379)
Population					
Seoul	63.2	63.7	62.3	58.7	50.7
Kyonggi	36.8	36.3	37.7	41.3	49.3
Total	100.0	100.0	100.0	100.0	100.0
(000 persons)	(9,959)	(12,275)	(14,783)	(17,526)	(20,189)

Source: Economic Planning Board, *Mining and Manufacturing Census* 1973, 1978, 1983, 1988, 1993
a. Manufacturing establishments with five or more employees.

Table 6.8 Changing commuter patterns of the Seoul metropolitan region

	1980	1990	1995
Average commuting distance	9.10 km	9.82 km	10.28 km
	%	%	%
Seoul → Seoul	65.3	55.3	45.8
Seoul → Kyonggi	3.9	4.7	4.8
Kyonggi → Seoul	5.9	10.1	11.1
Kyonggi → Kyonggi	24.9	30.2	38.2

Source: Economic Planning Board, *Population and Housing Census* 1980, 1990, 1995

increasing between Seoul and its outlying Kyonggi province. Inbound commuting from Kyonggi to Seoul, however, remains more significant than outbound (reverse) commuting from Seoul to Kyonggi. The former prevails primarily because commuting is less costly to suburban residents than housing. The latter occurs partly due to white-collar workers who have stayed in Seoul so that their children have access to high-quality education.

In general, cross-commuting represents a job/housing imbalance and the undesirable separation of home and workplace (Cervero 1989). The underlying cause of this separation in the SMR is inefficient land-use patterns and transportation networks. Metropolitan spatial structure is an important determinant of energy demand because it affects the separation of urban activities and therefore energy use (Breheny 1992). In the light of sustainable metropolitan development, it would be preferable to minimize the need for commuting through the creation of mixed land-use zoning laws and the "compact city" urban design model.

New towns and housing

During the 1970s, the population in Seoul grew rapidly while the supply of housing slowly followed. Mainly due to soaring land prices, Seoul has suffered from acute housing shortages since the 1970s, and little has changed since that time. In order to alleviate both the chronic housing shortages and population concentration in the city, the national government announced a bold development plan in 1989. The plan called for the construction of five new towns to be built in the SMR.

The five new towns are located within about 20 km of the city centre just beyond the outer edge of the green belt (Figure 6.2). Bundang and Ilsan were developed as self-contained independent towns for the middle-income classes, and the remaining three were similar to "new towns in town". As shown in Table 6.9, compared with other existing towns in the country, roads, parks, and open space made up a significantly larger por-

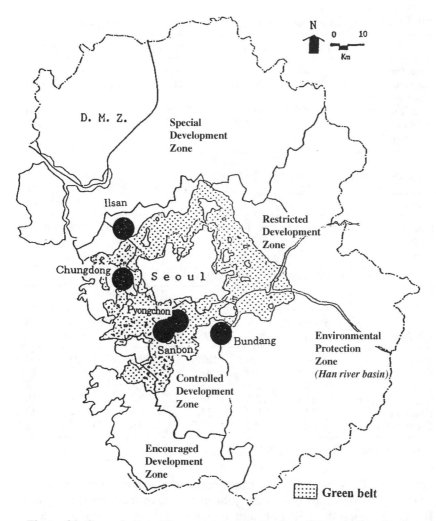

Figure 6.2 Green belt and five new towns in the Seoul Metropolitan Region
Source: Ministry of Construction 1984

tion of land use. Also noticeable was the application of a new technique
of urban design that included such land-use components as bikeways and
pedestrian facilities.

The five new towns not only successfully provided housing to a large
number of families, but the projects were completed rapidly, taking only
five years (1989–1993). Yet in terms of other indicators they have not
completely fulfilled their promises. Approximately 90 per cent of the
housing units built were high-rise apartments. These buildings have a
monotonous appearance, lack diversity, and have even been considered

Table 6.9 Profiles of five new towns in the Seoul metropolitan region

	Pundang	Ilsan	Chungdong	Pyongchon	Sanbon
Area (ha)	1,964	1,574	545	511	420
Planned population	390,000	276,000	170,000	170,000	170,000
Housing units	97,500	69,000	42,500	42,500	42,500
Gross population density	198	175	312	333	404
Floor area ratio (%)	184	169	226	204	205
Road space (%)	19.7	20.9	26.1	23.3	15.2
Parks and open space (%)	22.0	24.1	12.9	13.9	21.2

Source: Korea Research Institute for Human Settlements 1997; Lee and Kim 1995

Table 6.10 Job location of new town residents

Job location	New towns					
	Bundang %	Ilsan %	Chungdong %	Sanbon %	Pyongchon %	Total %
Total	100.0	100.0	100.0	100.0	100.0	100.0
Seoul	72.8	68.0	44.6	54.9	66.3	66.0
Incheon	0.5	2.7	13.7	1.9	0.4	2.9
Own new town	12.1	12.3	28.6	22.2	17.2	16.7
Kyonggi	11.8	7.7	11.4	21.6	15.3	12.9
Outside the SMR	2.8	0.4	1.7	0.6	0.8	1.5

Source: Chung and Lee 1996, p. 60

inhumane. They have created transportation problems, since two-thirds of new town residents have their jobs in Seoul. In the largest new town, Bundang, more than 70 per cent of workers commute daily to Seoul (Table 6.10). Lastly, there were enormous negative side-effects from their hasty and massive construction. These include such unintended macro-economic repercussions as labour cost inflation and skilled manpower and building materials shortages.

The new town construction provides a good example of the negative aspects derived from neglecting urban governance. Urban governance refers to the basic relationship between national, regional, and local governments in the management of mega-cities (Stubbs and Clarke 1996). However, "governance" as a concept is much broader than government, and includes partnerships between public, private, and voluntary sectors. Before the advent of local autonomy in the early 1990s, there were few opportunities for citizens' participation in such important decisions as constructing new towns in the SMR. Over last 30 years, Korea's central government's containment policy has prevented Seoul from proactively participating in its own urban development. Instead, central government corporations have monopolized almost all large-scale housing projects, even within the city's borders. Further, the active role of private developers in public works (such as industrial parks) has not been encouraged until recently. For sustainable metropolitan development, consensus and commitment of multi-stakeholders from both public and private sectors should be made through a variety of negotiation forms.

Globalization and the Seoul economy

The increase in international transactions

There has been enormous and consistent growth in the Korean economy since the 1980s. This growth is highly related to increases in international economic transactions. For example, the total amount of foreign trade as a share of GNP increased from 20.6 per cent in 1962 to 60.6 per cent in 1991 (SaKong 1993). Considering its poor natural endowments, limited market size, and the availability of capital and technology, Korea's success has been determined by access to international markets, foreign capital, and imported technology. For this reason, enhancing globalization could not but become a national policy objective for sustaining economic growth. The gateway functions to increase globalization have undoubtedly been given to Seoul. Accordingly, the globalization of the Korean economy has been directly related to transformations in Seoul's economy. Seoul has played a central role in servicing and financing international trade, investments, and headquarters operations. Nationally, Seoul continues to be the site of concentrated economic power,[1] while provincial cities continue to suffer from stagnant or relatively declining economies.

Since the 1988 summer Olympics, Seoul has gradually expanded its role as one of the key political and economic locations in the Asia Pacific region, and the nation has achieved an impressive increase in foreign trade. Table 6.11 shows an increasing volume of international flows of people and commodities into Seoul. Over the period 1985–1995, the number of foreign visitors and air passengers and the volume of airfreight almost tripled. More than half of the foreign visitors, however, originated from only three countries: Japan (46 per cent), the USA (9.3 per cent), and Hong Kong (3.4 per cent). It goes without saying that the destination countries of overseas travellers from Seoul follow exactly the same order.

Table 6.11 Seoul's international flows of people and commodities

	1985	1988	1990	1992	1994	1995
Foreign visitors (000)	1,446	2,172	2,720	3,009	3,375	3,565
Rate of increase[a]	100	150	188	208	234	247
International air passengers[b] (000 persons)	3,776	5,417	8,443	9,800	11,865	13,366
Rate of increase[a]	100	143	224	260	314	354
International air freight (000 tonnes)	317	477	746	807	1,080	1,256
Rate of increase[a]	100	150	235	254	340	395

Source: Korea Research Institute for Human Settlements 1997
a. Base: 1985 = 100.
b. Outgoing from and incoming to Kimpo airport only.

Table 6.12 Intra-Asian air freight

City	To			From		
	1983 tonnes	1990 tonnes	% change	1983 tonnes	1990 tonnes	% change
Bangkok	24,607	73,895	+200	44,310	132,232	+198
Beijing	2,602	1,815	−30	523	2,314	+342
Hong Kong	79,425	199,046	+151	87,883	227,911	+159
Jakarta	5,985	23,140	+287	6,615	37,540	+468
Kuala Lumpur	15,317	36,274	+137	10,170	44,651	+339
Manila	19,739	31,836	+61	14,657	40,863	+179
Seoul	49,595	267,149	+439	38,658	253,382	+555
Shanghai	667	1,045	+57	430	4,464	+938
Singapore	61,151	181,164	+196	41,285	164,380	+298
Taipei	29,246	116,593	+299	76,621	172,031	+125
Tokyo	111,475	344,089	+209	84,520	214,450	+154
Total volume	1983:	423,761	1990:	1,355,563	% change:	+220

Source: International Civil Aviation Organization 1984 and 1991, Rimmer undated

At the same time, Seoul's trade with Asian cities increased substantially in the 1990s. Table 6.12 shows dramatic increases in intra-Asian air freight traffic volumes. It is particularly worth noting that Seoul's high growth rate (four to five times between 1983 and 1990) and international linkages provide evidence of its deepening economic linkages with the Asian urban system.

A key feature of the globalization trend of Seoul in the 1990s is the

Table 6.13 Trends of foreign direct investment in Korea

Year	Total US$ million	Inbound US$ million	Outbound US$ million
1990	1,761.5	802.6	958.9
1991	2,511.0	1,396.0	1,115.0
1992	2,112.4	894.5	1,217.9
1993	2,306.3	1,044.3	1,262.0
1994	3,614.7	1,316.5	2,298.2
1995	5,008.1	1,941.4	3,066.7
1996	7,378.9	3,202.6	4,176.3

Source: Bank of Korea 1997

Table 6.14 Foreign direct investment in Seoul

	Japan US$ million	USA US$ million	Europe US$ million	Malaysia US$ million	Singa-pore US$ million	Hong Kong US$ million	Others US$ million
Manufac-turing	174	207	56	88	32	12	39
Service	1,705	921	1,106	271	52	50	223
Total	1,879	1,128	1,162	359	84	62	262
(%)	(38.0)	(22.8)	(23.5)	(7.3)	(1.7)	(1.3)	(5.4)

Source: Korean Ministry of Finance and Economy 1996

increase in the new types of international transactions. The growth in foreign direct investment (FDI) is one example of international economic flows related to Seoul's economy (Table 6.13). Generally speaking, the amount of inbound FDI into Korea is small and unstable compared with outbound FDI from Korea. In 1996, outbound FDI reached US$4,176 million. The largest portion, 38.4 per cent, was invested in South-East Asia, 37.7 per cent went to North America, and 15.6 per cent landed in Europe. The increasing share of Korean outbound FDI to South-East Asia draws special attention because intra-Asian FDI flows have been growing rapidly in recent years. Growing economic interdependence reflects Seoul's increasingly integrated production network with other mega-cities in the region (Lo and Yeung 1996). While this integration has benefited the country and city, it also has had a cost. Such close economic relationships played an important part in the crisis of 1997, particularly in terms of loan arrangements. Table 6.14 summarizes the total amount of the FDI that accumulated in Seoul from 1988 to 1996. Foreign capital came, by and large, from advanced countries and was mainly invested in

service industries. As a consequence, various locations of fast-food restaurants and convenience stores led the tendency of what has been called
McDonalization, which has been shaping the cityscape of Seoul.

Expansion of producer services

Another salient feature of the globalization of Seoul's economy is the
growing number of transnational corporations (TNCs) in the city. The
number of parent TNCs in Korea is the highest among developing countries. Most of Korea's TNCs are based in Seoul (Brotchie and Batty
1995). The advanced information and.telecommunications requirements
of TNC headquarters have a strong impact on the spatial organization of
Seoul. This is a new form of agglomeration of control and management
functions (CMFs) at both the national and international scales. Further,
the production of services for these headquarters is a growing part of the
economy in Seoul. These services include, *inter alia*, banking, finance,
insurance, real estate, legal services, accounting, economic consulting,
design, printing, and advertising. Seoul's dominance within the national
and regional urban system in these key activities is the source of its
new growth engine and new comparative advantage, replacing the once-
dominant manufacturing sectors.

Table 6.15 demonstrates that producer service employment has contributed to the great concentration of major economic activities and actors in Seoul. A recent survey reveals that Seoul alone accounts for over
45 per cent of all producer services in Korea, and 57 per cent of the most
specialized ones. Prior to the Asian financial crisis, globalization accelerated office development in downtown Seoul. The key location factors

Table 6.15 Expansion of producer service employment in Seoul

	1981		1986		1991		1996	
	No. (000)	%	No. (000)	%	No. (000)	%	No. (000)	%
Whole industry	2,378	100.0	2,869	100.0	3,629	100.0	3,612	100.0
Manufacturing	722	30.4	880	30.7	1,133	31.2	810	22.4
Tertiary industry	1,186	49.9	1,655	57.7	2,092	57.6	2,421	67.9
Producer services	208	8.7	298	10.4	418	11.5	515	14.3
Banking/finance	73	3.1	109	3.8	135	3.7	124	3.4
Insurance	39	1.7	55	1.9	82	2.3	101	2.8
Real estate	47	2.0	68	2.4	70	1.9	72	2.0
Business services	46	1.9	62	2.2	126	3.5	192	5.3

Source: Economic Planning Board, *Comprehensive Survey of Industries*, 1981,
1986, 1991, 1996

for international business activities were convenience of transportation and telecommunications and the supply of high-quality offices (Hahn 1997). It is also argued that information technologies actually contribute to spatial concentration (Sassen 1995). For these reasons, many corporation headquarters as well as their back offices have moved across the Han river to the newly formed "secondary CBDs" in south Seoul as described in the previous section.

Promoting urban competitiveness

The trend of globalization demands more advanced lifestyles and urban infrastructure. Highly educated professional workers (such as managers, scientists, and technicians) are extremely sensitive to the quality of living environment. If a high level of office rent prevails in Seoul, TNC headquarters functions and the growth of advanced business services and ancillary services cannot be accommodated. The high cost of housing and the lack of English-speaking people are comparative disadvantages in the competition for enhanced global flows among other cities in the region. Besides, Seoul has acquired the image of a non-cultural hard-working city. Image-making combined with various amenity[2] factors (such as clean air) are of critical importance to attract entrepreneurs and international investment. The perceptions of Seoul as a "world city" and the "mental images" held by visitors have become linchpins to its future economic success.

On the other hand, the provision of global infrastructure is a key ingredient used by governments to influence the new urban economy. One of the major urban strategies used by cities in the region to accommodate globalization flows has been the construction of large-scale international airports to function as hub airports to cities in East Asia. Seoul's Kimpo airport has a maximum capacity of 24 million passengers per year and, considering its current annual passenger growth rate of 17 per cent, it is expected to reach maximum capacity by the end of the 1990s. Plans for the new Seoul international airport on Youngjong island include an annual passenger load of 27 million at the initial stage, and eventually 100 million passengers per year by the final stage. There are also other mega-projects under consideration for the SMR, including the construction of a teleport, convention centres, and high-tech industrial parks.

Environmental sustainability

Despite the current focus on sustainable development, there is yet no agreement upon its definition.[3] Inherently, there is a problem with the concept since it will differ with community perception (Stocker and Young 1993). Despite the lack of rigour concerning the term, the important point to consider is that it is closely related to "environmentally friendly" development.

Cities are heavily implicated in the sustainability of the environment. Mega-cities are massive consumers of resources and generators of many forms of waste and pollution. Urban activities involving transport, the heating (or cooling) of buildings, and the fuelling of production processes contribute to global warming. The 1992 Rio conference increased public concern for the urban environment and "green" issues, but we are now only beginning to address the notion of sustainability and to consider the need for a full-scale environmental reappraisal of urban development.

Generally, increased economic growth translates into increased environmental concern and worries about quality of life for urban residents (Friedmann 1998). Seoul's citizens have begun to express dissatisfaction with the lack of parks and open space, and severe air pollution mainly caused by automobiles within the city. Today, imbalances between economic growth and environmental improvement are increasingly not tolerated by the public. In this connection, Seoul has three environmental sustainability issues: a CBD congestion toll, green-belt maintenance, and solid waste management.

CBD congestion toll

Of all modern technologies, the automobile has had the most profound impact on the urban environment. In Seoul, since 1988, car ownership has increased at the phenomenal annual rate of 20 per cent. Ironically, however, as people have attempted to increase their mobility by driving cars, they have also increased their travel time due to slower traffic flows (Wright 1992). The automobile society tends to consume most urban land in car-oriented uses, fuelling further demand for cars. The more lanes and parking lots supplied by governments, the more cars pour into streets. Notwithstanding the slow traffic, car congestion, and increasing land devoted to cars, automobile usage incurs social and amenity costs, accidents, noise, air contamination, and pedestrian sidewalk destruction.

Supply-side remedies to solve traffic congestion have generated a vicious circle of inadequate policy remedies that have created more traffic rather than decreased vehicle loads. Building more roads does not reduce the intensity of peak-hour traffic congestion, and increasing carrying capacity attracts more drivers (Downs 1992). Alternatively, transportation demand management (TDM) techniques have recently caught Seoul's policy-makers' attention. TDM has gained noticeable popularity because it aims to achieve the maximum utilization of existing transportation facilities without an additional financial burden. In order to discourage automobile use, a CBD congestion toll is now under implementation as one of the TDM programmes.

Beginning on 11 November 1996 a congestion price of 2,000 won was charged to all automobiles[4] with less than three passengers using the Namsan Tunnels Nos 1 and 3. These tunnels are main access roads to Seoul's CBD. The charge was levied from 7am to 9pm during weekdays and 7am to 3pm on Saturday. During the first four weeks of policy implementation, the average daily traffic volumes in Tunnel No. 1 decreased by 22.3–26.2 per cent and the flows through Tunnel No. 3 decreased by 22.4–25.8 per cent. For both tunnels, the traffic-depressing effects of congestion pricing were significant (Hwang and Son 1997). Accordingly, the daily average speed improved drastically after one month by 41.1 per cent from 25.3 km/h to 35.7 km/h for Tunnel No. 1 and by 77 per cent from 17.8 km/h to 31.5 km/h for Tunnel No. 3. Also, the number of cars with less than three passengers using the two tunnel corridors substantially decreased by 43 per cent from 36,062 cars to 27,429 cars after the implementation of congestion pricing.

During the four-week observation period, traffic volumes for the alternative roads to the CBD increased by only 5.3–7.3 per cent after the implementation of the congestion toll. This result invalidated some of the arguments against congestion pricing. Those against the policy suggested that congestion pricing would push traffic from toll roads to free roads without reducing the total volume of traffic.

Congestion pricing has proved to be very effective in reducing traffic volume and a powerful encouragement to car-pooling and the use of mass transit. The most serious shortcoming of the CBD congestion toll is its unintended effect on low-income groups (Lee 1998). Wealthy people now prefer to use the toll roads and can do so without significantly affecting their total incomes. Middle- and low-income drivers, however, suffer from the regressive charge from road pricing and yet need to use the system to take advantage of the time saved in travel. Thus, for equity measures, the government should use the revenue acquired under this policy to improve mass transportation and environmental quality. For political and technical reasons, however, it does not seem feasible to expand the toll roads to cover many parts of Seoul as originally planned.

Establishment of green belt versus high-density urban redevelopment

The first green belt, established in 1971, comprised approximately 143.4 square kilometres of open space surrounding Seoul (Figure 6.2). The green belt was implemented to restrict urban sprawl. Since that time, not only has the containment policy been firmly and consistently administered, but also the total area protected was expanded to cover 1,567 square kilometres. Landowners in the green belt are prohibited by law from constructing new buildings and changing existing land uses for purposes other than agriculture. While this policy has been a powerful and effective tool for controlling physical growth, such as encroachment upon farmland and forests, it also proved to be a 'strait-jacket' programme with its own social costs.

Residents in the green-belt area did not receive any compensation for the relative decline in their property values. This turned out to be a double disadvantage given that the pressure for housing development has increased over the years. Moreover, villages in the middle of the green belt have limited growth capacity and have missed an opportunity to reap economies of scale in providing public facilities. Furthermore, the protection of the green belt is costly. Enforcement through ground and aerial surveillance is a routine and high-priced operation. This responsibility has fallen into the hands of local authorities, becoming a source of inter-governmental conflicts. Lastly, because designations were made without detailed surveys, the boundaries of the green belt ignore the landscape and do not follow natural contour lines.

On the other hand, high-rise apartment blocks are being built, replacing mostly "squatter" houses on the hilly slopes in Seoul. Although various urban redevelopment methods had been employed, in the early 1980s massive renewal and rebuilding projects, called "partnership redevelopment", emerged as the most important housing development style.[5] As of 1996, 279 substandard housing redevelopment districts were designated for renewal, covering 2.2 per cent of the total city area. Among those planned for redevelopment, 128 districts are completed and 100 more are under construction. The remaining 51 districts have yet to submit project plans for approval. Although redevelopment itself takes four to five years, the overall process from district designation to project completion has taken more than 12 years on average (Kim 1997). The partnership method inevitably seeks high-density redevelopment to secure profits (Figure 6.3). This situation was enhanced by the government's blind policy to maximize housing supply.

Today, political and economic interests are shaping the skyline in Seoul. Urban design imperatives do not determine the city's growth. Poorly planned buildings are obstructing the beautiful mountain views surrounding the city. While Seoul's planners and citizens have advised against vertical sprawl, there is a lack of aesthetic control on urban redevelopment and improper conservation of historic areas within the city. The added population has contributed to traffic congestion, overcrowded

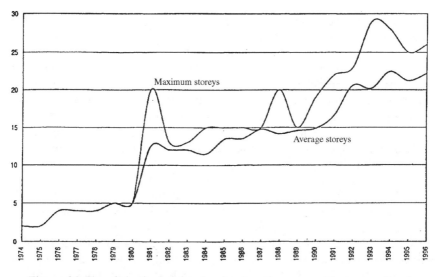

Figure 6.3 Trends in the height of redeveloped apartment houses in Seoul
Source: Kim 1997

schools, overloaded water supply and sewage facilities, and lack of parking and open space. In general there is a decline in the quality of life for
Seoul's population.

Many economists argue that the high-density urban redevelopment is
caused by the green belt. They insist on its immediate repeal to make up
for the lack of developable land within commuting distance. Seoul now
confronts the dilemma of whether to continue vertical sprawl or promote
horizontal sprawl. The green belt is increasingly becoming a controversial issue among stakeholders, not to mention landowners. Environmentalists and planners, by and large, would favour sustaining the green belt
with just compensation for its residents under strict regulations. Detailed
investigations by the government to review the benefit/cost of implementing the green-belt policy are currently under way. In view of environmental sustainability, any decision to harmonize the policy goals of preserving the green area and controlling high-density redevelopment deserves
attention.

Solid waste management

Solid waste management solutions include a flexible combination of source
reduction, recycling (and composting), waste incineration, and landfilling.
Among these, source reduction is high among environmentally sound

management practices because it avoids waste. Recycling is a waste reuse technique which saves landfill space, energy, and natural resources. Combustion is a volume reduction technique that is also designed to produce energy for beneficial use. Until the 1980s, waste was mostly dumped in landfills as Seoul lacked the necessary infrastructure for other more advanced solid waste treatment practices. It was only after 1992 that a state-of-the-art sanitary landfill for the SMR was built on reclaimed land (an area of 20.7 square kilometres) in the west coastal area. By sharing such a common metropolitan landfill site, Seoul has been able to cope efficiently with its solid waste problem.

The average amount of waste generation in Seoul is 1.22 kg per person/day. The substance of wastes varies a great deal from source to source. Of the total amount, half of domestic waste is food, whereas 61 per cent of office waste is paper. The total amount of food thrown away in a day reaches 27.8 per cent of all waste products. Koreans tend to have lavish meals, favouring soups with a high water content. This has created problems due to leakage at landfill sites. The best option would be to reduce food waste at home, and the best way to implement this strategy is through collaboration with housewives. Under food waste recycling projects implemented through a Local Agenda 21 programme, eight composting plants (total capacity 415 tonnes per day) have been constructed and put into operation so far.

The introduction of the "volume rate" system of waste reduction is one of the important programmes for environmental sustainability in Seoul. The system was enforced on 1 January 1995 as a means to reduce waste generation from domestic sources and encourage separation of recyclable wastes. All households must buy standardized bags of different volumes from the municipalities, and must buy as many bags as they need to remove all their domestic waste. Recyclable items can be put into these bags and disposed of as waste – at a cost – or separated out and recycled for free. This has made all households more conscious of volumes of domestic waste and more aware of the need to separate recyclable material; as a result, domestic waste was reduced by 8.4 per cent from 15,397 to 14,102 tonnes per day, while recyclable waste collection increased by 30 per cent (Tark 1998).

In an era of financial crisis, efficient use of wastes through diverse measures for thriftiness will become increasingly important. Government subsidies and technical assistance should be provided to small-scale recycling businesses in Seoul. Each municipality is currently building a treatment plant for recycling wastes. The successful promotion of markets for the recycled materials will be based on the new environmental ethic of sustainability. It should be remembered that sustainable urban development is simply a form of development that does not create negative environmental impacts.

Conclusions

The development of Seoul since the 1960s has been regarded as a symbol of the rapid economic growth of Korea. Seoul has served multiple social, economic, and cultural functions across national and international borders. At the same time, Seoul has experienced urban problems: traffic congestion, chronic housing shortage, pollution and environmental disruption, fiscal plight, and so on. Such problems called for better "management and planning", whether they be social (how to deliver public services *equitably*), economic (how to foster investment *efficiently*), or physical (how to regulate sprawl *effectively*). Seoul is said to be an emporium of urban problems; its locus occupies the midway between the advanced countries of the North and the developing countries of the South. In this context, Korea's experience in policy responses to urban transformation of Seoul yields a number of lessons.

- The containment policy of the primate city, Seoul, did not guarantee the automatic growth of provincial areas. Slowing down the rapid urbanization was like swimming against the tide. But it was worth attempting to catch up with urban infrastructure provision.
- The government placed too much emphasis on control measures simply because they do not involve any financial cost. A "more carrots, fewer sticks" policy scheme, which works with the market, would be preferable.
- Urbanization policy should incorporate "equity" considerations into population dispersal programmes. Particularly, industrial relocation and squatter housing removal plans discriminated against blue-collar jobs, the urban poor, and the informal sector.
- Spatial disparity within the national urban system tends to be exacerbated by globalization. The borderless economy weakens, to a great extent, government's power to regulate industrial locations and mitigate the excessive concentration of urban population.
- The real estate (capital) market played a more prominent role in the allocation of land uses than governmental development controls. Development by agreement needs "communication and negotiation" skills to resolve conflicting interests, along with people's participation.

In the present global economy, economic sustainability depends on the invisible financial flows around the world. Amid the ongoing Asian financial crisis, Seoul's development goals and strategies should inevitably be reoriented. Despite the successful match of "industrialization and urbanization" in the past decades, Seoul must embrace new forms of adaptation and transformation; it must keep pace with the globalization process, but also provide amenities for its citizens. To sharpen its competitiveness under the economic crisis in Korea, Seoul is challenged to bridge two seemingly divergent paths (to provide low cost of production factors and to create a high quality of life environment). There is a compelling need for a trade-off between restructuring the urban economy and creating environmental sustainability. In the past, environmental sustainability was often sacrificed to economic demands. At this moment in history, there is an opportunity to re-evaluate this focus and consider some of the shortcomings of these policies.

In small ways also, Seoul can make growth sustainable by promoting jobs that will help improve environmental conditions. Examples include employment geared to the maintenance and renewal of deteriorated public facilities; preservation of historic and cultural centres within the city; enhancement of the waste management and recycling systems; production of pollution control equipment; woodland protection and urban organic farming; and building databases for geographic information systems' analysis of environmental problems.

In other ways, attention must be focused on the provision of basic needs infrastructure, including adequate housing, public transportation, and open space. In this sense, making Seoul a humane city by enhancing people's QOL may be a more important factor to determine its competitiveness in the long run than upgrading its industrial structure.

Finally, Seoul was relatively low in its international contributions in comparison with its population size and export-oriented national economy. But the mega-city has enormous potential in terms of its geopolitical and geo-economic status. It can connect socialist economies and capital economies, as well as accommodate Western and Asian cultures. No doubt, in the new millennium, Seoul will continue to function as a major centre of regional cooperation in the Asia Pacific region.

Notes

1. As of 1995, Seoul city alone produced 24.2 per cent of the national GDP, while the Seoul metropolitan region (SMR) as a whole accounted for 46 per cent.
2. The term "amenity" includes an appreciation of quality in the natural environment or built environments of cities.
3. The followings are some components of "sustainability": *environmental capacity* – pursuing economic growth that does not permanently damage the environment, which in practice means travel, energy consumption, polluting industries, and waste; *quality of growth* – development must put more emphasis on the quality of growth, rather than the quantity of growth; *intergeneration equity* – planning decisions have to take into account

the needs of future generations as well as current generations; *social equity* – equity considerations should be made, because the poor almost always live in worse environments than the more affluent.
4. Taxis, all buses, vans, trucks, emergency cars, diplomatic vehicles, journalists' cars, and government cars are exempted.
5. Partnerships are contracts between landowners and a construction company, with the former providing land and the latter redevelopment costs.

REFERENCES

Bank of Korea. 1997. *Monthly Bulletin*, September. Seoul: Bank of Korea (in Korean).

Breheny, M. J. (ed.). 1992. *Sustainable Development and Urban Form*. London: Pion.

Brotchie, John and Mike Batty (eds). 1995. *Cities in Competition*. Melbourne: Longman House.

Cervero, Robert. 1989. "Jobs-housing balancing and regional mobility", *American Planning Association Journal*, Vol. 55, No. 2.

Choe, Sang-Chuel. 1990. "Growth management of mega-cities", *Journal of Environmental Studies*, No. 27, Seoul National University.

Chung, H. S. and D. S. Lee (eds). 1996. *Globalization and Housing Industry*. Seoul: Korea Housing Institute.

Downs, Anthony. 1992. *Stuck in Traffic*. Washington, DC: Brookings Institution.

Economic Planning Board. 1960, 1966, 1970, 1975, 1980, 1985, 1990, and 1995. *Population and Housing Census*. Seoul: Economic Planning Board (in Korean).

Economic Planning Board. 1973, 1978, 1983, 1988, and 1993. *Mining and Manufacturing Census*. Seoul: Economic Planning Board (in Korean).

Economic Planning Board. 1981, 1986, 1991, and 1996. *Comprehensive Survey of Industries*. Seoul: Economic Planning Board (in Korean).

Friedmann, John. 1998. "Rethinking urban competition and sustainability in East Asia", paper presented at SMF 1998, University of Seoul, Korea.

Hahn, Yeong-Joo. 1997. *Spatial Structure of Business Services in Seoul*. Seoul: Seoul Development Institute (in Korean).

Hong, S. W. 1997. *Building a Power House: Korea Experiences of Regional Development and Infrastructure*. Seoul: KRIHS Press.

Hwang, K. Y. and B. S. Son. 1997. "The effectiveness of congestion pricing in Seoul", *Journal of East Asian Transportation Society*, Vol. 1.

Kim, Kwang Joong. 1997. *Substandard Housing Redevelopment in Seoul (1973–1996)*. Seoul: Seoul Development Institute (in Korean).

Kim, Kwang-Sik. 1995. "Growth management measures and industrial location patterns in the capital region", in G. Y. Lee and H. S. Kim (eds) *Cities and Nation*. Anyang, Korea: KRIHS Press.

Klaassen, Leo, W. Molle and J. Paelink. 1981. *Dynamics of Urban Development*. New York: St Martins Press.

Korea Research Institute for Human Settlements. 1980. *Ad Hoc Survey on the Behaviour of Residential Location in Seoul*. Unpublished report (in Korean).

Korea Research Institute for Human Settlements. 1997. *Social Overhead Capital Statistics*. Anyang, Korea: KRIHS Press.

Korean Ministry of Construction. 1984. *Growth Management Plan for the Capital Region*. Seoul: Ministry of Construction (in Korean).

Korean Ministry of Finance and Economy. 1996. *Financial Statistics*. Various issues. Kwachon: Ministry of Finance and Economy (in Korean).

Kwon, Won-yong. 1981. "Seoul: A dynamic metropolis", in M. Honjo (ed.) *Urbanization and Regional Development*. Singapore: Maruzen Asia, pp. 297–329.

Kwon, Won-yong. 1987. "Population decentralization from Seoul and regional development", in H. W. Richardson and M. C. Hwang (eds) *Urbanization and Regional Policy in Korea and International Experience*. Seoul: Kon-kuk University Press.

Lee, Bun Song. 1998. "Land-use regulations and efficiency of Seoul's economy", paper presented at SMF 1998, University of Seoul, Korea.

Lee, Gun Young and Hyun-Sik Kim. 1995. *Cities and Nation*. Anyang, Korea: KRIHS Press.

Lo, Fu-chen and Yue-man Yeung (eds). 1996. *Emerging World Cities in Pacific Asia*. Tokyo: United Nations University Press.

Park, Sang-Woo. 1996. *A Study of Office Buildings in Large Cities*. Seoul: KRIHS Press (in Korean).

Rimmer, Peter J. Undated. "International transport and communications interactions between Pacific Asia's emerging world cities." Unpublished manuscript.

SaKong, Il. 1993. *Korea in the World Economy*. Washington, DC: Institute for International Economics.

Sassen, Saskia. 1995. "Urban impacts of economic globalization", in John Brotchie and Mike Batty (eds) *Cities in Competition*. Melbourne: Longman.

Seoul Metropolitan Government. 1997. *The Comprehensive Development Plan for Seoul*. Seoul: Seoul Metropolitan Government (in Korean).

Stocker, Gerry and S. Young. 1993. *Cities in the 1990s*. Harlow: Longman.

Stubbs, J. and G. Clarke (eds). 1996. *Megacity Management in the Asian and Pacific Region, Volumes I and II*. Manila: Asian Development Bank.

Tark, Byong Oh. 1998. "Waste reduction and recycling in Seoul", in *Proceedings of 1998 Metropolis Board of Directors Meeting (23–25 April)*, pp. 89–106.

Wright, C. L. 1992. *Fast Wheels, Slow Traffic*. Philadelphia: Temple University Press.

7

Urban population in Taiwan and the growth of the Taipei metropolitan area

Ching-lung Tsay

Introduction

The course of urbanization in Taiwan was shaped by trends in economic development and population growth. The country was fortunate in the timing of its stages of economic development relative to the timing of its post-war population growth. As detailed by Speare, Liu, and Tsay (1988), the "take-off" stage of development in the 1950s preceded the entry of the post-war baby-boom cohorts into the labour market. By the time these larger cohorts entered the labour force in the 1960s, Taiwan had proceeded to the "labour-intensive" stage of development. During the 1960s and 1970s, Taiwan developed sufficient infrastructure to provide for the rapid growth of manufacturing, which could take advantage of the sharp increase in the labour force. Since the late 1970s, Taiwan's development has been characterized as being in an "industrial upgrading" phase. In this stage, Taiwan had to adapt to increasing competition from lower-wage countries in export markets, and could no longer continue the rapid expansion of labour-intensive, export-oriented industries. In the meantime, the fertility declines of the 1960s began to have an effect on reducing the number of entrants into the labour force and keeping the labour supply in line with the declining demand for labour.

Economic development in Taiwan was accompanied by a significant rural-urban transition in the society. In this chapter, the urbanization process in Taiwan is assessed through the examination of growth in vari-

167

ous cities, the growth of urban population, and the changes in the Taipei metropolitan area. Emphases is placed upon how urban growth in Taiwan has led to a system of cities that approximates the ideal rank-size distribution and avoids the excessive growth of a single primate city as has happened in several countries. With regard to the Taipei metropolitan area, deconcentration of growth will be investigated. This process has helped avoid some of the problems that would have occurred if more of the growth had been concentrated in the central city.

Growth of cities in Taiwan

Compared with many developing countries, the growth of cities in Taiwan has been relatively smooth. While urbanization has kept pace with industrialization, the growth has been distributed over both time and space, so there have been few periods of very rapid growth and most cities have shared in the process. Urban growth in Taiwan was due to both the multiplication of cities and the growth of the population of existing cities. The data in Table 7.1 demonstrate that, in 1960, there were fewer than 10 cities in the country with a population of over 100,000. This number increased to 14 in 1970, 22 in 1980, and 30 in 1990. The national urban population increased from 1.6 million in 1950 to 5.3 million in 1970 and 11.3 million in 1990. It accounted for 21 per cent, 36 per cent, and 55 per cent of the total Taiwanese population in these three years, respectively.

In addition to population increases, the overall growth of cities also includes the reclassification of population resulting from the addition of new cities and the boundary expansion of existing cities. The expansion of Taipei city in 1931 and 1968 is partially responsible for the high growth rate of 11.8 per cent in the 1930s and 6.6 per cent in the 1960s (Table 7.1). The annual growth of these cities when measured within constant boundaries varied from 2.3 per cent to 5.6 per cent, with the most rapid growth occurring in the period from the end of the Second World War to around 1970. While growth during this period was high, it never exceeded 6.0 per cent and about half of this growth was due to the high rate of natural increase (Speare, Liu, and Tsay 1988). Considering the rapid industrialization during this period, the urban growth rate was quite modest.

Much of the urban growth was concentrated in the two major cities of Taipei and Kaohsiung, and in the cities and towns surrounding Taipei. However, there was also a considerable amount of growth in cities and urban areas elsewhere on the island. Unlike many Asian countries where the capital city has grown much more rapidly than other cities and has become a "primate city", the distribution of cities by size in Taiwan conforms

Table 7.1 Growth of the total population of Taiwan and cities of over 100,000 inhabitants, 1920–1990

Year	Total population (000s)	Average annual growth in previous period %	Number of cities over 100,000	Population (000s) in cities over 100,000	Average annual growth in preceding period		% of total population in cities
					Overall %	Constant boundaries %	
1920	3,655		1	163			4.5
1930	4,593	2.3	1	231	3.5	3.5	5.0
1940	5,872	2.5	4	701	11.8	4.2	11.9
1950	7,554	2.6	7	1,560	8.3	5.6	20.7
1960	10,792	3.6	9	1,795	6.0	5.3	25.9
1970	14,676	3.1	14	5,282	6.6	4.7	36.0
1980	17,805	2.0	22	8,396	4.7	3.5	47.2
1985	19,258	1.6	25	9,772	3.1	2.4	50.4
1990	20,359	1.1	30	11,287	2.9	2.3	55.4
1995	21,304	0.9	30	11,729	0.8		54.9

Sources: 1920–1985: Speare, Liu, and Tsay 1988
1990: MOE 1991
1995: MOE 1996

well to the ideal rank-size distribution (Speare, Liu, and Tsay 1988). One underlying reason for this distribution has been the development of intermediate cities.

Intermediate or secondary cities are typically defined as those ranging in size from 100,000 to about 500,000 inhabitants (Rondinelli 1983). Many intermediate cities are regional metropolises that play a key function in the national system of cities between the major functional cities and smaller cities. Others are industrial cities which are important centres of manufacturing but which are not as important in the coordination of regional economic activities (Meyer 1984). In this analysis, the focus is on the 17 cities that were officially designated as county-level cities in 1980. They correspond fairly closely to the list of places with populations of 100,000 to 500,000. The growth of this set of cities is presented in Table 7.2. Between 1960 and 1990, the population living in the 17 cities increased more than threefold from 1.3 million to 4.3 million.

The growth of the intermediate cities was about the same as that of the

Table 7.2 Population and growth, large and intermediate cities, 1980

	1960	1970	1980	1985	1990	1995
			Population in 000s			
Large cities[a]	2,435	3,845	4,945	5,477	5,880	5,988
Intermediate cities	1,306	2,093	3,430	3,923	4,290	4,505
Old cities	671	915	1,046	1,149	1,197	1,241
New cities						
Around Taipei	314	664	1,541	1,814	2,042	2,119
Other new cities	320	514	842	960	1,052	1,145
All cities	3,701	5,938	8,375	9,400	10,170	10,493
		Average % annual growth in preceding period				
Large cities		4.7	2.6	2.1	1.4	0.4
Intermediate cities		4.8	5.1	2.7	1.8	1.0
Old cities		3.2	1.3	1.9	0.8	0.7
New cities						
Around Taipei		7.8	8.8	3.3	2.4	0.7
Other new cities		4.8	5.1	2.6	1.8	1.7
All cities		4.7	3.5	2.3	1.6	0.6

Source: Speare, Liu, and Tsay 1988; MOE 1991, 1996
a. Large cities are Taipei, Kaohsiung, Taichung, Tainan, and Keelung. The population of all except Keelung exceeded 500,000 in 1980. The old intermediate cities include all of those classified as cities by 1960. These include Hsinchu, Chiayi, Pingtung, Changhwa, Ilan, and Hualien. The new cities around Taipei are Sanchung, Panchiao, Chungho, Yungho, Hsinchuang, and Hsintien. The other new cities are Fengshan, Taoyuan, Chungli, Fengyuan, and Taitung.

five large cities in Taiwan during the 1960s, when natural increase was high. With the decline in natural increase in the 1970s, the rate of growth of the large cities decreased to 2.6 per cent per year, while the intermediate cities grew at almost twice that rate. In the 1980s, growth rates for both large and intermediate cities declined, although the intermediate cities continued to grow more rapidly than the large cities.

The growth of the intermediate cities, however, was not entirely uniform. The old cities – those that had been designated as county-level cities by 1960 – grew much more slowly than the newer cities. During the 1970s, the old cities had an average annual growth rate of only 1.3 per cent, which was considerably below the national rate of natural increase (1.94 per cent). In late 1980s, the rate was below 1.0 per cent. Some of these cities, such as Hsinchu and Chiayi, were older manufacturing centres in which few expanding industries had located. Others, such as Pingtung, Hualien, and Ilan, were small regional centres in regions that did not attract much new economic activity during that period.

The new intermediate cities fall into two categories. Six of these cities are located around Taipei city. While the population of these satellite cities has grown significantly since 1960, they are more than residential suburbs. Much of the new industrial development in Taiwan has taken place in these cities. Between 1960 and 1990, the population of these cities increased almost sevenfold. The other five new cities are scattered throughout Taiwan. Two of these (Fengyuan and Fengshan) are satellite to other large cities (Taichung and Kaohsiung), while two others (Taoyuan and Chungli) are major manufacturing centres not far from Taipei. The other city, Taitung, is a regional centre on the east coast. As a group, these other new cities grew at rates about equal to the average for all the intermediate cities – much faster than the old cities, but considerably slower than the cities surrounding the Taipei municipality.

The urban population

Research and planning for urban and regional development requires accurate information on the volume and distribution of population by rural-urban classification. Due to the lack of a set of consistent urban definitions, previous studies in Taiwan usually adopted one of three criteria for categorizing the urban population: non-agricultural population; population of all the cities and urban townships designated by the administrative system; or population of cities and any townships over a specific size (for example, 50,000 inhabitants). While these classifications serve particular purposes, they are far from approximating a satisfactory definition (Tsay 1982). To develop a standard classification system of statistical areas for Taiwan, the government initiated two research projects employing data from 1972 and 1980 (Liu 1975; Tsay 1982).

The classification system was officially adopted on an experimental basis in July 1983. After some minor changes, the system was then formally implemented in June 1985. Using data from 1991, the first revised version of the standard classification system of statistical areas for Taiwan was published in 1993 (DGBAS 1993). Basically, the revised system followed the idea of classification developed by the two pilot studies. However, some criteria were changed and several procedures were refined (*ibid.*). This chapter utilizes the comparable part of the results from the three data sources to examine the growth patterns of the urban population in Taiwan and its four regions between 1972 and 1980 and between 1980 and 1991.

In the standard classification system, a locality is defined as one or more adjacent small administrative units of *lis* or *chuns*, which are within the boundaries of a city or township and meet at least one of the following four urban characteristics specified by the criteria. They must have a threshold proportion of employment in the secondary and tertiary industries of 60 per cent or above; at least three urban facilities such as kindergarten, school, park, hospital, clinic, post office, cinema, or township government; a density of 2,000 or more residents per square kilometre; or boundaries that are adjacent on three sides to other *lis* or *chuns*.

Under this system, any *li* or *chun* in Taiwan should either belong to a locality or be part of non-localities. By the new set of urban definitions, all the localities with populations of 500,000 or more registered inhabitants are the major cities, those with populations between 100,000 and 500,000 are the intermediate cities, and those with populations between 20,000 and 100,000 are the small cities. All the major, intermediate, and small cities as a whole are classified as the urban places of Taiwan. The other areas of Taiwan, including localities with less than 20,000 population and non-localities, are considered rural places. The cut-off point between what is considered urban and what is considered a rural locality is not fixed at 20,000, but is set at the point deemed most appropriate to a particular purpose.

According to the new scheme, the classification of rural-urban places is based upon major economic activities, population size, population density, and types of settlements, but is independent of the administrative status of places (a city, urban township, or rural township). Nevertheless, a city is always confined within the administrative boundaries of the officially delimited city or township to which the newly defined city belongs. It is evident that the new system covers a wide range of objective criteria. Using the new definitions, the data on Taiwan's urban population growth and distribution reveal a more precise picture of events than was known previously.

The growth and distribution of the urban population

Table 7.3 presents the number and population of all localities in Taiwan, by size and region, for the three years of 1972, 1980, and 1991. There were 67 cities (localities of more than 20,000 residents) with a total of 7.7 million people in 1972. The urban population accounted for half of the total for Taiwan. The total area of the 67 cities (1,914 square kilometres) was only 5.3 per cent of the total land surface, resulting in a density of almost 4,000 persons per square kilometre. By 1980, the number of cities grew to 90 with a total population of 11 million. This volume of registered residents raised the cities' share of the total population of Taiwan from 50.1 per cent to 62.1 per cent during the eight-year period. The total urban area encompassed 2,628 square kilometres (7.4 per cent of Taiwan's land surface), and increased the urban density to 4,177 persons per square kilometre.

The change in urban population from 7.7 million in 1972 to 11.0 million in 1980 indicates an increase of 43.3 per cent in eight years. The group of cities with 500,000 residents and over had the largest absolute population (1.7 million) while the category of 50,000–100,000 inhabitants enjoyed the highest growth rate (82 per cent). As noted above, this category is also the one which had the largest increase in the number of cities.

In terms of geographic distribution, Table 7.4 shows that the central region has the largest number of new cities (10), followed by the northern region (seven) and the southern region (five). Among the total urban population increase, the northern region absorbed 54.9 per cent. The central region had the second largest population increment of 742,412, and registered the highest growth rate (60 per cent) among the four regions. Both the southern and eastern regions increased their urban population by 31 per cent.

The data in Table 7.4 further reveal that the major increase of urban population in the northern region occurred in the category of intermediate cities of 100,000–500,000 people (an increase of almost 1.2 million). Both the central and southern regions share the same pattern of having most of their urban growth resulting from the entry of a city into the category of major cities with more than half a million population. Another pattern discovered for the two regions is that both have a significant growth in the category of minor cities of 50,000–100,000 residents.

Table 7.5 presents the results for Taiwan, using 1972, 1980, and 1991 data. The structure of size distribution of cities in the whole of Taiwan

Table 7.3 Number and population for cities and localities by size and region, 1972, 1980, and 1991

Size of locality (000s)	All Taiwan			Northern region			Central region			Southern region			Eastern region		
	No.	Population	%	No.	Population	%	No.	Population	%	No.	Population	%	No.	Population	%
1972															
500+	2	2,792,947	18.3	1	1,890,760	35	0	–	–	1	902,187	18.0	–	–	–
100–500	13	2,780,394	18.2	7	1,271,276	23.5	2	556,193	13.2	4	952,925	19.0	0	–	–
50–100	12	823,778	5.4	6	404,669	7.5	2	154,920	3.7	2	106,323	2.1	2	157,866	25.0
30–50	22	827,469	5.4	8	316,156	5.8	10	361,022	8.5	4	150,291	3.0	0	–	–
20–30	18	435,699	2.9	6	144,519	2.7	7	160,894	3.8	5	130,286	2.6	0	–	–
All cities	67	7,660,287	50.1	28	4,027,380	74.5	21	1,233,029	29.2	16	2,242,012	44.7	2	157,866	25.0
5–20	147	1,465,438	9.6	27	288,815	5.3	50	491,084	11.7	57	561,504	11.2	13	124,035	19.6
Less than 5	276	674,785	4.4	52	111,873	2.1	90	241,850	5.7	111	268,188	5.4	23	52,847	8.3
All localities	490	9,800,510	64.1	107	4,428,068	81.9	161	1,965,963	46.5	184	3,071,704	61.2	38	334,748	52.9
Non-localities	–	5,488,565	35.9	–	978,984	18.1	–	2,261,266	53.5	–	1,950,716	38.8	–	297,599	47.1
Total	490	15,289,048	100.0	107	5,407,052	100.0	161	4,227,229	100.0	184	5,022,420	100.0	38	632,347	100.0
1980															
500+	4	4,481,923	25.4	1	2,202,704	31.9	1	556,163	12.1	2	1,723,056	31.1	0	–	–
100–500	16	3,435,622	19.4	10	2,440,457	35.4	2	270,333	5.9	3	622,260	11.2	1	102,572	16.2
50–100	23	1,501,931	8.5	10	665,194	9.6	8	519,583	11.3	4	243,453	4.4	1	73,701	11.6
30–50	25	1,017,188	5.8	11	462,800	6.7	9	370,463	8	5	183,925	3.3	0	–	–
20–30	22	538,931	3	3	76,755	1.1	11	258,899	5.6	7	173,378	3.1	1	29,919	4.7
All cities	90	10,975,595	62.1	35	5,847,890	84.7	31	1,975,441	42.9	21	2,946,072	53.2	3	206,192	32.5
5–20	86	887,652	5	16	170,965	2.5	30	307,451	6.7	36	371,330	6.7	4	37,906	6.0
Less than 5	169	403,868	2.3	33	89,959	1.3	51	129,578	2.8	65	138,365	2.5	20	45,966	7.2
All localities	345	12,267,115	69.4	84	6,108,814	88.6	112	2,412,470	52.3	122	3,455,767	62.4	27	290,064	45.7
Non-localities	–	5,412,891	30.6	–	785,927	11.4	–	2,196,839	47.7	–	2,085,972	37.6	–	344,153	54.3
Total	345	17,680,006	100.0	84	6,894,741	100.0	112	4,609,309	100.0	122	5,541,739	100.0	27	634,217	100.0

1991

	No.	Population	%	No.	Population	%	No.	Population	%	No.	Population	%	No.	Population	%
500+	5	6,062,872	29.5	2	3,252,180	37.3	1	757,736	14.7	2	2,057,733	33.9	0	–	–
100–500	24	5,051,333	24.6	14	3,365,131	38.6	5	688,147	13.3	4	879,663	14.5	1	106,007	17.4
50–100	31	2,019,423	9.8	12	835,381	9.6	12	717,208	13.9	5	332,448	5.5	2	134,386	22.0
30–50	24	911,112	4.4	6	258,015	3.0	10	361,905	7.0	8	291,192	4.8	0	–	–
20–30	21	516,702	2.5	3	65,701	0.8	6	157,253	3.0	11	271,964	4.5	1	21,784	3.6
All cities	105	14,554,017	70.8	37	7,776,408	89.1	34	2,682,249	52.0	30	3,833,000	63.2	4	262,177	42.9
5–20	91	940,612	4.6	20	205,140	2.4	28	317,397	6.1	36	359,945	5.9	7	58,130	9.5
Less than 5	255	557,771	2.7	39	90,567	1.0	86	207,508	4.0	96	183,176	3.0	34	76,520	12.5
All localities	451	16,052,400	78.1	96	8,072,115	92.5	148	3,207,154	62.1	162	4,376,121	72.1	45	396,827	65.0
Non-localities	–	4,504,442	21.9	–	651,373	7.5	–	1,955,264	37.9	–	1,691,058	27.9	–	213,598	35.0
Total	451	20,556,842	100.0	96	8,723,488	100.0	148	5,162,418	100.0	162	6,067,179	100.0	45	610,425	100.0

Table 7.4 Indicators of urban growth by city size and region, 1972–1991

Region and city size (000s)	Increase in no. of cities		Population growth		Increase in proportion urban		Increase in urban area	
	No.	%	Persons	%	Points	%	km²	%
			1972–1980					
Taiwan	23	34.3	3,315,308	43.3	12.0	24.0	697	36.2
500+	2		1,688,976	60.5				
100–500	3		655,228	23.6				
50–100	11		678,153	82.3				
30–50	3		189,719	22.3				
20–30	4		103,232	23.7				
North	7	25.0	1,820,510	45.2	10.2	13.7	319	34.4
500+	0		311,944	16.5				
100–500	3		1,169,181	92.0				
50–100	4		260,525	64.4				
30–50	3		146,644	46.4				
20–30	–3		–67,784	–46.9				
Central	10	47.6	742,412	60.2	13.8	47.3	255	62.9
500+	1		556,163	N/A				
100–500	0		–285,860	–51.4				
50–100	6		364,663	235.1				
30–50	–1		9,441	2.6				
20–30	4		98,005	60.9				
South	5	31.3	704,060	31.4	8.4	18.8	81	14.7
500+	1		820,869	91.0				
100–500	–1		–330,665	–34.7				
50–100	2		137,130	129.0				
30–50	1		33,634	22.4				
20–30	2		43,092	33.1				
East	1	50.0	48,326	30.6	7.5	30.0	43	109.4
100–500	1		102,572	N/A				
50–100	–1		–84,165	–53.3				
30–50	0		–	–				
20–30	1		29,919	N/A				

1980–1991

Taiwan	15	16.7	3,585,847	32.7	8.7	14.0	549.0	20.9
500+	1		1,580,949	35.3				
100–500	8		1,615,711	47.0				
50–100	8		517,492	34.5				
30–50	−1		−106,076	−10.4				
20–30	−1		−22,229	−4.1				
North	2	5.7	1,928,498	33.0	4.4	5.2	122.9	9.9
500+	1		1,049,476	47.6				
100–500	4		924,674	37.9				
50–100	2		170,187	25.6				
30–50	−5		−204,785	−44.2				
20–30	0		−11,054	−1.4				
Central	3	9.7	706,808	35.8	9.1	21.2	87.7	13.2
500+	0		201,573	36.2				
100–500	3		417,814	154.6				
50–100	4		197,625	38.0				
30–50	1		−8,558	−2.7				
20–30	−5		−101,646	−39.3				
South	9	42.9	886,928	30.1	10.0	18.9	246.8	38.9
500+	0		334,677	19.4				
100–500	1		257,403	41.4				
50–100	1		88,995	36.6				
30–50	3		107,267	58.3				
20–30	4		98,586	56.9				
East	2	66.7	55,985	27.2	10.4	32.0	91.6	109.0
100–500	0		3,435	3.3				
50–100	1		60,685	82.3				
30–50	0		—	–				
20–30	1		−8,135	−27.2				

Table 7.5 Estimates of rank-size rule parameters for regions in Taiwan, 1972, 1980, and 1991

Year	Estimates	Taiwan	North	Central	South	East
1972	a′	1.05304	1.1774	0.84527	1.40952	–
	b′	6.23283	6.05126	5.38825	5.98764	–
	r	−0.9977	−0.9864	−0.9631	−0.9897	–
	R^2	0.9953	0.973	0.9277	0.9794	–
	n	67	28	21	16	2
1980	a′	1.02781	1.12034	0.81228	1.36757	–
	b′	6.36602	6.20015	5.5342	6.06372	–
	r	−0.9951	−0.9812	−0.978	−0.9911	–
	R^2	0.9902	0.9627	0.9566	0.9823	–
	n	90	35	31	21	3
1991	a′	1.05346	1.16382	0.81288	1.24619	–
	b′	6.520672	6.375983	5.64965	6.08448	–
	r	−0.9943	−0.9663	−0.9822	−0.9895	–
	R^2	0.9886	0.9336	0.9636	0.9792	–
	n	105	37	34	30	4

Note: a′ and b′ are the two parameters in $\log P = -a' \log R + b'$, where P is the population size of a city, and R is the rank of the city in the region. r represents the correlation coefficient between $\log R$ and $\log P$. n denotes the number of cities.

conforms to the rank-size rule for all three years. The estimated values for the slope of the regression line are rather close to negative unity. With the sole exception of the eastern region, the regional structures of city distributions are all of the rank-size rule type. The southern region has the highest degree of fit, followed by the northern and central regions. The eastern region has too few cities to permit a detailed analysis. Notwithstanding the inability to uphold the rank-size rule throughout Taiwan, the data clearly suggest that the rule does hold at least among the three major regions on the west side of the country.

The Taipei metropolitan area

The previous section has demonstrated that, during the 1970s, population increase in the major cities in Taiwan slowed while the intermediate and small cities continued to grow. The shift was most noticeable in the northern region, which contains the capital city of Taipei. Utilizing the unique data available, this section examines the patterns of population change in the various parts of the Taipei metropolitan area. The purpose is to study the Taipei case as an example of suburbanization. This case study is important since it provides, with rich data analysis, for a level of detail rarely found in the developing world.

The Taipei metropolitan area is an agglomeration of several administrative units, including Taipei municipality as the central city, a Taiwan provincial city named Keelung, and 12 county cities, four urban townships, and four rural townships in Taipei county, which encloses Taipei municipality (Figure 7.1). In the Taipei municipality, three rings can be conveniently distinguished according to the history of changes in the city boundaries. The historical area of the central business district, which comprises four precincts, was the originating core of the city. It was within this area that the seat of administration chosen by the Ching dynasty and the colonial government of Japan located. In 1931, the official boundaries of the city were pushed outward and six precincts were merged. Between 1954 and 1956, Taipei was the provincial capital of Taiwan. In 1967, the status of the city in administrative hierarchy was upgraded, and it became a municipality under the direct jurisdiction of the central government. It was in the following year that the municipal boundaries were expanded. As a result, six townships adjacent to the city on the north, east, and south-east lost their administrative affiliation with Taipei county and were converted to form precincts of the municipal city. This addition brought the total to 16 precincts for Taipei municipality.

The metropolitan areas outside the Taipei municipality are divided into two categories: the surrounding urbanized areas, and the surrounding metropolitan areas. The surrounding metropolitan areas include Keelung city and two urban townships. Keelung, a major harbour with 350,000 population, is a trade outlet 26 kilometres north-east of Taipei. One of the towns (Tanshui) is the site of a much smaller sea port north of Taipei, while the other (Juifang) is adjacent to Keelung in the east.

The set of urbanized areas surrounding on the southern, western, and north-eastern sides of the Taipei municipality are composed of six county cities and six townships. In the 1980s, the population of each of the six cities ranged from approximately 200,000 to 500,000. Administratively, only two of the six townships were designated as urban, and the rest were rural.

The data on the population of the Taipei metropolitan area and the various rings within the metropolis are presented in Table 7.6 for selected years from 1920 to 1984. The number of registered residents of the total metropolitan area was less than half a million in 1970. The population grew rather slowly, and did not reach 1 million until 1950. However, the population tripled its size in the 20 years after 1950, averaging an annual growth at the high level of 5–6 per cent. Between 1970 and 1980, the area

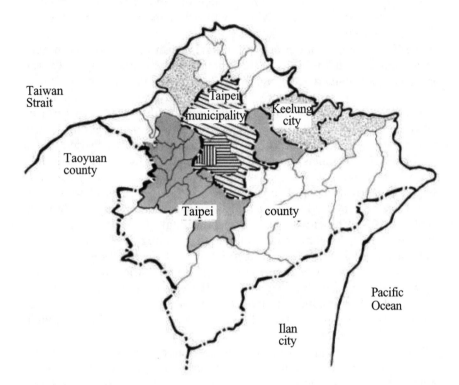

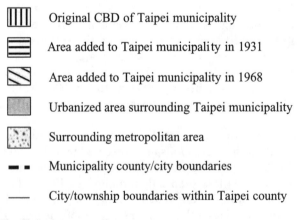

	Original CBD of Taipei municipality
	Area added to Taipei municipality in 1931
	Area added to Taipei municipality in 1968
	Urbanized area surrounding Taipei municipality
	Surrounding metropolitan area
▬ ▪	Municipality county/city boundaries
───	City/township boundaries within Taipei county

Figure 7.1 The Taipei metropolitan area

Table 7.6 Growth of the Taipei metropolitan area, 1920–1990

Year	Original central business district	Areas added in 1931	Areas added in 1968	Total Taipei city	Rest of urban area	Rest of metro-politan area	Total metro-politan area
	Population (000s)						
1920	109	66	49	224	116	89	428
1930	131	115	56	302	128	126	555
1940	^a	326	66	392	147	188	726
1950	213	291	112	616	210	221	1,046
1960	255	644	198	1,097	429	333	1,860
1970	262	1,113	394	1,770	853	447	3,070
1980	179	1,295	746	2,220	1,854	477	4,551
1985	173	1,397	938	2,508	2,227	484	5,219
1990	168	1,470	1,066	2,704	2,610	489	5,803
	% annual growth in preceding period[b]						
1930	1.8	5.7	1.4	3.0	1.0	3.6	2.6
1940	^a	2.9	1.6	2.7	1.4	4.1	2.7
1950	^a	4.4	5.5	4.6	3.7	1.6	3.7
1960	1.8	8.3	5.9	5.9	7.4	4.2	5.9
1970	0.3	5.6	7.1	4.9	7.1	3.0	5.1
1980	−3.7	1.5	6.6	2.3	8.1	0.6	4.0
1985	−0.8	1.5	4.7	2.5	3.7	0.3	2.8
1990	−0.6	1.0	2.6	1.5	3.2	0.2	2.1

Sources: 1920–1985: Speare, Liu, and Tsay 1988, p. 65
             1990: MOE 1991
a. Combined with population in areas added in 1931.
b. Based on the formula: $r = 100*(EXP(\ln(P2/P1)/n) - 1)$, where n denotes the number of years in the period.

increased its population size by 48 per cent from 3.1 million to 4.6 million at an average growth rate of 4 per cent per year. After 1980, the speed of growth declined to below 2.9 per cent per year. The population increased 12 per cent from 4.6 million in 1980 to 5.1 million in 1984. Table 7.7 shows that the share of the growth accounted for by net migration decreased from 52 per cent in 1973–1978 to 43 per cent in 1978–1983.

The population within the municipal boundaries was more than half the size of the total metropolitan areas in 1970 and before (Table 7.6). It is also clear that the municipal area grew faster than the metropolitan area before the 1950s. After 1960, the municipality growth slowed to a rate consistently lower than that of the whole metropolis, while the latter was declining as well. Undoubtedly, these changes in growth patterns

Table 7.7 Decomposition of population change for Taipei metropolitan area, 1973–1993

	Population change	Natural increase	Net migration
1973–1978			
CBD (pre-1930)	−41,218	16,147 (−39.2)	−57,365 (139.2)
Areas added in 1931	67,255	101,817 (151.4)	−34,562 (−51.4)
Areas added in 1968	179,172	58,242 (32.5)	120,930 (67.5)
Current municipality	205,209	176,206 (85.9)	29,003 (14.1)
Surrounding urbanized areas	555,264	153,975 (27.7)	401,289 (72.3)
Surrounding metropolitan areas	11,124	38,466 (345.8)	−27,342 (−245.8)
Total metropolitan area	771,597	368,647 (47.8)	402,950 (52.2)
Taoyuan-Chungli urbanized area	163,588	69,400 (42.4)	94,188 (57.6)
1978–1983			
CBD (pre-1930)	−19,721	12,003 (−60.1)	−31,724 (−160.1)
Areas added in 1931	59,093	91,995 (155.7)	−32,902 (−55.7)
Areas added in 1968	185,397	70,262 (37.9)	115,135 (62.1)
Current municipality	224,769	174,260 (77.5)	50,509 (22.5)
Surrounding urbanized areas	491,457	206,113 (41.9)	285,344 (58.1)
Surrounding metropolitan areas	11,542	36,717 (318.1)	−25,175 (−218.1)
Total metropolitan area	727,768	417,090 (57.3)	310,678 (42.7)
Taoyuan-Chungli urbanized area	184,707	82,687 (44.8)	102,020 (55.2)
1983–1988			
CBD (pre-1930)	−9,675	5,174 (53.5)	−14,849 (153.5)
Areas added in 1931	111,064	58,769 (52.9)	52,295 (47.1)
Areas added in 1968	192,094	59,209 (30.8)	132,885 (69.2)
Current municipality	293,483	123,152 (42.0)	170,331 (58.0)
Surrounding urbanized areas	363,946	166,567 (45.8)	197,379 (54.2)
Surrounding metropolitan areas	−3,189	24,278 (−761.3)	−27,467 (861.3)
Total metropolitan area	654,240	313,997 (48.0)	340,243 (52.0)
Taoyuan-Chungli urbanized area	127,917	85,234 (66.6)	42,683 (33.4)

were related to what happened in the three rings within the municipality and in the two component parts outside the boundaries of current Taipei city, as will be explained.

In the early years, the areas surrounding the city were rural in charac-

Table 7.7 (cont.)

	Population change	Natural increase	Net migration
1988–1993			
CBD (pre-1930)	–	–	–
Areas added in 1931	–	–	–
Areas added in 1968	–	–	–
Current municipality	−28,612	−25455 (89.0)	−3,157 (11.0)
Surrounding urbanized areas	290,836	165,640 (57.0)	125,196 (43.1)
Surrounding metropolitan areas	26,077	24,141 (92.6)	1,936 (7.4)
Total metropolitan area	288,301	418,590 (145.2)	−130,289 (−45.2)
Taoyuan-Chungli urbanized area	159,560	86,309 (54.1)	73,251 (45.9)

Note: Figures in parenthese denote the relative weights in percentages of natural increase and net migration to population change.

ter. The population of these areas did not start to increase significantly until the end of the Second World War (Table 7.6). During that era, they were presumably the areas of out-migration to Taipei. In the three decades following 1950, however, the urbanized areas had remarkably high rates of growth, ranging from 7.1 per cent to 8.1 per cent annually. From 1980 to 1984, the rate declined to 4.0 per cent, which is still higher than that of the metropolitan area or the municipality. In the two decades before 1970, the population residing in the urbanized areas accounted for less than a quarter of the metropolitan areas as a whole, even though the growth rate of the former was high. From 1980, the share increased dramatically to be over 40 per cent, due to the impact of population growth rates that reached record highs of 8.1 per cent in the 1970s.

During the period 1950–1980, Taiwan became a newly industrializing country. The urbanized areas surrounding Taipei were also the areas of concentrated manufacturing establishments. In the early stage, secondary industries provided employment opportunities for those who had been pushed out of the agricultural sector due to high population-land ratios resulting from demographic transition. In latter years, factories absorbed the excess labour released by agricultural mechanization and shrinkage in the primary sector. The surrounding urbanized areas were destinations for many migrants looking for off-farm jobs. As shown in Table 7.7, net migration accounted for 72 per cent of the population increase in the urbanized areas between 1973 and 1978, and for 58 per cent in the period from 1978 to 1983.

As noted earlier, the surrounding metropolitan areas include Keelung, Tanshui, and Juifang. The first two are harbours with long histories and the latter was a major site of mining in the early years. Before 1940, these three places grew faster than both the total metropolitan population and the population within the municipality boundaries (Table 7.6), suggesting some net inflow of people. In recent years, however, the areas increased their total population at an average rate of less than 1 per cent per year. This observation indicates a substantial amount of net out-migration, which almost offsets all the natural increase. Table 7.7 provides confirmation by giving the estimated net migration for 1973–1978.

The findings stated above conform to the fact that the three surrounding metropolitan areas were places developed rather early, and that at least two of them are unique in having quite specific limitations to growth. Before the 1970s, the population of Keelung city seemed to have reached a maximum under its given geographic constraints and easy access from Taipei municipality. Juifang has been in a stagnant stage in terms of development since the extinction of mines there in the 1960s.

The population growth of the pre-1930 central business district (CBD) was rather low and reached a level of almost no increase in the 1960s. Thereafter, the CBD population decreased at 3.7 per cent on average for each year in the 1970–1980 decade. In recent years, the rate of decrease declined dramatically and the population is currently, once again, approaching the zero growth level. The district will probably continue having a constant population size for the foreseeable future. The data in Table 7.6 reveal a significant net migration out of the historical CBD in the whole study period, especially after 1970. Table 7.7 further indicates that the net out-migration from the district was 3.6 times the natural increase in 1973–1978. The decline of this quotient to 2.6 times for 1978–1983 indicates the diminishing relative importance of net migration in population change. This finding is also evidenced by the substantial decrease in net out-migration away from the CBD (from 57,365 to 31,724).

As mentioned earlier, the historical CBD is composed of four precincts that make up the original Taipei, the so-called "Taipei inner city". Population growth brought the district to a level of overcrowding in the 1950s. From the 1960s, within this area the city implemented many projects to renew inadequate settlements, accompanied by various programmes to develop new communities in the outer rings of the city. These are some possible explanations for the sudden and temporary, but striking, rate of population decrease observed during the 1970–1980 period. As the centre of Taipei city moved towards the newly expanded areas in the east, the original CBD retained some of its importance by being filled with retail businesses.

The areas added to Taipei city in 1931 grew faster in terms of population than the current municipal areas during the years before 1970. In particular, the average annual growth rate of 8.3 per cent for 1960–1970 is the highest found in Table 7.6. After 1970, however, the increase rate became lower than that of the Taipei municipality, and has stayed at 1.5 per cent since then. Table 7.7 further shows that net migration offset one-third of the natural increase observed for the areas in the years after 1973. This is probably due to the complete development of the areas and the new expansion to the areas added to the municipality in 1968.

The six precincts which joined the city in 1931 are important parts of the Taipei municipality. As the original CBD became old and crowded, the centre of the city started to move eastwards in the 1960s. While the six precincts have many residential communities, two of them (Chung Shan and Sung Shan) have become new centres of commerce, finance, and modern service industries. Another two precincts (Ta-an and Ku-ting) have become mixtures of residential, commercial, and educational areas.

The areas mostly recently annexed to Taipei municipality in 1968 did not grow fast until 1940 (Table 7.6). In the decade during which the annexation occurred, the growth rate reached a high of 7.1 per cent per annum. It remained at a high level of 6.6 per cent in the 1970s, and then declined to 4.7 per cent for 1980–1984. Nevertheless, this rate is greater than that of any other part of the Taipei metropolitan area during the same period. It is almost twice as high as the growth rate of the municipality as a whole. According to Table 7.7, net migration accounted for three-fifths to two-thirds of the population growth in the decade 1973–1983. The migrants include those from the original CBD, the 1931 added areas, and places outside the municipality. The data, along with those discussed earlier, clearly indicate a dispersion of population within the municipality as well as intrametropolitan redistribution.

It should be noted that the six new precincts of 1968 are all large in size, including substantial hilly areas on the north, east, and south-east sides of Taipei basin. These precincts were developed mainly as residential and recreation areas as well as locations for schools. Given the high potential of these areas in terms of future development, the population growth rate is anticipated to continue at a higher level than those of other parts of the study site.

Globalization and urban development

As mentioned earlier, the pattern of urbanization in Taiwan has accompanied a similar path of industrialization within the country. The development of rural and agricultural industries in the early 1950s fostered the subsequent decentralized industrialization of labour-intensive import-substituting manufacturing (Ho 1979). This process was crucial in preventing the emergence of a primate city in Taiwan, as occurred in many other Asian countries. In later years, Taiwan quickly entered the stage of export-oriented industrialization to take advantages of the liberalization of world trade. The rapid industrialization was undoubtedly a key driving force behind urbanization and urban growth in Taiwan (Speare, Liu, and Tsay 1988; Tsai 1996). Urban development was characterized by the growth of existing major cities, the expansion to their surrounding areas, and the evolution of several intermediate cities.

In the process of economic development, the export-oriented industries sector was the engine of initial industrialization in Taiwan. Another source of industrialization is the transfer of technology via either technical cooperation with overseas companies or foreign direct investment. This type of industrialization has been particularly important in Taiwan since the 1980s. Both export-oriented manufacturing and technology-intensive industries are urban-centred and created employment opportunities mostly in major metropolitan areas. Consequently, urbanization in Taiwan was mainly induced by industrialization, while industrialization was driven by exports. In other words, the pattern of Taiwanese urban development is significantly influenced by the globalization of world economy (Tsai 1996).

Globalization and sustainable development

It is well known that the rapid development in Taiwan over the past few decades has been affected by trends of economic globalization. The success in import-substitution industrialization in the 1950s and the subsequent labour-intensive export growth is often cited as the most important example. The value of exports increased from US$1.5 billion in 1970 to US$19.8 billion in 1980, US$67.2 billion in 1990, and then reached US$110.6 billion in 1998. As a percentage of GNP, the importance of exports jumped from 30 per cent in 1970 to 53 per cent in 1980 and 60 per cent in 1998. Due to the expansion of exports, Taiwan has continuously enjoyed trade surpluses and a high level of foreign reserves. This capacity enabled the economy to develop further capital-intensive and technology-intensive industrialization in the late 1980s and 1990s. In the meanwhile, Taiwan has diversified its trading partners to enlarge the coverage of overseas markets.

While the inflow of capital is an important part of economic globalization, since the halt of US aid in 1965, neither FDI nor foreign debt has been an important source of capital in Taiwan (Tung 1999). The approved amount of FDI was only US$139 million in 1970 and US$466 million in 1980. It increased more in the late 1980s, to reach US$2.3 billion in 1990 and US$3.7 billion in 1998. In the period 1952–1997, the approved FDI accounted on average for only 4.2 per cent of the total fixed capital formation in Taiwan. Most of the FDI is involved in manufacturing industries, especially the electrical and electronics industry. The service sector did not receive much FDI until restrictions were gradually lifted in the late 1980s.

It has been argued that even though FDI was not the engine of development, it has undoubtedly expedited economic growth in Taiwan (Schive 1994). With FDI, export expansion and technology transfer are easily achieved. There are also both a theoretical base and empirical evidence for a positive effect of FDI in reducing urban unemployment (Yabuuchi 1999). These arguments are supported by the pattern of urban development presented in the previous sections.

The outward FDI from Taiwan did not become evident until the middle of the 1980s. Since then, the level of FDI has increased sharply. It surged from around US$11 million in the early 1980s to US$41 million in 1985, US$1.5 billion in 1990, and US$3.3 billion in 1998. The major reasons for the capital outflow include labour shortages and wage increases, the sharp appreciation of the Taiwanese currency during the 1985–1990 period, and rising production costs due to other factors. From 1952 to 1986, 60 per cent of the accumulated FDI went to the USA, while 32 per cent went to Asia. The US share began to decline after 1985, while the share going to ASEAN increased very rapidly. In 1993, China took over from the USA as the leading recipient of FDI from Taiwan. The relative importance of ASEAN started to drop in the early 1990s when Taiwan launched investment in China and Viet Nam (Tsay and Huang 1997).

In the 1990s, Taiwanese FDI to South-East Asia and China became very significant. For example, FDI to China in 1996 was 1.4 times the total inward FDI, while the total outward FDI was 2.3 times the FDI inflow. In terms of industrial composition, the FDI to South-East Asia headed mainly for traditional light industries, while that to China went disproportionately to labour-intensive manufacturing. Nevertheless, the share of heavy and chemical industries increased in both cases. While there are some concerns about the negative impacts of the outward capital flows, the outbound FDI facilitated industrial restructuring in the Taiwanese economy and upgrading from low-value-added to higher-value-added production (Schive 1994; Tung 1999).

In the past few decades, Taiwan has experienced dramatic change, including demographic transition, social diversification, economic liberalization, political democratization, and the legalization of importing foreign workers. After martial law was lifted in 1987, the transformation was particularly remarkable in the 1980s and 1990s. With these changes, the country has become more and more involved in the process of globalization. The evidence discussed above has pointed to the fact that globalization was important to economic development in Taiwan through fostering exports, industrial restructuring, technology transfer, and production upgrading. However, data on trade and FDI are not available for a further examination of the spatial aspect of the development process.

As professional transients are capital-assisted migrants and many foreign residents are involved in business, the phenomenon of human interactions is one major dimension of globalization. For this reason, the following presentation will focus on the distribution of foreign manpower in Taiwan. It is believed that the element of human resources from overseas can reflect the impacts of globalization in various regions of Taiwan. Table 7.8 provides the latest available data on foreign residents other than contract workers and missionaries in Taiwan by sex, occupation, and region. In 1999, the total number of employed foreign residents was 22,221, with 74 per cent females. Except for those in unspecified occupations, they are mostly traders, teachers, engineers, and technicians. There are only 216 professional managers, accountants, lawyers, reporters, physicians, and nurses.

It is not surprising to find that foreign professionals are unevenly distributed across Taiwan (Table 7.8). The northern region has the lion's share, 75 per cent, while the central and southern regions have 12 per cent each. It is also clear that the foreigners mostly live in major cities, especially Taipei municipality. The degree of concentration is particularly high in the traders group. Engineers and technicians are more spread out from the north to the centre of Taiwan. This fact reflects the pattern of industrial development and the process of urbanization, as discussed previously. In a study on the "reversal of brain drain" (Tsay and Lin 1999), it was also found that returning nationals with at least university education are highly concentrated in the northern region of Taiwan, especially Taipei city and prefecture.

The regional distribution of contract workers is very different from that of the professionals (Table 7.9). These migrant workers, mainly from Thailand, the Philippines, and Indonesia, are engaged in construction, manufacturing production, and care services (Tsay 2000). Consequently, they are not concentrated in cities, but are more spread out among the prefectures. The shares of the northern, central, and southern regions are 52 per cent, 27 per cent, and 19 per cent, respectively. The contract workers are important to the economic development of Taiwan in terms of supplying the needed workforce. They are expected to continue participating in the labour market of Taiwan in the foreseeable future.

It has been demonstrated that the northern region of Taiwan, especially the Taipei extended metropolitan area, will remain important in

Table 7.8 Spatial distribution of foreigners in Taiwan, 1990

Prefecture/city	All	Nationality			
		USA	Japan	South-East Asia	Others
	Number (persons)				
Whole Taiwan	**31,212**	**7,422**	**8,248**	**10,004**	**5,538**
Northern region	**22,127**	**4,905**	**5,765**	**7,154**	**4,303**
Taipei city (1)	16,832	3,932	5,136	4,383	3,381
Keelung city (2)	313	59	30	133	91
Hsinchu city (3)	450	202	45	108	95
Taipei prefecture (4)	3,062	464	226	1,862	510
Taoyuan prefecture (5)	1,118	170	264	545	139
Other two prefectures	352	78	64	123	87
Taipei metropolitan area (6)	**20,207**	**4,455**	**5,392**	**6,378**	**3,982**
Taipei EMA (7)	**21,325**	**4,625**	**5,656**	**6,923**	**4,121**
Central region	**3,942**	**1,384**	**977**	**1,053**	**528**
Taichung city	2,641	900	747	609	385
Other five prefectures	1,301	484	230	444	143
Southern region	**4,822**	**1,014**	**1,476**	**1,736**	**596**
Kaohsiung city	2,478	378	1,223	614	263
Tainan city	1,071	270	123	601	77
Chiayi city	177	76	38	47	16
Other five prefectures	1,096	290	92	474	240
Eastern region (two prefectures)	321	119	30	61	111
	(%)				
Whole Taiwan	**100.0**	**100.0**	**100.0**	**100.0**	**100.0**
Northern region	**70.9**	**66.1**	**69.9**	**71.5**	**77.7**
Taipei city (1)	53.9	53.0	62.3	43.8	61.1
Keelung city (2)	1.0	0.8	0.4	1.3	1.6
Hsinchu city (3)	1.4	2.7	0.5	1.1	1.7
Taipei prefecture (4)	9.8	6.3	2.7	18.6	9.2
Taoyuan prefecture (5)	3.6	2.3	3.2	5.4	2.5
Other two prefectures	1.1	1.1	0.8	1.2	1.6
Taipei metropolitan area (6)	**64.7**	**60.0**	**65.4**	**63.8**	**71.9**
Taipei EMA (7)	**68.3**	**62.3**	**68.6**	**69.2**	**74.4**
Central region	**12.6**	**18.6**	**11.8**	**10.5**	**9.5**
Taichung city	8.5	12.1	9.1	6.1	7.0
Other five prefectures	4.2	6.5	2.8	4.4	2.6
Southern region	**15.4**	**13.7**	**17.9**	**17.4**	**10.8**
Kaohsiung city	7.9	5.1	14.8	6.1	4.7
Tainan city	3.4	3.6	1.5	6.0	1.4
Chiayi city	0.6	1.0	0.5	0.5	0.3
Other five prefectures	3.5	3.9	1.1	4.7	4.3
Eastern region (two prefectures)	1.0	1.6	0.4	0.6	2.0

Source: Original records of the 1990 Taiwanese population census
Note: (6) = (1) + (2) + (4), (7) = (6) + (5).

189

Table 7.9 Regional distribution of contract workers from Thailand, the Philippines, Indonesia, and Malaysia, end February 1999

Region and city/prefecture	Persons	%
Whole Taiwan	**271,839**	**100.0**
Northern region	**142,454**	**52.4**
Taipei city (1)	24,305	8.9
Keelung city (2)	2,094	0.8
Hsinchu city (3)	8,263	3.0
Taipei prefecture (4)	37,513	13.8
Taoyuan prefecture (5)	57,798	21.3
Other two prefectures	12,481	4.6
Taipei metropolitan Area (6)	**63,912**	**23.5**
Taipei EMA (7)	**121,710**	**44.8**
Central region	**74,365**	**27.4**
Taichung city	8,037	3.0
Taichung prefecture	18598	6.8
Other four prefectures	47,730	17.6
Southern region	**51,991**	**19.1**
Kaohsiung city	11,494	4.2
Kaohsiung prefecture	11,715	4.3
Tainan city	3,784	1.4
Chiayi city	1,418	0.5
Other four prefectures	23,580	8.7
Eastern region (two prefectures)	**3,029**	**1.1**

Source: Council of Labour Affairs
Note: (6) = (1) + (2) + (4), (7) = (6) + (5).

linking economic growth and globalization. This statement can be further supported by the spatial distribution of industrial and commercial development in the past few years. As shown in Table 7.10, the northern region had 47 per cent of the total number of enterprises in Taiwan in 1996. In terms of employment and produce, however, the shares accounted for by the northern region were 54 per cent and 57 per cent, respectively. The important role played by Taipei city and the metropolitan area is evident. This finding holds true when the fixed capital growth in 1992–1996 is taken as a measure. Taipei city is important to Taiwan in terms of both development and globalization.

Taipei is also important to the regional city system in East and South-East Asia. This fact is reflected by the statistics on international air passengers presented in Table 7.11. Almost 19 million persons travelled to and from Taiwan in 1998, and 90 per cent of them used Taipei as the entry and exit port. As shown in Table 7.11, Taipei is well linked to major cities in East and South-East Asia as well as world cities in other contin-

Table 7.10 Spatial distribution of industrial and commercial development in Taiwan, 1996

Prefecture/city	Number of enterprises (establishments)	%	Number of workforce in 1996 (persons)	%	Yearly total produce in 1996 (100 million NT$)	%	Fixed capital growth in 1992–1996 (%)
Whole Taiwan	**891,661**	**100.0**	**6,578,562**	**100.0**	**134,215**	**100.0**	**100.0**
Northern region	**421,256**	**47.2**	**3,567,495**	**54.2**	**74,928**	**56.6**	**55.3**
Taipei city (1)	166,147	18.6	1,513,520	23.0	32,257	24.0	25.7
Keelung city (2)	15,179	1.7	93,727	1.4	1,481	1.1	1.2
Hsinchu city (3)	15,573	1.7	130,200	2.0	3,114	2.3	2.4
Taipei prefecture (4)	140,171	15.7	1,021,567	15.5	18,637	13.9	14.2
Taoyuan prefecture (5)	55,047	6.2	570,823	8.7	14,712	11.0	7.5
Other two prefectures	29,139	3.3	237,658	3.6	5,727	4.3	4.3
Taipei metropolitan area (6)	**321,497**	**36.1**	**2,628,814**	**40.0**	**52,375**	**39.0**	**41.1**
Taipei EMA (7)	**376,544**	**42.2**	**3,199,637**	**48.6**	**67,087**	**50.0**	**48.6**
Central region	**215,947**	**24.2**	**1,404,005**	**21.3**	**24,226**	**18.1**	**17.0**
Taichung city	50,904	5.7	352,906	5.4	5,658	4.2	4.6
Taichung prefecture	59,075	6.6	420,783	6.4	7,579	5.6	3.9
Other four prefectures	105,968	11.9	630,316	9.6	10,989	8.2	8.5
Southern region	**232,306**	**26.1**	**1,510,541**	**23.0**	**32,551**	**24.3**	**26.4**
Kaohsiung city	69,845	7.8	499,761	7.6	11,516	8.6	10.1
Kaohsiung prefecture	37,017	4.2	268,871	4.1	7,285	5.4	5.4
Tainan city	35,335	4.0	195,194	3.0	2,809	2.1	2.3
Chiayi city	13,055	1.5	66,676	1.0	1,168	0.9	0.7
Other four prefectures	77,054	8.6	480,039	7.3	9,773	7.3	8.0
Eastern region (two prefectures)	**22,152**	**2.5**	**96,521**	**1.5**	**1,510**	**1.1**	**1.3**

Source: 1996 Industry, Commerce and Service Census of Taiwan
Note: (6) = (1) + (2) + (4), (7) = (6) + (5).

Table 7.11 International air passengers to and from Taiwan, 1998

Destination	Taipei CCK		Kaohsiung		Total	
	Passengers	%	Passengers	%	Passengers	%
Grand total	**16,754,454**	**100.00**	**1,932,216**	**100.00**	**18,686,670**	**100.00**
East Asia						
Hong Kong	4,533,428	27.06	785,999	40.68	5,319,427	28.47
Macau	1,036,436	6.19	358,047	18.53	1,394,483	7.46
Tokyo	1,724,602	10.29	35,368	1.83	1,759,970	9.42
Osaka	823,825	4.92	17,974	0.93	841,799	4.50
Fukouka	462,210	2.76	–		462,210	2.47
Nagoya	369,422	2.20	–		369,422	1.98
Okinawa	227,215	1.36	–		227,215	1.22
Seoul	411,528	2.46	–		411,528	2.20
South-East Asia						
Bangkok	1,201,234	7.17	171,729	8.89	1,372,963	7.35
Singapore	882,440	5.27	149,936	7.76	1,032,376	5.52
Manila	611,422	3.65	89,154	4.61	700,576	3.75
Kuala Lumpur	426,371	2.54	48,867	2.53	475,238	2.54
Ho Chi Minh	424,172	2.53	77,814	4.03	501,986	2.69
Jakarta	189,348	1.13	8,333	0.43	197,681	1.06
Others	475,331	2.84	132,346	6.85	607,677	3.25
North American						
Los Angeles	1,039,571	6.20	34,002	1.76	1,073,573	5.75
San Francisco	589,976	3.52	–		589,976	3.16
Seattle	110,116	0.66	–		110,116	0.59
New York	189,496	1.12	–		189,496	1.00
Vancouver	374,192	2.23	–		374,192	2.00

Pacific						
Honolulu	117,849	0.70	—	—	117,849	0.63
Sydney	162,149	0.97	—	—	162,149	0.87
Brisbane/Cairns	132,706	0.79	—	—	132,706	0.71
Auckland	49,660	0.30	—	—	49,660	0.27
Others	59,773	0.36	22,647	1.17	82,420	0.44
Middle East (for Europe)						
Dubai	83,671	0.50	—	—	83,671	0.45
Abu Dhabi	46,311	0.28	—	—	46,311	0.25

Source: Ministry of Transportation and Communications 1998

ents. Hong Kong accounts for 27 per cent of the volume of passengers, reflecting the significance of business and personal connections between Taiwan and China. There are also close linkages between Taipei and such world cities as Tokyo, Bangkok, Singapore, and Los Angeles. The five cities mentioned above are also the intermediate points for Taipei to reach other parts of the world.

Conclusions

Taiwan is often mentioned as an exception to much of what has been written about development and urbanization in Asia. While many Asian countries have experienced urbanization without much industrialization, Taiwan has undergone a transformation from a predominately agricultural society to an industrial economy. The means of transformation is far more similar to the earlier experience in Western Europe and the USA than is the case in most other Asian nations. While this significant change in industrial structure was accompanied by rapid urbanization, the pattern of urban growth was reasonably balanced between large and small cities, and between different regions in Taiwan.

This chapter describes the process of urbanization in Taiwan from 1950 to 1995 using annual data from the household registration system and other statistical data. Two measures of urban growth are used. For the entire period, data are available on the growth of officially defined cities and townships. For 1972, 1980, and 1991, additional data are available for small units at village and city ward level that enable the construction of localities of 20,000 and over in a standardized manner. This technique can be used in many other developed countries. The locality data show that the percentage of the population living in towns/cities with 20,000 or more inhabitants increased from 50 per cent in 1972 to 62 per cent in 1980, and then to 71 per cent in 1991. Additional data indicate that the growth of the 10 major cities accounted for most of the urban growth in excess of natural increase up until 1970. Between 1920 and 1970, these cities grew at approximately twice the rate of growth of the remainder of Taiwan. However, in the 1970s these cities grew no faster than the rest of Taiwan.

During the 1970s, the growth of the larger cities slowed, while the "intermediate cities" continued to grow. This change in the pattern of urbanization was most noticeable in the northern region, which contains the capital city of Taipei. During the most recent past, Taipei has experienced deconcentration similar to many of the older cities in Western countries. The population in the original central business district has declined, and the greatest growth has occurred in the newly added precincts and in the surrounding urbanized areas. This shift in urban growth pattern has been accompanied by a shift in the growth of manufacturing away from the major cities into the surrounding areas and the "intermediate cities". The resulting distribution of urban population conforms to the "rank-size" rule for both Taiwan as a whole and within most regions.

Taiwan has been involved in the process of globalization in the past two decades, and gained benefits for its economic development and urban growth. The northern region, especially the Taipei extended metropolitan area, plays a key role in this evolutionary history, and will remain important in future development. As the political, social, and economic centre of Taiwan, Taipei is well integrated in the regional city system of East and South-East Asia and properly linked to the world city system. It is anticipated that Taipei will lead Taiwan into another stage of sustainable development.

Notes

1. As the regional statistics of employment are available by place of residence rather than by place of work, they are not able to reflect exactly the location of job opportunities.

REFERENCES

DGBAS. 1993. *Standard Classifications of Statistical Areas* (First Revision). Taipei: Directorate-General of Budget, Accounting and Statistics, The Executive Yuan.

Ho, Samuel P. S. 1979. "Decentralized industrialization and rural development: Evidence from Taiwan", *Economic Development and Cultural Change*, Vol. 28, No. 1, pp. 77–96.

Liu, Paul K. C. 1975. *A Study on Urban Definitions for Taiwan* (in Chinese). Taipei: Department of Urban Planning, Economic Research and Planning Council.

Meyer, David R. 1984. "Intermediate cities in the system of cities in developing countries", in *Conference on Urban Growth and Economic Development in the Pacific Region*. Taipei: Institute of Economics, Academia Sinica, pp. 141–159.

Ministry of Transportation and Communication. 1998. *1998 Statistical Abstract of Transportation and Communications*. Taipei: Department of Statistics, Ministry of Transportation and Communication.

MOE. 1991. *Taiwan-Fukien Demographic Fact Book, 1990*. Taipei: Ministry of the Interior.

MOE. 1996. *Taiwan-Fukien Demographic Fact Book, 1995*. Taipei: Ministry of the Interior.

Rondinelli, Dennis A. 1983. *Secondary Cities in Developing Countries: Politics for Diffusing Urbanization*. Beverly Hills, CA: Sage Publications.

Schive, Chi. 1994. "FDI and technology transfer", in Kuo-Hsu Liang (ed.) *Collected Articles on Taiwan's Economic Development in Memory of Professor Yen Hua*. Taipei: Times Publications (in Chinese), pp. 296–325.

Speare, Alden Jr, Parul K. C. Liu, and Ching-lung Tsay. 1988. *Urbanization and Development: The Rural-Urban Transition in Taiwan*. Boulder, CO: Westview Press.

Tsai, Hsung-hsiung. 1996. "Globalization and the urban system in Taiwan", in Fu-chen Lo and Yue-man Yeung (eds) *Emerging World Cities in Pacific Asia*. Tokyo: United Nations University Press, pp. 179–218.

Tsay, Ching-lung. 1982. "The growth and distribution of urban population in Taiwan", (in Chinese) in Chau-nan Chen, Yu-lung Kiang, and Kuanjeng Chen (eds) *Essays on the Integration of Social Sciences*. Taipei: Sun Yat-Sen Institute for Social Sciences and Philosophy, Academia Sinica, pp. 207–241.

Tsay, Ching-lung. 2000. "Trends and characteristics of migration flows to Taiwan", paper presented to Conference on International Migration and Human Resources Development, Chiba, Japan, Institute of Developing Economies, 20–21 January 2000.

Tsay, Ching-lung and Deng-shing Huang. 1997. "Taiwan FDI in East and South-East Asia: A perspective from the origin", paper presented to Conference on the Role of Thailand and Taiwan in Regional Economic Cooperation, Bangkok, Thailand, Thammasat University.

Tsay, Ching-lung and Ji-ping Lin. 1999. *Return Immigration and the Reversal of Brain Drain in Taiwan: A Preliminary Analysis Based on the 1990 Population Census*. Taipei: Institute of Economics, Academia Sinica.

Tung, An-Chi. 1999. "Taiwan's exports", in D. Das and A. Krueger (eds) *Asian Exports*. Hong Kong: Oxford University Press for Asian Development Bank.

Yabuuchi, Shigemi. 1999. "Foreign direct investment, urban unemployment and welfare", *Journal of International Trade and Economic Development*, Vol. 8, No. 4, pp. 359–371.

The entrepôt borderless cities

8

Increasing globalization and the growth of the Hong Kong extended metropolitan region

Victor F. S. Sit

Introduction: Globalization and urbanization in the form of extended metropolitan regions

Post-Second World War urbanization in the third world differs very much from experiences in Europe in the nineteenth century, and a number of explanations have been advanced as to why (Fuchs, Jones, and Pernia 1987; Cohen 1981; Harvey 1975; Castells 1977; Armstrong and McGee 1985). Among them, the dependency school, whose arguments hinge on the importance of external forces, including international capital, provides a laudable thesis. Those using this perspective see contemporary urbanization in the third world as the spatial expression of global capital accumulation and the dependency relation that has been derived from it. Urbanization in the third world is believed to be a spatial expression of the relationship between the exploiters (industrial core countries) and the exploited (third world countries). Castells (1977) identified three types or phases of domination. The latest round is one of "imperialist industrial and financial" domination. To him third world urbanization is a "dependency urbanization" which "in its forms and in its rhythms, is the concrete articulation of these economic and political relations". Armstrong and McGee (1985) and Harvey (1986) further described in detail the capital, information, and material flows involved in such articulation that are presently labelled as globalization. These influences take the form of increasing multinational corporation (MNC) control of trade and investment, the persistent dispersal of manufacturing to low-labour-cost countries, and diffusion of modern lifestyles and manipulation of consumer demand in these third world countries. Increasingly external influences are focused on the big cities, though they also reach down to small centres and even villages. Thus, urban centres in a peripheral society are believed to serve mainly as "theatres of accumulation" for international capital. The function and growth of each centre are arguably manipulated by international capital, which in turn determines whether it is a financing, production, or marketing and distributing centre. Similarly, the urban hierarchy of a third world country functions and develops according to the goals and manipulation of international capital based in world cities. Thus, the urbanization process and urban hierarchy formation in a peripheral society are processes subsumed under the hierarchy of control of international capital. Such a close relationship between capitalism and urban organization on a global scale has been echoed by Hymer (1975), who stated that the "TNC hierarchy and human settlements are two sides of the same coin".

Dependency urbanization is also linked to the concept of the new international division of labour (NIDL) (Cohen 1981). The gist of the NIDL concept is the rearrangement of the world economy into a set of more regionally based zones of production dependent on the dominant core industrialized countries; labour-intensive processes are performed in the periphery or semi-periphery, whereas the core countries retain and develop higher-level activities. The mode by and extent to which a city or place in the third world is integrated with the world economy through the NIDL will largely determine the structural change within it and provide a new basis for its urban growth. Thus Friedmann (1986) believes that in some less developed countries (LDCs), urbanization is for the most part a process of adaptation to changes externally induced. In addition, the NIDL also induces growth of new centres of corporate or national development in some peripheral or semi-peripheral countries. Nations or urban centres that serve as centres of corporate services also form part of the new international financial markets that support the NIDL.

In the past two decades, internal reforms of the People's Republic of China (PRC), combined with the massive influx of FDI into southern China, have produced drastic structural changes and rapid urbanization there. South China thus provides a case for studying the relationship between globalization and urbanization of a third world society. Sit and Yang's (1997a) study revealed how export-oriented and labour-intensive manufacturing, a result of south China's rapid integration with the world economy, has led to a process of "exo-urbanization". That study, however, did not include the core of the development process there – Hong Kong's emergence as a new servicing, financing, and coordinating centre

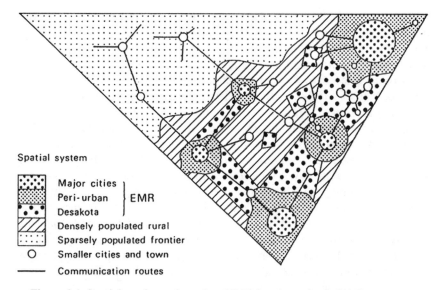

Spatial system

Figure 8.1 Spatial configuration of an EMR in a hypothetical Asian country
Source: Adopted from McGee 1991

for the expanded NIDL in south China. To be more specific, since the
1980s, Hong Kong, Macau, and the Pearl river delta (PRD) have been
developing rapidly into an integrated urban mass under the intensified
process of globalization (Zheng 1990). These areas are in reality an extended metropolitan region (EMR), like Jabotabek, or the Bangkok EMR.

As a new urban form, the EMR is comprised of a large core metropolis, its periphery, the desakota area of semi-urban and semi-rural character, and small towns and cities in the periphery and within the desakota
area (Figure 8.1). Sit (1996) believes that the growth of the EMR is primarily due to the forces of polarization and dispersal. In Asia, and possibly in other third world regions too, the major cities are the best locations for labour-intensive production as well as serving as the financing,
coordinating, and distributing centres in the NIDL. The presence in these
major cities, often the national capitals, of modern port and airport
facilities, the seat of the nation's or region's government, financial and
business services, well-developed communication and land transport infrastructure, accumulated capital and human resources, and so on have
contributed to polarization forces. Invariably, EMRs in Asia are based on
core metropolises which are national capitals, major regional ports, and
financial centres. These large metropolises are nevertheless equally im-
bued with problems of congestion, high land prices, relatively high labour
costs, and environmental degradation. These negative factors have pushed

labour- and land-intensive activities away from the core city into the rural-urban fringe or further afield. They constitute a spatial dispersal force. Thus, strengthened globalization in many Asian countries has led to a new form of urbanization around their core cities, and the EMRs in Asia are closely related to foreign direct investment (FDI) (Ginsburg 1991; Soegijoko 1996; McGee 1991; Chu 1996; Sit 1993, 1996). It is a new spatial configuration and functional division of labour in an enlarged urban region centred around the metropolis. In the metropolitan centre, FDI in banking and finance, MNC regional head offices, hotels, and international tourist businesses and convention centres, etc., is helping to promote or strengthen an existing Western central business district (CBD). Conventional and labour- and land-intensive manufacturing, wholesaling, and warehousing functions have been dispersed outwards into formerly rural areas around the core. These outer areas of the EMR have become intensively mixed in land uses to form a rural-urban transition zone or desakota area. Domestic investments follow a similar spatial pattern as the polarization and dispersal forces of the national capital or major city work on them as well.

The purpose of this chapter is to reveal the spatial pattern of urbanization and functional division of labour in different parts of the Hong Kong EMR. The macro dynamics are related to globalization, whereas local spatial dynamics are the opposing forces of polarization and dispersal. Rapid urbanization in the peri-urban and desakota areas has posed problems of administrative and infrastructural integration, coordinated planning, environment protection, and sustainability. It is hoped that the case study will give a new insight on globalization and the growth of major cities in the Pacific Rim as well as their relationship with the concept of the EMR.

Globalization and Hong Kong's economic growth

Global forces and the NIDL in manufacturing

Hong Kong is comprised of three separate pieces of territory formerly ceded or leased from the Ching government of China to Britain under the three Unequal Treaties of the nineteenth century. At present, its total area is 1,093 square kilometres (Figure 8.2), lying to the north of the mouth of the Pearl river, the largest navigable river in south China and the third largest in China. Since the start of British rule, Hong Kong gradually turned from a sleepy rural and fishing community of south China into an internationally renowned entrepôt of the late nineteenth century, handling a large part of trade between China and the rest of the world. This role persisted until the early 1950s, when the new PRC gov-

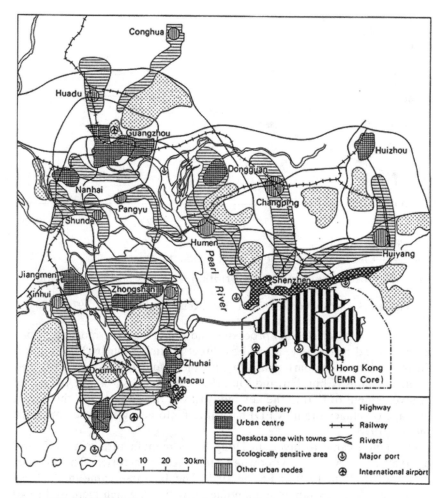

Figure 8.2 The Hong Kong extended metropolitan region

ernment of China (with the Soviet bloc) and the Western countries con-
fronted each other in the Cold War. With the capital, experience, and
entrepreneurship of the mainland Chinese (largely Shanghaiese), Hong
Kong's economy made a successful transition from dependence on entrepôt trade to being an export-oriented industrial (EOI) economy based
on labour-intensive light consumer goods manufacturing (Sit 1989, 1991;
Cheng 1977). Hong Kong set a good example of an EOI economy and led
the newly industrialized economies (NIEs) in an early success in globalization by engaging in export-oriented production (Sit 1989; Chiu, Ho,
and Lui 1997; Clark and Kim 1995). In this round of globalization, international technology was successfully transferred through original equip-

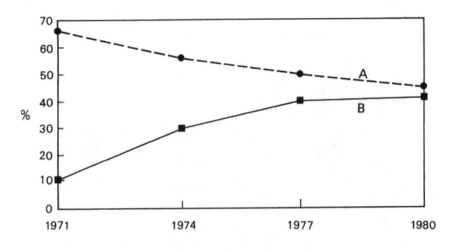

A : Electronics, textiles, metal products, toys

B : Chemicals, electricals, printing, watches and clocks, food

Figure 8.3 Distribution of FDI in Hong Kong manufacturing, 1971–1980

ment manufacturer (OEM) processes and imports of the most appropriate advanced machinery, as well as direct participation by MNCs in industrial production, particularly by Japanese and US industrialists and retailing chains (Chiu, Ho, and Liu 1997). Figure 8.3 shows the high level of involvement of FDI in the key industries of the early 1970s, the end of the take-off stage, and how FDI has shifted into new growth sectors since the mid-1970s.

US capital came to invest in Hong Kong manufacturing in 1955, and by 1959 there were six US-owned Hong Kong factories. The number increased to 27 in 1979 and 87 in 1995. The Japanese came in 1960. By 1963, there were 23 Japanese manufacturing firms, which increased to 40 in 1979. Japanese firms were smaller in scale, averaging HK$100 million in total assets compared to US firms that averaged assets of HK$150 million. During the 1970s and 1980s, the USA was the largest source of FDI in Hong Kong manufacturing, contributing an average of 35 per cent of total FDI into that sector. In 1988 the US share was 36 per cent, followed by Japan (27 per cent). The other significant sources were the UK (7 per cent) and mainland China (8 per cent). In 1996, Japan contributed 38 per cent and the USA 27 per cent, while mainland China contributed 5.5 per cent and the UK contributed 5 per cent of total FDI inflows (Wu 1997). The significance of FDI in Hong Kong's manufacturing growth can also be seen from a number of other perspectives. In 1988, it contributed to 12.7 per cent of all manufacturing employment and 20 per cent of total

Table 8.1 Foreign capital in Hong Kong manufacturing

	1955	1988	1995	1996
No. of factories	8	605	430	403
Total employees	N/A	108,082	65521	61,483
Investment (HK$ bn)	N/A	26.2	45.3	48.0
Output value (HK$ bn)	N/A	54.1		126.2
% output for export	N/A	69		60
% of total domestic export	N/A	20		36

Source: Compiled from Hong Kong government data

Table 8.2 Structure of ownership and source of orders for the two largest industries in Hong Kong, 1992

Characteristics	Garments %	Electronics %
Locally owned	94.2	82.0
Owner managed	92.8	74.0
Production for export: 50 per cent or more	57.8	62.0
Order from overseas directly: 50 per cent or more	10.4	42.0
Order from local import and export houses: 50 per cent or more	47.9	28.0
Order from local factories: 50 per cent or more	23.3	24.0
Order from own overseas outlets	2.8	8.0

Source: Compiled from Hong Kong government data

domestic export. In 1995, with the northward shift of most labour-intensive local manufacturing into the Pearl river delta, these contributions of FDI increased further, reaching 19 per cent and 36 per cent respectively (Table 8.1). The second important contribution has been the transfer of modern and advanced technologies, including management information systems, computer-aided design systems, and material requirement planning software systems. A survey of registered patents for 1970–1982 showed that foreign firms were responsible for 98 per cent of the total. There was also a high correlation between technological progress and the percentage share of foreign investment in any local industrial branch (Yu 1997: 148). Both Japan and the USA have targeted Hong Kong as a platform for globalized regional coordination of cross-border division of labour in the neighbouring regions of South-East Asia and south China, while Hong Kong also simultaneously serves as an important assembling and component production base for MNCs. The majority of domestic manufacturers are also dependent on the NIDL, as indicated by both their large export percentages and their heavy reliance on overseas distributors and local trade subsidiaries (Table 8.2).

Table 8.3 Cost of Hong Kong manufactured goods, 1973

Items	%
Consumption of materials	59.5
Fuel, water, and electricity	1.3
Industrial services	3.6
Non-industrial services	2.9
Labour cost	19.3
Rental and other payments	2.9
Depreciation of fixed assets	2.2
Net operation surplus	8.3

Source: Cheng 1977, p. 159

Such characteristics of high dependence on foreign market and supplies of raw materials, intermediate inputs, and equipment, with low value-added and the low skill requirements of OEM manufacturing, are further reflected in the cost structure of Hong Kong manufacturing (Table 8.3). Though computed from statistics of 1973, the situation presented in Table 8.3 remains more or less the same today. Local value-added is small and is made up mostly of labour inputs. Around the early 1970s, the first phase of export-oriented industrialization, which accounts for the labour-intensive segment of the NIDL, reached its peak in Hong Kong when manufacturing directly contributed 30 per cent of local GDP. As the Hong Kong economy improved, high costs of land and labour began to undermine the local comparative advantage to support this NIDL. In the early 1980s, the economy reflected such pains by registering almost no growth – 0.8 per cent in 1985. It was fortunate that at that time China was gradually opening up. While local manufacturing was under stress, the northward shift of some local manufacturing had already started. This has prolonged the growth of phase one of EOI and the spatial expansion of the NIDL into the delta, using Hong Kong as the coordinating centre.

Global forces in other sectors

Foreign capital is not only important in the industrial sector of Hong Kong, but also has a much longer history and great significance in Hong Kong's growth since it became a British colony. At first, foreign capital from the UK was invested mainly in activities related to entrepôt trade, such as shipping, warehousing, banking, and trading. It also monopolized utilities and dominated the property sector. At present, these are still areas where UK capital is concentrated in the Hong Kong Special Administrative Region. By the end of 1995, UK capital stock amounted to HK$145.4 billion, 27.3 per cent of the total stock of foreign capital in Hong Kong. Mainland China capital has become the second largest input, amounting to HK$107.5 billion, or 20.2 per cent. The third and fourth largest contributors are Japan (HK$88 billion) and the USA (HK$72 billion). The sectors targeted by US FDI were trading and wholesaling, followed by banking and insurance. About 15 per cent of it went into manufacturing. Hong Kong is the destination of the largest amount of Japanese FDI in Asia – 20 per cent of its total Asian FDI – about twice the size of its FDI in Indonesia. About 25 per cent of Japanese FDI went into banking and finance. In 1995, Japanese banks accounted for 15.6 per cent of total Hong Kong deposits and Japanese firms handled 15 per cent of Hong Kong turnover in the stock exchange. They are also active in trading and local retailing, besides being a key source of FDI in local manufacturing. In 1995, all told, non-manufacturing FDI stock accounted for 91 per cent of the total FDI stock. Thus, in recent years, globalization forces are operating increasingly in the tertiary sectors of Hong Kong, particularly in banking and finance, insurance, trading, and retailing, taking advantage of Hong Kong's free-trade policy as well as its position as the world's third largest financial centre, its ideal geographical location in Asia, its developed port and other infrastructure, its growing buying power and consumer market, and its relationship to the mainland Chinese market.

Hong Kong's post-1980 transition into a tertiary-sector-dominated economy is related to two major factors. The first is the northward shift and tremendous expansion of the NIDL as export-oriented phase one industries move into the PRD. The second is China's opening up, which has led to increased entrepôt activities and a rapid increase of China trade offices of foreign firms in Hong Kong. In 1980, regional headquarters of foreign firms numbered 136 and representative offices 253. By 1995 they had multiplied to 800 and 1,470 respectively. Close to 45 per cent of the increase occurred between 1991 and 1995 (Wu 1997) when the expansion of the NIDL into south China and the country's speed of opening up were both heightened after Deng Xiao-ping's further opening-up push in 1992.

Post-1980 globalization and new partnership with the PRD

Thus, globalization has been the prevailing force in Hong Kong's post-Second World War economic development. In the first three decades globalization forces took advantage of the city's NIDL in the form of labour-intensive manufacturing. After 1980, globalization forces promoted the transition of the economy into one predominantly driven by the tertiary sector. This process of transformation was intensified as China opened to the world its cheap labour, cheap land, and large domestic market. The situation was exploited by Hong Kong and foreign capital using Hong Kong as a base or bridgehead (Federation of Hong Kong Industries 1992; Hong Kong Trade Development Council 1997). In the process Hong Kong's manufacturing has not only largely shifted into south China, but has also expanded there. By the end of 1995, industrial enterprises with foreign ownership and FDI participation in Guangdong numbered 15,615 establishments which employed 2.8 million persons and produced a gross output value of 404.4 billion yuan, or 42.5 per cent of the province's total. Of all enterprises with some form of foreign equity, 83 per cent of FDI came from Hong Kong. The latter represented 54 per cent of total FDI for all sectors in the whole country (Niu 1998).

Hong Kong's extension of the NIDL workbench into Guangdong can also be measured from another perspective. Between 1985 and 1995, Hong Kong FDI in manufacturing in the province increased from an annual flow of US$0.5 billion to US$5.8 billion, with an annual average increase rate of 27.5 per cent. The total cumulative actualized Hong Kong FDI in manufacturing in the province for 1979–1995 amounted to US$25.1 billion, or 63.1 per cent of all FDI from Hong Kong. As Hong Kong FDI in manufacturing in the province is similar to Hong Kong's typical industries of the 1970s and 1980s, it is equally "trade creative". Such an effect is seen in both the large jump in foreign trade in Guangdong and Hong Kong's expansion in trade. Foreign trade in the province at the start of the opening and reform of 1978 was only US$1.4 billion. By 1995, it had risen to US$55.7 billion, with an annual growth rate of 24 per cent. At the same time, Hong Kong's trade expanded from HK$117 billion in 1978 to HK$2,835 billion in 1995, which raised its rank among the world's leading trading nations/regions from twenty-third to eighth. Of Hong Kong's total trade in 1995, re-exports accounted for 60 per cent, and 83 per cent of Guangdong's foreign trade went through Hong Kong. It is estimated by one source that the presence of China's re-exports has increased Hong Kong's total trade threefold (Wu 1997). A lot of these are, in fact, generated directly by Hong Kong's FDI in manufacturing in Guangdong (Table 8.4).

The impact of the extended workbench of Hong Kong on its internal

Table 8.4 Proportion of Hong Kong's trade involving outward processing in China, 1989–1995

	1989 %	1990 %	1991 %	1992 %	1995 %
Total exports to China	53.0	58.8	55.5	52.4	49.0
Domestic exports to China	76.0	79.0	76.5	74.3	–
Re-exports to China	43.6	50.3	48.2	46.2	–
Imports from China	58.1	61.8	67.6	72.1	74.0
Re-exports of Chinese origin (except to China)	–	–	74.1	78.3	82.0

Source: Hong Kong Government, *Annual Digest of Statistics*, various years

structural transformation, such as the growth of the trading, shipping, transportation, communication, and warehousing sectors, as well as finance and insurance, has been colossal. Take trading as an example. By the end of 1996, Hong Kong registered 105,000 trading firms which employed 530,000 persons or 23 per cent of the local labour force (11 per cent in 1980). Therefore while the NIDL has largely expanded across the border, tertiary activities that support the extended workbench have grown fast within Hong Kong and continued to draw in FDI and local investments. The situation may be represented by the "front shop, back factory" model (Figure 8.4).

The model portrays a new spatial division of labour in this latest round of globalization and represents a structural transformation within Hong Kong – the tremendous drop of the secondary sector with the growth of the tertiary sector (Table 8.5). On the surface, Hong Kong appears to have become a post-industrial economy, with the tertiary sector accounting for 79.2 per cent of its GDP and 71.5 per cent of the total labour force.

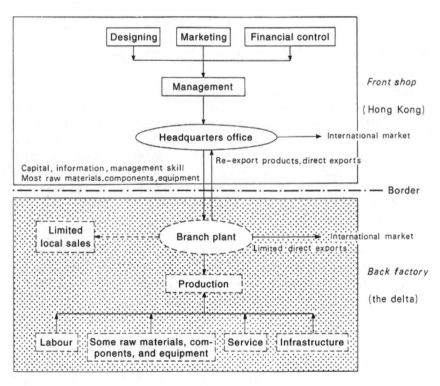

Figure 8.4 Hong Kong–Pearl river delta cross-border MNC model

Table 8.5 Structural transformation of Hong Kong's economy

Contribution to GDP	1970 %	1980 %	1990 %	1995 %
Primary	2.0	0.8	0.3	0.2
Secondary	37.3	32.0	25.3	16.0
manufacturing	30.9	23.8	17.6	9.0
construction	4.2	6.7	5.4	7.0
Services	60.1	63.2	74.5	79.2

Working population	1971 %	1981 %	1991 %	1996 %
Manufacturing	45.2	41.2	28.3	18.9
Construction	6.1	7.7	6.9	8.1
Wholesale, retail, trade, restaurants, hotels	16.7	19.2	22.5	24.9
Transport, storage, and communications	6.8	7.5	9.7	10.9
Finance, insurance, real estate, business services	2.6	4.8	10.5	13.4
Community, social, and personal services	14.7	15.6	18.9	22.3
Others	13.6	3.9	2.0	1.5
Total (000 persons)	1,534.6	2,404.1	2,715.1	3,043.7

Source: Hong Kong Government, *Annual Report*, various dates

In spatial terms, Hong Kong's urban land uses have equally undergone major changes. There has been a decline of industrial land, and an expansion of warehousing and other land uses related to the growth of trade and transport. The CBD has also expanded. Some of the increased land for tertiary functions has come from conversion of former industrial uses or their rezoning. Good examples of such are the rezoning of the third industrial zone in Shatin new town to warehousing, and the widespread conversion of vacant farmland in the New Territories into open storage for empty containers. Yet this is only part of the spatial and landscape change taking place under recent globalization dynamics. In the Pearl river delta of Guangdong, where most of the production activities of the expanded system of Hong Kong NIDL are taking place, drastic land-use transformations and urbanization have been registered in the same period, leading to the integration of the delta's isolated urban centres and surrounding rural areas into the new expanded metropolitan region of Hong Kong.

Taken in isolation, Hong Kong's development typified the formation of a world city (Friedmann 1986), as it has been rapidly transformed in both employment and economy due to increased integration with the world economy. It has been the base point in the spatial organization and articulation of production and markets used by international capital for the south China (and China) arena. Global control functions are evidenced by the large contingent of MNC regional headquarters and representative offices. It has generated class polarization within Hong Kong as well as within its immediate hinterland. Being an important port, with excellent airport and container terminals and communication facilities, it is also an important platform for the flow and management of a huge volume of international cargo. Yet Hong Kong's growth in the last two decades is, to a large measure, due to the opening up of China and the integration of south China into the global economy. It is therefore a fact that globalization has combined with the receptive policy of opening and reform in the PRC to create an enlarged urban unit in south China, the Hong Kong extended metropolitan region (HKEMR). The following section turns to examine how the forces of globalization in Hong Kong have extended into south China and effected its transformation into part of the HKEMR.

NIDL in the PRD

While post-Second World War Hong Kong was moving rapidly into export-oriented phrase one industrialization to become an NIE, its immediate hinterland, the PRD, was still predominantly rural and deeply locked in a situation of underdevelopment under socialist central planning, with little contact with the world economy and little relationship even with the blooming international city of Hong Kong next door (Kwok and So 1995; Sit and Yang 1995).

Figures 8.2 and 8.5 show the extent of the delta. It comprises 28 cities and counties around the mouth of the Pearl river, the third longest river in China. Geographically, the delta includes Hong Kong and Macau, though administratively these are under quite different systems. In 1997 Hong Kong changed to become a special administrative region (SAR) of the PRC, while Macau was Portuguese territory until December 1999. After China adopted the opening and reform policy in 1978, the delta soon became the testing ground for economic and administrative reforms. In 1979, two special economic zones (SEZs) were designated there. In 1984, Guangzhou was given the preferential status of an open city. In 1987, the whole delta was turned into a large open economic zone, thus it was opened to foreign investment much earlier than the rest of China. It has also been successful in utilizing foreign capital in attaining rapid economic growth based on preferential policies granted by the state, local initiatives in reform, improvements of infrastructure, and its geographical proximity to Hong Kong.

In 1982, however, the delta was still quite backward despite its inclusion

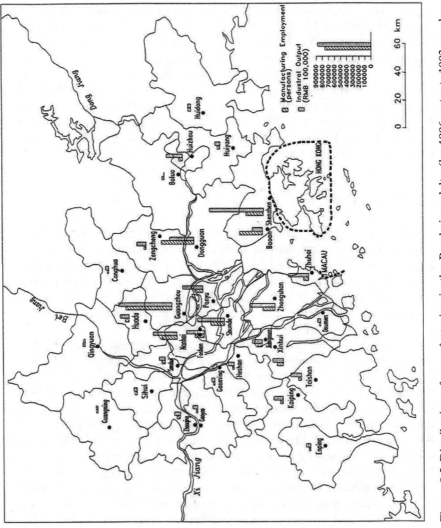

Figure 8.5 Distribution of manufacturing in the Pearl river delta (by 1996 output, 1993 employment)

Table 8.6 FDI in the delta, China, and LDCs, 1980–1995

Year	LDCs US$ million	China US$ million	Delta US$ million	Delta as % of China
1980	130	–	1.0	–
1986	250	46.5	7.5	16.1
1988	280	102.3	13.9	13.6
1990	310	102.9	15.8	15.4
1991	390	115.5	21.3	18.7
1992	510	192.0	32.4	16.9
1993	800	338.0	64.3	16.5
1994	870	375.0	83.0	22.1
1995	997	481.3	85.8	17.8
% average growth (1986–1995)	16.6	29.7	31.1	–

Source: Computed from UN and Chinese official statistics

within Guangzhou, the provincial capital and a millionaire city (a city with over 1 million population). Roughly 15.76 million people resided within the delta, giving it an urbanization level of approximately 15 per cent – much lower than the national average. Its gross agricultural output value then was 6 billion yuan, and gross industrial output value was 15 billion yuan.

Since 1979, the PRD has been able to transform itself largely because of the opening and reform policy that allowed it to integrate rapidly with the global economy through the NIDL. The pace and scale of development may be gleaned from a series of relevant statistics. Table 8.6 shows the inflow of FDI into LDCs, China, and the delta. The average rate of growth of the inflow into the PRD is 31.1 per cent for 1986–1995, much faster than the rates for China as a whole and all the LDC recipients. Although less than 1 per cent of China in territory and less than 0.1 per cent in population, the delta consistently accounted for 15–20 per cent of the FDI inflow into China, which in absolute amounts was equivalent to US$8.5 billion in 1995 (or 8.9 per cent of total FDI into all LDCs in that year).

Inflow of FDI, which amounted to 95 per cent of all forms of foreign capital inflow (including public and private loans, donations, etc.) became a major source of total investments in the 1980–1994 period (Table 8.7). While government and domestic funds went largely to basic and social infrastructure projects, FDI predominated in productive projects, particularly manufacturing projects. For the delta as a whole the distribution of FDI by sector in 1979–1992 shows a clear bias towards the secondary sector: primary, 2.6 per cent; secondary, 70.2 per cent; tertiary, 27.2 per cent. In 1995, the distribution shows some slight change in favour of the

Table 8.7 Foreign capital in total investment, 1980–1994

	1980 %	1985 %	1990 %	1994 %
Guangzhou	3.0	6.0	8.7	23.7
Shenzhen	16.1	13.8	23.7	34.6
Zhuhai	24.9	14.5	23.1	34.4
PRD	5.5	8.0	18.5	30.7

Source: Shen, Wong, and Chu 1998

tertiary sector, mainly due to real estate development, but the secondary remained predominant: 0.9 per cent for primary, 65.0 per cent for secondary, and 34.1 per cent for tertiary (Zheng, Wang, and Chen 1997).

Sit and Yang (1997a) demonstrated in detail that most of the FDI inflows into the delta came from Hong Kong. Indeed, by the end of 1995, Hong Kong still accounted for 53.5 per cent of the accumulated FDI in China (with Macau registering 1.2 per cent). By that year Hong Kong's accumulated FDI in Guangdong province amounted to US$50.3 billion, of which 70.5 per cent or US$35.5 billion went into the delta, where Hong Kong capital accounted for over 80 per cent of all foreign capital and its rate of increase in 1979–1995 was 31.1 per cent; 63.7 per cent of all capital was invested in manufacturing projects (Zheng, Wang, and Cheng 1997). Hong Kong's industrial FDI into the Pearl river delta is locally known as "out-processing", as it first took the form of the northward shift of some of the processing into the delta, taking advantage of the cheap labour and land and the open and preferential policies that started there in 1979. Thereafter, these investments grew into cooperative projects, joint ventures, and even greenfield, 100-per-cent-foreign-owned investments. The type of manufacturing and the scale of operations followed the general characteristics of Hong Kong manufacturing firms, and the majority of their products were exported through Hong Kong. Details of this expanded NIDL with the "shop" or coordinating centre in Hong Kong are not discussed here as they have been extensively documented elsewhere (Sit 1989; Sit and Yang 1995, 1997a; Hong Kong Trade Development Council 1997).

At the end of 1995, there were 8,044 industrial enterprises funded by foreign capital (*sam-zhi*) in the delta, employing 2.14 million workers. A large number of small to medium-sized factories owned and run by village community offices known as "collectives" were also predominantly engaged in out-processing. They numbered 44,571 establishments with a total workforce of 2.46 million. Thus the number of persons directly employed by the northward-shifted Hong Kong-based NIDL may number

Table 8.8 Industrial employment and output of the cities and counties of the Pearl river delta

Case/year	Manufacturing employment (persons)		Industrial output (RMB 10,000 yuan)	
	1982	1990	1980	1996
Guangzhou	748,645	759,829	843,293	8,824,642
Huaxian	42,062	67,796	18,397	1,501,368
Conhua	12,224	21,099	5,725	536,545
Zengcheng	14,967	29,101	9,181	1,451,085
Panyu	69,426	125,133	35,715	3,371,102
Shenzhen	13,738	286,269	5,121	8,963,858
Baoan	10,714	378,071	4,266	1,660,927
Zhuhai	9,382	85,097	7,452	3,340,830
Doumen	0	24,620	10,363	522,894
Huizhou	17,529	61,207	7,273	2,737,426
Huidong	11,972	46,132	5,178	521,283
Huiyang	7,292	45,229	4,315	818,680
Boluo	12,789	37,629	7,100	69,678
Dongguan	121,163	545,268	55,111	4,021,701
Zhongshan	97,005	206,726	63,553	4,185,524
Jiangmen	56,964	76,275	63,168	1,626,003
Xinhui	77,702	101,934	36,559	1,756,320
Taishan	42,596	50,648	21,659	1,778,756
Kaiping	25,284	45,337	19,973	1,556,538
Enping	14,397	27,770	9,004	744,436
Heshan	10,821	27,163	8,101	983,217
Foshan	93,828	149,491	86,141	2,922,628
Nanhai	135,304	248,672	70,112	3,916,192
Shunde	121,033	226,095	70,415	4,458,750
Gaoming	5,210	22,636	3,677	533,742
Sanshui	18,436	54,784	10,613	1,000,233
Zhaoqing	30,888	55,298	19,210	980,967
Gaoyao	22,069	27,918	10,899	843,297
Guangning	11,031	24,503	7,863	277,294
Sihui	18,848	37,479	9,463	521,877
Qingyuan	22,679	37,404	10,988	260,879
Total	1,897,980	3,934,603	1,541,868	66,688,662

Source: Guangdong Provincial Government, *Statistical Yearbook of Guangdong*, various dates

5.5 million persons. Their rough spatial distribution is indicated in Table 8.8 and Figure 8.5. In 1995 they produced a total gross output value of 253 billion yuan and contributed to about 30 per cent of the gross industrial output value and 71 per cent of the total exports (US$39.5 billion) of the province (Zheng, Wang, and Cheng 1997). In terms of total employ-

Table 8.9 Composition of rural products and rural labour force in the delta, 1978–1993

	Rural products			Rural labour force			Annual growth %
	1978 %	1985 %	1993 %	1980 %	1985 %	1993 %	
Agriculture	68.4	56.2	27.8	89.5	76.4	59.6	−0.8
Industry	20.6	23.3	53.4	4.4	7.8	13.2	11.2
Building	4.1	10.7	8.3	3.0	5.0	6.8	9.0
Tertiary	6.9	9.8	10.5	3.1	10.8	20.4	17.6
Total	100.0	100.0	100.0	100.0	100.0	100.0	2.4

Source: Guangdong Provincial Government, *Guangdong Agricultural Statistical Yearbook 1993*

ment and gross output by industry, they represent 34.4 per cent and 68 per cent of the delta's employment and output, respectively. It is therefore clear that FDI-financed NIDL forms the backbone of the delta's new export-oriented industrial economy.

The impact of FDI-financed NIDL is felt in manufacturing for the local Chinese market and in other non-agricultural sectors in the delta as well. Export-oriented manufacturing in the labour-intensive mode has a large multiplier effect on trade, transport, retailing, commerce, and real estate activities. The direct and indirect effects culminated in rapid structural transformation of the delta. Table 8.9 documents the movements of the rural labour force from agriculture into manufacturing. In the rural part of the delta, an "invisible urbanization" has thus been taking place as non-farm employment increased and the rural labour force engaged in agriculture decreased from 89.5 per cent in 1980 to 59.6 per cent in 1993. The countryside has become a landscape of juxtaposed farms and industrial estates (Lin 1997). In short, FDI, taking the form of NIDL expansion from Hong Kong, has transformed the PRD structurally as well as converting it into a large and rapidly urbanizing desakota area.

The Hong Kong EMR

As globalization forces that centred at Hong Kong gradually incorporated the PRD, an EMR that includes Hong Kong as the metropolitan core (covering 1,075 square kilometres and with a population of 6.3 million), Macau (20 square kilometres; population 0.45 million), and Shenzhen (2,020 square kilometres; population 3.58 million) as its urban periphery, and the Pearl river delta (45,005 square kilometres; population 21.7 million) as the desakota area emerged.

The metropolitan core

In 1980, Hong Kong was already a large metropolis with 5.04 million inhabitants. By the end of 1996, it registered 6.41 million inhabitants. At present, the figure should be very close to 6.6 million. As more than 70 per cent of the territory is on a steep gradient (between 1:5 and 1:2), developable land is limited. At present, built-up/developed land occupies 16 per cent of the entire territory, with fishponds and agricultural land occupying another 10 per cent, leaving only medium-gradient slopes undeveloped. Many of these are, however, already included in a system of country parks that covers 40 per cent of the territory. Hong Kong is therefore highly developed and urbanized, with about 60 per cent of the population concentrated in the main core of Hong Kong island and Kowloon, and another 40 per cent in the seven new towns. The latter are planned urban developments connected to the main core by modern mass transits with average commuting time of less than one hour. Though narrow strips of green belt separate the new towns and provide some open space in the main core area, the city is a packed urban mass of very high density (the overall population density of Hong Kong is about 6,000 persons per square kilometre).

The problems generated by high population density and congestion include the high cost of land and inadequate space for a number of important urban functions, such as leisure and recreation. Hong Kong turned to Macau as its leisure resort early on. Macau has also served as its extended NIDL workbench since the 1970s (Sit, Cremer, and Wong 1990). Since China opened up in the late 1970s, it has absorbed much of the cheap labour as well as the recreation demands of Hong Kong. The latter role is particularly well developed in Shenzhen.

The physical expansion of Hong Kong into its immediate neighbourhood in EMR formation is not simply a function of population increase, however. Rather, it is due more to the interplay of two sets of forces that have been mentioned earlier. First were the opportunities for adapting the NIDL in Hong Kong as part of an international market, China's opening up, and the existence of readily utilizable cheap land and labour in the delta next to Hong Kong. Second, problems of congestion, high land and environmental costs, high labour costs, and labour shortages in the core made Hong Kong lose its cost-effectiveness. Further, it became spatially and physically unmanageable in terms of further growth of labour-intensive manufacturing. The golden opportunity offered by China's opening up and the delta's preferential status in launching programmes to attract foreign capital and joint ventures has enabled Hong Kong to attain rapid economic expansion. From 1980 to 1994, Hong Kong's GDP grew at an average annual rate of 15.1 per cent in real terms. The secondary sector grew at a rate of 9.9 per cent (manufacturing at 7.6 per cent), and the tertiary sector at 16.7 per cent. While manufacturing's share of GDP declined from 23.7 per cent to 9.3 per cent during the period, the tertiary sector's share increased from 67.5 per cent to 84 per cent, of which the import-export sector grew from a total GDP share of 10.7 per cent to 17.9 per cent. The import-export sector's huge growth was good proof of the increased servicing need associated with the expansion of the NIDL, although about 80 per cent of it is spatially located outside Hong Kong, mainly in the delta. It was estimated that, in 1990, 25.7 per cent of Hong Kong's GDP was derived from the "China factor" – the NIDL in the mainland and other trading and tertiary business there. By 1996, Hong Kong's dependence ratio on the "China factor" had moved up to 40 per cent. Similar ratios for trading and shipping reached 60 per cent. In total, the "China factor" was said to be responsible for 20 per cent of Hong Kong's economic growth in the first half of the 1990s (Wu 1997: 96).

The above analysis indicates that Hong Kong has since 1980 moved towards intensified development of the tertiary sector, which has its most important role in servicing, supporting, and coordinating a much-expanded NIDL in the delta (Table 8.5). In the process, Hong Kong's employment in trading, finance and banking, transport, storage, and communications activities has increased rapidly as well. Urban land uses, influenced by such dynamics, moved towards an expanded CBD along the northern coastal strip into Wanchai and Causeway Bay and in Tsimshatsui as well. Declines in industrial land and the expansion in warehousing and port land uses took place rapidly. The expansion included the grand proposals in the Hong Kong government's (1989) Port and Airport Development Strategy, which have been partly implemented in the new replacement airport at Chek Lap Kok and huge commercial and office developments in the western Kowloon and Central District–Wanchai reclamation areas. Upgrading of residential areas and the urban environment, together with large-scale new developments in urban transport infrastructure, have also taken place since 1980.

In short, the opening and reform policies in China, in particular the offering of cheap land and labour in the capitalistic-style market in southern China, have intensified and extended globalization processes to the entire Hong Kong EMR. These processes have been manifested partially as polarization in the core, Hong Kong, because of the city's experience in international business and marketing, superb infrastructure, and huge stock of capital and human resources. Yet congestion and shortages of land and labour there have led to a logical spatial division of labour, whereby Hong Kong concentrates and has grown much in "front-shop" activities while most of the enlarged "back factory" has moved into the delta.

The peri-urban areas

Macau

Macau, located on the western flank of the mouth of the Pearl river opposite to Hong Kong (Figure 8.2), has been a small Portuguese colony since the sixteenth century. In the days of sailing boats, its location made it the entrepôt of southern China as it benefited from the onshore and offshore monsoon winds. However, its small and shallow harbour could not accommodate large steamships, and hence its China trade and significance as an entrepôt in south China declined. In the early twentieth century, the urban economy was dependent on the manufacture of joss-sticks and fire-crackers, salt-fish, and on gambling. From the mid-1950s, it survived on gambling, supplemented by Hong Kong investments in export-oriented manufacturing which tapped the cheaper land and labour there as well as its separate export quota (Sit, Cremer, and Wong 1990). In 1997, its property values and labour costs were still only about 10 per cent and 50 per cent respectively of those in Hong Kong. The gambling-cum-tourist sector remains the pillar of its economy. In 1995, it provided for 30 per cent of the local employment, 50 per cent of the government revenue, and 40 per cent of the GDP. In 1996, 8.15 million visitors came to Macau, of whom 5.2 million were from Hong Kong, indicating that this highly urbanized territory functions largely as a peri-urban area of Hong Kong as a specialized resort (Macau Census and Statistics Department 1997).

In 1994 Macau had 1,587 factories that employed 478,507 workers (Lui and Wang 1997). Most of the factories are branches of Hong Kong factories. Thus the size of this part of Hong Kong's extended workbench is small, being restricted by the size of its population as well as a comparatively (to the delta) higher labour cost. Yet it was the first cross-border peri-urban area of Hong Kong before China opened up.

Macau returned to China in 1999. It is expected to move gradually from the Portuguese colonial system to a Hong Kong system of law and administration, after which its integration with Hong Kong as part of the EMR will be much more solid.

Shenzhen

Shenzhen before 1978 was a small border township of less than 50,000 inhabitants, mainly engaged in agriculture. Although next door to Hong

Kong, the border served as both a political and an economic divide. At that time, the population of the entire territory of the present municipality of Shenzhen (2,020 square kilometres; Table 8.10 and Figures 8.2 and 8.5) was less than 300,000. The southern part of the municipality of about 370 square kilometres, right next to Hong Kong, was made a special economic zone in 1979 and given special privileges in economic autonomy and dealing with FDI. It has since attracted a large-scale inflow of FDI from Hong Kong. When the NIDL expanded further, in the 1990s, it was extended into the rest of the delta where labour and land costs were even lower. In the meantime, Shenzhen's transport, communication, port and airport, and other infrastructure were constructed or improved, and it therefore also attracted domestic and international capital for developing higher value-added industries and the tertiary sector. By 1996, Shenzhen's manufacturing had grown from almost nothing to a major sector that employed more workers than Hong Kong's industries, and about 10 times the number of those so employed in Macau. In gross output, manufacturing in Shenzhen, at present, is about half the size of that in Hong Kong. Thus despite some diversification of Shenzhen's economy since the late 1980s, it is still a substantial extension of the Hong Kong workbench, and manufacturing there accounted for 41 per cent of the local GDP (Table 8.10). Rapid growth, as measured by local GDP, amounted to 40.8 per cent averaged annually for 1980–1994. Per capita GDP has also grown tremendously, at 18.5 per cent annually. Foreign capital, more precisely Hong Kong's globalization dynamic, was behind such colossal growth. Table 8.11 shows clearly that FDI forms as much as 78.8 per cent of all capital investment in the Shenzhen SEZ, and close to half for the entire municipality.

Rapid growth in Shenzhen has attracted, and is facilitated by, mass immigration from the rest of the delta and much further afield. Table 8.12 indicates the pace and absolute number of increases between 1980 and 1995. The SEZ grew by more than 15 times to become a millionaire city, and the entire municipality registered a population of 3.45 million. Of the increases, a large proportion is a "temporary" population that have no household registrations, though some may have lived in the city for more than 10 years. The majority of the "temporary" population are unskilled and work on two-year employment contracts. After completing their contracts, they return to their home village/town (Sit and Yang 1995).

Rapid economic growth and large-scale domestic and foreign capital have also transformed Shenzhen, especially the SEZ, into a modern multifunction city. Though the border still separates it from Hong Kong in many respects and ensures a significant differential in the level of economic development, it is definitely a modern metropolis in cityscape and function. Thus it may be regarded as Hong Kong's peri-urban area, and is

Table 8.10 Hong Kong and adjacent areas, 1996

	Hong Kong	Macau	Shenzhen	PRD	Whole EMR	
					Total	Hong Kong %
Population (10,000)	631.1	41.5	358.5	2,170 (31.5)[a]	2,843	20.2
% urban population	100.0	100.0	76.4	32.8	63.8	–
Territory (km²)	1,095	21	2,020	45,005 (25.3)	46,119	2.3
GDP (billion)[b]	1,199	58	95	450 (69.5)	1,677	71.4
GDP per capita	189,985	116,107	26,051	20,889	58,924	322
GDP growth rate (%) (1990–1996)	5.4	5.0	23.4	22.1	–	–
Industrial output as % of GDP	7.8	N/A	41.0	42.6	–	–
Industrial output (US$ bn)	300.0	13.4	142.7	684.6 (77.7)	655.3	45.8
Manufacturing workers (000)	32.5	4.8	42.7	611.6 (80.0)	648.9	5.0
FDI (US$ bn)	33.0	N/A	2.4	9.9 (70.5)	–	–
Import and export (US$ bn)	376	3.7	52.2	N/A	–	–
Exports (US$ bn)	179	1.9	30.4	53.7 (91.1)	234.6	76.3
Export/person (US$)	28,398	4,863	8,498	2,476	–	–
Retail sales/person	30,552	N/A	9,559	7,900	–	–
Revenue/person	33,015	19,203	3,675	1,401	–	–
Savings/person	389,519	N/A	16,242	17,929	–	–
Actualized FDI/person (US$)	5,361	N/A	676	454	–	–
Fixed capital investment/person	7,420	N/A	9,137	6,724	–	–

a. Bracketed figures are percentages of Guangdong province.
b. All currency in RMB yuan unless specified.

221

Table 8.11 FDI in Shenzhen, 1981–1995

Year	FDI (US$ million)	FDI share of total investment (%)
1981	112.8	70.1 (86.5)[a]
1985	329.3	29.0 (98.5)
1990	518.6	42.8 (91.9)
1995	1,735.5	52.5 (60.2)
1981–1995 total	9,397.4	43.3 (78.8)

Source: Shen, Wong, and Chu 1998
a. Bracketed figures refer to the SEZ.

Table 8.12 Population growth in Shenzhen, 1980–1995

	Total population (000)	Temporary population as % of total	Population growth over last year (000 persons)	Growth over last year as % share of migration
1980	333 (94)[a]	96.4 (89)	18	73.4
1985	882 (470)	54.3 (49)	140	97.1 (98)
1990	2,019 (1000)	34.0 (39)	103	91.4 (.63)
1995	3,451 (1511)	28.7 (40)	961	88.5 (80)

Source: Shen, Wong, and Chu 1998
a. Bracketed figures refer to the SEZ.

increasingly becoming part of the metropolitan core. Fast development of the airport and container terminals, and tourist and trading activities, have already enabled it to share some of Hong Kong's "front-shop" role.

The desakota area

In 1978, there was only one "millionaire" city in the delta, Guangzhou, no large city of between 500,000 and 1 million inhabitants, one medium-size city of 200,000–500,000 inhabitants and only three small cities of less than 200,000 inhabitants. As previously stated, the area's urbanization level was 15.7 per cent: with the exception of Guangzhou, the delta was a largely rural region with few urban centres. After the opening and reform, in 1980–1994, the non-agricultural population in the delta (China's commonly used definition for urban population) increased rapidly from 4.81 million to 9.04 million, with an annual rate of increase that reached 5 per cent, much higher than the national rate of 3.5 per cent. The level of urbanization of the delta thus moved up rapidly from 15.78 per cent in 1978 to 45.8 per cent in 1994, and was 21.7 percentage points higher than the national urbanization level. The number of cities there had also increased from five in 1978 to 26 in 1994. These improvements have turned it from a region of low-level urbanization, about 2 per cent lower than the national average, to one of the most urbanized regions in the nation, comparable to the Yangtze delta and the Bohai rim region (Sit and Yang 1997a).

Sit and Yang's (1997a) study documented that the driving force behind economic transformation and growth, as well as rapid urbanization, has been Hong Kong capital. Indeed, in 1996, manufacturing – which is mainly low value-added, low-skill, export-oriented, and trade-creative in nature – still predominated in the delta's economy, accounting for 42.6 per cent of the local GDP with an absolute output value of 684.6 billion yuan and employing 6.12 million workers. Respectively the size of the output is about 2.5 times and the employment figure 20 times those of Hong Kong (Table 8.10).

Export-oriented manufacturing and its related supporting services and activities have led to massive growth of population, besides a significant structural transformation of the indigenous population as mentioned earlier. Between 1982 and 1990, the population in the delta grew at an average rate of 3.1 per cent, whereas between 1964 and 1982 the rate was only 1.7 per cent. Some of the administrative units, like Shenzhen, Zhuhai, and Dongguan, grew much faster: 19.1 per cent, 12.1 per cent, and 18.4 per cent respectively between 1982 and 1990. Such growth was supported mainly by large-scale immigration of young and unskilled labour from other provinces. Unlike the desakota regions of Jakarta or Bangkok, where the labour or population increases are mainly caused by rural-urban migration at the local level, the increase of population in the delta happened both at the level of the original townships, which have now become seats of the new municipalities that cover all former rural counties of the delta, and in the rural periphery of these "municipal" cores. By 2010, it is expected that the proportion of temporary population to total population in some of these newly created municipalities will be as high as 50 per cent in places such as Huizhou, Huiyang, Huidong, and Bolo, and between 25 per cent and 50 per cent in many other municipalities, such Zhuhai, Nanhai, Xihui, Zhongshan, Huadu, and Zhangzhen. Even Guangzhou is expected to have a temporary population that reaches 24.6 per cent (Guangdong Construction Committee 1996: 132).

Besides the above, this so-called "exo-urbanization" in the desakota area has some additional characteristics. First, it is small-centre biased, in that the smaller urban centres have been growing much faster than larger centres (Table 8.13). For example, small cities have increased from five to 15 in number during the 1980–1993 period, and their share of the total urban population in the delta increased from 14.6 per cent to 38.7 per cent over the same period. Second, it is border-oriented: centres and

Table 8.13 The changing urban hierarchy in the delta and Hong Kong EMR, 1980–2010

Year	Extra-large city		Large city		Medium city		Small city		Total urban pop. (10,000s)
	No.	Population (10,000s)	No.	Population (10,000s)	No.	Population (10,000s)	No.	Population (10,000s)	
1964	1	–	–	–	–	–	–	–	–
1980	1	228.9 (78.4)[a]	–	–	1	20.3 (7.0)	5	42.6 (14.6)	291.8
1985	1	257.0	–	–	1	24.5	6	70.9	352.4
1990	1	291.4	1	35.1	2	53.4	6	90.4	470.3
1993	1	303.7 (37.2)	1	64.1 (7.8)	5	133.7 (16.3)	15	316.4 (38.7)	817.9
Average annual % increase (1980–1993)		2.2				15.6		16.7	1.0
2010 (projected)	4	1,148.0	9	821.0	13	419.0	–	–	–
HK EMR 1993	2	903.7	1	64.1	5	171.7	15	316.4	1,455.9
2010 (projected)	5	1,968.0	9	821.0	14	499.0	–	–	3,288.0

Source: Guangdong Construction Committee 1996; plus author's estimations for Hong Kong and Macau for 2010.
a. Bracketed figures refer to % share of total urban population.

locations that are close to the border with Hong Kong and Macau have registered faster and higher levels of growth, showing the significant influence of Hong Kong as the capital source, the coordinating centre, and the platform for the globalization dynamics of exo-urbanization. Third, there is widespread "invisible" urbanization – former rural counties of the newly created municipalities registered very high degrees of non-agricultural employment as well as non-agricultural contribution to local GDP (Sit and Yang 1995). Finally, with the exception of Guangzhou and Zhuhai, the delta shows an internal division of labour. The urban centres there function as seats of administration and have other central-place functions, besides having some industrial functions. They are, in fact, field coordinating centres for the expanding NIDL. Over the 1980–1993 period, the countryside or "rural" periphery recorded high levels of employment and a higher ratio of employed people in labour-intensive, export-oriented manufacturing. The delta has bands of highly mixed agricultural and industrial, rural and urban land use following major transport corridors leading to Hong Kong and Macau, or around and adjourning river ports in the mouth of the Pearl river.

The delta (excluding Shenzhen and Guangzhou) may be regarded as a desakota area that has become highly urbanized due to the northward shift of the NIDL from Hong Kong and its *in situ* expansion there. This is manifested spatially as a spreading-out process from Hong Kong's border following the major transport routes. In the area there are highly mixed rural-urban land uses and large-scale conversion of rural land into urban uses. In the 1980–1993 period, farm land in the delta declined from 1.04 million ha to 0.71 million ha, with an average annual loss rate of 2.2 per cent. Shenzhen's SEZ and its Boan district registered a loss of 14.2 per cent and 11.9 per cent respectively (Sit and Yang 1997b). This shows that despite the border, the process of the outward spatial extension of Hong Kong's globalization processes has been vigorous. Thus, a huge desakota area, a major part of the Hong Kong EMR, has emerged. This desakota area "thins" out in the north, east, and west, as these locales are more remote from Hong Kong.

The Hong Kong EMR or world city and its future growth

Projection of growth to 2010

From the above description and Table 8.10, it is obvious that by 1996 the Hong Kong EMR had become a huge urbanized area of 46,119 square kilometres with a total urban population of 18.14 million and an urbanization level of 63.8 per cent. The core, Hong Kong, accounted for 22.2

per cent of its total population, or 34.9 per cent of its total urban population. An additional 3.25 million, or 17.9 per cent, of the urban population were amassed in the peri-urban areas of Shenzhen and Macau. The balance of 8.58 million were mainly found in Guangzhou, the five medium-sized cities and 15 small cities, though over 1.5 million were in the urban-rural transition areas. Judging from the urbanization level, population quantum, per capita GDP, per capita FDI, per capita revenue, and per capita retail sales, there is a steep gradient descending from the core to the peripheral or desakota areas (Table 8.10). The huge economic and urbanization gradients that exist indicate that the Hong Kong EMR possesses much potential for further development.

The significance of manufacturing in the economies of Shenzhen and the desakota area and their clear link to Hong Kong FDI and the use of Hong Kong as the entrepôt highlight the dependency relationship of these outer areas to the metropolitan core. In turn, Hong Kong's import-export trade is largely made up of re-exports to and from the desakota area, which also provides business to Hong Kong's tertiary sector in general. Official estimates by local governments stress the importance of cooperation in the future growth of the EMR. As Table 8.13 illustrates, by 2010 the Hong Kong EMR will have five millionaire cities, nine large cities, 14 medium cities, and a total population of around 32.9 million. By then, the core – Hong Kong – will have a population of over 8 million, the threshold for a "mega-city". Although there is general agreement that the EMR will continue to grow and develop, there are differences in opinion as to the qualitative aspects of the future round of growth, and hence the above-estimated huge increase in population of the EMR has been much debated. In short, there are two main issues involved in such discussions. First is the nature of next round of globalisation; second is the sustainability of development of the EMR.

Next round of globalization

Since 1997, there are clear symptoms of a slowing down of the NIDL based on EOI phase one in the entire HKEMR. Saturation and protectionism in the major market (the USA), rising costs, especially labour costs in the delta, and increasing international competition from alternative suppliers – such as Viet Nam and India – are factors challenging the sustainability of the present set of growth forces. As a result, most governments in the Hong Kong EMR are planning to move into high-tech and high-value-added industries. For example, in 1994 the Guangdong government set up a special task force led by the head of the Planning Bureau to study the future development strategy of the urban agglomeration of the PRD economic region (Guangdong Construction Commission 1996). In broad terms, the findings of the team were that the PRD was divided into an inner ring, which embraces Guangzhou, Shenzhen, Zhuhai, and the areas that lie between, and an outer ring, which comprises the rest of the economic region. In 1993, the inner ring had a territory of 11,740 square kilometres and a population of 17.14 million. It produced about 80 per cent of the gross industrial output of the PRD by value. The major future growth directions for the inner ring are development of high-tech industries and improvement of infrastructures that link with the outside world. The much larger outer ring of 31,840 square kilometres, with a 1993 population of 9.15 million, will maintain some degree of EOI phase one industries, but its main effort will lie in the development of recreational and weekend resorts, as well as commercial and large-scale specialized agriculture. Based on further improvements of the basic infrastructure, including the airports, express roads, and deep-water ports, several large-scale heavy industrial and high-tech projects have either started construction or are in planning stages, to broaden the industrial and economic base of the inner ring. For example, an oil refinery and petrochemical complex has been approved by the State Council, which will annually utilize 10 million imperial tons of imported oil. A new electronics city is unfolding in Huiyang in Shenzhen, while an iron and steel plant will be built next to the large port at Zhuhai.

In the core, Hong Kong, the new SAR government has set up a new strategic planning committee to draw up plans for developing Hong Kong into a coordinating centre of a new "bay area" of high-tech industries, making use of the complementary comparative advantages of the delta. In 1998, stressing the need to improve transport and communication links and integration of Hong Kong with the delta, the SAR government announced plans to spend HK$200 billion on such major infrastructure projects. In 1997, a joint committee between the SAR and mainland Chinese officials on infrastructure development and a committee on strategic economic cooperation between the SAR and Guangdong were formed. Thus governments in the HKEMR are keen on forging closer cooperation to promote globalization. It is quite obvious that the EMR is aiming to raise its technological and skill levels so as to provide new drive to promote globalization-related growth even further. Continual efforts to woo FDI and maintain a strong export orientation have been key elements in future plans of the relevant governments. The political "return" of Hong Kong and Macau to China in 1997 and 1999 provided or will provide the political and administrative setting for better cooperation and coordination as well as raising the HKEMR's overall attractiveness to FDI. The current Asian financial crisis forms an additional push for its governments to search for new means and strategy for growth.

Supported by the general success and rapid progress as a whole in

1980–1997, in economic and infrastructural development as well as in reform and opening up, the EMR is better poised for the next round of globalization. The core, Hong Kong, with its accumulated land fund and budgetary surpluses of over HK$400 billion, can take the lead in inducing new high-tech and heavy industries into the EMR. Major local groups such as HK Wharf, HK Bank, Hutchison Whampoa, New World, and Cheungkong are already significant Asian MNCs which cast their production, distribution, and servicing nets worldwide, but which emphasize China and the Asian arenas. They will play an important role in this new round of globalization in terms of investment and coordinating activities that spread over the EMR, China, Asia, and further afield. With the services of the core and new and improved infrastructure and relevant policies in the delta, the Hong Kong EMR will serve as a base point for international capital for exploiting the Chinese market and its comparative advantages.

A world city

In the past round of globalization, the emphasis was on the role of the market, the predominant sector being EOI phase one industries. Though Hong Kong provided some degree of tertiary services in banking, financing, and trading for the rest of China, its mainstay activities were bound in space by the "front-shop, back-factory" model. It was thus inappropriate to label it a world city or global city (cross-continents), as it was more of an international city (cross-national influence within the region). In the coming round of globalization, Hong Kong will serve as a coordinating centre for activities much further afield. For example, there are plans to develop Zhuhai airport into a global transpark with large-scale industrial activities producing components or assembling products from various parts of the world, including the EU, Japan, and the USA, for the car and pharmaceutical industries in various parts of China. A major international hub of tourism and recreation is also planned to combine the traditional gambling attraction of Macau, the shopping and scenic attractions of Hong Kong, a major Oriental Disneyland, and the coastal resort charms of south China. This will serve both the international and the domestic Chinese markets. Hong Kong's role as an international cultural and fashion centre can also be enhanced by major plans to attract local investment and FDI. Based on its long tradition and experience in textiles and garments, and its leading position in the media and the cinema industry in Asia, the possibility for Hong Kong to achieve the status of a major cultural hub is considerable.

While there will still be a division of labour between its various parts, the Hong Kong EMR will most probably function as a world or global city, at least for its core based on its financing, data-processing, information, and decision and control functions. The EMR already has five major international airports (Chek Lap Kok, Guangzhou, Shenzhen, Macau, and Zhuhai) within its boundaries, all only 20–40 km distance from each other. Their present passenger throughput is currently 40 million a year, with a projected 2010 capacity of 110 million. Container port throughput at present is over 17 million TEU a year, making it the world's largest container terminal area. The capacity around 2010, with the development of major ports at Golang, Yiantien, and Chiwan, will be close to 50 million TEU a year. It certainly satisfies Rimmer's (1996) requirement for a global platform on which a world city should be based.

Hong Kong's development into a world city was previously constrained by its limited space, colonial status, and an economic strategy hinged on EOI phase one. The past two decades have provided a transition period in which Hong Kong has breached some of these former confinements to gain in tertiary-sector development and forged growth of the EMR. Its world city status and role will soon materialize with deepened growth and cooperation between it and the delta.

Issues, policies, and sustainable development

Being only 1,093 square kilometres in size, Hong Kong's post-war success in becoming an NIE and major financial and shipping hub owes much to its geography and free-trade policy. Together they offered the right environment for FDI, and hence Hong Kong's integration with the world economy under globalization forces in EOI phase one development. As previously shown, the past two decades saw the extension of such globalization dynamics into the delta, extending the NIDL Hong Kong workbench. This induced rapid structural transformation and urbanization in the delta while Hong Kong enjoyed the benefit of rapid growth in tertiary services, the so-called "front-shop" activities. The opening and reform policies of China and the pioneer and preferential status enjoyed by the delta from 1980 to 1997 allowed and facilitated this new economic partnership. Thus globalization dynamics that incorporated the activities of Hong Kong after the end of the Second World War were able to extend into the delta. In the process Hong Kong and the delta became integrated economically as well as in urban growth and land use to become an EMR. The process, however, has resulted mainly from market forces and China's new receptive policy environment. There has been little official guidance, coordination, and planning. Such is typical to EOI phase one. In the delta, this promoted what is known as "red capitalism" (Lin 1997), which underlines the inexperience of cadres in the delta on one hand and their pent-up desire for quick profits with minimum regard to societal well-being on the other. Physical expansion, which took the form of massive immigration of unskilled young manual workers and rapid conversion of farmland into built-up areas, has degraded the vast desakota area and part of the peri-urban area, while reinvestment in human capital and new industries has been scant. Zhuhai, as the only exception, has maintained and implemented set standards for urban development, such as a cap on urban density at 8,000 persons per square kilometre, implementing a policy of one-third green coverage for all developments, and promoting adequate provision of space for transport. It is therefore worthwhile to discuss further a number of related issues: wasteful use of farmland, pollution, inadequate planning and its coordination, and cross-border cooperation.

Issues

Wasteful use of farmland

The loss of farmland has been averaged at 2.2 per cent annually from 1980 to 1993. In some areas, the figure is much higher – for example, in the peri-urban area of Shenzhen, the SEZ registered a rate of 14.2 per cent per year, and the outskirts of Boan recorded 11.9 per cent. Such loss was mainly due to conversion of agricultural land into urban land, particularly industrial land. The process was bolstered by rampant speculation, fuelled by a lack of planning and a related system of control, as well as the zest of officials for quick returns. On average, the built-up areas of all the towns and cities of the delta increased by 1.5 times during the 1980–1997 period. Shenzhen increased 3,710 per cent, Zhongshan 480 per cent, Nanhai 230 per cent, Huizhou 210 per cent, and Guangzhou 180 per cent (Sit and Yang 1997a). These figures, however, do not reflect the extent that good-quality farmland was wasted when hot-headed local officials bulldozed much more good land into construction sites, many of which are still lying vacant. In applying GIS (geographic information system) techniques to the study of loss of agricultural land in Dongguan, the central part of the delta, during the 1988–1993 period, Yeh and Li (1998) found that actual land loss was 21,285 ha, much higher (two to nine times) than the "expected" loss for meeting the area's expansion needs. Further, it was found that 80.1 per cent of the actual land conversion fell outside optimal locations from the point of view of transport infrastructure and suitable urban development. Thus conversion costs were unnecessarily high and spatially inefficient. What is more, the total amount of construction site increased by an astonishing 96.9 per cent, much higher than the 13.7 per cent increase in built-up area reported

(Yeh and Li 1997). Dongguan's example is certainly duplicated in other areas of the delta. As conversion of agricultural land into urban land, or leaving it to lie vacant for a number of years after being bulldozed, will remove the land from food production capacity for ever, the goal of sustainable land allocation therefore becomes an important issue. Good planning to ensure the minimum loss of good-quality farmland, as well as the selection of less important plots for conversion from the point of view of ecology and food production, become imperative.

Pollution

Large-scale in-migration of unskilled manual workers into the delta and rapid expansion of NIDL industries that utilized land extensively and brought in heavy traffic, together with insignificant attention to and spending on preserving the environment, have combined to yield a serious pollution problem in the delta. It was reported in 1990 that 55.4 per cent and 55.3 per cent of Guangdong province's areas exceeded national standards for air and water pollution. Pollution data for the PRD as a whole are difficult to collect, but Guangzhou and Shenzhen provide illustrations (Guangdong Construction Committee 1996). Guangzhou's air quality standards in 1993, measured in TSP, SO_2 and NO_x, were respectively three, 2.3, and three times worst than those of Hong Kong, and all have exceeded national standards. Noise pollution at 74.8 dBA was found near all major traffic arteries of the city, which is much higher than the national standard. In this city, where attention to the environment is much higher than in the rest of the delta, funds for combating pollution were equivalent to 0.84 per cent of local GDP (Lin 1996). Inadequate funding is a larger problem in the rest of the delta. In Shenzhen, factories are a major source of water pollution. The composite P value used to monitor water pollution of streams in the city increased from 1.89 in 1986 for the SEZ to 4.06 in 1990. The P value for Shenzhen river, its major watercourse, increased from 2.39 to 3.46 in the same period. Pollution worsened since increases in pollutants were not been matched with treatment facility development. From 1982 to 1990 the volume of sewage increased at an annual rate of 38 per cent, but in 1990 the treatment capacity could handle only 14 per cent of the volume. Solid waste increased from 50.5 imperial tons per day in 1981 to 721 tons per day in 1990, and poses another pollution problem. There were increases in noise pollution, from 54.5 dBA in 1986 to 61.3 dBA in 1990, in the entire built-up area of the city (Lai and Yang 1996).

   Water pollution poses a serious threat to the major source of fresh water supply for a larger part of the EMR, including Hong Kong. NIDL factories and the large number of temporary workers associated with them have deteriorated the source of the East river and its numerous storage reservoirs, particularly Shenzhen reservoir, which has drawn critical attention from both the Guangdong and Hong Kong governments.

Inadequate planning and its coordination

The rapid growth of the NIDL in the delta and its export orientation are both unparalleled in PRC history. These changes also happened shortly after China started to modify its central planning system. Hence, planning inadequacy and lack of reasonable inter-bureau and inter-metropolitan coordination were logical consequences. Short-term problems and interests as well as the actions of FDI investors replaced or greatly modified rational long-term considerations. Viewed across the delta as a whole, hot-headedness in opening and in catching up with the NIEs, accompanied by the devolution of power to governments, fuelled the rush towards short-term interests and localism and led to increasing problems related to inadequate planning and coordination (Lin 1997). Excessive waste of valuable agricultural land and the rapid increase of the built-up area are just two of the results of inadequate planning for land conversion and the pricing of land at too low a level.

The coordination of individual urban centres in a regional development strategy was lacking clear definition. Functional duplication and lack of reasonable division of labour were common. Some urban centres tried blindly to develop their own facilities, leading to duplication of major infrastructure projects, their inappropriate siting, and much waste. These faults are easily observable in transport infrastructure. The inter-urban expressway system is fragmented. The connectivity of major highways is unsatisfactory, while state and provincial highways are often reduced to intra-urban roads once they enter the urban centres, putting severe constraints on the efficiency and safety of these major intra-regional conduits.

Poor coordination is also seen in the division of the administrative units, particularly so for the newly formed municipalities. Often, one municipality is almost surrounded by another. The territories of some municipalities zig-zag, or even cross over or leap-frog into one another, creating confusion and unnecessary conflicts and difficulties. Strong localism has sometimes led to refusals to agree to the siting of major regional basic infrastructure.

Cross-border cooperation

Growth and development of the EMR also hinges on cross-border coordination, as the EMR comprises China, Britain and Portugal's authorities before 1997, and, post-1999, governments that will straddle the "two systems" under one country. Thus far, there is no permanent official channel between Hong Kong and Macau dealing with cross-border cooperation. Between Macau and the delta there was a diplomatic channel, the Joint Liaison Committee between the PRC and Portugal, which handled both transitional and cross-border infrastructure and cooperative problems. The committee was not successful because the Portuguese government lacked initiative. Between Hong Kong and the delta, before 1997, under the Joint Liaison Committee of the PRC and the UK, there was a special subcommittee to handle cross-border infrastructural issues. After September 1997, the committee was transformed into the Coordinating Committee for Cross-border Infrastructure between Hong Kong and the mainland to handle major cross-border infrastructure issues. Thus the present cross-border coordination in the EMR is unsatisfactory, limited to infrastructural issues, and fragmented and incomplete in its coverage. The proposal for a bridge linking Hong Kong directly with the western flank of the Pearl river mouth is a case in point (Figure 8.2). Zhuhai and Macau have made different proposals. Zhuhai's proposal made its way to the Infrastructure Coordinating Committee between the UK and China (pre-June 1997), whereas Macau's proposal could not be tabled because of a diplomatic technicality as it was still under Portuguese rule in 1999.

Cross-border cooperation in economic and sectoral strategies and policies, immigration, export-import, customs, and taxation matters have not yet been considered in these committees. While the NIDL under EOI phase one may proceed smoothly within a free-market framework, exploitation and development of comparative advantages to meet the next round of globalization will require coordinated and much stronger input from various governments in the EMR. Thus the HKEMR lags much behind the Singapore growth triangle in setting up the right milieu for cross-border coordination (Krumar 1994).

Sustainable development and policies

China has already adopted "sustainable development" as one of its major national development targets, following the principles of the UN's "Programme for the Twenty-first Century". Future planning and development strategies of Guangdong province and the delta have also promoted sustainability as a major goal. The Hong Kong SAR, in its first policy statement, equally stressed sustainability in drawing up its long-term economic and physical planning strategies. The basic consideration for the HKEMR in achieving sustainable development may be seen as the maximization of the efficiency and benefits of three interrelated systems, the ecological, the social, and the economic (Tang 1996). In more realistic terms, plans should include:

- protection of the natural environment and natural resources;
- restriction on population growth and activity patterns of the population through good management and technological improvement for maintaining an ecological balance;
- improvement in quality of life;
- minimization of non-renewable resource use.

Future growth of the EMR cannot simply be based on its ability to attract FDI and other globalization forces – economic efficiency alone is not enough. New policies and measures should be devised through coordinated efforts of various governments to face a number of challenges:

- protect the water resources;
- protect and minimize the loss of good farmland;
- protect the ecologically sensitive areas;
- enhance efficiency and minimize loss of non-renewable resources by coordinated efforts in road, bridges, and railways building, and the construction and utilization of major infrastructure such as ports, airports, and sewage treatment facilities;
- control the growth of population;
- attain the right sectoral policies for enhancing efficient use of facilities and human resources.

Farmland and the green environment form a major part of the EMR. Farmland does not only have economic value, it is also part of the natural ecology. Vast tracts of farmland together with protected green areas can improve the efficiency of the EMR as an urban ecological system. Guangdong province has proposed new legislation for the Pearl river delta to provide the legal enforcement power and a system of control over the planning of development at various levels of the delta. It will also be the legal basis for a new series of plans to supersede existing and outdated plans adopted in 1989. A new household registration reform is also proposed to give urban resident status to all residents within the built-up areas and put all land under national ownership. Under the new legislation, a Delta Planning Committee is to be formed under the provincial government for coordinating physical planning, managing and implementing the various plans, and coordinating and arranging finance for major infrastructural and investment projects. To aid the work of the committee, a development fund is to be set up with contributions from budget revenues, part of the returns from land sales, and fees from the utilization of the basic infrastructure. A new land policy is also proposed which will include curbing the rights of local authorities, public enterprises, and work units in transferring land and changing its present or designated use; this policy will reduce many of the unreasonable fees related to land transactions and ensure that all developable land is disposed of by public auction (Guangdong Construction Committee 1996).

Though new developments to solve present problems, to develop future comparative advantages, and to enhance sustainability have been discussed at various local governments, a pan-EMR strategic committee to pool ideas and resources of the entire EMR has not yet been developed. Such a pan-EMR committee should include members from the governments of the Hong Kong SAR, Macau, Shenzhen, Zhuhai, and Guangdong. The experience of the Singapore growth triangle (Krumar 1994) has shown that pan-regional cooperation can be achieved between governments of different sovereignties, so a similar or even closer cooperation under the "one country, two systems" regime should be realizable.

Conclusion: Lessons of the HKEMR

Detailed examination of the formation and nature of the HKEMR provides new insights on how globalization forces are concentrated in core urban centres that provide facilities, resources, and a good geographical location, and serve as the platform, hub, or front shop to support globalization. Globalization based on EOI phase one has also been selective in its location, much affected by sources of cheap labour and land. Strengthened globalization in the EOI phase one type of NIDL has led to the development of supercities around core urban centres in Asia – these are invariably port cities and national/regional administrative centres. The combination of polarization and dispersal forces in the criss-crossing of global and local dynamics is best illustrated in the "front-shop, back-factory" model found in the HKEMR. However, contrary to McGee's belief (Chapter 14 in this volume), the dynamics for growth in the case of the HKEMR, and to some extent in other EMRs such as Jabotabek, are largely externally induced. In addition, the structural transformation leading to the emergence of the desakota area has little to do with commuting between this area and the core urban centre. The growth of the entire EMR has a noticeable causal relationship with a rural economy of wet paddy and a dense rural population. For many EMRs in Asia, these two observable "background" elements may most likely be a coincidence. In the case of the HKEMR, long-distance immigration has supplied a good proportion of the labour force demanded by the NIDL, and this constitutes a larger proportion of the non-agricultural population in the desakota area. It may therefore be inferred that EMR formation is linked more to globalization and shows no causual relationship with a past/present rural economy based on wet paddy. It can reasonably be expected that in other areas of the third world, globalization forces combined with the right local physical and policy milieu will lead to rapid urbanization and rural-urban transition around core urban centres.

In many respects, EMRs compete fiercely with each other and other major world metropolises in the globalization process. Rapid structural and physical transformation over a large space and spanning different administrative units are logically difficult to understand properly. It is even more difficult to manage and coordinate further or deepened development in the future. A number of issues and policy solutions have been discussed here using the example of the HKEMR. Further study is required to understanding this new form of urbanization before governments can plan for its sustainable development.

REFERENCES

Amstrong, W. and T. G. McGee. 1985. *Theatres of Accumulation – Studies in Asian and Latin American Urbanization*. London: Methuen.

Castells, M. 1977. *The Urban Question*. Cambridge, MA: MIT Press.

Cheng, T. Y. 1977. *The Economy of Hong Kong*. Hong Kong: Far East Publications.

Chiu, S., K. C. Ho, and T. Lui. 1997. *City-states in the Global Economy*. Boulder, CO: Westview Press.

Chu, D. Y. K. 1996. "The Hong Kong-Zhujiang delta and the world city system", in F. C. Lo and Y. M. Yeung (eds) *Emerging World Cities in Pacific Asia*. Tokyo: United Nations University Press, pp. 465–497.

Clark, G. L. and W. B. Kim. 1995. *Asian NIEs and the Global Economy*. Baltimore: John Hopkins University Press.

Cohen, R. B. 1981. "The new international division of labour, multinational corporations and urban hierarchy", in M. Dear and A. J. Scott (eds) *Urbanization and Urban Planning in Capitalist Societies*. New York: Methuen, pp. 287–315.

Federation of Hong Kong Industries (FHKI). 1992. *Hong Kong's Industrial Investment in the Pearl River Delta*. Hong Kong: FHKI.

Friedmann, J. 1986. "The world city hypothesis", *Development and Change*, Vol. 17, No. 1, pp. 69–84.

Fuchs, R. J., G. W. Jones, and E. M. Pernia (eds). 1987. *Urbanization and Urban Policies in Pacific Asia*. Boulder, CO: Westview Press, pp. 88–111.

Ginsberg, N. 1991. "Extended metropolitan regions in Asia: A new spatial paradigm", in N. Ginsberg, B. Koppel, and T. G. McGee (eds) *The Extended Metropolis: Settlement Transition in Asia*. Honolulu: University of Hawaii Press.

Guangdong Construction Committee. 1996. *The Planning for Urban Agglomeration of the Pearl River Delta Economic Region*. Beijing: China Construction Industry Press (Chinese text).

Guangdong Provincial Government. Various dates. *Guangdong Agricultural Statistical Yearbook*.

Guangdong Provincial Government. Various dates. *Statistical Yearbook of Guangdong*.

Harvey, D. W. 1975. "The Political Economy of Urbanization in Advanced Capitalist Societies", in G. Gappert and H. Rose (eds) *The Social Economy of Cities*. Beverly Hills: *Urban Affairs Annual Review*, Vol. 9.

Harvey, D. W. 1986. *The Urbanization of Capital*. Oxford: Blackwell.

Hong Kong Government. Various dates. *Annual Digest of Statistics.*

Hong Kong Government. Various dates. *Hong Kong Annual Report.*

Hong Kong Government. 1989. "Hong Kong's Port and Airport Development Strategy." Unpublished report.

Hong Kong Trade Development Council. 1997. "Grasp the present, cooperate to build the future", in One Country Two Systems Economic Research Institute (OCTSERI) (ed.) *The Ninth Five Year Plan: The Long-term Target for the Year 2010 and the Hong Kong Economy.* Vol. 1. Hong Kong: OCTSERI, pp. 37–70 (Chinese text).

Hymer, S. 1975. "The multinational corporation and the law of uneven development", in H. Radice (ed.) *International Firms and Modern Imperialism: Selected Readings.* Harmondsworth: Penguin, pp. 37–62.

Krumar, S. 1994. "Johor-Singapore-Riau growth triangle: A model of subregional cooperation", in M. Thant, M. Tang, and H. Kakuza (eds) *Growth Triangles in Asia.* Hong Kong: Oxford University Press, pp. 175–217.

Kwok, P. R. and A. Y. So (eds). 1995. *The Hong Kong-Guangdong Link.* Armonk: M. E. Sharpe, pp. 163–188.

Lai, X. Y. and Z. Yang. 1996. "Preliminary analysis on the relation between population increase and environmental impacts in Shenzhen", in Geographical Association of Guangdong (ed.) *1994 Annual Conference Essays.* Guangzhou: South China Polytechnic University Press (Chinese text), pp. 108–114.

Lin, G. C. S. 1997. *Red Capitalism in South China.* Vancouver: University of British Colombia Press.

Lin, M. Z. 1996. "Comprehensive treatment of Guangzhou's environment and sustainable development", in Geographical Association of Guangdong (ed.) *1994 Annual Conference Essays.* Guangzhou: South China Polytechnic University Press (Chinese text), pp. 52–55.

Lui, Z. and H. D. Wang. 1997. "Hong Kong and Macau's economic relationship after 1997", *Asian Studies* (Hong Kong), No. 24, pp. 228–252 (Chinese text).

Macau Census and Statistics Department. 1997. *Macau in Figures.* Macau: Macau Government.

McGee, T. G. 1991. "The emergence of Desakota regions in Asia: expanding a hypothesis", in N. Ginsberg, B. Koppel and T. G. McGee (eds) *The Extended Metropolis: Settlement Transition in Asia.* Honolulu: University of Hawaii Press.

Niu, Y. F. 1998. "Study on the economic integration of Hong Kong, Macau and Guangdong." Mimeograph, Chinese text.

Rimmer, P. 1996. "International transport and communications interactions between Pacific Asia's emerging world cities", in F. C. Lo and Y. M. Yeung (eds) *Emerging World Cities in Pacific Asia.* Tokyo, United Nations University Press, pp. 48–97.

Shen, J. F., K. Y. Wong and D. Chu. 1998. "Shenzhen model." Mimeograph, Chinese text.

Sit, V. F. S. 1989. "Hong Kong's new industrial partnership with the Pearl river delta", *Asian Geographer*, No. 8, pp. 103–115.

Sit, V. F. S. 1996. "Mega-city, extended metropolitan region, desakota, exo-urbanization: An introduction", in V. F. S. Sit and X. Xu (eds) *Rural Urban Transition and the Growth of Mega Urban Regions in China.* Special issues, *Asian Geographer*, Vol. 15, Nos 1 and 2, pp. 1–14.

Sit, V. F. S., R. D. Cremer, and S. L. Wong. 1990. *Entrepreneurs and Enterprises in Macau*. Hong Kong: Hong Kong University Press.

Sit, V. F. S. and C. Yang. 1995. "Integration of the socialist market economy and world markets: Foreign investment in the Pearl river delta", *Asian Profile*, Vol. 23, No. 1, pp. 1–15.

Sit, V. F. S. and C. Yang. 1997a. "Foreign-investment-induced exo-urbanization in the Pearl river delta, China", *Urban Studies*, Vol. 34, No. 4, pp. 647–677.

Sit, V. F. S. and C. Yang. 1997b. "Foreign capital: New urbanization dynamic of developing countries – Case study of the Pearl river delta", *Geography Journal*, Vol. 50, No. 3, pp. 193–206 (Chinese text).

Soegijoko, B. T. 1996. "Jabotabek and globalization", in F. C. Lo and Y. M. Yeung (eds) *Emerging World Cities in Pacific Asia*. Tokyo: United Nations University Press, pp. 377–414.

Tang, H. Z. 1996. "Issues on sustainable development of the Pearl river delta economic region", in Geographical Association of Guangdong (ed.) *1994 Annual Conference Essays*. Guangzhou: South China Polytechnic University Press (Chinese text), pp. 18–28.

Wu, L. M. L. 1997. *Hong Kong Economic Towards the 21st Century*. Hong Kong: Joint Publishing (Chinese text).

Yeh, A. G. and X. Li. 1997. "An integrated remote sensing and GIS approach in the monitoring and evaluation of rapid urban growth for sustainable development in the Pearl river delta, China", *International Planning Studies*, Vol. 2, No. 2, pp. 193–210.

Yeh, A. G. and X. Li. 1998. "Sustainable land development model for rapid growth areas using GIS", *International Journal of Geographical Information Science*, Vol. 12, No. 2, pp. 169–189.

Yu, T. F. 1997. *Entrepreneurship and Economic Development in Hong Kong*. London: Routledge.

Zheng, P. K., Wang, L. W., and Chen, X. H. 1997. "Hong Kong Investment in Guangdong and its Future", in One Country Two Systems Economic Research Institute (OCTSERI) (ed.) *The Ninth Five-Year Plan: The Long-Term Target for the Year 2010 and the Hong Kong Economy*. Hong Kong: Trade Development Council, pp. 95–124.

Zheng, T. X. 1990. "Accelerating the emergence of megalopolis with the centre of Hong Kong and Macau in the Pearl river delta", *Gangao Jingji*, No. 8, pp. 15–21 (Chinese text).

9

Singapore: Global city and service hub

Chia Siow Yue

Introduction

In the study of cities, Singapore occupies a peculiar place. It is a city-state, which is a city as well as nation. As a city, it is only medium-sized by Asian standards, overshadowed in population and land area by capital cities such as Tokyo, Beijing, Seoul, Taipei, Manila, Bangkok, and Jakarta. As a nation, it has one of the smallest populations and land areas in the world, and in South-East Asia it has the second smallest population (after Brunei) and the smallest land area. However, in economic size it is not small, as its GNP (gross national product) is the third largest in South-East Asia (after Indonesia and Thailand). Its small geographical size appears not to have been a limiting economic handicap, as the city-state has made remarkable economic strides since it gained political independence in August 1965. By 1998 the World Bank ranked Singapore as the richest country in the world in terms of purchasing-power-adjusted per capita income (World Bank 1998). When compared with other metropolitan cities, however, Singapore's per capita GNP ranking would be much lower.

Unlike other cities, many of the issues that confront Singapore are national rather than municipal in character. First, Singapore faces the unique problem of being geographically constrained by political borders and not being able to extend physically into the hinterland. This constraint has prompted Singapore's policy-makers and urban planners to plan ahead, well in anticipation of demand. Physical expansion must take place largely through the expansion of vertical space. At the same time, economic expansion sees the city-state developing its regional and global roles, extending its economic hinterland through trade and investment flows. Second, the city-state has a single-tier government. This has minimized urban-rural conflicts in allocation of government finance, infrastructure development, and environmental protection, thus facilitating physical planning and the implementation of policies.

Singapore is the hub city of South-East Asia. It is the regional entrepôt and South-East Asia's intraregional trade is largely with or through Singapore. It is the major shipping and air transport node of the region, linked by land, sea, and air to all parts of South-East Asia. Singapore is the region's financial centre, providing an ever-widening range of financial services. Singapore's foreign workers and tourists are also largely from South-East Asia. The flows of goods, services, and people have been reinforced by Singapore's outward investments to the region. As a South-East Asian nation, Singapore's regional role and membership in the ASEAN (Association of South-East Asian Nations) regional grouping are crucial for its political security.

As a regional hub city, Singapore serves as the regional headquarters of many American, European, and Japanese multinationals. However, Singapore is more than a regional hub city. It is also a global city, as it has extensive global commercial, financial, transportation, telecommunication, and information links. It serves as the conduit for global commercial and financial penetration into South-East Asia and for South-East Asian goods entering the world market. Singapore's manufactured goods are destined largely for markets in North America and Western Europe rather than South-East Asia. Singapore plays host to some 5,000 foreign multinationals and international companies; they find Singapore an attractive location for manufacturing and service functions as well as headquarters functions. As a global city, the world is Singapore's hinterland, and its physical smallness and lack of natural resources and sizeable domestic market have not been insurmountable obstacles.

The globalization of the Singapore economy, however, renders it highly vulnerable to external developments. Therefore, it has to be informed and tuned into global developments and it must have the economic flexibility to adjust and adapt to expected and unexpected changes in global and regional conditions. To survive and thrive, Singapore must remain internationally competitive and relevant. Likewise, with globalization, Singapore society is exposed to social and cultural changes taking place elsewhere in the world; being a global city as well as a nation, Singapore's leaders are challenged to create strong socio-cultural roots for its citizens.

With the return of Hong Kong to Chinese sovereignty, Singapore is the only city-state left in Asia. This chapter highlights the physical and economic constraints of the city-state, and how these constraints have been overcome through careful physical planning and the strategy of integrating the city-state with the region and the global economy. As a city, it is physically constrained, unable to spill over into the hinterland. However, as an economy it has become borderless, with the region and world as its economic hinterland. The economic strategy has enabled the city-state to achieve one of the highest living standards in the world and to become one of the world's largest trading nations.

City-state and constraints

As a city-state, Singapore suffers from both severe physical constraints, particularly shortages of land and water, and economic vulnerabilities from having to depend on the external world for natural resources and markets.

Managing physical constraints

With a population of 3.9 million in 1998 (including 633,000 non-residents) and a land size of only 648 square kilometres, Singapore has one of the highest population densities among nations in the world, though not among cities. Physical smallness has created intense competition for land and space, resulting in high prices for residential, commercial, and industrial space, and high costs of public utilities and land transport. Physical smallness, however, is not without advantages – a compact city-state with a one-tier government allows speedy and effective implementation of policies and contributes to social cohesion. Singapore has attempted to overcome its land constraint through land reclamation, more effective land-use planning, high-rise development, and stringent measures to control road congestion and environmental pollution, as well as globalization and regionalization strategies.

Land is a non-tradeable asset that Singapore cannot import, unlike other commodities. Extensive land reclamation in recent decades has increased the total land area by 11 per cent from 581 square kilometres. The planned target is eventually to reclaim land to 730 square kilometres to accommodate a population size of 4 million. Further reclamation faces increasing cost and shortage of fill materials (as most hills have been levelled and sand fill has to be imported). The focus is on more intense land utilization by expanding space – that is, vertical upward expansion of high-rise residential buildings, office blocks, flatted factories, and multi-storey carparks, and multi-tier roads and use of underground space, including for transport systems.

Land scarcity places a high premium on land-use planning and management. This has been facilitated by control of urban land demand through immigration restrictions and by control of urban land supply through land acquisition. Singapore does not face the rural-urban migration problem that confronts other city planners; migration is essentially cross-border and subject to border controls, making it easier to project population size. Singapore's Land Acquisition Act gave the government legal power to acquire land speedily and at low cost, which has enabled Singapore to implement its public housing, urban renewal, urban infrastructure, and industrialization projects. For example, since 1960 the Housing and Development Board has succeeded in providing high-rise public housing for 85 per cent of the population. New towns have developed into comprehensive communities, each with recreation facilities, open spaces, schools, and light industries. Non-light industries have been located in industrial estates to maximize the benefits of agglomeration and cluster development and to minimize industrial pollution effects.

In the 1960s, Singapore's city planners were preoccupied with the tasks of meeting the housing demands of a rapidly growing population, and with urban renewal to clear the slums, revitalize the city centre, and improve the living environment. To accommodate the rapid demographic and economic changes, the master plan of the 1950s was replaced in 1971 by the concept plan which guided Singapore's physical growth over the next two decades, providing for high-density residential areas, industries, and urban centres in a ring formation around the central catchment, linked together by a high-capacity and efficient transportation network. The public sector built new towns, airport expressways, main roads, and the mass rapid transit (MRT), and corridors of urbanized areas stretched along the southern part of the island.

In 1991 Singapore launched "The Next Lap", outlining the directions for long-term national development. The concept plan was reviewed, with the objectives of improving the quality of living and working environments and developing Singapore as an Asian tropical city of excellence and an international investment hub (Singapore Urban Redevelopment Authority 1991). Under a strategy of decentralization, new regional centres were planned in the east, north, north-east, and west, each serving up to 800,000 people, to reduce congestion in the central area and bring jobs closer to homes (see Figure 9.1). Within the central region, a new downtown area, incorporating hotels, offices, shopping centres, and nightlife facilities, was created to meet the needs of new and expanding businesses requiring a central location. Technology corridors were planned to contain business parks to meet the needs of new information-based and high-tech industries. Within these, workplaces are interspersed with housing and recreational facilities to build a scientific and business community.

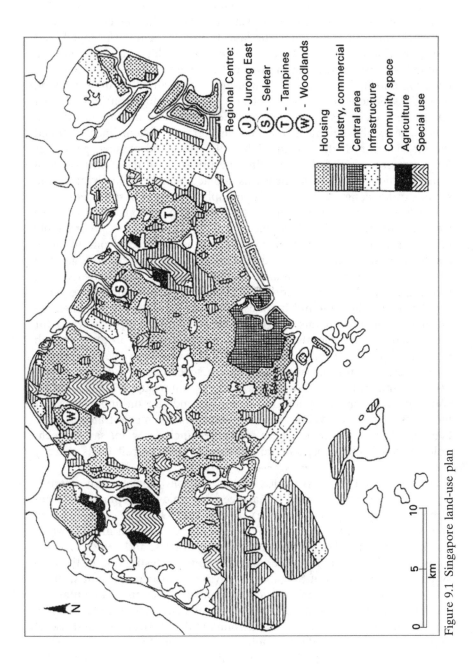

Figure 9.1 Singapore land-use plan

243

Singapore's transportation system makes heavy demands on its limited land resources for port and airport activities which link the city-state with the world, as well as for domestic land transport. A multi-pronged land transportation policy includes curbs on car ownership and usage that are among the most stringent in the world. Car ownership is subject to quota licensing and high taxes, while car usage is restrained by high taxes on petrol, restrictions on entry of vehicles into the central business district under the area licensing scheme, and electronic road pricing on expressways. The establishment of the mass rapid transit system since 1990 and the gradual introduction of the light rail system and planned passenger ferry services are aimed at reducing the pressure on the motor car as a transport mode. With these measures in place, Singapore has avoided the serious traffic congestion that is commonplace in many Asian cities.

Ensuring adequate water supply is a continuing challenge. With limited water catchment areas, only about half of Singapore's fresh water supply originates from domestic sources. The rest is imported from Johor in south Malaysia, and is governed by two bilateral agreements signed in 1961 and 1962 that will terminate in 2011 and 2061 respectively. With growing demand, there are continuing efforts to secure alternative water supplies from Malaysia and Indonesia. Recently, Singapore has been exploring desalination plants to provide a more secure supply of water for future needs. Three desalination plants are planned to produce enough water to replace the water supplied by Johor when the 1961 agreement terminates. The first desalination plant is scheduled to be built on reclaimed land in the north-west by 2003. As water supply extension becomes increasingly costly and the heavy dependence on imported water increases Singapore's vulnerability, demand management strategies have become more important. These strategies include water-saving technologies and campaigns, and raising water prices to reflect its scarcity value.

A limited land area has made Singapore's policy-makers and planners highly conscious of the need to balance economic development with environmental protection and conservation (Chia 1997). The environmental concerns of the city-state are mainly urban and focus on air and water quality, disposal of household and industrial wastes, and vehicular emissions, as well as sustainable land use to minimize destruction of the ecosystem. Key elements of Singapore's environment management strategy are long-term planning and preventive control; strict environmental legislation and effective enforcement; comprehensive monitoring of environmental quality; provision of environmental infrastructure; and use of appropriate environmental technology. As a result, Singapore has developed a reputation as a garden city with high environmental standards. Air and water pollution levels are low when measured against standards set

Table 9.1 Singapore economic structure, 1997

GDP by sector	S$million	% distribution
Total GDP	143,014	100.0
Agriculture and fishing	200	0.1
Quarrying	42	0.0
Manufacturing	34,744	24.3
Utilities	2,671	1.9
Construction	12,907	9.0
Commerce	26,878	18.8
Transport and communications	15,803	11.1
Financial and business services	44,254	30.9
Other services	15,302	10.7
Adjustments	−9,787	−6.8

Source: Singapore Department of Statistics 1998b

by the World Health Organization. The pollution standards index (PSI) is usually in the good to moderate range, except for periods of haze caused by land and forest fires in neighbouring Indonesia. Air in the city-state is free of photochemical smog. Water from the taps is drinkable. Rivers and streams are relatively pollution free and support aquatic life. The whole population enjoys modern sanitation and there is low incidence of food-, water-, and vector-borne diseases. All wastewater and sewage are collected and treated. Singapore's experience with environmental management has shown that despite rapid population growth, urbanization, and industrialization, negative impacts on the environment can be effectively controlled and managed through appropriate policy planning and implementation.

Economic vulnerability and sustainability

Singapore is a country with an atypical economic structure with no primary sector, reflecting its city-state status and its integration into the global economy. As shown in Table 9.1, manufacturing accounted for 24.3 per cent and services (commerce, transport and communications, and financial, business, and other services) for 71.5 per cent of GDP (gross domestic product).

Singapore's lack of natural resources is compensated for by its strategic geographical location and natural harbour, which gave it an initial competitive advantage. However, geographical location has to be buttressed by ease of transportation and telecommunications. Comprehensive air and sea transport and telecommunications networks link the city-state with major cities and ports in the region and around the world. First, the advantageous location astride major sea and air routes linking East Asia with Europe and across the Pacific, together with a natural sheltered deep harbour, have led to the growth of port and shipping activities and marine-related industries such as shipbuilding, ship repairing, and oil-rig construction. Singapore is a major distribution and transhipment hub for the Asia Pacific region. The city-state is close to the region's leading business centres, being within three hours' flying time of the ASEAN capitals, and eight hours' flying time of Beijing, Tokyo, Seoul, Taipei, and Hong Kong in the north, Sydney in the south, and New Delhi in the west. It is a regional distribution and transhipment hub with an advantageous location for time-sensitive shipments. Second, Singapore straddles the time zones of Asia and Europe, which, together with efficient telecommunications, enables its financial markets and institutions to carry on transactions with Japan, Europe, and the USA within official working hours. As a result, Singapore has emerged as an important regional financial centre. Third, Singapore is located in the heart of South-East Asia, a region rich in natural resources and with a market size of nearly 500 million people. The formation of the ASEAN Free Trade Area (AFTA) and the ASEAN Investment Area (AIA) has increased ASEAN's attractions for investors.

Early in the post-colonial years, there were concerns over the city-state's economic viability which led its political leaders, keen to wean Singapore from British colonial rule, to seek political merger and economic union in the larger Federation of Malaysia in September 1963. The merger failed due to political and economic differences, and Singapore became a separate nation in August 1965. In the early post-independence years there were many sceptics who doubted Singapore's political and economic viability. However, by plugging into the global economic system, Singapore was able to establish its economic viability and consequently maintain its political independence.

The economic strategy for the independent city-state is to ensure ready access to global and regional sources of food, water, energy, and industrial goods and develop an export competitiveness in manufacturing and services so as to ensure the capacity to import. The policy emphases are on maintaining free trade, efficient trade infrastructure, adequate foreign exchange reserves, and friendly and cooperative relations with neighbours and major trading partners. Singapore's official foreign reserves, at US$81 billion in 1997, are among the largest in the world, and adequate to finance over seven months of imports (including imports for the entrepôt trade).

Prior to the 1960s, the entrepôt trade and British military base were major sources of export earnings. Since the late 1960s, export manufacturing became increasingly important. When Singapore embarked on an industrialization process in 1960, it faced enormous challenges – the small domestic market inhibited the establishment of industries with scale economies; the lack of natural resources inhibited the development of resource-based industries, although some did emerge by utilizing the raw materials of surrounding countries; and with relatively high wage levels, there was no competitive advantage in labour-intensive industries. However, Singapore was not without advantages for industrialization – industrializing started from a commercial rather than agricultural base, and Singapore had the advantage of a well-developed infrastructure and commercial and financial expertise and could exploit its geographical location. Import substitution was the initial strategy, due to difficulties of developing export capability for infant industries and the promise of a Malaysian common market. Following political secession from Malaysia and the consequent collapse of the common market proposal, Singapore moved rapidly into export manufacturing. Attracting foreign multinational corporations (MNCs) was seen as a necessary strategy for Singapore to achieve industrial competence and market access quickly. Since the early 1980s, service exports have become increasingly important.

Sustained economic growth since the mid-1960s led to extensive job creation, while a stringent population control policy limited the growth in the domestic labour supply after the 1960s; thus emerging labour shortages in the late 1970s led to loss of competitiveness in labour-intensive industries and services. The economic strategy switched to the promotion of high-tech manufacturing and high-value-added services. This industrial restructuring was interrupted by the 1985–1986 recession.

The post-recession strategy as outlined in *The Singapore Economy: New Directions* (Singapore Economic Committee 1986) and *The Strategic Economic Plan* (Singapore Economic Planning Committee 1991) called for the development of high-tech manufacturing and high-value-added services as twin engines of growth and Singapore as a total business centre. Domestically, Singapore as a production base was increasingly constrained by its small economic size, limited land and labour, and weak technological base. Externally, globalization trends were accelerating and competing production centres were multiplying. Singapore needed to develop beyond manufacturing to encompass other parts of the business value chain, such as research, product development and design, process engineering, international marketing and distribution, and operational headquarters. The "Manufacturing 2000" programme, under the Strategic Economic Plan (SEP), affirms the continuing importance of manufacturing for the Singapore economy and targets the share of manufacturing at no less than 25 per cent of GDP, in recognition of the strong linkage between modern manufacturing and services, while the SEP's "International Business Hub 2000" programme promotes a parallel strategy to develop Singapore as a global city and a hub for business and finance, logistics and distribution, and telecommunications and information.

Global and regional links

Singapore has one of the most outward-oriented economies in the world, with extensive global and regional links. The extent to which Singapore has become a global city is evident from the size of its international trade and international financial transactions, the daily movements of aircraft and ships, and contacts made by telecommunications.

Trade and investment links

Singapore's international trade in goods and services is more than three times the size of its GNP. The high international trade orientation reflects a poor resource base and small population size, as well as Singapore's entrepôt role and free-trade policy. Table 9.2 shows the geographical pattern of external trade for 1997. Of total trade, Asia accounted for a 61.6 per cent share; this share would be higher if data on trade with Indonesia were available for inclusion. Within Asia, the trade is mainly with Malaysia and Japan, and to a lesser extent Hong Kong, Taiwan, and Thailand. Outside Asia, the main trading partners are the USA (Singapore's second largest trading partner after Malaysia) and the European Union.

Singapore has served as the regional entrepôt of South-East Asia since the early nineteenth century, providing the functions of trading, financing, transhipment, storage, breaking of bulk, sorting, grading, and processing. Historically the entrepôt function was largely one of importing manufactures from the Western industrial countries for bulk-breaking and redistribution to countries in South-East Asia, and collecting the primary produce of South-East Asia for sorting, grading, processing, and re-export to the Western industrial countries. The initial advantages of a strategic location, a natural deep harbour, and the free-port policy under British colonial rule were reinforced over the decades by the development of transportation, telecommunications, financial, and commercial infrastructure and the accumulation of expertise in trade and finance. As the economic hinterland was located in other countries, this entrepôt trade has always been vulnerable to disruption by external developments and policies. The external threat became serious in the 1950s, as countries in the region established their own national governments and sought to develop their own ports, direct trading, and processing industries, thus undermining Singapore's traditional entrepôt role. However, the entrepôt trade continued to expand with the growth and industrialization of South-East Asian economies. Instead of an intermediation role for South-East Asian primary produce, Singapore increasingly plays an intermediation

Table 9.2 Geographical pattern of Singapore's external trade, 1997

	Total trade	Imports	Exports	Total trade	Imports	Exports
	S$million			% distribution		
Total	**382,218**	**196,605**	**185,613**	**100.0**	**100.0**	**100.0**
America	**74,226**	**36,297**	**37,929**	**19.4**	**18.5**	**20.4**
Brazil	1,008	385	623	0.3	0.2	0.3
Canada	1,595	1,028	568	0.4	0.5	0.3
USA	67,135	33,017	34,117	17.6	16.8	18.4
Asia	**235,316**	**124,271**	**111,045**	**61.6**	**63.2**	**59.8**
Bahrain	245	201	44	0.1	0.1	0.0
Bangladesh	897	71	825	0.2	0.0	0.4
Brunei	2,337	271	2,067	0.6	0.1	1.1
China	14,484	8,447	6,038	3.8	4.3	3.3
Hong Kong	23,629	5,780	17,848	6.2	2.9	9.6
India	4,846	1,548	3,297	1.3	0.8	1.8
Iran	1,071	873	198	0.3	0.4	0.1
Japan	47,688	34,564	13,125	12.5	17.6	7.1
Korea, Republic of	11,539	6,056	5,483	3.0	3.1	3.0
Kuwait	1,870	1,769	101	0.5	0.9	0.1
Malaysia	61,953	29,548	32,405	16.2	15.0	17.5
Pakistan	495	88	407	0.1	0.0	0.2
Philippines	7,335	2,954	4,382	1.9	1.5	2.4
Saudi Arabia	8,529	7,974	555	2.2	4.1	0.3
Sri Lanka	661	69	591	0.2	0.0	0.3
Taiwan	16,575	8,208	8,367	4.3	4.2	4.5
Thailand	18,613	10,080	8,532	4.9	5.1	4.6
United Arab Emirates	3,823	2,430	1,393	1.0	1.2	0.8

249

Table 9.2 (cont.)

	Total trade	Imports	Exports	Total trade	Imports	Exports
	S$million			% distribution		
Europe	**60,574**	**31,944**	**28,630**	**15.8**	**16.2**	**15.4**
France	9,080	5,431	3,648	2.4	2.8	2.0
Germany	12,101	6,723	5,378	3.2	3.4	2.9
Italy	3,675	2,903	771	1.0	1.5	0.4
Netherlands	6,253	1,695	4,558	1.6	0.9	2.5
Switzerland	2,664	2,292	373	0.7	1.2	0.2
UK	11,703	5,513	6,190	3.1	2.8	3.3
Commonwealth of Independent States (CIS)	1,571	394	1,176	0.4	0.2	0.6
Oceania	**8,878**	**3,111**	**5,767**	**2.3**	**1.6**	**3.1**
Australia	6,997	2,668	4,328	1.8	1.4	2.3
New Zealand	895	335	559	0.2	0.2	0.3
Africa	**3,223**	**982**	**2,241**	**0.8**	**0.5**	**1.2**

Source: Singapore Department of Statistics 1998b

role for South-East Asian trade in machinery, equipment, and industrial parts and components. Table 9.3 shows the commodity composition and geographical destination of Singapore's entrepôt exports. The destinations are mainly Malaysia, Hong Kong, Japan, Thailand, and the USA; although no data are available, it is generally recognized that entrepôt trade with Indonesia is also sizeable.

Apart from trade, further evidence of Singapore's link with the global economy is the concentration of foreign multinational corporations. Singapore is home to about 5,000 foreign MNCs that use the city-state as a base for their global and regional operations. MNC presence has enabled Singapore to expand industrially beyond its small domestic market, linking it to world markets. UNCTAD (1997) data show that Singapore has one of the highest foreign direct investment (FDI) penetrations in the world, whether measured in terms of the ratio of inward FDI flows to gross fixed capital formation or the ratio of inward FDI stock to GDP. And until 1990, when overtaken by China, Singapore was the largest recipient of FDI in the developing world. In the early years FDI was needed to close the savings-investment gap, but increasingly FDI has augmented the scarcer resources of technology, management, and marketing expertise.

The number of foreign-controlled companies (that is, with at least 50 per cent foreign equity) reached 11,290 by 1995, accounting for 18.1 per cent of total companies in Singapore's corporate sector, 28.3 per cent of corporate shareholders' equity, and 58.6 per cent of corporate assets (Singapore Department of Statistics 1998a). Data on the inward stock of foreign equity investments in Singapore are shown in Table 9.4. An overwhelming 85 per cent of foreign investment in Singapore has taken the form of FDI, with only 15 per cent in portfolio investments. Sectorally, the largest concentrations of FDI are in financial and business services (45 per cent), manufacturing (36.3 per cent), and commerce (13.9 per cent), reflecting Singapore's role as a financial centre, manufacturing base, and transportation and trading hub. Singapore is heavily dependent on FDI from the "triad", with the European Union (20.6 per cent), Japan (20.1 per cent), and the USA (16.9 per cent) accounting for a combined 57.6 per cent share. ASEAN sourcing accounted for only 6.7 per cent.

Singapore's outward investments have been growing rapidly in the past decade, although still substantially below the growth levels of inward investments. By 1995 (latest available figures), the stock of equity investments abroad by the Singapore corporate sector had reached S$48.5 billion (US$34.2 billion), of which 76.0 per cent were direct equity and 24.0 per cent were portfolio equity investments. As shown in Table 9.5, the direct equity investments were concentrated in finance (51.5 per cent),

Table 9.3 Singapore's entrepôt exports, 1997

Destination	S$million	% distribution
Total	**78,078**	**100.0**
America	**8,736**	**11.2**
Brazil	316	0.4
Canada	248	0.3
USA	7,268	9.3
Asia	**56,009**	**71.7**
Bahrain	21	0.0
Bangladesh	453	0.6
Brunei	1,662	2.1
China	2,439	3.1
Hong Kong	7,312	9.4
India	1,918	2.5
Iran	151	0.2
Japan	5,169	6.6
Korea, Republic of	2,716	3.5
Kuwait	50	0.1
Malaysia	18,408	23.6
Pakistan	238	0.3
Philippines	2,174	2.8
Saudi Arabia	329	0.4
Sri Lanka	337	0.4
Taiwan	4,144	5.3
Thailand	4,491	5.8
United Arab Emirates	1,007	1.3
Europe	**9,270**	**11.9**
France	1,128	1.4
Germany	1,799	2.3
Italy	308	0.4
Netherlands	1,409	1.8
Switzerland	248	0.3
UK	1,633	2.1
Commonwealth of Independent States (CIS)	873	1.1
Oceania	**2,763**	**3.5**
Australia	2,199	2.8
New Zealand	303	0.4
Africa	**1,298**	**1.7**

manufacturing (25.6 per cent), commerce (8.9 per cent), and real estate (6.9 per cent). Firms with foreign-equity capital spearheaded the outward investment drive. While inward FDI is largely global, outward FDI is mainly regional. The main destinations are Malaysia (mainly manufacturing, finance, and commerce), Hong Kong (mainly finance), and Indonesia (mainly manufacturing).

Table 9.3 (cont.)

Commodity	S$million	% distribution
Total	**78,078**	**100.0**
Food	1,945	2.5
Beverages and tobacco	2,359	3.0
Crude materials	1,235	1.6
Mineral fuels	307	0.4
Animal and vegetable oils	193	0.2
Chemicals	4,486	5.7
Manufactured goods by material	7,467	9.6
Machinery and transport equipment	49,629	63.6
Miscellaneous manufactures	8,243	10.6
Miscellaneous transactions	2,214	2.8

Source: Singapore Department of Statistics 1998b

Manufacturing platform and service hub

FDI penetration is highest in the manufacturing sector, where foreign investors own around two-thirds of total equity capital. Foreign investments are mainly targeted at high-capital-intensive industries such as electronics, chemicals, and petroleum refining. Foreign firms (100 per cent and majority equity) made an overwhelming contribution to the growth, widening, and deepening of Singapore's manufacturing sector and to its international competitiveness, contributing the bulk of manufacturing output, value added, and exports.

For most of the 1960s, foreign investors in manufacturing were attracted by Singapore's ready access to South-East Asian raw materials, the protected (albeit small) domestic market, and textiles and garments not being subject to export quota restrictions under the international multifibre arrangement. However, the largest FDI investments were in capital-intensive petroleum refineries by American, British, and Dutch companies to meet the market demand for petroleum products in the Asia Pacific. Singapore's geographical location and the large petroleum bunkering demand, as well as the trend of locating refining facilities near market areas, led to the establishment of refineries in the country using imported crude. Refining capacity expanded rapidly to exceed 1 million barrels per day, and Singapore became the third largest refining centre after Rotterdam and Houston. By the 1980s, development extended into downstream petrochemicals. Since the late 1960s there had also been a surge of Japanese and American investments in shipyards and in the electrical and electronics industry. The rapid development of shipbuilding, ship repairing, and oil-rig construction facilities was in response to

Table 9.4 Singapore's stock of inward foreign equity investment, 1995

Country source	S$million	% distribution
Direct equity investment	**84,267**	**100.0**
USA	14,253	16.9
Australia	3,132	3.7
Europe	24,816	29.4
European Union	17,385	20.6
UK	6,666	7.9
Germany	1,895	2.2
Netherlands	4,397	5.2
Others	4,427	5.3
Switzerland	7,107	8.4
Other Europe	324	0.4
Asia	28,388	33.7
Japan	16,970	20.1
Hong Kong	3,910	4.6
Taiwan	928	1.1
ASEAN	5,677	6.7
Malaysia	3,524	4.2
Indonesia	788	0.9
Philippines	357	0.4
Thailand	802	1.0
Brunei	206	0.2
Other Asia	904	1.1
Other countries	13,678	16.2
Portfolio and other equity	**14,949**	
Total equity investment	**99,216**	
Sector	S$million	% distribution
Direct equity investment	**84,267**	**100.0**
Agriculture and fishing	34	0.0
Mining and quarrying	−2	−0.0
Manufacturing	30,626	36.3
Construction	969	1.1
Commerce	11,697	13.9
Transport and storage	2,655	3.2
Financial and business services	38,238	45.4
Other services	50	0.1
Portfolio and other equity	**14,949**	
Total equity investment	**99,216**	

Source: Singapore Department of Statistics 1998b

the world boom in shipping and the regional boom in oil prospecting. In the electrical and electronics industry, American MNCs increasingly sought offshore production locations for products and components to offset rising

Table 9.5 Singapore's stock of outward equity investment, 1995

Country source	S$million	% distribution
Direct equity investment	**36,866**	**100.0**
Asia	21,511	58.3
ASEAN	12,467	33.8
Brunei	37	0.1
Indonesia	3,448	9.4
Malaysia	7,305	19.8
Philippines	521	1.4
Thailand	860	2.3
Viet Nam	296	0.8
Hong Kong	5,089	13.8
Taiwan	530	1.4
China	2,445	6.6
Japan	382	1.0
Other Asia	598	1.6
Europe	3,844	10.4
Netherlands	456	1.2
UK	2,435	6.6
Other Europe	953	2.6
Australia	1,116	3.0
USA	2,036	5.5
Other countries	8,359	22.7
Portfolio and other equity	11,632	
Total equity investment	48,498	
Sector	S$million	% distribution
Direct equity investment	**36,866**	**100.0**
Manufacturing	9,424	25.6
Construction	320	0.9
Commerce	3,289	8.9
Transport and storage	861	2.3
Financial	18,997	51.5
Real estate	2,535	6.9
Business services	1,084	2.9
Others	356	1.0
Portfolio and other equity	**11,632**	
Total equity investment	**48,498**	

Source: Singapore Department of Statistics 1998b

labour costs at home; the American investments in Singapore were soon followed by European and Japanese MNCs (Chia 1997). Japanese investments in Singapore industries grew rapidly in the 1980s, reflecting the rising trend in offshore production by Japanese firms. After 1985, following the sharp appreciation of the yen, Japan became the leading source of new foreign investment in Singapore manufacturing. Foreign investments in Singapore industries are largely targeted for the export market, both for the foreign investors' home markets and third-country markets.

Singapore remains a highly attractive location for foreign MNCs despite eroding cost competitiveness *vis-à-vis* neighbouring countries and cities – for projects with high value-added and technological content, the benefits are the availability of professional and skilled manpower and efficient and modern infrastructure; projects of high capital intensity and long gestation benefit from political stability and a conducive operating environment; projects requiring quick operational start-ups benefit from the availability of efficient industrial infrastructure and support services; and for projects serving the regional and global markets, the attractions are the strategic location and regional and global links.

Apart from manufacturing, Singapore's economic strategy also focused on the development of high-value-added services. It is a regional trading, financial, transport, and telecommunications hub. Competitive advantage arises from its strategic location, the development of physical infrastructure and human resources, and a trade policy that imposes minimal restrictions on the movement of goods, services, and production factors. The hub strategy is based on the notion that key economic activities such as finance, shipping, air transport, telecommunications, and information are increasingly concentrated in a few strategic centres around the world, each one acting as a hub to service its extended hinterland and link it with the rest of the world. Singapore seeks to secure the "first mover" advantage by developing world-class physical infrastructure, providing the institutional and incentive frameworks, and building good relations with regional countries through political diplomacy, outward investment, and joint ventures to combine the competitive strengths of Singapore and its regional and international partners.

Singapore is the world's busiest seaport in terms of shipping tonnage, cargo tonnage, and volume of bunkers sold. In 1997, 130,333 ships called at the port, with shipping tonnage of 808.3 million gross tonnes, carrying cargo of 327.5 million tonnes, and giving rise to bunker sales of 16.9 million tonnes. It is also the world's second largest port in terms of container throughput, with 14.1 million 20-foot equivalent units (TEUs) in 1997. Ships from all over the world, carrying goods and passengers, call at Singapore. Singapore services some 400 shipping lines which provide links to over 700 ports worldwide. The frequency of shipping calling at the port as well as the range and efficiency of port and port-related services have enabled Singapore to maintain its position as a leading global and regional port (Maritime and Port Authority of Singapore 1998).

In air transport, Singapore's Changi airport has been ranked among the world's top 10 airports, and in 1997 it served 86,276 aircraft, 25.2

million passengers, and 1.3 million tonnes of air cargo. Also, 70 scheduled airlines provide over 3,300 flights a week, linking Singapore directly to 133 cities in 54 countries. Singapore has bilateral air service agreements with 89 countries and in April 1997 signed a historic open-skies agreement with the USA. When Changi's Terminal 3 and ancillary facilities are completed by the year 2004, the airport will be able to handle over 60 million passengers a year (Civil Aviation Authority of Singapore 1997). The flight frequency and the efficiency and quality of services provided by Changi airport and Singapore Airlines have contributed to Singapore being a major air transport hub in the Asia Pacific. Changi was named the best airport in 1997 by eight travel magazines. Table 9.6 shows the geographical distribution of air cargo and air passenger traffic. For cargo traffic, North-East Asia is the most important, followed by South-East Asia and Europe, with Japan, Australia, and the USA being the leading countries. For passenger traffic, South-East Asia is the most important, followed by North-East Asia and Europe, with Malaysia, Indonesia, Thailand, Japan, and Australia as the leading countries.

In telecommunications, Singapore is connected by telephone to almost every country in the world. Operator-connected calls provide links to more than 226 destinations. Singapore is also in touch with the world through Singapore Telecom's 001 IDD service, which has direct connections to 220 countries. The emphasis is on communications infrastructure and information technology education. All of Singapore is to be networked by fibre-optic cable, linking households and institutions into a giant information system.

While the export manufacturing strategy requires the active role of foreign MNCs, the hub strategy means attracting international business, including regional headquarters. Many of the thousands of foreign MNCs in Singapore have divisions performing various regional headquarters (RHQ) functions. Government policy in recent years has encouraged the establishment of RHQs in Singapore by global companies, performing wide-ranging functions including business planning and coordination, treasury and risk management, personnel management and human resource development, R&D, production engineering and product design, technical support, marketing and sales service, and procurement of raw materials and components. The advantages of Singapore for RHQs include its strategic geographical location in the dynamic East Asian region; world-class transport and telecommunications infrastructure, logistics, and financial services; established Western legal and accounting systems; availability of human resources and widespread use of English; political stability, a conducive business environment, and comfortable living environment; and low transactions costs for movement of goods, services, persons, and funds.

Table 9.6 Geographical pattern of Singapore's air cargo and air passengers, 1997

	Air cargo (tonnes)			Air cargo % distribution			Air passengers (000s)			Air passengers % distribution		
	Total	Discharged	Loaded	Total	Discharged	Loaded	Total	Arrivals	Departures	Total	Arrivals	Departures
Total	**1,336,348**	**696,778**	**639,570**	**100.0**	**100.0**	**100.0**	**23,799**	**11,916**	**11,883**	**100.0**	**100.0**	**100.0**
South-East Asia	**314,140**	**168,936**	**145,204**	**23.5**	**24.2**	**22.7**	**10,388**	**5,235**	**5,153**	**43.6**	**43.9**	**43.4**
ASEAN	N/A	N/A	N/A	N/A	N/A	N/A	10,215	5,145	5,070	42.9	43.2	42.7
Brunei	N/A	N/A	N/A	N/A	N/A	N/A	278	139	139	1.2	1.2	1.2
Indonesia	N/A	N/A	N/A	N/A	N/A	N/A	3,288	1,610	1,678	13.8	13.5	14.1
Malaysia	58,209	26,945	31,264	4.4	3.9	4.9	3,543	1,820	1,723	14.9	15.3	14.5
Philippines	41,290	16,500	24,790	3.1	2.4	3.9	645	326	319	2.7	2.7	2.7
Thailand	89,174	51,049	38,125	6.7	7.3	6.0	2,200	1,121	1,079	9.2	9.4	9.1
Viet Nam	N/A	N/A	N/A	N/A	N/A	N/A	262	130	132	1.1	1.1	1.1
North-East Asia	**462,868**	**229,292**	**233,576**	**34.6**	**32.9**	**36.5**	**5,909**	**2,947**	**2,962**	**24.8**	**24.7**	**24.9**
Hong Kong	102,873	46,764	56,109	7.7	6.7	8.8	1,598	816	782	6.7	6.8	6.6
Japan	154,315	71,259	83,056	11.5	10.2	13.0	2,189	1,086	1,103	9.2	9.1	9.3
Taiwan	100,278	54,607	45,671	7.5	7.8	7.1	964	456	508	4.1	3.8	4.3
South Asia	**70,540**	**38,684**	**31,856**	**5.3**	**5.6**	**5.0**	**1,452**	**755**	**697**	**6.1**	**6.3**	**5.9**
India	43,209	22,394	20,815	3.2	3.2	3.3	877	458	419	3.7	3.8	3.5
Pakistan	N/A	N/A	N/A	N/A	N/A	N/A	82	44	38	0.3	0.4	0.3
Sri Lanka	N/A	N/A	N/A	N/A	N/A	N/A	208	107	101	0.9	0.9	0.8
West Asia	**23,501**	**9,869**	**13,632**	**1.8**	**1.4**	**2.1**	**253**	**133**	**120**	**1.1**	**1.1**	**1.0**
Oceania	**127,252**	**72,437**	**54,815**	**9.5**	**10.4**	**8.6**	**2,412**	**1,172**	**1,240**	**10.1**	**9.8**	**10.4**
Australia	110,320	64,314	46,006	8.3	9.2	7.2	2,082	1,010	1,072	8.7	8.5	9.0
New Zealand	15,592	7,808	7,784	1.2	1.1	1.2	306	150	156	1.3	1.3	1.3
Europe	**217,710**	**116,040**	**101,670**	**16.3**	**16.7**	**15.9**	**2,518**	**1,259**	**1,259**	**10.6**	**10.6**	**10.6**
France	26,388	14,455	11,933	2.0	2.1	1.9	220	109	111	0.9	0.9	0.9
Germany	29,643	15,413	14,230	2.2	2.2	2.2	457	228	229	1.9	1.9	1.9
Netherlands	31,951	16,824	15,127	2.4	2.4	2.4	233	116	117	1.0	1.0	1.0
Scandinavia	18,576	12,335	6,241	1.4	1.8	1.0	119	58	61	0.5	0.5	0.5
Switzerland	23,392	14,549	8,843	1.8	2.1	1.4	233	113	120	1.0	0.9	1.0
UK	33,641	16,295	17,346	2.5	2.3	2.7	919	472	447	3.9	4.0	3.8
North America	**109,564**	**57,087**	**52,477**	**8.2**	**8.2**	**8.2**	**614**	**287**	**327**	**2.6**	**2.4**	**2.8**
USA	108,171	56,275	51,896	8.1	8.1	8.1	576	269	307	2.4	2.3	2.6
Other regions	**10,773**	**4,433**	**6,340**	**0.8**	**0.6**	**1.0**	**253**	**127**	**126**	**1.1**	**1.1**	**1.1**

Source: Singapore Department of Statistics 1998b

Regional financial centre

Singapore is the third largest financial centre in Asia (after Tokyo and Hong Kong). While Singapore has developed financial services to serve its entrepôt trade and manufacturing, it was only in the 1960s that the idea emerged to promote it as a regional financial centre. 1968 saw the establishment of the Asian Dollar Market (ADM), collecting offshore funds for offshore lending. Banks were encouraged to set up Asian currency units (ACUs) to handle these foreign currency deposits and loans. The main users of the ADM are the world's leading commercial and merchant banks, supranational bodies, governments, and MNCs. The ADM has played a key role in financing regional trade and economic development by acting as a channel for international capital flows into the region. The assets of ACUs had reached US$557 billion by 1997. Over the years, the strategy has also been to establish Singapore as a risk management centre with active foreign exchange trading, money market operations, and trading in capital market instruments, equities, and futures.

A wide variety of foreign financial institutions are located in Singapore, linking it to the international financial network and other global cities. In 1997 there were 152 commercial banks, 80 merchant banks, 65 representative offices of banks and merchant banks, and nine international money brokers. Of the 152 commercial banks, 140 were foreign banks, with 22 having full banking licences, 13 having restricted banking licences, and 105 having offshore banking licences. Of these, 144 were granted ACUs to transact in the Asian Dollar Market (Monetary Authority of Singapore 1998). Foreign financial institutions based in Singapore enjoy time-zone advantages (straddling Asia and Europe), efficient transport and telecommunications facilities, the transparent legal framework and financial regulations, ready availability of professional manpower, attractive investment incentives, and political, social, and economic stability.

Regionalization and the Indonesia-Malaysia-Singapore growth triangle

Regionalization strategy

A maturing economy, changing factor endowments (capital surpluses and labour shortages), and rising costs have increasingly pushed Singapore to invest abroad. Particularly in manufacturing, outward investments complement domestic industrial upgrading and productivity improvements to overcome land and labour constraints and a strong Singapore dollar so as to maintain international competitiveness. And as foreign MNCs in

Singapore relocated some of their electronics operations to neighbouring countries such as Malaysia and Thailand, subcontractors followed their MNC clients abroad. The outward investments were also attracted by the improving investment opportunities in East Asia. Choice of investment location depended on market and cost considerations; proximity to Singapore was a key factor for some, as it facilitated procurement of inputs and shipment of outputs, and provided ready access to support staff based in Singapore. Investments in finance, commerce, and real estate were more attracted by investment and business opportunities in host countries than by the cost push factor.

In early 1993, the Singapore government launched its regionalization strategy in response to domestic and regional developments, and actively encouraged private enterprises in Singapore to invest in Asia. There were a number of push and pull factors. First, on the push side, a maturing Singapore economy was facing severe land and labour constraints and rising costs, necessitating outward investments to sustain its growth performance. Second, on the pull side, Singapore wished to take advantage of the economic boom in East Asia, a region offering abundant natural resources, low-cost labour, and rapidly expanding markets, providing opportunities for Singapore to invest in manufacturing, services, and infrastructure projects. Third, domestic enterprises with limited outward investment experience found it easier to regionalize than to go global; geographical proximity and cultural and linguistic familiarity helped to reduce information and transaction costs, while for small and medium-sized enterprises with limited managerial resources, nearby investments facilitated management supervision from the home base. Fourth, Singapore also wanted to share with the region its expertise in economic management, infrastructure development, and human resource development. The regionalization strategy included cooperative joint ventures by the Singapore government and Singaporean firms with foreign government agencies, foreign MNCs, and companies in host countries.

Thus, Singapore development agencies and state-owned enterprises have entered into partnership with foreign authorities and private enterprises to develop regional infrastructure projects such as the Batam industrial park, Bintan industrial estate, Bintan Beach international resort and Karimun marine and petroleum complexes in the Indonesia-Malaysia-Singapore growth triangle; the Suzhou township and industrial park project and Wuxi industrial park in China; the Bangalore information technology park in India; and the Viet Nam-Singapore industrial park. In the China-Singapore Suzhou industrial park, state-owned Jurong Town Corporation oversees the master planning, infrastructure, engineering, and building design and project management works for the 7,000 ha project as well as developing the low-rise and high-rise factory buildings; a total of

83 projects have been secured with investment commitments exceeding US$2.3 billion. The information technology park in Bangalore is a S$680 million joint venture with Indian partners; Phase I of development, covering 27 hectares, has been completed, providing office and production facilities for lease and sale. These industrial parks provide quick and effective start-up platforms for companies, as they are generally self-contained, with ready-built factories and industrial land located near commercial, medical, educational, residential, recreational, and other facilities. The next section case studies one such regionalization venture.

Indonesia-Malaysia-Singapore growth triangle

The Indonesia-Malaysia-Singapore growth triangle (IMS-GT) is a metropolitan spill-over from Singapore into neighbouring Malaysia and Indonesia (Figure 9.2). It has been described as an extended metropolitan region by McGee and McLeod (1992), a natural economic territory by Scalapino (1992), and one of three types of subregional economic zones in East Asia by Chia and Lee (1993). Since the inception of the IMS-GT around 1990, other ASEAN growth triangles have sprung up, namely the northern Indonesia-Malaysia-Thailand growth triangle (IMT-GT), the Brunei-Indonesia-Malaysia-Philippines east ASEAN growth area (BIMP-EAGA), and the greater Mekong subregion (GMS). The ASEAN growth triangles are the outcome of political cooperation, economic complementarity, and geographical proximity.

Unlike a free-trade area that focuses on market sharing and trade liberalization among member countries, the growth triangle (GT) emphasizes resource pooling and investment cooperation among contiguous geographical provinces and states of countries. The objective of the GT is to combine the factor resources of geographically contiguous areas to exploit the economies of scale and agglomeration and differences in comparative advantage and cost structures for cluster development, so as to attract more regional and foreign investments and achieve greater competitiveness in regional and world markets. Such economic cooperation is a positive-sum game in which all the constituent areas benefit.

In December 1989, Singapore proposed the formation of a growth triangle linking the contiguous areas of Singapore, Johor (in south Malaysia), and the Riau islands (in west Indonesia). The growth triangle, initially known as Sijori, was formalized in December 1994 and its name changed to the Indonesia-Malaysia-Singapore growth triangle. In 1996, the geographical coverage was extended to include the contiguous states of Malacca, Negri Sembilan, and Pahang in Malaysia, and the province of Western Sumatra in Indonesia. In 1997, the coverage was further extended to include the Indonesian provinces of Jambi, Bengkulu, Southern

Figure 9.2 Singapore-Johor-Riau growth triangle

Sumatra, Lampung, and West Kalimantan. As such, the IMS-GT now encompasses a geographical area of about 565,000 square kilometres and a population of over 35 million, respectively 870 times and 10 times the size of Singapore.

Political cooperation was crucial in launching the IMS-GT in 1990. In the 1970s, Indonesia had promoted Batam, a Riau island close to Singapore and on the northern periphery of Indonesia with a sparse population of only a few thousand and undeveloped infrastructure, as an oil base and a duty-free zone to compete with Singapore. The Batam strategy met with limited success, so Indonesia then shifted its strategy to twinning with Singapore. Subsequent Singapore government support and Singapore investments in infrastructure and a relaxation of foreign investment regulations by Indonesia were instrumental in the surge of investments from Singapore companies and foreign MNCs based in Singapore. The Singapore government helped develop and manage the Batamindo industrial park (BIP) and persuaded Singapore companies to invest; Sumitomo, the first major tenant in the BIP, attributed its investment to the urging of the Singapore government. Development cooperation in Batam has since been extended to Bintan and other Riau islands. Bilateral agreements between Indonesia and Singapore provide for the joint development of Riau, including water resources, part of which will meet Singapore's future water needs. For the Singapore-Johor side of the GT, traditional bilateral political and economic links had been very strong, due to common historical ties under British colonial rule, geographical proximity cemented by a causeway, Johor supplying Singapore with raw water and Singapore in turn supplying Johor with treated water, and friendly relations between the two governments. Cross-border flows of people, trade, and investments are dependent on friendly relations. Political frictions in 1997–1998, as well as the imposition of currency controls by Malaysia since September 1998, have impacted negatively on these cross-border transactions.

There are strong economic complementarities in the IMS-GT, specifically between Singapore on the one hand, and the Malaysian states and Indonesian provinces on the other. The growth triangle combines Singapore's abundant financial and commercial resources, managerial and professional expertise, and world-class transportation and telecommunications infrastructure with Malaysian and Indonesian land, natural resources, and labour resources. Both Riau and Johor explicitly twin their attractions with those of Singapore to attract investments and link with the global economy through Singapore's world-class financial, shipping, and communications facilities. Within the GT, investors can distribute their activities to take full advantage of the entire mix of resources available so as to develop industrial clusters and value chains. In particular, as the Indonesian government faces severe budgetary constraints, the bilateral joint ventures for infrastructure development – the Batamindo industrial park and the Bintan integrated development project (BIDP) – help to develop industrial and tourism facilities and promote the economic development of the Riau islands.

Geographical proximity to Singapore is a critical factor for Singaporean investors and foreign MNCs in Singapore relocating to the Riau islands of Batam-Bintan and Johor. Production costs in terms of wages, rentals, and utilities in Johor and Batam-Bintan are lower than in Singapore, no doubt, but higher than in many other Asian locations, including locations in Malaysia and Indonesia which are geographically further from Singapore. Moreover, Johor and Batam have no abundant labour and are themselves dependent on in-migration from other neighbouring states. The crucial attraction of Johor and Batam for Singapore investors lies in geographical proximity and ready access to Singapore's world-class airport, seaport, telecommunications network, and financial and commercial infrastructures, which lower transaction costs and facilitate value-chain and just-in-time manufacturing for MNCs. And for businesses in Batam-Bintan and Johor, doing business with and through Singapore is much more cost-efficient and time-saving than doing business through their own metropolitan cities and ports. Batam is conveniently linked to Singapore by a 30–45 minute ferry ride and Johor is linked to Singapore by causeway and bridge, with minimal immigration restrictions. Singaporean and foreign investors in Batam-Bintan and Johor can be based in Singapore and commute daily or periodically to supervise operations and attend to production and distribution problems. The Singapore office provides the financial, technical, logistical, and administrative support for the operations in Batam-Bintan and Johor. Singapore also offers a more comfortable and convenient living environment (albeit more expensive) for business executives and their families, as it is an ultra-modern metropolis with a wide range of efficient urban facilities and services, including health and education.

The launching of the IMS-GT has led to increased flows of goods, people, and capital between Singapore and Johor-Batam-Bintan. Actual statistics on cross-border flows of goods and people within the GT are not readily available. For Singapore and Johor, to facilitate cross-border flows of goods and people, a second link in the form of a land bridge was completed in 1997 to supplement the increasingly congested causeway. Malaysian authorities have estimated that 40 per cent of Malaysia's exports were channelled through and to Singapore and thus pass through Johor customs. Also, some 25,000 residents of Johor cross into Singapore daily to work, with a reverse flow of Singaporeans who visit Johor weekly for shopping, eating, and recreation. For Singapore and Batam-Bintan, there have been sharp increases in ferry services and the introduction of smartcards allow businessmen and professionals from Singapore a quicker transit time through Batam immigration. In recent years, annual tourist visits to Batam exceeded 1 million, mostly from Singapore. Batam exports have grown rapidly since the inception of the GT, reaching

US$4.9 billion by 1997, and mostly shipped to or through Singapore. Singaporeans are also flocking to the tourist resorts in Bintan.

Without doubt, Johor, Riau, and Singapore have all benefited from the GT. Johor and Riau have benefited from the accelerated inflows of investment from Singapore and elsewhere for infrastructural, resource, industrial, and commercial development, and from expenditures of Singapore tourists and shoppers, with positive effects on business development, economic growth, employment, skill development, and technology transfer. In Johor, Singaporean visitors contribute significantly to the business turnovers of shopping centres, eateries, and recreation establishments, to the dismay of the Singapore retail sector. Singapore investments in Johor in over 650 manufacturing projects between 1990 and 1996 amounted to RM$5.85 billion. The investments were mainly for electrical and electronic products, wood products, basic metal and fabricated metal products, chemical products, food products, and printing and publishing. Recent measures by the Malaysian government have adversely affected the bilateral flows. Malaysian exporters are discouraged from exporting via Singapore and directed to use Malaysian ports; Malaysian shippers have been reluctant to heed their government's directive, complaining about the differences in port efficiency and the lesser frequency of shipping calling at Malaysian ports as compared to Singapore. Currency controls introduced by Malaysia to help resolve the country's financial and economic crisis have also posed barriers for the movement of both goods and people.

In Batam, total investments reached US$6.7 billion by 1997, of which foreign investment accounted for US$2.9 billion, with investments from Singapore (including MNCs based in Singapore) as the major source. The Batamindo industrial park (BIP) project is a joint venture of Singapore's state-owned Jurong Town Corporation and Singapore Technologies, and Indonesia's private sector. The BIP has involved an infrastructure investment of S$500 million. The industrial park is over 320 hectares, with 82 manufacturers generating annual exports exceeding US$1 billion. The Bintan industrial estate (BIE) project started later and involves an investment of approximately S$200 million to develop 106 hectares of land. The Bintan Beach international resort (BBIR) is a S$3.5 billion effort to develop tourism facilities. Several resort facilities have started operations, with investments of about S$1.7 billion.

Like Johor and Riau, Singapore also benefited from the IMS-GT. First, the relocation of labour-intensive industries and processes to Johor and Riau help shift scarce domestic resources into new areas of comparative advantage in manufacturing and services, including securing Singapore as a regional commercial, financial, and transportation hub and base for MNC regional headquarters. There are half a million foreign workers in

Singapore, and there are social limits to the further absorption of foreign workers for labour-intensive industries. Expansion into Riau helps diversify the traditional dependence on Johor alone. Second, indigenous Singaporean enterprises, both private small and medium-sized firms as well as large state-owned enterprises, faced growing land and labour constraints and saturated domestic markets, and needed outward investment for expansion. Johor and Riau offer opportunities to expand offshore to gain experience for eventual globalization. Third, Singapore is critically dependent on Johor for its water supply. Investing and spending in Johor will promote Johor's economic development, while cooperative development of Riau will help tap the water resources in Bintan and secure an additional source to meet Singapore's future water needs. Fourth, the rising affluence of Singaporeans has led to a growing demand for leisure and recreational facilities. Availability of such facilities in nearby areas provides a consumer convenience for Singaporeans.

Conclusions

Although Singapore's economic and financial fundamentals and its corporate and financial institutions are sound, the city-state could not escape the regional contagion as the financial storm swept through East Asia in the second half of 1997. While the regional financial crisis had led to increasing questioning regarding the benefits and costs of globalization among policy-makers and analysts in the region, Singapore's policy-makers remain convinced that globalization offers real opportunities and benefits, and that the city-state has to stay plugged into the global economy and must meet the challenges of globalization and international competition head on. Small size and physical constraints leave the Singapore city-state with no other viable choice.

The regional financial crisis has impacted on Singapore negatively as its currency and stock markets also came under attack (albeit less seriously than several other countries), regional demand for its goods and services have dropped sharply, and the sharp devaluations of regional currencies have eroded its cost competitiveness. Rather than engage in competitive devaluation, however, the city-state is seeking to restore cost competitiveness through reining in business costs by way of cuts in wages and employers' contributions to the Central Provident Fund, rentals, and a wide range of government user charges and taxes.

In May 1997, even before the onset of the regional crisis, the Singapore government convened the Committee on Singapore's Competitiveness to review Singapore's competitiveness for the forthcoming decade in the light of global trends and existing and emerging competition, and to propose strategies and policies. Due to the onset of the regional crisis and the need to factor in the impact of the crisis and provide offsetting and remedial measures, the committee's report was delayed until November 1998. The report (Committee on Singapore's Competitiveness 1998) noted that Singapore's competitiveness could no longer depend on cost but must increasingly be based on capability, as with other advanced industrial economies. It recommended eight key long-term strategies for Singapore to realize its vision to be an advanced and globally competitive knowledge economy: maintain manufacturing and services as twin engines of growth; strengthen the external wing to complement the domestic economy as a source of growth; build world-class companies with core competencies to compete in the global economy; nurture and strengthen local enterprises; develop human and intellectual capital with cost-competitive and outstanding capabilities; leverage on science, technology, and innovation as competitive tools; optimize resource management by promoting alternative supply and efficient usage; and use the government as a facilitator of the private sector by providing sound economic policies and a good regulatory environment for the conduct of business.

REFERENCES

Chia, Siow Yue. 1997. "Singapore: Advanced production base and smart hub of the electronics industry", in Wendy Dobson and Siow Yue Chia (eds) *Multinationals and East Asian Integration*. Canada and Singapore: International Development Research Centre and Institute of South-East Asian Studies.

Chia, Siow Yue and Lee Tsao Yuan. 1993. "Subregional economic zones: A new motive force in Asia-Pacific development", in C. Fred Bergsten and Marcus Noland (eds) *Pacific Dynamism and the International Economic System*. Washington, DC: Institute of International Economics.

Civil Aviation Authority of Singapore. 1997. *Listening: Annual Report 97/98*. Singapore: Civil Aviation Authority.

Committee on Singapore's Competitiveness. 1998. *Report*. Singapore: Ministry of Trade and Industry.

Maritime and Port Authority of Singapore. 1998. *The Making of an International Maritime Centre – Seeing the Big Picture. Annual Report 1997*. Singapore: Maritime and Port Authority.

McGee, Terry G. and Scott McLeod. 1992. "Emerging extended metropolitan regions in the Asian Pacific urban system: A case study of the Singapore-Johor-Riau growth triangle", paper presented at the workshop on the Asian Pacific Urban System: Towards the 21st Century, held at the Chinese University of Hong Kong, 11–13 February.

Monetary Authority of Singapore. 1998. *Annual Report 1997/98*. Singapore: Monetary Authority.

Scalapino, Robert A. 1992. "The United States and Asia: Future prospects", *Foreign Affairs*, Winter 1991–1992, pp. 19–40.

Singapore Department of Statistics. 1998a. *Singapore's Corporate Sector 1986–1995*. Singapore: Department of Statistics.

Singapore Department of Statistics. 1998b. *Yearbook of Statistics, Singapore 1997*. Singapore: Department of Statistics.

Singapore Economic Committee. 1986. *The Singapore Economy: New Directions*. Singapore: Ministry of Trade and Industry.

Singapore Economic Planning Committee. 1991. *The Strategic Economic Plan: Towards a Developed Nation*. Singapore: Ministry of Trade and Industry.

Singapore Urban Redevelopment Authority. 1991. *Living the Next Lap: Towards a Tropical City of Excellence*. Singapore: Urban Redevelopment Authority.

United Nations Conference on Trade and Development (UNCTAD). 1997. *World Investment Report 1997*. New York and Geneva: United Nations.

World Bank. 1998. *World Development Report 1998*. New York: Oxford University Press.

The industrial cities

10

Globalization and the sustainable development of Shanghai

Ning Yuemin

Introduction

Since the 1950s, the new technological revolution accompanied by the rapid development of multinational corporations, multinational financial institutions, and international regional blocs have facilitated global economic integration. These trends, called globalization, have resulted in a series of impacts on the world economic system and the world urban system. One result is the formation of world cities (Cohen 1981; Friedmann and Wolff 1982; Friedmann 1986; Sassen 1991). In the Pacific Asia region, some large cities, such as Seoul, Bangkok, and Jakarta, are now emerging as world cities (Yeung and Lo 1996; Hong 1996; Krongkaew 1996; Soegijoko 1996; McGee 1997).

Compared to other nations and localities involved in the various processes of global economic integration, China has only recently felt the impacts of globalization. It was isolated from the world economic system from the 1950s to the 1970s. During that period, China implemented a planned economy strategy and held firmly to the policy of "maintain independence and self-reliance" for national development. The country was proud that it had no foreign debt, after it had paid off loans from the former Soviet Union, and that it was able to stimulate economic progress. By the end of the 1970s, however, it faced a series of economic problems due to a lack of the advanced technology and capital (especially hard currency) that were needed to develop its national economy further.

The year 1978 was a key turning point in the history of Chinese development. In December of that year, at the third plenary meeting of the eleventh central committee of the Chinese Communist Party, the government declared a change in China's economic policy to one of reform and openness. This important measure allowed the country to reopen its door to the outside world. Undoubtedly, the reform and openness policy has brought profound change to Chinese social and economic development. Not only has it facilitated the articulation of the nation to processes of globalization, but in doing so it promoted national growth at historically and globally unprecedented rates.

This growth has been based upon China's competitive advantages, which have attracted massive amounts of foreign investment. These advantages include China's abundant and cheap labour force resources, which greatly reduce this factor cost. During the 1980s, labour costs in the country were among the lowest in the world. The country's attractiveness has not been lost on overseas Chinese, as capital from Hong Kong, Taiwan, and other Chinese abroad has recently poured into its cities. Also, an important attraction for foreign direct investment (FDI) is China's large and growing domestic market.

The year 1992 was another major turning point in Chinese development history. At that time the national government declared the establishment of a socialist market economic system and the adoption of a several new open policies. Rather than a few select places, the new policy opened the entire country to investors. Since that time China has become the world's second largest FDI recipient.

The reform and openness policy has greatly promoted the process of urbanization (Yeh and Xu 1996). Before 1978, China successfully controlled urban development, particularly the growth of its large cities. During the Cultural Revolution (1966–1976), the process of urbanization was almost completely stopped as 30 million people from cities migrated to the countryside (Ning, Wudong, and Jingxi 1994). Since the 1980s, however, Chinese cities have experienced rapid growth and development. Not only has the total number of cities increased, but the country's urbanization level has also risen from 17.9 per cent in 1978 to 29 per cent in 1995. When the government loosened the household registration system, a large floating population of approximately 80 million emerged (see later sections). This massive population moves around China in search of employment.

Rapid economic development and population pressures have been accompanied by serious environmental problems, such as air, water, and solid waste pollution. Meanwhile, a great quantity of cultivated land has been converted to urban and infrastructure areas, economic development zones, and housing estates. These changes have prompted Chinese leaders to support a strategy of sustainable development. For example, in 1994 China published *China's Agenda 21: China's White Paper on Population, Environment, and Development for the 21st Century*. This document outlined the country's overall strategy, policy, and implementation plans for promoting the coordinated development of the economy, society, natural resources, environment, population, and education. It will hopefully guide development decisions made at all levels of government within their medium- and long-term national economic and social development programmes (Deng 1995).

Shanghai has taken a leading role in China's economic and urban development. As a site of FDI is has experienced a dramatic growth and transformation since the opening of the country. As an important location for the "floating" population and being a city with a high concentration of industrial pollution, it also provides a poignant example of some of the contradictions of globalization-driven growth.

This chapter attempts to document the recent development of Shanghai. The first section presents the background conditions to its development. The second section identifies the trends and character of FDI inflows. The third section analyses the impacts of globalization on the economic transition of the city. The final section examines the structural and spatial dimensions of resident and floating populations and analyses the sources of growing environmental problems.

Development background of Shanghai as an emerging world city

Shanghai is an ancient city whose origin dates back some 700 years. During the Ming and Qing dynasties (AD 1344–1840), the city became one of the major ports for domestic and international trade and shipping, not only within the Yangtze delta but also for the entire Chinese coastal area.

The end of the Opium Wars brought profound changes in Shanghai. In 1843, the Treaty of Nanjing opened the city as one of the treaty ports. Because of the city's accessibility to the Yangtze river, Shanghai's harbour activities thrived. It was at that time that modern industrial and financial sectors established themselves. By 1930, through continued trade-related growth and development, Shanghai had become one of the world cities of the Far East (Ning 1995).

After 1949, the dominant economic activities within the city shifted from international trade to industrial production. Shanghai became one of the centres of industrial output for China. While manufacturing growth held a privileged status, however, the planned economy neglected the development of tertiary industries. Foreign banks and the city's securities exchange closed. Many of the major Chinese banks moved to Beijing. Thus, by the 1950s, the city had lost its position as the financial centre of the country. Meanwhile, the growth of industrial production was brought to the attention of policy-makers. Interested in equitable distributions of activities, they promulgated a set of policies to develop other parts of the country. Through these successful attempts to distribute economic activities, Shanghai gradually lost its position as the largest commercial centre of China (Ning and Yan 1995).

After 1978, the Chinese government initially adopted a gradual strategy for implementing reform and an openness policy. The original four pilot areas designated in 1979 as special economic zones (SEZs) were Shenzhen, Zhuhai, Shantou, and Xiamen, all of which were located in the southern areas of Guangdong and Fujian provinces. During the period 1980–1983, Shanghai did not grow as fast as cities within these zones. It was only able to attract 18 projects worth US$124 million in investments. In 1984, however, the central government extended the openness policy to 14 coastal cities, and established a number of economic and technological development zones (ETDZs) in "open cities". While this was a boost, SEZs still enjoyed more preferential policies than the open cities. For example, income taxes on foreign enterprises in SEZs were below those in ETDZs. The SEZs are also much larger in size than the ETDZs. For example, Shanghai developed three ETDZs, namely Minhang, Caohejing, and Hongqiao, with a combined area of eight square kilometres. The smallest ETDZ was a little more than half a square kilometre, and the largest was about five square kilometres.

In order to restore its original status as the economic centre of China, the Shanghai municipal government formulated Shanghai's "Economic Development Strategy" in 1984 (Shanghai Municipal People's Government 1989). The strategy identified five priorities. Most important among these was the need to relax restrictive investment policies in order to attract foreign investment. These investments were anticipated in the construction of luxury hotels and office buildings, and the improvement of municipal engineering and communication facilities. It was also hoped that FDI would help to introduce advanced technology into the country. Lower-order priorities included the need to remodel the city to promote high-technology industrial development, and the physical renewal of old city urban areas and infrastructure. This strategy did not anticipate the impacts that opening up to globalization forces would have on the city. Indeed, theories of globalization and world city formation had not been introduced into China at that time. The strategy thus naïvely promoted the goal of making Shanghai the economic centre of China.

In 1990, the Chinese government announced the opening of Shanghai's Pudong area to development. This policy marked the extension of the openness policy and provided Shanghai with the opportunity for rapid

Table 10.1 Growth and globalization of China's economy

	1980	1985	1990	1995	1997
GDP (RMB bn)	451.8	896.4	1,854.8	5,826.1	7,477.2
Total value of foreign trade (US$ bn)	38.1	69.7	115.5	280.9	325.1
Imports (US$ bn)	20.0	42.3	53.4	132.1	142.4
Exports (US$ bn)	18.1	27.4	62.1	148.8	182.7
Value of FDI (US$ bn)	–	1.66	3.49	37.52	45.26
Overseas tourists (million persons)	5.7	17.83	27.46	46.39	–

Source: China Statistics Press 1997

growth. To stimulate this policy, in 1992 the central government empha-sized the goal of building Shanghai into an international economic, finance, and trade centre. Together these policies determined the development tra-jectory of the city.

Shanghai is currently well situated to accommodate the growth related to world city formation. First, the rapid take-off of the Chinese economy has provided a solid foundation for Shanghai's development into a world city. Currently, the country maintains the highest economic growth rates in the world. Its GDP increased from RMB 451.8 billion in 1980 to RMB 7,477.2 billion in 1997 (US$900 billion), and with that growth it increased its world ranking from eleventh in 1993 to seventh in 1997. The total value of foreign trade was US$38.1 billion in 1980, and this level increased to US$325.1 billion in 1997. China is now ranked tenth in world foreign trade. Export values reached US$182.7 billion in 1997, which demon-strates China's industrial strength. By 1997, the total value of FDI stock was US$221.9 billion (Table 10.1).

Second, Shanghai possesses unique location advantages. As a port at the mouth of the Yangtze river basin, it is a hub for connecting China and its vast hinterland to the outside world. It also lies in the centre of the eastern development zones. As the focal point of a great "T", it benefits from the convergence of flows from and to these areas. The coastal eco-nomic belt has been shaped into the most important development axis of China. Economic activity within this belt accounts for 53.3 per cent of the national GDP. At the same time, the Yangtze river, 6,300 kilometres long, runs through the east, central, and west parts of China with an extensive hinterland of 1.8 million square kilometres. The Yangtze river valley also has tremendous development potential (Table 10.2). In combination, these development belts serve as the new economic propeller for the country. Situated at the crucial axis between the two belts, Shanghai's role is seen as the "dragon head" leading the entire country's development.

Third, the new Pudong development area has provided increased inter-

Table 10.2 Share of coastal and Yangtze river economic activity in the national economy of China, 1993

Region	Area %	Population %	GDP %	Foreign trade %	FDI used %
Coastal economic belt	13.3	40.1	53.3	85.7	85.9
Yangtze river economic belt	15.1	38.5	37.3	27.0	24.9

Source: China Statistics Press 1994
Note: Some areas are included in both the coastal economic belt and the Yangtze river economic belt, thus percentages may total more than 100.

national economic linkages. In the 1980s, the southern parts of China, particularly Guangdong province, were the keys to its growth. As a coastal open city, Shanghai's three small economic development zones were unable to provide the foundation for the city's future development. The Pudong New Area, however, is a large and comprehensive development zone with an original area of 350 square kilometres, later enlarged to 522 square kilometres. Its large area has enticed investments, making it the foundation for links to the world market (Shanghai Pudong New Area Administration 1993). The size and variety of inflowing investments have greatly enhanced Shanghai's ability to provide comprehensive services. They increasingly underlie the city's ability to link to both the region and the world.

Fourth, reform and opening has enabled Shanghai to continue its growth by stimulating both secondary and tertiary industries. During the 1990s, the economy of Shanghai maintained rapid growth led by tertiary industries. Finance, commerce and trade, transport, telecommunications, and real estate were the main components of the new economic growth sector. In the secondary industrial sector, a number of new pillar industries, such as motor vehicles, telecommunication equipment, and power station equipment, also developed. This dual-sector-driven growth model is in stark contrast to the past, when economic growth was provided for by manufacturing. Further, the government has intensified infrastructure development through a number of major projects. Together, these transformations form the frame of the increasingly modern city.

In 1994, the Shanghai municipal government formulated a new development strategy (Shanghai Municipal People's Government 1995). It announced that by 2010, Shanghai will be an international economic, financial, and trade centre and that Pudong will become a first-class, export-oriented, multifunctional, and modernized area. There is no doubt that, if achieved, these goals will raise Shanghai to the status of an international economic city.

The features of foreign direct investment in Shanghai

Growth trends of FDI

The history of foreign investment growth in Shanghai can be divided into three stages (Table 10.3). The first period started around 1984. Previous to this stage there was little foreign capital attracted to the city. For example, in 1981 Shanghai established its first international joint venture firm since it closed its doors to the outside world in the early 1950s. By the end of 1983, however, as mentioned previously, Shanghai was failing to attract foreign investment because most investors preferred the opportunities in southern China. In 1984, with its designation as an "open city" by the central government, FDI began to flow inwardly. The second stage, however, was characterized by a reversal of the first surge. Shortly after the open city designation, in 1986, FDI inflows began to wane, and the fall in numbers and dollar investment amounts continued to 1991. By 1992, however, this stage ended and FDI inflows picked up again. From this time to the present, Shanghai has experienced a second surge period that has marked its third stage of FDI inflows.

The initial attempt to attract foreign capital began with the implementation of the openness policy, especially the establishment of the three ETDZs in Hongqiao, Caohejing, and Minhang in 1984. FDI inflows to Shanghai increased rapidly between 1984 and 1985. By 1985, the accumulated number of contracts signed reached 153, and total value of FDI reached US$1.26 billion. Investments were mainly in hotels, motor vehicle manufacturing, textiles, and some services. At that time, the government encouraged foreign firms to invest in luxury hotels and office buildings to meet the demands of foreign firms and tourists. Also during this period, the Shanghai Automotive Company and German Volkswagen jointly established the Shanghai Volkswagen Automotive Corporation to produce cars for the domestic market. This was the first large joint-venture firm established by Shanghai with a famous transnational corporation. It almost immediately provided benefits to the ailing motor vehicle manufacturing sector in the city through updating and remodelling.

After 1986, foreign firms decreased their investment in Shanghai. Both the number of contracts and the total value of FDI inflows during 1986 and 1987 were lower than those in 1985. From 1987 to 1991, the numbers of contracts increased, but only gradually. The total value of investment during these periods was still lower than that of 1985. A decreasing average scale of investment for each project also marked this trend. Small foreign companies continued to establish firms in Shanghai, while transnational corporations did not.

In 1992, in order to establish a socialist market economy, China imple-

Table 10.3 Growth of FDI in Shanghai

	By 1983	1984	1985	1986	1987	1988	1989	1990	1991	1992	1993	1994	1995	1996
Number of contracts signed	18	41	94	62	76	219	119	203	365	2,012	3,650	3,802	1,845	2,106
Total value of contracted FDI (US$ m)	124	425	715	300	247	334	359	375	449	3,357	7,016	10,030	10,540	11,070
Actually used FDI (US$ m)	N/A	N/A	102	148	212	364	422	177	175	790	2,318	3,231	3,250	4,716

Source: Shanghai Municipal Statistics Bureau 1985–1998

mented a land leasing system. It was at this time that Shanghai's foreign capital inflows entered the third stage and the second surge period began. For example, between 1994 and 1996, the contracted FDI in Shanghai during each year continuously exceeded US$10 billion. Further, transnational corporations increased their investments in the city. FDI expanded to include the tertiary sector, such as banking, insurance, real estate, foreign trade, and retail establishments. Spatially, it diffused into the Pudong and suburban areas. By the end of 1996, the total amount of contracted FDI in Shanghai has accumulated to US$45.3 billion, accounting for 9.7 per cent of total FDI in the country. The total amount of foreign capital actually used reached US$16 billion, giving Shanghai a 9.1 per cent share of China's utilized FDI. However, due to the Asian financial crises, FDI inflows to Shanghai have contracted since then, such that in 1997 inflows were 48 per cent of what they were in 1996.

Distribution of FDI

Shanghai is China's largest city and has a massive industrial base. Beginning in the 1980s, through a series of preferential policies implemented by the central government, Shanghai developed a solid foundation for investment through infrastructure development for foreign manufacturing.

Recent investors have not overlooked this opportunity. By the end of 1996, Shanghai had signed agreements on 15,692 investment projects. Approximately two-thirds of these projects were manufacturing related, while the remainder were tertiary industrial developments. Among contractual investments, the tertiary industry accounted for 58.8 per cent while manufacturing's share amounted to 41 per cent. However, actual tertiary-industry investments made up only 47 per cent of the total actual FDI while actual manufacturing investments made up 52.8 per cent of the total (Table 10.4).

Table 10.4 Industrial distribution of FDI in Shanghai, 1996

	Contracts		Total value of contracted FDI		Total value of actually used FDI	
	Number	%	US$ bn	%	US$ bn	%
Total	15,692	100.00	45.34	100.00	15.96	100.00
Manufacturing	10,643	67.8	18.08	39.9	8.31	52.1
All services	4,387	28.0	26.68	58.8	7.50	47.0
Retail	758	4.8	1.94	4.3	1.92	12.0
Real estate	651	4.1	17.31	38.2	3.64	22.8
Social services	1,021	6.5	3.44	7.6	1.15	7.2

Source: Shanghai Municipal Statistics Bureau 1985–1998

Among various manufacturing sectors, foreign investment has concentrated in garments, shoes, transportation equipment, electric equipment, electronics and telecommunications, and chemical industries, among others. Investors are attracted to the cheap labour and land resources available within the city. The impacts of these investments are moulding Shanghai into a new production node within the global production system. This is further enhanced by foreign investment in Shanghai's tertiary industry, especially those service sectors that enhance the city's industrial structure.

Sources of FDI

Among various investor countries and regions, Hong Kong has historically played a key role with Shanghai's investment community. In 1996, Hong Kong investments accounted for 46 per cent of Shanghai's contractual investment and 48.8 per cent of Shanghai's actual investment. But both percentages are lower than the nation's average level (over 60 per cent). Other Asian countries and regions have also invested in Shanghai. For example, Japan, Singapore, Taiwan, and the Republic of Korea are the second, fourth, sixth, and eighth largest investor economies in the city, respectively. Some Western countries are also becoming important investment sources for Shanghai. For example, the USA, the UK, and Germany ranked third, fifth, and seventh in terms of contractual investment, while the USA is currently the second largest actual investor (Table 10.5).

Table 10.5 Source distribution of FDI in Shanghai, 1996

Countries and regions	Projects		Contractual investment		Actual investment	
	Number	%	US$ bn	%	US$ bn	%
Hong Kong	6,594	42.0	20.85	46.0	7.79	48.8
Taiwan	2,180	13.4	2.09	4.6	0.90	5.6
Republic of Korea	140	0.9	0.65	1.9	0.09	0.6
Japan	1,977	12.6	4.96	10.9	1.61	10.1
Singapore	636	4.1	2.86	6.3	0.43	2.7
Thailand	104	0.7	0.42	0.9	0.09	0.6
Germany	165	1.1	0.93	2.1	0.36	2.3
UK	257	1.6	2.26	5.0	0.51	3.2
France	81	0.5	0.22	0.5	0.12	0.8
Italy	57	0.4	0.13	0.3	0.07	0.4
USA	1,991	12.7	4.04	8.9	2.36	14.8
Canada	305	1.9	0.49	1.1	0.19	1.2
Australia	252	1.6	0.57	1.3	0.07	0.4

Source: Shanghai Municipal Statistics Bureau 1985–1998

Spatial distribution of FDI

The area of Shanghai is 6,358 square kilometres and can be divided three zones, namely the central city, Pudong New Area, and the suburban districts or counties. Between 1991 and 1996, contracted FDI within the three zones reached US$12.1 billion, US$12.5 billion, and US$11 billion, respectively. While the investment levels are fairly equal, each zone demonstrates specific attractions.

The central city consists of 10 districts laid out over 280 square kilometres. Its traditional industrial sectors were manufacturing and commerce. The development of industry since the 1950s resulted in an inefficient land-use pattern. There were nearly 10,000 factories and workshops in the central area, and these brought serious environmental problems to the city. The centre was also the location of shabby housing and many narrow roads, which created traffic congestion. Thus, the central city was in urgent need of urban renewal. Housing needed upgrading, roads needed widening, and factories needed to be relocated to other areas. During the 1980s, however, the municipal government lacked the financial resources to improve infrastructure and housing.

Since the late 1980s, the reform of the land-use system and a new policy of "two levels of governments, two levels of administration" have provided some help. The new policy devolves the power of land leasing and some powers of urban planning down to the district level. These new policies have sped urban renewal. For example, from 1988 to 1996, 103 million square metres of land in Shanghai were transferred to developers. The government charged US$8.51 billion and RMB 10.03 billion for the transfer of land-use rights. The transferred land is mainly located in Huangpu, Jing'an, Xuhui, and Luwan, which are the traditional commercial areas. In the Huangpu district, the government charged US$1.01 billion for the transfer of 210,000 square metres of land. This accounted for 45.5 per cent of the total foreign investment within the district (Li 1998). Hongkou district charged US$1.2 billion for the transfer of land-use rights that accounted for 82.2 per cent of the total foreign investment in that district. In addition to the investment in real estate, foreign capital has also invested in retail establishments, catering, and small industries.

Since the central government announced its intention to develop and open Pudong New Area in 1990, Pudong has become the most important element for attracting FDI into Shanghai. In 1990, Pudong attracted only 28 foreign projects worth US$34 million, accounting for 10.4 per cent and 5.8 per cent of the total number and value of investments in Shanghai respectively. From 1993 onwards, however, FDI in Pudong has accounted for between 25 per cent and 30 per cent of the total foreign projects and investments flowing into the city (Table 10.6).

Table 10.6 FDI in Pudong New Area and its proportion in Shanghai

Year	Projects		Contractual investment	
	Number	%	US$ million	%
1990	28	10.4	34	5.8
1991	92	18.1	101	10.7
1992	567	26.1	1,353	30.6
1993	924	24.8	1,757	25.0
1994	1,035	26.4	2,593	24.8
1995	838	29.5	3,256	30.9
1996	802	38.1	3,309	29.9

Source: Shanghai Municipal Statistics Bureau 1985–1998

There is a close relationship between Pudong's development and the transformation of Shanghai's economic structure, although the investment structure of Pudong has been different from that of the city. FDI in the tertiary sector accounted for 66.9 per cent of the total contractual invest- ment, which was higher than the 58.8 per cent of Shanghai's average. Industrial FDI inflows into Pudong accounted for 31.3 per cent of the total, which was lower than Shanghai's average share of 39.9 per cent. Among manufacturing investments, foreign enterprises were concentrated in the chemical, textile, and ordinary machine-building industries at the beginning of the 1990s. Since 1993, foreign enterprises, especially large transnational corporations, have begun to invest in automobiles, pharmaceutical prod- ucts, electrical equipment, electronics, and communication equipment in- dustries. In the tertiary sector, foreign firms have invested chiefly in real estate and public utilities, which accounted for 46.6 per cent of the total. Other investments in this sector include retail establishments, tourism, and so on.

Because Pudong has become one of the most famous open areas in China, it has attracted many large transnational corporations. Currently almost all of the large investment projects (those over US$100 million) within Shanghai are located in Pudong. This includes the Shanghai Gen- eral Motor Automobile Company, which has invested US$1.56 billion, the Huahong Micro-Electronic Company (with NEC), and Shanghai Stainless Steel Company, which have each invested more than US$1 billion. Other investments include the Global Financial Centre, the tallest office build- ing in the world at 460 metres, with an investment of US$800 million, and Shanghai Suoguang Electronic Company (with Sony), which includes an investment of US$410 million.

Shanghai's suburban areas possess cheap labour and land and, since 1992, they have also become a new location for investment. For instance, land lease fees for industrial land in Pudong are approximately US$97 per square metre, while they are only US$30–40 per square metre in the economic development zones in suburban areas and US$20 per square metre in the rural towns. These preferential investment policies not only attract foreign medium-sized and small firms, but also large transnational corporations. Industrial projects accounted for over 80 per cent of the total investment projects in these areas. By the end of 1997 there were 8,633 foreign-funded manufacturing enterprises, accounting for 44 per cent of the total, located in Shanghai suburban locations. Contractual investments reached US$14.79 billion, accounting for 27 per cent of the total, and actual investment reached US$5.26 billion. There are 5,780 enterprises in production and their sales values reached RMB 42.8 billion (Feng 1998). Among nine suburban districts and counties, Minhang, Qingpu, Songjiang, and Jiading, which are near Hongqiao international airport and easily accessible by expressways or high-class highways, have each attracted US$2 billion or more of foreign capital. Other counties have attracted less foreign capital due to their location disadvantages. This feature of FDI demonstrates that the suburban areas have a different division of labour from the central city and Pudong New Area. Further, the suburban areas are becoming a principal industrial location for multinational investment within Shanghai. In the future, the economic strength of the suburban areas will become more powerful.

Investments from multinational corporations

Increasingly, multinational corporations are finding the huge Chinese market attractive and are attempting to access this market via Shanghai. Forty-three of the world's top 100 industrial giants came to Shanghai in 1995. Among these, 17 are American, nine are Japanese, and eight are German corporations. In 1999, this number increased to 67. Moreover, among the world's top 50 service corporations, 13 have invested in the city.

Generally, there are four common characteristics of multinational corporations investing in Shanghai. First, and most obvious, is the large average size of investment projects. Because the target of the multinational corporations is long-term investments, the average scale of investment projects is generally larger than those of medium-sized and small enterprises. The average investment per project is approximately US$20 million, and some projects reach as high as US$1 billion. For example, the average investment from multinationals is US$27.6 million (based on the total investment capital) and US$12 million (based on contractual foreign capital). While multinationals have taken a prudent attitude to large-scale investment, after initial successes quite a number of them increased their input. General Motors started from automobile parts and components and then expanded to car production, while General Electric started from lighting and moved to power plant equipment and Johnson & Johnson moved from health articles to pharmaceuticals.

Secondly, most investments match Shanghai's industrial policies. In order to speed up the restructuring of Shanghai's industries, the local government has emphasized the development of automobiles, telecommunications facilities, oil and chemicals, household appliances, iron and steel, and equipment for power-station-related manufacturing as six pillar industries. During the 1990s, Shanghai further promoted pharmaceutical products, bio-engineering, and the computer industry as a high-tech industrial development strategy. Most multinational investment projects fall into the set of industrial development categories, including the projects of GM and Volkswagen in the automobile industry, Sharp, Hitachi, National, and Sony in the household appliance industry, and Bell and Siemens in the telecommunications facilities industry.

Third, investment projects from multinational corporations are import-substituted industries with advanced technologies. Among foreign investment in Shanghai, the enterprises from Hong Kong and Taiwan mostly invest in clothing, textiles, and the metalwork industry. These industries prioritize export production, as do small enterprises from Japan and the USA. However, some enterprises invested in by multinational corporations make high-tech products, such as large-scale IC (integrated circuit) communication equipment, wide-screen TVs, medicines, and chemical reagents (others produce air conditioners, microwave ovens, chemical fibres, etc.). These industries are import-substituted enterprises. The multinational enterprises are competitive because of their level of technology and production efficiency.

Fourth, many multinational corporation enterprises are assembly plants and need to import components. In order to penetrate the Chinese market as quickly as possible and make use of the preferential policies of Shanghai, many multinational corporations import spare parts and components from abroad and then assemble them in Shanghai. After notification, it takes about one year for a factory to start operation. Once the product has achieved a certain level of consumption, multinational corporations usually expand their investments. For example, initially Shanghai Sharp Air-conditioner Company invested US$29.5 million in May 1992. Their second investment of US$8.6 million was made in 1994, and they made a third investment of US$140 million in 1995.

There are different explanations for the determinants of FDI trends. One important theory concerns the product cycle. This theory classifies product development and production into three stages, namely innovation, maturation, and decline (Vernon 1966). In the first stage, production concentrates in the country where the innovation developed, and enterprises enter international markets by way of export and trade. In the second stage, the product is standardized, thus reducing costs while product competition increases. This facilitates the outward expansion of the production process. In the third stage, when foreign production costs are lower than domestic production costs, products will be made abroad and returned for sale in the domestic market.

Another theory relies on the concept of the new international division of labour (NIDL). It maintains that automation and standardization of production and the modernization of transportation and communications enhance the role of labour costs in determining investment decisions. Making use of the labour in developing countries is one of the primary determinants for a multinational corporation's overseas investments (Frobel, Heinrichs, and Kreye 1980; Cohen 1981).

For the large multinationals in Shanghai, the primary investment motive is the attractiveness of the huge Chinese market. Though China is a developing country, the Chinese market has tremendous potential for making profits. Its large population and quick development pace have been the factors attracting investment. The per capita GDP of China rose from US$342 in 1990 to US$678 in 1996, and some large cities in the country achieved an even higher per capita production index. Shanghai's per capita production exceeded US$3,000 in 1997. After plants start to operate, their products easily occupy the Chinese market, as evidenced by Volkswagen cars, Sharp and Hitachi air conditioners, and Siemens mobile telephones. A survey of foreign investment in Shanghai also demonstrated that the huge market potential in China is the first consideration for location decisions. The second determinant for FDI inflows into Shanghai is to take advantage of the cheap labour supply, land resources, and preferential policies of China. Other factors, such as good infrastructure, quick access to information and transportation (airports and ports), sound investment laws and regulations, and the efficiency of administrative bureaucracies also play important roles (Nyaw 1996).

Although many multinationals have factories or firms in Shanghai, most of them have regional headquarters in Hong Kong or other Asian cities. By 1995, Shanghai had only six headquarters of multinationals, all of which were Chinese and only three were industrial corporations (the others were service providers). In recent years, an increasing number of multinationals have established a China regional office, but most are in Beijing. Shanghai is currently not as attractive as the capital city in this respect, and this has implications for the world city formation process.

Globalization and the economic transition of Shanghai

Economic growth of Shanghai since the 1980s

From 1952 to 1979, Shanghai experienced comparatively rapid economic growth. Over nearly three decades, its gross domestic product increased at an average growth rate of 8.7 per cent per year. Because governmental policy prioritized the development of industry, Shanghai's gross industrial output value registered a annual growth rate of 10 per cent, just below the 11.3 per cent national average (State Statistics Bureau of PRC 1995; Shanghai Municipal Statistics Bureau 1985–1998). With the economic reform and opening of the 1980s, Shanghai's economic development faced serious challenges. Between 1980 and 1991, its annual average growth rate fell to 7.4 per cent. Several factors help to explain this drop, including the rapid development of industrialization in other provinces, the opening of southern provinces, the burden of revenue requirements of the central government, and the shortage of infrastructure and housing (Ning 1995). After the central government announced its plan to develop and open Pudong in 1990, and especially after 1992, Shanghai's economy started a new period of rapid development fuelled by domestic and foreign investments. During the 1992–1996 period, the annual average growth rate in Shanghai reached 14.2 per cent, surpassing the nation's average of 11.7 per cent (State Statistics Bureau of PRC 1997; Shanghai Municipal Statistics Bureau 1985–1998). In 1997, Shanghai's gross production totalled RMB 336 billion, and was growing at the rate of 13 per cent. The per capita production index of the city surpassed US$3,000, which gave Shanghai the highest per capita level among the 31 provincial units in mainland China. The Pudong New Area also achieved high levels of production, rising to RMB 60.8 billion in 1997 from RMB 6.02 billion in 1990. Per capita levels rose to US$4,800 in 1997, four times the levels of 1990.

Porter has divided national competitive development into four stages: factor-driven; investment-driven; innovation-driven; and wealth-driven (Porter 1990). According to this scenario, Shanghai is currently in the second stage, for its economic growth is mainly driven by investments. Table 10.7 compares the growth of actual FDI and total investment in fixed assets. The proportion of FDI accounting for total investment demonstrates the contribution of FDI to growth. In 1991, FDI accounted for only 3.6 per cent of growth. By 1996, this had risen to over 20 per cent, meaning that one-fifth of the economic growth of Shanghai was directly driven by FDI.

Table 10.7 Contribution of FDI to the economic growth of Shanghai

Year	1991	1992	1993	1994	1995	1996
FDI used (RMB bn)	0.93	4.35	17.97	27.85	27.05	39.14
Total investment (RMB bn)	25.83	35.74	65.39	112.33	160.18	195.21
FDI/total investment (%)	3.6	12.2	27.5	24.8	16.9	20.1

Note: FDI is counted in terms of the exchange rate of RMB against US$.
Source: Shanghai Municipal Statistics Bureau 1985–1998

Shanghai's urban economic transition

Shanghai had been the economic centre of China before the 1950s, and it had a relatively advanced tertiary sector at that time. The proportions of the primary sector, secondary sector, and tertiary sector in GDP in 1952 were 5.9 per cent, 52.4 per cent, and 41.7 per cent, respectively. However, the overemphasis on industrial development and the neglect of services resulted in an unbalanced economic structure during the later years of the planned economy. By 1978, the proportions of the three sectors had changed to 4 per cent, 77.4 per cent, and 18.6 per cent. This trend demonstrated that Shanghai was gradually became a manufacturing centre instead of being a centre of economic management and control. The less-developed tertiary sector not only prevented Shanghai from developing as a comprehensive economic metropolitan centre, but it also reduced job opportunities. At the time, Shanghai faced another set of problems. On the one hand, some industrial sectors established in the period of industrialization had lost their competitive abilities. On the other hand, there was a surplus of rural labour which was pressuring the economy to shift to other industrial sectors.

The government's development strategy of 1984 mandated the restructuring of Shanghai's economy. One of the priorities was to re-establish an advanced tertiary sector so as to restore the status of the city to being a national economic centre. During the 1980s, the development of tertiary-sector activities focused on transportation, commerce, and tourism. Another priority was to enhance the six pillar industries mentioned previously. It was believed that the development of these six industries would remodel the industrial structure of Shanghai and make it both more efficient and vital. Third, township industries were encouraged to absorb the surplus labour force in rural areas.

The policy programme was effective, as can be seen by the structure of the economy. By 1990, the proportions of the primary, secondary, and tertiary sectors in GDP had altered to 4.3 per cent, 63.8 per cent, and 31.9 per cent. The push for both secondary- and tertiary-sector developments allowed the city to maintain a high economic growth pace from 1992 onwards. From 1990 to 1997, the city's production levels increased by RMB 336 billion, of which the tertiary sector accounted for 49.5 per cent. Compared to 1980, the contribution of the tertiary sector increased by 24.4 percentage points (Table 10.8).

Structural changes in employment were slightly different from those of production. With the process of rural industrialization, the rural surplus labour force shifted to the secondary sector. The proportion of employment in the secondary sector rose from 48.6 per cent to 59.3 per cent during the 1980s. This share has since decreased, and in 1997 it stood at 49.7

Table 10.8 Changes of the sectors in GDP of Shanghai

	GDP RMB bn	Primary sector		Secondary sector		Tertiary sector	
		RMB bn	%	RMB bn	%	RMB bn	%
1980	31.19	1.01	3.2	23.61	75.7	6.57	21.1
1990	75.65	3.26	4.3	48.27	63.8	24.12	31.9
1997	336.02	7.58	2.3	175.44	52.2	153.00	45.5

Source: Shanghai Municipal Statistics Bureau 1985–1998

Table 10.9 Percentage changes of the sectors in employment of Shanghai

	Primary sector	Secondary sector	Tertiary sector
1980	29.0	48.6	22.4
1990	11.1	59.3	30.6
1997	10.1	49.7	40.3

Source: Shanghai Municipal Statistics Bureau 1985–1998

per cent. The decrease was largely due to the reduction of some traditional industries, such as textiles. In order to solve the growing unemployment problem, the government produced a plan that emphasized the absorption capacity of the tertiary sector, and as a result employment in the tertiary sector has a risen rapidly (Table 10.9).

Banking and insurance, wholesale and retail sales, transportation and telecommunications, and real estate are the largest four sectors in the tertiary sector, classified by production levels. Classified by employment, however, wholesale and retail sales, social services, transportation and telecommunications, and education are the largest four sectors in the tertiary sector. Employment in banking, insurance and real estate, brokerage, and information services stood at 151,000, accounting for only 5 per cent of the total employment in the tertiary sector and 1.9 per cent of the total employment of Shanghai. This demonstrates that the scale of Shanghai's advanced tertiary sector is still limited.

Within manufacturing the six pillar industries accounted for most output. Their share of gross industrial output accounted for 52.3 per cent of the total of Shanghai's industry, and their pre-tax profit share reached as high as 55.8 per cent. Automobile industries, mainly through Sino-German investments, have become Shanghai's number-one pillar industry. In 1997, the production capacity of Shanghai Volkswagen reached 230,000 cars, and it now occupies 48 per cent of China's car market. Moreover, Shanghai's high-tech industrial output value accounted for 15.1 per cent of Shanghai's total industrial output (*Jiefang Daily* 1998). Through industrial restructuring, a new labour division between Shanghai and other cities in the

Yangtze delta is emerging. This spatial division of labour, it is hoped, will continue to promote the sustainable development of Shanghai's industry.

Development of producer services and office centres

Since Shanghai opened its doors to the international community, its producer services have rapidly developed. Finance has become the most important sector among services. There are currently 2,722 financial service enterprises, among which are 16 head offices and branches of Chinese capital banks, six head offices and branches of Chinese capital insurance companies, four trust investment companies, and five securities companies. There are also approximately 272 institutions that do not have legal status but were established by securities dealers from other parts of the country. Shanghai houses one headquarters of a national bank and two headquarters of local banks. Shanghai's Stock Exchange and China's Foreign Exchange Trading Centre are also located in the city. Within mainland China, the only other city with a stock exchange is Shenzhen. The Shanghai Stock Exchange was established in 1989 and already stocks from 400 companies are traded daily. Shanghai Stock Exchange issues two kinds of shares: "A" shares and "B" shares. "A" shares are issued in the domestic market using RMB, and "B" shares are issued in the foreign financial markets using US dollars and transacted in the Shanghai Stock Exchange. All of these are domestic companies, as no foreign company has yet been listed on the exchange. The China Foreign Exchange Trading Centre is the only institution of its type on the mainland. US dollars, the Japanese yen, and Hong Kong dollars are the currencies traded in the centre. The volume of transactions for one working day is about US$260 million. China has limits on foreign currency exchange and has not established an offshore financial market.

Since the 1990s, China has gradually opened its financial market. Shanghai is one of the cities where foreign financial institutions can establish branches within the country. At the end of 1996 there were 36 foreign financial institutions from 14 countries in the city. Among these, nine foreign banks have received approval to deal in RMB. Moreover, 149 representative offices of foreign financial institutions have picked Shanghai as a location in which to conduct business. Among these are 61 representatives of banks, 27 representatives of securities dealers, 36 representatives of insurance companies, and 24 representatives of other financial institutions.

Besides financial services, China has also opened up to other parts of the service sector, such as advertising, trade, retail, law, consultancy services, etc. By the end of 1995 there were 4,174 foreign representative offices from these sectors. Of these, 875 were in trading, financial services, transportation liaison, aviation, and tourism. In order to meet the demands of pro-

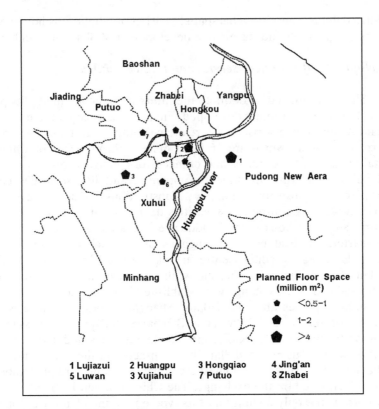

Figure 10.1 Distribution of office centres in Shanghai

ducer services, Shanghai has constructed high-class office buildings, chiefly located in the Lujiazui new CBD, the Bund, in Hongqiao, and along Huai-hai Road, among other places. In the future Shanghai plans to construct eight office centres in three different parts of town (Figure 10.1). The first phase of the plan called for development of a new CBD for Shanghai in Lujiazui. Total office space for buildings in the CBD will reach 4 million square metres. The second phase includes plans for the Bund and Hong-qiao. These are the former CBD of Shanghai and a new economic develop-ment zone; floor space of office buildings in these two areas will be 1.5 and 2.0 million square metres respectively. The third phase includes construc-tion in Luwan, Jing'an, Xujiahui, Putuo, and Zhabei. Total planned floor space will be between 0.5 and 1.0 million square metres in each area.

Economic and technological development zones

With Shanghai's 1984 designation as an "open city", it established three economic and technological development zones. The ETDZs were recognized as pilot areas of the reform and opening programme. The chief objectives of ETDZs were to attract foreign capital, to introduce advanced technology and management skills to China, and to provide the basis for international economic and technological cooperation. After the Pudong New Area development was announced, four new ETDZs were established, namely the Lujiazui financial and trade zone, Waigaoqiao free-trade zone, Jingqiao export-processing zone, and Zhangjiang high-tech park. The ETDZs provide sound infrastructure and preferential policies, and an effective administrative bureaucracy. They have therefore been successful in attracting foreign capital, and have been recognized as an effective means of promoting the local economy. At present, Shanghai has eight national-level ETDZs (the earliest seven ETDZs and Mount She national tourist and leisure development zone), 13 city-level ETDZs (12 industrial zones and Sunqiao modern agricultural development zone), and nearly 200 county- or town-level development zones (Figure 10.2).

Table 10.10 summarizes the main features of the ETDZs. As shown, Minhang, located about 30 km south of the central city, is Shanghai's first industrial satellite town. In the north-western part of Minhang, an ETDZ was originally designated as 2.3 square kilometres. Later, its area expanded to cover 4.0 square kilometres. The main industrial sectors within the zone are electronic instruments, machine manufacturing, fine chemical products, soft beverages, construction materials, and textiles, among others. In 1996, the sales value of these enterprises reached RMB 14.1 billion, the profit value was RMB 1.55 billion, and the export value was US$900 million (Yearbook of Shanghai Foreign Economic Relations and Trade 1997).

Hongqiao has a location advantage, as it is only five kilometres from Hongqiao international airport and eight kilometres from the city centre. The planned area of the zone is 65.2 ha, and it is divided into three sub-areas with 34 building sites. At present, four hotels, seven office buildings, two exhibition halls, two shopping centres, and five comprehensive apartment buildings have started to operate in the zone.

Caohejing, located to the south-west of the central city, was the first high-tech development zone among the coastal ETDZs approved by the State Council in June 1988. As a high-tech industrial zone, the main sectors include microelectronics, computer software, and new engineering materials. It is the largest scientific innovation centre in Shanghai, and over 50 foreign-funded enterprises have established their R&D centres in the zone. In 1996, its gross industrial output value was RMB 7.5 billion, with foreign-funded enterprises accounting for 56.6 per cent of all production.

Lujiazui is the only financial and trading zone in China, and faces the Bund across the Huangpu river. The area of the zone is 28 square kilometres. By 1997, the zone was over one-third developed, with buildings covering approximately 9.92 square kilometres of land. The zone is di-

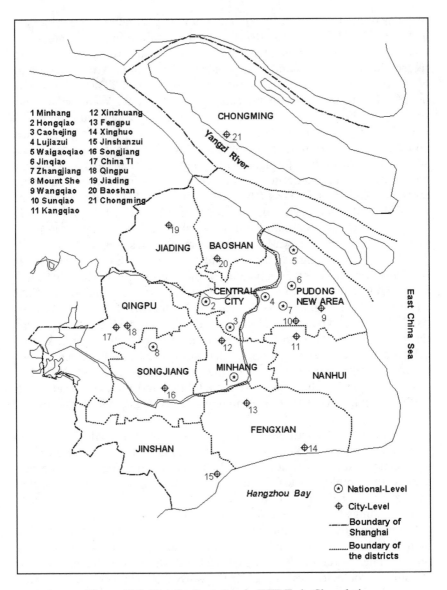

Figure 10.2 Distribution of main ETDZs in Shanghai

vided into three subareas: the finance centre area, the Zhuyuan trade and commerce area, and the Zhangyang Road commercial centre. Plans for the finance centre area include 22 high-rise financial buildings with a total floor space of 2 million square metres. At present, there are 24 branches of foreign banks and over 20 branches of domestic financial institutions

Table 10.10 Main economic and technological development zones in Shanghai, 1996

ETDZ	Level	Planned area (km²)	Total amount of investment (US$ bn)	Contracted FDI (US$ bn)	Main industrial sectors or functions
Minhang	National	3.5	1.68	1.14	machinery, medicine, beverages
Hongqiao	National	0.65	2.06	1.66	offices, hotels, exhibitions
Caohejing	National	12	1.21	0.81	high-tech park, electronic
Lujiazui	National	28	5.22	7.0	finance, trade, retail sales
Waigaoqiao	National	10	3.46	3.91	free-trade zone
Jingqiao	National	19	6.8	2.98	automobiles, electronics and communications, electrical equipment
Zhangjiang	National	16	0.58	0.45	high-tech park, medicine
Xinghuo	City	16.8	0.72	0.44	medicine, textiles
Xinzhuang	City	13.65	0.4	N/A	electric equipment, electronics and communications
Jiading	City	24.8	N/A	0.60	automobile parts, electronics, garments
Songjiang	City	20.6	1.45	1.20	electrical equipment, beverages, medicine
China textile industrial zone	City	0.2	0.49	N/A	synthetic fibres
Kangqiao	City	26	0.58	0.23	automobiles, garments, building materials

Source: Yearbook of Shanghai Foreign Economic Relations and Trade 1997

located in the area. It is hoped that Lujiazui will form the core of a future CBD for Shanghai.

Jinqiao, located in the central part of Pudong New Area, is 19 square kilometres, with a current built-up area of 8.5 square kilometres. The main functions of the ETDZ are manufacturing and housing. By 1997, this zone had successfully attracted 302 projects, with over 158 projects already in operation. In that year, the total output value of industry in the zone reached RMB 17 billion and export values reached RMB 3.12 billion.

Waigaoqiao, located in the estuary of the Yangtze river, is 20 km away from the city proper. By the end of 1997, the area within the ETDZ covered 6.4 square kilometres and had attracted 3,239 projects worth US$3.91 billion. During that year, the gross production output reached RMB 4.8 billion, the export volume was US$600 million, and the port of Waigaoqiao handled 4.5 million tonnes of goods (439,000 TEU).

Zhangjiang, another high-tech park in Shanghai situated in the central part of Pudong New Area, has the mandated function of becoming a bio-engineering technology and industrial zone. Currently, four national bio-engineering R&D centres operate in this industrial park, along with the Chinese bases of some famous pharmaceutical multinationals.

Songjiang, the county seat, is 35 km south-west of the central city, and the first city-level ETDZ in Shanghai was established here in 1992. The planned area is 20.56 square kilometres, with nine square kilometres of land already developed. Because it possesses a sound location advantage with easy access to transportation routes (it is close to the Shanghai-Hangzhou expressway and railway), and lower land transfer fees (US$30 per square metre for industrial land), it has attracted many famous multinationals from Western countries. By the end of 1997, there were 180 projects in the zone worth a total of US$1.2 billion in FDI. This level of investment exceeds some national-level ETDZs, such as Caohejing and Zhangjiang. Among 32 large industrial projects, 15 are Japanese investments, seven are American, two are German, two are British, and the others are from France, Denmark, Switzerland, and Canada.

The ETDZs have become a successful instrument in attracting FDI. However, there are some problems in the development of the ETDZs. First, because so many ETDZs have been established, there is keen competition among them for limited FDI, especially among industrial ETDZs. Some have been forced to provide very inexpensive terms of investment, including lower land transfer fees. Second, some ETDZs have relatively disadvantageous locations so that they not only attract a small amount of FDI, but they often occupy a large quantity of land, resulting in the conversion of prime agricultural land. Third, because of the South-East Asia financial crises, it has recently been difficult for the ETDZs to attract FDI. The Shanghai municipal government had to reduce its plans for attracting

FDI in 1997. In order to counteract the fall of FDI from Asian economies, Shanghai has focused attention on attracting foreign investment from the Western multinationals.

Growth of foreign trade

During the planned economy period, China had a closed economic system and foreign trade was therefore an unimportant sector. As the country's largest industrial city, the total value of foreign trade of Shanghai was only US$3.03 billion in 1978. This accounted for 14.6 per cent of the total trade for China. Since the 1980s, with the development of an export-oriented economy, foreign trade has taken on special significance, as reflected in the import and export values of Shanghai. In 1996, the total value of exports and imports for the city reached US$22.26 billion (Table 10.11).

Foreign-funded enterprises have played an important role in the growth of Shanghai's exports. In 1996, total exports from this group of businesses rose to US$4.05 billion and accounted for 30.25 per cent of the total export capacity of the city. Textiles and other light industrial products accounted for 65 per cent of foreign-funded enterprise exports, while machinery, electrical equipment, and instruments accounted for 19 per cent.

The processing trade, however, has also developed rapidly. In 1978, annual processing fees were only US$300,000, but they had skyrocketed to US$313.81 million by 1995 (Shanghai Economy Yearbook 1996). Further, the value of processing contracts amounted to US$1.52 billion in 1995. The products of processing have changed from labour-intensive textiles and other light industrial goods to those produced with advanced technology. These include high-added-value goods such as electronics, garments, instrument and meters, chemicals, and shipbuilding.

China's trading partners are mainly located in the Asia Pacific region. Japan is the largest trade partner, followed by Hong Kong; only then come North America and the European Union. Directly thereafter in ranking

Table 10.11 Growth of export and import in Shanghai

Year	Total value of import and export (US$ bn)	Value of export (US$ bn)	Value of import (US$ bn)
1980	4.50	4.27	0.24
1985	4.99	3.36	1.63
1990	7.43	5.32	2.11
1995	19.06	11.58	7.48
1996	22.26	13.24	9.03
1997	24.76	14.70	10.06

Source: Shanghai Municipal Statistics Bureau 1985–1998

Table 10.12 Main trade partners of Shanghai, 1996

	Export (US$ bn)	Import (US$ bn)	Total (US$ bn)
Hong Kong, Taiwan, Macao	2.72	1.48	4.20
East Asia	5.04	3.35	8.39
Japan	4.52	2.89	7.41
Korea	0.51	0.45	0.96
South-East Asia	0.83	0.30	1.13
European Union	1.79	1.62	3.41
North America	2.40	1.00	3.40
USA	2.18	0.90	3.08
Oceanic and Pacific islands	0.25	0.28	0.53
Total	13.49	9.31	22.80

Source: Shanghai Municipal Statistics Bureau 1985–1998

are South-East Asian countries (Table 10.12). In 1997, the total value of foreign trade to the Asia Pacific region reached US$18.35 billion and accounted for 72.7 per cent of the total value of foreign trade of Shanghai.

With the growth of foreign trade, the Shanghai port handles increasingly larger numbers of international containers. In 1990, it handled 456,000 containers; in 1998 this number rose to 3,050,000 containers. Currently, the Shanghai container port has become the largest in China. According to Shanghai customs figures, the total value of import and export commodities rose from US$17.29 billion in 1990 to US$63.64 billion in 1998.

Sustainable development challenges for Shanghai

For Shanghai, the strategy of sustainable development translates chiefly to three issues: strengthening population control; managing the floating population; and protecting the environment. Besides maintaining economic growth, these are the three most important issues facing the city in the twenty-first century.

Population trends

Natural growth

By the end of 1949, the total population of Shanghai was approximately 5.02 million. The spatial distribution of this population concentrated around the city's urban districts. Approximately 4.19 million (83.3 per cent) lived in these areas. The other 0.84 million people (16.7 per cent) were located in the suburban districts. After 10 counties within Jiangsu province were

Table 10.13 Population growth of Shanghai, 1950–1996

Year	Population (000)	Births Number (000)	Births Rate (%)	Deaths Number (000)	Deaths Rate (%)	Natural growth rate
1950	4,927.3	–	24.2	–	8.5	15.7
1954	6,627.1	–	52.6	–	7.1	45.5
1960	10,563.0	–	27.6	–	6.8	20.8
1963	10,736.4	–	30.3	–	7.0	23.3
1970	10,725.5	–	13.9	–	5.0	8.9
1975	10,767.2	–	9.4	–	6.0	3.4
1980	11,465.2	143.1	11.8	73.9	6.5	5.3
1982	11,805.1	216.8	18.5	73.5	6.3	12.2
1985	12,166.9	154.3	12.7	81.0	6.7	6.0
1990	12,833.5	131.2	10.2	86.3	6.7	3.5
1993	12,947.1	84.0	6.5	94.0	6.3	−0.8
1996	13,044.3	67.9	5.2	97.7	7.5	−2.3

Source: Shanghai Municipal Statistics Bureau 1985–1998

merged into Shanghai in 1958, the total population of the city increased to 10.28 million.

The city's natural growth has experienced fluctuations between the 1950s and the early 1990s (Table 10.13). Despite this, some trends can be identified. First, the birth rate of the population between the 1950s and the early 1960s was very high, peaking at 52.6 per thousand in 1954. Thereafter, in 1963, the municipal government set up a family planning committee to control rapid population growth and the governments at the district and county levels also established similar organizations. As a result, the birth rate declined after 1964. However, because of the increase in the numbers of women of child-bearing age, the city's birth rate rose again in the early 1980s. In 1982, it climbed to 18.5 per thousand. Since that point the birth rate has declined, and in 1997 it stood at 4.9 per thousand. Second, the death rate has increased since the 1990s, as Shanghai has entered the ageing society phase of development. Third, natural growth rates have followed a similar trend to that of the birth rates: they increased between the 1950s and the early 1960s and then gradually decreased, rose again in the early 1980s, but recently have slowed and since 1993 have dipped to negative growth rate levels as the birth rate declined and the death rate rose. Shanghai has become the first Chinese city with a negative natural population growth rate.

Migration

Migration has contributed to Shanghai's population growth. Similar to the natural growth of population, Shanghai's migration pattern has experienced a marked fluctuation. For example, during the period 1968–1972,

881,100 educated youths were moved to the countryside through the policies of the Cultural Revolution. After the revolution ended, a large number of young educated people returned to the city. Between 1978 and 1983 the large in-migration brought a net increase of 614,000 persons to Shanghai. This was equal to two-thirds of the city's net population growth during this period.

The household registration regulation has been the most important tool in China for restricting migration from inner provinces to coastal provinces and between towns and countryside (see the section on the floating population). It was because of this policy that the growth rates of Shanghai have been maintained at a low level since the early 1980s. However, because of the thousands of migrants moving into the city every year, the total population of Shanghai has increased gradually and by 1997 had reached 13.07 million.

Starting from the beginning of the 1980s, international migration has become an important feature of Shanghai's population trend. Between 1986 and 1990, 111,700 Shanghai inhabitants migrated to other countries. The main destinations for migrants were Japan, Australia, the USA, Canada, and European countries. With the establishment of foreign-funded enterprises in Shanghai, the number of foreign residents (including those from Hong Kong, Taiwan, and Macao) has also grown, reaching over 20,000 persons.

Population distribution

The Shanghai municipality has experienced several administrative changes since the 1960s. Currently, Shanghai consists of 15 districts and five counties. They are arranged in concentric rings around the core. The first ring consists of the central city including 10 urban districts. The second ring consists of four inner suburban districts: Pudong New Area, Baoshan, Jiading, and Minhang. The outer ring consists of five exurban counties, namely Qingpu, Songjiang, Nanhui, Fengxian, and Chongming, and Jinshan district.

Shanghai is a compact city with a high average population density. In 1982, the density of the central city was 43,000 persons per square kilometre. The density of some districts exceeded 60,000 persons per square kilometre, while some subdistricts reached densities of between 150,000 and 160,000 persons per square kilometre. The average density of the suburbs is much lower, at approximately 929 persons per square kilometre. In order to upgrade the environmental quality and improve the spatial structure of the central city, the area of the central city has been continuously enlarged. The effect of this enlargement has been a decrease in average density. In 1996, its population accounted for 48.6 per cent of the total population of Shanghai (Table 10.14).

Table 10.14 Population distribution of Shanghai, 1996

Region	Area (km^2)	Total population (000)	Population density (persons per km^2)
Central city	280.08	6,339.3	22,634
Inner suburbs	1,776.93	3,270.9	1,841
Exurbs	4,283.49	3,434.1	802
Total	6,340.50	13,044.3	2,057

Source: Shanghai Municipal Statistics Bureau 1985–1998

The characteristics of the floating population

China has had a household registration system policy since the 1950s. Registered permanent residents are divided into two categories: the agricultural population and the non-agricultural population, and the latter has obviously dominated the urban population. The government has granted the urban population a series of social welfare benefits, such as employment, housing, medical treatment, and education. At the same time, they strictly controlled the shift of the agricultural population into non-agricultural employment. They also controlled the migration of rural population to urban areas. Before the 1980s, due to these policies, there was a relatively small floating population in China's cities.

The large-scale rural-urban floating of the population in China is a new phenomenon which developed after the implementation of reform policies. This population movement is characterized by its ability to float from rural to urban areas and from inland to coastal areas. A survey in 1993 revealed that Shanghai's floating population reached 3.3 million, of whom 2.51 million are immigrants from other provinces. The floating population 10 years earlier, in 1983, was only 0.5 million (Wang 1995), thus the non-native population of the city increased fourfold over the course of the decade.

The cause of floating population formation

Internal population migrations to Shanghai result from both pull and push forces operating between urban and rural areas. The pulling force has two components. First, Shanghai's rapid economic development created a huge non-native labour market. In 1984, Shanghai migrant population was 0.7 million. At that level it accounted for approximately 5.8 per cent of the city's total registered residents. The proportion of those employed in this population was only 6.6 per cent. The number of migrants and their share of the total registered resident population increased with Shanghai's rapid economic development. Further, the share of those employed within this population also rose to 75.6 per cent (Table 10.15). Second, the local labour

Table 10.15 Growth of migrants and investment in Shanghai

Year	1984	1985	1986	1988	1993
Migrants (10,000)	70	134	165	141	251
Employment proportion of migrants (%)	6.6	–	22.9	61.4	75.6
Investment of fixed assets (million RMB)	9,230	11,856	14,693	24,527	65,391
Foreign investment in real utilization (million US$)	–	148	286	1,322	3,175

Source: Wang 1995; Shanghai Municipal Statistics Bureau 1985–1998

force is ageing. Shanghai was China's first city to adopt family planning. By the end of the 1970s, Shanghai had begun to practise the policy of "one family, one child". The implementation of this policy not only resulted in a negative population growth for the city, but also provided for an ageing society. In 1993, the average age of Shanghai's population was 35.5 years. A sample survey of the floating population revealed that the 18–30-year-old group accounted for 57.3 per cent of the all migrants. The 31–40 age group's share was 25.3 per cent of the total. The conclusion of this research was that the non-native labour force was effectively filling a demand for young and middle-aged labourers (Ning 1997).

Social status of floating population

Since the 1990s, the policy of the household registration system in China has undergone change. This change can be seen in the growing distinctions within the floating population. For example, in Shanghai the floating population can be divided into four groups. The first group consists of blue-card household registration holders. The blue-card policy, implemented in 1993, is for any enterprise or any individual from another province or city who has invested at least 1 million yuan in Shanghai. An amendment to the policy in 1996 allowed any enterprise or individual having purchased a house valued at over 0.4 million yuan in the city to apply for up to three blue cards. Currently, professional technical personnel can also apply for blue cards. With the card, residents can enjoy social welfare benefits equal to those of Shanghai's permanent residents. After holding the card for five years, the migrant can apply for Shanghai permanent resident status. There are currently approximately 1,500 people holding blue cards in Shanghai.

The floating population in suburban rural areas is the second group. The non-native population that marries into the local agricultural population can apply for agricultural household registration. Non-native persons doing business in small cities and towns, after paying urban construction fees at 10,000 yuan, can then apply to become a registered permanent resident of the town they live in.

Non-native people who marry urban residents comprise the third group. When non-native males marry urban females their children are afforded the right to apply for local registered permanent resident status. But non-native females who marry urban males are not given the same privileges. They and their children will not enjoy Shanghai's registered permanent resident status. Social welfare benefits are also not available to this group. According to a survey of registered Shanghai residents, those married to non-native persons account for 15 per cent of all married couples. Over 90 per cent of these types of marriages are a non-native female married to an urban male (Wang 1995). This policy was enforced until 1998; since then children, whether their parents are native or non-native people, can apply for local registered permanent resident status when they are six years old.

The fourth group includes the ordinary non-native population. The local government does not provide education, housing, or other services to this group. These individuals secure jobs as contract workers. The contract period usually lasts between two to six years, but not more than eight. After the contract expires they must seek new jobs. Their income is only half that of the formal workers and staff members. Often, enterprises provide them with a medical treatment subsidy. Further, the non-native population with this type of informal employment cannot access any social security benefits.

Management of migrants

Without a doubt, the non-native floating population of Shanghai has contributed to the economic development of the city. This great influx of people, however, has also brought about many social problems. The management of the floating population has thus become one of the most important issues for Shanghai's social sustainability.

Shanghai is a city with a high population density. With its 2.5 million non-native population, Shanghai's average population density has increased by 21.7 per cent. This is especially true of the inner suburban districts, where the density has increased by 35.4 per cent (Table 10.16). This increased density exerts pressure on the city's transportation, water supply, electricity supply, and sanitation. Since Shanghai's non-native population has surpassed the demand of the local labour market, part of the non-native population has to be engaged in informal jobs. Further, the non-native population commits approximately 57 per cent of Shanghai's criminal acts. This last fact has facilitated a negative perception of this population.

China's local government possesses limited fiscal revenues for social programmes. It can only provide social welfare benefits and infrastructure

Table 10.16 Actual population density of Shanghai, 1995

	Permanent population density (person/km^2)	Non-native population density (person/km^2)	Actual population density (person/km^2)
Central city	22,873	4,463	27,336
Inner suburbs	1,730	613	2,343
Country	809	110	919
Average	2,042	443	2,485

Source: Wang 1995; Shanghai Municipal Statistics Bureau 1985–1998

for permanent residents. Because of recent structural adjustments within the local economy, Shanghai's actual unemployment rate has risen. In order to secure employment for local residents, the local government has adopted a new policy to limit the non-native population engaging in specific professions. While the various policies of the household registration system are still being implemented, the local government has the opportunity to limit the number of non-native persons attempting to become local residents. In order to achieve some control, local government should consider allowing all non-native people who marry local residents, and their children, to transform gradually into local permanent residents.

Environmental quality

One of Shanghai's greatest challenges is to maintain a sound environment quality. For a long period of time, the environmental quality in Shanghai was satisfactory, but over the last few decades it has developed a multitude of problems, including air and water pollution and growing solid waste production.

The major air pollutants affecting life in the city include total suspended particulate (TSP) and sulphur dioxide (SO$_2$). Shanghai had the dubious honour of being China's leading emitter of both TSP and SO$_2$ during the 1970s. Both TSP and SO$_2$ levels were in excess of the national secondary air quality standards until the early 1990s. The results from air quality monitoring indicated that 80–90 per cent of the time the daily TSP levels exceeded the World Health Organization's criterion by as much as two to three times between 1981 and 1987 (Lam and Tao 1996). Recently, this problem has been compounded by the rise in automobile usage. Vehicular emissions are increasingly becoming a new pollution source.

Water pollution has long troubled Shanghai. The main pollutants are heavy metals, phenol, phosphorus, petroleum waste, and those that create chemical oxygen demand. These chemicals emanate mainly from agriculture run-off, industrial point sources, and domestic sewage. Only 85 per cent of industrial effluent and 14 per cent of domestic sewage were treated prior to discharge in the early 1990s. Because some small rivers in and around the city have received these outflows for a long time, they have become extremely polluted. The lower reach of Suzhou creek, one tributary of the Huangpu river, has been grossly polluted since the 1950s. The water quality is so poor that the river no longer supports fish life. The lower reaches of the Huangpu river have also been seriously polluted since the 1970s. The annual number of days that the river emitted offensive smells increased from 28 in 1975 to 229 days in 1988.

Another problem that the city faces is the disposal of waste. Solid waste generated from industrial sectors has more than doubled over the last 15 years. In 1980s the total annual amount was 5.8 million tonnes, and in 1996 it reached 13.1 million tonnes. At the same time, the amount of municipal garbage reached 4.18 million tonnes. The city has promoted a programme of solid waste and industrial waste reduction and reuse. The results are that 84 per cent of these waste streams are currently being treated in this manner. Further, a large garbage landfill was constructed at the mouth of the Yangtze river. This facility, however, has not eliminated the use of thousands of temporary and inadequate sites on the outskirts of the city.

Besides attempting to implement increased pollution control and sanitation services, Shanghai faces underlying structural problems that affect the city's environmental quality. For example, Shanghai is and has been an industrial city. Environmental quality was not a consideration when the older factories were built. Further, lack of adequate land-use planning has resulted in an undesirable mixing of residential and industrial land uses. During the 1980s there were 10,000 factories and workshops located in the urban districts, and these have generated a great quantity of industrial waste gases, wastewater, solid waste, and noise pollution.

Since the 1950s, Shanghai has promoted heavy and chemical industries. These industries require large energy inputs. In order to meet this demand the city has attempted to update its electricity production with the development of new large power plants with a total generating capacity of over 6,000 MW. These modern facilities, however, have not eliminated the city's industrial use of coal as a main fuel. In 1995, the consumption of coal reached 35 million tonnes (Shanghai Municipal Statistics Bureau 1996). Both SO_2 and TSP are the by-products of coal combustion, and the discharges of these pollutants continue to climb. For example, SO_2 production increased from 390,000 tonnes in 1989 to 510,000 tonnes in 1996.

Lastly, investments for environment protection have been inadequate, being only 0.85 per cent of Shanghai's total production output in 1991. It is no wonder that the city has poor waste collection and disposal facilities.

Table 10.17 Investments in Shanghai's environmental protection and its proportion of GDP, 1991–1996

Year	1991	1992	1993	1994	1995	1996
Environmental protection investments[a]	1.00	2.00	4.23	5.14	6.12	–
Proportion of GDP (%)	0.85	1.36	2.13	1.98	1.89	2.40

Source: Shanghai Environment Protection Bureau 1996
a. The environmental protection investment in 1991 is regarded as 1.00.

Policies and measures for environmental protection

According to the laws and regulations on environmental protection and resources management in China, Shanghai has set up a system of environmental controls. The main components of the programme include:
• formulation of local laws and regulations for environmental protection;
• implementing an environmental impact assessment system;
• creating discharge registration reports and a pollutant discharge permits system;
• collecting pollution charges;
• developing a system of environmental pollution treatment facilities.
These policies and measures are not strictly for domestic firms but have been implemented citywide for all firms, including foreign-funded enterprises. Polluting foreign-funded projects have not been given permission to operate in the city. Generally, large multinational corporations are attentive to environmental protection demands. They usually build sewage treatment facilities when they invest in projects in Shanghai. Most of the small foreign-funded factories belong to labour-intensive sectors that generate low levels of industrial wastewater.

The funds used for environmental protection have been increasing ever year, albeit slowly (Table 10.17). These funds are mainly used for the control of old pollution sources (including the relocation of some polluting factories), development of new projects and urban environmental infrastructure, the comprehensive management of the regional environment, and the implementation of environmental protection departments.

Achievements in environmental protection

Through the management of environmental pollution, Shanghai has made great progress in the improvement of its environmental quality. In the national comprehensive urban environmental quality and management assessment exercise undertaken by 37 cities, Shanghai ranked tenth and seventh in 1994 and 1995 respectively (Table 10.18). The assessment is based on 21 criteria, which can be divided into three groups. The first group focuses on air, water, and noise pollution. The second group is based on

Table 10.18 Shanghai's scores and positions in the national comprehensive urban environmental quality and management assessment exercises, 1989–1996

Year	1989	1990	1991	1992	1993	1994	1995
Score	54.30	57.40	70.33	69.33	77.53	80.99	83.93
Position	15	24	13	20	13	10	7

Source: Shanghai Environment Protection Bureau 1996

Table 10.19 Environmental quality in Shanghai: Density of TSP and SO_2, 1991–1996

Year	1991 mg/m^3	1992 mg/m^3	1993 mg/m^3	1994 mg/m^3	1995 mg/m^3	1996 mg/m^3
SO_2	0.106	0.093	0.089	0.073	0.053	0.059
TSP	0.324	0.333	0.295	0.281	0.246	0.241

Source: Shanghai Environment Protection Bureau 1996

the measures adopted to control pollution, and the third group refers to the provision of basic municipal infrastructure and waste treatment facilities. In 1995, Shanghai's scores in these three groups were 18.83, 44.69, and 15.33, respectively. Within the 37 cities, Shanghai ranked thirty-first, first, and seventh for its scores in these groups. The results indicate that in the aspects of pollution control and infrastructure construction, Shanghai was leading the country. In terms of improving the indexes of environmental quality, however, Shanghai still has a long way to go.

With respect to air pollution control, some polluting factories (workshops) in the central city have been given orders either to close, stop their polluting activities, or merge with other companies and transform their production processes. Various activities have promoted cleaner air. For example, deadlines have been set for the completion of remedial works, household gas usage and central heating technology have been popularized, smog- and dust-controlling districts have been built, the control of dust generation on construction sites has been strengthened, and the examination of automobile emissions has been implemented. Due to these measures, although the amount of air pollution discharges increased, the air quality in Shanghai actually improved between 1991 and 1996 (Table 10.19). Compared to 1994, the amount of coal consumption and industrial waste gas emission in 1995 increased 0.3 per cent and 10.5 per cent respectively, but the average density of SO_2 and TSP was reduced by 0.02 mg/m^3 and 0.035 mg/m^3. The frequency of acid rain was also reduced by 2.6 per cent, the amount of average dust fall was reduced by 1.45 tonnes per month per square kilometre compared to figures for the previous year (Shanghai Environment Protection Bureau 1996).

In respect of water pollution control, Shanghai's environmental protection agencies have started routinely to check the upper reaches of the Huangpu river. Further, monitoring of pollution sources and management of the environmental protection facilities have been strengthened. The largest wastewater control project in Shanghai, Suzhou creek's phase one wastewater project, funded by the World Bank, has been completed. Shanghai's water quality has thus been steadily improved. In 1995, discharged volumes of industrial wastewater reached 1.16 billion tonnes. The discharged volume of domestic sewage reached 1.08 billion tonnes in 1995, and the treatment rate for these discharges was up to 41.07 per cent. The water quality of the upper reaches of Huangpu river is at national secondary or third-class water quality standards.

New goals for Shanghai's environmental protection

In 1995, Shanghai's ninth five-year plan (1996–2000) and environmental protection long-term plan for 2010 were put into action. The environmental plan's main objectives and tasks have been adopted into Shanghai's overall urban planning, and into the ninth five-year plan and long-range plan for 2010 for Shanghai's national economic and social development.

According to this plan, the general aim of Shanghai's environmental protection is to develop an urban environment suited to the standards of an international city. In addition to its continued growth, Shanghai wants to readjust its urban layout and industrial structure, perfect the city's infrastructure and pollution treatment, control environmental pollution, and enable each environmental functional area to meet environmental quality standards.

The city's long-range targets for 2010 include the development of a highly coordinated environmental system and the complete establishment of environmental functional areas. Broadly speaking, the plan's implementation will move Shanghai towards creating a sound ecological environment and the realization of its goal of sustainable development.

In order to realize these goals, Shanghai's environmental protection agencies have formulated a green project plan. The main objectives of this plan include the protection of water and air and improvement of solid waste management. Water pollution controls will include the construction of a comprehensive treatment facility for Suzhou creek and the construction of a sewage disposal system. In addition, a system for the disposal of night soil from chicken and stock farms will be developed. Efforts for the protection of the air include the construction of a natural gas project, the construction of a central heating project, the control of automobile emissions, and a project for removing power-station-related sulphur dioxide. Efforts to control the disposal of solid waste include the construction of landfill and garbage incinerators.

In addition to these main thrusts, the new environmental policies of the city will include the treatment of industrial pollution and nature preservation. Industrial pollution control efforts will include the further implementation of policies for environmental protection and the promotion of measures for clean production. Nature preservation attempts will include reafforestation efforts and the creation of a green belt, nature reserves, and ecological agriculture.

Approximately 30 environmental projects have already been initiated in the city, among which some of the most important are the initiation of the second phase of Suzhou creek's wastewater project, the central heating project, the project for removing power-related sulphur dioxide, the comprehensive disposal of chicken and stock night soil, domestic garbage incineration, and the hazardous solid waste dump site project.

Conclusions

Over the last two decades, Shanghai has made great strides in economic development. Since the 1980s, globalization of the world economy and China's reform and openness policy have combined to affect the growth of the city beneficially. While the development of Shanghai has been considerable, however, it still has a long way to go before it attains its goal of becoming a regional city and world city. On the path to this goal, three important challenges await the city.

First, although Shanghai has begun to play a role as a domestic economic centre, most Chinese national company and bank headquarters are still located in Beijing. As Shanghai provides a more open investment environment it will attract an increasing number of regional headquarters of multinationals. This may lead to unhealthy competition between cities. Currently, as Beijing is the capital of China, representative and investment offices of foreign companies prefer this city to Shanghai. As the environment for investment changes, so might the centre for headquarters location. Therefore, a rational division of functions between Beijing and Shanghai must be established. This also must occur between Shanghai and Hong Kong.

China has a large population, and because of its economic development Shanghai is attracting an increasing number of the floating population. With this migration has come heavy pressure on the environment and the ability of the city to maintain sustainable development. Shanghai's second challenge is therefore to manage this population correctly and control its growth. The goal of population management should be to meet the equilibrium of supply and demand in the labour market.

Third, Shanghai must improve its infrastructure. Compared to other

world cities, Shanghai still faces a shortage of infrastructure. In turn this
has greatly affected the environment. Indeed, the quality of the environment is still unsatisfactory. Although Shanghai has already put a great
quantity of funds into environmental protection, it must continue to do so
for the long-run benefit of the population and the future of the city. It will
be a long-term task to improve the environmental quality of Shanghai. In
order to meet this challenge, Shanghai must insist on a strategy of sustainable development.

REFERENCES

China Statistics Press. 1994. *China Statistical Yearbook*. Beijing: China Statistics
    Press.
China Statistics Press. 1997. *China Statistical Yearbook*. Beijing: China Statistics
    Press.
Cohen, R. 1981. "The new international division of labour, multinational corpo-
    rations and urban hierarchy", in M. Dear and A. Scott (eds) *Urbanization and
    Urban Planning in Capitalist Society*. London: Methuen, pp. 287–315.
Deng, Nan. 1995. "Report on China's Agenda 21", paper presented to the Third
    Meeting of China Council for International Cooperation on Environment and
    Development, Beijing.
Feng, Guoqin. 1998. "New round development of Shanghai's rural areas" (in
    Chinese), *Shanghai Rural Economy*, No. 2, pp. 4–9.
Friedmann, John. 1986. "The world city hypothesis", *Development and Changes*,
    Vol. 17, No. 1, pp. 69–83.
Friedmann, John and Goetz Wolff. 1982. "World city formation: An agenda for
    research and action", *International Journal for Urban and Regional Research*,
    No. 3, pp. 309–404.
Frobel, F., F. Heinrichs, and O. Kreye. 1980. *The New International Division of
    Labour*. Cambridge: Cambridge University Press.
Hong, Sung Woong. 1996. "A global city in a nation of rapid growth", in Fu-chen
    Lo and Yue-man Yeung (eds) *Emerging World Cities in Pacific Asia*. Tokyo:
    United Nations University Press, pp. 144–178.
Jiefang Daily (Shanghai). 1998. 9 February.
Krongkaew, Medhi. 1996. "The changing urban system in a fast-growing city and
    economy: The case of Bangkok and Thailand", in Fu-chen Lo and Yue-man
    Yeung (eds) *Emerging World Cities in Pacific Asia*. Tokyo: United Nations
    University Press, pp. 286–334.
Lam, Kin-che and Tao Shu. 1996. "Environmental quality and pollution control",
    in Yue-man Yeung and Sung Yun-wing (eds) *Shanghai, Transformation and
    Modernization under China's Open Policy*. Hong Kong: Chinese University
    Press, pp. 469–492.
Li, Xiaomei. 1998. "Land use of Huangpu district" (in Chinese), *Shanghai Land*,
    No. 3, pp. 7–10.

McGee, Terry G. 1997. "Globalization, urbanization and the emergence of sub-global regions: A case study of the Asia Pacific region", in R. F. Watters and T. G. McGee (eds) *New Geographies of the Pacific Rim.* Vancouver: University of British Columbia Press, pp. 29–45.

Ning, Yuemin. 1995. "Case study of Shanghai, China", in United Nations Centre for Human Settlements (eds) *Metropolitan Planning and Management in the Developing World: Shanghai and Guangzhou, China.* Nairobi: UNCHS, pp. 27–70.

Ning, Yuemin. 1997. "An approach to the floating population in Shanghai in the 1990s", *Population and Economics* (in Chinese), No. 2, pp. 9–16.

Ning, Yuemin, Zhang Wudong, and Qian Jingxi. 1994. *The History of Chinese Cities* (in Chinese). Hefei: Anhui Science and Technology Press.

Ning, Yuemin and Yan Zhongmin. 1995. "The changing industrial and spatial structure in Shanghai", *Urban Geography*, Vol. 16, No. 7, pp. 577–594.

Nyaw, Mee-Kau. 1996. "Investment environment: Perceptions of overseas investors of foreign-funded industrial firms", in Yue-man Yeung and Sung Yun-wing (eds) *Shanghai, Transformation and Modernization under China's Open Policy.* Hong Kong: Chinese University Press, pp. 249–272.

Porter, Michael. 1990. *The Competitive Advantage of Nations.* New York: Free Press.

Sassen, Saskia. 1991. *The Global City, New York, London, Tokyo.* Princeton: Princeton University Press.

Shanghai Economy Yearbook. 1996. *Shanghai Economy Yearbook.* Shanghai: Shanghai Academy of Social Science Press.

Shanghai Environment Protection Bureau. 1996. *Environmental State Bulletin of Shanghai* (in Chinese). Shanghai: Shanghai Environment Protection Bureau.

Shanghai Municipal People's Government. 1989. "On the report outline of the economic development strategy of Shanghai", in *Industrial Yearbook of Shanghai* (in Chinese). Shanghai: Shanghai Dictionary Press, pp. 5–12.

Shanghai Municipal People's Government. 1995. *Shanghai Towards the 21st Century* (in Chinese). Shanghai: Shanghai People's Publishing House.

Shanghai Municipal Statistics Bureau. 1985–1998. *Statistical Yearbook of Shanghai.* Beijing: China Statistical Publishing House.

Shanghai Pudong New Area Administration. 1993. *Shanghai Pudong New Area, Investment Environment and Development Prospect.* Shanghai: Shanghai Pudong New Area Administration.

Soegijoko, Budhy Tjahjati S. 1996. "Jabotabek and globalization", in Fu-chen Lo and Yue-man Yeung (eds) *Emerging World Cities in Pacific Asia.* Tokyo: United Nations University Press, pp. 377–416.

State Statistics Bureau of PRC. 1994, 1995, 1997, 1998. *China Statistical Yearbook.* Beijing: China Statistical Publishing House.

Vernon, R. 1966. "International investment and international trade in the product cycle", *Quarterly Journal of Economics*, Vol. 80, pp. 190–207.

Wang, Wuding (ed.). 1995. *Floating Population in Shanghai in the 1990s* (in Chinese). Shanghai: East China Normal University Press.

Yearbook of Shanghai Foreign Economic Relations and Trade. 1997. *Yearbook of Shanghai Foreign Economic Relations and Trade, 1997.* Shanghai: Shanghai Academy of Social Science Press.

Yeh, Anthony Gar-on and Xu Xueqiang. 1996. "Globalization and urban systems in China", in Fu-chen Lo and Yue-man Yeung (eds) *Emerging World Cities in Pacific Asia.* Tokyo: United Nations University Press, pp. 219–267.

Yeung, Yue-man and Fu-chen Lo. 1996. "Global restructuring and emerging urban corridors in Pacific Asia", in Fu-chen Lo and Yue-man Yeung (eds) *Emerging World Cities in Pacific Asia.* Tokyo: United Nations University Press, pp. 17–47.

11

Globalization and the sustainability of Jabotabek, Indonesia

Budhy Tjahjati S. Soegijoko and B. S. Kusbiantoro

Introduction

While globalization trends and structural changes in the world economy have benefited some regions and cities around the world, in general these trends have impacted on the development of both the global spatial economic system and the world urban system (Cohen 1981; Friedmann and Wolff 1982; Friedmann 1986). Cities have increasingly linked into the global economy and at the same time have undergone dramatic physical, economic, and social transformations, affecting both their development patterns and their functional roles within the regional and global system. As the world system develops, cities articulated to each other are becoming more specialized in their functions and complementary in their economic relationships.

Important elements underlying economic globalization are the expansion of trade, capital flows (particularly foreign direct investment), and a wave of new technologies. Through a growing network of flows in goods and services, capital, finance, people, and information, the world is becoming "borderless" as nations become linked through the activities performed in their major urban centres. The role of cities as the major sites of production, distribution, and consumption cannot be underestimated in the new global economy.

Since the Asian financial crisis, however, scholars have been re-evaluating the role of the new global economy as a means of development.

One way in which to view the impacts of globalization is through the vague but powerful notion of sustainable development. This strategy includes the management of all assets – natural resources and human resources as well as financial and physical assets – with the goal of increasing long-term wealth and well-being. Sustainable development policies and practices include those that support current and future living standards without depleting the resource base. Sustainable development is an approach that maximizes the net benefits of economic development, subject to maintaining the services and quality of natural resources over time (Pearce and Kerry 1990). As such, the concept of sustainability is not limited to environmental protection, but also embraces economic and social well-being. A sustainable city, therefore, is a city where achievements in economic, social, and physical development are made to last. The key elements of sustainable development include economic efficiency in the use of development resources (including goods and services provided by the natural environment); social equity in the distribution of development benefits and costs (with special emphasis on the needs of low-income groups); and the avoidance of unnecessary environmental hazards that could threaten or foreclose future development options.

Through these key elements, the sustainable development concept can be used to evaluate the impacts of economic globalization not only in terms of the economics of scale and competitive advantage, but also in social and environmental terms. Economic efficiency is one of the critical issues for the development of the global city. In the current economic environment, in order to be sustainable a city must be globally competitive, meaning that it must be integrated into the global network of flows. Integration into the global economy will, in turn, strengthen international functional links that further enhance functional regional or international urban systems. Degradation of the social and environmental character of the city not only impacts on economic efficiency, but also on the quality of life experienced by citizens.

DKI Jakarta is an example of a city that has been both positively and negatively impacted by integration into the global economic system. Jakarta, Indonesia's capital and gateway to the world, has experienced rapid economic development over the past 10 years during the economic boom in East and South-East Asia. The economic development has spread out to the adjacent areas surrounding DKI Jakarta, namely Bogor, Tangerang, and Bekasi (referred to as the Botabek region). Jakarta and the Botabek region, together known as Jabotabek, make up the largest metropolitan area and the most dynamic region in Indonesia. The rapid development of the Jabotabek area started at the end of the 1980s with increasing inflows of foreign direct investment and the development of large-scale industrial and housing estates. Thus, Jabotabek's rapid physical, social, and economic changes reflect its integration process into the system of global cities. Recently, however, Jabotabek suffered as the Asia financial crisis took hold and wreaked havoc on Indonesian economic and political structures. The abrupt halt in the growth process that accompanied the crisis and the current mood within the country have stimulated a re-evaluation of the role of globalization in urban and regional development.

This chapter will illustrate the impacts of the globalization process on Jabotabek by demonstrating the relationship between global flows of goods, services, FDI, people, and information and the spatial and functional transformation of the region. Furthermore, it will illustrate how the globalization and sustainability of Jabotabek, in terms of economic, social, and environmental aspects, are associated. The three main tasks required to achieve this are identifying how the processes of globalization developed within the region; identifying the impacts of these processes at both spatial and functional levels; and evaluating these impacts in terms of the economic, social, and environmental sustainability of Jabotabek. The results of these analyses suggest general policy directions that minimize negative impacts of the globalization process and support sustainability in the region.

The chapter is organized into five sections. Following the introduction, section two describes the urbanization process of Jabotabek and its role within the Indonesian economy. Section three illustrates urban development trends, including the increase of globalization/economic internationalization in the Jabotabek region. It also shows how global forces have transformed the region spatially as well as functionally. Section four analyses the impact of the Asian economic crisis, referred to as the next round of globalization, in terms of the sustainability of the Jabotabek region. Section five describes the challenges that will be faced by the urban managers as they attempt to promote sustainable economic, social, and environmental trends. It presents recommendations for the general policy for the Jabotabek region as we enter the twenty-first century. It is hoped that the region will continue to grow by becoming both a sustainable and a globally competitive world city.

The role of Jabotabek in Indonesia

Jabotabek is the largest metropolitan area and the most dynamic region in Indonesia (Figure 11.1). It is located in the northern part of the province of West Java. Originally a small harbour city called Sunda Kelapa, the Special Region of Jakarta (DKI Jakarta) is the seat of the provincial government and lies at the heart of the metropolitan area. The entire area now encompasses six other administrative units that surround Jakarta, includ-

Figure 11.1 Jabotabek region, Indonesia

ing the municipalities and administrative districts of Bogor, Tangerang, and Bekasi.

Recently, the development of Jabotabek has spilled over to Serang in the west and Karawang in the east. Since the 1980s, Jabotabek has experienced rapid growth in both population and economy. Despite its small relative size (638,273 ha or 0.33 per cent of the total area of Indonesia), Jabotabek is the nation's area of highest population concentration, housing 21.68 million inhabitants (10.61 per cent of the country's population). Furthermore, in terms of a number of indicators (concentration of banks' head offices, money circulation, credit expansion, flow of export-import goods, etc.), Jabotabek has become the engine of national economic development (Table 11.1).

Table 11.1 The role of Jabotabek in the Indonesian economy

	Year	Number	Jabotabek as % of Indonesia
Area (ha)	1998	638,273	0.33
Population (million)	1998	21.68	10.61
GRDP (billion Rp)	1995	83,847	21.83
Tertiary sector	1995	45,749	28.40
Secondary sector	1995	36,281	22.40
Labour force (million)	1995	10.40	12.10
Financial institutions, real estate, and business services	1995	0.66	84.50
Manufacturing	1995	1.53	15.10
Trade, hotels, and restaurants	1995	1.80	12.90
FDI (number of projects) in Jakarta	1996	294	36.30
Export-import through Tanjung Priok seaport			
Non-oil export (billion US$)	1997	16.70	39.90
Non-oil import (billion US$)	1997	22.30	59.00
International aircraft movement/year from/to Soekarno-Hatta, Jakarta international airport			
Arrivals	1997	22,734	47.41
Departures	1997	22,833	46.32
Circulation of money			80.00
Expansion of credit			75.00
Number of banks (head office in Jakarta)			
State banks	1997	7	100.0
Private national banks	1997	122	84.72
Foreign and joint banks	1997	34	77.27

Source: Central Bureau of Statistics 1996c, 1999d; Jakarta Statistical Office 1999a; West Java Statistical Office 1999

Social conditions in Jabotabek

Jabotabek is currently the most urbanized region in the country and is likely to continue to be so in the future. Based on the 1995 Intercensal Population Survey, the urbanization level in Jabotabek has reached 82.6 per cent, compared to 37.4 per cent for all of Indonesia. This difference in urbanization levels is enhanced by the political position of DKI Jakarta as the nation's capital. The urban area has not only become the centre of various economic activities such as manufacturing, trade, shipping, finance, and services, but it is also the location of national government services headquarters and education facilities. Given its privileged position within the country's economic and political structure, it is not surprising that the region's annual population growth rate (2.7 per cent) far exceeded that of Indonesia overall (1.7 per cent) during the 1990–1995 period.

The population of Jabotabek is not only more concentrated, more economically active, and growing faster than the rest of the country, but the average Jabotabekian enjoys a higher level of education than the average Indonesian (Table 11.2). People who have completed their education to the level of college/university, senior high school, and junior high school in Jabotabek constitute 5.07, 23.15, and 17.16 per cent of the total population, respectively. Compare this to the national averages of 3.58, 15.22, and 11.25 per cent for the same categories. While almost 54.62 per cent of those in Jabotabek still have a relatively low level of educational attainment (reflected in the percentage of the population who completed primary school), the portion of low educational attainment is much lower

Table 11.2 Social and economic indicators in Jabotabek and Indonesia

	Year	Jabotabek %	Indonesia %
Educational attainment			
College/university	1995	5.07	3.58
Senior high school	1995	23.15	15.22
Junior high school	1995	17.16	11.25
Primary school and lower	1995	54.62	69.95
Population growth (per year)	1990–1995	2.70	1.70
Urbanization level	1995	82.60	37.40
Economic growth	1995	8.50	8.20
GRDP/capita (million Rp/person/year)	1995	6.69	2.00
	1996	8.30	7.30
Per capita revenue/year (US$)	1996	3,600	1,155

Source: Central Bureau of Statistics 1996c, 1997a; Jakarta Statistical Office 1997b; West Java Statistical Office 1999

than the national average, 69.95 per cent. In general, those living in the urban region have better access to education than those in other parts of the country. This relatively better-educated population is one of Jabotabek's comparative advantages.

The role of Jabotabek within the national economy

As mentioned previously, Jabotabek is the engine of the Indonesian economy. In 1995, Jabotabek's contribution to the GDP of the country was 21.8 per cent (double its share of national population). The region's tertiary and secondary sectors contributed the greatest to the GDP at 28.4 and 22.4 per cent, respectively.

Regarding economic productivity, special mention must be made of the centre of the region, DKI Jakarta. The GRDP per capita of DKI Jakarta has always been the highest among all provinces in the country. In 1995, the GRDP per capita of DKI Jakarta (excluding oil and its products) totalled 6.68 million rupiah (Rp). The figure was almost 10 times that of the poorest region in the country, East Nusa Tenggara, which reached Rp 0.69 million during that year (Jakarta Statistical Office 1997b; Central Bureau of Statistics 1997c). Even with the inclusion of all its oil and primary commodity production and its lower population concentration, the GRDP per capita of East Kalimantan could not match that of DKI Jakarta. Within the city, the sectors of manufacturing, trade, hotels and restaurants, financial and business, and construction are those that made the greatest contribution to the GRDP.

In 1995, the labour force in Jabotabek amounted to 10.4 million, or 12.1 per cent of the total labour force in Indonesia. Concentrated employment is experienced within the service, manufacturing, and tourist sectors. Banks and other financial institutions, insurance agencies, real estate, and business services in Jabotabek attracted 85 per cent of all workers in those sectors in Indonesia. The manufacturing sector absorbed 15 per cent and trade, hotels, and restaurants absorbed 13 per cent of the national workers within their respective sectors (Table 11.1).

For the most part because of the activities in those sectors, the economic growth of Jabotabek reached 8.5 per cent in 1995 and 8.3 per cent in 1996. Its growth was higher than Indonesia's total growth of 8.2 per cent in 1995 and 7.3 per cent in 1996. Under these economic conditions, in 1996 the annual per capita revenue of Jabotabek was US$3,600, over three times greater than the US$1,155 national average.

Another indicator of the importance of Jabotabek's role in the national economy was the concentration of various infrastructure developments that facilitate Indonesia's international linkages. For example, Tanjung

Priok, Indonesia's major seaport, is located in Jabotabek. In 1997, the seaport received approximately 59 per cent of the total import value and 40 per cent of the total export value in Indonesia. Soekarno-Hatta airport, Indonesia's major international airport that transports people and goods to almost any place in the world, is also located in Jabotabek. The airport services approximately 50 per cent of the total international airlines entering and exiting Indonesia every year. Until 1997, the airport provided 70 international trips per day to and from Indonesia.

Jabotabek has also become the centre for a variety of service, financial, and international institutions. Almost all head offices of state banks, private national banks, and foreign and joint banks are located in the region, and more particularly in DKI Jakarta. All the head offices of the state banks, 85 per cent of private national banks, and 77 per cent of foreign/joint banks have locations in DKI Jakarta. Similarly, the offices of international tele-communications and information services providers are located in the core urban area along with embassies, consulate generals, foreign aid offices, and other foreign institutions. The Jakarta Stock Exchange (JSX), which has become the centre of stock exchange activities in the country, is also located in DKI Jakarta.

The concentration of these activities in the city has impacted on the circulation of money and credit. The concentration of financial activities in Jakarta has encouraged the concentration of money circulation within the city. Almost 80 per cent of the total circulation of Indonesian money flows within the borders of DKI Jakarta. The expansion of credit in Jakarta was almost 75 per cent of that in Indonesia (Table 11.1).

Because of these comparative advantages, a large amount of foreign direct investment (FDI) flows into the Jabotabek region. FDI inflows into Indonesia have dramatically increased since the mid-1990s. In 1988, annual FDI-related developments in Indonesia stood at around 125 projects averaging US$4 billion in total. In the early years of the economic boom (1990–1994) annual project numbers jumped to more than 400 projects per year with a total value of around US$20 billion. Jabotabek attracted about 50 per cent of all FDI projects in Indonesia, the value of which fluctuated between 15 and 30 per cent of the country's annual investment approvals during that period.

Jabotabek has a position of significant economic power within Indonesia. Internationally its comparative advantages associated with finance, trade, and investment have helped to enhance this power. These linkages, however, have also made the urban region susceptible to changes in global flows. Jabotabek is Indonesia's gateway to the world and therefore is highly affected by changes in regional and global conditions. Globalization processes have impacted on the region's spatial form and functional role.

Globalization processes and the Jabotabek region

The globalization process in Jabotabek can be traced through its international linkages, particularly through flows of goods and services, capital, finance, people, and information. Although these flows are the consequences of global and regional economic structural adjustments, they have affected the development of the urban region. They have allowed Jabotabek to internationalize, in terms of spreading economic activities across borders and facilitating the functional integration of these activities with other localities, and have also impacted on its internal workings by changing the physical structure of the region.

Global forces

As the nation's capital and the main gateway to the international economy, it is most likely that what was experienced by Jabotabek is a reflection of its integration into the system of global cities. The economic internationalization has increased the links of large cities in the world, including Jabotabek. This situation can be seen from several indicators, as discussed below.

Flows of goods and services

Trade

The amounts, sources, and destinations of exports and imports are important indicators of the extent to which a country is linked to others. The activities of export-import to and from Jabotabek are mainly carried out through Tanjung Priok, with a minor proportion of activities taking place at Soekarno-Hatta airport and the seaports of Kali Baru and Pasar Ikan. In general, during 1986–1997 DKI Jakarta's export-import seaport activities increased although the city's import functions remained more important than those of its exports. During 1985 the seaports in DKI Jakarta, mainly Tanjung Priok, exported only 10 per cent of the total national export value while handling 47 per cent of the total value of Indonesian imports. By 1997, the share of the national value of exports flowing through Tanjung Priok increased to 40 per cent (US$16.7 billion) and the share of the national value of imported goods increased to 59 per cent (US$22.3 billion) (Table 11.3).

Destinations of the largest shares of Indonesian exported goods were the USA, Singapore, Japan, and Hong Kong (Soegijoko 1996). Most of the imported goods came from Japan, the USA, the Republic of Korea, Taiwan, and Singapore. Textiles were the largest export commodities, followed by metal products, other industrial products, mining products, chemicals, and

Table 11.3 Comparison of non-oil trade flows through Jakarta and Indonesia, 1986–1997

| | Jakarta | | Indonesia | |
Year	Export US$ bn	Import US$ bn	Export US$ bn	Import US$ bn
1986	1.5	5.0	6.5	9.6
1990	5.1	14.0	14.6	19.9
1994	9.7	16.5	30.4	29.6
1996	14.8	25.8	38.1	39.3
1997	16.7	22.3	41.8	37.8

Source: Central Bureau of Statistics 1999b

wood. In terms of imported commodities, during 1990–1993 most of DKI Jakarta's imports from foreign countries consisted of metal products and machinery, chemical products, basic metals, and textile products. Indonesian estimates suggest that despite the current economic crisis, the trade patterns in terms of destinations and sources remain the same for the country.

Services

Studies on "global city" formation suggest that the internationalization of the economy is accompanied by the emergence of related facilities and services that support manufacturing activities (Soegijoko and Kusbiantoro 1998). In addition to the agglomeration of manufacturing activities, large cities in developing countries, including Jabotabek, are characterized by a high concentration of service-sector activities, particularly in the central business district. These activities include not only banking, finance, and the supply of high-quality offices, but also the availability of amenities such as convention centres, hotels, open spaces, and restaurants that accommodate local citizens, domestic tourists, and international visitors.

Not only is Jakarta the central location for banks, financial institutions, and money transactions, but that concentration has increased over the last decade (Table 11.4). From 1985 to 1997 the total number of state, national private, and foreign banks, including both head offices and branches, located in DKI Jakarta increased from 193 to 806, over a 300 per cent increase. During this period, while the number of state banks' head offices remained the same, the number of branch offices increased from 90 to 187. As the government allowed the operation of private and foreign banks through deregulation packages that were launched in 1988, the number of these banks has increased rapidly. The number of head offices of private banks increased from 45 in 1985 to 137 in 1996, then dropped to 122 in 1997. The number of branch offices increased from 40 in 1985 to 402 in 1996 and 446 in 1997. The number of foreign banks also increased dra-

Table 11.4 Growth in number of banks in DKI Jakarta, 1985–1997

Year	State banks		National private banks		Foreign banks	
	Head office	Branch office	Head office	Branch office	Head office	Branch office
1985	7	90	45	40	1	10
1990	7	173	87	196	28	10
1995	7	193	138	382	31	10
1996	7	182	137	402	31	10
1997	7	187	122	446	34	10

Source: Jakarta Statistical Office 1997b, 1999a

Table 11.5 Growth in office space in DKI Jakarta, 1988–1997

Year	Prime offices[a]		Secondary offices[a]	
	Supply (000 m^2)	Occupancy rate (%)	Supply (000 m^2)	Occupancy rate (%)
1988	30	95	26	78
1989	88	99	32	90
1990	155	96	56	85
1991	240	90	64	87
1992	280	86	102	84
1993	175	88	133	82
1994	180	89	158	86
1995	250	90	N/A	N/A
1996	200	93	N/A	N/A
1997	250	91	N/A	N/A

Source: Soegijoko 1996
a. Offices built in the central part or CBD of Jakarta are categorized as prime offices; offices built in the subcentral part of Jakarta are categorized as secondary offices.

matically, from only one head office located in the city in 1985 to 31 in 1996 and 34 in 1997.

The fast-growing economy of Jabotabek has been supported by the expansion of office space, particularly in DKI Jakarta. Offices have been built not only in the CBD of Jakarta but also in the subcentres of the region. Offices built in the central part or CBD of Jakarta are categorized as prime offices, and those built in the subcentres are secondary ones. Most of these offices were designed according to international standards so that they can accommodate the demands of international companies. A booming prime office development sector has operated in the city since the late 1980s (Table 11.5). Until the financial crisis began in 1997, the rate of growth for office space was 28 per cent annually. From 1988 to 1997, the total increase in prime office floor space exceeded 1,800,000 square metres (180 ha). Since 1992, similar to the rapid growth of the Botabek region, secondary office space development has also been increasing in these subcentres of the Jabotabek region.

Flows of capital and finance – FDI

Indonesia has been one of the targets for the Asian and world foreign investment community. According to the United Nations Conference on Trade and Development, in 1995 Indonesia was the fourth largest recipient of FDI among developing countries, after China, Malaysia, and Singapore (UNCTAD 1996).

Much of the FDI flowing into the country finds a location in Jabotabek. Within the region, FDI has grown rapidly since the mid-1980s (Table 11.6). Within Jabotabek, the number of project approvals increased three times from 71 in 1988 to 213 in 1994. Project approvals continue to increase, and in 1997 the number of FDI approvals in DKI Jakarta alone was approximately 246. Both the absolute number of projects and the value of these projects have increased. In 1988, the total value of inflowing investments to Jabotabek was US$0.60 billion. By 1994 this value had increased fivefold, reaching more than US$3.03 billion. In 1997, in DKI Jakarta, the value of investment reached US$6.14 billion.

Although more than half of the total number and value of FDI projects within the region were located in the centre, DKI Jakarta, the largest increases in foreign investment were found in the outer areas of Botabek. From 1983 to 1994 the average annual growth rate of FDI in Botabek was 51.4 per cent, almost seven times higher than that of DKI Jakarta. While DKI Jakarta has maintained itself as an attractive location for FDI, the appeal of Botabek for investment has increased. This in turn caused the increasing development of secondary offices in the Botabek region, as mentioned earlier.

Notwithstanding the exact location of FDI within the region, investment

Table 11.6 FDI in Jabotabek and Indonesia, 1988–1997

Year	Jakarta		Jabotabek		Indonesia	
	Number of projects	US$ bn	Number of projects	US$ bn	Number of projects	US$ bn
1988	34	0.24	71	0.60	129	4.43
1990	108	1.62	266	2.56	432	8.75
1994	115	1.83	213	3.03	449	23.72
1997	246	6.14	N/A	N/A	790	33.83

Source: Central Bureau of Statistics 1991, 1992, 1996c, 1998; Jakarta Statistical Office 1999a

has come from a large number of foreign countries. Among the nations that are attracted by the advantages offered by the Jabotabek region, there are seven major financers: Japan, Singapore, Hong Kong, the Republic of Korea, the UK, the Netherlands, and Taiwan. Together investors from these countries contributed 87 per cent of the total FDI in Jabotabek during the 1990–1994 period (Soegijoko 1996).

Among investment sectors, Jabotabek was most attractive to manufacturing FDI. From 1990 to 1994, manufacturing-related FDI within the region totalled 128 projects with a cumulative value of US$1 billion. Following manufacturing investments were property; trade, hotels, and restaurants; and services (education, health, social and community, personal and household services, etc.) – amounting to US$0.5 billion; US$0.33 billion, and US$0.15 billion, respectively.

These facts suggest that Jabotabek has increasingly become part of the global economy, and that the linkages between Jabotabek and foreign companies include a high degree of integration. Through investment by foreigners in manufacturing, property (trade-related, hotels, and restaurants), and services, Jabotabek has been increasingly linked to economic activities in other nations. Further, the connections to global capital have demonstrated a spatial pattern. DKI Jakarta has become the location for countries that placed most of their investments in the tertiary sector, while Botabek has developed economic bonds with countries that placed most of their investments in the secondary sector. Together these linkages have not only globalized Jabotabek, but they have also helped shape its form.

Flows of capital and finance – The Jakarta Stock Exchange

The existence of a stock market reflects the fact that cities function as a hub of domestic and international capital flows. The Jakarta Stock Exchange (JSX), established in 1977, began its rapid development around 1989. From 1977 to 1988, the average annual value of trading was Rp 7 billion per year. By 1989, the value of total trading was slightly less than Rp 1 trillion. From 1989 to 1997, trades increased to an annual average of 6.32 trillion and by the end of that period the value of total trading reached Rp 120 trillion (Table 11.7).

Similarly market capitalization, defined as the worth of listed companies, has accelerated since 1989. Market capitalization increased from Rp 4.3 trillion in 1989 to Rp 152.2 trillion in 1995 as the number of listed companies increased from only 56 in 1989 to 282 in 1997. Within the JSX in 1994, 61 per cent of the transactions (trading values) occurred mainly in manufacturing (basic industries and chemicals, consumer goods industries, miscellaneous industries), while 14.5 per cent were in finance and 16 per cent were in construction, property, and real estate (Soegijoko 1996).

Table 11.7 Jakarta Stock Exchange activity, 1977–1997

Year	US rate	Value of total trading (Rp bn)	Market capital-ization (Rp bn)	Listed com-panies	Number of listed shares (millions)
1977	421	0.15	2.73	1	0.26
1980	634	5.73	41.04	6	14.59
1983	994	10.10	102.66	23	48.01
1986	1,641	1.82	94.23	24	58.35
1989	1,800	964.27	4,309.44	56	432.84
1992	2,062	7,953.30	24,839.45	153	6,253.92
1995	2,308	32,357.50	152,246.46	238	45,794.66
1997	N/A	120,385.17	N/A	282	N/A

Source: Central Bureau of Statistics 1996c, 1998

Flows of people – Jabotabek as a foreign tourist gate

The flow of foreign visitors through Jakarta is another indicator that demonstrates Jakarta's international network development. The number of tourists arriving in Indonesia through the Soekarno-Hatta airport has gradually increased since the early 1980s. Until 1989, the average number of tourists arriving in Jakarta was 426,500 per year. This flow increased to more than 1 million per year from 1990 to 1996. The number of foreign tourists arriving in the Soekarno-Hatta airport in 1996 was about 38.8 per cent of the total foreign tourist arrivals in Indonesia.

Since the early 1980s, the centrality of Jakarta as a point of entry for foreign visitors has increased. For instance, in 1985 more than half of the tourists from nine countries (India, the Philippines, Singapore, Thailand, Taiwan, Italy, France, Germany, and Switzerland) entered Indonesia through DKI Jakarta. In 1994, the centrality of Jakarta became stronger because it functioned as an entry port for tourists from 12 countries: Japan, India, Malaysia, the Philippines, Taiwan, Thailand, the USA, Canada, Italy, France, Germany, and Switzerland (Soegijoko 1996).

Flows of people – International air traffic

The intensity of flows of people and goods through air traffic provides a further indication of the international links between Jabotabek and other countries. Jakarta airport served about 50 per cent of the total frequency of international airlines exiting and entering Indonesia every year (Table 11.8). The number of international aircraft arrivals and departures to and from Jakarta international airport (JIA) increased from approximately 17,000 aircraft movements/year in 1982 to 45,000 aircraft movements/year

Table 11.8 International aircraft traffic, Jakarta international airport and Indonesia, 1982–1997

Year	JIA		Indonesia	
	Departures	Arrivals	Departures	Arrivals
1982	8,418	8,586	14,287	14,391
1986	8,449	7,447	12,843	11,502
1990	10,264	10,303	22,996	23,201
1996	20,796	21,030	46,273	46,112
1997	22,833	22,734	49,295	47,947
% to Indonesia				
1982	58.92	59.66	100.00	100.00
1986	65.79	65.01	100.00	100.00
1990	44.63	44.41	100.00	100.00
1996	44.84	45.61	100.00	100.00
1997	46.32	47.41	100.00	100.00
Annual % growth/year				
1982–1986	0.09	−3.32	−2.53	−5.02
1986–1990	5.37	9.45	19.76	25.43
1990–1996	17.10	17.35	16.87	16,46

Source: Central Bureau of Statistics 1996c, 1997b, 1999d; Jakarta Statistical Office 1999a, 1999b

in 1997 (until September). The expansion mainly occurred during the 1990–1996 period, when the annual growth rate per year exceeded 17 per cent for both categories.

The number of international aircraft passengers who departed from or arrived at Soekarno-Hatta in 1982 was approximately 1.7 million (Table 11.9), or 72 per cent of the total number of international aircraft passengers entering and leaving Indonesia. In 1997 (until September), the number reached 4.2 million. By this time, however, the airport's share of the total international passengers to and from the country had dropped to 54 per cent. The decrease in share is related to improvements in international airports in other parts of the country. The majority of air traffic coming from and heading to JIA, including passengers, cargo, and mail, has destinations or origins within Asia (Soegijoko 1996).

The impact of globalization

Changes of functional (socio-economic) structures

One of the most important social structural changes to affect Jabotabek has been the rapid urbanization of the region. The process has been char-

Table 11.9 International aircraft passenger traffic, Jakarta international airport and Indonesia, 1982–1997

	JIA		Indonesia	
	Departures	Arrivals	Departures	Arrivals
1982	867,154	865,452	1,191,527	1,188,082
1986	919,255	801,515	1,229,644	1,084,157
1990	1,292,803	1,359,582	2,179,198	2,183,323
1996	2,520,923	2,854,470	4,674,379	4,930,092
1997 (until September)	2,093,115	2,130,875	3,880,916	3,922,964
% to Indonesia				
1982	72.78	72.84	100.00	100.00
1986	74.76	73.93	100.00	100.00
1990	59.32	62.27	100.00	100.00
1996	53.93	57.90	100.00	100.00
1997 (until September)	53.93	54.32	100.00	100.00
Annual % growth/year				
1982–1986	1.50	−1.85	0.80	−2.19
1986–1990	10.16	17.41	19.31	25.35
1990–1996	15.83	18.33	19.08	20.97

Source: Central Bureau of Statistics 1996c, 1997b, 1999d; Jakarta Statistical Office 1999a, 1999b

acterized by three important features: Jabotabek's central position within the national urban system; the changing dynamics between DKI Jakarta's and Botabek's rate of urban growth; and as a consequence of the second factor, the spatial dispersion of the urban population within Jabotabek from DKI Jakarta to the surrounding areas (Soegijoko 1996). Evidence demonstrates that DKI Jakarta is still very attractive for migrants, although an increasing number of migrants have chosen and continue to prefer Botabek as a place to live (Table 11.10).

Jabotabek has undergone rapid urbanization. In 1995, urbanization in Jabotabek reached 82.6 per cent – 16.7 million of the 20.2 million population resided in urban areas – up from the 1971 level of 58.3 per cent (Central Bureau of Statistics 1996a, 1996b). The centre is completely urbanized, and for more than two decades (1971–1995), DKI Jakarta's population has been classified as urban. It has also increased rapidly during that period, rising from 4.5 million to 9.1 million. In Botabek there were only 290,000 urban dwellers in 1971, giving a 7.8 per cent urbanization level, but by 1995 the number of urban dwellers had increased dramatically to 7.5 million or 68.3 per cent of Botabek's total population (Table 11.10). During the same period, the rural population in outer areas remained constant in size, totalling 3.5 million people, but obviously decreased in terms of its share of the total population.

Table 11.10 Urbanization levels in Jabotabek, 1971, 1980, 1990, and 1995

Year	DKI Jakarta		Botabek			Jabotabek		
	Number of population (millions)	Urbanization level (%)	Number of population (millions)	Number of population resided in urban area (millions)	Urbanization level (%)	Number of population (millions)	Number of population resided in urban area (millions)	Urbanization level (%)
1971	4.55	100	3.76	0.29	7.79	8.31	4.84	58.25
1980	6.50	100	5.40	1.30	24.03	11.90	7.80	65.51
1990	8.25	100	8.87	4.86	54.84	17.12	13.11	76.60
1995	9.11	100	11.05	7.55	68.29	20.16	16.66	82.63

Source: Soegijoko 1996; Central Bureau of Statistics 1996c; Jakarta Statistical Office 1997a

Changes in the structure of the GRDP

In 1988, the contribution of Jabotabek to the GDP of the country was 20.2 per cent. This share increased to almost 24.0 per cent in 1995. Most of Jabotabek's GRDP was the result of activities in DKI Jakarta. In 1988, 70.0 per cent of the GRDP of Jabotabek came from DKI Jakarta, whereas 30.0 per cent originated from Botabek. However, the annual growth rate of Botabek's GRDP was twice as high as that of DKI Jakarta. Botabek's importance as a contributor to the GRDP of West Java increased from 37.0 per cent in 1988 to 40.0 per cent in 1995 (Jakarta Statistical Office 1997b, 1997c; Central Bureau of Statistics 1997c).

Since 1988, economic production in the region is increasingly less concentrated in the primary sector (agriculture, mining, and livestock). The share of this sector within the economy decreased from 5 per cent in 1988 to 3 per cent in 1995. At the same time, secondary-sector production has risen while the structure of the tertiary sector has undergone transformations. The contribution of the service sector (tertiary sector) to the Jabotabek GRDP has declined slightly from 58 per cent to 55 per cent between 1988 and 1995. The slight drop in share, however, masks interesting changes. In 1988, most service-sector activity was in trade and government services. By 1995, most tertiary-sector activity was still in trade, but banking and other financial sources of wealth creation now doubled the input of government services. Trade and other financial institutions are now the dominant contributors to the service sector. In 1995 their shares of total production were 21 per cent and 17 per cent, respectively.

The region's industrial sector has grown considerably. In 1988, secondary-sector production contributed 37.1 per cent to the regional economy, but by 1995 its share had increased to 42.4 per cent. Manufacturing and construction-related activities have contributed significantly. Manufacturing rose from a 26.3 per cent share in 1988 to a 28.3 per cent share in 1995. Construction activities' share almost doubled from 7.7 per cent to 12.2 per cent during the same period. This structural transformation of the Jabotabek GRDP can be seen in Table 11.11.

Changes in employment

Jabotabek's large low-wage workforce has helped to make it a target for foreign investment, particularly in labour-intensive industrial activities. As much as 52 per cent of the region's total workforce population (10.4 million people) fall into this category. Analysis of employment distribution demonstrates that employment changes followed the structural changes in the economy mentioned above. In 1971, Jabotabek employment was stronger in the primary (19.9 per cent) than the secondary (16.2 per cent) sector, while the tertiary activities accounted for around 63.9 per cent of

Table 11.11 Structural transformation of the Jabotabek GRDP and Indonesia GDP

Sectors	Distribution (%)		
	1988	1992	1995
DKI Jakarta	**100.00**	**100.00**	**100.00**
Total primary sector	1.43	0.64	0.20
Total secondary sector	34.33	36.82	37.45
Total tertiary sector	64.24	62.54	62.35
Botabek	**100.00**	**100.00**	**100.00**
Total primary sector	17.09	14.19	10.36
Total secondary sector	35.96	40.35	55.42
Total tertiary sector	46.95	45.46	34.22
Jabotabek	**100.00**	**100.00**	**100.00**
Agriculture	4.07	3.69	2.17
Mining and quarrying	0.82	0.10	0.85
Total primary sector	**4.89**	**3.79**	**3.01**
Manufacturing	26.25	26.26	28.31
Electricity, gas, and water supply	3.13	4.01	1.87
Construction	7.72	7.37	12.24
Total secondary sector	**37.10**	**37.64**	**42.42**
Trade	22.08	22.12	20.99
Transportation and communication	10.35	10.30	7.73
Banking and other financial	11.46	12.41	17.18
Government and other services	14.12	13.74	8.67
Total tertiary sector	**58.01**	**58.57**	**54.56**
Indonesia	**100.00**	**100.00**	**100.00**
Agriculture	24.09	19.52	16.12
Mining and quarrying	11.61	11.51	9.25
Total primary sector	**35.70**	**31.03**	**25.38**
Manufacturing	18.52	21.76	23.88
Electricity, gas, and water supply	0.60	0.83	1.12
Construction	5.01	5.89	7.61
Total secondary sector	**24.13**	**28.48**	**32.60**
Trade	17.33	16.44	16.74
Transportation and communication	5.78	6.58	7.12
Banking and other financial	3.77	4.81	8.94
Government and other services	13.45	12.19	9.23
Total tertiary sector	**40.33**	**40.02**	**42.02**

Source: Central Bureau of Statistics 1997c; Jakarta Statistical Office 1997b

employment. From 1971 to 1980, the percentage of employed workers in the secondary sector increased while the percentage decreased in the tertiary sector (Table 11.12). The latter fall probably resulted mostly from the decreasing percentage of people employed in informal-sector services.

These trends continued throughout the early 1990s and by 1995 em-

Table 11.12 Structural transformation of Jabotabek and Indonesian employment

Sectors	Distribution (%)			
	1971	1980	1990	1995
DKI Jakarta	**100.00**	**100.00**	**100.00**	**100.00**
Total primary sector	4.03	2.67	1.70	4.13
Total secondary sector	17.73	22.23	27.63	23.28
Total tertiary sector	78.24	75.09	70.67	72.59
Botabek	**100.00**	**100.00**	**100.00**	**100.00**
Total primary sector	44.29	45.74	29.21	10.81
Total secondary sector	13.84	15.73	25.24	33.74
Total tertiary sector	41.87	38.52	45.56	55.45
Jabotabek	**100.00**	**100.00**	**100.00**	**100.00**
Agriculture	19.52	20.57	14.95	5.62
Mining and quarrying	0.36	0.78	0.85	1.99
Total primary sector	**19.88**	**21.35**	**15.80**	**7.62**
Manufacturing	9.63	13.19	19.65	21.99
Electricity, gas, and water supply	0.43	0.40	0.51	0.73
Construction	6.14	5.82	6.24	6.02
Total secondary sector	**16.20**	**19.41**	**26.40**	**28.74**
Trade	24.45	21.10	23.55	25.74
Transportation and communication	8.51	6.51	6.68	6.47
Banking and other financial	1.88	2.24	4.38	8.01
Government and other services	29.08	29.39	23.19	23.42
Total tertiary sector	**63.92**	**59.24**	**57.80**	**63.65**
Indonesia	100.00	100.00	100.00	100.00
Agriculture	66.00	54.77	51.67	43.98
Mining and quarrying	0.09	0.72	0.81	0.80
Total primary sector	**66.09**	**55.49**	**52.48**	**44.78**
Manufacturing	6.66	6.56	8.61	12.64
Electricity, gas, and water supply	0.66	1.75	1.75	0.27
Construction	0.03	3.07	3.64	4.70
Total secondary sector	**7.35**	**11.38**	**14.00**	**17.61**
Trade	12.00	12.93	14.01	17.33
Transportation and communication	2.09	3.10	3.64	4.32
Banking and other financial	2.00	1.92	2.78	0.82
Government and other services	10.46	15.17	13.09	15.13
Total tertiary sector	**26.55**	**33.12**	**33.52**	**37.60**

Source: Central Bureau of Statistics 1997c; Jakarta Statistical Office 1997b

ployment was mainly concentrated in tertiary and secondary sectors at 63.7 per cent and 28.7 per cent, respectively. The increased percentage of people employed in the tertiary sector was mainly related to employment in the formal as well as the informal sector.

In the area surrounding DKI Jakarta, the Botabek region, employment in the tertiary sector, especially trade and government services, increased during the 1971–1995 period. Before 1980, the primary sector was a major source of employment for people in this part of the urban region (45.7 per cent of the workforce). After 1980, manufacturing activities increasingly absorbed a larger part of the workforce. The secondary sector's contribution to employment increased from approximately 13.8 per cent in the 1970s to 33.7 per cent in 1995. Within the core, DKI Jakarta, employment in the tertiary and secondary sectors has dominated since the early 1970s. Service-sector employment has generated over 70 per cent of all jobs since that time. Government and other services, trade, restaurants, and hotels have always been important for generating work. However, manufacturing, banking/finance, and construction have increased their relative shares, and by 1995 held the positions of third, fourth, and fifth, respectively, in the hierarchy of job generation.

The dramatic changes for the Botabek region were especially effective in reducing the role of the primary sector from 44.3 per cent (1971) to 10.8 per cent (1995) and increasing the role of the secondary sector from 13.8 per cent (1971) to 33.7 per cent (1995) of the employment. Since 1995, the percentage of employment in the secondary sector has been even higher in Botabek (33.7 per cent) than in Jakarta (23.3 per cent).

Changes in spatial structure

The impact of economic internationalization on Jabotabek has also been experienced in terms of physical development. This includes positive as well as negative impacts. Changes in land uses and the emergence of new centres and subcentres, supported by the development of a regional transportation network, are the major impacts of the increasing links between Jabotabek and the international economy on the urban physical form of the city.

Until the mid-1970s, the urban structure of DKI Jakarta was characterized as a uni-polar system, with the suburban town of Kebayoran Baru in south Jakarta planned as a residential area for those who worked in the centre of the city. In early 1983, the government started to impose limits on urban development in the south, an area believed to be the water recharge area for the region. Since then, although some development in that part of the region has occurred, the expansion of physical development is most obvious along the east-west axis from Jakarta to Tangerang in the west and Bekasi in the east. Since the late 1980s the development of Jabotabek has been characterized by the emergence of new centres in the Botabek region, with a radius of 60 kilometres, and new or rebuilt subcentres in DKI Jakarta. Overall, many new urban centres in Jabotabek have developed. While DKI Jakarta maintains the position of main centre, the cities of Bogor, Tangerang, and Bekasi in addition to other fast-growing centres such as new towns and industrial estates in Botabek have impacted on the region's urban character.

Development of built-up areas and land-use change

In the early 1980s, the built-up areas in DKI Jakarta already covered around 48 per cent of the city's total land area. However, since that time the expansion of built-up areas in the city has continued to increase, and by 1994 they covered at least 82.1 per cent of the city. In contrast to DKI Jakarta, the amount of built-up area in the Botabek region has always been smaller. Lately, however, the rate of expansion of developed areas has been much faster than that of the centre. The amount of built-up area in Bogor, Tangerang, and Bekasi accounted for approximately 10 per cent of total land areas in these cities in the early 1980s. By 1994, the amount of built-up area had doubled to 19.0 per cent of the total for Bogor and 18.4 per cent for Bekasi. It tripled in Tangerang, rising to 34.5 per cent by 1992 (Table 11.13).

The change of land use is another indicator reflecting restructuring of urban physical patterns. From 1980 to 1994, the average annual growth rate of settlement areas in Botabek was 4.8 per cent, resulting in an expansion from 70,794 ha in 1980 to 118,800 ha in 1994. This expansion accompanied the decrease of land used as paddy fields, multicrop fields, plantation areas, and forests as land was converted from these activities to more urban-related uses (Table 11.14). In DKI Jakarta, the proportion of land devoted to residential uses also increased from 1987 to 1996. At the start of this period, residential land use accounted for approximately 59.6 per cent of the total, but by 1996 it had risen to 67.3 per cent (Table 11.15). Directly related to this rise in the growth of residential land use is the rise of land used for industrial, office, and service purposes.

The amount of agriculture land converted into different land uses can

Table 11.13 Built-up area development in Jabotabek, 1979–1994

	DKI Jakarta %	Bogor %	Tangerang %	Bekasi %
1979	48.03	–	–	–
1980	–	13.05	10.95	9.64
1987	–	17.67	–	–
1988	61.46	–	–	10.71
1989	–	–	27.00	–
1992	–	–	34.49	–
1993	–	–	–	18.44
1994	82.05	18.99	–	–

Source: Soegijoko 1996

Table 11.14 Land use in Botabek, 1980 and 1994

Year	Village %	Wet rice fields %	Mixture garden %	Dry agri-cultural fields, plantation %	Forest, meadow, underbrush %	Embank-ment, lake, marsh %	Others %	Total %
1980	11.41	39.76	20.28	12.23	12.99	2.75	0.58	100.00
1994	19.17	34.46	18.44	9.97	12.06	3.16	2.74	100.00

Source: Soegijoko 1996

333

Table 11.15 Land use in DKI Jakarta, 1987, 1994, and 1996

Year	Housing %	Offices %	Industry %	Services %	Vacant %	Other %	Total %
1987	59.63	5.02	4.59	6.35	8.90	15.51	100.00
1994	60.00	5.75	6.38	6.89	9.07	11.91	100.00
1996	67.37	10.77	4.93	N/A	N/A	16.93	100.00

Source: Soegijoko 1996; Jakarta Statistical Office 1997b

be seen in Table 11.16. The proportion of land conversion in Bekasi is the highest among the cities in the region. Within Bekasi, industrial conversion has been the dominant land use preferred. In general, the table demonstrates that, along with the economic boom, there has been a decrease in the amount of land used for agriculture. These land conversions have not only changed the structure of the physical development of the outer administrative districts, but they are also directly related to increased pollution levels from industrial activities.

Large-scale housing and new town developments

New town developments and large-scale housing developments have changed the regional spatial structure in Jabotabek dramatically. In the recent past, hundreds of residential areas of various sizes have been developed in the region. Some of these developments were greater than 1,000 ha (Table 11.17), and include new towns. Although new towns are not a new phenomenon in Indonesia, as they have been developed since the 1950s, their rate of growth accelerated during the late 1980s. By 1996, there were 61 residential area developments with land coverage of less than 500 ha and around another 28 areas with more than 500 ha. From 1990 to 1995, developers were permitted to build on 121,631 ha of land within the region. Land acquisition, however, covered only 38 per cent of the total permits allocated. What is more, by the end of 1995, developers had built on only 16,609 ha of this land.

For the foreseeable future DKI Jakarta will remain the main centre of the Jabotabek region. Many subordinate new centres, however, continue to develop in the outlying areas. These new subcentres form a new pattern of development and are increasingly linked by transportation networks. However, the new towns are highly dependent on Jakarta as the main centre of economic activity, and more or less function as residential suburbs.

Industrial estate development

The development of industrial estates has also affected the urban structure of Jabotabek. Table 11.18 presents data on the number and location

Table 11.16 Agriculture conversion into non-residential uses

Region	Total region area (000 ha)	Area of conversion								Total area of conversion	
		Residential		Industrial		Offices		Other			
		(000 ha)	(%)	(000 ha)	(%)	(000 ha)	(%)	(000 ha)	(%)	(000 ha)	(%)
Bekasi	148.44	1.73	30.7	3.79	67.4	0.08	1.4	0.02	0.4	5.62	100
Tangerang Regency	123.53	1.54	36.9	1.55	37.1	0.11	2.5	0.98	23.5	4.18	100
Tangerang Municipality	18.38	2.04	62.1	1.18	35.8	0.06	1.9	0.01	0.2	3.28	100
Total	290.35	5.31	40.6	6.51	49.8	0.25	1.9	1.01	7.7	13.08	100

Source: West Java Statistical Office 1998

Table 11.17 Housing and new town development projects in Jabotabek, 1996

	DKI Jakarta	Botabek	Jabotabek
50–99 ha	10	18	28
100–249 ha	10	15	25
250–499 ha	3	5	8
500–999 ha	4	9	13
>1,000 ha	2	13	15

Source: *Property Indonesia Bulletin* 1996

Table 11.18 Industrial estate distribution in Indonesia, 1995

Region	Ha	Number of enterprises
DKI Jakarta	3,196	8
Tangerang	3,550	16
Bekasi	3,062	12
Karawang	9,028	18
Purwakarta	200	6
Others in West Java	2,602	13
Central Java/Jogya	2,691	15
East Java	6,019	29
Riau	5,554	14
Others	3,187	14
Total	39,088	145

Source: *Property Indonesia Bulletin* 1995

of these structures. Approximately 25 per cent of all industrial estates in Indonesia are located in Jabotabek, and together they cover an area of 9,808 ha. The activities within these estates generate thousands of jobs and subsequently promote the expansion of new settlements and increase the densities of the existing settlements directly adjacent to them. Moreover, commercial and service activities have also mushroomed as demand from workers for everyday needs has increased.

The development of industrial estates has increased the regional traffic intensities. Many industrial estates built new roads to connect them with the existing regional highway and railway systems. Regional traffic flows from these industrial estates, not to mention from industries located outside industrial estates, to the seaport of Tanjung Priok have intensified.

Shopping malls and shopping centres

The development of shopping centres in DKI Jakarta began in 1978. However, growth accelerated during the early 1990s. Before 1990 there

Table 11.19 Development of shopping centres in Jabotabek, 1981–1995

Year	Number of buildings	Area (ha)
pre-1980	6	N/A
1981–1985	5	7.6
1986–1990	10	23.3
1991–1995	46	199.59
Total	67	230.49

Source: Soegijoko 1996

were 21 shopping centres, including shopping malls, in Jabotabek; within five years, during the early 1990s, 46 new shopping centres were built. In total, these centres cover over 230.49 ha (Table 11.19). The new malls are located a distance away from Jakarta and closer to the newly built residential complexes. While they have helped to accommodate the demand created by these new developments, they have also been the stimulus for increased flows of consumers from the centre of the city. Consequently, this has changed the overall pattern of population shopping movement and helped to generate traffic congestion.

Development of the CBD and subcentres

Jakarta is the main centre for all urban economic activities in Jabotabek. Its position as the nation's capital and its high levels of infrastructure and social facilities have not only helped it to maintain that status but have helped to maintain its central position within the country. The emergence of new commercial, government, and private offices as well as service centres in the golden triangle of Sudirman-Kuningan-Gatot Subroto CBD has strengthened its central role. The area surrounding the CBD, which was intended to function as housing, has developed instead as a centre of commercial activity. These commercial offices service the demands of the region's new economy. Although the importance of this commercial activity is less than that of the CBD, it has diverted traffic from the centre.

Enhanced by the comparative advantages of its factor endowments, Jabotabek has been the target for trade and investments associated with globalization processes. These growing linkages have connected the region to a system of global cities. In turn, the flows associated with global forces have transformed Jabotabek spatially as well as functionally. Recently, however, due primarily to the Asian financial crisis, the imbalances that accompanied the region's rapid growth have become apparent. Necessary supporting infrastructure has not been constructed over the last 20 years. This gap has exacerbated the creation of pollution and other environmental problems.

The next round of globalization: Sustainable development in Jabotabek

Jabotabek has played a central role in linking Indonesia to other countries in and outside the Asia Pacific region. Through the restructuring of the urban economy as a result of regional and global integration, Jabotabek has also provided a large share of the increases in the national economy. Yet not all the impacts of globalization were positive. First and foremost of the negative consequences of globalization was the devastation caused by the Asian financial crisis, which hit Indonesia and especially Jabotabek after September 1997. Second, for future development, or what can be termed the next round of globalization, Jabotabek must incorporate aspects of sustainable development if any of the benefits bestowed upon the urban area by these processes are to last.

Although the Asian economic crisis also hit other countries in the Asian region, such as Thailand, Malaysia, and Korea, the negative aspects of the crisis were experienced at their strongest in Indonesia. In 1996, the economic growth rates for Indonesia, Thailand, and Malaysia were 7.8 per cent, 6.7 per cent, and 8.8 per cent, with inflation rates of 6.5 per cent, 5.9 per cent, and 3.5 per cent, respectively. However, in 1998 the figures were −13.7 per cent, 6.6 per cent, and 2.0 per cent for economic growth rates and 77.6 per cent, 11.6 per cent, and 7.5 per cent for inflation (Table 11.20). How strongly the Asian crisis hit Indonesia is also reflected in the unemployment rate figures (Table 11.21). Indonesia was hit worst in the unemployment sector, reaching a rate of 21 per cent compared to only 6.7 per cent in Korea, 6.0 per cent in Thailand, and 3.5 per cent in Malaysia. While other countries have started to recover from the crisis, Indonesia is still experiencing unstable conditions. This is reflected in fluctuation of the exchange rate of the US dollar to the rupiah (Table 11.22). Before the crisis, the rate was approximately 2,500 (US$1 = Rp 2,500), whereas after the crisis the rate fluctuated, reaching a high of 14,800 in July 1998 before dropping to approximately 6,500 one year later; in September 1999 the rates rose again to more than 8,000 per US$1.

Granted that growth will return to the country and urban region through the return of the positive aspects of globalization, sustainable development practices, for example good transportation infrastructures, are required to mediate against its negative impacts. Creation of adequate transportation and other urban infrastructures did not accompany the rapid development in the Jabotabek region over the past decade. This gap will become a constraint for the future development of Jabotabek. At the same time, the rapid development in the urban region has negatively impacted on the environmental conditions in the region. For future generations of Jabota-

Table 11.20 Economic growth rate and inflation rate of the world, industrial countries, developing countries, those in transition, and ASEAN, 1996–1998

Groups of country	Economic growth rate %			Inflation rate %		
	1996	1997[a]	1998[a]	1996	1997[a]	1998[a]
World	4.1	4.2	N/A			
Industrial countries	2.7	3.0	N/A	2.4	2.2	N/A
Seven main industrial countries	2.4	2.8	N/A	2.2	2.1	N/A
Japan	3.5	0.9	−0.7	0.1	1.7	1.0
USA	2.8	3.8	2.8	2.9	2.3	1.5
Germany	1.4	2.3	N/A	1.5	1.9	N/A
UK	2.3	3.3	N/A	2.9	2.6	N/A
France	1.5	2.2	N/A	2.0	1.1	N/A
Italy	0.7	1.2	N/A	3.9	1.8	N/A
Canada	1.5	3.8	3.4	1.7	1.6	1.0
Others	3.7	3.9	N/A	3.3	2.7	N/A
Developing countries	6.5	6.2	N/A	13.2	10.0	N/A
Africa	5.2	3.7	N/A	25.0	14.8	N/A
Asia	8.2	7.6	N/A	6.6	5.8	N/A
Latin America	3.4	4.1	2.3	20.5	13.5	N/A
Europe and Middle East	4.8	4.6	N/A	24.8	22.1	N/A
Countries in transition	0.1	1.8	N/A	40.0	32.0	N/A
East and Middle Europe	1.5	2.1	N/A	32.0	41.0	N/A
Russia	−2.8	0.4	−1.0	48.0	11.0	10.0
Middle Asia and Trans-Caucasus	1.6	1.3	N/A	70.0	43.0	N/A
ASEAN countries[b]						
Malaysia	8.8	7.8	2.0	3.5	2.7	7.5
Philippine	5.5	5.6	3.0	8.4	5.0	3.0
Singapore	7.0	7.8	4.0	1.4	2.0	2.8
Thailand	6.7	6.1	6.6	5.9	5.6	11.6
Brunei	3.0	4.0	N/A	2.0	3.0	N/A
Indonesia	7.82	4.91	−13.68[c]	6.47	11.05	77.63
Viet Nam	9.5	9.0	7.5	6.0	3.6	8.5

Source: Central Bureau of Statistics 1999c
a. Estimation.
b. Excludes Laos and Myanmar.
c. Tentative rate.

bekians, environmental aspects must become one of the major concerns of city and regional administrators.

This section investigates the impacts of the economic crisis on the Jabotabek region and the challenges that it must face in order to remain com-

Table 11.21 Estimated unemployment rate of selected countries during the Asian crisis

Country	Estimated unemployment rate (%)
China	3.10
Japan	4.10
Taiwan	2.42
Malaysia	3.50
Philippines	8.40
Republic of Korea	6.70
Hong Kong	3.90
Indonesia	21.00
Thailand	6.00
Singapore	2.20

Source: *Kompas* 1998c

Table 11.22 Fluctuation of the exchange rate, US dollar to rupiah, April–December 1998

Month	Exchange rate (rupiah per unit)	
	Sell	Buy
April	8,061.96	7,398.00
May	11,304.05	9,896.84
June	14,469.04	13,220.04
July	14,821.32	14,067.72
August	12,908.57	12,389.10
September	11,323.81	10,739.29
October	8,853.52	8,418.91
November	8,039.56	7,466.55
December	7,671.13	7,307.79

Source: Central Bureau of Statistics 1999a

petitive globally. While most of the focus is on current economic aspects of development, there is also a review of the impacts of the economic crisis on the social and environmental conditions of the region.

Economic impacts

As mentioned, the Asian economic crisis hit the Indonesian economy severely (Table 11.23). The national economic growth rate (including oil and gas products) fell from 8.22 per cent in 1995 to 4.91 per cent in 1997 and −13.68 per cent in 1998. Excluding oil and gas products, the national economic growth rate fell from 9.24 per cent in 1995 to 5.45 per cent in

Table 11.23 General economic indicators before and after the economic crisis for Indonesia and Jabotabek

Indicator	Before			After	
	1994	1995	1996	1997	1998
Indonesia					
Economic growth (%)	7.54	8.22	7.82	4.91	−13.68
Gross domestic product (Rp bn) at constant 1993 market prices including oil and gas	354,640.8	383,792.3	414,418.9	434,095.5	374,718.7
Inflation rate (%)	9.24	8.64	6.47	11.05	77.63
Foreign trade (US$ bn)					
exports	40.05	45.42	49.81	53.44	50.06
imports	31.98	40.63	42.93	41.68	26.95
FDI (US$ bn)	23.72	39.91	29.93	33.83	8.34
Interest rate (%)	12.42	16.72	16.92	23.01	60.38
Exchange rate (Rp/US$)	N/A	N/A	2,500	13,500	10,688
Income per capita (US$)	N/A	N/A	1,155	1,055	436.3
The poor (%)	13.67	12.50	11.34	17.77	24.2
Open unemployment (%)	N/A	7.24	4.86	4.68	5.46
Jabotabek/DKI Jakarta					
Economic growth (%) (Jabotabek)	N/A	8.47	8.32	N/A	−7
Gross domestic product (Rp bn) at constant 1993 market prices including oil and gas (DKI Jakarta)	55,505.3	60,638.2	66,201.8	69,479.4	N/A
Inflation rate (%) (DKI Jakarta)	10.56	9.54	7.25	11.70	74.42
The poor (%)	5.65	4.06	2.48	N/A	N/A
Open unemployment (%) (Jabotabek)	N/A	16.61	N/A	N/A	37.89

Source: Central Bureau of Statistics 1996c, 1997b, 1999c; Jakarta Statistical Office 1997b

1997 and −14.78 in 1998. Economic growth in DKI Jakarta also hit negative figures (−19.39 per cent), showing the worst economic growth among all Indonesia's provinces (Central Bureau of Statistics 1999c, 1999d).

The worsening economy has affected almost every sector. The depreciation of the rupiah coupled with high interest rates make it difficult for the private sector to continue business activities. Similar to the overall Indonesian situation, the inflation rate in Jakarta was only 7.25 per cent before the crisis (1996), then reached 11.70 per cent in 1997 and 74.42 per cent in 1998 (Central Bureau of Statistics 1999c). At the same time, with the further decline of the rupiah's value against the US dollar, per capita income levels dropped from US$1,055.4 in 1997 to US$436.3 in 1998 (*Pilar Bulletin* 1998).

The current economic crisis has created massive unemployment in Indonesia and the Jabotabek region. Before the crisis (1996), the open unemployment rate in Indonesia was approximately 4.86 per cent, but the crisis increased the rate to 5.46 per cent or 5.06 million people in 1998 (Central Bureau of Statistics 1997c, 1999d). However, the Jabotabek region was hit even more dramatically than the nation as a whole, as the region's unemployment rate climbed as high as 16.61 per cent, affecting 1.5 million people. The worst-hit areas were in the centre, as DKI Jakarta experienced an unemployment rate of 21.51 per cent in the first quarter of 1999 (URDI 1998).

If the critical unemployment rate (those who work less than 14 hours/ week) is added to the open unemployment rate, by March 1998 the total number of unemployed in Indonesia surpassed 31.8 million persons – 34 per cent of the labour force. Before the crisis, this figure stood at 13.6 million people or 15 per cent of the working population. For DKI Jakarta (no data are available for critical unemployment within Jabotabek), a total of 2.6 million people were unemployed in March 1998: 1.1 million experienced open unemployment and 1.5 million experienced critical unemployment. Based on these data, the proportion of open and critical unemployment to the total labour force for the Jabotabek region is estimated at approximately 65 per cent.

Finance

The crisis started with the depreciation of the rupiah's value against the US dollar, which severely hit banks and financial institutions with exposure to the US dollar and companies with large US dollar loans. Since most banks within the banking system in Indonesia overextended loans during the preceding few years, the depreciation of the rupiah created havoc. Moreover, most of the banks used short-term funds for long-term investments in the property market. When the crisis began the banking and financial institutions quickly felt the crunch. The failing banking and financial system slowed down the rate of lending and thereby prevented the economy from recovering.

Goods and services

The banking-sector crisis quickly spread to the production sectors. The price of production escalated due to the depreciation of the rupiah against the US dollar, the high inflation rate, the scarcity of some input materials (especially imported materials) for production, and the decreasing purchasing power of residents. Manufacturers within the region either could not produce goods due to the scarcity of input materials or, if they were still producing the goods, in order to secure profits they had to increase the price of items dramatically. However, the purchasing power of residents declined due to the high inflation and unemployment rates, making the selling of higher-priced goods difficult. These events, in turn, have affected factory production lines and forced some factories to close or cut down their worker numbers, as reflected in the unemployment figures.

The manufacturing companies which are surviving are mainly the export-oriented companies and those that do not rely heavily on imported components. This group is small, however, since most middle-sized and large manufacturing companies in Indonesia rely heavily on imported components as a major input for production. Between 25 and 60 per cent of all medium-sized and large manufacturing companies in Jabotabek are highly dependent on import materials and hence have had to cut down or even stop production. The closing of these import-dependent manufacturing companies not only affects their workers directly, but also affects other small companies which were suppliers or users of their products.

Research from Akatiga (1999) suggests that even small-scale industries, such as traditional textiles, snacks, ketchup, etc., have imported components. Textiles, yarn, colouring enzymes, polyester, rayon, cotton, etc. are imported. In making snacks, plastic and chemical flavourings and preservatives are imported components. The research revealed that in Indonesia only food-related companies and wood-related industries have a relatively low imported input content, at 9.5 per cent and 2.9 per cent, respectively.

Service industries, such as airlines, property developers, and construction companies, were also severely hit by the crisis. The property and construction sectors are normally driven by the growth of other sectors. Declining purchasing power has lowered the demand for property and construction activities, depressed property prices, and significantly affected developers. The situation worsened when interest rates rose (60.38 per cent in 1998), because most of these companies need financing mechanisms in order to deliver their products. Most of the construction sites within the region have been abandoned and hundreds of thousands of construction workers have been laid off. The repercussions of the collapse of the construction industry extended to other sectors, because private construction firms produced almost 70 per cent of the infrastructure in Jabotabek.

Capital

Political instability following the economic crisis has discouraged the return of foreign direct investment in Indonesia and Jabotabek. Total FDI approved in Indonesia by June 1998 was US$8.3 billion, a drop of over 75.3 per cent from the previous year when it reached US$33.8 billion (Central Bureau of Statistics 1999c). Many foreign companies have cancelled or delayed their investment plans, and some existing developments have pulled out of the country. Indonesia's position among developing countries receiving FDI has dropped significantly (*Kompas* 1998b).

Movements of people

Foreign visitor arrivals to Indonesia and especially to the Jabotabek region also dropped drastically after the social unrest and riots in May 1998. Travel agencies report that many foreign visitors cancelled their plans to visit Indonesia in 1999. Some countries, especially the USA, Australia, France, Italy, and Japan, advised their citizens not to come to Indonesia for safety reasons. The negative international press coverage concerning social and political conditions in the country added to the economic crisis, as all the services involved with foreign visits (conventions, hotels, restaurants, and travel industries) in Indonesia and particularly in Jabotabek experienced a drop in business.

Social impacts

The wide economic gap between income groups in DKI Jakarta already existed during the economic boom period, but the situation worsened with the growing economic crisis. Within Indonesia, DKI Jakarta has one of the highest economic gaps among its citizens – only Surabaya has a wider economic gap. Within the capital city, the distribution among the quartiles of income groups (defined by expenditure) is polarized. The incomes of the first quartile (the highest) were almost seven times greater than the incomes of the fourth quartile (the lowest). The high concentration of investment and high percentage of GRDP contribution to national GDP in DKI Jakarta have not been a guarantee of more equality between income groups.

Growing income inequality is currently a serious problem for the Jabotabek region. During the period of economic boom, social unrest was not a serious threat to society. The widening income gap and falling economic conditions after the financial crisis exacerbated already established inequities, however, particularly in DKI Jakarta, and led to social unrest in mid-May 1998. The riots destroyed much of the positive results of the economic developments accumulated in the past 10 years and have hampered government efforts to move the urban region towards a sustainable development strategy.

Urban poverty

Following the World Bank (*Pilar Bulletin* 1998), the United Nations defines poverty as an income of less than US$1 a day (using purchase power parity). People below the poverty line live in poor environments and slum areas. Moreover, they do not have access to health services and their children have little opportunity for proper education.

The free fall of the rupiah against the US dollar that has devastated per capita incomes has also affected the numbers of those living in poverty. For instance, the minimum regional wage, ranging from Rp 3,000 to Rp 8,000, was previously over the poverty threshold but is currently equal to US$0.3–0.8. This brought a new large group into the absolute poverty category. However, the situation does not merely affect marginal populations. For example, the new groups joining the absolute poverty figures do not include primary and junior high-school teachers, nor do they include the two lowest civil servant levels, but due to the current situation, these workers may also fall in this category. The rupiah's fall in valuation along with price hikes of staple goods have caused Indonesians with annual incomes of less than Rp 500,000 to fall into this group. Those with higher incomes experienced a significant drop in their quality of life. By the end of June 1998, Jakarta had more than 0.86 million people living below the poverty line (*Pilar Bulletin* 1998). There is evidence that since the economic crisis and the fall of incomes, there have been more burglaries and sexual harassment cases throughout the Jabotabek region (*Kompas* 1998a).

Social unrest

The poor felt the heavy burden of the economic crisis most severely, and the widening gap between income groups created social unrest. The riots that took place in several cities in Indonesia, particularly in Jakarta, have increased awareness of the dangers of social unrest to enclave communities. These are residential sites that provide housing for middle- and upper-income groups, and became easy targets for angry people during the riots. Poor neighbourhoods and slum areas surround many of these exclusive residential sites.

Persistent inequity within the country and the urban region has had a negative impact, especially on unfortunate groups. For example, the government's regulation that private developers must provide six low-priced housing units and three medium-priced units for every one luxury unit built (known as 1:3:6) has not been applied adequately in real estate development. The current situation suggests urgent and real consideration must be given to this area. The diversity of the community in residential sites has become an important aspect for achieving social cohesion and avoiding social divides. Based on theory, communities of this type will experience less social unrest in the future.

The financial and property losses generated by the last riots in Jakarta (mid-May 1998) are huge. Approximately 5,547 shops, 504 office buildings, and 1,028 houses were destroyed during the riots. Many businesses closed down after the riots and many business players encountered difficulties in starting over again due to financial problems and the fear of possible riots in the near future. Further, the riots have lead to psychological impacts as people experience a sense of lower personal safety and security.

Impacts on the development of urban infrastructure

Notwithstanding the progress made over the past 10 years during the economic boom, there still continues to be a lack of public-oriented urban infrastructure in the Jabotabek region. Compared to other metropolitan regions, especially in industrialized countries, Jabotabek has a much lower urban public infrastructure per capita level. This lower level of development influences the competitiveness of the urban economy. Further, the imbalances between supply and demand of infrastructure services have also contributed to pollution and the degradation of the environment.

During the economic boom, most of the infrastructure development in Jabotabek – toll roads, etc. – was built exclusivity for middle- and upper-class residents. The recent economic crisis, particularly the rupiah depreciation, has made some infrastructure such as transportation (especially public transport), water, electricity, and telephones more expensive, thus making them less affordable to the urban poor. Therefore, increasingly fewer people within the region are benefiting from the region's previous growth.

Transportation

The public transportation facilities in Jabotabek are far from sufficient. For example, the ratio of road to urban area for Jakarta is less than 10 per cent, compared to around 15 per cent for Tokyo or Paris. Furthermore, these two cities are supported by mass transit systems that are lacking even in the core of Jakarta (Kusbiantoro 1996, 1998). The road system in Botabek is worse than that of Jakarta (Table 11.24). The imbalance between the growth rates in the number of vehicles and the extensions to the road system is increasingly becoming problematic. Between 1991 and 1996, the road length in DKI Jakarta grew by 1.7 per cent per year while the growth rate of the number of private motor vehicles, including cars and motor

Table 11.24 Length of roads in Jakarta and Jabotabek, 1996

	Area (km^2)	Length of road (km)	km/km^2
DKI Jakarta	661.63	5,061	7.65
Botabek	5,977	4,451	0.74
Jabotabek	6,638	9,512	1.43

Source: Central Bureau of Statistics 1997c; West Java Statistical Office 1998

Table 11.25 Growth in vehicle numbers and road length in Jakarta, 1991–1996

	Number		Annual % growth 1991–1996
	1991	1996	
Public vehicles			
Bus	2,594	3,539	7.29
Microbus	4,428	4,914	2.20
Microlet	8,751	10,498	3.99
Bemo	1,080	1,096	0.30
Bajaj	14,612	15,112	0.68
Taxi	15,366	18,815	22.40
Total	46,831	53,974	15.25
Private vehicles			
Motor cycle	865,026	1,775,153	21.04
Car	535,216	967,229	16.14
Total	1,400,242	2,742,382	19.17
Roads	1989	1996	Annual % growth
Length of road (km)	4,534	5,061	1.66

Source: Jakarta Statistical Office 1997b
Note: A microlet is a four-wheel public vehicle with a capacity of 14 passengers; a bemo is a three-wheel public vehicle with a capacity of seven passengers; a bajaj is a three-wheel public vehicle with a capacity of two passengers.

cycles, reached 19.71 per cent per year. Public transportation did not make up for the difference, growing at a rate of 15.25 per cent per year during that period (Table 11.25).

DKI Jakarta lacks adequate public transportation provision. In 1996, only 53,974 units of public transportation, including para-transit services, were available for a population of 9.3 million people. Due to the inadequate public transportation and the absence of mass transportation, citizens are increasingly opting to purchase private vehicles. This trend contributes directly to the increase of air pollution in the region. The recent hike in fuel prices and the increasing prices for spare parts, due to the depreciation of the rupiah, have significantly increased the price of public transporta-

Table 11.26 Electricity connections in Jabotabek, 1996

	Number of electricity connections	Number of households	% households served by connections
DKI Jakarta	1,824,721	2,117,000	86.19
Bogor	825,980	935,725	88.27
Tangerang	457,203	749,266	61.02
Bekasi	399,751	558,098	71.63
Jabotabek	3,507,655	4,360,089	80.45

Source: Jakarta Statistical Office 1997b; West Java Statistical Office 1998

Table 11.27 Telephone connections in Jabotabek, 1996

	Number of telephone connections	Number of population	Telephone per head of population
DKI Jakarta	2,117,504	9,341,400	0.23
Bogor	246,636	4,261,116	0.06
Tangerang	N/A	3,624,139	N/A
Bekasi	164,584	2,914,153	0.06

Source: Jakarta Statistical Office 1997b; West Java Statistical Office 1998

tion. Not only is this affecting the transportation sector, but it is also being reflected in the prices of goods and services as transportation costs in general are higher. Further, many local public transportation companies are no longer able to afford to operate and maintain their fleets, placing more stress on the economy and the population in general.

Electricity and telephone

Jabotabek has adequate electricity facilities with over 80 per cent of all households connected to the system (Table 11.26). However, telephone facilities are still far from adequate. In 1996, the total number of telephone lines available was 2.1 million for the central city and slightly over 411,000 for all of Bogor and Bekasi. For the region, the telephone line per individual access rate is 20 per cent. In addition, there is a discrepancy between the level of service in DKI Jakarta and that in its surrounding areas. Whereas in Jakarta there are 23 telephone lines for every 100 persons, in Botabek and Bekasi there are only six for every 100 persons (Table 11.27).

Water supply

Although the region receives ample rainfall, water supply problems have escalated because wells over a very wide area have become polluted. Shallow wells throughout the urban area suffer from high levels of pollu-

Table 11.28 Piped water connections in Jabotabek, 1996

	Households with piped water connection	Total households	% with piped water
DKI Jakarta	396,707	2,117,000	18.74
Bogor Municipality	33,447	144,305	23.18
Bogor Regency	54,584	791,420	6.90
Tangerang Regency	16,108	524,830	3.07

Source: Jakarta Statistical Office 1997; West Java Statistical Office 1998

tion resulting from lack of proper treatment of wastewater. Further, these shallow wells are being overexploited, so that in several areas the water table levels fluctuate greatly, with wells drying up during certain times of the year (particularly the dry season from March until August). One alternative, pumping from deep wells, is unsustainable since it is both expensive (in terms of infrastructure investment) and has lead to land subsidence.

By 1996, piped water connections within Jakarta were delivering service to 18.7 per cent of the population or approximately 396,000 out of 2.1 million households (Table 11.28). The level of service by PDAM (Indonesian Water Company) varies for other areas. For example, water connections reached less than 7.0 per cent of the total households in the Bogor Regency, while over 23.2 per cent of the households in Bogor Municipality had service connections. Only 3.07 per cent of all households in the Tangerang Regency had water connections.

This lack of connectivity has been one source of water supply problems within the region. Although there is adequate quantity, water quality has deteriorated. A recent study predicted that the current clean water supply would be outstripped by demand in the city of Jakarta by the year 2005 (Department of Public Works 1997a). It is urgent to develop coordination between the DKI Jakarta government and the West Java provincial government to improve the water supply management techniques used by the city and also develop community participation (such as for maintenance and changing behaviour in water use).

Inequity in water supply provision still persists in Jabotabek, and has become major issue. Most piped water connections deliver water to residential areas that are in middle- to upper-income neighbourhoods. However, most isolated and poor neighbourhoods are not served by piped water connections. People within these communities must therefore buy water from vendors. Since the vendors usually charge higher prices for water than the prices paid by the middle- and upper-income groups, the poor are not only suffering from poor service but must also pay a higher price for this vital good.

Table 11.29 Garbage disposal and transport capacity in Jakarta and surrounding areas

	Volume (m³/day)	Capacity of transportation (m³/day)	Service rate (%)
DKI Jakarta	25,715	21,744	84.56
Bogor Municipality	1,329	1,010	76.00
Tangerang Municipality	3,012	602	20.00
Tangerang Regency			
Balaraja	213	21	9.86
Ciputat	720	187	26.02
Bekasi Regency	1,797	557	31.00

Source: JICA 1998b

Wastewater and waste disposal

More than 70 per cent of all houses in DKI Jakarta have a septic tank, but about 22 per cent do not have an adequate wastewater discharge system. As a result people use fields, rivers, holes, etc. as toilet facilities. Wastewater contamination of pure water sources is one reason for the deterioration of the water supply system.

The solid waste disposal system in the Jabotabek area consists of a fairly substantial programme in Jakarta with less extensive programmes in Bogor, Tangerang, and Bekasi. A significant amount of waste continually goes uncollected. In DKI Jakarta, the system services 84.6 per cent of total garbage volume produced every day, whereas in Bekasi and Tangerang only 31 per cent and 20 per cent, respectively, of the garbage produced daily is serviced (Table 11.29). The rest is disposed into rivers and canals.

Environmental impacts

With the rapid economic growth in the Jabotabek region, the urban environment has suffered significantly. The unprecedented number of people who have come to the Jabotabek region over the past decade and were not supported by adequate urban infrastructure underpins the increased environmental pollution levels, traffic congestion, and environmental disaster potentials in the entire Jabotabek region.

The current economic situation is exacerbating environmental conditions. While the city and region continue to grow, government funds to finance urban infrastructure have decreased. The current crisis has forced the government to cut their budget for urban environmental projects. The delay in investment in these and other development projects may continue for an extended period.

Drainage and flooding

DKI Jakarta lies in the flood plain zone of a number of rivers and streams, such as Cengkareng drain, Cakung drain, Kali Karang, Kali Pekapuran, Kali Sentiong, Kali Sunter, Kali Blincong, Kali Angke, Kali Kamal, and Kali Ciliwung (the largest river). The drainage and flood problems experienced within the city and outer regions are the result of overflow from inadequate and disintegrating drainage systems and inefficient flood-control systems on rivers.

The main reason for flooding within the city and the region is the lack of a strategic drainage plan. Uncontrolled development around the lower river banks has impeded flow and reduced river capacity, causing water to back up and flood upstream areas. The developed drains and canals have also become dumping places for solid waste and construction debris, all of which causes flooding. New developments, for example real estate and toll roads, have failed to provide adequate drainage and to integrate into albeit inadequate but existing drainage systems. As a consequence, these developments suffer from flooding or cause extensive flooding in other already developed areas, some of which had never previously experienced floods. Further, many residential sites are located on lower ground than the wetlands that cause flooding, and as water seeks the lowest ground, these sites often find themselves inundated. Lastly, Jabotabek receives rainwater run-off from the entire watershed. As the city expands, the amount of run-off increases, as it is not soaked into the soil but carried on the surface of concrete and asphalt roads and developments. Following storms, increasing amounts of water are flowing into the region's rivers and canals, and at times of high tide the water fails to flow out into the bay and instead spreads out over neighbouring lands.

Lakes

The acceleration of Jabotabek's development has not been supported by proper natural resource preservation, particularly in terms of the protection of water catchment areas. Water catchment areas have an important role in preserving the water supply and preventing flooding. Originally, within its borders, Jabotabek had 193 lakes with a total surface area of 2,282 ha. By 1997, however, only 1,492 ha of lakes could be found, translating into a loss of 790 ha (Table 11.30). The remaining lakes are in poor condition. The transformation and reduction of lakes within the region are directly related to population pressures (Department of Public Works 1997b). Many lakes have been drained or filled to become residential sites, toll roads, industrial areas, etc. Further, some lakes have suffered as their water sources have been diverted for other means. Those that remain have been the destinations of industrial and other wastes.

Table 11.30 Lakes in Jabotabek

Location	Original number	Problem
DKI Jakarta	9	N/A
Bogor	122	Total lake surface area decreased from 561 ha to 361 ha. Seven lakes dried and functionally changed to other uses
Tangerang	45	Two lakes (370 ha) have functionally changed to wet rice fields and settlement areas
Bekasi	17	Eight lakes (123 ha) disappeared
Jabotabek	193	

Source: DKI Jakarta Planning Agency 1997

Air pollution

According to studies conducted by the Japan International Cooperation Agency and DKI Jakarta's Urban and Environment Research, Jakarta ranked third after Mexico City and Bangkok as the city with the worst air pollution (JICA 1998a). The transportation and industrial sectors are the major contributors to air pollution (Table 11.31). In Jakarta, the transportation sector contributed 40 per cent of the total SPM (suspended particulate matter), 69 per cent of the NO_x (nitrogen oxide), and 15 per cent of the SO_x (sulphur oxide). In DKI Jakarta, with 3,021,138 vehicles, the pollutant level reaches approximately 232.3 tonnes per day. At the same time, health bills reach almost Rp 1.3 billion per day. Health costs alone, however, are not sufficient in accounting for the impact of air pollution. The degradation of air quality also affects the condition of buildings, pollutes vegetation, corrodes infrastructure, and impacts on levels of greenhouse gases.

The largest sources of air pollution in Jabotabek are vehicle emissions, followed by industrial emissions (BAPEDAL 1994). Without any pre-

Table 11.31 Sources of air pollution emissions in Jakarta

Sources	SO_x %	NO_x %	SPM %
Factories	76	26	57
Automobiles	15	69	40
Households	8	3	3
Ships	1	1	0
Aircraft	0	1	0
Total	100	100	100

Source: JICA 1998a

ventive actions the level of air pollution in DKI Jakarta caused by motor vehicle emissions will worsen. The level of air pollutants in DKI Jakarta's artery roads has far exceeded the maximum threshold according to the Indonesian State Ministry of Environment Act. For example, on Jalan M. H. Thamrin, one of the major roads in Jakarta, the proportion of NO_x reached 40.6 per cent, which is three times the maximum threshold. Fortunately, many indicators of air quality within Jakarta's residential neighbourhoods are below standard harmful levels, except for particle parameters such as dust, mist, fumes, and total suspended particulates (TSP). In these cases the amount of pollutants exceeds health thresholds by 2.4 per cent to 45.5 per cent. This indicates that the health consequences of air pollution, such as TSP mortality, asthma, increased blood pressure, decreases in children's IQ, and bronchitis in children, will be greater, and will increase the health costs further.

River pollution

River pollution has also worsened over the past 10 years, due mostly to household waste and industrial wastewater inputs. The primary source of river pollution is household waste. Generally, septic tanks are not emptied regularly and many public facilities, housing estates, and private toilet owners bypass effluent pipes and send wastewater directly to drains that empty into rivers. Table 11.32 demonstrates the sources of pollution and distribution of total biological oxygen demand load in the Sunter river which flows through northern Jakarta.

Within the industrial sector, inadequate waste recycling systems in some industries in Jabotabek have created river pollution. Many times waste is disposed of into the river without meeting the required threshold set by the Indonesian State Ministry of Environment Act. There is a general water shortage in Jakarta and Botabek every dry season, but the situation could

Table 11.32 Distribution of total BOD load in the Sunter river

Source	%	BOD/day (tonnes)
Industry	10.00	5
Domestic sewage and septage[a]	19.00	9
Domestic sullage[a]	50.00	24
Solid waste leachate	15.00	7
Unaccounted	6.00	3
Total	100.00	48

Source: JICA 1998b
a. Septage = the liquid waste from septic tanks; sullage = other household wastewater from washing, etc.

be avoided if the 13 rivers in Jakarta were preserved for water supply to these areas rather than maintaining the water debit for provision to Jabotabek. Most upper-stream areas are in worse condition; their water is polluted and their debit decreases during the dry season because most people use the rivers as their garbage disposal facilities due to lack of adequate solid waste disposal infrastructure/facilities.

Coastal pollution

The increasing intensity of manufacturing and other activities in Jabotabek has accompanied coastal pollution in Jakarta Bay. At the end of 1997, the level of pollution in Jakarta Bay had reached 10 kilometres from the seashore. The zones nearest the seashore reached above the average values for chemical oxygen demand (COD), biological oxygen demand (BOD), ammonium, metal, and sediment contents. The quality of water in all probability will get worse in the future before it gets better. It will further worsen if the increasing intensity of activities is not controlled. The causes of pollution, among other factors, are domestic waste disposal, water vessel traffic, oil waste, and pollution from mining and seaport activities.

Land subsidence

As mentioned previously, the use of groundwater in newly urbanized area has exceeded the limits of natural aquifer recharge. The lowering of the level of groundwater causes land subsidence. In areas of high groundwater obstruction, particularly from deep aquifers, the water is squeezed out from between clay layers. This results in substantial compression of the overlying solid mass and it sinks. On the surface the result is noticeable land subsidence.

Land subsidence in DKI Jakarta has been reported by previous studies (Department of Public Works 1993; JICA 1998b) (Table 11.33). Since 1989, DKI Jakarta's government and other interested agencies have been

Table 11.33 Land subsidence in Jakarta

Location	Drop in elevation from 1974/1978 to 1993/1994	Drainage system
Jl. Daan Mogot (west Jakarta)	0.6 m to 1.0 m	Mookervaart canal
Jl. Pangeran Jayakarta (central Jakarta)	0.6 m to 0.9 m	Ciliwung river
Jl. Perintis Kemerdekaan (east Jakarta)	0.6 m to 0.7 m	Sunter river

Source: JICA 1998b

monitoring wells, while levelling surveys on the elevation of existing benchmarks in Jakarta have been carried out periodically. Research has revealed that the burden of the rapid urbanization and the land subsidence has led to seawater penetration of the groundwater (JICA 1998b).

The question of sustainability

Based on the above analysis of the present conditions in Indonesia, Jabotabek, and particularly DKI Jakarta, development within the country, urban region, and city is not sustainable. Jabotabek's development has not been progressing along sustainable lines in economic, social, or environmental terms. All economic activities in the Jabotabek region have suffered great losses as a result of the financial crisis, and the city is not capable of supporting and maintaining the previous economic activities. The large number of unemployed workers in the Jabotabek region remains a threat to society. From the environmental point of view, Jabotabek is unsustainable since the environmental cost created by both the past and present economic development strategies has been extremely high. These costs are now placing a heavy burden on both economic recovery and the quality of life in the region.

Investing in the real estate sector, previously regarded as a money machine for Jabotabek's economy, turned out to be a bad business decision. Many real estate developments were not planned. Moreover, they were not constructed to meet real market demands, rather, they were part of a giant land speculation gambit. Industrial sectors were overly dependent on import content. In general, while globalization has lead to positive growth and development, it also has a dark side. This side revealed itself as the financial crisis deepened and economic growth became negative.

The economic crisis in the country later turned into a social and political crisis. Instability within the country has affected a variety of other activities, as seen in the decline of the tourism sector. Other obvious and clear impacts of political instability include the reluctance of foreign investors to bring their investment back into the country and the continuous rupiah depreciation. Accordingly, many companies, factories, and other economic activities are going bankrupt. The huge number of unemployed has exacerbated the problems and has become a national issue.

It is evident that the past and current development trends within Jakarta and Jabotabek are not sustainable. The positive indicators mentioned in the previous section which have strengthened over the past decades have masked some growing problems. The economic crisis brought them to light. While all have paid dearly through the impacts of the crisis, those who pay most are those who can least afford it, the poor.

The world city

The impacts of rapid development during the decades before the economic crisis demonstrate that some of the development patterns for the Jabotabek region were unsustainable. The crisis has brought these issues to light as living conditions and the environment continue to deteriorate. Furthermore, currently limited government funds are unable to keep up with maintenance and improvement costs for the region's infrastructure. The challenge for the government is twofold: to solve the existing "sustainability" problems, and to enhance the position of Jabotabek as a "world city" within the regional and global city system. This section will conclude the chapter with an analysis of the competitive advantages of the urban region within the world economy, and the policy directions the government intends to take in order to move the region to become both a more sustainable and a more globally competitive urban area.

Comparative versus competitive advantage

Almost every economic sector in the Jabotabek region has been severely hit by the current crisis. Besides the closure of many industrial plants, tertiary industries, such as those in the property sector and its related services, have suffered tremendous losses. Many service-sector players, such as consultancy services, transportation, banks, hotels, and restaurants, are no longer able to continue their businesses since the buying power of the people has greatly reduced due to inflation and the depreciation of the rupiah. Further, the informal sectors have also felt the burden caused by the economic crisis, as the reduced buying power of consumers has affected their activities. Jabotabek suffers from low economic efficiency within many of its systems for wealth creation. This has greatly affected the social structure and environmental conditions of the region. While this lack of efficiency could be overlooked during the period of rapid growth, it can no longer be ignored. The current situation in the urban region can be described as a condition of non-competitiveness within the regional and world city system.

Research has indicated that the rapid development in the Jabotabek region over the past decade did not rely on competitive or product/output advantages, but more on comparative or input advantages. The comparative advantage of the region were the results of access to cheap labour; decision-makers in charge of regulating the region; infrastructure to support export and import activities (particularly within Jabotabek); the domestic market; and domestic and international transportation and communication networks. Under these conditions the region was considered a good location as a host for other activities which define globalization.

For example, the large percentage (over half) of the population included in the low-wage workforce, as compared to other locations, made Jabotabek a commendable location for labour-intensive industrial investments. However, the majority of this large pool of cheap labour were not able to learn new skills, and remain low-skilled to this day. While this situation bodes well for some types of activities, it is not sustainable under the current situation. Jabotabek's labour force is currently not competitive in the global market. Furthermore, its internal characteristics have made it difficult for the region to move up the comparative advantage ladder.

Another factor that also goes hand in hand with globalization and the comparative advantages that have helped to make the Jabotabek region's development unsustainable is the fact that most of the industrial activities rely on high import content as inputs for production. Continuous rupiah depreciation has forced many companies to halt their production and consequently lay off their employees. Many industrial activities that were once the stimulus of national economic growth had to discontinue their production. The Asian financial crisis has had effects across the region: while many industries are located within developing countries, these firms still rely heavily on imported parts and materials. These were the industries hit first and hardest by the crisis. They are vulnerable to foreign currency fluctuations and are weak competitors within the global economy, thus during the economic crisis most of these industries collapsed.

The provision of infrastructure during the economic boom leaned more towards the middle and upper classes. These infrastructure developments included exclusive facilities such as golf courses, shopping malls, apartments, condominiums, luxury hotels and resorts, and other facilities of a similar sort. Moreover, the development of toll roads created inequities, since they benefit people who can afford to have private motor vehicles. The tremendous investments in exclusive and expensive facilities were at the expense of those living in slum areas. The *kampungs* of Jakarta are still in need of basic infrastructure and the provision of public transportation. This oversight has weakened the city's competitiveness in the global economy, since much of the primary and important infrastructure such as water provision, waste disposal facilities, road systems, and public transportation are crucial to the function of the urban region. As the economy declined, the effect of these omissions grew more critical.

One important lesson learned from the present economic crisis is that Jabotabek must improve its competitive advantages instead of its comparative advantages. In order to be part of an integrated and/or interconnected world city system, Jabotabek must be more competitive globally and more sustainable economically, socially, and environmentally. Competitive advantages that are more dynamic and flexible should then become the object of government policies in guiding the economic recovery in Jabotabek in particular and in Indonesia in general.

Directions of government policies

Which policy directions should the Jabotabek government embrace in order to move the region to more sustainable development and increase global competitiveness? What lessons could be learned from the first and second phases of globalization? How could development be achieved based on comparative advantages or competitive advantages?

Inward- versus outward-looking policies

In order to be more competitive in the global market the government must integrate the inward- and outward-looking strategies. The government must not be biased towards outward-looking policies, as they have been, but must also promote the development of internal strengths. On one hand, the government must promote globalization, but it must also prepare strategic plans to mitigate the negative aspects of spatial transformations and accompanying dynamic changes. Investment opportunities must be reviewed to suit local knowledge and resources. The government must focus on the development of local industries to support foreign direct investment. In the case of Jabotabek, development must be tailored to benefit and support the hinterland, small-scale industries, and the informal sector. The government should initiate job-creation programmes and induce investors into the region for more than just the benefits of a low-skilled, cheap labour force.

Regarding the inward-looking approach, it is important to develop the human resources and promote the transfer of technologies. Human resources are a prime determinant factor for a country's success in economic development. In the information-age society, successful members of the society are those who can fully access and utilize knowledge at all levels. The government must provide better access to education for all people. Through an effective education system, people will benefit from higher skills and be able to meet the demands of the coming era. In doing so, the government could also focus on skills that fit the changing demands of the global economy. Both formal education and technical training systems must be adjusted. Future workers are expected to continue advancing their work-based skills, and the workplace must also be viewed as a place of learning. In this way, education and on-the-job training can be linked.

Social integration

The social integration of Indonesian society is of critical concern today, and this is an area in which the government could play an active role. Indeed, politicians and bureaucrats play an important part in creating social integration among the population, both socio-economically and socio-culturally. For example, the development of large-scale residential and housing estates must be based on the mixed development concept and the 1:3:6 housing development rule. The government must eliminate the development of exclusive housing estates and must encourage the construction of large housing estates for the general public. It must work with the private sector to develop affordable housing, and must also develop settlement policies and plans according to the distribution of population and workplaces, and promote controlled use of land. Importantly, there is a role for government in the promotion of controlled land values. Land speculation may be discouraged.

Another important policy needed to create greater equality and social cohesion is the improvement of urban infrastructure, as well as living conditions in the rural areas and city village (*kampung*) areas. In this case, the government must give priority to the rehabilitation of dense and environmentally degraded settlement areas through redevelopment programmes and *kampung* improvement programmes (KIPs). Social safety-net programmes can be devised and implemented with the assistance of the World Bank. The government must also promote regulations, permits, and retribution systems that encourage the development of housing for the low- and middle-income groups.

Development of urban public infrastructure

During the past decade infrastructure development was mainly for the benefit of middle- and upper-income groups – for example, most of the poor have no access to piped water. In the future, the government must review the development of urban infrastructure so that it covers a greater share of society. The provision of basic needs should be a target for infrastructure development.

In order to become more competitive globally, the government must improve the urban public infrastructure in Jabotabek, such as public and mass transportation systems, road networks, telecommunication lines, water, electricity, and other urban infrastructure. In the case of transportation, the government must reduce traffic and promote the usage of mass public transportation systems, and increase the efficiency of road use. At the same time the government must also pay more attention to the improvement of the service level of passenger and freight transportation systems and warehouses in order to be globally competitive. Low-cost solutions to urban infrastructure problems and strategic infrastructure management must be prioritized.

Good governance

Last but not least, it seems that the absence of good governance is one of the major reasons why Indonesia – compared with its neighbouring countries – has not been able to recover sooner from its economic, social, and political crisis. The government must deal seriously with the "KKN" issue (corruption, collusion, and nepotism). The government must regain the trust and confidence of the people, first domestically and then internationally. If the government regains trust and confidence, new investments and businesses will come back to Indonesia and the Jabotabek area in particular. Fresh funds from both foreign and domestic investors are needed to restore economic growth.

In general, to regain trust and confidence from the people, the government must change the behaviour of the community as a whole to become more honest, capable, and highly dedicated. The new government then must review and amend all regulations that previously catered only to certain levels and parts of the society. The new government must also show their full commitment to the improvement and implementation of the legal system. The new government must provide signs of a strong political will to abolish all corruption, collusion, and nepotism – which became a part of the old government system – without tolerating any form of misconduct or misbehaviour in the future. Only then will the system be called good and clean governance.

Specifically, the government must improve the banking and financial system. Strategic financial resource management for the needs of small and medium-scale industries will benefit the economy as a whole. The government must assist small and medium-sized enterprises and include them integrally in the national economic system. General banking and financial regulations must be reviewed, rewritten, and implemented prudently. One way to save the banking and financial system is through a recapitalization programme with the assistance of the IMF and the World Bank.

Considering the magnitude of the problems that Jabotabek currently faces, the government must seriously consider institutional changes. A new structure of local governance that includes partnerships among the government, private sector, and community in the development process is warranted. Traditional government-centred top-down planning is no longer appropriate or effective for managing development. These types of changes not only require changes in attitudes but transparency and better mechanisms to allow the active participation of the private sector and community groups. It also requires restructuring of the basic ways in which the government operates.

Acknowledgements

The authors would like to acknowledge the contributions of Edmund Parengkuan, Evi Hermirasari, Indira Sari, Ernawati, and Woro Srihastuti.

Their thoughtful comments, suggestions, and input helped to strengthen the chapter. All errors are the sole responsibility of the authors.

REFERENCES

Akatiga (Centre for Social Analysis), Asia Foundation, and USAID. 1999. *Study of Monitoring on Crisis Impact on Small-Scale Enterprises.* Bandung: Akatiga.

Central Bureau of Statistics. 1991. *Statistical Year Book of Indonesia 1990.* Jakarta: CBS Printing.

Central Bureau of Statistics. 1992. *Statistical Year Book of Indonesia 1991.* Jakarta: CBS Printing.

Central Bureau of Statistics. 1996a. *Population of DKI Jakarta Based on Results of the 1995 Intercensal Population Survey.* Jakarta: CBS Printing.

Central Bureau of Statistics. 1996b. *Population of West Java Based on Results of the 1995 Intercensal Population Survey.* Jakarta: CBS Printing.

Central Bureau of Statistics. 1996c. *Statistical Year Book of Indonesia 1995.* Jakarta: CBS Printing.

Central Bureau of Statistics. 1997a. *Mobilization and Urbanization in Indonesia Based on 1995 Intercensal Population Survey.* Jakarta: CV Putra Jaya Printing.

Central Bureau of Statistics. 1997b. *Monthly Statistical Bulletin, Economic Indicators September 1997.* Jakarta: CBS Printing.

Central Bureau of Statistics. 1997c. *Statistical Year Book of Indonesia 1996.* Jakarta: CBS Printing.

Central Bureau of Statistics. 1998. *Monthly Statistical Bulletin, Economic Indicators July 1998.* Jakarta: CBS Printing.

Central Bureau of Statistics. 1999a. *Foreign Exchange Rates In Indonesia 1998.* Jakarta: PD Mutiara Karang Printing.

Central Bureau of Statistics. 1999b. *Foreign Trade Statistical Bulletin: Imports March 1999.* Jakarta: CV Husna Printing.

Central Bureau of Statistics. 1999c. *Indonesia Economy Report 1998.* Jakarta: CV Hendrika Printing.

Central Bureau of Statistics. 1999d. *Statistical Year Book of Indonesia 1998.* Jakarta: CBS Printing.

Cohen, R. 1981. "The new international division of labour, multinational corporations, and urban hierarchy", in M. Dear and A. Scott (eds) *Urbanization and Urban Planning in Capitalist Society.* London: Methuen.

Department of Public Works, Directorate General of Human Settlements. 1993. *Jabotabek Metropolitan Development Plan Review and the Context of North Land of Java (Pantura).* Jakarta: Department of Public Works Printing.

Department of Public Works, Directorate General of Human Settlements. 1997a. *Final Report of Study on Jabotabek Area Development Strategies.* Jakarta: Department of Public Works Printing.

Department of Public Works, Directorate General of Human Settlements. 1997b. "Study on comprehensive river water management plan in Jabotabek", in Japan International Cooperation Agency (JICA) and State Ministry of Housing and

National Land Agency, Republic of Indonesia, *Study on Land Provision for Housing and Settlements Development through Kasiba and Land Consolidation in Jakarta Metropolitan Area, Progress Report 1*. Jakarta: JICA and State Ministry of Housing and National Land Agency, Republic of Indonesia.

DKI Jakarta Planning Agency (Bappeda DKI Jakarta). 1997. *Interim Report of Study on Integrating of Jabotabek Spatial Planning*. Jakarta: Bappeda DKI Jakarta.

Friedmann, John. 1986. "The world city hypothesis", *Development and Change*, Vol. 17, No. 1.

Friedmann, John and Goetz Wolff. 1982. "World city formation: An agenda for research and action", *International Journal for Urban and Regional Research*, No. 3, pp. 309–404.

Government of Indonesia, State Ministry of Environment and Environmental Impact Control Agency (BAPEDAL). 1994. *Third Jabotabek Urban Development Project (JUDP III), Phase II Report*. Jakarta: BAPEDAL Printing.

Jakarta Statistical Office. 1997a. *Analysis of Migration in DKI Jakarta Based on 1995 Intercensal Population Survey*. Jakarta: Jakarta Statistical Office Printing.

Jakarta Statistical Office. 1997b. *Jakarta in Figures 1997*. Jakarta: Jakarta Statistical Office Printing.

Jakarta Statistical Office. 1997c. *Regional Income of Jakarta 1993–1996*. Jakarta: Jakarta Statistical Office Printing.

Jakarta Statistical Office. 1999a. *Jakarta in Figures 1998*. Jakarta: Jakarta Statistical Office Printing.

Jakarta Statistical Office. 1999b. *Wealth Indicators of DKI Jakarta People 1998*. Jakarta: Jakarta Statistical Office Printing.

Japan International Cooperation Agency (JICA). 1998a. "Study of the integrated air quality management for Jakarta metropolitan area", in JICA and State Ministry of Housing and National Land Agency, Republic of Indonesia, *Study on Land Provision for Housing and Settlements Development through Kasiba and Land Consolidation in Jakarta Metropolitan Area, Progress Report 1*. Jakarta: JICA and State Ministry of Housing and National Land Agency, Republic of Indonesia.

Japan International Cooperation Agency (JICA) and State Ministry of Housing and National Land Agency, Republic of Indonesia. 1998b. *Study on Land Provision for Housing and Settlements Development through Kasiba and Land Consolidation in Jakarta Metropolitan Area, Progress Report 1*. Jakarta: JICA and State Ministry of Housing and National Land Agency, Republic of Indonesia.

Kompas. 1998a. January, http//www.kompas.com.

Kompas. 1998b. *Kompas*, 7 June.

Kompas. 1998c. *Kompas*, 17 June.

Kusbiantoro, B. S. 1996. "Transportation problem in rapidly developing new town areas", paper presented at the Fourth PRSCO of the RSAI, Tsukuba, Japan, 7–8 May.

Kusbiantoro, B. S. 1998. "Some notes on urban transportation problems in Indonesia: The case of Jabotabek", paper presented at Conference on Transportation in Developing Countries, University of California at Berkeley, April.

Pearce, David W. and R. Kerry. 1990. *Economics of Natural Resources and Environment.* Baltimore: Johns Hopkins University Press.

Pilar Bulletin. 1998. "Poverty changes the lifestyle", *Pilar Bulletin,* No. 19, 23 September–6 October.

Property Indonesia Bulletin. 1995. "Industrial Estate Association 1994", *Property Indonesia Bulletin.*

Property Indonesia Bulletin. 1996. "Map of housing development in Jabotabek", *Property Indonesia Bulletin.*

Soegijoko, Budhy Tjahjati S. 1996. *Impact of Strengthening in International Urban Linkage. The Case of Jabotabek, Indonesia.* Jakarta: NLI Research Institute (Bappenas Joint Research).

Soegijoko, Budhy Tjahjati S. and B. S. Kusbiantoro. 1998. "Globalization and the sustainability of cities in Pacific Asia: The case of Jabotabek, Indonesia", paper presented at UNU-IAS/UBC workshop on Globalization and the Sustainability of Cities in Pacific Asia, Vancouver, 24–26 June.

UNCTAD. 1996. Paper in Soegijoko, Budhy Tjahjati S. *Impact of Strengthening in International Urban Linkage. The Case of Jabotabek, Indonesia.* Jakarta: NLI Research Institute (Bappenas Joint Research).

Urban and Regional Development Institute (URDI). 1998. *Study on the Impact of Indonesia's Economic Crisis on Job Losses in Jabotabek.* Jakarta: URDI.

West Java Statistical Office. 1998. *West Java in Figures 1997.* Bandung: West Java Statistical Office Printing.

West Java Statistical Office. 1999. *Social Economy Figures of West Java People Based on Intercensal Population Survey 1998.* Bandung: West Java Statistical Office Printing.

12

The extended Bangkok region: Globalization and sustainability

Sauwalak Kittiprapas

Introduction

The Asia Pacific region has become an important centre in the global economy. Within this region, Thailand has emerged as a strategic location for the destination of foreign direct investment (FDI) and flows of trade, information, and people. These transnational movements have affected the social behaviour of the Thais and the spatial economy of the country and its cities. In particular, the capital city, Bangkok, and its extended periphery have undergone extensive transformations over the past three decades. The provinces most affected by the economic boom and recent bust are contained within the "extended Bangkok region" (EBR), which consists of the Bangkok metropolitan region (BMR)[1] and the core eastern seaboard (ESB).[2] This region remains important for the national economy, despite the current economic crisis, and continues to transform in function and form.

This chapter describes the overall trends in urban and regional development in Thailand and the recent changes to the EBR. Further, it outlines the extensive changes in the national urban regional system due to the rapid urbanization experienced during the last three decades. These pressures and the current economic crisis require a re-evaluation of Thailand's urban and regional development strategies. Of interest are the role of the EBR within the regional economy, and the growth of the functional city system and how that has impacted on Thailand's development. Attention is also paid to the obstacles to sustainable urban development and policy implementation.

The first section of the chapter presents an overview of the internal and external factors impacting on spatial development and urban transformation in Thailand, while also addressing problems resulting from the current economic crisis. The second section examines migration and industrial location trends over the recent past. The third section presents the urbanization trends in Thailand and the EBR. The fourth section focuses on the urban systems within the EBR's subregions (Bangkok, the five surrounding provinces, and the three core eastern seaboard provinces), and the impacts of linkages to the global and regional economy. A discussion of problems and policy responses for sustainable development are presented in the fifth section. Finally, the chapter concludes with a discussion of policy options.

Spatial development in Thailand: Internal and external factors

No matter what geographical scale is considered, the role of Bangkok and its surrounding area within the national economy is evident. For example, the share of the city of Bangkok in national GDP is currently approximately 40 per cent (Table 12.1). In 1995, the per capita income of the metropolitan area of Bangkok was about four times the national average. Figure 12.1 demonstrates that until the mid-1990s the regional income disparity between the EBR and the rest of the nation increased. Trends of per capita income in the five surrounding provinces and the three core ESB provinces also continue to increase, demonstrating faster growth than the national average. These trends confirm the role of the capital area and the continuing regional divergence within the country.

Impact of internal factors on Thailand's spatial development

While the central role of Bangkok in Thailand's growth has been attributed to its geographical location[3] and advantages of economic agglomeration, governmental policies have also played an important role in concentrating economic activities in the area. Since the first Five-Year National Economic and Social Development Plan (1961–1966), development policies promoting industrialization (starting with import substitution and, later, export promotion), international trade, and growth poles have enhanced urban-based industrialization and led to a high concentration of economic

Table 12.1 Trends of Bangkok's GPP share to national GDP at constant 1988 prices

Year	1989	1990	1991	1992	1993	1994	1995
BMR GPP (baht)	656,995	778,604	843,330	811,612	1,018,432	1,080,302	1,156,225
National GDP (baht)	1,749,952	1,945,379	2,111,862	2,288,865	2,481,278	2,702,078	2,941,183
Share of GPP BMR/ nation (%)	37.54	40.02	39.93	35.51	41.04	39.98	39.31

Source: Data collected from the office of the National Economic and Social Development Board (NESDB)
Note: GPP stands for gross provincial products. The sum of GPP of all provinces equals to the national GDP.

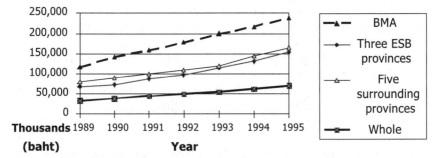

Figure 12.1 Per capita GDP by region at constant 1988 prices
Source: Statistical data from office of National Economic and Social Development Board (NESDB), 1991–1995

activities in Bangkok, which was the only international trade point and a centre of domestic transportation hubs.

As the earlier national plans (from the first to the third), adopted from the 1960s to the mid-1970s, emphasized accelerated growth through industrialization in areas with the highest "potential", such as Bangkok, regional development of provinces and cities throughout the rest of the country was neglected. Through these development plans Bangkok received most of the national public investment disbursements.

Sectoral international trade policies implemented throughout these earlier plans favoured industries through tariff protection while taxing agricultural exports (particularly rice), thus biasing growth against agriculture and towards industrial development. This sectoral policy bias also enhanced urban-rural disparity, since a majority of Thai people living in outlying rural regions are engaged in agriculture. At the same time, the concentration of promoted industries in Bangkok enabled the city to grow at a much faster rate than the rest of the country, widening regional income disparities.

Later plans (from the fourth to the current eighth plan) focused some attention on regional development outside Bangkok. After political instability and social disorder reached a peak in 1975–1976, the fourth plan (1977–1981) attempted to balance regional development by targeting regional urban centres outside Bangkok. Attempts at deconcentrating population and industries from Bangkok began seriously during the fifth plan (1982–1986), with the launching of the ESB programme. Through the provision of industrial infrastructure, the programme aimed at moving industrial development eastward. Since that time, the concept of a more balanced development has been adopted. The sixth (1987–1991), seventh (1992–1996), and eighth (1997–2001) plans identified more regional (secondary) urban centres, promoted regional clusters, and focused on regional network development. Because previous regional initiatives before the sixth plan had not been very successful due to limited budget allocation and insufficient local institutional authority at regional levels, the recent policies in the seventh and eighth plans have focused more on capacity-building of local governments in regional urban centres and on encouraging private sector participation. These spatial development strategies also aim to enhance regional comparative advantages and linkages, in order to promote regional economic growth.

The global economy and the spatial development in Thailand

Since the Second World War period, Thailand has been linked into the world economy and the growth of Bangkok has expanded. Since that time, all imports and exports have streamed through the Bangkok port, and as a result all trading-related activities were based in Bangkok. At the same time, Bangkok was the centre of education, government, and the economic development of the nation. Thus, Bangkok had emerged as Thailand's largest concentrated urban area and one of the world's largest primate cities.

However, industrial development from the mid-1980s to the early 1990s, when the Thai economy expanded drastically with double-digit growth, led to the spatial restructuring of Bangkok and the EBR. Resulting from the so-called "flying geese" pattern of development, Thailand, which had comparative advantages in location-specific endowments (labour, raw materials, and basic infrastructure) and macroeconomic policies (investment promotion, exchange rate stability, etc.), emerged as an important manufacturing centre in East and South-East Asia in the mid-1980s. At the same time, costs of operations, particularly land and labour, in Bangkok continued to rise. Peripherial regions (the BMR and the ESB) eventually became more competitive, affecting industrial location choices domestically.

While before the mid-1980s global investments concentrated in the city of Bangkok as a destination, during the later years of the decade they dispersed to its periphery. The shifts in the investment location, however, are still limited to the EBR, because Bangkok and it surrounding regions have the nation's best-quality infrastructure, social facilities, and human capital. With this concentration of attributes, the Bangkok region continues to garner the highest share of FDI and industrial investment. In 1994 the EBR accounted for 33 per cent of all new firms and 40 per cent of new investments; however, the location of manufacturing establishments within the EBR shifted from Bangkok proper to the ESB. Thus, while most industrial growth continued to take place within the EBR, the direction of new manufacturing establishments shifted to the eastern corridor. This accompanied the development of major infrastructure (such as ports and industrial estate facilities). At the same time, Bangkok's core area became a centre for services and small-scale manufacturing activities. The dispersal phenomena within the EBR was somewhat similar to that which had taken place in Jabotabek, Indonesia, in the late 1980s (see Chapter 11 in this volume).

Global links and the current financial and economic crisis

Thailand's severe financial crisis started in early 1997. Financial liberalization in the early 1990s without effective supervision resulted in increasing amounts of short-term investment, which largely went to speculation and "non-productive" sectors. This overinvestment created a "bubble economy". Furthermore, financial scandals and loan mismanagement added to the economic instability. Increasingly, speculation on the baht resulted in large foreign-reserve spending by the Bank of Thailand (more than US$30 billion was spent on defending the baht). In late June 1997, Thailand had just US$2.8 billion in usable foreign-exchange reserves (after subtracting dollars that had been committed in forward transactions). The government had no choice but to unpeg the baht, which had been tied to a basket of currencies, with a consequent drastic devaluation on 2 July 1997. Domestic financial turmoil subsequently triggered an economic crisis in the entire East and South-East Asian region.

Even after the floating of the baht, the Thai export sector remained sluggish. On the one hand, the country's production structure had relied heavily on external sources of capital, and a weakened baht increased the costs of imported capital goods and production inputs. On the other hand, the Asian regional economy, Thailand's main export market, faced both recession and falling or unstable local currency trends. These factors led to the decline in export demand and a drop in international competitiveness. As the Thai crisis grew into an Asian regional crisis, the country was faced with the difficulty of exporting increasingly expensive goods to declining markets. The economy plunged further downward. By the end of 1998, the national GDP growth was approximately −8 per cent.

Given the role of the EBR in the national economy, the current East Asian financial turmoil and economic recession have significantly affected the area. The crisis has resulted in unemployment (1.48 million people or 4.6 per cent of the total labour force in February 1998[4]), particularly in the construction, industrial, financial, and banking sectors, which are heavily concentrated in the EBR. Of the 1.48 million unemployed persons in the national economy, 13 per cent are in the EBR. Progress in the major public infrastructure projects planned previously has either slowed or stopped altogether. In general, the 1998 budget was cut 15.7 per cent from the 1997 budget,[5] affecting a large number of development programmes.

During 1998 the Thai banking sector faced a severe crisis; non-performing loans accounted for approximately 40 per cent of total loans, and entrepreneurs were hurt by high interest rates and a credit crunch. As a result, many factories closed down. As banking and real estate sector crises accumulated, the government implemented the so-called "comprehensive" scheme of financial restructuring in August 1998. This restructuring scheme included bank mergers, privatization, capital write-down, and recapitalization; it resulted in a smaller number of local commercial banks and ultimately a large number of worker lay-offs in the financial sector (including the 1997 staff lay-offs when 56 financial companies were closed).

The lay-offs in the financial and manufacturing sectors added to the rising unemployment rate throughout the EBR. Thirty-five per cent of about 700,000 laid-off workers nationwide in 1998 were in the EBR.[6] Private companies experienced downscaling, the public sector froze hiring, and, in general, economic and business opportunities decreased dramatically. The EBR had a total of 192,990 unemployed as of February 1998, accounting for about 13 per cent of the total for the country. The construction sector was among the most seriously hit, dropping by almost 1 million workers and accounting for 32 per cent of total employment reduction (February 1997–1998). The heavy drop in construction-sector employment severely affected unskilled workers.

In Bangkok, the decline in construction activities largely resulted from a stagnant real estate sector. Office vacancy rates in Bangkok climbed to 20 per cent in 1997 and reached 40 per cent during the 1998–1999 fiscal year (Renaud, Zhang, and Koeberle 1998).

The current economic crisis resulted in lower levels of investment by both the public and private sectors as well as affecting the distribution of urban population growth. The urban growth of Bangkok has slowed down, while that of other regional urban centres has increased, largely because of reverse migration. Those workers who were affected by the closure of operations in Bangkok have been returning to stay with their families in their home towns, despite few job opportunities there.

Although the adverse impacts of the crisis have spread to all regions of the country, the EBR has been the most affected in terms of income reduction. The EBR has the greatest income reduction[7] (−13 per cent in Bangkok, −17 per cent in the BMR periphery, and −24 per cent in the core ESB) compared the national average (−11 per cent). Thus, in Thailand, the EBR is the region most affected by the Asian regional economic boom and bust.

Patterns of deconcentration: Migration and industrial location

The migration pattern has shifted within the BMR and, to a larger extent, within the EBR. Even before the launch of the ESB, the BMR had been the nation's major destination of migrant labour from the 1960s to the 1980s. From 1970 to 1986, roughly 44 per cent of the population growth in Bangkok was attributed to in-migration (Ichikawa 1990). Although migration to the BMR is still the highest among cities in the country, the core city of Bangkok is no longer the key destination. From 1985 to 1990, growth of migration to Bangkok's five surrounding provinces was higher than that to Bangkok itself (NESDB 1991). Table 12.2 demonstrates that the net migration to the surrounding provinces and the ESB was higher than the net migration to Bangkok during the period 1990–1995. The table also forecasts growth of net migration in each province for five-year periods. These projections portray a continual decline in the net migration to Bangkok while suggesting an increase to the BMR periphery and the ESB, with the ESB achieving the highest net migration growth rates.

These patterns are consistent with the deconcentration of manufacturing activities from Bangkok. During the 1980s, manufacturing of value-added goods in the BMR accounted for more than three-quarters of the national total. However, since the late 1980s the growth rate of industrial establishments in the five surrounding provinces has been higher than that in Bangkok (Biggs *et al.* 1990). Large manufacturing firms are moving out. The early 1990s saw a significant shift of the industrial location from the BMR to the ESB. For example, during 1991–1996, the percentage of Board of Investment (BOI) approved projects and capital investment in the ESB region increased from 21 per cent to 34 per cent and from 23 per cent to 63 per cent, respectively. At the same time, the number of projects and total investment percentages in the BMR declined. Table 12.3 shows that, in 1997, the ESB region accounted for the largest shares of BOI approval projects (66 per cent), investment (75 per cent), and foreign-registered capital (82 per cent) in the country.

The concentration of non-agricultural employment, especially manufacturing employment, in Bangkok has also declined significantly. Industrial employment is mainly found in the five surrounding provinces, followed by the central and eastern regions (Kittiprapas 1995; Kittiprapas and McCann 1999a, 1999b). This trend in the deconcentration of non-agricultural activities is consistent with the decline in Bangkok's primacy index (Figure 12.2).

Bangkok is losing its primacy within the Thai urban system, primarily because of increasing regional factor price differentials as well as other agglomeration diseconomies (high land prices, traffic congestion, pollution,

Table 12.2 Net migration by region

Province	1990–1995	1995–2000	Growth (%)	2000–2005	2005–2010	Growth (%)
Bangkok	123,879	116,346	–6.08	109,418	99,477	–9.09
BMR	223,308	254,126	13.80	277,754	285,363	2.74
Nonthaburi	71,720	81,136	13.13	84,168	85,681	1.80
Pathum Thani	61,125	65,062	6.44	70,395	73,337	4.18
Samut Prakran	74,979	87,260	16.38	98,706	100,929	2.25
Samut Sakhon	7,335	9,950	35.65	11,478	12,344	7.54
Nakhon Pathom	8,150	10,716	31.48	13,008	13,071	0.48
Core ESB	105,949	137,779	30.04	150,737	176,446	17.06
Chonburi	34,230	38,272	11.81	40,553	41,388	2.06
Cha Choengsao	26,895	39,037	45.15	44,379	62,446	40.71
Rayong	39,120	42,864	9.57	45,144	53,006	17.42

Source: NESDB 1995

Table 12.3 BOI approval projects in each subregion, 1997

	No. of projects	Investment (million baht)	Registered capital (million baht)	Foreign capital (million baht)
Bangkok	69	18,344	3,853	594
Five surrounding provinces	66	45,296	8,023	3,275
Samut Prakarn	31	19,150	4,007	2,579
Patumthani	24	4,513	333	324
Samut Sakorn	7	1,177	623	356
Nontaburi	3	20,426	3,010	4
Nakorn Pathom	1	30	50	12
Core ESB provinces	260	195,674	54,228	21,530
Chonburi	60	39,567	8,914	2,821
Chachoengsao	43	14,736	2,276	930
Rayong	157	141,371	43,038	17,779
Total	395	259,314	66,104	25,399

Source: Data collected from Office of the Board of Investment

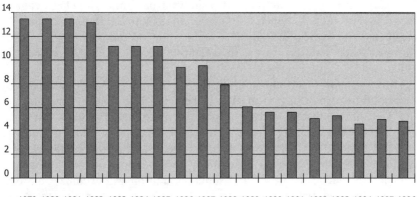

1979 1980 1981 1982 1983 1984 1985 1986 1987 1988 1989 1990 1991 1992 1993 1994 1995 1996

Figure 12.2 Primacy index of Bangkok

etc.). As production costs in Bangkok increased and firms faced trade-offs between agglomeration advantages in Bangkok and cheaper factor prices in other regions, non-Bangkok areas have become more competitive. However, the decentralization of employment from Bangkok has mainly been to the surrounding provinces within the EBR rather than to outlying areas. Thus, interregional inequality between the EBR and the outlying regions remains high. Similar to the case of Jabotabek in Indonesia, the

EBR dominates the national economy and is the strategic point for the country's global linkages.

Trends of urbanization in Thailand

Thailand experienced rapid urbanization during the last two decades. The nation's urban centres grew by an average of 5.0 per cent annually compared to a 2.7 per cent rural population growth rate. From 1990 to 2010, the country's urban population growth is forecast to increase to approximately 3.0 per cent while rural population growth is expected to be negative (NESDB 1991).

Accurate measurement of urbanization in Thailand is still a problem, however, because of urban boundary definitions. This problem arises primarily from the fact that local governments often "underbound" actual built-up urban areas (Norconsult International 1996). Actual urban areas geographically are usually larger than the administrative boundaries. Table 12.4 shows that within the definition of urban municipalities and sanitary districts (population over 5,000), Thailand's urbanization rate was 28.5 per cent in 1992. The table also shows urbanization levels by region. Apart from Bangkok, which is 100 per cent urbanized, Bangkok's vicinity region has the highest urbanization level, about 46 per cent in 1992, while the north-east has the lowest urbanization level, about 16 per cent in 1992.

Future growth of urbanization in the BMR and ESB will be driven by in-migration responding to market forces, and Bangkok's domination in the Thai urban system will be weakened. Although Bangkok currently accounts for the highest percentage share of urban population in Thailand – 36 per cent in 1995 – the proportion has been declining. This decline will continue as other regions in the country become more attractive for business and residence. Table 12.5 presents population and urbanization forecasts for the country by region. By 2010, the eastern, north-eastern, and northern regions are expected to experience high urbanization rates and the north-east will have the highest urban growth rate (Norconsult International 1996).

Table 12.6 presents the current and predicted urbanization levels for each province of the EBR for five-year periods until 2010. Apart from Bangkok, the most urbanized EBR provinces are Nonthaburi (residential communities) and Samut Prakarn (industrial areas), both bordering Bangkok. High urbanization in the eastern region may be experienced by Chonburi, where there are currently high concentrations of services and industrialization, and Rayong, which boasts a growing industrial base.

Table 12.4 Percentage of urban population, by region and urban definition, 1990–1992

Urban definition	Whole country		Bangkok vicinity		Central		Eastern		Western		North-east		Northern		Southern	
	90	92	90	92	90	92	90	92	90	92	90	92	90	92	90	92
Municipality and sanitary population over 5,000	28.35	28.46	41.96	46.32	24.27	24.80	26.57	27.08	25.81	25.45	15.62	16.42	20.85	19.65	17.58	17.22
Municipality and sanitary population over 5,000 and greater than 1,000 persons per km^2	24.63	24.52	35.39	40.08	19.39	19.50	16.84	19.74	17.50	16.11	13.60	13.79	15.32	14.09	15.92	15.06
Urbanization projection for seventh plan																
Administrative definition	30.01		46.88		24.86		27.67		26.52		16.27		21.70		18.00	
Geographical definition	32.32		55.24		27.40		33.26		29.24		17.92		23.76		20.20	

Source: Norconsult International 1996

Table 12.5 Population and urbanization forecasts for Thailand

	1995 (millions)	2000 (millions)	2005 (millions)	2010 (millions)
Whole country	59.4	62.4	65.0	67.2
Urban	21.9	25.8	30.6	35.3
Rural	37.5	36.8	34.5	31.7
Percentage urban	36.9	41.0	46.9	52.8
Bangkok	8.0	9.1	10.3	11.5
BMR perimeter	3.3	3.6	4.2	5.0
North-east	19.4	19.9	20.0	20.1
Urban	3.4	4.5	5.9	7.5
Rural	16.0	15.4	14.1	12.6
Percentage urban	17.5	22.6	29.5	37.4
South	7.8	8.2	8.6	8.7
Urban	1.5	1.7	2.0	2.2
Rural	6.3	6.5	6.6	6.5
Percentage urban	19.1	20.8	23.2	25.2
North	10.9	11.1	10.8	10.6
Urban	2.6	3.0	3.4	3.7
Rural	8.3	8.1	7.4	6.9
Percentage urban	23.8	27.1	31.6	35.0
ESB II	5.8	6.3	6.9	7.2
Urban	2.0	2.7	3.5	4.0
Rural	3.8	3.6	3.4	3.2
Percentage urban	34.5	42.9	50.7	55.6
West and upper central	4.2	4.3	4.3	4.2
Urban	1.1	1.2	1.3	1.4
Rural	3.1	3.1	3.0	2.8
Percentage urban	26.1	28.1	30.2	33.0

Souce: Norconsult International 1996

In sum, Bangkok city has dominated Thai urbanization during the past three decades, but the degree of domination has started to decline. Currently, Bangkok is losing its share in Thailand's urbanization to other areas, but particularly to its surrounding provinces in the EBR. Thus, the urban growth remains concentrated within the EBR, particularly residential and industrial communities, and the inequality between the EBR and the outlying regions remains high.

Table 12.6 Predicted urbanization levels among provinces within the extended Bangkok region, 1990–2010

Province	1990	1995	2000	2005	2010
Bangkok	100.00	100.00	100.00	100.00	100.00
Nonthaburi	81.40	86.48	90.33	93.17	95.22
Pathum Thani	52.62	61.19	69.12	76.07	81.86
Samut Prakran	66.65	72.82	78.22	82.80	86.58
Samut Sakhon	40.88	44.67	48.53	52.40	56.24
Nakhon Pathom	24.41	28.81	33.64	38.85	44.32
Chonburi	61.76	67.69	73.09	77.89	82.04
Cha Choengsao	21.73	26.77	32.49	38.78	45.48
Rayong	39.61	47.72	55.95	63.87	71.10

Source: NESDB 1995

The extended Bangkok region: Interaction within subregions

Global forces are driving structural changes in the economy of the EBR. With the increasing industrial FDI inflows to Thailand, and more specifically into the EBR, the region underwent spatial and economic restructuring. At first manufacturing firms chose Bangkok as a location, but as the costs of land and labour in the city rose and major infrastructure investment projects in the ESB developed, new large firms, especially those in heavy industries, chose to locate in surrounding provinces or in the ESB region. Transportation infrastructure improvements now make the trip from Bangkok to the ESB convenient. Bangkok, however, continues to be the home of a large number of small-scale industries[8] and has the highest concentration of workers. Consequently, Bangkok's economy is increasingly dominated by service-sector and small-scale operations.

Figure 12.3 presents the structure of the economy within Bangkok, its five surrounding provinces, and the core ESB. The figures demonstrate the importance of the service sector to the Bangkok economy and the importance of industry to both the five surrounding provinces and the ESB. This is consistent with the findings of a study of regional specialization through the use of sectoral location quotients of employment[9] (LQs) (Kittiprapas 1995). The Bangkok service-sector LQ has dominated its industrial-sector LQ since the late 1980s. The five surrounding provinces have specialized in industrial production since 1977, while in the eastern region the industrial sector has clearly dominated since 1989, correlating with the development of the ESB. Although the five surrounding provinces and the ESB specialize in manufacturing industry, their sectoral characteristics are quite different. Industries in the five surrounding provinces are mainly

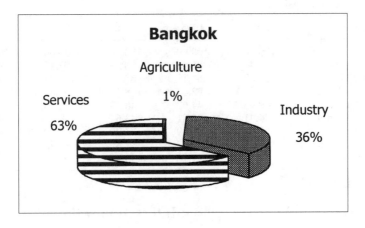

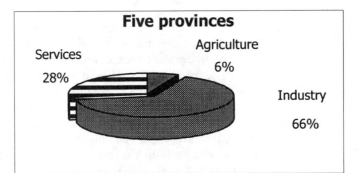

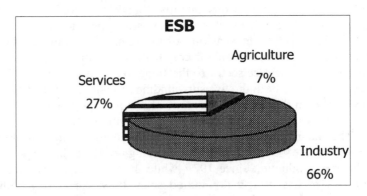

Figure 12.3 Structural GDP share of Bangkok, five surrounding provinces, and the core ESB region, 1995

Indexes

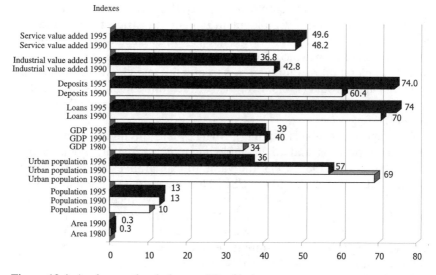

Figure 12.4 Agglomeration indexes of Bangkok

light industries such as electronics and textiles, while industrial clusters in the ESB are heavy industries such as petrochemicals, oil refineries, and steel.

Among the service subsectors in Bangkok, retail and wholesale trade, banking and finance, and transportation and utilities are the most important in terms of GDP share. In 1995, these sectors accounted for 46.3 per cent of the Bangkok GDP (outweighing the manufacturing-sector share, which contributed 31.1 per cent). During the bubble period of 1989–1993, within the BMR's GDP the banking, insurance, and real estate sectors had increased the fastest, reaching annual growth rates up to 150.46 per cent. Manufacturing growth rates followed these trends, with 63.7 per cent annual increases. Bangkok city dominates the business and professional services sector of the country, with all of the nation's commercial banking headquarters located within its borders. Agglomeration indexes shown in Figure 12.4 demonstrate Bangkok's domination in service sectors (indicated by variables of service value added, and commercial banks' loans and deposits). All of the indicators increased from 1990 to 1995, demonstrating continuing concentration of service activities, while the industrial value-added component declined. Bangkok's share in the nation's urban population also declined, from 57 per cent in 1990 to 36 per cent in 1995.

For the five surrounding provinces and the ESB, manufacturing GDP share dominates other components of the economy. The subregions gained the highest share of new employment in BOI-approved industries during the 1988–1993 period.[10] Employment in light industries, textiles and garments, services, and agro-industries were the engines of growth for the five surrounding provinces, while the ESB's employment gains were highest in metal fabrication and parts, ceramics and glassware, and chemical and paper products. The ESB also attracted the highest percentage of new BOI-approved foreign-registered capital (approximately 70 per cent in 1995).

Although the five surrounding provinces had the highest share of the number of projects and total employment in BOI-approved industries during the period 1988–1993, the value of capital investment still lagged behind that of Bangkok and the ESB. This reflects the fact that large-scale capital investment projects (heavy industries) have recently been located in the ESB, and production units in Bangkok are likely to be high value-added functions. As industries located in the five surrounding provinces are mostly light and labour-intensive industries, the area has not dominated capital investment but rather has increased the number of large-scale labour employment projects in the region.

Although Bangkok accounted for the highest share of factory establishments, its share had declined even before the rapid economic growth of the late 1980s and early 1990s (from 59 per cent in 1984 to 54 per cent in 1989) and, at the same time, the five provinces and the eastern region achieved positive growth rates from 1985 to 1989 (12.1 per cent and 4.5 per cent, respectively).

Bangkok has passed the industrial development stage and its economy has restructured toward higher-value services activities. The five surrounding provinces absorbed the economic sprawl as manufacturing production moved away from the city. The core ESB region is increasingly becoming an important centre for heavy industries. Its future depends on accessibility to the global economy and increasing investments in infrastructure, agglomeration economies from existing industrial clusters, and national promotion programmes. The developing specialization among these regions, driven by their unique comparative advantages, has lead to structural interdependence within the entire EBR.

The EBR's global linkages

The EBR is, no doubt, Thailand's strategic point of international linkages for both trade and people. The interaction of the EBR with the global economy and the Asia Pacific region can be viewed, for example, from the figures for international trade flows and tourist visitors.

Table 12.7 Inbound/outbound containers via the last port of call at Bangkok port, 1996–1998

	1996					
	Inbound		Outbound		Total	
Country	TEU	tonnes	TEU	tonnes	TEU	tonnes
Singapore	299,297	2,893,820	319,613	3,741,413	618,910 50%	6,635,233 51.3%
Hong Kong	131,022	1,116,108	129,718	1,752,326	260,740 21%	2,868,434 22.2%
Japan	115,957	921,609	108,644	1,209,136	224,601 18.2%	2,130,745 16.5%
Taiwan	39,528	364,999	30,093	411,606	69,621 5.6%	776,605 6%
Viet Nam	23,427	153,471	28,077	294,476	51,504 4.2%	447,947 3.5%
Europe	248	935	65	114	313 0%	1,049 0%
Korea	551	5,253	387	4,172	938 0%	9,425 0%
China	57	533	863	10,603	920 0%	11,136 0%
Africa	15	368	0	0	15 0%	368 0%
Malaysia						
Laem Chabang (Chonburi, Thailand)						
Others	31	275	5,017	56,184	5,048 0%	56,459 0%
Total	610,133	5,457,371	622,477	7,480,030	1,232,610	12,937,401

Source: Data collected from Port Authority of Thailand

Table 12.7 demonstrates the international trade flows through Bangkok's port (Klong Toey). The table shows that the port has been highly integrated with Asian ports, especially Singapore, which accounts for more than 50 per cent of the total trade volume, followed by Hong Kong and Japan. Table 12.8 shows international trade flows to Laem Chabang port in Chonburi in the ESB. Similar to the flows at the Bangkok port, most of trade is from Asian ports, particularly Singapore, Japan, and Hong Kong.

The Bangkok international airport (Don Muang) is an important transportation hub in the Asia Pacific. Serving global visitors, the airport is the most important tourist gateway to Thailand. Table 12.9 shows that the majority of tourists visiting Thailand during 1995–1998 were from East

Table 12.7 (cont.)

	1997					
	Inbound		Outbound		Total	
Country	TEU	tonnes	TEU	tonnes	TEU	tonnes
Singapore	274,834	2,299,910	306,998	3,556,507	581,832 53%	5,856,417 52.1%
Hong Kong	121,634	883,190	116,645	1,624,886	238,279 22%	2,508,076 22.3%
Japan	97,675	710,681	98,537	1,105,610	196,212 18%	1,816,291 16.2%
Taiwan	39,534	386,006	29,766	457,652	69,300 6%	843,658 8%
Viet Nam	7,904	51,683	7,514	88,719	15,418 1%	140,402 1.2%
Europe	93	282	10	20	103 0%	302 0%
Korea	711	4,175	909	10,581	1,620 0%	14,756 0%
China	644	7,993	791	13,927	1,435 0%	21,920 0%
Africa	508	514	0	0	508 0%	514 0%
Malaysia	192	2,124	743	11,069	935 0%	13,193 0%
Laem Chabang (Chonburi, Thailand) Others	316	2,651	1,197	19,946	1,513 0%	22,597 0%
Total	544,045	4,349,209	563,110	6,888,917	1,107,155	11,238,126

Asia (60 per cent or more), indicating the high mobility of people within the region.

Indicators of trade flows and movement of people suggest that Bangkok is strongly linked to East Asian countries. Thus, transportation infrastructure development in cities in the EBR would enhance the development of the region as a whole.

Towards liveable cities and sustainable development

The Bangkok Metropolitan Administration (BMA) government has plans to make the city "liveable" by providing a clean and safe environment through public and social services, recreational opportunities, and pre-

Table 12.7 (cont.)

Country	1998					
	Inbound		Outbound		Total	
	TEU	tonnes	TEU	tonnes	TEU	tonnes
Singapore	274,240	2,226,683	319,370	3,770,430	593,610 55%	5,997,113 52%
Hong Kong	135,089	1,151,883	120,291	1,774,607	255,380 24%	2,926,490 25.4%
Japan	75,024	601,620	94,842	1,153,009	169,866 16%	1,754,629 15.2%
Taiwan	22,079	274,452	15,092	248,994	37,171 3%	523,446 5%
Viet Nam	5,484	80,708	6,183	80,425	11,667 1%	161,133 1.4%
Europe						
Korea						
China						
Africa						
Malaysia	3,452	28,861	7,224	99,715	10,676 1%	128,576 1%
Laem Chabang (Chonburi, Thailand)	379	8,008	924	11,991	1,303 0%	19,999 0%
Others	351	406	463	7,149	814 0%	7,555 0%
Total	516,098	4,372,621	564,389	7,146,320	1,080,487	11,518,941

ferred amenities. Limited formal authority of the local governments, sectoral fragmentation among government agencies, and intergovernmental relationships, however, limit the ability of the BMA government to improve liveable conditions of the city directly. Notwithstanding these limitations, however, progress has been made in three areas that have been constraining Bangkok's development: infrastructure development, especially for transportation improvement, environmental quality, and human resources development for high-value production and knowledge-intensive activities.

Infrastructure development

Communication infrastructure is the key to future global competitiveness in the information age, and privatization and sectoral reform regulations

Table 12.8 Numbers of containers in and out at Chonburi, Laem Chabang port, 1997–1998

Country	August 1996–July 1997	%	August 1997–July 1998	%
Singapore				
Inbound	59,159	26.27	53,458	21.93
Outbound	95,575	30.47	97,541	30.02
Total	154,734	28.71	150,999	26.56
Hong Kong				
Inbound	19,350	8.59	25,301	10.38
Outbound	30,776	9.81	34,809	10.71
Total	50,126	9.30	60,110	10.57
Japan				
Inbound	38,045	16.89	41,962	17.22
Outbound	45,991	14.66	50,561	15.56
Total	84,036	15.59	92,523	16.27
Taiwan				
Inbound	14,515	6.45	18,359	7.53
Outbound	15,865	5.06	18,152	5.59
Total	30,380	5.64	36,511	6.42
Indonesia				
Inbound	8,651	3.84	8,669	3.56
Outbound	9,493	3.03	8,720	2.68
Total	18,144	3.37	17,389	3.06
Spain				
Inbound	12,025	5.34	15,885	6.52
Outbound	13,751	4.38	15,982	4.92
Total	25,776	4.78	31,867	5.60
Italy				
Inbound	11,417	5.07	14,465	5.93
Outbound	12,631	4.03	14,915	4.59
Total	24,048	4.46	29,380	5.17
France				
Inbound	10,140	4.50	11,539	4.73
Outbound	11,096	3.54	11,418	3.51
Total	21,236	3.94	22,957	4.04
Sweden				
Inbound	9,521	4.23	9,701	3.98
Outbound	10,466	3.34	9,987	3.07
Total	19,987	3.71	19,688	3.46
American				
Inbound	17,507	7.77	18,673	7.66
Outbound	36,932	11.77	31,929	9.83
Total	54,439	10.10	50,602	8.90

Table 12.8 (cont.)

Country	August 1996– July 1997	%	August 1997– July 1998	%
Others				
Inbound	24,859	11.04	25,732	10.56
Outbound	31,103	9.92	30,860	9.50
Total	55,962	10.39	56,592	9.95
Total inbound containers	225,189	100.00	243,744	100.00
Total outbound containers	313,679	100.00	324,874	100.00
Total inbound/ outbound containers	538,868	100.00	568,618	100.00

Source: Data collected from Port Authority of Thailand

are under way in this area. Telecommunications projects within Bangkok include the expansion of telephone lines, national satellite projects, cable networks, and new high-technology installations such as an integrated service digital network (ISDN) and fibre optic networks. In terms of basic telephone service, there has been a great increase in the number of telephone lines since the late 1980s (Figure 12.5) and the waiting lists for new telephones have declined since 1993 (Lueprasitsakul 1998), after the Telephone Organization of Thailand (TOT) granted concessions for providing new telephone lines and services to private companies, which facilitated the installation. In 1995 it could take up to 1.9 years to get a telephone line from TOT (International Telecommunication Union 1997), but now services can be installed in some localities by a private concessionaire (Telecom Asia or TT&T) and TOT within a week. Within the country as a whole, Bangkok city has the highest "teledensity" at approximately 50 units per 100 persons (Telephone Organization of Thailand 1997).

Presently, many of the advanced communication services, including mobile phones, paging services, ISDN, leased circuits, data communications, and Internet connections, are allocated through build-transfer-operate (BTO) concessions given to private sector investors. Two state organizations, TOT for domestic services and the Communications Authority of Thailand (CAT) for international services, monopolize the allocation of concessions. Private investment, including foreign joint ventures through BTO, has led to a drastic expansion in telecommunications infrastructure, which allows the country, and Bangkok in particular, to move higher up the ladder of development into a more value-added manufacturing and service-based economy. According to WTO regulations, all telecommunications businesses must be liberalized by 2006, after TOT and CAT are

Table 12.9 International tourist arrivals to Thailand by residence, 1996–1998

Country of residence	1995 arrivals		1996 arrivals		1997 arrivals		1998 arrivals	
	Number	%	Number	%	Number	%	Number	%
Total	6,951,566	100.0	7,192,145	100.0	7,221,345	100.0	7,764,930	100.0
East Asia	4,358,354	62.7	4,513,315	62.8	4,568,837	63.3	4,583,160	59.0
ASEAN	1,793,374	25.8	1,713,616	23.8	1,767,316	24.5	1,765,488	22.7
Brunei	5,842	0.1	6,668	0.1	6,938	0.1	12,569	0.2
Indonesia	93,274	1.3	85,757	1.2	89,110	1.2	69,474	0.9
Laos	94,056	1.4	24,288	0.3	28,301	0.4	49,738	0.6
Malaysia	1,077,005	15.5	1,056,172	14.7	1,046,029	14.5	918,071	11.8
Philippines	69,046	1.0	77,732	1.1	76,727	1.1	78,181	1.0
Singapore	430,824	6.2	437,103	6.1	492,089	6.8	586,113	7.5
Viet Nam	23,327	0.3	25,896	0.4	28,122	0.4	51,342	0.7
China	375,564	5.4	456,912	6.4	439,795	6.1	571,061	7.4
Hong Kong	346,254	5.0	396,679	5.5	472,325	6.5	517,966	6.7
Japan	814,706	11.7	934,111	13.0	965,454	13.4	986,264	12.7
Korea	456,228	6.6	488,669	6.8	411,087	5.7	202,841	2.6
Taiwan	492,189	7.1	447,124	6.2	448,280	6.2	457,360	5.9
Others	80,039	1.2	76,204	1.1	64,580	0.9	82,180	1.1
Europe	1,574,491	22.6	1,605,113	22.3	1,585,916	22.0	1,888,673	24.3
Americas	357,674	5.1	383,925	5.3	388,190	5.4	448,761	5.8
South Asia	270,478	3.9	271,269	3.8	229,571	3.2	258,815	3.3
Oceania	223,953	3.2	251,876	3.5	271,442	3.8	348,346	4.5
Middle East	119,358	1.7	119,198	1.7	126,427	1.8	165,078	2.1
Africa	47,258	0.7	47,449	0.7	50,963	0.7	72,097	0.9

Source: Data collected from Tourism Authority of Thailand

Number of telephone lines

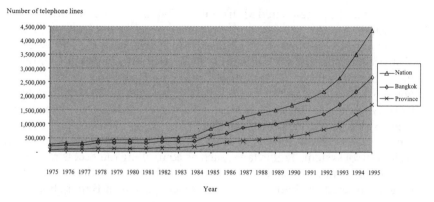

Year

Figure 12.5 Telephone line capacity for Thailand, 1975–1995

privatized. A more competitive structure within these industries as well as technological innovation in the future would bring lower costs and offer people easier access to information. Currently, the cost of mobile phone handsets[11] from privately owned mobile phone companies ranges between 10,000 and 50,000 baht, and call fees are three baht a minute for local calls plus a lump-sum service fee of 500 baht a month. These costs are relatively high for ordinary Thais. With a more competitive structure in this industry, these telecom services could be offered to people at lower costs and be made available to broader groups of customers. With market liberalization the costs may be more affordable, and should enhance the economic growth of the city and the Asia Pacific linkages.

The main infrastructure bottleneck in Bangkok continues to be in the area of transportation. Traffic congestion has been a serious problem for Bangkok for several decades. Time-consuming commutes and wasted energy are responsible for significant losses of economic production[12] and negative health effects.[13] The root cause of these problems is the city's lack of efficient public and mass transportation systems. Though many mass transit systems have been planned over the past 25 years, they were not implemented. Mass transit systems and expressways were uncoordinated, and fell within the jurisdictions of various government agencies. For example, several different mass transit plans were designed or constructed in Bangkok in 1990 (Unger 1998), and required coordination between the Highways Department within the Ministry of Transport and Communications, the State Railways of Thailand, the Expressways and Rapid Transit Authority, and the Bangkok Metropolitan Administration, among others.

Current efforts to relieve the problems have met with mixed success. Positive signs, however, include the construction of a subway and elevated rail systems. The state-owned Metropolitan Rapid Transit Authority grants concessions for the subway and skytrain project operations to private companies, and presently the rail mass transit system in the city is under construction. The first 20 kilometres of the city subway (Hua Lumpong-Queen Sirikit National Convention Centre-Bangsue) is a private sector endeavour and is expected to be fully operational by 2004 (*The Nation* 1999). Other major infrastructure projects are proceeding, despite stalled progress due to the current economic crisis. Also, the Bangkok government has successfully improved traffic flows with a computerized aerial traffic control system. Traffic laws, such as controlling the access routes for heavy trucks and traffic lane regulations, have been strengthened. Options being considered for improving mass transit systems in Bangkok are bus and van systems, river and canal transportation using boats, transit links with future metropolitan rail systems, and mass transit for tourists (tourist trams and open-deck buses).[14]

Before the financial crisis, the ESB was slated to be the location for a variety of transportation-related major infrastructure developments. Projects included expansion of the major port (Laem Chabang Port Phase II), a high-speed train system, a dual-rail train system, the second Bangkok international airport (at Nong Ngu Hao), and a global transpark at U-Tapao. Most of these projects have to be financed through private means rather than government investment. The major deep-sea ports in the ESB will continue to draw shipping activities away from Bangkok. The global transpark facility can provide interconnections between air, land, sea, and telecommunications systems, facilitating the delivery of components on "just-in-time" schedules. As a result of the financial crisis, some projects have been delayed (such as the high-speed train), while some are planned for scaling down (such as the global transpark project). The second Bangkok international airport construction, financed by Japanese aid loans, will proceed as planned. The new airport, expected to begin operation by 2004, will serve an estimated 40 million passengers annually.

Infrastructure development projects require strong institutional arrangements for their swift and successful completion. Within Thailand, while many agencies are involved in projects within overlapping areas, conflicts between different agencies frequently occur. Proposals, planning, and construction coordination (of mass transit systems, for example) are under the authority of different agencies. Needless to say, these agencies are not coordinating their efforts. Local governments have no authority to manage major development projects in their jurisdictions because most such projects are under the authority of central government agencies. For example, expressway, subway, and elevated rail systems in Bangkok city are under the Ministry of Interior; utilities such as piped water and electricity in

Bangkok are also operated by state enterprises under the Ministry of Interior. The BMA has no authority to manage or integrate development plans for these infrastructure investments in the city. When problems arise, it is difficult for the local agency to respond to problems quickly. Traffic in Bangkok, for example, is a long-term problem handled by more than 10 central government agencies, which has led to the delay and difficulties in solving the problem.

As Thailand's local governments still lack authority in managing local infrastructure and in integrating development plans in their own jurisdictions, decentralization of administration from the central government is recommended. The Bangkok government in particular faces a big obstacle in integrating development plans and has limited capability to respond to problems. Therefore, in addition to clarifying the functions of different government agencies, decentralization and giving more authority to local government is needed to speed up Bangkok's development and enhance efficient management.

Environmental control

A serious obstacle to Bangkok's sustainable development is the high level of urban environmental degradation. A summary of environmental problems in Bangkok is shown in a "radar graph" in Figure 12.6 (Kruger Consult 1996). The most serious problems (level 5) are those of air quality, traffic, shortage of open space (public parks), slums, sewerage services, and ground pollution (due to dumping of chemical pollutants and hazardous substances). However, it is generally agreed that the most serious environmental problem in Bangkok is air pollution, mainly from traffic congestion; approximately 60–70 per cent of air pollution in Bangkok is the product of the city's traffic (Kaothien and Webster 1995). Locations of high congestion within the city have dust and noise pollution levels above the maximum permissible standards.[15] Rising levels of suspended particulate matter have become an increasingly serious issue, as levels continue to increase over acceptable limits. Figure 12.7 shows that 14 roadside stations in Bangkok report higher levels of suspended particulate matter (dust and smoke) than the standard level of 0.33 mg/m^3, with dust levels ranging from 0.4 to 1.3 mg/m^3. While vehicle emissions are the largest source of air pollution, emissions from industrial sources are also important, particularly for the ESB, where heavy industry is a significant contributor to declining air quality.

Traffic-related noise levels are also a problem within Bangkok. In places the noise levels are above 80 decibels, compared to the 70 decibels standard. As truck traffic contributes significantly to the noise problem, mea-

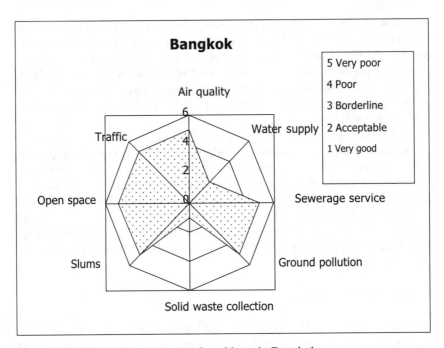

Figure 12.6 Levels of environmental problems in Bangkok
Source: Kruger Consult 1996

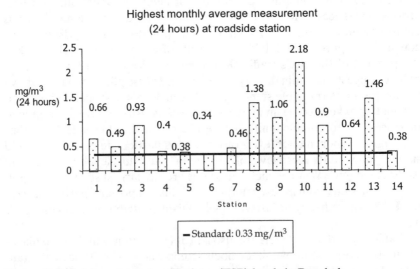

Figure 12.7 Total suspended particulates (TSP) levels in Bangkok
Source: Kruger Consult 1996

sures to control the access routes of truck traffic to the inner city during certain times may help reduce this problem.

The second most serious environmental problem within Bangkok is water pollution caused by domestic waste. Although as of 1995 only 2.0 per cent of the population in Bangkok was served by a sewerage network (Setchell 1995), vigorous efforts are under way to connect as much as 20 per cent of the Bangkok metropolitan area's population by early in the twenty-first century (Kaothien and Webster 1995). In addition, there are water resource problems such as insufficient piped water supply in some areas, flooding, and land subsidence. Flooding seems to be a perennial problem for Bangkok because there is no long-term flood control plan for this city with low elevation and high land subsidence.

Another problem generated by rapid industrialization-led urbanization is the creation of poor working environments for employees. Many factories contribute to work-related injuries or have dangerous working conditions. Of particular concern is the potential danger of accidents due to hazardous chemicals. Most of the nation's chemical firms, some 75 per cent of such factories, are located in the BMR (Phantumvanit 1989). This problem requires effective enforcement of accident prevention regulations.

The BMA has emphasized environmental improvement of the city, and has recently been successful in increasing "green" spaces (more public parks and roadside trees), in addition to improving dust control (from trucks and construction).

As the city's industrial base shifts to services and light industry, the type of urban environmental stress will change. Traffic and its related harmful emissions continue to be a problem in the city. At the same time, however, major industrial problems and health risks have shifted to the ESB. Industrial zones, especially those with petrochemical plants or oil refineries, are blamed for health problems in their neighbourhood. As evidenced by the contemporary history of Bangkok, these problems are difficult to solve once land development has taken place. Relocating industries or communities is costly. Obviously, new forms of urban management and regulation are needed to tackle these issues, for they will be with us way into the twenty-first century.

Human resource development

The new "knowledge" society of the twenty-first century places a premium on human resources as a determining factor for a country's successful economic development. Important tools for competition are related to the ability to turn new ideas into marketable products or services, and international competition is increasingly based upon quality.

As the Thai economy is highly integrated into the global economy, the country's workforce must be prepared with skills fit for the rapidly changing needs and demands of the global market. Education and training systems must adjust to meet these dynamic challenges so that the country can climb up the comparative advantage ladder.

To be competitive in the global economy, Bangkok needs to offer various kinds of effective training in order to prepare people for dynamic changes and a modern economy. The nature of modern technologies also demands high skills acquired through both education and on-the-job training. Shortage of skilled labour is a major constraint for Thailand in climbing up to the "late industry" stage of development. Currently, major high-tech industries still import high-skilled labour from abroad. For example, in the ESB, petrochemical industries in which investment in training for production is very costly have to hire additional skilled workers from the NICs, particularly Taiwan. In the future global economy, timely responses will be more critical than cheap labour. Human capital training has to be supported by information technology infrastructure as well. Education systems must increasingly produce high-level competence in basic skills such as languages, sciences, mathematics, and information technology, as well as promoting creativity and imagination. Thus, local institutions and policy planners will have to deal seriously with the preparation of human resources for the dynamic changes predicted for the region.

Conclusions and recommendations for strategic roles for Bangkok and the EBR

With the increasing importance of global linkages, it is expected that the subregions within the EBR will face more economic restructuring and more specialization in economic functions. These trends in specialization are expected to increase along with increasing trade flows among regions and nations.

Flows of international trade as well as human resources will affect economic growth in the subregions. The strategic roles of Bangkok, the five surrounding provinces, and the core ESB region should be based on their comparative advantages, both nationally and internationally. While Bangkok's surrounding provinces and the ESB emerge as important industrial bases for multinational operations, Bangkok city has more advantages in attracting a number of service sectors.

Concerning constraints in Bangkok's development so far, the city should strengthen its roles in the sectors in which it has comparative advantages. Bangkok city may well serve the Asia Pacific region in a number of service functions. Apart from manufacturing-support service functions, Bangkok has been famous for excellent tourism-related services (such as hotel accommodation, food, shopping, etc.), and still attracts foreign tourists from virtually every part of the world. Increasing flows of global visitors along with the relatively greater freedom of the Thai media (compared to other South-East Asian countries) may also enable the city to support and develop international mass media, given the provision of good infrastructure like telecommunications networks.

As Bangkok is a strategic location for international transportation within the Indochina region, the city can strengthen its position as a regional transportation hub as well as playing a leading role in the development of the region in areas such as education, trade, and tourism services. With further development of transnational transport links, Bangkok can serve as a gateway to the Indochinese region. The ESB can also serve as an important manufacturing centre and a major port in the region.

Given the current limited government revenue, more private sector involvement is necessary to finance prioritized projects for urban infrastructure and the environment. Currently, regulation reforms for the privatization of state enterprises and infrastructure projects are in process. Many infrastructure projects in Bangkok have been planned for privatization, such as expressway systems, the state-owned Bangkok Metropolitan Transit Authority, the metropolitan rail transit system, community trains, and elevated highway projects, as well as many telecommunications projects.

To finance the needed urban environmental infrastructure, privatization of environmental management activities (such as solid waste disposal and wastewater treatment) is recommended. Also, methods such as the cost-recovery pricing of environmental infrastructure (for wastewater and solid waste management) would help to supply the environmental facilities to meet demand.

In addition to environmental regulations, policy options should take the costs of environmental degradation into account through pricing policies. Similar to the case of infrastructure development, local government has limited authority in dealing with local environmental pricing policies and regulations. The implementation of pollution pricing (fuel tax, charges on old vehicles) would be an effective way to reduce traffic-related pollution. To that end, local governments, which currently have no authority, should be empowered to implement local pricing policies. Energy prices and taxes, for example, are fixed nationally with the same rates across the board, but the cost of environmental degradation locally cannot be taken into account without local pricing policies.

Bangkok also has to move forward in upgrading products and services. To be competitive in the future global economy of the Asia Pacific region, products and services have to be approved to reach globally acceptable standards of quality, with competitive production costs. The ability to use modern technology and information is essential for cost-competitive quality manufacturing production as well as for advanced business services.

It is thus important to prepare people, planners, and policy-makers for the future changing environment. This also calls for increasing public and private participation and the empowerment of local authorities. In managing city development, for example, decentralization of management administration to local authorities is essential. Education systems should be able to adjust training programmes to respond to the rapid dynamic changes. Only with global thinking, knowledge, and ideas will Bangkok have the capability to manage challenges and take advantages of new opportunities, and adjust better to the global economy of the twenty-first century.

Notes

1. The BMR includes Bangkok and its five surrounding provinces, Nontaburi, Pathum Thani, Samut Prakarn, Samut Sakorn, and Nakorn Prathom. The BMR is not a legal or governing entity, however, as there are no regional governments in Thailand.
2. The ESB includes the core eastern seaboard provinces of Chachoengsao, Chonburi, and Rayong.
3. Bangkok is located on the delta plain of the Chao Praya river, and has historically been the centre hub in the interregional transportation system. The river was formerly the main commercial transportation route within the country and the delta port, on the Gulf of Thailand, promoted international linkages. Thus, since the early nineteenth century the city has dominated the urban system of the country.
4. These data were calculated from the Labour Force Survey, Round 1 of the National Statistical Office, Office of Prime Minister (1998).
5. Budget Bureau, Office of Prime Minister.
6. Labour Force Survey, August 1998.
7. Calculated from the Labour Force Survey, August 1997–1998.
8. In 1995, Bangkok was the location of approximately 48 per cent of all factories in the country.
9. The employment index reflects the cluster of workers within each sector.
10. Board of Investment (BOI).
11. The estimate was true as of early 1999.
12. A study sponsored by the Japanese government suggested that Bangkok was losing about a third of its potential production due to the impact of traffic congestion (Unger 1998).
13. Results of a study by Trakannuwatkul (1996) suggest that suspended particulate matter in Bangkok is significantly related to respiratory morbidity in Bangkok. This is significant since respiratory morbidity accounts for as much as 13 per cent of total morbidity within the city.
14. From an interview with the BMA government, Planning Division.
15. Pollution Control Department, Ministry of Science, Technology, and Environment.

REFERENCES

Biggs, Tyler, Peter Brimble, Donald Snodgrass, and Michael Murray. 1990. *Rural Industry and Employment Study: A Synthesis Report*. Bangkok: Thailand Development Research Institute.

Ichikawa, Nobuko. 1990. "Foreign and direct investment in Thailand: A regional analysis", Background Report Nos. 1–4, National Urban Development Policy Framework. Bangkok: Thailand Development Research Institute.

International Telecommunication Union. 1997. *World Telecommunication Development Report 1996/97*. Geneva: International Telecommunication Union.

Kaothien, Utis and Douglas Webster. 1995. "Bangkok: Regional form, economic restructuring, and changing social expectations", paper presented to International Symposium on Regional Cities, Cambridge, MA.

Kittiprapas, Sauwalak. 1995. "Regional concentration and the location behaviour of manufacturing firms in the electronics and automobile industries in Thailand", PhD dissertation, University of Pennsylvania, Philadelphia.

Kittiprapas, Sauwalak and Philip McCann. 1999a. "Industrial location behaviour and regional restructuring within the fifth tiger economy: Evidence from the Thai electronics industry", *Journal of Applied Economics*, Vol. 31, No. 1, pp. 37–51.

Kittiprapas, Sauwalak and Philip McCann. 1999b. "Regional development in Thailand: Some observations from the Thai automotive industry", *ASEAN Economic Bulletin*, Vol. 16, No. 2, pp. 190–207.

Kruger Consult. 1996. *Urban Environmental Management in Thailand: A Strategic Planning Process*. Bangkok: NESDB/DANCED.

Lueprasitsakul, Pipat. 1998. "An empirical study of network externality: The case of Thailand's telephone system", PhD dissertation, Temple University, Philadelphia.

National Economic and Social Development Board (NESDB). 1991. *National Urban Development Policy Framework*. Bangkok: NESDB/UNDP/TDRI.

National Economic and Social Development Board (NESDB). 1995. *Metropolitan Regional Structure Planning Study*. Bangkok: NESDB.

Norconsult International. 1996. *A Spatial Development Framework for Thailand*. Bangkok: NESDB/NORAD.

Phanthumvanit, Dhira. 1989. "Coming to terms with Bangkok's environment problems", *Environment and Urbanization*, Vol. 1, No. 1, pp. 31–39.

Renaud, Bertrand, Ming Zhang, and Stefan Koeberle. 1998. "How the Thai real estate boom undid financial institutions – What should be done now?" paper presented at the Conference on Thailand's Dynamic Economic Recovery and Competitiveness, Bangkok: NESDB/World Bank.

Setchell, Charles A. 1995. "The growing environmental crisis in the world's megacities: The case of Bangkok", *Third World Planning Review*, Vol. 17, No. 1, pp. 1–17.

Telephone Organization of Thailand. 1997. *Telephone Statistics 1997*. Bangkok: Telephone Organization of Thailand.

The Nation. 1999. 6 April.

Trakannuwatkul, Maneerut. 1996. "Economic analysis of air pollution and health: A case study of Bangkok", MA thesis, Thammasat University, Bangkok, Thailand.

Unger, Danny. 1998. *Building Social Capital in Thailand: Fibres, Finance, and Infrastructure.* Cambridge: Cambridge University Press.

The amenity cities

13

Globalization and the sustainability of cities in the Asia Pacific region: The case of Sydney

Peter A. Murphy and Chung-Tong Wu

Introduction

Economic globalization simultaneously challenges and provides new opportunities for the sustainable development of cities in the Asia Pacific region. The term "sustainability" refers to economies, societies, and biophysical environments, all of which are interrelated. With respect to ecologically sustainable development (ESD), the decreased financial capacity of elected governments – resulting from lower per capita levels of economic growth in such Asia Pacific nations as Australia and Canada – may lead to underinvestment in urban infrastructure and/or impel a shift to private provision. Such trends may, in turn, entail ecological opportunity costs. In many of the cities of East and South-East Asia – such as Bangkok, Taipei, Seoul, and Shanghai – globalization has propelled economic growth at rates far in excess of the political and financial capacities of governments to cope. The economic downturn of the late 1990s in East and South-East Asia could see governments regressing to a "growth at all costs" strategy just when a shift in favour of the environment had been gathering momentum. Despite such scenarios, economic globalization in principle provides the basis for a shift to ecologically sustainable cities. First, there is the standard argument that when economic development has produced a sufficiently high level of per capita welfare, political acceptance of the need to clean up the environment will be forthcoming. Second, there is the argument that for post-industrial cities (such as Sydney and Vancouver) a high-quality environment is an essential element of their competitive advantage in attracting tourists and business investment. A high-quality environment, in this sense, requires high levels of "amenity" deriving from both the natural and the built environment. In the case of the natural environment (the focus of ecologically sustainable development), amenities such as clean air and water (for personal consumption and recreational uses) are critical. High amenity in the built environment entails the conservation of heritage values, good urban design, low levels of traffic congestion, and the like.[1] So ecological sustainability is integral to economic sustainability. Economic sustainability is also critical to social sustainability, although – it will be argued in this chapter – measures to promote economic development, especially measures involving city planning, create an uneven pattern of benefits and costs for those living in different parts of the city.

As an economically advanced nation with a high average welfare level and a pronounced shift towards a post-industrial economic structure, at least in its cities, Australia might be expected to have high levels of urban environmental quality and strong governance to support this. In fact, while things are obviously better than in many other cities in the Asia Pacific, they are still far from adequate. The particular spatial structure of Australian cities, their social composition, their forms of governance, and their varying economic prospects result in a complex mixture of opportunities and constraints that, in general, is not optimal for the achievement of ecological sustainability.

This chapter addresses the relationship between globalization and the ecological sustainability of Australia's largest and most globalized city, metropolitan Sydney. In terms of its spatial structure and governance, Sydney is arguably representative of Australian cities as a class. However, among major metropolitan areas in Australia, Sydney most sharply represents the challenge of achieving sustainability, because of its large size and unique physical setting. The chapter's focus on ecological sustainability reflects the particular importance of environmental amenity (deriving from both the biophysical and built environments) to cities like Sydney, as the basis for their economic sustainability. Indeed, it is this dependence on amenity-driven economic development that gives Sydney a particular niche in the system of Asia Pacific cities. It should also be noted that in producing ecologically sustainable development Sydney's governance has to deal with significant questions of social sustainability. The first part of the chapter gives details Sydney's globalization, especially in the context of the system of cities in the Asia Pacific region. Interconnected aspects of the city's internal spatial structure, its governance, and environmental quality – and how these have been influenced by, or mediate, the pressures of globalization – are then characterized. The second part of the chapter addresses financial and political constraints on achieving sustainability, with specific attention being given to direct and indirect effects of globalization.

Before proceeding, however, three key terms – globalization, governance, and ecological sustainability – need to be defined.

As an economic phenomenon, globalization refers to the increasing interdependence of national and subnational economies. Since interdependence may be economically either beneficial or detrimental (or some combination of both), governments seek to blunt negative impacts and to grasp opportunities for development. While for the purposes of this chapter globalization is regarded as being an essentially economic phenomenon, there are important social, cultural, and political ramifications. Especially significant in an urban context are the vast short- and long-term movements of people responding to opportunities, which consequently generate change in the cities of the world.

In the language of political studies, urban governance is produced from the intersecting domains of elected government, the private sector, and civil society, with elected government ultimately (in theory) being the arbiter and mediator of changes in cities. Urban managerial governance is centrally concerned with the regulation of land use and the provision of infrastructure. Urban entrepreneurial governance, on the other hand, seeks to capture geographically mobile consumption and investment flows. Since the latter may involve land use and infrastructure issues, managerial and entrepreneurial governance may be intertwined, and that relationship is strengthening in cities like Sydney and Vancouver (Murphy and Wu 1998). The interest of both forms of urban governance is sustainable development in its ecological, social, and economic senses.

In an urban context, ecologically sustainable development (ESD) is obviously concerned with air and water quality, plant and animal populations and ecosystems, agricultural land, and ecological footprints. In practice, ESD means halting and/or reversing environmental degradation. ESD principles include the maintenance of intergenerational equity, intragenerational equity, and biodiversity. They also require implementation of the precautionary principle in decisions that may impact negatively on the biophysical environment.

The Sydney region

In order to assess the relationship between Sydney's ecological sustainability and its incorporation into the global economy, aspects of the city's development, spatial structure, governance, and environmental quality need to be considered. The first section of this part of the chapter demonstrates why Sydney is regarded as being Australia's most globalized city, particularly in the context of the Asia Pacific region. The implications of this for the maintenance and improvement of environmental amenity, including investment in urban infrastructure, are stressed. The structures of Sydney's managerial and entrepreneurial governance are then outlined prior to presenting key indicators of levels and trends in environmental quality. Finally, the influence of Sydney's urban form on ecological sustainability is discussed and linked with key contemporary challenges faced by managerial governance.

Sydney in the Asia Pacific region

Sydney is the capital city of the Australian state of New South Wales (NSW). Figure 13.1 is a regional map that may be referred to at various points throughout the text. Sydney's population – approaching 4 million – represents 21 per cent of the Australian total. The city also contains 62 per cent of the NSW population and thus dominates the state's economy and politics. Population growth rates fluctuate, primarily in response to levels of immigration, but currently stand at less than 1 per cent per annum. Gross residential densities of about 18 persons per hectare are low by European, and very low by Asian, standards (Newman and Kenworthy 1991).

Sydney is Australia's most globalized city (NSW Department of State and Regional Development 1997; NSW Government 1997). As one index of this status, Sydney has captured a much higher share of regional headquarters (RHQs) of transnational corporations serving the Asia Pacific region than has its strongest Australian competitor, Melbourne, which is Australia's second largest city. Thus of the 259 international companies with RHQs or major operating centres in Australia that were established between 1990 and 1998, 163 located in Sydney, 59 in Melbourne, and 37 in other Australian cities (unpublished data from the Commonwealth Department of Industry, Science, and Tourism). In particular, Sydney hosts headquarters and RHQs of three-quarters of the international and domestic banks operating in Australia. It also has Australia's largest stock exchange and the country's only futures exchange, the latter rivalling competitors – such as Tokyo and Hong Kong – in the Asia Pacific region. Sydney's employment structure reflects this trend. Thus jobs in the finance, professional services, and property sector increased by 119,537 between 1971 and 1991 and now represent 15.4 per cent of the city's employment. In strong contrast, manufacturing jobs decreased by 140,000 over the same period, and declined from 28 to 14 per cent of the labour force.

Sydney's competitive advantage over other Australian cities derives

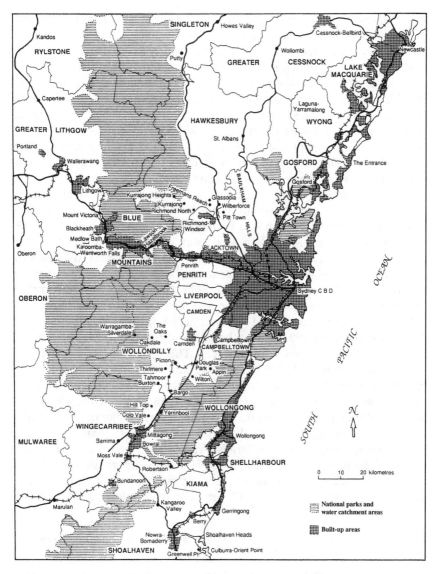

Figure 13.1 The Sydney region

partly from Kingsford Smith airport's (KSA) dominance as the hub of
air traffic into and out of Australia. KSA is serviced by more than 37 international airlines, offering 408 direct flights a week to more than 100
destinations – non-stop to the USA, Japan, the Republic of Korea, Hong
Kong, and South-East Asia, and one-stop to the UK and Europe (NSW

Department of State and Regional Development 1997). This compares with Melbourne's 26 airlines and 142 direct weekly international flights. Figures for other Australian cities are also much lower than for Sydney.

The city's environmental amenity and multicultural character are also key competitive advantages. Environmental amenity is based on an equable climate (warm summers and mild winters), a large and beautiful harbour, and renowned ocean beaches. Cultural connections between actual or potential trading partners are also considered to be an important element of competitive advantage (Anderson 1993). An example is the symbiotic relationship that is evolving between Hong Kong, a command and control centre and/or conduit of investment capital, and the explosive growth of manufacturing in the adjacent Pearl river delta of China. There is a parallel relationship between the USA and Mexico. Less tightly symbiotic, and not as strongly based on shared culture, is the relationship between Australian and Asian economies. Here, discourses of multiculturalism and the high number of Asian migrants to Sydney, in particular, are deployed by commonwealth and NSW state governments to stress cultural continuities. These links are enhanced by Australia's proximity to Asia relative to Europe and the USA.

Immigration to Sydney and Melbourne has always dominated other Australian cities. In 1991 Sydney had 28.5 per cent and Melbourne 23.7 per cent of total persons born overseas. The figures for recent overseas born – those who settled between 1986 and 1991 – were, respectively, 36.2 per cent and 23.5 per cent. Sydney has thus opened up a marked lead over Melbourne that contrasts with the 1950s and 1960s when Melbourne had a lead over Sydney.[2] This trend is emphasized by the figures in Table 13.1, which show shares of growth in overseas born with shares of national population growth for the five largest Australian cities. The geographical source of immigrants to Australia, as with other international linkages, has shifted markedly in favour of Asia. At the peak of the last immigration boom, in the late 1980s, 42 per cent of immigrants were Asian,

Table 13.1 Capital city shares of growth in total Australian population and overseas-born population, 1971–1991

City	Share of total population growth (%)	Share of growth in overseas born (%)
Sydney	14.4	30.1
Melbourne	11.7	17.2
Perth	10.5	13.6
Brisbane	3.6	5.6
Adelaide	4.2	2.6

Source: Australian Bureau of Statistics 1971 and 1991

whereas in the late 1960s India was the only Asian nation ranked in the top 10 list of source countries, and its position was tenth. The precise reasons for Sydney's capturing a disproportionate share of recent immigrants are uncertain, but apart from the influence of earlier settlers, which should favour Melbourne as much as Sydney, Sydney's greater integration with the global economy is clearly influential (Burnley, Murphy, and Fagan 1997).

Tourism has become Australia's most important service export. In the 1980s numbers doubled from a base of about a million annually. The Australian Tourism Forecasting Council (NSW Government 1997) extrapolated a doubling of in-bound tourist expenditure from A$6 billion in 1995 to A$15 billion by 2003. Alongside this explosive growth has been a marked shift in favour of Asian sources. In 1980, as a percentage of total tourists, Japan accounted for 5.4 per cent and the rest of Asia 9.9 per cent. The respective figures in 1990 were 21.7 per cent and 15.7 per cent, although in 1998 the Asian economic crisis resulted in a sharp downward revision of expectations.

Of the Australian capital cities Sydney attracts a disproportionately large share of tourists. In 1995, 30 per cent of international visitor nights were spent in Sydney (26 million nights), compared with 15 per cent in Melbourne and less than 10 per cent in each of Perth and Brisbane (NSW Government 1997). Sydney's dominance is accounted for by KSA's gateway function to Australia, together with the city's disproportionate share of internationally oriented businesses and immigrants, both of which generate tourism (Forsyth et al. 1993). Very important, too, is the fact that Sydney is the one Australian city that is widely known in Asia (Murphy and Watson 1997).

Another type of "people movement" that has become economically important to Australia is education exports. Around 60,000 international students are now studying in Australia. Unlike tourism and immigration, however, foreign students are distributed more in proportion to population. Indeed, Brisbane, Perth, and Adelaide have shares of international students somewhat larger than their shares of national population (Murphy 1999).

Compared with cities in East and South-East Asia, Sydney's competitive advantage derives from its high environmental amenity, cheap professional labour, and low rents for housing and commercial floor space. Hong Kong and Singapore have the obvious advantage of being in the midst of the Asian region and have low personal and company taxation levels compared with Australia. But these advantages are offset by ever-reducing telecommunications costs, by high-quality air links from Australia, and by cost disadvantages compared with Sydney. As the journalist Peter Smark (1994) wrote of Singapore: "as the local currency strengthens, rents soar and local skilled salaries jump, the supermarket with a scent of satay offers few bargains for outsiders". The general liveability of Sydney is also much higher than many Asian cities. Illustrating this, Peter Smark (*ibid.*) wrote of Bangkok: "[i]n pollution, traffic congestion and availability of top education and medical services, it may not be Hell but it certainly gives Purgatory a nudge".

While Sydney lags well behind Hong Kong and Singapore as a site for RHQs, in the field of business services Sydney is now the preferred location for multinational companies in the Asia Pacific. Of the regional head offices of the top 20 firms in four sectors – accounting, advertising, management consulting, and international real estate – 39 per cent are in Sydney. Ten per cent are in the other Australian states and the remainder are split between Hong Kong (32 per cent), Tokyo (13 per cent), and Singapore (6 per cent) (Blue 1990). In 1994, of 32 RHQs setting up in Australia, 21 chose Sydney and seven chose Melbourne (NSW Department of State and Regional Development 1994).

Infrastructure investment

With the aim of capturing globally mobile investment and consumption flows, Sydney, in common with other cities with similar pretensions, has invested heavily in certain forms of infrastructure. Because of its particular situation in the Asia Pacific region, much of that investment in Sydney has aimed directly and indirectly to influence the city's amenity as a place to visit, to live, and to do business. Various examples of this are discussed below, but the types of development include pollution control infrastructure; road improvements; increased capacity at KSA; and refurbishment of the built environment adjacent to the popular ocean beaches. There has also been redevelopment and preservation of inner-city areas such as Darling Harbour and The Rocks. The latter is a historic precinct at the northern edge of Sydney's central business district, consisting of nineteenth-century workers' housing and port buildings. The locality has been refurbished and is now a major tourist attraction with many restaurants and hotels. It is analogous to Vancouver's "Gas Town" (Hutton 1998). Darling Harbour, on the western margin of the central business district, is a waterfront redevelopment of derelict industrial land and was also designed to attract tourists with its shops, restaurants, and entertainment facilities. The locality is larger in scale but in other respects very similar to Granville Island in Vancouver (*ibid.*). Investment in each of these categories has been controversial because of opportunity costs and negative impacts on parts of the city's population. The most obvious example of a negative impact is noise pollution from increased air traffic through the airport. Opportunity costs arise when one form of investment is preferred over another, as, for example, when government money is used to expand an airport rather than to improve roads.

Governance

The commonwealth (Australian) government lacks constitutional authority to intervene directly in the governance of cities. Indirectly, however, it exerts influence through funding programmes administered by the states, via the construction of commonwealth-owned infrastructure (notably airports and defence facilities), and by means of policies that impact on the cities as by-products (such as immigration and microeconomic reform). Commonwealth interest in urban affairs waxes and wanes. Politically conservative governments are typically uninterested in urban affairs and regard them as state responsibilities.

It is thus state governments which have constitutional authority to regulate land use and provide infrastructure in the cities. In addition, although there has been a pronounced trend to corporatization and privatization, urban infrastructure has traditionally been provided by state agencies. In NSW the central agent of managerial governance is the Department of Urban Affairs and Planning (DUAP). While it has statewide responsibilities, the DUAP is effectively the metropolitan planning agency for Sydney. In the two phases of city planning – generally known in Australia as strategic planning and development control – consideration of the implications of development for ecological sustainability is mandated. At the strategic level, for example, large areas of land earmarked for urban development in Sydney's west and south-west were put on hold in the early 1990s due to concerns about air pollution. At the level of specific projects, environmental impact assessment is well entrenched as an aspect of governance. It applies to both government agencies (including those providing urban infrastructure) and private developers. Citizens and non-governmental organizations (NGOs) are not always happy with the weight given to environmental factors in governmental decision-making, but at least the processes are explicit and relatively transparent. Pollution control, at source, is addressed in legislation and regulations deployed by the NSW Environment Protection Authority (EPA), an agency that also conducts environmental research. There is also a long history of NGO involvement in environmental matters in Sydney. While much of this has involved criticism of actions, or inaction, by governments, there are also cases of constructive relationships between NGOs and governments. A good recent example of a constructive relationship is the National Roads and Motorists' Association's "Clean Air 2000" campaign (National Roads and Motorists' Association 1997). Ironically, the campaign is spearheaded by an organization that represents private automobile owners and has thus, historically, encouraged governments to build more roads. Also of interest is the fact that "Clean Air 2000" is headed by a prominent private sector promoter of Sydney, and includes in its task force representatives of government departments; normally governments prefer to set their priorities without acknowledging the direct influence of NGOs.

Entrepreneurial governance in NSW is based in the Department of State and Regional Development. Its role is to bargain with potential job-creating investors to encourage them to set up in Sydney rather than in some other country or Australian state. The NSW Tourism Commission also has an important entrepreneurial role. Business interests of course support these functions, with the recently formed Committee for Sydney – an NGO comprising business interests from the "top end" of town – acting as a lobby group to keep governments on track in their efforts to promote the economic development of the city.[3]

In Australia, local government has an important regulatory and strategic planning role, but it is circumscribed by state legislation (Farrier 1993). This represents a key difference compared with the USA, where strong regional planning is inhibited by the relative weakness of state planning power *vis-à-vis* local government. Local government is bound – by state legislation – to take environmental factors into account in all of its decision-making. But, as is the case with state government, it is constrained by limits to knowledge and the *realpolitik* of development pressures.

Environment

Air and water quality

The impacts of urbanization on the environment go beyond the effects on air and water quality, but it is these that are most readily monitored and which generate the greatest level of community concern. Air and water pollution are more significant problems in Sydney than in other Australian capital cities, with the exception of Melbourne where levels of certain air pollutants are as high as Sydney (Australian Academy of Technological Sciences and Engineering 1997). This situation is substantially a by-product of Sydney's pre-eminence as Australia's largest city, since with patterns of economic production and consumption held constant, as they more or less are across Australia, pollution is ultimately a matter of population size. The particular physical characteristics of the Sydney region (see below) add significantly to the problem (NSW Department of Urban Affairs and Planning 1997).

Wastewater and sewage goes into either the Pacific Ocean or the

Hawkesbury-Nepean river on Sydney's western perimeter (Figure 13.1). While disposal to the ocean has adverse impacts on aquatic fauna and flora, it also threatens Sydney's beach culture. It is common, after storms, for the ocean beaches to be declared too polluted for swimming. The threat to water quality from sewage, and to a lesser but still significant extent stormwater drainage, became a major political issue in the 1970s. As a result, the NSW government committed millions of dollars to build deep-water ocean outfalls at three locations (North Head, Bondi, and Malabar). These were (and are) the main sewage treatment works on the coast. The NSW EPA (1997) now regards "[p]ollution on Sydney's beaches as being relatively uncommon since the introduction of deep ocean outfalls, except after rainfall events when stormwater pollution can be evident". Before the outfalls were commissioned, raw sewage – screened only for "solids" – was dumped into the ocean at the base of sandstone cliffs. Sun and salt were left to kill bacteria and viruses and to dilute effluent in the water. As Sydney's population grew after the Second World War conditions gradually worsened, with more effluent being discharged to the ocean. It included toxic effluent from factories that blossomed in the industrial areas in the 1950s and 1960s. But it is not only the residents of Sydney who find pleasure at the beach, so increasingly do international tourists. The maintenance of high environmental quality is – and will increasingly be – crucial in sustaining the tourism expenditure that has come to be so important to Australia, and especially Sydney.

The Hawkesbury-Nepean river supplies most of Sydney's drinking water. It is a precious habitat for aquatic flora and fauna and a popular recreational resource. The river draws on a very large catchment – about 22,000 square kilometres – bounded by Goulburn to the south-west, Lithgow to the west of the Blue Mountains, and the Broken Bay plateau to the north between Hornsby and Gosford (Figure 13.1). The catchment is 65 per cent forested but there are also extensive agricultural uses and increasing urban and industrial development. Sydney's population growth is now almost entirely contained within the catchment of the Hawkesbury-Nepean river, which means that sewage and wastewater will increasingly be disposed of in the river. For years environmental activists have been drawing attention to worsening water quality, especially problems of viral and bacterial pollution. There is also the problem of plant nutrients – nitrogen and phosphorous – getting into the river from sewage and run-off from farms located on the river flood plain. These nutrients cause plant growth – notably of the toxic blue-green algae – and threaten eutrophication of the river with fish kills and strong odours of decaying vegetation.

The NSW government responded by deferring large areas of land previously designated for urban development and implementing higher-technology effluent disposal. New housing at Rouse Hill in Sydney's north-west – an area which will be developed over 30 years and will ultimately yield 70,000 housing allotments (averaging 600 square metres) – will, for example, have two water supplies, with separate plumbing. One will be potable water for household drinking, cooking, and washing; the other will be recycled water for toilet flushing, car washing, and garden watering. This is the first time such a recycling system has been available in Australia on anything but a trial scale. It will help reduce the demand for potable water – thus delaying the need for further dams – and will reduce the volume of wastewater entering the Hawkesbury-Nepean river system. A new sewage treatment works is also being developed at Rouse Hill. Dewatered sludge will be sold to fertilizer manufacturers and the treated water will be recycled or treated in on-site wetlands. As well as reducing the treatment plant's environmental impact, the wetlands will provide a sanctuary for birds and small wildlife and a recreation site for residents. These systems are expensive to construct and are arguably only possible because the land releases will attract predominantly upper- and middle-income purchasers. In the generally cheaper areas of the west and south-west such technology means higher costs to lower-income earners unless they compensate by buying smaller parcels of land and living at higher densities (Murphy and Watson 1997).

Sewage effluent has been the major source of pollutants that affect water quality in the Hawkesbury-Nepean. In the 1980s levels of nutrients and plant growth measured by the NSW EPA (1997) showed reductions. But excessive levels still exist in sections of the river that receive discharges, with phosphorous, nitrogen, faecal coliforms, and algae sometimes exceeding guidelines. The NSW EPA believes that there is general downwards pressure on pollutant levels – especially improved water treatment, with long-term effluent quality objectives expected to be achieved by 2000. Diffuse sources of water pollution continue to be a problem, and the NSW EPA is shifting its focus to these. Environmental groups naturally distrust the sanguine rhetoric of government and call for a ban on further urbanization of the catchment. The problem is that there are as yet no clear alternatives. To ban development would lead to price increases, and these would especially affect first-time home-buyers who are struggling to get a foothold in the housing market.

The main air pollutants in Sydney are lead compounds, nitrogen oxides, carbon monoxide, ozone, particulate matter, sulphur dioxide, and other acid gases. The NSW EPA monitors the sources, levels and trends in Sydney's air quality. In its latest summation (1997) it made the following assessments.

• Acid gases: Since 1980 levels have fallen and are well below long-term health goals. Industry contributes 77 per cent.

- Particulates (basically dust): Levels peaked in central and suburban Sydney in 1985 and declined since then to below the National Health and Medical Research Council (NHMRC) annual average goal. Forty per cent are from motor vehicles. Suburban levels are well below World Health Organization guidelines; levels in the central business district are higher but still below those guidelines.
- Nitrous oxides: 80 per cent are from motor vehicles. Of these, heavy-duty diesel-powered vehicles account for 25 per cent. Levels have exceeded NHMRC guidelines for years but introduction of three-way catalyst technology in new cars appears to have been effective. The trend has been down, but it is not clear for the future.
- Ozone and smog: In the 1970s, Sydney was Australia's most smog-bound capital. The situation has improved in recent years and the occurrence of photochemical smog has decreased. Future trends are unclear.
- Lead: Unleaded gasoline was introduced in 1985 and lead levels have declined below the NHMRC standard. Whilst 60 per cent of gasoline sold is still leaded, the proportion will decline to zero in the foreseeable future as older motor vehicles are retired.

These trends are encouraging but, in a report by the Australian Urban and Regional Development Review (1995), the NSW EPA was reported as judging that "in the absence of further controls on vehicle emissions, the combination of population growth, urban expansion and increased use of motor vehicles will result in declining air quality in the medium to long term". NGOs such as the Total Environment Centre (1992) are less constrained in their assessment of what they regard as an "emerging air pollution crisis in western Sydney":

Air protection in Western Sydney has a history of neglect and secrecy by all NSW Governments over the last two decades. In an educated and progressive society the public have a democratic right to be properly informed of matters that affect their health and lifestyle. With regard to air quality, this right has not yet been recognised by our politicians and bureaucrats.

Air pollution in Sydney is largely the product of motor vehicle exhausts. There are no electric power stations operating in the region and, although industry is a significant source of pollutants, Sydney is not a specialized heavy industrial city. High levels of car ownership and the regional topography exacerbate the problem. High levels of car ownership, especially in the western and south-western areas of highest population growth, are linked to low residential densities. This is because low densities ensure that public transport, especially buses, cannot be provided economically; the lack of public transport then induces car ownership. Although the "quarter acre block", which gave Australian cities the

Table 13.2 Annual contributions of motor vehicles (private and commercial) to anthropogenic pollution in major Australian capital cities

	Carbon monoxide Kt (%)	Volatile organic compounds Kt (%)	Nitrous oxides Kt (%)	Suspended particulates Kt (%)
Sydney	711 (89)	78 (45)	80 (80)	6.1 (24)
Melbourne	621 (79)	79 (46)	62 (75)	4.4 (16)
Brisbane	329 (83)	43 (52)	52 (75)	3.9 (18)
Perth	214 (80)	27 (44)	23 (51)	N/A

Note: Kt = kilotonnes of pollutant produced annually by motor vehicles in the designated city; % = the proportion of the given pollutant produced by motor vehicle emissions.
Source: Australian Academy of Technological Sciences and Engineering 1997

lowest residential densities in the Western industrialized world, is long gone for most home-buyers, the massive suburbanization of the population that commenced in the 1950s has not abated. The outer areas of the city remain poorly served by public transport. Furthermore, the numbers of jobs in these areas remain significantly lower than resident populations. Journeys to work are thus long and typically made by car. Cars that were initially luxuries have become necessities. The cycle of car dependence is thus perpetuated.

The situation is exacerbated by topography. Sydney is ringed by higher terrain: the southern highlands south of Campbelltown; the Blue Mountains west of Penrith; and the plateau country between Hornsby and Gosford (Figure 13.1). The effect is that much of the region is poorly ventilated by prevailing winds. Instead of polluted air being dispersed away from the city, it tends to accumulate for long periods. Concentrations are especially high to the south-west along one of Sydney's growth axes. From a global perspective even if wind clearance of pollutants were high, pollutants produced by Sydney's car-dependent population would be an environmental problem of considerable magnitude because of their contribution to greenhouse gases.

Table 13.2 compares Sydney with other Australian cities with respect to pollutants from motor vehicles. Except for volatile organic compounds, Sydney produces the largest quantity of pollutants and this is directly related to the number of vehicles in the city. While Melbourne (3.2 million) has a smaller population than Sydney, on a per capita basis pollution is much the same. Of the smaller cities it is noteworthy that Brisbane (population 1.5 million) produces, per capita, more pollutants from motor vehicles than either Sydney or Melbourne. This signals that the planning of growth in the newer "sunbelt" cities is no better than it has been for the older larger cities, although the situation in Perth (population 1.3 million) is marginally better.

Table 13.3 Transport emissions averaged across 37 cities in world regions, 1990

Regions	Carbon monoxide kg per capita	Volatile organic compounds kg per capita	Nitrous oxides kg per capita	Suspended particulates kg per capita	Sulphur dioxide kg per capita
Australia	185.8	23.0	21.9	1.4	0.6
USA and Canada	204.5	22.3	22.3	1.0	1.6
Europe	72.6	11.6	13.0	0.8	2.0
Asia I					
Tokyo	14.3	2.0	4.4	N/A	0.8
Hong Kong	25.2	2.4	8.0	1.1	1.7
Average	19.8	2.2	6.2	1.1	1.3
Asia II					
Kuala Lumpur	90.0	22.8	11.2	1.0	1.0
Bangkok	84.6	23.2	3.6	9.1	1.8
Manila	67.5	11.2	9.2	1.5	1.5
Average	61.8	13.6	8.7	3.4	1.3

Source: Kenworthy *et al.* 1997

Table 13.3 compares air pollution in Australian cities with the rest of the world. Regarding the latter, the Australian Academy of Technological Sciences and Engineering (1997) concluded as follows: "Comparing Australian cities with those overseas shows that, in general, air quality is relatively good in all the major capitals ... But on a per capita basis, transport emissions in Australia are very significantly greater than European and Asian levels." The contrast with Europe is interpreted by Newman and Kenworthy (1991) as reflecting higher levels of patronage of public transport. This in turn results, they argue, from higher residential densities in Europe that make provision of public transport financially viable. The contrast with Asian cities results from relatively low per capita car ownership, but explosive growth in demand will no doubt radically increase these figures in the twenty-first century – at least in megacities such as Bangkok and Manila – unless governments take strong countermeasures. Table 13.3 also includes data for North American cities. Per capita pollution on the five indicators closely match the Australian scores, reflecting similar patterns of low-density cities combined with the affluence required to promote high rates of motor vehicle ownership.

Urban form and environmental quality

For the past 15 years or so Australian state governments have attempted to engineer higher residential population densities in the main cities (Troy 1996). This trend is popularly referred to as "urban consolidation", and involves the construction of residential apartment buildings, town houses, villa units, and similar medium-density dwelling units. There are several reasons for this effort to promote higher densities, but a particularly important one is to reduce air pollution. The argument goes that Australians are highly car dependent, at least partly because public transport – especially buses – in the outer areas of cities is poorly developed. Bus services are poorly developed partly because population densities are too low to generate profits to private providers or acceptable levels of cost recovery for government services. This cycle of car dependency might thus in principle be breached if population densities were higher.[4]

Most of the effort to promote higher densities has involved land-use regulations and public education. These should be regarded as necessary but not sufficient conditions for policy effectiveness. An important consideration here is that urban services have historically been priced at levels below cost recovery. Prime examples are commuter rail and bus transport in Sydney. A recent study by the NSW Independent Regulatory and Pricing Tribunal (1996) concluded that while "State Government funding of public transport's operating costs has declined, it still costs taxpayers some AU$361m per annum". As part of its inquiry into taxation and financial policy impacts on urban settlement, the Commonwealth Industry Commission (1993) concluded that in Sydney cost recovery on water and sewerage services per housing allotment fell short by an average of A$3,900. Given costs of an average A$25,000 per allotment this implies that charges would have to increase by about 16 per cent in order to remove the estimated subsidy. Subsidies of this order exist in other Australian cities. An inference from this sort of information is that population densities are lower than would have otherwise been the case. Full cost recovery for urban services, or privatization of services, which amounts to the same thing – and both are now inexorable trends – will arguably do more, as an unintended by-product, to increase residential densities over the next couple of decades than regulation and education could ever hope to achieve. This is because if such subsidies are removed and household incomes do not increase, it is likely that people will purchase smaller housing allotments so as to maintain housing affordability.

The pattern of expansion of cities into surrounding farmland and countryside also has significant implications for their ecological sustainability. There is a connection here with the question of population densities, inasmuch as increases in density are theoretically capable of reducing rates of fringe expansion; the more people that are accommodated within the confines of the existing city the less land needs to be converted to suburbs. Realistically, however, eliminating lateral expansion of cities when demand for housing is increasing is a very long-term prospect. Most growth in cities like Sydney will therefore continue to be on the fringe. Redirection of growth away from sensitive air sheds and water catchments, while desirable, is similarly unlikely to make a major short-run contribution to environmental management because people will simply not be prepared to live in localities that are inaccessible to jobs and services. It has to be understood that cities are very complex systems and have tremendous inertia to change. Like an ocean liner at full speed, changing direction takes enormous effort over a sustained period of time. Controlling the environmental effects of lateral expansion must therefore rely on behavioural changes engineered over long periods of time.

Regarding air pollution, apart from low residential densities, the separation of workplaces from homes is a key contributing factor. Getting a better balance between where people live and where they work has several potential benefits but, in the present context, potential reductions in travel distances mean reduced air pollution. Like other aspects of urban form, patterns of work and housing location are largely the product of market forces responding to prices, especially transport prices. Where prices do not reflect the full (private and social) costs of the activities the tendency is to overconsume. This is the root cause of long journeys to work. Like other aspects of urban form, things cannot be changed overnight. Regulation and education will only go so far in achieving change, and pricing must be accepted as an integral part of the solution. Supporting the argument that regulation in itself will do little to produce ecologically sustainable forms is the unconvincing performance of metropolitan planning in Sydney:

Successions of (State Government produced) metropolitan planning strategies have reiterated concern about imbalance between jobs and housing and the long journeys to work which result. Whilst over the years large numbers of jobs have been created within, and have relocated to, the outer city, the imbalance compared to residential populations remains large and has worsened. (NSW Department of Urban Affairs and Planning 1996)

Constraints on achieving sustainability

The ecological sustainability of cities is a complex outcome of population levels and growth rates, human behaviour, geographical context, and urban form. Public policy has to influence one or all of these variables via the pricing of urban goods and services, regulation of environmentally destructive behaviour, and public education; in other words, the standard triad of resource economics.

Achieving an ecologically sustainable city is not a technical but a political problem. The question here is the extent to which globalization has exacerbated or enhanced the political tractability of environmentally sound governance in Sydney. The city's environmental problems obviously do not have their genesis in globalization, but are embedded in a specific biophysical environment upon which a particular economy, spatial structure, and system of governance has evolved over many years. But over the past quarter of a century – the period of contemporary economic globalization – while some gains have been recorded and the deterioration in environmental quality has been widely politicized, the tractability of environmental problems has not notably improved.

The capacity of government to act effectively is always constrained by the agendas of different parts of civil society and their relative influence. Political constraints on environmentally sound governance derive from three key elements of Sydney's civil society: immigrant groups; the social justice lobby; and environmentalists. These groups have agendas that conflict, and this makes it difficult for governments to act optimally in support of the environment. Environmentalists, for example, argue for reduced immigration because they regard population numbers as a key factor in environmental decay. They also argue for pricing measures to suppress demand for environmentally damaging activities, such as driving motor vehicles. On the other hand, immigrant groups want to see more migration, especially of friends and relatives, while welfare groups argue that pricing will produce inequitable outcomes. The technical capacity of government to deal with environmental degradation depends on knowledge and financial resources. While knowledge may be regarded as a relatively minor constraint, financial capacity is not.

This part of the chapter, building on the context of information established in the first part, considers three key constraints on governments wishing to encourage ecologically sustainable urban development. First there is the question of financial capacity, since sustainability requires, amongst other things, investment in infrastructure. Second, there is the question of population growth, a critical issue in Sydney (and in Vancouver) since environmentalists claim that growth is the main cause of environmental decay. Third, there is the question of the implications of measures to maintain environmental amenity for social welfare.

Financial capacity of governments

In common with other Western industrialized nations, the financial capacity of all levels of government (federal, state, and local) in Australia has been reduced by slowed rates of economic growth that in turn have reduced rates of increase in tax bases (Kirwan 1990). Coupled with higher costs of borrowing and increased demands arising from refurbishment needs and environmental contingencies, this has meant that governments have deferred expenditures and shifted to cost-recovery pricing and privatization of urban infrastructure. Cost-recovery pricing has the potential directly and indirectly (through its influence on urban form) to improve environmental quality but, as is discussed below, may have marked negative welfare outcomes as well. So too might privatization, when governments, keen to secure private investment, soften standards of environmental assessment. Specifically, over the last two decades governments in Sydney have encouraged private sector investments in a cross-harbour tunnel, motorways, airports, and other essential services. The state, having adopted the strategy of relying on the private sector to provide infrastructure, becomes less capable of making the hard decisions required to develop a public transportation system that can alleviate some of the environmental problems brought about by the pressure of population growth at the urban fringe. In examples such as this, private sector providers of infrastructure have thus negotiated favourable terms that limit the state's ability to implement strategies which might impinge on the pecuniary interests of those who invested in the infrastructure.[5]

Immigration and the city size debate

As noted above, Sydney's population size has been a key element in contemporary debate about environmental quality. The following quotations, one from the NSW Premier and the other from a respected economist, give a flavour of the polarized positions in this debate:

In line with the Premier, Mr Carr's views that Sydney is "bursting at the seams", the NSW Government will take a proactive role in trying to cut the number of migrants settling in the city ... "I want Sydney interests to figure larger when the national immigration intakes are considered," Mr Carr said. "It might suit Perth or Adelaide to have maximum intakes, but it's not in the interest of Australia's largest city." (Humphries and Sharp 1995)

On the environmental issues that are specific to Australia, there seems no case to restrict immigration in order to overcome identified environmental problems, which seem to be overstated in any event. These problems appear to be capable of solution, or at least of alleviation, by appropriate adjustments to environmental and resource management policies, including by giving emphasis to property rights and to proper pricing of resources. (Moore 1993)

If human behaviour and urban form remain constant, then slowing rates of population growth, even curtailing growth completely, in cities will contribute to their ecological sustainability. But questions of how to achieve such objectives arise. So too do questions of the relative effectiveness of population control compared with controls over urban form and environmentally damaging behaviour. The particular attraction of population control in Australia, and especially in cities like Sydney, which appears to have the most deteriorated environment, is that growth is strongly driven by immigration. Compared with the movement of people within Australia and natural increase through the excess of births over deaths, controls over immigration are relatively straightforward. Technically the Australian government could stop immigration overnight – although of course political realities are such that this is implausible. Controls over natural increase and internal migration are nevertheless far less feasible.

From a purely technical viewpoint, reducing immigration to achieve sustainable cities is a second-best option (Tolley and Crihfield 1987). First, if immigration is halted this will not stop population growth overnight. This is partly because the population will continue to grow through natural increase. In the case of Sydney, it has been noted that when population growth from immigration is high, more people move to other parts of Australia (Burnley, Murphy, and Fagan 1997). Conversely, when immigration is low the outflow of people from Sydney declines. The implication of this relationship is that if immigration is reduced the effect on Sydney's population growth will be much less than proportional. A second reason why controls over population growth are a second-best option for dealing with environmental problems is that such a strategy will only defer attacks on the more fundamental issue of environmentally damaging behaviour.

Because such a high percentage of Australia's population was born overseas, or was born of immigrants, there is quite naturally a vital interest in permitting substantial family reunion migration. The overseas born are likely to give more weight to this concern than to improvements in urban environmental quality. Apart from an "ethnic" backlash if governments seek to cut back too hard on immigration, there is also the consideration that multiculturalism is part of Sydney's competitive advantage. Ethnic diversity is sold "at a million miles an hour" by agencies like the NSW Department of State and Regional Development and the NSW Tourist Commission in their efforts to attract investment and tourists. The marketing of Sydney's 2000 Olympics made strong play on the multicultural advantage.

Cost-recovery pricing and social justice

From a policy viewpoint, the most direct and effective means of maintaining ecologically sustainable cities is to dampen behaviour that works against sustainability. If the aim is to lower air pollution, for example, cars must be driven less. The most direct method of achieving this is to make cars more expensive to drive. Air pollution is a social cost, or negative externality in economic jargon. Its existence means that people are not being required to take the pollution they generate into account when they make decisions to drive. Were they required to do so they would drive less, with the result that emissions would be reduced to sustainable levels. Price increases may be most effectively achieved by higher taxes on fuel. An issue that must be contended with here is that modest price increases do not have much of an impact on demand for gasoline (see, for example, Wachs 1996). The same approach applies to the case of water pollution. If the objective, for example, is to produce effluent free of plant nutrients so as to prevent eutrophication of enclosed water bodies, then people may be discouraged by higher prices from using products such as detergents and fertilizers that contain those compounds. Again, "externality" pricing imposed by regulation is the most direct and effective means of achieving the objective. It is worth reiterating that externality pricing (together with the full recovery of private costs of supplying urban infrastructure) will result in behaviour changes that in turn will produce environmentally beneficial modifications to urban form, namely increased residential densities, reduced rates of lateral expansion, and shorter distances between where people live and where they work. Those shifts will, in the long term, enable people to compensate for the inconvenience and financial costs that they incur in making changes to their behaviour.

The problem for governments is that whilst the "social justice lobby" may concede immigrant and environmentalist viewpoints, it rejects – on equity grounds – this most effective of means to maintain ecological sustainability. As far as it goes this perspective is valid. The case of leaded versus unleaded gasoline is illustrative. To encourage owners to retire rapidly the stock of cars that burn leaded gasoline would require a much larger differential in gasoline prices than exists now. But it is older cars that burn leaded gasoline and poorer people who predominantly own these. Another example concerns tolls on urban freeways in Sydney. Equity, it is claimed, demands that tolls be removed since it is longer-distance commuters from the outer suburbs of Sydney who use these roads most and such people are assumed – because of Sydney's particular socio-spatial structure – to be poorer than average. There is also a matter of intergenerational equity, one of the principles of ecologically sustainable development, because those who live in the established parts of the city have available roads for the development of which they did not pay.

Thus socio-spatial divisions within Sydney will unquestionably exacerbate the equity impacts of a shift towards externality pricing and cost-recovery pricing in general. Sharpening this concern, globalization has – as in other cities around the world – entailed economic restructuring that has widened the gap between more and less affluent parts of the population (Murphy and Watson 1994). The spatial outcome in Sydney is a widening gap in welfare levels between the inner and outer city. The more attractive residential locations near the harbour and the central city are desirable for those who can afford to pay, with low-income earners tending to be displaced at an increasing rate to the outer parts of the city. Given that a significant portion of Sydney's employment opportunities are still located within the central area, commuting from the outer parts of the city to the central city is the way of life for many on low incomes. In a city in which public transport is not as well developed as it could be, this situation means that people on lower incomes have, on average, to drive the furthest to get to their places of employment.

Equity impacts need not be unmanageable if implemented properly over reasonable periods of time. The interim report of the Economic Planning and Advisory Council's Task Force on Private Infrastructure (1995) discusses the distributional impacts of user pays and, by extension, externality pricing. There are indirect and direct means to compensate those least able to absorb increased costs of living resulting from measures to protect the environment.[6]

Externality pricing, and more generally cost-recovery pricing for urban infrastructure, are clearly the linchpins of ecologically sustainable cities. Properly conceptualized and implemented, their use is capable of defusing conflicting social justice, environmentalist, and ethnic agendas. Equity effects need to be and can be identified. Where appropriate those who are adversely affected need to be compensated. Externality pricing will, of course, satisfy environmentalists; ecological sustainability will be rapidly and efficiently achieved – and as part of this process urban form and city size will adapt to more sustainable parameters. Immigrants should also be content in so far as immigration need not be curtailed or, if it is as a complementary measure, reductions can be modest. But neither immigrants nor environmentalists will be happy, any more than the rest of the population, with the shifts in behaviour which cost-recovery pricing will induce. They too will be differentially affected by pricing. To the extent that immigrants and environmentalists are poor – though just how poor is an issue – then compensation eases or eliminates the burden. If they are not poor then the challenge is for them to accept enforced shifts in behaviour for the common good.

Conclusions

The question addressed in this chapter is the manner in which economic globalization and its correlates have impacted on the capacity and willingness of governments to implement ecologically sustainable development objectives in metropolitan Sydney.[7] The structure of the argument is summarized in Figure 13.2. In the effort to attract globally mobile

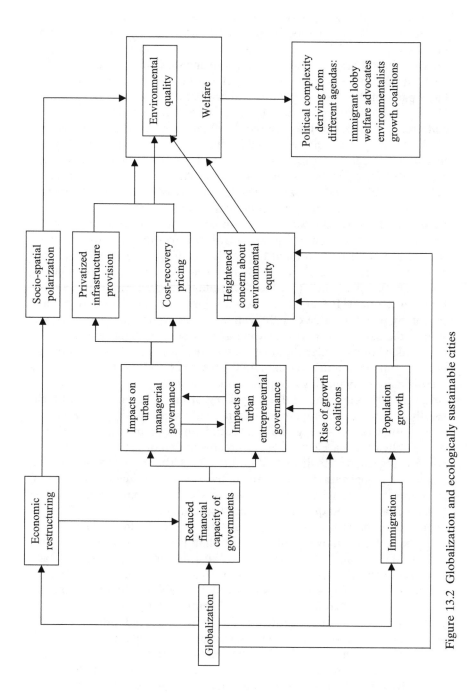

Figure 13.2 Globalization and ecologically sustainable cities

investment and consumption flows, the enhancement of environmental quality is clearly understood by governments as adding to the city's competitive advantage. But because such flows impact in restricted parts of the city (central business district/downtown and surrounds, eastern beaches, harbour foreshores, the more affluent eastern and northern suburbs), large parts of the city's population do not benefit directly – or may even lose out – if resources are diverted from their localities. The diversion of state funds to support the Olympics 2000 facilities is a prime case of this tendency. In general, however, achievement of managerial objectives of urban governance has not been facilitated, or has actually been made more difficult, by Sydney's becoming enmeshed in "the global space of flows" (Castells 1996). Private infrastructure provision and ownership can have perverse effects for environmental quality, as road investments in particular demonstrate. Another example – relevant primarily to noise pollution – is the currently raging controversy over the need for and location of a second international airport for Sydney. The Australian government, which currently owns Sydney's KSA airport, has conflicting goals. On the one hand, it wishes to maintain the asset value of KSA before privatizing it. It fears that by establishing a second international airport in Sydney the value of KSA will decline. On the other hand, expansion of the existing airport is causing a great deal of anger on the part of residents who live under the flight paths. This is a classic case of conflict between financial and environmental objectives and, in addition, shows the difficulty of managing complex modern cities.

Externality pricing and full-cost pricing of urban services should technically enable the elimination of urban "bads" such as air and water pollution. Indeed, because globally induced financial pressures (and also treaty obligations) are driving governments in that direction, the outcome could be regarded as environmentally beneficial. But the income-polarizing effects of globalization – reinforced by Sydney's specific socio-spatial structure – have heightened resistance to such environmentally desirable outcomes and raised questions of social sustainability. A key correlate of economic globalization is immigration. Because of Sydney's high degree of globalization relative to other Australian cities it has attracted a disproportionate share of immigrants to Australia over the past 20 years. Because of the city's size and its relatively degraded environment, environmentalist NGOs – whose views reflect a good slice of community opinion and are therefore politically influential – have argued that immigration-driven population growth is the cause of degradation and should be terminated. Given the voting power of immigrants, many of whom wish to sponsor the migration of relatives to Australia, governments thus face a dilemma, especially since immigration is the basis for "multicultural advantage", a key theme in city marketing. So, in sum, globalization has directly and indirectly affected urban management in ways that seem generally to have been unconducive to the maintenance, let alone improvement, of Sydney's environmental quality.

As always, of course, management takes place within a political framework, and the particular mix of agendas of environmentalists, rational managers, immigrants and their Australian-born relatives, and lower-income groups makes the task increasingly difficult. At least, though, Australia is affluent and has strong, relatively transparent urban management systems and government. Provided economic growth strengthens in the medium to longer term – as a result of globally driven economic restructuring – the basis for bearing down significantly on urban environmental problems exists. The potential economic advantage of doing so, as Sydney seeks to position itself in competition with other Asia Pacific cities, should heighten awareness of environmental amenity as a key dimension of competitive advantage. In other words, ecological, social, and economic sustainability are inextricably linked in specific combinations unique to Sydney.

Notes

1. This chapter is concerned with "ecologically sustainable development" and how it interacts with social and economic sustainability. So while it is recognized that the notion of "amenity" refers to both the biophysical and the built environments, the focus is on the former. The term "environmental quality" is used interchangeably with ecological sustainability except where meanings differ slightly in context.
2. Between 1991 and 1996 the numbers of overseas-born persons increased in Sydney by 148,919 and in Melbourne by 70,611. Shares of the total Australian overseas born to be found in these cities remained, however, more or less constant, with the big increases in shares over that period being elsewhere, especially in Perth and to a lesser extent Brisbane (Australian Bureau of Statistics 1991 and 1996).
3. The strengthening of entrepreneurial governance and its implications for managerial governance are explored in Murphy and Wu (1998). Trends in Sydney echo, in perhaps a more subdued fashion, what has been noted elsewhere; see Hall and Hubbard (1996), Jewson and MacGregor (1997), Newman and Thornley (1997).
4. Data on urban private motor vehicle usage presented in Australian Urban and Regional Development Review (1995) compare urban passenger kilometres per capita in Australia (10,729), the USA (12,586), Canada (9,850), and Europe (5,600).
5. An excellent example of how private infrastructure provision may subvert the broader process of managerial governance is the "Eastern Distributor" in central Sydney. This is a toll road and tunnel – under construction at the time of writing – that will connect the southern exit from Sydney Harbour Bridge to Southern Cross Drive, which is the main freeway access to Sydney airport. Airport Motorway Limited won the tender to finance, design, construct, operate, and maintain the distributor. In its performance audit report, the NSW Audit Office (1997) was critical of the state government's handling of the project on a number of points. Regarding the strategic planning context of the development, the report said:

As part of this audit, the authorities responsible for Transport and Roads were asked for details of the transport policies within which the Eastern Distributor is being developed ... None [of the responses received] offers a comprehensive policy framework to guide transport planning and development across the region.

RTA [NSW Roads and Traffic Authority] justifies the Eastern Distributor in terms of providing "a key strategic transport link to support the Government's initiatives and objectives to complete a Sydney Orbital identified in the various strategy documents". However the audit can find no clear government policy or plan supporting the implementation of the Orbital and no evaluation of the effects of doing so. Certainly it is not made explicit in the 1994 State Road Network Strategy. And at least one State agency involved in the integrated planning process has questioned the concept in its submission to the EIS [environmental impact statement]. The concept of the Orbital itself needs to be justified if RTA is to rely on it to help justify the Eastern Distributor proposal.

In the absence of integrated plans, and in response to policies to reduce debt and have no new taxes, an opportunistic approach has been adopted by RTA, and by other agencies. They have sought to take advantage of private debt sources (and private tolls) and match them to specific agency priorities. Such arrangements tend to encourage "insert" schemes, like the Eastern Distributor, which are narrowly defined to developments of private sector interest within an agency's sphere of influence. This makes achieving integrated solutions for the land use and transportation system as a whole (both public and private) more difficult. Individual agencies are left to grapple continually with wider issues, and with each other, on individual projects, without a useful framework to resolve them.

The Audit Office was also critical of the cost-benefit analysis undertaken in relation to the project. For any major public infrastructure project like the Eastern Distributor, an investment appraisal (CBA) is required before the project can proceed in NSW:

... the process gives the impression of being driven by the private sector's ability to undertake road improvements on the RTA's behalf, without a cost to the RTA, rather than by the State's wider road-building, transport and environment priorities. The limitations in cost benefit methodology [regarding traffic implications and environmental effects], and the lack of clarity in the State's agreed strategies and plans to implement these priorities, have contributed to this shortcoming.

The production of an environmental impact statement (EIS) has been the major new feature of land use and transport planning in the last 20 years in NSW. The Audit Office was also critical of the environmental impact assessment conducted in relation to the project:

In the absence of an appropriate strategic planning process, the EIS is the predominant means by which the public is in a position to consider and comment on a proposal. The Audit Office considers that the EIS for a particular project is not the most appropriate means to gauge public reaction to proposals.

Following from these concerns the performance audit made a number of recommendations regarding the planning process associated with major infrastructure projects. They emphasize the need for:
• a clearer definition of transport policy;
• a better-integrated transport plan which clarifies and reconciles strategic and policy objectives and so provides an agreed framework within which individual agencies, and individual schemes, can proceed with more certainty;
• applying the EIS process to transport policies and plans as well as specific proposals;

- promoting improvements in the methods used to assess local and regional impacts on traffic and the environment.

6. Two categories of indirect means of compensation may be identified. First, as higher levels of resource costs for infrastructure provision are recovered, governments may be able to decrease taxes or to increase spending elsewhere. A second option arises when reductions in charges for business users (for example of water), consequent upon the removal of cross-subsidies, may be partly passed on to consumers in the form of lower prices. Three direct means of compensation may be deployed by governments when people are adversely affected by externality pricing, and cost-recovery pricing generally. First, direct payments may be made to individuals designated through means testing. Second, payments equal to the differences between the full costs of service provision and the subsidized price which governments deem appropriate for designated groups may be made to service providers. A third compensatory option is for public sector providers to reduce the required rate of return on their assets, thereby reducing government dividend requirements.

7. Parenthetically, while it is beyond the scope of the chapter to compare and contrast the situation in Sydney with that in Vancouver, it can be casually observed that much of what has been argued regarding Sydney is likely to apply to Vancouver. The cities are very similar in important respects. Both rely heavily, and increasingly, on the maintenance of environmental amenity to underpin their attractiveness to investors and tourists. Yet the population of both is driven heavily by immigration and this is promoting growth pressures. Both cities have immaculate physical settings that constitute a key element of their attraction. The most obvious difference is in their size, with Greater Vancouver having only around half of Sydney's population. Vancouver's growth has also been much more recent than Sydney's which – casual observation by the authors suggests – seems to have enabled a modern planning system to control growth more effectively than has been the case in Sydney, where much of the urban fabric was constructed before effective metropolitan planning began to be established after the Second World War. Another significance difference is that Sydney has been a major industrial city, and this has resulted in diminished environmental quality. The potential to explore the implications of these similarities and differences for governance in two prominent post-industrial cities of the Asia Pacific region seems great. It is now conventionally observed, by those addressing the topic, that the impacts of globalization cannot simply be "read off" on to the system of cities. Rather, the forces of globalization interact with local economic, political, and physical circumstances. It is the resolution of such interactions that encourage or inhibit – to varying degrees – ecologically sensitive governance.

REFERENCES

Anderson, G. 1993. *Creating Competitive Economic Regions: The New Economics of Competitive Advantage*. SRI International Business Intelligence Programme.

Australian Academy of Technological Sciences and Engineering. 1997. *Urban Air Pollution in Australia*. Canberra: AATSE.

Australian Bureau of Statistics. 1971 and 1991. *Censuses of Population and Housing*. Canberra: ABS.

Australian Bureau of Statistics. 1991 and 1996. *Censuses of Population and Housing*. Canberra: ABS.

Australian Bureau of Statistics. 1998. *Migration 1996–97*. Canberra: ABS, Cat. 3412.0.

Australian Urban and Regional Development Review. 1995. *Green Cities.* Strategy Paper No. 3. Canberra: AURDR.

Blue, Tim. 1990. "Nation's powerhouse leads the recovery", *Business Review Weekly,* 5 June.

Burnley, Ian, Peter Murphy, and Robert Fagan. 1997. *Immigration and Australian Cities.* Sydney: Federation Press.

Castells, Manuel. 1996. *The Information Age: Economy, Society, and Culture, The Rise of the Network Society.* London: Blackwell.

Commonwealth Department of Industry, Science, and Tourism. 1998. Unpublished data on regional headquarters of transnational corporations establishing in Australia. In-house list supplied to authors.

Commonwealth Industry Commission. 1993. *Taxation and Financial Policy Impacts on Urban Settlement.* Draft Report, Vol. 1. Canberra: AGPS.

Economic Planning and Advisory Council. 1995. *Private Infrastructure Task Force Interim Report.* Canberra: AGPS.

Farrier, David. 1993. *The Environmental Law Handbook: Planning and Land Use in New South Wales.* Sydney: Redfern Legal Centre Publishing.

Forsyth, Peter, Larry Dwyer, Ian Burnley, and Peter Murphy. 1993. "The impact of immigration on tourism flows to and from Australia." Discussion Paper No. 232, Centre for Economic Policy Research, Australian National University, Canberra.

Hall, Tim and Phil Hubbard. 1996. "The entrepreneurial city: new urban politics, new urban geographies?", *Progress in Human Geography,* Vol. 20, No. 2, pp. 153–174.

Humphries, Dennis and Marion Sharp. 1995. "Carr wants migrant intake cut", *Sydney Morning Herald,* 22 May.

Hutton, Thomas A. 1998. *The Transformation of Canada's Metropolis: A Study of Vancouver.* Montreal: Institute for Research on Public Policy.

Jewson, Nick and Susanne MacGregor (eds). 1997. *Transforming Cities: Contested Governance and Spatial Forms.* London: Routledge.

Kenworthy, J., F. Laube, P. Newman, and P. Barter. 1997. *Indicators of Transport Efficiency in 37 Global Cities.* Perth: Report for the World Bank, Institute for Science and Technology Policy, Murdoch University.

Kirwan, Richard. 1990. "Infrastructure finance: Aims, attitudes and approaches", *Urban Policy and Research,* No. 8, pp. 185–193.

Moore, Des. 1993. "Australia's carrying capacity: How many people to the acre?", address to the CSIRO Seminar at the National Press Club, Canberra, 7 April, *Significant Speeches,* Winter, pp. 34–39.

Murphy, Peter. 1999. "Sydney now: Going global in the space of flows", *Monash Papers in Geography: Chris Maher Memorial Collection.* Melbourne.

Murphy, Peter and Sophie Watson. 1994. "Social polarisation and Australian cities", *International Journal of Urban and Regional Research,* No. 18, pp. 573–590.

Murphy, Peter and Sophie Watson. 1997. *Surface City: Sydney at the Millennium.* Sydney: Pluto Press.

Murphy, Peter and Chung-Tong Wu. 1998. "Governing global Sydney: From managerialism to entrepreneurialism", unpublished paper presented to Intercity Networks Meeting, Taipei, April.

National Roads and Motorists' Association. 1997. *Clean Air 2000: Strategic Action Plan, 1997–2000*. Sydney: NRMA.

Newman, Peter and Jeffrey Kenworthy. 1991. *Cities and Automobile Dependence: An International Sourcebook*. Aldershot: Avebury Technical.

Newman, Peter and Andy Thornley. 1997. "Fragmentation and centralisation in the governance of London: Influencing the urban policy and planning agenda", *Urban Studies*, Vol. 34, No. 7, pp. 967–988.

New South Wales Audit Office. 1997. *Performance Audit Report. Review of Eastern Distributor*. Sydney: NSWAO.

New South Wales Department of State and Regional Development. 1994. "RHQs announced/established since last year", in-house list supplied to authors.

New South Wales Department of State and Regional Development. 1997. *Sydney Investment Profiles*. Sydney: SRD.

New South Wales Department of Urban Affairs and Planning. 1996. *Journey to Work*. Sydney: DUAP.

New South Wales Department of Urban Affairs and Planning. 1997. *A Framework for Growth and Change: The Review of Strategic Planning*. Sydney: DUAP.

New South Wales Environment Protection Authority. 1997. *New South Wales State of the Environment Report*. Sydney: EPA.

New South Wales Government. 1997. *Tourism Strategy for Sydney*. Sydney: NSWG.

New South Wales Independent Pricing and Regulatory Tribunal. 1996. *Inquiry into the Pricing of Public Passenger Transport Services. Final Report*. Sydney: IPRT.

Smark, Peter. 1994. "Australia is as cheap as chips: Just ask IBM", *Sydney Morning Herald*, 16 June.

Tolley, G. and J. Crihfield. 1987. "City size and place as policy issues", in E. S. Mills (ed.) *Handbook of Regional and Urban Economics*. Vol II. Amsterdam: North Holland, pp. 1285–1311.

Total Environment Centre. 1992. *Newsletter*, Vol. 11.

Troy, Patrick Nicol. 1996. *The Perils of Urban Consolidation*. Sydney: Federation Press.

Wachs, M. 1996. "The evolution of transport policy in Los Angeles", in Edward W. Soja and Allen J. Scott (eds) *The City: Los Angeles and Urban Theory at the End of the Twentieth Century*. Berkley and Los Angeles: University of California Press.

14

From village on the edge of the rainforest to Cascadia: Issues in the emergence of a liveable subglobal world city

Terry G. McGee

Prologue

In the introductory chapter of his recent book, *The Rumour of Calcutta*, Jon Hutnyck cites a comment of one of his respondents: "Everyone thinks that Calcutta is saying something; that it is a message, a sign, and all we need to do is crack the code" (Hutnyck 1996: 1). He then explores how Calcutta has been inserted into global consciousness as the archetypal example of urban poverty. Levi-Strauss's famous quote concerning Calcutta is typical of this trope.

Filth, chaos, promiscuity, congestion, ruins, huts, mud, dirt, dung, urine, pus, humours, secretions and running sores: all the things against which we expect urban life to give us protection, all these things we hate and guard against, at such great cost, all these by-products of cohabitation do not set any limitation on its spread. On the contrary they constitute the natural setting which the town must have if it is to thrive. (Levi-Strauss 1962: 3)[1]

When we come to investigate issues of sustainability within the Asia Pacific region, we are exploring the same generic issue, but instead of poverty, governments are focused on how they increase the efficiency of cities as generators of wealth.[2] This central issue is not only analysed actually in terms of wealth generation but how cities/city regions can be represented as sites where wealth can be created more effectively than in some other competing urban site. A recent essay by Lindfield and Stimson (1999) attempts to quantify this concept of competitiveness by using a variation of the Swiss-based World Competitiveness Project to measure the competitiveness of Melbourne against other cities in the Pacific Rim such as Auckland, Sydney, Jakarta, Kuala Lumpur, Los Angeles, and Bangkok. The WCP criteria are almost entirely economic and make no effort to measure intangible qualities such as perceptions of attractive environment and liveability. In an era of globalization, what image or combination of images is needed? Efficient urban management; quality of life; urban settings; cheap labour and land; supportive institutional milieu; access to global systems of communication; and so on. How can one describe such material characteristics as images? Easily, since the representation of these material characteristics (the creation of the trope of wealth) becomes in many ways more important than the material characteristics themselves; thus the festivals like the Olympics and the Expos. In the case of Vancouver and the urban region of which it is part, there are some special features of the interlocking process of images and materialism which position it in a certain matrix of the interconnected urban places of the Pacific Rim.

In another publication which lays out many of the ideas that underpin this volume, Lo and Yeung (1996: 2) present the idea of a functional city system which is a "network of cities" that are linked, often in a hierarchical manner based on given economic or socio-political functions at the global or regional level. Scott (1996) has argued that the emergence of this "network of cities" is characterized by "a significant reallocation of economic coordination and steering functions away from the sovereign state up to international and down to regional levels". One issue that is of importance for urban liveability is what effect this process of functional reallocation has on the component cities of the network. In particular, one may argue that the effects are twofold. First, the allocation process is highly competitive and therefore all levels of government, often in partnership with the private sector, are forced to make strategic decisions that enhance their cities' competitiveness within the system. Second, this allocation process, which involves the redirection of resources to increase the international attractiveness of cities, may reduce liveability because of less investment in the environment and sustainable features, both of which benefit the local inhabitants. There is an ongoing tension between the need to position cities competitively in economic networks and the goal to make them liveable. This chapter chooses to emphasize the liveability of cities and living as a prime goal. This term is often conflated with sustainability, in the sense that both assume careful management of growth in order to ensure the preservation of future resources. In fact, the author would argue that the message (to use Hutnyck's term) of Vancouver is that "liveability" will create an "amenity environment" which will be attractive to the post-industrial economy of the twenty-first century. This case study of the Vancouver urban region shows that city regions can develop strategic planning processes that provide liveability and also reinforce the competitive strength of urban regions.

A second point to be made about Vancouver is that it is a very recent urban development, being established for less than 150 years. In the early part of the nineteenth century, at a time when many other subglobal cities had been established for centuries, Vancouver was still a "native place" in which Indian bands controlled most of the territory. The small European trading posts clung to the edge of the rainforest, and it was not until 1867 that British Columbia (BC) entered the Canadian Federation. From that time onwards, Vancouver became defined by its role as the port and principal urban centre of a "staples frontier" (Innis 1933) involving the harvesting and exportation of salmon, timber and pulp, and minerals. Vancouver's economy was primarily oriented to servicing those activities. Finance, retailing, and small industries such as mechanical repairing were all oriented to this purpose. This led to a highly dualistic class structure in which the élite that governed and managed BC primarily consisted of the managers and owners of the large corporate entities which controlled the "staples economy", and a working class laboured in the timber mills, the mines, and the clerical jobs of the service economy. The upper class was highly concentrated in the core of Vancouver city; the working class largely on the edge of the city and resource frontier.[3]

But in the post-war period, increasing urbanization and the growth of producer services have fuelled a spatial expansion of the built environment into surrounding areas, including agricultural regions like the Fraser valley. Today the built environment of the Vancouver urban region is very new. A considerable proportion (approximately 80 per cent) of the commercial and residential buildings have been built since 1945. This newness provides an architectural setting that encourages innovation and willingness to accept change on the part of the urban managers. This is a necessary quality for building strategic networks.

However, this desire for change must be constantly balanced against the physical environment of the Vancouver region, squeezed between the Rocky Mountains and the Pacific coast on east and west. To the north, the coastal mountains limit expansion, and in the south, the US boundary is less than 30 kilometres from downtown Vancouver. Thus there is a constant tension between the push for urban growth and global status and the protection of the natural environment – a dialectic that becomes increasingly obvious as British Columbia and Vancouver position themselves to become one of the major tourist amenity regions in the world. The fact is supported by the declining role of staple exports and the great increase in tourism earnings. The response to this pressure in Vancouver has been to develop a particular system of "growth management" that is focused on creating a "liveable region". This chapter focuses on the features of this system of management.

Vancouver in its regional context

It is important to stress that Vancouver is part of a wide region of "geographical affinity" which stretches from southern Oregon to the ski resort of Whistler (120 km north of Vancouver). This region includes metropolitan Portland, Seattle, and Vancouver as its major points, and has been termed "Cascadia" (Schnell and Hamer 1993; *The Economist* 1994; Pivo 1996) (Figure 14.1). Some commentators would wish to see this region

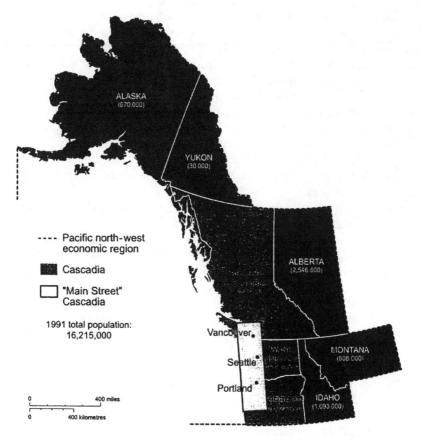

Figure 14.1 Pacific north-west region

further extended to include the US north-western states of Alaska, Idaho, and Montana as well as the Canadian province of Alberta and territory of the Yukon in what has been called the Pacific north-west economic region.[4] Supporters of this concept point out that if this "region were a country, then with a combined population approaching 15 million and a 1991 GNP of nearly US$300 billion, it would rank as the third largest economy in the world behind the United States and other G7 countries" (Edgington 1995: 333). Within this wider region, the main urban focus is the urban corridor that stretches from Eugene, Oregon, through Seattle, Tacoma, and Greater Vancouver north to the ski resort centre of Whistler. A major international highway, intensive air traffic routes, and a railroad artery characterized by daily trips all link this urban corridor. These three centres act as the major gateways for the exports of the western region of Canada and the USA. An increasing proportion of business is with Asia Pacific countries. Almost half the region's exports cross the Pacific Ocean, and urban foreign investment from Asian Pacific countries is a major source of capital. But not all exports are raw materials. This corridor is the home of three of the largest world multinationals: Boeing and Microsoft in Seattle and Nike in Portland. Vancouver is now popularly known as Hollywood North and is host to the second largest number of movie productions in North America. It is no coincidence that these industries represent the leading edge of the post-industrial age – entertainment, leisure, transportation, and information. This Asia Pacific linkage has been further reinforced by the movements of new migrants from the Asia Pacific nations, most markedly to the central part of the Greater Vancouver region. Mobility within the urban corridor is high; over 14 million American tourists enter BC each year by land (most from the urban corridor "Main Street Cascadia") and over 10 million Canadians enter the USA from BC each year.

Within the corridor, the urban cores form part of an extended metropolitan region encompassing approximately 50 per cent of the state or province's population. They are central points of economic articulation generating more than 50 per cent of the GDP of their respective province/state. It is important to note that Vancouver forms part of a wide region of urban interaction or extended metropolitan region (EMR). This EMR stretches across the Georgia Strait to Vancouver Island and includes Victoria (the capital) and a string of towns that stretch along the north-south island highway as far north as Parksville. In the south, the EMR follows the IR5 thoroughway linking Vancouver to Bellingham (Figure 14.2). One of the largest ferry systems in the world moves people and goods between the internal centres of Nanaimo, Victoria, and Vancouver. Local air (intraregional) transportation is available on an hourly basis.

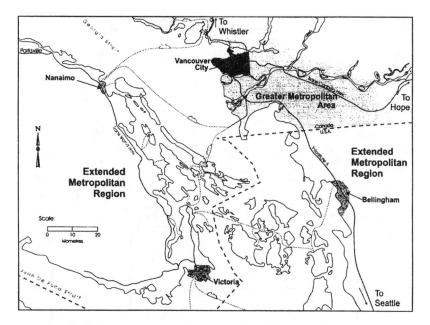

Figure 14.2 Vancouver extended metropolitan region

Narrowing the scale of investigation, the next focus is the urban region of Vancouver. Today this is defined as the Greater Vancouver Regional District (GVRD) which is the focus of this chapter (Figure 14.3). It consists of a partnership of municipalities and two electoral areas that make up the metropolitan area of Greater Vancouver. One municipality outside the GVRD takes advantage of services offered by the GVRD. In 1996, the total GVRD area contained 1.9 million people. The major portion of the population is located in Vancouver city, which had a population of 514,007 in 1996. The city and the adjacent municipalities of Burnaby (179,209), New Westminster (49,350), North Vancouver City (41,475), North Vancouver District (80,418), West Vancouver (40,882), and Richmond (148,867) make up 49 per cent of the total population of the GVRD. The GVRD is expected to grow by another million to 3 million by 2020.

Administration, power, and governance

Each of these spatially nested urban scales is in a sense a constructed space. The regions of "Main Street Cascadia" and the extended metropolitan region of Vancouver-Victoria, while they may have some economic validity, are not recognized politically. Political control and responsibility

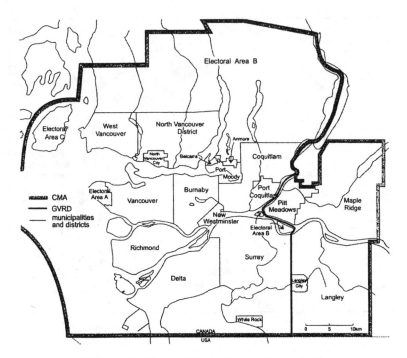

Figure 14.3 Greater Vancouver regional district

in Canada is essentially three tier. The federal government is responsible for national and external affairs. The provinces have responsibility for most provincial administration, and municipalities and districts operate at the lowest level.

The main political power is exercised at the national/provincial level, and within the urban setting at the level of municipality or city and outside cities as smaller units of administration such as districts. These administrative powers are also regulated by both the province and a partnership of political units called the Greater Vancouver Regional District. At the topmost level, the federal government has exercised considerable influence through national agencies such as the Canadian Municipal and Housing Authority. The province is also involved in municipal affairs through the Ministry of Municipal Affairs and shared transfer payments to the GVRD. Because it is a useful model for the mega-urban regions of the Asia Pacific (McGee and Robinson 1996), this chapter will concentrate on the organization of the GVRD and its members (Figure 14.3).

The vision of the GVRD is fivefold, as follows:

To make the Lower Mainland the first urban region in the world to combine in one place, the things which humanity aspires for on a global basis. A place where:

- human activities enhance rather than degrade the natural environment;
- the quality of the built environment approaches that of the natural setting;
- the diversity of origins and religions is a source of social strength rather than strife;
- people controlling their own destiny;
- the basics of food, clothing, shelter, security, and useful activity are accessible to all. (Marr 1996)[5]

The GVRD is part of 30 regional districts in the province created in 1965 that are essentially regional service and coordinating bodies.[6] The GVRD provides regional services for its municipal members in the areas of drinking water quality and supply; liquid waste collection and treatment; solid waste disposal; environmental controls, particularly through pollution control; regional park management; administration of the 911 emergency phone system; hospital planning and capital financing; labour relations with local government employees; ownership and management of 47 rental housing developments; strategic planning for land use and growth management; and economic development and transportation.

The GVRD is administered by a board on which each municipality is represented by one director for 100,000 people. Each director has a vote for every unit of 20,000 people (up to five votes) if votes are requested. The various services are administered through service districts such as the Greater Vancouver Water District, etc. To describe these as "service districts" is in fact imprecise. They are separate legal corporations which share a common administrative staff, and each has virtually the same board of directors as the GVRD. The most recent creation is the Greater Vancouver Transportation Authority, now named Trans Link. It took over responsibility for the public transportation systems from the provincial government on 1 April 1999. From the GVRD's point of view this is a significant development because it enables their overall land-use planning and management to be closely coordinated with transportation plans. In the past, provincial priorities, for example the rapid rail system, were forced on the region as a provincial initiative despite opposition from municipalities and NGOs at the local level. The GVRD is largely financed by funds paid by the municipalities it services. In 1996, the GVRD had an annual budget of C$428 million. Approximately 77 per cent of its funds come from taxes collected by municipalities for the provision of services. Other income comes from government levies, transfers, interest, etc. Most of the GVRD expenditures are operating expenses for the services provided and loan servicing for capital projects. This system of funding ensures that the local political units which belong to the GVRD are committed to the idea of consensual planning for the overall land-use and transportation planning of the region.

The municipalities that are members of the GVRD are administered by elected councils for the entire municipality. There is no ward system; the political parties that control the councils of the municipalities, while not aligned (in most cases) with provincial parties, represent broadly a coalition of pro-business groups and more socially concerned labour-supported parties.[7] At present, the pro-business parties control most councils. But the planning systems operating in most of the municipalities generally allow local-level opposition to be represented through the appeal process; an example of this is in land rezoning. The municipalities are responsible for most local-level source provision, including fire, police, and other such services.

Given the three tiers of government (province, regional district, and municipality), it must be obvious that there are considerable opportunities for conflict, particularly over growth goals and the allocation of government funds for regional initiatives. However, the existence of a regional authority that can deal with the inevitable emergence of the large urban region is seen as creating a leading edge in the competition between cities for global economic activity.

For this reason this chapter focuses on the aspects of strategic planning for land use, economic development, and transportation in the GVRD, which has developed a "liveable region strategic plan" to be completed by 2001 (Greater Vancouver Regional Authority 1990). This involved an intense effort at public participation before it was approved in 1996. Basically the plan for the region has five main components. First, the intensification of population within the central metropolitan region covering Vancouver, Burnaby, New Westminster, Richmond, and North Vancouver. Second, the growth of regional town centres in the districts of New Westminster, Lonsdale, Surrey, Richmond, Metrotown, Coquitlam, Langley, and Haney. Third, implementing a transportation system involving a mixture of private and public systems that will link these major centres. Fourth, committing more than two-thirds of the GVRD's land base to a green zone to protect watersheds, parks, ecologically important areas, working forests, and farmland from uncontrolled urban development. Already half the region's developable land is included, with 233,214 hectares designated as green space. This makes the fourth component of the plan the most advanced. Fifth, the GVRD will continue to implement environmentally acceptable policies of waste removal and treatment, water provision, and pollution control.

The implementation of this strategic plan is no easy task. The GVRD is mandated to operate through a consensus partnership/process and must negotiate with the province, districts, and member municipalities. At the same time each of the municipalities has its own strategic plan that has to be incorporated into this overall regional vision. However, over the last five years the province of British Columbia has developed a series of planning measures which are designed to put in place planning procedures to reduce conflict between the various levels of government within all regional districts, including the GVRD. This Growth Strategies Act (GSA) was introduced as an amendment to the Municipal Act (Part 28-1) in October 1995. The Act is administered by the Ministry of Municipal Affairs for British Columbia and is thus a provincial responsibility; it requires local governments (regional districts and municipalities) to prepare three planning instruments.

A regional growth strategy (RGS) is a statement that commits government to a regional vision of development for the next 20 years. It must include:

- a statement on the future of the region, including social, economic, and environmental objectives and population and employment projections;
- actions to meet the needs of future residents in relation to housing, transportation, regional district services, parks and natural areas, and economic development.

The RGS is to be prepared in consultation with the public, First Nations organizations, which include many of the tribal bands of native Indians who were the first residents of Vancouver, and interested groups including school districts, regional health boards, and regional service delivery organizations such as the water districts.

Once the RGS is prepared it must to go through public hearings. The first phase involves the setting up of an intergovernmental committee, the IAC, to advise on the development of the strategies and help coordinate provincial and local government involvement. The IAC includes senior staff of relevant local governments as well as representatives of provincial ministries involved (public works, transportation, environment etc.). Thus, the RGS process provides the opportunity for several regional districts to be involved in this process. The Growth Strategies Act recognizes that regional districts throughout the province will have different capacities to develop RGSs and therefore does give some latitude for regional districts to take varying times in the preparation of the RGS. The completed RGS is then submitted to all local governments within the GVRD as well as adjacent regional districts. All parties have 120 days to lodge objections, and if mediation does not produce an agreement the province may initiate a binding settlement process by arbitration.

The second phase is one of implementation, in which municipalities have up to two years to prepare a regional context statement (RCS) that forms part of the official community plan. The RCS describes the relationship between the RGS and the municipality's plan. If the RCS is not acceptable to the regional district, the same dispute resolution processes described above are put in place.

The third and final phase of the RGS is an implementation agreement (IA) – a partnership agreement between the regional district and various levels of government, which spells out how, for example, the RGS will be carried out. The administered IA might include agreements between various levels of government about sharing sewage costs, etc. Since this process is very new (dating only from 1995), its impact is difficult to gauge. In the case of the Vancouver Regional District Authority, the IA has been moving forward quite rapidly despite substantial disagreements with three municipalities (Burnaby, Surrey, and Richmond).

RGS plans are generally presented in terms of broad conceptual statements about land use, transportation, etc. For the GVRD, they incorporate the principles set out in the RGS. They do not have any formal binding capacity as law until they become by-laws of the Municipal Act. There appears to be ample opportunity for negotiation in the process between various levels of government, and effective measures for resolution of disputes.

While this process may seem complex and perhaps bureaucratic, it affords an opportunity to create liveable urban regions.

Immigration and economic change

The extended metropolitan region of which the GVRD is part is one of the most rapidly growing urbanizing regions of North America. Much of this growth has been focused within the GVRD. Between 1911 and 1941, the area encompassed by the GVRD grew in population from 120,000 to 350,000; and between 1941 and 1981 from 350,000 to 1.2 million. By 1996, this population had increased to 1.9 million; an increase of almost 50 per cent in 15 years. Of this, 600,000 people, almost one-third, arrived in the years 1991–1994. The changes in sources of population growth greatly accentuated trends that had begun in the decade of the 1980s. Natural increase declined from 35 per cent to 25 per cent, and net migration from other Canadian provinces and other regions of BC decreased from 32 per cent to 16 per cent. Most significantly, net international migration increased its share of population growth in metropolitan Vancouver[8] from 33 per cent in the 1980s to 59 per cent during 1991–1994. There were a total of 115,000 net immigrants to the region between 1991 and 1994 (about 85 per cent of all international immigrants to BC). Future projections of population growth suggest that the Vancouver metropolitan region will reach almost 3 million population by 2020, roughly 60 per cent of the entire BC population. When this projected population is added to that projected for the rest of Cascadia, the region will have a population of approximately 30 million by 2020; roughly the current size of Greater Tokyo!

The changes in the Vancouver EMR during the decades of the 1980s and 1990s have been characterized by three demographic trends. First, the core of the region, Vancouver city, has continued to grow in size and has not experienced the inner-core population decline so typical of North American cities during the post-war period. Second, the surrounding municipalities have grown at a much faster rate as the suburban frontier has expanded. Third, accompanying these trends are striking differences in ethnic, gender, and age structure.

In the 1960s, nearly two-thirds of the population in metropolitan Vancouver were of British or French background and another 28 per cent claimed European ancestry. Less than 6 per cent were described by the 1961 census as non-European. But this situation began to change in the 1970s following the publication of a 1966 white paper on immigration, which led to changes in the Immigration Act with respect to the classification of immigrants from "preferred" and "non-preferred" nations to a points system.[9] As a result, Vancouver began to attract growing numbers of non-European immigrants. By 1981 this group had grown to 150,000, and reached almost 250,000 by 1986. In 1991 this figure had risen to 300,000, and in the four years 1991–1995 it is estimated to have grown by another 38,000. The majority of these immigrants are of Chinese background, coming from Hong Kong, Taiwan, and China. Others come from the Philippines, Viet Nam, and India. They have added a distinct element to the social geography of the metropolitan region: the Chinese clustering in the municipalities of Vancouver, Richmond, and Burnaby, while the South Asians are more dispersed. There is also ethnic clustering among certain retailing and service occupations (Ley, Hiebert, and Pratt 1992: 234–266).

A second trend relates to the gender aspects of these demographic trends. Ley, Hiebert, and Pratt (*ibid.*: 239) state that: "In the last 35 years, there have been radical transformations in the types of work that individuals do, the number of workers per household, and the arrangement of work within households, family stability, the very idea of what constitutes a family, and in gender and sexual identity." This has led to a radical redistribution of demographic groups in the internal space of the GVRD. In 1960, the GVRD seemed to conform to the model of North American cities where the central city was made up of renters, ethnic minorities, the elderly, the poor, the single, and the marginalized as well as those living alternative lifestyles. Around this centre stretched suburbs characterized by simple family households. But in the next 20 years a growing diversity of household types emerged, especially a growing number of single-person households that is partly related to the increasing housing costs in the core of the GVRD.

These demographic trends are associated with changes in the economic structure of the GVRD, characterized by a shift in the type of industry and rapid growth of producer services, many of them directed to markets in the Pacific Rim and aided by the role of Vancouver as a major gateway to the Pacific Rim.

There has been a dramatic increase in the services component of the labour force as well as continuing growth in the size of the manufacturing and construction sector. While the reasons for the restructuring of the urban labour force have been well researched, the specific causes in Vancouver are more complex than previously stated. Many commentators feel that the turning point in the Vancouver economy occurred with the decision to sponsor the Expo 1986 held at the end of the early 1980s' recession. The decision of the provincial government to invest in major public works, a recovery in staple prices, the continuing investment in gateway facilities, including a "cruise ship facility", new container facilities, and the extension of the airport have made Vancouver a major competitive destination for international tourism. Thus, the number of conventions held in Greater Vancouver increased from 291 (with 117,000 delegates) in 1981 to 358 in 1995 (with 164,000 delegates). The number of overnight visitors increased from 5.9 million in 1991 to 7.0 million in 1995, and international visitors (including those from the USA) rose in number from 675,000 to 1.1 million during the same period. The industrial structure has also changed, with an emphasis on consultancy, software development, biotechnology, and new innovation industries. Vancouver is becoming a major centre for architectural services and the multimedia industry; other developments include film and television production.

All these developments have been accompanied by a surge in office and hotel construction.[10]

Intercity network circulation and the Asia Pacific region

Clearly, the Vancouver extended metropolitan region has benefited from its geographical location on the Pacific Rim and the implementation of policies to ensure its position within the transactional world of the Asia Pacific.

Of course, the concept of the Asia Pacific region is an abstraction constructed ideologically to facilitate the interaction between the various national units which are part of it.[11] In traditional geographic terminology, it should be described as a "functional region" held together by the mutual benefits gained from the exchange of people, goods, capital, and ideas. This concept will be used as the frame for the analysis of various kinds of circulation which demonstrate Vancouver's links to the Pacific Rim and the importance of those linkages to the Vancouver EMR. In particular, the movements of people (immigration and tourism), goods (trade and transport), and information (culture, education, services) are vital to Vancouver.

An important geographical development affecting trends in circulation is that which has been called "time-space" collapse. This term simply refers to the reduction in the time it takes to cover a given distance (the world is getting smaller). Time-space collapse (for example, due to jet aircraft) has made the circulation of goods, people, capital, and ideas around the world and around the Asia Pacific region much more fluid and rapid, with major repercussions for the cities of the region, like Vancouver.

The movement of people

The major element in the movement of people to Vancouver has been the increasing presence of Asian immigrants. This makes Vancouver a cosmopolitan city, and forms part of its allure. Immigration has brought ethnic groups from all over the world to intermingle in myriad ways in the city's unique setting. The development of Vancouver cannot be separated from trends in immigration and resultant ethnic relations.

The growth in the Asian community is critically important to the development of the GVRD for a number of reasons. First, it is important because these immigrants provide a channel for linkages between Vancouver and the rest of the world (through family networks, investment preferences, cultural interchange, political allegiances, etc.).[12]

Second, ethnic groups affect the nature of the city as community through residential segregation, ethnic politics, and cultural efflorescence/diffusion, etc. Ethnic divisions and differences between the traditionally dominant Anglos and the Asian community are perhaps the key issues which animate the city today.

The school system provides one window on the dimensions of this change. Currently, in the Vancouver school system, most children use English as a second language, and the majority of those speak an Asian tongue as their first language. In 1998 at the University of British Columbia, 41 per cent of the freshman class came from Asian-language homes compared to 10 per cent in 1990.

Today, Vancouver's immigration profile has become more clearly fragmented and variegated. This short section introduces three of the new types of immigration that occur in Vancouver. The first conforms to a new and emerging norm, a type of immigration especially noted by Saskia Sassen (1994) and others. It concerns the migration of workers from the developing world to industrialized metropoles to perform tasks below the wage threshold of locals. These immigrants tend to be females engaged in lower-order services. In Canada, this type of immigrant operates under contracted labour agreements, exemplified by the Filipino nanny in Vancouver. The number of Asian women imported to care for the city's children has increased considerably over the last few years, and the playgrounds of Vancouver's wealthier neighbourhoods are witness to the magnitude of this recent trend.

Many of these Filipino nannies return home after their contract expires, forming the movement pattern that underlies the second new genre of immigrant, the "circular migrant". Circulatory migration is very evident in certain Asian source areas, such as Hong Kong. Many Hong Kong business immigrants actually still live in Hong Kong (where their businesses may be) but have sought to establish their families in Vancouver. This form of migration has a number of repercussions. It tightens the bonds between Vancouver and Asia (enhanced by the fax machine and e-mail, an essential part of life for many Vancouver/Hong Kong families). It also indicates that Vancouver may be seen more as a bedroom community rather than a potential business centre, at least in the near term. Another factor contributing to this lifestyle is the fact that many immigrants from Hong Kong and Taiwan state that the most important reasons for moving to Vancouver are the availability of education for their children and an unpolluted environment. Thus, the "liveability" of the Vancouver region emphasizes its role as an amenity location.[13]

The third and the most striking departure from past immigration patterns is the newly constituted "business or entrepreneurial immigrant" (examined in Fladell 1989). This class of immigration is set aside for people who are either able to invest C$250,000 or create new jobs for a Canadian citizen. This policy has come under much fire. It has raised concerns among some sections of the populace about allowing "queue jumping" by wealthy Asians. It has also been criticized because there have been a number of cases in which unwary Asian investors have been fleeced of their savings by duplicitous "immigration consultants". Despite the local impression that the entrepreneur category is awash in people from Hong Kong and Taiwan, it makes up only 6 per cent of the total immigration. The business or entrepreneurial immigrant class has brought two new types of immigrants to Vancouver. First there is the new immigrant to the city: relatively wealthy, successful immigrants with families moving into any and all areas of the city. These people, occasionally called "astronauts", defy the stereotyped descriptions of Asian immigrants grounded in the past. They are buying valuable property and goods, particularly on the west side of Vancouver and Richmond, and sending their children to the best schools (Edgington and Goldberg 1991). Second, there is a more numerous group of small-business people from various parts of Asia, including Hong Kong, Korea, India, and other countries in South-East Asia. Travel agencies, restaurants, insurance offices, and other small businesses can now be found dominating the commercial fronts along Kingsway, Main Street, Fraser Street, and in new shopping malls in Richmond.

At the macro scale, patterns of family residence and immigration provide the skeletal framework for a network of familial investment. This is especially true of Chinese investment patterns (Goldberg 1985; Edgington and Goldberg 1991). A good deal of Asia Pacific commerce goes on within networks of *"waisheng"*, overseas Chinese. These activities occur throughout the Asia Pacific region. In this way, immigration levels are directly linked to increasing Asia Pacific interdependence and directly affect the Vancouver region.

Advances in transportation technologies have not only brought more immigrants to Vancouver, but have greatly increased the number of short-term visitors: tourists. Tourism is now the province's second major industry, and is a mainstay of the burgeoning Vancouver service sector. Hotel occupancy rates in Vancouver are the highest of any Canadian city. A key reason for the success of the hotel sector is the growing presence of Asian tourists. Since the collapse of the Japanese "bubble economy" and the onset of the Asian economic crisis in 1997, the number of Asian tourists has been falling, particularly from Japan. However, this shortfall has been taken up by the increased movement of tourists from Europe and the USA, attracted by the low Canadian dollar and the "amenity" characteristics of the Vancouver region and its surrounding areas. The growth of the Whistler ski resort has played a major role in these developments.

The movement of goods

As elaborated in earlier parts of the chapter, over the last 20 years BC has experienced a dramatic shift in its trade from the USA and Europe to the Pacific Rim. Perhaps the most important feature of these developments is the growing importance of Japan. Japanese-Canadian trade has increased with the growth of trading companies called *sogo shosha*.

In contrast to US patterns of investment, whereby corporations endeavour to purchase Canadian companies outright or obtain equity control through direct investment, Japanese corporate strategy has, up until recently, involved minority investment or loans. Japanese trading companies and their clients (such as steel mills and power utilities) have had no qualms about surrendering organizational control to Canadian or other foreign timber, mining, or other resource companies, as long as they could be assured of a stable flow of supplies.

Due to the need to secure very large quantities of Canadian agricultural and industrial resources, 11 of Japan's major general trading companies established subsidiaries in Canada from the late 1950s onwards. Five of these companies chose Vancouver as their local headquarters. Ontario by itself comprises about 45 per cent of the Canadian economy, yet approximately 60 per cent of the *sogo shosha's* trade is done through the port of Vancouver. This is due to both BC's Pacific Rim location and the particular focus of the trading houses' Canadian activities on BC's and Alberta's resources.

Japanese trade with Canada expanded immensely between 1960 and 1990, and the Canadian-based branches of the Japanese *sogo shosha* generated most of the business. For Japan, Canada has continued to remain within the list of its top 10 or so trading partners. Conversely, Japan has been Canada's second trading partner, after the USA, since the 1960s, when it overtook the UK. Over the last three years, the decline of the Japanese economy has led to a dramatic reduction in the demand for BC raw materials, which has contributed to a slowdown in the BC economy. Continuing demand for the agricultural products of the prairies from Asia (particularly China) and an increase in exports to the booming USA has enabled Vancouver to keep an important gateway function. However, it is clear that these developments have further accentuated the divide in the province between the "depressed resource frontier" and the "post-industrial" Vancouver region.

The movement of ideas and information

Orchestrating the movement of large amounts of material across the Pacific requires effective communication linkages. These channels of communication weave a thick web that increasingly brings Asia closer to North America and to Vancouver. But it does so in uneven ways. The flow of information across the Pacific occurs along a number of channels, ranging from "telematic" (satellite computer-based communications systems) and mass media to education and cultural exchanges and immigration. This is a wide range of phenomena, but two components, namely, educational and cultural linkages and telematics, are especially illustrative of Vancouver's orientation.

Asia increasingly pervades the cultural fabric and educational institutions of the city of Vancouver. The provincial Ministry of Education is deeply committed to increasing British Columbians' awareness of Asia, in an effort to enhance the provincial competitiveness abroad and to ameliorate racial tensions at home. There are a great many Asia-related programmes in elementary and high schools. These primary and secondary school programmes are supported by major institutes of Asian research at the three provincial universities. The University of British Columbia has by far the largest programme of research and teaching on Asia of any university in Canada. The federally funded Asia Pacific Foundation is also located in Vancouver, and reinforces the city's primacy as a depository of Asian knowledge in Canada. These programmes are foundations of the city's Pacific destiny. It is in the classrooms of the city that the "nuts and bolts" of change in the city's geographical orientation are forged.

Vancouver has also developed an appetite for news from Asia. The local newspapers have daily columns from Asia, along with listings such as the Hong Kong stock exchange. There are new television shows on business in Asia, and a proliferation of Asian-language newspapers such as *Sing Tao* and *Ming Bao*.

The interest shown within the Vancouver educational system for "things Asian" is reciprocated by Asian interest in the city. Vancouver is the destination of rapidly increasing numbers of students from Asia. These students intensify links between Vancouver and Asia. It is estimated that there are some 20,000 graduates of Vancouver educational institutions in Hong Kong. The growth in educational exchanges has accompanied a growth in cultural interchange through a variety of activities. These range from film festivals and the extremely popular dragon-boat races in False Creek to the daily interactions among children of different background in the city's playgrounds. Tangible evidence of the cultural impression of Asia within the city is the new landscapes formed by outstanding examples of formal Japanese and Chinese gardens. Asian-oriented cultural events and/or projects are often the result of the work of one of the city's many Asia-Canada business organizations. These organizations work to enhance communications between the Vancouver business community and those of Asian countries (often in concert with government agencies). Some of these groups (for example, the Dr Sun Yat Sen Classical Gardens Committee) are important networking frameworks of the city's élite. A number of these business/cultural groups are very large; all are growing. For example, the Vancouver chapter of the Hong Kong-Canada Business Association has 800 members, second in size only to the Vancouver Board of Trade, and is an organization linking Vancouver to almost all of the countries of Asia.

At the other end of the scale from the personal level of interchange evinced in educational and cultural exchanges lies the global telematic information system. This set of formal structures define the avenues through which much of the world's business is carried on. The term "telematics" refers to the combination of computer and telecommunication technologies that permits very rapid communication. This allows long-range control of corporate activities. In many ways breakthroughs in this area underpin the emergence of the Asia Pacific as an economic dynamo, because they negate some of the friction of distance (time-space collapse) which was for so long the barrier to links across the Pacific. The system of networks is composed of fax lines, public databases, and the private dedicated control-communications systems of large corporations.

Where does Vancouver sit within these networks? Despite the efforts of the Canadian and BC governments to establish Vancouver as a "hub" for international communications networks, in terms of financial transactions this has not been successful. Generally, it may be argued that Vancouver remains peripheral to the business communication networks, which still concentrate their activities in Toronto and New York. As communication links diminish the role of distance, they diminish the locational advantage of Vancouver's position on the edge of the Pacific.

The city, while becoming increasingly bound to Asia, has been unable to engage fully in the complete spectrum of opportunities found within the Asian region. Vancouver occupies an awkward niche. It is partially integrated into the Asia Pacific economic system, but is also peripheral. This mix is also evident in the present phase of economic volatility in Asia, which has exposed Vancouver's and BC's reliance upon Asian markets.

Conclusion: Future scenarios and the tension of liveability

This chapter has examined the various contexts in which the metropolitan region of Vancouver is situated. Four main points emerge. First, the Vancouver region is developing as a somewhat fragile component of the subglobal regional system that is defined as the Asia Pacific. While it still relies upon its territorial hinterland of western Canada, increasingly the flows of goods, information, and people are being articulated through networks of cities located throughout the Pacific Rim. A simple example will suffice to illustrate this point. Most of the western US and Pacific Rim cities can be reached by direct flights from Vancouver; most flights to New York involve transfers, as does any Latin American destination apart from Mexico City. The "gateway" functions of Vancouver have been greatly enhanced to facilitate this interaction with intercity networks in the Pacific Rim.

Second, Vancouver city is at most a subglobal node. Within the Asia Pacific, the dominant world cities in terms of volumes of transactions and/ or power are Tokyo, Singapore, Hong Kong, and Los Angeles. But if Vancouver becomes more integrated in the Cascadia corridor of Seattle and Portland, the area's concentration of post-industrial industry and services could propel the region to a world-class status by 2020. Such a

scenario assumes that the NAFTA (North American Free Trade Association) agreement will increasingly create more permeable borders between the USA and Canada.

But this push to world city status is a controversial one, because it means
changes for Vancouver that can potentially challenge the concept of a
sustainable "liveable region". In 1998, the author attended a meeting of
the Dunbar Residents Association (his neighbourhood in Vancouver) at
which Vancouver's most celebrated architect, Arthur Erickson, admon-
ished single-family-housing residents for wanting to keep "low-density
nirvanas". We should be ready, he said, for not 3 million by 2020 but 20
million. The only way to do this was to densify existing single-family-
housing areas if the existing "liveable region" of the GVRD was to be
maintained. This is the tip of an escalating debate over the region's future.
On one side are supporters of the "development business" who argue
that government should "use top-down brutality" to intervene and ensure
that the community groups do not undermine efficient land use (*The
Vancouver Sun* 1997). On the other side are the community groups which
have had some success in reducing these densification processes. This
situation is further exacerbated by the rapid growth of Asian immigration, and value conflicts surrounding the size and style of houses and
retention of landscapes in which trees and gardens are important. Mr
Erickson left the meeting with comments that the audience's lack of support for his point of view was "not being realistic".

The push to world city status is a controversial one, which in the Vancouver context encapsulates many of the dualities between small-town
"liveable region" advocates and the mega-urban growth position supporters. Despite this division, there is no doubt that the main economic
change faced by the Vancouver region is "globalization". Globalization is
in many ways the flip side of the world city phenomenon. Now, more than
ever, one needs to speak of global markets of capital, labour, products,
and services (as the preceding sections have suggested). This new economic context has a number of interrelated repercussions for Vancouver
and its region.

First, the city's arrival on the world stage in the mid-1980s meant an
extension of aggregate demand for real estate. As Vancouver's land prices
were notably below world city levels (especially those in Asia), there was
an influx of investment into "undervalued properties" in the city. The disparity in pricing levels invites the flow of capital to Vancouver, especially
during a switching crisis, as illustrated by the overaccumulation crisis in
Japan. While this situation has now changed, in that Vancouver prices are
much higher, they are still relatively cheaper than most global cities in the
Pacific Rim.

Second, globalization means global competition among jurisdictions for the investments that create jobs. This leads to the emergence of what David Harvey (1989) has called a "place market", where cities as political units sacrifice their autonomy to attract capital. Vancouver reflects this trend in its push to world city status in at least two ways. In order to attract circulating capital, cities need to develop characteristics attractive to capital or at least to capitalists. This means lowering regulatory restrictions or enhancing local amenities, thus reworking the fabric of the city to a post-industrial landscape. This landscape is basically one of consumption (for example, the transformation of Granville Island from industrial to commercial uses). Yet though the city may attain some more seawalks and markets, or perhaps improvements to "Robson Strasse" with its franchise boutiques (such as Laura Ashley and Ralph Lauren), these developments cost the city money. In the context of neoconservatism and a declining tax base, this means that improvements in these areas are attained at the cost of social programmes and services for the city's poor. Thus, one sees in Vancouver the evolution of a key trait of world cities: a dual society. This further accentuates the tension between the supporters of low-key development and the promoters of mega-urban growth, and creates a paradoxical image of the Vancouver region of wealth and poverty.

The third set of repercussions relates to the scale of business enterprises and the emergence of a two-tiered economic structure. A few very large global corporations and a multitude of smaller dependent enterprises will characterize this structure. Such a business structure has deep roots in Asia (especially in Japan, but also in Hong Kong and Taiwan). The development of global markets has occurred symbiotically with the growth of very large global corporations that orchestrate the flow of goods, people, capital, and ideas on a massive scale (the classic case being Japan's *sogo shosha*). The growth of very large global corporations is at the expense of regional firms. Thus, one sees a shift from local diffuse control, which tended to funnel wealth into Vancouver, to a more centralized and often offshore control of the province's resource sector. This sector is increasingly controlled by companies from resource-hungry Asian economies (for example, North-East Coal and Nippon Steel).

Counterpoised to the development of behemoth global corporations is the proliferation of very small local firms. These firms are spawned by the processes of vertical disintegration whereby larger corporations subcontract facets of their business to cut risk and increase flexibility. These small firms need to be extremely flexible in meeting the demands of the quickly changing global marketplace and the large corporations which purchase their products or services (many of which want products or services immediately). They are a dynamic but very unstable side of the economy. The number of such firms is growing rapidly in Vancouver. The "dynamism" of this small, flexible sector also comes to be reflected in the fabric of the city with the proliferation and concentration of small, white-collar businesses engaged in producer services. These "post-industrial" workers tend to work and reside near the urban core and demand specific urban amenities (such as gentrification).

To succeed in a fluid, competitive, and global marketplace it seems necessary to keep government regulation and labour organization to a minimum. The pull in this direction comes from two areas. Small busi-nesses and large corporations are aided and encouraged by the various levels of government (municipal, provincial, and federal), a potent polit-ical mix that is reshaping the city. The primary ethic of the city thus be-comes establishing its competitiveness in the global economy, a driving outward ethos that seems to clash with the ideas of a comfortable, eco-logically correct "village on the edge of the rainforest".[14]

This is the issue Manuel Castells so consistently hammers away at in much of his more recent work (Castells 1996). Cities are faced with an unpleasant choice. In order to succeed it seems cities must engage the world economy. To "opt out" does not appear to be an option; thus, it seems the city must accept the impingement of international forces and all the social, political, and economic strains this entails.

The strain of this seemingly abstract model can be seen in Vancouver. Stress has been a consistent theme in this section: it underlies the love/hate relationship with Asia, the pro/anti-development rift, and the split over the move to world city status. It is also at the base of the socio-political structure of the city. Vancouver will, like all cities, continue to be the outcome of struggle. What is clear from this admittedly sketchy analysis is that the various levels of government have put in place a strategic plan for the managing of a sustainable scenario for the future of the Van-couver metropolitan region that offers some grounds for optimism.[15]

The changes discussed here encompass some piercing political ques-tions. Where will the region go from here? Will the region attain the vision of its premier architect, Arthur Erickson, and some day reach 22 million people, or will the traditional love of the city for its environment provoke a revulsion for the ecological costs of economic development and lead the city more towards the model of a kind of "ecoville"?

The answer is as yet unclear, but one can certainly conclude that the creation of a "liveable region" will be an important part of the com-petitiveness of the Vancouver region in the twenty-first century. It is also clearly established that Vancouver is no longer on the edge of the rain-forest but is now part of the Asia Pacific region. Is the "code" already cracked?

Notes

1. For much the same reason the author inserted the same quote in *The Southeast Asian City* published in 1967. He was, of course, much more concerned with inserting the idea of third world poverty into the mind of the reader than in analysing why this idea had to be inserted.
2. Although in view of the current fiscal crisis in Asia, it may well be that in cities such as Jakarta and Bangkok this goal will have to be postponed in order to cope with the more pressing tasks of alleviating poverty and creating a macro-environment which will aid economic recovery (see McGee 1999).
3. The exception to this was the "Chinatown" located close to the core of the city.
4. The earliest representation of the region occurred in Callenbach's (1975) novel. It was popularized in Garreau (1981).
5. The GVRD has an excellent website with up-to-date factual information on the Vancouver region: ⟨http.www.gvrd.bc.ca⟩.
6. Personal discussion with Ken Cameron, regional planner of the Greater Vancouver Regional District.
7. Recent revisions to the BC Municipal Act recognize that municipalities now take on many more responsibilities than before. Some public groups have argued that low rates of voter participation in municipal elections could be remedied by the introduction of a ward system.
8. Note that recent population projections provide data at the level of the Vancouver metropolitan region, which encompasses a small area of the lower Fraser valley outside the GVRD.
9. Under the new system, prospective immigrants were given preferential ranking under a points system that included professional skills and family reunion. This eliminated the "racial bias" of the earlier immigration provisions.
10. See Hutton 1997 for a more detailed discussion of economic change in the Vancouver EMR.
11. For a discussion of the ideological rationale for the Asia Pacific region, see Watters and McGee 1997.
12. See for example, Paul Yee (1986) on the Sam Kee Company of Vancouver at the turn of the century, or the work of Chadney (1984) on Indo-Canadian links to their homelands. Robinson 1988 could also be consulted.
13. Goldberg (1985) presents the first evidence for this "amenity" factor in immigration in the Vancouver case study.
14. This phrase has been attributed to a *New York Times* article that was commenting on the loss of the New York Cosmos (including at that time the famous Pele) to the Vancouver Whitecaps in the final of the North American soccer competition.
15. By contrast, the historical, cultural, institutional, and political features of many Asian urban regions make the task of establishing regional management authorities extraordinarily difficult (see McGee and Robinson 1996; Rüland 1996).

REFERENCES

Callenbach, E. 1975. *Ecotopia: The Notebooks and Reports of William Weston*. Berkeley: Banyan Tree Books.

Castells, Manuel. 1996. *The Information Age: Economy, Society, and Culture, The Rise of Network Society*. Vol. 1. London: Blackwell.

Chadney, J. 1984. *The Sikhs of Vancouver*. New York: AMS Press.

Edgington, David. 1995. "Trade, investment and the new regionalism: Cascadia and its economic linkages with Japan", *Canadian Journal of Regional Science*, Vol. XVIII, p. 3.

Edgington, David and M. Goldberg. 1991. "Vancouver, Canada's gateway to the rim", in E. J. Blakely and R. J. Stimson (eds) *New Cities of the Pacific Rim*. UC Berkeley: Institute of Urban and Regional Development.

Fladell, M. 1989. "The immigration boom: Business immigration to Canada", *Lifestyle* (Chinese edition), pp. 29–34.

Garreau, Joel. 1981. *The Nine Nations of North America*. Boston: Houghton, Mifflin.

Goldberg, M. A. 1985. *The Chinese Connection: Getting Plugged into the Pacific Rim Real Estate, Trade and Capital Markets*. Vancouver: University of British Columbia Press.

Greater Vancouver Regional Authority. 1990. *Creating our Future*. Vancouver: Greater Vancouver Regional Authority.

Harvey, David. 1989. *The Condition of Post Modernity*. Oxford: Oxford University Press.

Hutnyck, Jon. 1996. *The Rumour of Calcutta. Tourism. Charity and the Poverty of Representation*. London: Zed Books.

Hutton, Tom. 1997. *The Transformation of Canada's Pacific Metropolis: A Study of Vancouver*. Montreal: Institute for Research on Public Policy.

Innis, H. A. 1933. *Problems of Staple Production in Canada*. Toronto: Ryerson.

Levi-Strauss, Claude. 1962. "Crowds", *New Left Review*, No. 15, pp. 3–6.

Ley, David, Daniel Hiebert, and Geraldine Pratt. 1992. "Time to grow up? From urban village to world city, 1996–91", in Graeme Wynn and Tom Oke (eds) *Vancouver and its Region*. Vancouver: University of British Columbia Press.

Lindfield, Michael and Robert Stimson. 1999. "Urban economic development and globalization linkages in the Pacific Rim", in John Brotchie, Peter Newton, Peter Hall, and John Dickey (eds) *East-West Perspectives on 21st Century Urban Development*. Aldershot: Ashgate.

Lo, Fu-chen and Yue-man Yeung. 1996. "Introduction", in Fu-chen Lo and Yue-man Yeung (eds) *Emerging World Cities in Pacific Asia*. Tokyo: United Nations University Press, pp. 1–13.

Marr, B. E. 1996. "The Greater Vancouver Regional District: Its purpose, programs and administrative structure", unpublished paper, GVRD.

McGee, T. G. 1967. *The Southeast Asian City. A Social Geography of the Primate Cities of Southeast Asia*. London: G. Bell and Sons.

McGee, T. G. 1999. "Urbanization in an era of volatile globalization: Policy problematiques for the 21st century", in John Brotchie, Peter Newton, Peter Hall, and John Dickey (eds). *East-West Perspectives on 21st Century Urban Development*. Aldershot, Ashgate.

McGee, T. G. and Ira Robinson (eds). 1996. *The Mega-Urban Regions of Southeast Asia*. Vancouver: University of British Columbia Press.

Pivo, Gary. 1996. "Towards sustainable urbanization on mainstream Cascadia", *Cities*, Vol. 13, No. 5. pp. 339–354.

Robinson, J. L. 1988. "Vancouver – Changing geographical aspects to a multi-cultural city", *B.C. Studies*, Autumn, pp. 59–80.

Rüland, Jürgen (ed.). 1996. *The Dynamics of Metropolitan Management in Southeast Asia*. Singapore: Institute of Southeast Asian Studies.

Sassen, Saskia. 1994. *Cities in a World Economy*. Thousand Oaks, CA: Pine Forge Press.

Schnell, P. and J. Hamer. 1993. "What is the future of Cascadia? Discover Institute Inquiry", Occasional Paper No. 2. Seattle: Discovery Institute.

Scott, Allen J. 1996. "Regional motors of the global economy", *Futures*, Vol. 28, No. 5, pp. 391–411.

The Economist. 1994. "Welcome to Cascadia", *The Economist*, 21 May.

The Vancouver Sun. 1997. 12 March.

Watters, R. F. and T. G. McGee (eds). 1997. *Asia Pacific: New Geographies of the Pacific Rim*. London: Hurst.

Yee, Paul. 1986. *Saltwater: An Illustrated History of Chinese in Vancouver*. Vancouver: Douglas & McIntyre.

Conclusion

15

Globalization and the sustainability of cities in the Asia Pacific region

Peter J. Marcotullio

Introduction

As has been mentioned several times in chapters of this volume, urban sustainability can only be achieved, at the minimum, through addressing the economic, ecological, and social health of the city. At the same time, scholars have recognized that urban areas are not autonomous units, but rather part of a larger development milieu. As mentioned in the Introduction, there is a body of literature that problematizes urban sustainability, in terms of the social, economic, and environmental development of cities, at the international scale (see, for example, Harris 1992; Stren, White, and Whitney 1992; Burgess, Carmona, and Kolstee 1997; Low *et al.* 2000). This chapter also attempts to associate the concepts of urban sustainability and globalization. Using the Asia Pacific region as a case study, the "functional city system" concept of Lo and Yeung (1996) is used to distinguish urban environmental and social issues among types of cities, categorized by their role within the regional production system. The argument implicates the emergence of the regional system as a condition for addressing urban environmental and social sustainability, and therefore directs attention to the role of supra-local policies.

This is not to imply that globalization forces are the only important influences on urban development. While transnational flows have been particularly strong within cities in the Asia Pacific, local factors play a crucial role in growth. Globalization-driven progress has not translated

455

into a single path of development, rather localities have demonstrated contextually specific paths. That is, addressing urban sustainability will require both local and international policies.

This chapter is divided into five sections. The first section presents an overview of urban sustainability perspectives, stressing the importance of placing cities within a broad development context. The second section provides a brief review of social and environment urban development in the Asia Pacific region, demonstrating the relationships between these issues and globalization forces. The third section discusses the recent Asian financial crisis and its social impacts on urban centres around the region. At the same time, it provides an opportunity to review the benefits and costs of previous development aims. As a result of reassessment, a new perspective, based on sustainability, is emerging. The fourth section distinguishes among various pressures related to the role of cities within the regional city system, and the variety of urban social and physical conditions experienced by types of urban centres. In the fifth and last section the chapter addresses how local conditions affected the world city formation process and influenced these circumstances.

Connecting the discourse on urban sustainability to globalization

As Graham Haughton (1999a, 1999b) suggests, among the visions of urban sustainability there are at least four competing perspectives – in his terms, "free-market", "redesigned", "self-reliant", and "fair shares" cities models. Of these visions, two (the "self-reliant" and the "redesigned" city) either do not explicitly address an external orientation or restrict their resource usage to a bio-region. Their focus is on improving individual components of the city, preserving natural assets, and encouraging small decentralized communities. While providing insights into aspects of urban development and how to make cities more equitable and environmentally friendly, they are limited in that they suggest that cities are/should be autonomous self-dependent units. Indeed, the idea of self-sufficient cities within ecologically defined regions or green cities efficiently planned for local transportation, residence, and industrial and commercial activities is not aligned to global current trends. Increasingly, urban growth in the region is dependent upon non-local forces (flows of trade, investment, people, information, etc.) and actors (transnational corporations, multinational financial institutions, international non-governmental organizations, etc.).

The two remaining visions attempt to combine global and local factors into sustainable urban growth. They reject attempts to divorce cities from their broader development context. One model, the "free-market" city, posits that urban centres undergoing economic development will inevitably overcome both environmental and social challenges as they grow in wealth. Thus, while growth is a transnational issue, a good social and physical environment is strictly a local one. Liberalization of trade and investment, therefore, are the preferred national policies, and preparing cities for increased transnational linkages forms the basis of desired local planning strategies. Further, this model suggests that wealth will trickle down to lower classes as incomes increase.

One interpretation of the relationship described by advocates of the "free-market" sustainable urban vision is the environmental "Kuznets" curve, named after an economist who studied the relationship between economic growth and income inequality. This curve describes a functional relationship between environmental problems and income, and is similar to an inverted "U" shape. It predicts that as nations and cities grow, environmental problems increase until a point in their development when societal changes in institutions and ideologies force changes in environmental management. The results, some argue, will be a transition from low to high to low environmental pollution levels.

A comparison of conditions among sets of cities has provided evidence as to whether cities do indeed undergo an "urban environmental transition". This research attempts to understand if and how increasing wealth (in terms of GDP) can be used to distinguish the environmental performance of cities. Rather then finding a simple relationship, however, researchers have found two important results. First, as wealth increases, "urban problems become spatially more extensive and priorities shift from environmental health to sustainability" (McGranahan and Songsore 1994: 7). With urban growth, environmental problems spill over to larger and larger geographical areas. Second, with growth different types of pollution and environmental problems increase and decrease. For example, in low-income communities, poverty-related and sanitary issues are of most importance, but quickly decrease with increasing income. At the same time, manufacturing-production-related pollution increases with industrialization (later to decrease with expanding wealth and increased interest in the environment). Finally, in developed countries, despite investment in pollution-related infrastructure, consumption-related pollution levels increase (Pugh 1996). The "urban environmental transition" thus consists of several environmental stages defined by changes in conditions associated first with poverty, then with manufacturing production, and finally with consumption (Bai and Imura 2000). Therefore, highly developed urbanized nations still face severe environmental challenges.

A study of Japan's experience with air pollution instructively demonstrates the later half of the stage model. The first stage of air pollution control ended in 1973. By that time the nation's industrial air pollution was dramatically reduced by governmental regulation, the procurement of low-sulphur crude oil, and the planning and introduction of heavy oil desulphurization facilities. Thereafter, the battle shifted to urban and domestic air pollution caused by nitrogen oxide emissions. Based on the techniques used before 1973, and with some help from the oil shocks that encouraged energy conservation measures and hastened a structural transformation from heavy to machine assembly and information industries, Japan achieved further success. In the transportation sector, however, policy measures related to manufacturing production, distribution, and land use were not effective and the pollution situation remains unsatisfactory. The lack of success, despite massive investments (at 1990 prices, Japan spent US$46.7 billion from 1960 to 1995 on air pollution control technologies), has been attributed to both renewed energy demand increases and lifestyle consumption-related activities (automobile ownership tripled from 21.2 million in 1971 to 68.1 million in 1994).

The studies of environmental transition in nations and cities have been instructive, in that they have demonstrated that growth does not automatically and naturally produce beneficial environmental conditions and therefore have exposed weaknesses in the "fair shares" urban sustainable model.

Haughton's final vision of urban sustainability is the most complex and least developed. It proposes that while city regions are restricted by carrying capacity, trade and other flows should be encouraged (but only if guided by social and environmental concerns). This model takes features from the redesigned and the self-reliant city models (for example, increased regional autarky, greater urban compaction, and improved use of market tools for engaging in more equitable trading relationships with other areas), and it also recognizes that global and regional flows are important for development. It therefore engages the issues of scale so important to urban centres in the region. This perspective recognizes the importance of international flows associated with globalization, but also advocates policies to address imbalances.

The challenge of fleshing out the relationships between globalization and changing conditions within urban settings calls for an analysis of international urban systems. With globalization as the backdrop to development, the entire growth milieu of nations and their cities is changing. For example, rather than finding that growth brings prosperity for all, incomes in nations that are globalized are polarizing. Further, social, criminal, and spiritual influences are also moving across borders, affecting developing countries. Cities, under increased pressure of competition, are carving out particular functional roles at different levels within the international, regional, or global economy. Given the enormous task of uncovering the variety of ways in which globalization is impacting on urban development, it is no surprise that research has only just begun to address globalization and urban sustainability. Within the literature on "sustainable cities" there are limited international comparative studies currently available and even fewer on the influences of globalization.

As opposed to a strictly conclusory chapter that brings together the points made in other chapters in the text, this piece attempts this additional analysis, but only partially. The proposed framework used to construct this research suggests that within the Asia Pacific region, globalization influences the environmental and social performance of metropolitan urban regions articulated to the regional city system. This issue is argued in parts throughout the text, but not in each chapter. This particular section of the book will present the functional city system as increasingly defining urban economic activities and social/environmental trends; it can therefore help to distinguish among types and causes of urban environmental and social conditions. At the same time, it presents the world city formation process as a local process that allows for a variety of developmental paths. Indeed, globalization forces only set the general context for transformations in states and societies as they adapt to greater interconnectedness (see for example Held *et al.* 1999).

Urban social and environmental development in the Asia Pacific region

The physical urban transformations described in great detail in various chapters throughout the text were accompanied by dramatic social changes, including increases in per capita incomes (Table 15.1). Rapid and prolonged wealth creation for nations and their societies prompted some analysts to call Asian development a "miracle" (World Bank 1993). The economic indicators alone, however, do not capture the social transformations in the region. It was not only wealth that was increased, but also the quality of life in Asia dramatically improved, as manifested in reductions in shares of population below basic-needs poverty lines, longer life expectancy, reductions in birth mortality, increases in access to basic services, and greater literacy (ADB 1997).

Levels of poverty within the region dropped substantially. From 1987 to 1993, the Asia Pacific experienced decreases in both numbers of people living absolute poverty (a drop from 464 million to 446 million) and the percentage of total population living in absolute poverty (28.8 per cent to 26.0 per cent), while Europe, Central Asia, Latin America, the Middle

Table 15.1 Trends in GDP per capita in selected economies

Country	GDP per capita (1987 US$)				
	1960	1970	1980	1990	1995
Japan	4,706	11,892	16,384	22,928	24,104
Hong Kong	1,631	3,128	5,939	9,897	11,911
Singapore	1,510	3,067	5,907	9,877	13,451
Korea	520	967	1,953	4,132	5,663
Thailand	300	487	718	1,291	1,843
Malaysia	708	1,001	1,688	2,301	3,108
Indonesia	190	211	349	537	720
Philippines	2,043	887	1,483	1,759	587
China	75	92	138	285	481
Argentina	2,701	3,533	3,996	3,150	3,793
Mexico	938	1,363	1,949	1,839	1,724
Brazil	823	1,145	2,049	1,952	2,051
World	1,951	2,660	3,116	3,298	3,417
Developing	330	474	685	736	867
Industrialized	7,097	9,344	11,169	12,310	12,764

Source: UNDP various years

East, North Africa, South Asia, and sub-Saharan Africa all experienced increases in the number of people in poverty (World Bank, 1999). In Hong Kong, Taiwan, and Singapore, poverty has disappeared. It has almost been eliminated in the Republic of Korea and Malaysia. For example, in Malaysia poverty levels dropped from 49 per cent in 1970 to 21 per cent in 1980 and 9 per cent in 1995. In Indonesia, the incidence of poverty was halved from 60 to 29 per cent during the 1970s. By 1990 it had dropped by half again to 15 per cent. The Philippines and Thailand, however, made less progress in this area (ADB 1997).

Over the last 30 years, Asian nations have experienced increased life expectancy rates (Table 15.2) while birth mortality declined (Table 15.3). No doubt these trends are related to better nutrition and healthcare services. As Asians' chances for their own survival and the survival of their children increased, so fertility has dropped. While there is dramatic variation among nations in the region, between 1950 and 1990 the general trend for the number of children per typical Asian woman has fallen from six to three (ADB 1997). The region has undergone a rapid demographic transition.

The United Nations Development Programme (UNDP) has integrated various development indicators into a "human development index".[1] Notwithstanding the general nature of these indicators, their trends for

Table 15.2 Life expectancy trends in selected countries

Country	Expectancy in years	
	1960	1997
Japan	72	80
Korea	54	72
Taiwan		
Hong Kong	66	79
Singapore	65	78
Indonesia	41	65
Thailand	52	69
Philippines	53	68
Malaysia	54	72
China	47	70
Argentina	65	73
Brazil	55	67
Mexico	57	72
World	50	67
Developing	46	64
Industrialized	69	78

Source: UNDP 1998

countries in the region confirm a significant level of social and economic advances over the last three to four decades (Table 15.4).

Up until recently this was the model for urban development within the region. In 1997 and 1998, however, countries in Asia that had enjoyed high growth rates, maintained full employment, and were making significant strides in reducing poverty suffered severe economic contractions. The speed and intensity with which the crisis mounted within country after country surprised the world. Some have commented that during this period, globalization took a step backwards (ADB 1999).

The impacts of the Asian financial crisis

Some of the details of the Asian financial crisis were discussed in the Introduction and various chapters throughout the text. Across the region, the social consequences of the crisis include increases in unemployment and prices of goods, drops in human development and social capital, and increases in poverty (Lee 1998; ADB 1999; Gupta et al. 1998). Of course the consequences vary across countries, but in general those most often hurt were the poor and vulnerable (women, children, and migrant workers).

Table 15.3 Infant mortality trends in selected countries

Country	Deaths per thousand	
	1960	1997
Japan	14*	4
Korea	85	6
Singapore	36	4
Taiwan		
Indonesia	139	45
Thailand	103	31
Philippines	79	32
Malaysia	72	10
China	150	38
Argentina	60	21
Brazil	116	37
Mexico	95	29
World	129	58
Developing	149	64
Industrialized	39	6

Source: UNDP 1998
* = 1970

Unemployment rates have risen in Indonesia, Thailand, Korea, and the Philippines. In Indonesia, the rate rose to 5.5 per cent in 1998, up from 4.7 per cent the previous year. In Thailand it reached 5.3 per cent, compared with just about 1 per cent in 1997. The unemployment rate in Korea more than doubled to 6.8 per cent, while in the Philippines it climbed to 9.6 per cent. The condition of underemployment also increased markedly. Standards of living have fallen as inflation outstripped any increase in income. The crisis has reduced household expenditures on health and nutrition, education, and family planning. It also set back strides made in decreasing poverty. Large numbers of people are falling below poverty levels. The environment has also suffered serious degradation related to the crisis, exacerbated by the needs of poor households. Those families attempting to obtain additional income during this period have resorted to environmental destruction. Further, many countries are experiencing an increase in crime and violence, including domestic violence (ABD 1999).

The crisis has been most deeply felt in Asia's cities (Chatterjee 1998; Gould and Smith 1998; Douglass 1998a; Firman 1998, 1999). Impacts include economic, political, and physical changes to all sizes of urban

Table 15.4 Trends in human development

Country	Human development index				
	1960	1970	1980	1990	1995
Japan	0.686	0.875	0.906	0.983	0.939
Hong Kong	0.561	0.737	0.830	0.913	0.909
Singapore	0.519	0.682	0.780	0.849	0.896
Korea	0.398	0.523	0.666	0.872	0.894
Indonesia	0.223	0.306	0.418	0.515	0.679
Philippines	0.419	0.489	0.557	0.603	0.677
Thailand	0.373	0.465	0.551	0.715	0.838
Malaysia	0.330	0.471	0.687	0.790	0.834
China	0.248	0.372	0.475	0.566	0.650
Brazil	0.392	0.507	0.673	0.730	0.809
Argentina	0.667	0.748	0.790	0.832	0.888
Mexico	0.517	0.642	0.758	0.805	0.855

Source: UNDP 1998

centres in the region. Most commentators have noted the closed businesses, increases in unemployment and urban poverty, reduced public expenditures on infrastructure and service provision, growing vacant lands, and empty high-rise buildings and partially finished construction sites. Among the hardest hit was Jakarta. The related crises, both economic and political (Robison and Rosser 1998; Haut 1999), have turned Jabotabek from a "global city" into a "city of crisis" (Firman 1999).

The speed and sustainability of the current recoveries are uncertain, and problems may emerge elsewhere in the region (UNCTAD 1999). It appears, however, that the worst of the crisis is over. As Palanivel and Lo (1999: 11–12) have noted "The recovery, led by South Korea and hotly followed by Thailand, Malaysia, Singapore, and the Philippines, does look genuine and quite vigorous." The IMF (1999) predicted that growth will turn positive for the various groups of Asian economies in the year 2000 (Table 15.5). The full social effects of the crisis and the sustainability of current conditions can only be measured after some time has passed.

The impact of the crisis on regional policy theory has been heightened by the social problems accompanying the crisis and by pollution levels that have increased faster than GDP even during the most rapid growth periods (Brandon 1994).[2] The 1997–1998 crisis has forced scholars and decision-makers to view the region's globalization-driven growth in a significantly different light (McGee 1998; Douglass 1998b). The old model, based on the Japanese experience of "grow now, clean later", has been

Table 15.5 World economic output projections

Country/region/area	Annual % change			
	1997	1998	1999	2000
World	4.2	2.5	2.3	3.4
G7	3.0	2.2	1.9	2.0
Japan	1.4	−2.8	−1.4	0.3
Asian NIEs	6.0	−1.5	2.1	4.5
Developing countries	5.7	3.3	3.1	4.9
Africa	3.1	3.4	3.2	5.1
Asia	6.6	3.8	4.7	5.7
ASEAN-4	3.8	−9.4	−1.1	3.0
China	8.8	7.8	6.6	7.0
Countries in transition	2.2	−0.2	−0.9	2.5

Source: IMF 1999

proven faulty and is being replaced by one that includes immediately
mitigating environmental and social problems (Webster 1995; Kato 1998;
Cruz, Takemoto, and Warford 1998). Sustainability is increasingly included as an important component in development strategies.

Globalization and urban sustainability in the Asia Pacific

When surveying the state of the urban environmental across Asia, damage is often aggregated and compared across different cities to demonstrate difficult conditions. Asia's environmental performance has not
matched its economic or human development progress. Indeed, pollution
is one of the greatest challenges for the region. In general, Asian environmental quality has deteriorated to the extent that the region is one of
the world's most polluted. Environmental conditions in many countries
are severe (Table 15.6).

Conditions in urban Pacific Asia have been referred to as an "urban-
industrial environmental crisis" (Douglass and Ooi 1999). Water, air, and
solid waste conditions in urban areas have reached extreme levels. Asian
rivers contain three to four times the level of faecal pollutants than the
world average (ADB 1997). The water supplies within most metropolitan
regions in Pacific Asia are at or nearing crisis points (Douglass and Ooi
1999). Rapidly growing urban populations have accompanied increasing
physical coverage by cities, leading to a loss of ground cover, deforestation of uplands around cities, contamination of aquifers, and seepage of
seawater into water supply sources.

The air in Asia's cities is among the dirtiest in the world. The levels of

Table 15.6 Relative severity of environmental problems in Asia

Pollutant	East Asia	South-East Asia	China
Air pollution			
Sulphur dioxide	XXX	XX	XX
Particulates		XX	XX
Lead		XXX	X
Water pollution			
Suspended solids		XX	XXX
Faecal coliforms		XXX	XX
Biological oxygen demand		XXX	
Nitrates	XX	X	XX
Lead	XX	XXX	X
Access to water and sanitation			
Lack of access to safe water		XXX	X
Lack of access to sanitation		XXX	XXX

X: Moderage but rising
XX: Severe
XXX: Very severe
Source: Asian Development Bank 1997

ambient particulate matter – smoke particles and dust, which are a major cause of respiratory diseases – are generally twice the world average and more than five times as high as in industrial countries. Ten of Asia's 11 megacities exceeded WHO guideline values for particulate matter by a factor of at least three, four exceed acceptable lead levels, and three exceed acceptable ozone and sulphur dioxide levels (WHO and UNEP 1992).[3] Lead causes blood poisoning and significantly impairs children's cognitive development in cities such as Bangkok. Indeed, young populations throughout the region's urban centres have been affected negatively. Ambient levels of sulphur dioxide – an important cross-border pollutant that contributes to acid rain, which in turn damages crops and eats away at synthetic structures – are 50 per cent higher in Asia than in either Africa or Latin America (ADB 1997). Some Asian cities are so thickly covered with air pollutants that they are not visible on satellite photographs (Elsom 1996).

The local governmental responses to urban problems are inadequate. For example, sanitary collection of waste services within some individual cities remains low, with only 50 to 70 per cent of resident receiving any service (Cointreau-Levine 1994; UNEP 1993; Dua and Esty 1997). Some estimates suggest that only 2 per cent of waste is treated in cities in some developing countries in the region (*FEER* 1997). Potentially more dangerous than ordinary municipal solid wastes are the growing quantities of hazardous and toxic wastes that hospitals, certain factories, and households generate. Surprisingly, the PRC (which generates 50 million tonnes per year) and India (which generates 40 million tonnes per year) produce 10 times more hazardous waste per person annually than Korea, Hong Kong, or Singapore and 100 times more per person annually than Japan (ESCAP 1995). In Asia, 60–65 per cent of hazardous waste is put in dumpsites or landfills, 5–10 per cent is dumped in the ocean, and the rest is incinerated or chemically treated (UNEP 1993). In most cases, proper safeguards are absent or largely ineffective (ADB 1997).

These descriptions, however, do not hold for all cities. Indeed, as many chapters in the volume demonstrated, the concerns of a city such as Tokyo are not the same as for Vancouver or Shanghai, for example.

The regional city system and urban sustainability in the Asia Pacific

As is argued throughout this text, in the Asia Pacific a functional city system has emerged. Theoretically, not only does this functional city system impact on the economic growth of cities, but the roles that urban centres play within the larger regional system also significantly relate to the environmental and social conditions within the city. Indeed, it is increasingly difficult to distinguish between industrial and urban impacts on the environment (Douglass and Ooi 1999). The two processes are linked at the mega-urban regional level through a set of activities that are increasingly cross-border in nature (McGee and Robinson 1995). That is, the growth of these large regions and increasing investment, capital flows, and other transnational activities are occurring simultaneously. In part, therefore, understanding the urban macro-development trends helps to explain their costs. The context for understanding "urban sustainability" in this region will vary not only with the level of national development, but also with the functional role of the urban centre in the regional economy.

Below is a brief description of the topology of urban environmental and social problems found in cities in the region, based upon their functional roles in the international city system (Table 1.4). In general, distinct patterns can be ascertained that are associated with different economic functions and activities. In the case of air pollution indicators, for example, the highest concentrations of particulate matter are in the industrial cities (Table 15.7). Not only are environmentally related conditions categorized by urban type, but there are predictable social distinctions appearing in cities of different functional attributes (Table 15.8). Further speculative evidence is provided for the relationship between the social and environmental conditions in cities and the cities' regional/global functions.

Table 15.7 Suspended particles in selected Asian cities

City	Concentration of particles (ug/m^3)
Tokyo	45
Seoul	72
Taipei	55
Singapore	35
Hong Kong	79
Jakarta	140
Bangkok	330
Shanghai	215

Source: Choong 1999

Table 15.8 Infant mortality in selected cities in Asia

City	Infant mortality (deaths/1,000)
Tokyo	5
Seoul	12
Taipei	5
Hong Kong	7
Singapore	7
Bangkok	27
Jakarta	40
Metro Manila	36
Shanghai	14
Sydney	10

Sources: Population Crisis Committee 1990; UNCHS Habitat 2000

Capital exporters (post-industrial cities)

As mentioned in Chapter 2, the post-industrial city, such as Tokyo, Seoul, and to a lesser extent Taipei, is dominated by the processing of information and knowledge and the production of advanced business services. In the Asia Pacific region, the capital exporters are on the top of the hierarchy. These cities are the sites of concentrations of TNC headquarters, multinational banks, and producer and business services. At the same time these cities are expanding outward, leaving inner-city workers with longer commutes as many of the jobs remain in the inner-city area, despite large and efficient mass transit systems (Chapters 6 and 7). Manufacturing industries have decentralized while advanced services are concentrated in the core regions of the city. The urban population is wealthy and increasingly polarized in terms of income (see for example Sassen 1994). Contemporary development pressures have positioned consumption-related pollution, open space/quality of life issues, and issues pertaining to sprawl high on the list of policy priorities.

These cities have effectively reduced poverty and industrial pollution, and they are now struggling with consumption-related pollution and quality of life issues. While cities such as Tokyo and Seoul have been able to control air pollution from their point sources, they are still attempting to control the increase in air pollution that has accompanied lifestyle changes (increased automobile usage) (Sawa 1997; TMG 1999; Korean Ministry of Environment 1999), water pollution from household waste effluents, and neighbourhood noise pollution (TMG 2000). In Seoul, for example, automobile ownership has increased from 60,000 vehicles in 1970 to over 2.2 million in 1999, bringing with it congestion, noise, and air pollution (SMG 2000). Related to high levels of consumption are pollution emissions from waste treatment. For example, dioxin levels and a recent accident at a nearby nuclear power plant in Tokyo have raised concerns of citizens.

Urban strategies in post-industrial capital exporters that deal with consumption-related pollution levels have increasingly included new environmental strategies, demand management, and recycling strategies. In Tokyo, recent attempts to combat pollution from incinerator plants, for example, include achieving ISO 14,001 certification for environmental quality performance (*Tokyo Metropolitan News* 1999). Seoul has recently set up a pricing system for the *namsan* tunnels (that feed into the CBD) in an attempt to reduce traffic (Chapter 6). Japan, Korea, and Taiwan have adopted strict regulations on separating household waste for municipal pick-up, which has facilitated recycling efforts. Seoul's new waste management plan focuses on reducing the source of waste by approximately 1 per cent and increasing recycling of waste to 53 per cent by the year 2002 (SMG 2000). Tokyo's water plan promotes the use of rainwater and the recycling of wastewater (*Tokyo Metropolitan News* 1999).

Also high on the policy agenda of these cities is maintaining a high quality of life for wealthy groups of citizens, including increasing open space, waterfront access, urban entertainment, and cultural activities (Kato 1998). Among large cities in the developed world, Tokyo's comparatively low level of land designated as public open space has prompted the city's planners to promote laws to increase "greenery" (TMG 2000). Seoul residents are also increasingly expressing dissatisfaction with the lack of parks and open space (Chapter 6). One current and acrimonious debate within the city is how to reform the green-belt policy that since the early 1970s has attempted to maintain a belt of controlled development and open space around the city (see for example Choe 1998).

In general, Japan and Korea are responding vigorously through legislation to their individual environmental problems neglected in the early decades of their economic development. In Korea, almost the entire body of environmental legislation now in use has been adopted or updated since the early 1990s (OECD 1997). Korea's Green Vision 21 focuses on creating high-quality environments throughout the country by investing about US$66 billion in environmental infrastructure, among other actions (Korean Ministry of Environment 1999). In Tokyo, several new laws including the Tokyo Metropolitan Basic Environment Plan (1997) and the new Environmental Impact Assessment (1998) are attempts to improve the city's environmental quality.

Lastly, capital-exporting cities have recently experienced increases in land values within the city centres, such that working populations have sought residences further away from the centre. Seoul, in an effort to control housing development, launched a 2 million-unit housing construction programme in 1989 and about 80,000 new homes have been built in the city every year since 1980. In 1985, the housing supply ratio (the proportion of households requiring housing units which actually have a unit) was down to approximately 58 per cent; with government efforts it has increased to over 70 per cent (SMG 2000). Tokyo's land demand pressures have created two problems. Younger residents have moved out to the suburban fringes, where as commuters they have notoriously long and congested journeys to work. Despite an excellent and expanding public rail and subway system, passenger boarding rates are around 197 per cent of capacity (TMG 1996). Some workers must travel one-and-a-half to two hours each way in these conditions to get to work. An increasing proportion of those remaining in the city area are elderly, and by 2015 Tokyo will face the situation where almost 25 per cent of the population will be over 65 years of age (TMG 1999).

Capital-exporting cities are reaching a level of maturity associated with a deconcentration of manufacturing industries and population. In the case of Tokyo, it has already been through an environmental transition, although the city is finding it increasingly important to control consumption-related pollution and strike a balance among the many different urban functions and the quality of life issues demanded by the higher-income segment of an increasingly polarized society. Seoul is not that far behind. Vast amounts of public infrastructure have been developed in and around these cities, which has helped to put them on top of both their national and regional urban hierarchies.

Sites of FDI: Industrial cities

Industrial manufacturing processes are vitally important to the growth and development of the region, and hence manufacturing centres play an important role in the functional city system. Global integration has affected the pattern of development by encouraging the concentration of a ring of manufacturing plants in a doughnut fashion around the city cores (Chapter 2, Chapters 10–12). With rapid industrialization and uncontrolled population growth, these cities have been characterized by "unsustainable" processes affecting both environmental (see, for example, Douglass 1991) and social spheres (see, for example, Jellinek 2000).

As manufacturing production has become an increasingly important part of the urban economies of these cities, levels of air and water pollution and concentrations of hazardous wastes are rising. Air pollution is a major problem in industrial cities. Vehicles (particularly two-stroke motorcycles, three-wheel taxis, and diesel buses and trucks) are the major contributors. Cities such as Jakarta, Bangkok, and Shanghai are currently struggling to overcome these types of problems, but increases in vehicle ownership outpace even economic growth, doubling every three years in Thailand and every four years in China (Douglass and Ooi 1999). Air quality continues to deteriorate in cities such as Bangkok and Jakarta as total suspended particulates (TSP) and carbon monoxide increase, primarily from traffic congestion (Webster 1995). The resultant health and productivity effects of pollution cost billions of dollars a year in these cities. For example, the annual cost of air pollution is estimated at US$1.3–3.1 billion in Bangkok, US$1.0–1.6 billion in Kuala Lumpur and the Klang valley, and US$400–800 million in Jakarta (Brandon 1994; World Bank 1992). The human cost is tragic. Bangkok's children have the highest blood lead levels in the world (Setchell 1995). In cities in China, coal-driven electrical generators, used for about three-quarters of the country's energy consumption, have had tremendous impacts on the urban air quality. For example, SO_2 concentrations is cities such as Chongqing, Taiyuan, Qingdoa, and Guiyang (northern cities) substantially exceed the high end of the WHO guidelines for 24-hour exposure scenarios (Lo and Xing 1999). Shanghai's level of SO_2 is well over the annual standard WHO minimum exposure levels.

Water pollution is primarily caused by domestic wastewater flowing into open pits and canals without treatment, but industries are increasingly contributing substantially to the problem. In areas that are served with sewerage, more than 90 per cent of the wastewater is discharged without treatment (WHO 1992). In both Jakarta Bay (Jellinek 2000) and around Bangkok (Phantumvanit and Liengcharensit 1989), harmful industrial wastes are being dumped into waterways. The Chao Praya river running through Bangkok no longer supports life (the dissolved oxygen level in parts of the river is zero at certain times of the year) (Setchell 1995). The city's *klongs*, the storm drainage system, are extremely dirty as much of the city's grey water makes its way directly into these water bodies without treatment of any kind (Daniere 1996). In the mid-1990s sewers served only 2 per cent of the city's population (Webster 1995), although plans were being made to construct wastewater treatment facilities that would handle up to 30 per cent of the population's wastewater (ADB 1996). In the meantime, however, 6 per cent of annual deaths in Bangkok are due to such water-borne plagues as typhus, dysentery, and encephalitis (Annez and Friendly 1996). In Shanghai, river pollution cost the city US$300 million as municipal water intakes were moved 45 kilometres upstream. In the currently developing Pudong New Area, surface water pollution levels are already very serious (Wu 1999).

Solid waste has become a problem associated with inadequate garbage collection. In Jakarta, for example, only between 20 and 25 per cent of the garbage is collected (Pernia 1992; Webster 1995). In the BMR about 20 per cent of solid waste goes uncollected (Daniere 1996).[4] Hazardous waste treatment, particularly hospital wastes and toxic substances, is generally not adequately handled. Sanitary landfills are rare in Kuala Lumpur, Manila, Jakarta, and Bangkok, and much of the municipal garbage is eliminated by less sanitary means such as open burning and dumping into rivers and canals or into abandoned mine sites and swamp areas (Lee 1994).

Many of these major cities are founded on the coast where large rivers run into the ocean. Urban and industrial water contamination is seriously impacting the coastal zone ecology. For example, the effluents in Jakarta Bay include mercury such that levels in the bay are second only to the concentration once recorded in Japan's Minamata Bay (Douglass and Ooi 1999). In Bangkok, approximately 1.5 million cubic metres of untreated domestic and industrial pollutants are discharged directly into the waterways on a regular basis, with significant adverse impacts on water quality (Setchell 1995; Kaothien 1995).

Further, general environmental degradation in and around these cities has created problems of extreme water shortages in dry seasons and dangerous flooding in wet seasons (Douglass and Ooi 1999). Recently problems related to slash-and-burn farming in combination with water shortages during the dry season helped to create the 1997 massive fires in Indonesia which affected an estimated 7 million people (*FEER* 1999). Recent flooding in China, due to deforestation, has claimed over 3,000 lives and cost billions of dollars in property damage.

In terms of transnational flows and environmental conditions, there are at least three important considerations that need further examination. The first implicates global flows in altering the environmental transition in serious ways, creating "environmental risk overlaps". Kirk Smith (1993) suggests that within an urban setting, when there are significant amounts of both traditional and modern risks occurring at the same time, several classes of problems emerge. For example, Smith (*ibid.*) points out that about 40 per cent of the people in China still use crop residues for cooking, creating a traditional risk in homes (smoke from burning bio-fuels).

Now, however, the pesticide residues left on the crops compound the problems associated with the traditional forms of cooking and heating. These risk overlaps are important for large populations in rapidly growing developing countries. Further, in the past, citizens of developing cities might experience environmental risks mostly around the home or within the neighbourhood. Currently, however, significant populations are affected by these risks and in addition have to cope with consumption-related risks that affect larger areas, such as vehicle pollution. These conditions are related to the increasing flows of goods between countries.

The second consideration concerns the role of FDI in environmental pollution. In industrial cities the major environmental pollution sources are manufacturing firms. In industrialized parts of China, for example, 70 per cent of environmental pollution is caused by industry (Liu 2000). Global flows of manufacturing investment contribute to this process. Manufacturing FDI has taken on a clear spatial pattern and sector patterns. A large percentage of FDI stock into nations with industrial cities is in the "pollution-intensive industries" (chemicals, pulp and paper, petroleum and coal processing, and basic metals industries). For example, in 1996, 68.0, 44.1, and 27.4 per cent of all manufacturing inward FDI stock to Indonesia, the Philippines, and Thailand, respectively, were in these types of industries (UNCTAD 1999; see also Brandon 1994). Further, while commercial FDI is located in the central part of the city, most manufacturing investment is directed to the outer edges of the city. The case of Jabotabek is a good example (see Table 2.12). This consequence may be related to lax environmental regulation enforcement in outer areas of the city, among a variety of other location-based decisions. Larger firms tend to locate in explicit industrial zones or industrial estates where their activities are easier to notice.

While foreign direct investment has been one of the most important drivers in the global economy (Dicken 1998), systematic "pollution haven" activities of developed countries have been difficult to establish.[5] Indeed, some have argued that foreign firms tend to be better environmental citizens than locally owned firms, and the challenge for industrial cities is to improve the environmental behaviour of small and medium-sized enterprises (Webster 1995). Notwithstanding the debate, the fact is that many Asian governments see industries as the backbone of economic growth in the coming century. Car manufacturers, for example, create skilled jobs and some companies, such as General Motors, Volkswagen, and Toyota, have invested heavily in countries like Thailand. Other countries, such as Malaysia and Indonesia, have developed their own models (the Proton and Timor). Naturally, all manufacturers are looking forward to a continued growing market for cars. Total automobile sales in China and South-East Asia reached 2.5 million in 1996 and are expected to in-

Table 15.9 Automobile sales in selected Asian countries

Country	1992	1993	1994	1995	1996	2000
Thailand	179,994	230,363	227,587	247,767	261,103	*850,000*
Indonesia	171,898	214,298	326,471	378,704	326,157	*675,000*
Malaysia	138,831	148,284	190,145	272,259	345,134	*457,000*
Philippines	60,417	83,936	99,136	120,340	162,096	*280,000*
China	882,301	1,177,650	1,250,949	1,423,612	1,438,559	*2,210,000*

Source: Doven *et al.* 1997
Note: Italics are estimates

crease by 85 per cent by 2000 (Table 15.9) (Doven *et al.* 1997). Thus, the globalization of the automobile industry not only impacts on urban environments through production processes, but also affects urban air quality when the cars hit the streets. Given the importance of manufacturing in industrial cities and the growing market for cars, the result may be increased pollution.

Third, an important factor for a developing world city's capacity to deal with environmental problems is the contribution of international donors. Increasingly, however, private investment is growing while official development assistance is not. Between 1985 and 1995, average annual bilateral ODA to developing countries remained between US$50 billion and US$60 billion (Esty and Gentry 1997), while during the same period private investment to these economies increased from US$24.7 billion to US$96.3 billion (UNCTAD 1997). Further, donors such as the World Bank have not focused project development on urban environmental issues. Although there have been recent changes to the trend, over the past 15 years substantially less then one-fifth of all spending has been on sewerage and sanitation components (Briscoe 1993; World Bank 1992). This has made private development increasingly important to creating environmentally sustainable third world cities. Unfortunately, privatization in the area of basic infrastructure has been more of a non-event than a panacea (Gilbert 1994).

In terms of social issues, globalization forces together with pro-growth policies in these cities have created a severe wealth gap that has generated social tensions, which by and large are only addressed rhetorically by the local and national states (Schmidt 1998). One basic need that has remained largely unmet in these cities, particularly for low-income families, is housing (Pernia 1992). This problem is most visible in the continuing presence and proliferation of squatters and slum dwellers. In many of these cities a sizeable proportion of the population lives in slum communities. In Bangkok approximately 1.2 million people are slum dwellers, and in Manila approximately 30 per cent of the population live in slums.

While real per capita income increased in Bangkok by 9 per cent a year from 1987 to 1995, for example, Thailand's regional inequality also increased, largely because most of the growth was limited to the city region. Further, despite the impressive gains, poverty also increased in the BMR (Daniere 1996). Between 1984 and 1994 slum housing within 10 kilometres of the city centre declined by 20,376 housing units, but at the same time slum housing in the BMR overall increased by 69 per cent (Setchell 1995). This may be due to evictions caused by globalization-led development pressures (Jellinek 2000). Certainly, in cases of rapidly urbanizing areas, increases in per capita income are not necessarily associated with increases in well-being (Satterthwaite 1995). In Shanghai, the large migrant population has compounded social problems. Approximately 3.3 million temporary migrants and transients are now working and living in the city, and most are not counted as part of the resident population, thus taxing infrastructure and creating significant social pressures (Wu 1999).

While the traditional centre of the city is increasing in population, the outer areas are expanding much more rapidly (Clarke 1996; Douglass 1991; Chapter 11 in this volume). Increasingly, those in the outer rings are the poor, but the population is far from homogeneous. The middle classes are also increasingly part of the fringe (Browder, Bohland, and Scarpaci 1995). In their case, they choose to live in protected developments necessitated by rising social tensions (Leaf 1994; Firman 1997; Jellinek 2000).

Industrial cities may have some of the most severe environmental and social conditions among those in the regional city system. Air, water, and ecosystem damages are widespread and severe. Globalization flows have fuelled the deteriorating state of the environment and helped to create new sets of risks, by-products associated with both traditional and modern lifestyles. Rising social inequalities have resulted in violent explosions, demonstrated in some places during the financial crisis (Haut 1999). Indeed, Indonesia, the state with possibly the greatest regional imbalances, continues to disintegrate. One question of grave importance for these cities is whether growth will bring better environments.

The entrepôts: Borderless cities

Economic globalization has stimulated subregional economic cooperation in several locales, while still others are being planned for implementation. Growth triangles, a development pattern that started in the 1980s, are localized economic zones involving several countries and can be viewed as "borderless" economies where the international division of labour has developed to the city's advantage (Thant, Tang, and Kakazu 1995). An existing and successful "borderless" economy has grown between Singapore, Malaysia (Johor), and Indonesia (Riau islands), called

Sijori (Macleod and McGee 1996; Chapter 9 in this volume). It revolves around the city-state of Singapore, which has recently reached out to acquire the benefits that rural industrialization can provide. The growth of the outer reaches of Singapore's core was directly related to Singapore's maturing economy. The flows of people and goods from the city to the outlying areas accompanied an increasing level of cross-border capital flows. Another example of cross-border cooperative development, involving capital, technological, and managerial inputs, is the integration of Hong Kong, Taiwan, and China's southern provinces of Guangdong and Fujian. Hong Kong is the centre of the Zhujiang delta and has emerged as a financial and headquarters centre (Chapter 8 in this volume). A large proportion of the manufacturing production in Hong Kong relocated to southern Guangdong after China began its policy of economic reform in 1978.

For these cities, achieving a high quality of life has become an important concern (see for example, Foo 2000; ESCAP 1995). While their economies changed from labour-intensive industries in the 1960s and 1970s to high-tech, service, and finance industries in the 1980s and 1990s, they have seen the migration of manufacturing and other related activities across their borders.

Indeed, one of the most successful policy areas for Singapore has been environmental management (Ooi 1995; ESCAP 1995). It has certainly provided a model for traffic control (Webster 1995). Because of this emphasis both Hong Kong and Singapore appear on the list of the 10 most liveable cities in the region (Choong 1999). Singapore has not only overtaken the USA in terms of per capita GDP,[6] but is also Asia's "cleanest city" (ESCAP 1995).

In Singapore, a series of public campaigns for a cleaner environment began in 1959. By 1995, 21 different campaigns had been initiated (ESCAP 1995). At the same time rural-urban migration has been tightly controlled. Together these policies have enabled the city to increase the quality of its environment. Further, the relationship of a city to its borders (the ability to move industrial firms to outside the city boundaries) has played a significant role in keeping these cities clean (see, for example, Chapter 8 in this volume). The command-and-control and high-tech functions have remained in the centres, while the manufacturing and other pollution-related activities have been sent across borders.

Other services, such as water supply, are delivered at the highest of standards. In Singapore water loss stands at 8 per cent (Briscoe 1993), which is comparable to levels experienced by cities in the developed world. All homes receive piped potable water. Wastewater and refuse are collected daily and treated, and the air quality is within international standards.

Social sustainability in these cities started with public housing programmes. The improvement of low-income communities has taken place through massive provision of housing by government in both Singapore and Hong Kong. In Singapore, 86 per cent of the population live in housing built by the public sector, and over three-quarters of the population own their homes. Further, despite its globalized economy Singapore has not experienced social polarization, rather there is strong evidence of a trend towards a professionalized occupation structure with a growing middle-upper class (Baum 1999). This trend, no doubt, was enhanced by both Singapore's and Hong Kong's ability to control property development successfully during this period (Haili 1999).

Amenity cities

According to this perspective, globalization pressures can provide the impetus for the development of ecologically "sustainable" policies in some cities. In cities such as Sydney and Vancouver, the argument suggested in this volume is that governments have been encouraged to enhance their environments as part of strengthening their international comparative advantage. Good environmental quality, according to this theory, can be an important element in attracting investment and promoting local economic development. These two cities have three important aspects in common: post-industrial economies integrated into the regional economy; "inviting" natural environments or high concentrations of "amenities"; and economic development accompanied by a sufficiently high level of per capita welfare and political acceptance to maintain and enhance the environment. What Chapters 13 and 14 demonstrated, however, is that while amenity plays an important role in development, local governments have not been encouraged by globalization forces to enhance its importance. Rather, current conditions associated with globalization, including densification in Vancouver and lack of resources for infrastructure in Sydney, are in fact impeding the creation of "liveable" cities. This is not to say that Vancouver and Sydney do not have certain similarities in their patterns of growth. It does suggest, however, that globalization-driven growth will not also drive localities towards sustainability.

Globalization forces impacting on Vancouver and Sydney include financial and capital flows consistent with their post-industrial economic structures, trade in goods (for Vancouver), and immigration flows. Sydney is the capital of New South Wales and Australia's most global city. Vancouver, as part of "Cascadia", has been considered an emerging "sub-global world city" (Chapter 14). Each city's environmental amenities (climate, harbour, beaches, mountains, low levels of pollution) and multicultural character are key to their competitive advantage. Vancouver is part of a wide region of "geographical affinity" which stretches from southern Oregon to the ski resort of Whistler, 120 km north of Vancouver (Chapter 14). One problem for Vancouver is managing growth, as city expansion is sandwiched between the ocean and the foothills of the Rocky Mountains. In response the Greater Vancouver Regional District, a partnership of 20 municipalities and two electoral areas, has produced a "liveable region" plan that includes the protection of a green zone encompassing two-thirds of the entire area (GVRD 1996). This green zone is intended to protect the natural assets, including major parks (of which there are more than 22, covering 11,400 hectares) (GVRD 1997), watersheds, ecologically important areas, and farmland (GVRD 1996).

Sydney has many beaches, a beautiful harbour, and climate attractions considered an important part of the city's environmental amenities. The state of New South Wales and many local governments within the area are at pains to protect these amenities. Struggles have focused on how to keep the beaches clean, for example. In large part, this is because Sydney is a major tourist stop and the beach area is a important attraction (Chapter 13).

In terms of social issues, both of these cities are facing social tensions due to the large migrant population. Vancouver and Sydney have recently been the sites of Asian immigration. In 1991, Sydney had 28.5 per cent of the total number of persons born overseas within Australia, and 42 per cent of all immigrants to the country were from Asia. For Sydney the growth in the number of foreign-born residents is twice as fast as the growth of the total population (Chapter 13). Vancouver is one of the most rapidly growing urbanized regions in North America. Between 1981 and 1996 the population of the region increased from 1.2 million to 1.9 million. Of these, 600,000 people, almost one-third, arrived in the years 1991–1994. Most significantly, net international migration increased from 33 per cent in the 1980s to 59 per cent during 1991–1994. Many of these migrants are from Asia (Chapter 14). The rapid influx of migrants has not been without problems. Both cities have faced assimilation problems and immigrant backlash issues.

In both Sydney and Vancouver, according to the studies performed, increasing articulation to the regional city system is threatening the quality of life in these cities, or at least bringing with it concern from a variety of different groups. Rather than globalization as the force behind sustainability, the hope of the authors lies in the character, willingness, and political power of local groups.

World city formation and localization

The conditions described so far were created by multidimensional and complex sets of international forces. While on the one hand, maintaining

Table 15.10 Indicators of decentralization for selected countries

Country	Fiscal decentralization (1997)		Electoral decentralization (1999)		
	Share of subnational government (%)		Local elections	Number of elected subnational tiers	Number of local jurisdictions
	Total public expenditure	Total tax revenue			
USA	46.4	32.9	Yes	3	70,500
Japan[a]	–	37.8	Yes	2	3,233
Korea	–	–	Yes	2	204
Malaysia	19.1	2.4	No	0	143
Indonesia	14.8	2.9	No	0	–
Thailand	9.6	5.5	Yes	1	149[b]
Philippines[a]	6.5	4.0	Yes	2	1,541
China	55.7	51.4	No	0	–
Argentina	43.9	41.1	Yes	2	1,617
Brazil	36.5	31.3	Yes	1	4,642
Mexico	26.1	20.6	Yes	2	2,418

Source: World Bank 1999
a. Fiscal decentralization figures for 1990.
b. Thailand currently has elected municipal governments governing 149 cities. In addition there are 1,050 sanitary districts, which provide services in densely populated areas outside cities; each is governed by a board composed of appointed and elected members. There are up to 7,823 *tambon* administrative organizations, which provide basic services in rural areas and are governed by elected assemblies and appointed executives.
Italics are estimates.

growth, striving for equity, and sustaining the urban environment will necessarily require policies at the international level, local dynamics also matter. The world city formation process must be produced, and therefore local actors play an important role in shaping the future of their cities (Sassen 1994).

Local government decisions, however, are shaped by a variety of influences, including the drive to increase competitiveness and institutional capacity. Both national priorities and institutional limitations have affected the ability of local governments to delivery urban services and regulate private activities.

Decentralization[7] of government has not been a strong or common political trend in countries of East and South-East Asia (Table 15.10), although it has been common in other developing countries. For example, according to one study, of 75 countries with developing and transitional economies and a population exceeding 5 million, 63 had transferred additional powers to local government (Dillinger 1994).

A lack of or delay in decentralization in the post-war period in East

Asia resulted in an overwhelming concentration of state power in the hands of central governments, as well as a massive accumulation of rules and regulations and overlapping agency responsibilities (UNDP 1993). Many Asian countries have attempted to compensate for the lack of decentralization by implementing regulatory liberalization policies. However, an inability to move quickly and efficiently and adjust policies in the light of rapid urbanization has impacted on the development of many cities. Often national agencies compete over the development of infrastructure, fragmenting the implementation process, and metropolitan planning agencies have not been effective in coordinating and enforcing metropolitan development policies (Edralin 1998).

Notwithstanding some of the variations in the extent that local authorities across countries in the region depend on national government's financial support, the lack of political decentralization often allowed for high levels of central government intervention. While Seoul's local government, for instance, has been largely self-financed, from 1961 to 1991 there was no political decentralization in Korea and the central government controls local financial management and budgeting. Since 1991, local control has remained nominal. Hence, the Capital Region Management Law, providing guidelines for infrastructure provision, was prepared by the National Ministry of Construction and Transportation (Kim 1998). In Indonesia, the involvement of the central government and provincial administrations resulted in relatively weak local authorities. Until recently, central government met over 70 per cent of costs, and local taxes typically yielded insignificant levels of revenue. In Thailand, parallel systems of territorial administration and local self-government exist. A department of the Ministry of Interior administers local self-government through provincial, municipal, and district structures. Each is responsible for local government affairs within its area. Central government grants and assigned revenues, however, account for approximately 95 per cent of all local government revenues.

Two results of national financing for urban infrastructure are evident. First, infrastructure development has been centred in national capitals to the detriment of other cities. Second, infrastructure projects have been geared toward large items associated with international linkages, as opposed to basic services. Major metropolitan centres in the region have benefited from their national government's largesse. For example, spending on water supply in Bangkok exceeded that for all other urban areas in the country combined (Kaothien, Webster, and Vorathanyakit 1996). In post-war Japan, the national government consistently made massive infrastructure developments in and around Tokyo, including the country's first international airport, largest dam, first *Shinkonsen* route (from Tokyo to Osaka), and the majority of harbour projects (constructed in the coastal strip from Tokyo to Nagoya) (Uzawa undated).

At the metropolitan level many Pacific Asian cities have privileged large regional and global linkage infrastructure without appropriate attention to basic infrastructure needs. Infrastructure was often geared towards large projects dedicated to increasing capital accumulation processes rather than providing basic services to the expanding population. For example, during the 1980s and early 1990s, while telecommunications and transportation projects received 30 per cent of Indonesia's infrastructure development expenditures, housing and water supply received only 6 per cent (Bulkin 1996). In Thailand, transportation and telecommunications infrastructure spending increased from 43.5 per cent during the 1982–1986 period to 57.8 per cent during the 1992–1996 period, while expenditures on utilities (water supply, wastewater, and solid waste) fell from 9.6 per cent to 7.7 per cent over the same time (Kaothien, Webster, and Vorathanyakit 1996). Royston Brockman suggests that "Asia failed to anticipate and plan for the massive urbanization of the last decade. Urbanization has brought prosperity for many millions but still more live in conditions that are similar to those of the Middle Ages instead of the close of the millennium." (*FEER* 1996: 69) To overcome some of the problems mentioned above, in the future developing Asian cities will need to invest US$2.5–3 billion a year on sanitation, waste, and wastewater infrastructure alone (Ghooprasert 1996).

Typically, cities at different development levels experience different levels of expenditure on basic services (Table 15.11). It is not surprising, therefore, that an international comparison demonstrates different levels of provision and maintenance. In terms of water supply system maintenance, an important management issue is leakage (Table 15.12). Some of the industrial cities have poor records in this regard, while other cities in the hierarchy perform better. For example, in terms of water supply one-third of Bangkok's population has no access to public water (Lee 1994), and in Jakarta less than one-half of the population has direct connections to the municipal water supply system (ADB 1996), while in Shanghai only 7 per cent of the population are not connected to faucets (Wu 1999). Further, poor maintenance of systems has led to high water leakage rates.

Table 15.11 Government expenditures per person on water supply, sanitation, drainage, garbage collection, roads, and electricity

Income grouping (cities in)	US$ per person
Low-income countries	15.0
Low-mid-income countries	31.4
Middle-income countries	40.1
Mid-high-income countries	304.6
High-income countries	813.5

Source: Low *et al.* 2000

Table 15.12 Unaccounted-for water by utilities in selected cities of the Asia Pacific region

City	Unaccounted for water (%)
Tokyo	<10
Seoul	>40
Hong Kong	>20
Singapore	<10
Bangkok	>30
Jakarta	>50
Manila	>50
Shanghai	>35

Source: ESCAP 1995; TMG 2000

In many systems leakage is over 45 per cent. A reduction to 30 per cent would, in Jakarta alone, retrieve 45 million cubic metres of water annually, enough to provide for 800,000 people a year (Serageldin 1999). In Manila leakage accounts for over 55 per cent of withdrawals while around 1.5 million people in the metropolitan area are not served by a public water supply (ADB 1996).

Before the financial crisis, Brockman (1996) estimated that Asia would need US$6.9 trillion in infrastructure investment (US$280 billion annually) to meet its needs. Compare this with an annual investment of US$250 million in all developing countries throughout the world (Briscoe 1999). In the 1980s about 10 per cent of total public investment in developing countries or about 0.5 per cent of GDP was for water supply and sanitation (Briscoe 1993). During the financial crisis national governments cut funds for many infrastructure projects around the region, and the economic situation has made extracting revenues from local populations difficult. The questions remain if, how, and when these cities will be able to provide money for an environmental clean-up. When Japan began to clean up the environment in the early 1970s, pollution abatement investment surged to up to approximately 11.4 per cent of total private capital investment (Kato 1998). Will nations in developing Asia be able, under current growth conditions, to follow this path?

The way forward?

Despite the high cost these systems must be financed. Those hurt most by the lack of infrastructure are the poor, and just as urban centres cannot afford to isolate themselves from the global economy, so they cannot afford to isolate their poorest neighbourhoods from wider urban societies and economies. The handicap imposed on the poor by the lack of clean water, effective sanitation, sufficient drainage, and decent roads impedes the growth of entire cities (Annez and Friendly 1996).

Addressing the issues within cities across the region requires appropriate coordinated, integrated responses among a variety of agencies and institutions that work at different levels. Successful cities, such as Singapore and Hong Kong, have planned at the mega-urban regional level.[8] They were helped, no doubt, by wise leadership, their size, the city-state political system, which made city priorities national priorities, and the ability to reach across borders when expanding their economies. Given the specific context of its success, not all aspects of the Singapore environmental model may be transferable to developing world cities.

If neither the Japanese nor the Singapore model is available to most developing world cities, what are the alternatives? One argument is for a complement of policies based upon the "fair shares" city model articulated by Haughton (1999a). This includes both policies at the local level and those that deal with international flows. This would require new forms of governance: subnational, regional arrangements with institutional capacities and authority over the large urban regions. These may take the form of more collaborative styles of governing, both between the public, private, and NGO sectors and between different public administrative regions. This type of governance pattern is emerging in some urban areas in the region (Chapter 14). Regional development strategies that accompany adequate private property laws, appropriate tax regimes, and shared infrastructure development will prevent a "race to the bottom" or "bidding-down" syndrome, where localities will lower environmental standards or enforcement as a means to attract domestic and foreign investments (Douglass and Ooi 1999).

At the international scale there is also a need for new arrangements. Policy responses to enhance urban environmental and social conditions must therefore include international actors and institutions.

Despite the growing number of actors (governments, NGOs, private sector groups, etc.) that have responded at the international level, the environment has continued to degrade and the gap between what has been done and what is needed is widening (UNEP 1997).

Currently, the international actors attempting to manage environmental issues are multilaterial financial institutions, regional trade and investment institutions, and developed nations which provide overseas development funding. Dua and Esty (1997) have argued that to cure the Asia Pacific region's environmental problems, the Asia Pacific Economic Cooperation forum (APEC) is the optimal institutional response, since no other forum covers all the relevant actors and attempts by other actors have fallen short. These institutions, however, have neither the capacity nor the expertise for this assignment. Forcing the IMF or the WTO to include environmental concerns in their decision-making may not be as effective as strengthening international environmental institutions such as the United Nations Environment Programme (UNEP), the UNDP, or the United Nations Centre for Human Settlements (UNCHS-Habitat). Trade-offs within the APEC region between liberalization and the environmental agenda include conflicting priorities between trade, investment, and the environment. International trade and financial institutions may not be in the appropriate position to be the only decision-makers in this arena. Further, the differing urban environmental and social conditions of cities must be given high priority, meaning that blanket policies for all cities may be mis-specified, as each has a set of dominant environmental problems that should be addressed in specific ways. Such a complex task of policy development must be coordinated between local, national, and international levels.

Conclusions

As Graham Haughton (1999b: 234) has noted, "it is futile and indeed meaningless to attempt to create a sustainable city in isolation from its broader hinterland area". David Satterthwaite (1999: 6) has highlighted this point, noting that "the key issue is not 'sustainable cities' but cities whose built form, government structure, production systems, consumption pattern and waste generation and management systems are compatible with sustainable development goals for the city, its wider region and the whole biosphere". The increasing scale of development influences demands for more studies on the relationship between the regional and global economy and the urban social and physical environment. The Asia Pacific region provides a good case study with which to sketch out some speculations.

The concept of the functional city system, which defines urban development patterns by the particular roles that cities play within the increasingly interdependent regional economy, also provides for a differentiation of environmental and social conditions. Not only is the functional city system defining economic activity, but it is also penetrating physical and social realms. While this framework is helpful in understanding the current development of cities and the challenges they face in terms of environmental and social issues, it does not imply a single model for development. Certainly, globalization processes that are historically unprecedented are driving forces in contemporary development. But globalization is a contingent process; it is not only dynamic but also open-ended. There is no future trajectory for globalization. It is a long-term process that can be shaped by its own internal contradictions along with a host of other factors (Held *et al.* 2000). The impacts on urban communities can be shaped to a large extent by the political will of the community. In terms of environmental performance and development, Singapore stands out as an excellent example of overcoming many of the problems associated with rapid development. The city-state has overcome negative environmental trends that have accompanied development in other urban centres in Asia. It is a clean and efficiently run city, demonstrating that politics and political culture can make a difference. This is not to underplay the role of the small size of the city (approximately 3 million inhabitants) and its ability to control cross-border migration of people and economic activities; rather it points out that different trajectories are possible.

Lastly, this perspective has shed light on the ability of global forces to create conditions for cities. Even in the best situations (in developed world cities with high levels of amenity and post-industrial societies), globalization is failing to be a force behind environmentally sustainable development. Obviously, further work must be done to support or refute this thesis, including systematic data-gathering for the confirmation of the linkages between transnational flows and impacts on urban conditions. Notwithstanding the tentative nature of the results, the implications are consistent with current policy studies that suggest effective "sustainable" policies for urban environmental and social development must be constructed at all levels of governance.

Notes

1. The UNDP human development index (HDI) "is based on three indicators: longevity, as measured by life expectancy at birth; education attainment, as measured by a combination adult literacy (two-thirds weight) and combining primary, secondary and tertiary enrolment ratios (one-third weight); and standard of living, as measured by real GDP per capita (PPP$)" (UNDP 1995).
2. The impacts of the crisis have brought environmental (*FEER* 1999) and urban issues (Walton 1997) into focus for policy-makers.
3. There is currently no air quality guideline threshold for PM_{10} and $PM_{2.5}$. Instead curves have been constructed that fix an acceptable risk for some health endpoint. The guideline value for respirable particulate matter, however, was fixed and was based upon the knowledge established in the epidemiological literature.
4. In the slum settlements, approximately 68 per cent of all households benefit from regular solid waste collection (Daniere 1996).
5. Anecdotal evidence suggests that it has occurred in selected locations. Douglass and Ooi (1999), for example, discuss how TNC textile companies around Bandung, Indonesia, have not only depleted groundwater but have also fouled it to the point that it causes skin irritations. For reviews of the literature in this area, see for example UNCTAD 1999: 298; Esty and Gentry 1997.
6. As of 1998, Singapore's GDP per capita was US$30,060, compared to that of the USA, US$29,340, making it the ninth highest GDP per capita in the world (World Bank 1999).

7. Decentralization usually includes either a horizontal or a vertical disbursement of power. The more important circumstance is when lower-level bodies acquire responsibilities previously left to higher, centralized government institutions. However, decentralization can also signal a transfer of responsibilities from the public sector into the hands of private actors. Although there are many different forms this process may take, in general it involves the greater allocation of authority to local governments (UNDP 1993).
8. Examples of strategic environmental plans for entire urban regions have been developed by Hong Kong's Environmental Protection Department and Singapore's Ministry of Environment.

REFERENCES

Asian Development Bank (ADB). 1996. *Managing Water Resources to Meet Megacity Needs, Proceedings of Regional Consultation.* Manila: ADB.

Asian Development Bank (ADB). 1997. *Emerging Asia: Challenges and Changes.* Hong Kong: ADB and Oxford University Press.

Asian Development Bank (ADB). 1999. *Asian Development Outlook.* Hong Kong: ADB and Oxford University Press.

Annez, Patricia and Alfred Friendly. 1996. "Cities in the developing world: Agenda for action following Habitat II", *Finance and Development*, Vol. 33, No. 4 (December), pp. 12–14.

Bai, Xuemei and Hidefumi Imura. 2000. "A comparative study of urban environment in East Asia: Stage model of urban environmental evolution", *International Review for Environmental Strategies*, Vol. 1, No. 1, pp. 135–158.

Baum, Scott. 1999. "Social transformation in the global city: Singapore", *Urban Studies*, Vol. 36, No. 7, pp. 1095–1117.

Brandon, Carter. 1994. "Reversing pollution trends in Asia", *Finance and Development*, Vol. 31, No. 2, pp. 21–23.

Briscoe, John. 1993. "When the cup is half full: Improving water and sanitation services in the developing world", *Environment,* Vol. 35, No. 4, pp. 7–15 and 28–37.

Briscoe, John. 1999. "The changing face of water infrastructure financing in developing countries", *Water Resources Development*, Vol. 15, No. 3, pp. 301–308.

Brockman, Royston A. C. 1996. "Overview of urban finance in the region", in Royston A. C. Brockman and Allen Williams (eds) *Urban Infrastructure Finance.* Manila: ADB, pp. 47–88.

Browder, John O., James R. Bohland, and Joseph L. Scarpaci. 1995. "Patterns of development on metropolitan fringe, urban fringe expansion in Bangkok, Jakarta and Santiago", *Journal of the American Planning Association*, Vol. 61, No. 3 (Summer), pp. 310–327.

Bulkin, Imron. 1996. "Indonesia", in Royston A. C. Brockman and Allen Williams (eds) *Urban Infrastructure Finance.* Manila: ADB, pp. 393–420.

Burgess, Rod, Marisa Carmona, and Theo Kolstee. 1997. *The Challenge of Sustainable Cities.* London: Zed Books.

Chatterjee, Patralekha. 1998. "A new economic reality on Asian city streets", *Urban Age*, Vol. 5, No. 4 (Spring), pp. 5–9.

Choe, Sang Cheol. 1998. "Toward reform of Korea's green belt policy: Issues and adjustment", in *Proceedings of the International Seminar on Management of Green Belt Area*. Korean Research Institute for Human Settlements and Ministry of Construction and Transportation.

Choong, Tet Sieu. 1999. "Presssure points", *Asiaweek*, 17 December, pp. 44–48.

Clarke, Giles T. R. 1996. "Megacity management: Trends and issues", in Jeffry Stubbs and Giles Clarke (eds) *Megacity Management in the Asian and Pacific Region*. Manila: ADB, pp. 53–95.

Cointreau-Levine, Sandra. 1994. "Private sector participation in municipal solid waste services in developing countries", Urban Management Programme Discussion Paper No. 13. Washington, DC: World Bank.

Cruz, Wilfrido, Kazuhiko Takemoto, and Jeremy Warford. 1998. "Relevance for developing countries", in Wilfrido Cruz, Kazuhiko Takemoto, and Jeremy Warford (eds) *Urban and Industrial Management in Developing Countries: Lessons from Japanese Experience*. Washington, DC: World Bank, EDI Learning Resources Series, pp. 47–51.

Daniere, Amrita. 1996. "Growth, inequality and poverty in South-East Asia: The case of Thailand", *Third World Planning Review,* Vol. 18, No. 4, pp. 373–395.

Dicken, Peter. 1998. *Global Shift, Transforming the World Economy*, 3rd edn. New York: Gilford Press.

Dillinger, William. 1994. "Decentralization and its implications for urban service delivery", Urban Management Programme Discussion Paper No. 16. Washington, DC: World Bank.

Douglass, Michael, 1991. "Planning for environmental sustainability in the extended Jakarta metropolitan region", in Norton Ginsburg, Bruce Koppel, and Terry G. McGee (eds) *The Extended Metropolis, Settlement Transition in Asia*. Honolulu: University of Hawaii Press, pp. 239–273.

Douglass, Michael. 1998a. "Urban and regional policy after the era of naïve globalism", paper presented at the UNCRD Global Forum on Regional Development Policy, 1–4 December, Nagoya.

Douglass, Michael. 1998b. "Globalization, inter-city networks and rural-urban linkages: Rethinking regional development theory and policy", paper presented at the UNCRD Global Forum on Regional Development Policy, 1–4 December, Nagoya.

Douglass, Michael and Goik-ling Ooi. 1999. "Industrializing cities and the environment in Pacific Asia: Towards a policy framework and agenda for action", found at http://www.usaep.org/policy/framing1.html.

Doven, Ben, Pamela Yatsko, S. Jayasankaran, Rodney Tasker, Julian Baum, John McBeth, Sachiko Sakamaki, Michael Laris, Charles S. Less, and Nigel Holloway. 1997. "Asia's car crush", *Far Eastern Economic Review*, 8 May, pp. 42–47.

Dua, Andre and Daniel C. Esty. 1997. *Sustaining the Asia Pacific Miracle: Environmental Protection and Economic Integration*. Washington, DC: Institute for International Economics.

Economic and Social Commission for Asia and the Pacific (ESCAP). 1995. *State of the Environment in Asia and the Pacific*. Bangkok: ESCAP.

Edralin, Josefa S. (ed.). 1998. *Metropolitan Governance and Planning in Transition: Asia-Pacific Cases*. UNCRD Research Report Series No. 31.

Elsom, Derek. 1996. *Smog Alert: Managing Urban Air Quality*. London: Earth-scan Publications.

Esty, Daniel and Bradford S. Gentry. 1997. "Foreign investment, globalization and the environment", in *Globalization and Environment, Preliminary Perspectives*. Paris: OECD, pp. 141–172.

Far Eastern Economic Review (FEER). 1996. "Population", in *Asia 1996 Yearbook: A Review of Events of 1995*. Hong Kong: FEER, pp. 69–72.

Far Eastern Economic Review (FEER). 1999. "Environment", in *Asia 1999 Yearbook: A Review of Events of 1998*. Hong Kong: FEER, pp. 58–61.

Firman, Tommy. 1997. "Land conversion and urban development in the northern region of West Java, Indonesia", *Urban Studies*, Vol. 34, No. 7, pp. 1027–1046.

Firman, Tommy. 1998. "The restructuring of Jakarta metropolitan area: A 'global city' in Asia", *Cities*, Vol. 15, No. 4, pp. 229–243.

Firman, Tommy. 1999. "From 'global city' to 'city of crisis': Jakarta metropolitan region under economic turmoil", *Habitat International*, Vol. 23, No. 4, pp. 447–466.

Foo, Tuan Seik. 2000. "Subjective assessment of urban quality of life in Singapore", *Habitat International*, Vol. 24, pp. 31–49.

Ghooprasert, Wenchai. 1996. "Environmental services", in Royston A. C. Brockman and Allen Williams (eds) *Urban Infrastructure Finance*. Manila: ADB, pp. 273–297.

Gilbert, Alan. 1994. "Third world cities: Housing, infrastructure and servicing", *Urban Studies*, Vol. 29, Nos 3/4, pp. 435–460.

Gould, B. and D. Smith. 1998. "Labor and society in urban Southeast Asia: An introduction", *Third World Planning Review*, Vol. 20, No. 2, pp. iii–vii.

Greater Vancouver Regional District (GVRD). 1996. *Livable Regional Strategic Plan*. Burnaby, BC: GVRD.

Greater Vancouver Regional District (GVRD). 1997. *The Livable Region*. Burnaby, BC: GVRD.

Gupta, Sanjeev, Calvin McDonald, Christian Schiller, Marinus Verhoeven, Zejko Bogetic, and Gerd Schwartz. 1998. "Mitigating the social costs of the Asian crisis", *Finance and Development*, Vol. 35, No. 3, pp. 18–21.

Haila, Anne. 1999. "City building in the East and West", *Cities*, Vol. 16, No. 4, pp. 259–267.

Harris, Nigel. 1992. "Wastes, the environment and the international economy", *Cities*, August pp. 177–185.

Haughton, Graham. 1999a. "Searching for the sustainable city", *Urban Studies*, Vol. 36, No. 11, pp. 1891–1906.

Haughton, Graham. 1999b. "Environmental justice and the sustainable city", *Journal of Planning, Education and Research*, Vol. 18, No. 3 (Spring), pp. 233–243.

Haut, Chua Beng. 1999. "Global economy/immature polity: Current crisis in Southeast Asia", *International Journal of Urban and Regional Research*, Vol. 23, No. 4, pp. 782–795.

Held, David, Anthony McGrew, David Goldblatt, and Jonathan Perraton. 1999. *Global Transformations, Politics, Economics and Culture*. Stanford: Stanford University Press.

International Monetary Fund (IMF). 1999. *World Economic Outlook May 1999*. Washington, DC: IMF.

Jellinek, Lea. 2000. "Jakarta, Indonesia: *Kampung* culture or consumer culture?", in Nicholas Low, Brendan Gleeson, Ingemar Elander, and Rolf Lidskog (eds) *Consuming Cities*. London: Routledge, pp. 265–280.

Kaothien, Utis. 1995. "The Bangkok metropolitan region: Policies and issues in the seventh plan", in Terry G. McGee and Ira M. Robinson (eds) *The Mega-Urban Regions of Southeast Asia*. Vancouver: University of British Columbia Press, pp. 329–340.

Kaothien, Utis, Douglas Webster, and Voravit Vorathanyakit. 1996. "Thailand", in Royston A. C. Brockman and Allen Williams (eds) *Urban Infrastructure Finance*. Manila: ADB, pp. 539–578.

Kato, Kazu. 1998. "Grow now, clean up later? The Japanese experience", in Wilfrido Cruz, Kazuhiko Takemoto, and Jeremy Warford (eds) *Urban and Industrial Management in Developing Countries: Lessons from the Japanese Experience*. Washington, DC: World Bank, EDI Learning Resources Series, pp. 41–46.

Kim, Hyun-Sik. 1998. "Seoul metropolitan area, Republic of Korea", in Josefa S. Edralin (ed.) *Metropolitan Governance and Planning in Transition: Asia Pacific Cases*, UNCRD Report No. 31. Nagoya: UNCRD, pp. 101–112.

Korean Ministry of Environment. 1999. *Green Korea 1999: Environmental Vision for a Sustainable Society*. Kwacheon: Ministry of Environment.

Leaf, Michael. 1994. "The suburbanization of Jakarta: A concurrence of economics and ideology", *Third World Planning Review*, Vol. 16, pp. 341–356.

Lee, Eddy. 1998. *The Asian Financial Crisis, The Challenge for Social Policy*. Geneva: ILO.

Lee, Yok Shiu F. 1994. "Urban water supply and sanitation in developing countries", in James E. Nickum and K. William Easter (eds) *Metropolitan Water Use Conflicts in Asia and the Pacific*. Boulder, CO: Westview Press, pp. 19–35.

Liu, Chong-long. 2000. "China", Country Report for the Environmental Management Seminar (Asian Countries) sponsored by the Osaka International Centre and Japan International Cooperation Agency (June).

Lo, Fu-chen and Yu-qing Xing. 1999. *China's Sustainable Development Framework: Summary Report*. Tokyo: UNU/IAS.

Lo, Fu-chen and Yue-man Yeung (eds). 1996. *Emerging World Cities in Pacific Asia*. Tokyo: United Nations University Press.

Low, Nicholas, Brendan Gleeson, Ingemar Elander, and Rolf Lidskog (eds). 2000. *Consuming Cities, The Urban Environment in the Global Economy after the Rio Declaration*. London: Routledge.

McGee, Terry G. 1998. "Rethinking regional policy in an era of rapid urbanization and volatile globalization", paper presented at the UNCRD Global Forum on Regional Development Policy, 1–4 December, Nagoya.

McGee, Terry G. and Ira Robinson (eds). 1995. *The Mega-Urban Regions of Southeast Asia*. Vancouver: University of British Columbia Press.

McGranahan, Gordon and Jacob Songsore. 1994. "Wealth, health and the urban household", *Environment*, Vol. 36, No. 6, pp. 4–11 and 40–45.

Macleod, Scott and Terry G. McGee. 1996. "The Singapore-Johore-Riau growth triangle: An emerging extended metropolitan region", in Fu-chen Lo and Yue-man Yeung (eds) *Emerging World Cities in Pacific Asia*. Tokyo: United Nations University Press, pp. 417–464.

Organization for Economic Cooperation and Development (OECD). 1997. *Environmental Performance Reviews: Korea*. Paris: OECD.

Ooi, Goik-ling (ed.). 1995. *Environment and the City: Sharing Singapore's Experience and Future Challenges*. Singapore: Institute of Policy Studies/Times Academic Press.

Palanivel, T. and Fu-chen Lo. 1999. "India's economic reforms: Lessons from the East Asia", paper presented to international conference on India's Second Generation Reforms, sponsored by the Australian National University South Asia Research Centre and Madras School of Economics, 8–10 December, Chennai.

Pernia, Ernesto M. 1992. "Southeast Asia", in Richard Stren, Rodney White, and Joseph Whitney (eds) *Sustainable Cities: Urbanization and the Environment in International Perspective*. Boulder, CO: Westview Press, pp. 233–257.

Phantumvanit, Dhira and Winai Liengcharensit. 1989. "Coming to terms with Bangkok's environmental problems", *Environment and Urbanization*, Vol. 1, No. 1, pp. 31–39.

Population Crisis Committee. 1990. *Life in the World's Largest Metropolitan Areas*, Statistical Appendix. Washington, DC: World Population Committee.

Pugh, Cedric. 1996. "Sustainability and sustainable cities", in Cedric Pugh (ed.) *Sustainability, the Environment and Urbanization*. London: Earthscan Publications, pp. 135–177.

Robison, R. and Rosser, A. 1998. "Contesting reform: Indonesia's new order and the IMF", *World Development*, Vol. 26, No. 8, pp. 1593–1609.

Sassen, Saskia. 1994. *Cities in a World Economy*. Thousand Oaks, CA: Pine Forge Press.

Satterthwaite, David. 1995. "Viewpoint – The underestimate of urban poverty and of its health consequences", *Third World Planning Review,* Vol. 17, No. 4, pp. iii–x.

Satterthwaite, David. 1999. "The key issues and works included", in David Satterthwaite (ed.) *Sustainable Cities*. London: Earthscan Publications.

Sawa, Takamitsu. 1997. *Japan's Experience in the Battle Against Air Pollution*. Japan: Pollution-Related Health Damage Compensation and Prevention Association.

Schmidt, Johannes Dragsbaek. 1998. "Globalization and inequality in urban South-East Asia", *Third World Planning Review*, Vol. 20, No. 2, pp. 127–145.

Seoul Metropolitan Government (SMG). 2000. *Waste Management in Seoul*. Seoul: SMG.

Serageldin, Ismail. 1999. "Looking ahead: Water, life and the environment in the twenty-first century", *Water Resources Development*, Vol. 15, Nos 1/2, pp. 17–28.

Setchell, Charles, A. 1995. "The growing environmental crisis in the world's mega-cities: The case of Bangkok", *Third World Planning Review*, Vol. 17, No. 1, pp. 1–17.

Smith, Kirk R. 1993. "The most important chart in the world", UNU Lecture Series No. 4, June, United Nations University.

Stren, Richard, Rodney White, and Joseph Whitney (eds). 1992. *Sustainable Cities: Urbanization and the Environment in International Perspective*. Boulder, CO: Westview Press.

Thant, Myo, Min Tang, and Hiroshi Kakazu (eds). 1994. *Growth Triangles in Asia: A New Approach to Regional Economic Cooperation.* Hong Kong: Oxford University Press.

Tokyo Metropolitan Government (TMG). 1996. *Urban White Paper on Tokyo Metropolis 1996.* Tokyo: Bureau of City Planning, TMG.

Tokyo Metropolitan Government (TMG). 1999. *Tokyo Current Issues.* Tokyo: TMG.

Tokyo Metropolitan Government (TMG). 2000. *Environment in Tokyo.* Tokyo: Bureau of Environment, TMG.

Tokyo Metropolitan News. 1999. "Suginami incineration plant wins ISO environmental certification", *Tokyo Metropolitan News*, Vol. 49, No. 2 (Summer), p. 5.

United Nations Centre for Human Settlements (Habitat). 2000. Urban Indicators Database, www.urbanobsevatory.org/indicators/database.

United Nations Conference on Trade and Development (UNCTAD). 1997. *World Investment Report 1997.* New York: United Nations.

United Nations Conference on Trade and Development (UNCTAD). 1999. *World Investment Report 1999: Foreign Direct Investment and the Challenge of Development.* New York: United Nations.

United Nations Development Programme (UNDP). 1993. *Human Development Report 1993.* New York: Oxford University Press.

United Nations Development Programme (UNDP). 1995. *Human Development Report 1995.* New York: Oxford University Press.

United Nations Development Programme (UNDP). 1998. *Human Development Report 1998.* New York: Oxford University Press.

United Nations Environment Programme (UNEP). 1993. *Environmental Data Report 1993–94.* Oxford: Blackwell.

United Nations Environment Programme (UNEP). 1997. *Global Environmental Outlook.* Oxford: Oxford University Press and UNEP.

Urban Indicators database: http://www.urbanobservatory.org/indicators/database.

Uzawa, Hirofumi. Undated. "Infrastructure in Japan: Issues and lessons", UNU/IAS Working Paper No. 60. Tokyo: UNU/IAS.

Walton, Michael. 1997. "The maturation of the East Asian miracle", *Finance and Development*, Vol. 34, No. 3, pp. 7–10.

Webster, Douglas. 1995. "The urban environment in Southeast Asia: Challenges and opportunities", in *Southeast Asian Affairs*. Singapore: Institute of Southeast Asian Studies, pp. 89–107.

World Health Organization (WHO). 1992. *Our Planet, Our Health.* Geneva: WHO.

World Health Organization (WHO) and United Nations Environment Programme (UNEP). 1992. *Urban Air Pollution in Megacities of the World.* Oxford: Blackwell.

World Bank. 1992. *World Development Report.* New York: World Bank and Oxford University Press.

World Bank. 1993. *The East Asian Miracle, Economic Growth and Public Policy.* New York: Oxford University Press and World Bank.

World Bank. 1999. *World Development Report.* New York: World Bank and Oxford University Press.

Wu, Weiping. 1999. "Shanghai", *Cities*, Vol. 16, No. 3, pp. 207–216.

Acronyms

ACU	Asian currency unit
ADB	Asian Development Bank
ADM	Asian Dollar Market
AFTA	ASEAN Free Trade Area
AIA	ASEAN investment area
APEC	Asia Pacific Economic Cooperation
ASEAN	Association of South-East Asian Nations
BBIR	Bintan Beach international resort
BC	British Columbia
BCC	business core city
BIDP	Bintan integrated development project
BIE	Bintan industrial estate
BIMP-EAGA	Brunei-Indonesia-Malaysia-Philippines east ASEAN growth area
BIP	Batamindo industrial park
BMA	Bangkok Metropolitan Administration
BMR	Bangkok metropolitan region
BOD	biological oxygen demand
BOO	build-own-operate
BOT	build-operate-transfer
BTO	build-transfer-operate
CAT	Communications Authority of Thailand
CBA	cost-benefit analysis
CBD	central business district
CMF	control and management functions
COD	chemical oxygen demand

DUAP	Department of Urban Affairs and Planning (New South Wales)
EBR	extended Bangkok region
EIS	environmental impact statement
EMA	extended metropolitan area
EMR	extended metropolitan region
EOI	export-oriented industrialization
EPA	Environment Protection Authority (New South Wales)
EPZ	export processing zone
ESB	eastern seaboard (Thailand)
ESD	ecologically sustainable development
ETDZ	economic and technological development zone (China)
EU	European Union
FDI	foreign direct investment
GATT	General Agreement on Tariffs and Trade
GCC	Gulf Cooperation Council
GDP	gross domestic product
GIS	geographic information system
GMS	greater Mekong subregion
GNP	gross national product
GSA	Growth Strategies Act (British Columbia)
GT	growth triangle
GVRD	Greater Vancouver Regional District
HDI	human development index
HKEMR	Hong Kong extended metropolitan region
IA	implementation agreement
IC	integrated circuit
IMF	International Monetary Fund
IMS-GT	Indonesia-Malaysia-Singapore growth triangle
IMT-GT	Indonesia-Malaysia-Thailand growth triangle
IQ	industrial quotient
ISDN	integrated service digital network
JDB	Japan Development Bank
JETRO	Japan External Trade Organization
JIA	Jakarta international airport
JSX	Jakarta Stock Exchange
KIP	*kampung* improvement programme
KSA	Kingsford Smith airport (Sydney)
LDC	less developed country
LQ	location quotient
M&As	mergers and acquisitions
MITI	Ministry of International Trade and Industry (Japan)
MNC	multinational corporation
MRT	mass rapid transit
NAFTA	North American Free Trade Association
NCR	national capital region (Tokyo)
NCRDP	national capital region development plan (Japan)

NDP	national development plan (Japan)
NGO	non-governmental organization
NHMRC	National Health and Medical Research Council (Australia)
NIC	new industrial city (Japan)
NIC	newly industrializing country
NIDL	new international division of labour
NIE	newly industrializing economy
NLA	National Land Agency (Japan)
NO_x	nitrogen oxide
NPO	non-profit organization
NSW	New South Wales
NV	new vehicle
ODA	official development assistance
OECD	Organization for Economic Cooperation and Development
OEM	original equipment manufacturer
OJT	on-the-job training
OPEC	Organization of Petroleum Exporting Countries
PKM	person kilometre miles
PRD	Pearl river delta
PSI	pollution standards index
QC	quality control
QOL	quality of life
R&D	research and development
RCC	regional core city
RCS	regional context statement
RGS	regional growth strategy
RHQ	regional headquarters
RTC	research and training centre
RTP	research and training programme
SAR	special administrative region (China)
SEP	Strategic Economic Plan (Singapore)
SEZ	special economic zone (China)
SIC	standard industrial code
SID	special industrial district
SMR	Seoul metropolitan region
SO_2	sulphur dioxide
SO_x	sulphur oxide
SPM	suspended particulate matter
TDM	transportation demand management
TEU	20-foot equivalent unit
TMA	Tokyo metropolitan area
TMG	Tokyo metropolitan government
TMR	Tokyo metropolitan region
TNC	transnational corporation
TOT	Telephone Organization of Thailand
TSP	total suspended particulates

UNCHS	United Nations Centre for Human Settlements
UNCRD	United Nationa Centre for Regional Development
UNCTAD	United Nations Conference on Trade and Development
UNDP	United Nations Development Programme
UNEP	United Nations Environment Programme
UNESCO	United Nations Educational, Scientific, and Cultural Organization
UNIDO	United Nations Industrial Development Organization
UNU/IAS	United Nations University Institute of Advanced Studies
WCP	World Competitiveness Project
WTO	World Trade Organization

List of contributors

Fu-chen Lo (editor)
Representative
Taipei Economic and Cultural Representative Office in Japan.

Peter J. Marcotullio (editor)
Fellow
United Nations University
Institute of Advanced Studies.
Assistant Professor
Department of Urban Engineering
Faculty of Engineering
University of Tokyo.

Chia Siow Yue
Director
Institute of Southeast Asian Studies
Singapore.

Sung Woong Hong
President
Construction and Economy Research
  Institute of Korea (CERIK)
Korea.

Kidokoro Tetsuo
Associate Professor
Department of Urban Engineering
Faculty of Engineering
University of Tokyo.

Sauwalak Kittiprapas
Vice President and Research Director
Good Governance for Social Development and the Environment Institute
  (GSEI)
Bangkok
Thailand.

B. S. Kusbiantoro
Director
Center for Urban and Regional Development Studies
Institute of Technology
Bandung
Indonesia.

Won-yong Kwon
Professor
University of Seoul
Office of Planning and Development
Korea.

Terry G. McGee
Professor
Institute of Asian Research

University of British Columbia
Canada.

Peter A. Murphy
Professor
Head, School of the Built Environ-
  ment
Associate Dean, Research
Faculty of the Built Environment
University of New South Wales
Sydney, Australia.

Ning Yuemin
Professor and Director
Institute of Urban and Regional
  Development Studies
East China Normal University
Shanghai
China.

Onishi Takashi
Professor
Department of Urban Engineering
Faculty of Engineering
University of Tokyo.

Victor F. S. Sit
Professor
Department of Geography and Geology
University of Hong Kong
Hong Kong
China.

Budhy T. S. Soegijoko
Deputy Chairman for International
  Economic Cooperation
National Development Planning
  Agency
Indonesia.

Ching-lung Tsay
Professor
Institute of Economics
Academia Sinica
Taiwan.

Chung-Tong Wu
Dean
Faculty of the Built Environment
University of New South Wales
Australia.

Index

497